Novels
for Students

National Advisory Board

Novels for Students

Presenting Analysis, Context, and Criticism on Commonly Studied Novels

Volume 19

Jennifer Smith, Project Editor

Foreword by Anne Devereaux Jordan

Detroit • New York • San Francisco • San Diego • New Haven, Conn. • Waterville, Maine • London • Munich

Novels for Students, Volume 19

Project Editor
Jennifer Smith

Editorial
Anne Marie Hacht, Ira Mark Milne, Maikue Vang

Rights Acquisition and Management
Margaret Abendroth, Edna Hedblad, Ann Taylor

Manufacturing
Rhonda Williams

Imaging
Leitha Etheridge-Sims, Lezlie Light, Mike Logusz, Daniel W. Newell

Product Design
Pamela A. E. Galbreath

ISBN 0-7876-6942-3
ISSN 1094-3552

Printed in the United States of America
10 9 8 7 6 5 4 3 2 1

Table of Contents

The Informed Dialogue: Interacting with Literature

When we pick up a book, we usually do so with the anticipation of pleasure. We hope that by entering the time and place of the novel and sharing the thoughts and actions of the characters, we will find enjoyment. Unfortunately, this is often not the case; we are disappointed. But we should ask, has the author failed us, or have we failed the author?

We establish a dialogue with the author, the book, and with ourselves when we read. Consciously and unconsciously, we ask questions: "Why did the author write this book?" "Why did the author choose that time, place, or character?" "How did the author achieve that effect?" "Why did the character act that way?" "Would I act in the same way?" The answers we receive depend upon how much information about literature in general and about that book specifically we ourselves bring to our reading.

Young children have limited life and literary experiences. Being young, children frequently do not know how to go about exploring a book, nor sometimes, even know the questions to ask of a book. The books they read help them answer questions, the author often coming right out and *telling* young readers the things they are learning or are expected to learn. The perennial classic, *The Little Engine That Could, tells* its readers that, among other things, it is good to help others and brings happiness:

> "Hurray, hurray," cried the funny little clown and all the dolls and toys. "The good little boys and girls in

the city will be happy because you helped us, kind, Little Blue Engine."

In picture books, messages are often blatant and simple, the dialogue between the author and reader one-sided. Young children are concerned with the end result of a book—the enjoyment gained, the lesson learned—rather than with how that result was obtained. As we grow older and read further, however, we question more. We come to expect that the world within the book will closely mirror the concerns of our world, and that the author will *show* these through the events, descriptions, and conversations within the story, rather than *telling* of them. We are now expected to do the interpreting, carry on our share of the dialogue with the book and author, and glean not only the author's message, but comprehend how that message and the overall affect of the book were achieved. Sometimes, however, we need help to do these things. *Novels for Students* provides that help.

A novel is made up of many parts interacting to create a coherent whole. In reading a novel, the more obvious features can be easily spotted—theme, characters, plot—but we may overlook the more subtle elements that greatly influence how the novel is perceived by the reader: viewpoint, mood and tone, symbolism, or the use of humor. By focusing on both the obvious and more subtle literary elements within a novel, *Novels for Students* aids readers in both analyzing for message and in determining how and why that message is communicated. In the discussion on Harper Lee's *To*

Kill a Mockingbird (Vol. 2), for example, the mockingbird as a symbol of innocence is dealt with, among other things, as is the importance of Lee's use of humor which "enlivens a serious plot, adds depth to the characterization, and creates a sense of familiarity and universality." The reader comes to understand the internal elements of each novel discussed—as well as the external influences that help shape it.

"The desire to write greatly," Harold Bloom of Yale University says, "is the desire to be elsewhere, in a time and place of one's own, in an originality that must compound with inheritance, with an anxiety of influence." A writer seeks to create a unique world within a story, but although it is unique, it is not disconnected from our own world. It speaks to us *because* of what the writer brings to the writing from our world: how he or she was raised and educated; his or her likes and dislikes; the events occurring in the real world at the time of the writing, and while the author was growing up. When we know what an author has brought to his or her work, we gain a greater insight into both the "originality" (the world of the book), and the things that "compound" it. This insight enables us to question that created world and find answers more readily. By informing ourselves, we are able to establish a more effective dialogue with both book and author.

Novels for Students, in addition to providing a plot summary and descriptive list of characters—to remind readers of what they have read—also explores the external influences that shaped each book. Each entry includes a discussion of the author's background, and the historical context in which the novel was written. It is vital to know, for instance, that when Ray Bradbury was writing *Fahrenheit 451* (Vol. 1), the threat of Nazi domination had recently ended in Europe, and the McCarthy hearings were taking place in Washington, D.C. This information goes far in answering the question, "Why did he write a story of oppressive government control and book burning?" Similarly, it is important to know that Harper Lee, author of *To Kill a Mockingbird,* was born and raised in Monroeville, Alabama, and that her father was a lawyer.

Readers can now see why she chose the south as a setting for her novel—it is the place with which she was most familiar—and start to comprehend her characters and their actions.

Novels for Students helps readers find the answers they seek when they establish a dialogue with a particular novel. It also aids in the posing of questions by providing the opinions and interpretations of various critics and reviewers, broadening that dialogue. Some reviewers of *To Kill A Mockingbird,* for example, "faulted the novel's climax as melodramatic." This statement leads readers to ask, "Is it, indeed, melodramatic?" "If not, why did some reviewers see it as such?" "If it is, why did Lee choose to make it melodramatic?" "Is melodrama ever justified?" By being spurred to ask these questions, readers not only learn more about the book and its writer, but about the nature of writing itself.

The literature included for discussion in *Novels for Students* has been chosen because it has something vital to say to us. *Of Mice and Men, Catch-22, The Joy Luck Club, My Antonia, A Separate Peace* and the other novels here speak of life and modern sensibility. In addition to their individual, specific messages of prejudice, power, love or hate, living and dying, however, they and all great literature also share a common intent. They force us to *think*—about life, literature, and about others, not just about ourselves. They pry us from the narrow confines of our minds and thrust us outward to confront the world of books and the larger, real world we all share. *Novels for Students* helps us in this confrontation by providing the means of enriching our conversation with literature and the world, by creating an *informed* dialogue, one that brings true pleasure to the personal act of reading.

Sources

Harold Bloom, *The Western Canon, The Books and School of the Ages,* Riverhead Books, 1994.

Watty Piper, *The Little Engine That Could,* Platt & Munk, 1930.

Anne Devereaux Jordan
Senior Editor, TALL
(Teaching and Learning Literature)

Introduction

Purpose of the Book

The purpose of *Novels for Students (NfS)* is to provide readers with a guide to understanding, enjoying, and studying novels by giving them easy access to information about the work. Part of Gale's "For Students" Literature line, *NfS* is specifically designed to meet the curricular needs of high school and undergraduate college students and their teachers, as well as the interests of general readers and researchers considering specific novels. While each volume contains entries on "classic" novels frequently studied in classrooms, there are also entries containing hard-to-find information on contemporary novels, including works by multicultural, international, and women novelists.

The information covered in each entry includes an introduction to the novel and the novel's author; a plot summary, to help readers unravel and understand the events in a novel; descriptions of important characters, including explanation of a given character's role in the novel as well as discussion about that character's relationship to other characters in the novel; analysis of important themes in the novel; and an explanation of important literary techniques and movements as they are demonstrated in the novel.

In addition to this material, which helps the readers analyze the novel itself, students are also provided with important information on the literary and historical background informing each work. This includes a historical context essay, a box comparing the time or place the novel was written to modern Western culture, a critical essay, and excerpts from critical essays on the novel. A unique feature of *NfS* is a specially commissioned critical essay on each novel, targeted toward the student reader.

To further aid the student in studying and enjoying each novel, information on media adaptations is provided, as well as reading suggestions for works of fiction and nonfiction on similar themes and topics. Classroom aids include ideas for research papers and lists of critical sources that provide additional material on the novel.

Selection Criteria

The titles for each volume of *NfS* were selected by surveying numerous sources on teaching literature and analyzing course curricula for various school districts. Some of the sources surveyed included: literature anthologies; *Reading Lists for College-Bound Students: The Books Most Recommended by America's Top Colleges;* textbooks on teaching the novel; a College Board survey of novels commonly studied in high schools; a National Council of Teachers of English (NCTE) survey of novels commonly studied in high schools; the NCTE's *Teaching Literature in High School: The Novel;* and the Young Adult Library Services Association (YALSA) list of best books for young adults of the past twenty-five years.

Input was also solicited from our advisory board, as well as from educators from various areas.

From these discussions, it was determined that each volume should have a mix of "classic" novels (those works commonly taught in literature classes) and contemporary novels for which information is often hard to find. Because of the interest in expanding the canon of literature, an emphasis was also placed on including works by international, multicultural, and women authors. Our advisory board members—educational professionals—helped pare down the list for each volume. If a work was not selected for the present volume, it was often noted as a possibility for a future volume. As always, the editor welcomes suggestions for titles to be included in future volumes.

How Each Entry Is Organized

Each entry, or chapter, in *NfS* focuses on one novel. Each entry heading lists the full name of the novel, the author's name, and the date of the novel's publication. The following elements are contained in each entry:

- **Introduction:** a brief overview of the novel which provides information about its first appearance, its literary standing, any controversies surrounding the work, and major conflicts or themes within the work.

- **Author Biography:** this section includes basic facts about the author's life, and focuses on events and times in the author's life that inspired the novel in question.

- **Plot Summary:** a factual description of the major events in the novel. Lengthy summaries are broken down with subheads.

- **Characters:** an alphabetical listing of major characters in the novel. Each character name is followed by a brief to an extensive description of the character's role in the novel, as well as discussion of the character's actions, relationships, and possible motivation.

  Characters are listed alphabetically by last name. If a character is unnamed—for instance, the narrator in *Invisible Man*—the character is listed as "The Narrator" and alphabetized as "Narrator." If a character's first name is the only one given, the name will appear alphabetically by that name.

  Variant names are also included for each character. Thus, the full name "Jean Louise Finch" would head the listing for the narrator of *To Kill a Mockingbird,* but listed in a separate cross-reference would be the nickname "Scout Finch."

- **Themes:** a thorough overview of how the major topics, themes, and issues are addressed within the novel. Each theme discussed appears in a separate subhead and is easily accessed through the boldface entries in the Subject/Theme Index.

- **Style:** this section addresses important style elements of the novel, such as setting, point of view, and narration; important literary devices used, such as imagery, foreshadowing, symbolism; and, if applicable, genres to which the work might have belonged, such as Gothicism or Romanticism. Literary terms are explained within the entry but can also be found in the Glossary.

- **Historical Context:** This section outlines the social, political, and cultural climate *in which the author lived and the novel was created.* This section may include descriptions of related historical events, pertinent aspects of daily life in the culture, and the artistic and literary sensibilities of the time in which the work was written. If the novel is a historical work, information regarding the time in which the novel is set is also included. Each section is broken down with helpful subheads.

- **Critical Overview:** this section provides background on the critical reputation of the novel, including bannings or any other public controversies surrounding the work. For older works, this section includes a history of how the novel was first received and how perceptions of it may have changed over the years; for more recent novels, direct quotes from early reviews may also be included.

- **Criticism:** an essay commissioned by *NfS* which specifically deals with the novel and is written specifically for the student audience, as well as excerpts from previously published criticism on the work (if available).

- **Sources:** an alphabetical list of critical material used in compiling the entry, with full bibliographical information.

- **Further Reading:** an alphabetical list of other critical sources which may prove useful for the student. It includes full bibliographical information and a brief annotation.

In addition, each entry contains the following highlighted sections, set apart from the main text as sidebars:

- **Media Adaptations:** a list of important film and television adaptations of the novel, including source information. The list also includes stage adaptations, audio recordings, musical adaptations, etc.

- **Topics for Further Study:** a list of potential study questions or research topics dealing with the novel. This section includes questions related to other disciplines the student may be studying, such as American history, world history, science, math, government, business, geography, economics, psychology, etc.

- **Compare and Contrast Box:** an "at-a-glance" comparison of the cultural and historical differences between the author's time and culture and late twentieth century/early twenty-first century Western culture. This box includes pertinent parallels between the major scientific, political, and cultural movements of the time or place the novel was written, the time or place the novel was set (if a historical work), and modern Western culture. Works written after 1990 may not have this box.

- **What Do I Read Next?:** a list of works that might complement the featured novel or serve as a contrast to it. This includes works by the same author and others, works of fiction and nonfiction, and works from various genres, cultures, and eras.

Other Features

NfS includes "The Informed Dialogue: Interacting with Literature," a foreword by Anne Devereaux Jordan, Senior Editor for *Teaching and Learning Literature* (*TALL*), and a founder of the Children's Literature Association. This essay provides an enlightening look at how readers interact with literature and how *Novels for Students* can help teachers show students how to enrich their own reading experiences.

A Cumulative Author/Title Index lists the authors and titles covered in each volume of the *NfS* series.

A Cumulative Nationality/Ethnicity Index breaks down the authors and titles covered in each volume of the *NfS* series by nationality and ethnicity.

A Subject/Theme Index, specific to each volume, provides easy reference for users who may be studying a particular subject or theme rather than a single work. Significant subjects from events to broad themes are included, and the entries pointing to the specific theme discussions in each entry are indicated in **boldface.**

Each entry may have several illustrations, including photos of the author, stills from film adaptations, maps, and/or photos of key historical events, if available.

Citing Novels for Students

When writing papers, students who quote directly from any volume of *Novels for Students* may use the following general forms. These examples are based on MLA style; teachers may request that students adhere to a different style, so the following examples may be adapted as needed.

When citing text from *NfS* that is not attributed to a particular author (i.e., the Themes, Style, Historical Context sections, etc.), the following format should be used in the bibliography section:

"*Night*." *Novels for Students*. Ed. Marie Rose Napierkowski. Vol. 4. Detroit: Gale, 1998. 234–35.

When quoting the specially commissioned essay from *NfS* (usually the first piece under the "Criticism" subhead), the following format should be used:

Miller, Tyrus. Critical Essay on *Winesburg, Ohio*. *Novels for Students*. Ed. Marie Rose Napierkowski. Vol. 4. Detroit: Gale, 1998. 335–39.

When quoting a journal or newspaper essay that is reprinted in a volume of *NfS*, the following form may be used:

Malak, Amin. "Margaret Atwood's *The Handmaid's Tale* and the Dystopian Tradition," *Canadian Literature* No. 112 (Spring, 1987), 9–16; excerpted and reprinted in *Novels for Students*, Vol. 4, ed. Marie Rose Napierkowski (Detroit: Gale, 1998), pp. 133–36.

When quoting material reprinted from a book that appears in a volume of *NfS*, the following form may be used:

Adams, Timothy Dow. "Richard Wright: Wearing the Mask," in *Telling Lies in Modern American Autobiography* (University of North Carolina Press, 1990), 69–83; excerpted and reprinted in *Novels for Students*, Vol. 1, ed. Diane Telgen (Detroit: Gale, 1997), pp. 59–61.

We Welcome Your Suggestions

The editor of *Novels for Students* welcomes your comments and ideas. Readers who wish to suggest novels to appear in future volumes, or who have other suggestions, are cordially invited to contact the editor. You may contact the editor via e-mail at: **ForStudentsEditors@thomson.com.** Or write to the editor at:

Editor, *Novels for Students*
Gale
27500 Drake Road
Farmington Hills, MI 48331–3535

Literary Chronology

1802: Alexandre Dumas is born on July 24 in Villers-Cotterts in France.

1840: Thomas Hardy is born on June 2 in Higher Bockhampton, Dorset, England.

1843: Henry James is born on April 15 in New York City, U.S.A.

1844–1845: Alexandre Dumas's *The Count of Monte Cristo* is published.

1870: Alexandre Dumas dies of a stroke on December 5 at Puys, near Dieppe, in France.

1873: Willa Cather is born on December 7 in Back Creek Valley, Virginia, U.S.A.

1874: Thomas Hardy's *Far from the Madding Crowd* is published.

1876: Jack London is born on January 12 in San Francisco, California, U.S.A.

1881: Henry James's *The Portrait of a Lady* is published.

1885: Sinclair Lewis is born on February 7, 1885 in the prairie town of Sauk Centre, Minnesota, U.S.A.

1890: Jean Rhys is born on August 24 in Roseau, Dominica.

1896: Francis Scott Key Fitzgerald (F. Scott Fitzgerald) is born on September 24 in St. Paul, Minnesota, U.S.A.

1902: John Steinbeck is born on February 27 in Salinas, California, U.S.A.

1905: Arthur Koestler is born on September 5 in Budapest, Hungary.

1906: Jack London's *White Fang* is published.

1916: Henry James dies on February 28 in London, England.

1916: Jack London dies of an overdose of morphine on November 22 in Glen Ellen, U.S.A.

1922: Sinclair Lewis's *Babbitt* is published.

1923: Willa Cather is awarded the Pulitzer Prize for fiction for *One of Ours*.

1926: Sinclair Lewis is the first writer ever to turn down a Pulitzer Prize.

1927: Willa Cather's *Death Comes for the Archbishop* is published.

1928: Thomas Hardy dies on January 11.

1930: Sinclair Lewis is awarded the Nobel Prize for literature.

1934: F. Scott Fitzgerald's *Tender Is the Night* is published.

1939: Margaret Atwood is born on November 18 in Ottawa, Ontario, Canada.

1940: John Steinbeck is awarded the Pulitzer Prize for his novel *The Grapes of Wrath*.

1940: Arthur Koestler's *Darkness at Noon* is published.

1940: F. Scott Fitzgerald dies of a sudden heart attack on December 21.

1947: Willa Cather dies from a cerebral hemorrhage on April 24.

1951: Sinclair Lewis dies of heart troubles on January 10.

1952: John Steinbeck's *East of Eden* is published.

1957: Arthur Golden is born in Chattanooga, Tennessee.

1962: John Steinbeck receives the Nobel Prize in literature.

1966: Jean Rhys's *Wide Sargasso Sea* is published.

1968: John Steinbeck dies of a sudden heart attack on December 20 in New York City.

1979: Jean Rhys dies on May 14 in Exeter.

1983: Arthur Koestler dies in a joint suicide pact with his wife on March 3 in London, England.

1992: Lilian Lee's *Farewell My Concubine* is published.

1996: Margaret Atwood's *Alias Grace* is published.

1997: Arthur Golden's *Memoirs of a Geisha* is published.

Acknowledgments

The editors wish to thank the copyright holders of the excerpted criticism included in this volume and the permissions managers of many book and magazine publishing companies for assisting us in securing reproduction rights. We are also grateful to the staffs of the Detroit Public Library, the Library of Congress, the University of Detroit Mercy Library, Wayne State University Purdy/Kresge Library Complex, and the University of Michigan Libraries for making their resources available to us. Following is a list of the copyright holders who have granted us permission to reproduce material in this volume of *Novels for Students (NfS)*. Every effort has been made to trace copyright, but if omissions have been made, please let us know.

COPYRIGHTED MATERIALS IN *NfS*, VOLUME 19, WERE REPRODUCED FROM THE FOLLOWING PERIODICALS:

American Studies, v. 34, fall, 1993 for "Babitt as Veblenian Critique of Manliness" by Clare Virginia Eby. Copyright © 1993 by the Mid-American Studies Association. Reproduced by permission of the publisher and the author.—*Bronte Society Transactions*, v. 21, 1996. Copyright © 1996 by The Bronte Parsonage Museum. Reproduced by permission.—*Cather Studies*, v. 4, 1999. Copyright © 1999 by The University of Nebraska Press. Reproduced by permission.—*Christianity and Literature*, v. 52, spring, 2003. Copyright 2003 by Conference on Christianity and Literature. Reproduced by permission.—*Classical and Modern Literature: A Quarterly*, v. 8, winter, 1988 for "Classical Allusion in *The Count of Monte Cristo*" by Emily A. McDermott. Copyright © 1988 by *CML*, Inc. Reproduced by permission of the author.—*Critique: Studies in Modern Fiction*, v. 28, summer, 1987. Copyright © 1987 by Helen Dwight Reid Educational Foundation. Reproduced with permission of the Helen Dwight Reid Educational Foundation, published by Heldref Publications, 1319 18th Street, NW, Washington, DC 20036-1802.—*Henry James Review*, v. 22, winter, 2001. © 2001 The Johns Hopkins University Press. Reproduced by permission.—*Journal of Popular Culture*, v. 33, fall, 1999. Copyright © 1999 by Blackwell Publishers Ltd. Reproduced by permission of Blackwell Publishers.—*Modern Age*, v. 29, fall, 1985. Copyright © 1985 by *Modern Age*. Reproduced by permission.—*Partisan Review*, v. 67, summer, 2000 for "Sex and Race in *Wide Sargasso Sea*" by Elizabeth Dalton. Copyright © 2000 by *Partisan Review*. Reproduced by permission of the author.—*Religion and the Arts*, v. 3, March, 1999. Copyright © 1999 by Koninkltjke Brill NV. Leiden. Reproduced by permission.—*Steinbeck Quarterly*, v. 14, no. 1–2, winter/spring, 1981 for "Alienation in *East of Eden*: 'The Chart of the Soul'" by Barbara McDaniel; v. 26, no. 3–4, summer/fall, 1993 for "Steinbeck's Exploration of Good and Evil: Structural and Thematic Unity in *East of Eden*" by Barbara A. Heavilin. Copyright 1981, 1993 by *Steinbeck Quarterly*. Both reproduced by permission of the copyright owner and the respective authors.—*Texas Studies in Literature and*

Language, v. 25, 1983 for "*Tender Is the Night* as a Tragic Action" by Robert Merrill. Reproduced by permission of the publisher and the author.—*Twentieth Century Literature*, v. 42, fall, 1996. Copyright 1996 by Hofstra University Press. Reproduced by permission.—*The World & I*, v. 12, February 1, 1997. Copyright © 1997 by News World Communications, Inc. Reproduced by permission.—*World Literature Today*, v. 73, April 15, 1999. Copyright 1999 by the University of Oklahoma Press. Reproduced by permission of the publisher.

COPYRIGHTED MATERIALS IN *NfS*, VOLUME 19, WERE REPRODUCED FROM THE FOLLOWING BOOKS:

Carpenter, Richard. From "Fiction: The Major Chord," in ***Thomas Hardy***. Twayne Publishers, 1964. Copyright © 1964 by Twayne Publishers, Inc. Reproduced by permission of the Gale Group.—Etheridge, Charles L., Jr. From "Changing Attitudes toward Steinbeck's Naturalism and the Changing Reputation of *East of Eden*: A Survey of Criticism since 1974," in ***The Steinbeck Question: New Essays in Criticism***. Edited by Donald R. Noble. The Whitston Publishing Company, 1993. Copyright © 1993 by Donald R. Noble. Reproduced by permission of the author.—Morrell, Roy. From "*Far from the Madding Crowd* as an Introduction to Hardy's Novels," in ***Critical Essays on Thomas Hardy: The Novels***. Edited by Dale Kramer, with the assistance of Nancy Marck. G. K. Hall, 1990. Copyright © 1990. Reproduced by permission of the Gale Group.

PHOTOGRAPHS AND ILLUSTRATIONS APPEARING IN *NfS*, VOLUME 19, WERE RECEIVED FROM THE FOLLOWING SOURCES:

Archbishop Jean Baptiste Lamy, statue located in Santa Fe, New Mexico, photograph. Copyright © Royalty-Free/Corbis. Reproduced by permission.—Atwood, Margaret, 2001, photograph. Copyright © Christopher Felver/Corbis. Reproduced by permission.—Cathedral of Saint Francis, photograph. Copyright © Corbis. Reproduced by permission.—Cather, Willa, photograph. AP/Wide World Photos. Reproduced by permission.—Chevaliers de Fortune prospector's camp, where tens of thousands of hopeful people began the wary trek to the gold fields of the Yukon in Canada, photograph. Hulton/Archive/Getty Images. Reproduced by permission.—Dominica, illustration. The Library of Congress.—Dumas, Alexandre, c. 1850, photograph. Hulton/Archive/Getty Images. Reproduced by permission.—Edmond Dantès and the

Abbé Faria from *The Count of Monte Cristo*, illustration by Alexandre Dumas. Hulton/Archive/Getty Images. Reproduced by permission.—Fitzgerald, F. Scott, photograph. The Library of Congress.—Fitzgerald, F. Scott, with wife Zelda, c. 1921, photograph. Hulton/Archive/Getty Images. Reproduced by permission.—Geisha girls being instructed by their teacher, c. 1955, photograph. Hulton/Archive/Getty Images. Reproduced by permission.—Geisha girls entertaining a group of men, photograph. Hulton/Archive/Getty Images. Reproduced by permission.—Golden, Arthur, c. 1999, photograph. AP/Wide World Photos. Reproduced by permission.—Hardy, Thomas, photograph. Corbis-Bettmann. Reproduced by permission.—James, Henry, photograph. The Library of Congress.—Koestler, Arthur, photograph. Barnabas Bosshart/Corbis. Reproduced by permission.—Lewis, Sinclair, 1929, photograph. AP/Wide World Photos. Reproduced by permission.—London, Jack, photograph. The Library of Congress.—Prisoners laboring outside the Kingston penitentiary, located in Toronto, Canada, 19th century illustration, photograph. The Library and Archives of Canada. Reproduced by permission.—Rhys, Jean, photograph by Jerry Bauer. © Jerry Bauer. Reproduced by permission.—Salinas Valley, California, photograph. The Library of Congress.—Scene from the film version of Alexandre Dumas's *The Count of Monte Cristo*, starring Richard Chamberlain, directed by David Greene, 1974, photograph. Norman Rosemont Productions/The Kobal Collection. Reproduced by permission.—Scene from the film version of F. Scott Fitzgerald's *Tender is the Night*, starring Jason Robards and Joan Fontaine, directed by Henry King, 1961, photograph. 20th Century Fox/The Kobal Collection. Reproduced by permission.—Scene from the film version of Henry James's *The Portrait of a Lady*, starring Nicole Kidman, directed by Jane Campion, photograph. The Kobal Collection. Reproduced by permission.—Scene from the film version of Jack London's *White Fang*, starring Ethan Hawke, directed by Randal Kleiser, photograph. Walt Disney/The Kobal Collection. Reproduced by permission.—Scene from the film version of Jean Rhys's *Wide Sargasso Sea*, starring Nathaniel Parker, 1993, photograph. New Line/Laughing Kookaburra/The Kobal Collection/Wright, Kimberly. Reproduced by permission.—Scene from the film version of John Steinbeck's *East of Eden*, starring Julie Harris, Richard Davalos, and James Dean, photograph. Warner Bros/The Kobal Collection. Reproduced by permission.—Scene from the film version of Lillian Lee's

Farewell My Concubine, starring Leslie Cheung, directed by Kaige Chen, photograph. Tomson Films/China Film/Beijing/The Kobal Collection. Reproduced by permission.—Scene from the film version of Thomas Hardy's *Far from the Madding Crowd*, starring Julie Christie and Terence Stamp, directed by John Schlesinger, 1967, photograph. Vic/Appia/The Kobal Collection. Reproduced by permission.—Steinbeck, John, photograph. The Library of Congress.—Trotsky, Leon, photograph.—Workers at a recreation center in Wuhan (Hankow) watch a free open-air play, photograph. Hulton/Archive/Getty Images. Reproduced by permission.

Contributors

Bryan Aubrey: Aubrey holds a Ph.D. in English and has published many articles on nineteenth-century literature. Entries on *The Count of Monte Cristo* and *East of Eden*. Original essays on *The Count of Monte Cristo* and *East of Eden*.

Jennifer Bussey: Bussey holds a master's degree in interdisciplinary studies and a bachelor's degree in English literature, and is an independent writer specializing in literature. Entries on *Death Comes to the Archbishop* and *Memoirs of a Geisha*. Original essay on *Death Comes to the Archbishop*.

Kate Covintree: Covintree is a graduate student and expository writing instructor at Emerson College. Original essay on *Memoirs of a Geisha*.

Curt Guyette: Guyette received a bachelor's degree in English writing from the University of Pittsburgh and is a longtime journalist. Original essay on *Farewell My Concubine*.

Joyce Hart: Hart is a freelance writer and author of several books. Entries on *Alias Grace* and *Wide Sargasso Sea*. Original essays on *Alias Grace* and *Wide Sargasso Sea*.

David Kelly: Kelly is an instructor of creative writing and literature. Entry on *Far from the Madding Crowd*. Original essay on *Far from the Madding Crowd*.

Candyce Norvell: Norvell is an independent educational writer who specializes in English and literature. Entries on *The Portrait of a Lady* and *White Fang*. Original essays on *The Portrait of a Lady* and *White Fang*.

Ryan D. Poquette: Poquette has a bachelor's degree in English and specializes in writing about literature. Entry on *Farewell My Concubine*. Original essay on *Farewell My Concubine*.

Scott Trudell: Trudell is a freelance writer with a bachelor's degree in English literature. Entries on *Babbitt* and *Darkness at Noon*. Original essays on *Babbitt* and *Darkness at Noon*.

Mark White: White is the publisher of the Seattle-based Scala House Press. Entry on *Tender Is the Night*. Original essay on *Tender Is the Night*.

Alias Grace

Margaret Atwood

1996

In the novel *Alias Grace*, author Margaret Atwood retells the story of Grace Marks, a real nineteenth-century Canadian woman who was accused of, and spent thirty years in jail for, the murder of two people. These murders were the most sensationalized story of the mid-1800s, and accounts of the trial and aspects of Marks's life were well publicized. Atwood was first attracted to this story through the works of so-called Canadian journalist Susanna Moodie, who wrote about a wildly crazy Grace Marks. Atwood admits that at first she believed Moodie's recounting of the circumstances that surrounded this famous murderess. In fact, Atwood wrote a collection of poems called *The Journals of Susanna Moodie* and also a television script based on Moodie's version of Grace Marks's life. Atwood's interest in Marks waned for several years, but when it resurfaced, she dug deeper into the story. That was when she discovered numerous discrepancies in Moodie's work and decided to write her own version of Marks's story.

In real life, Grace Marks, a sixteen-year-old Irish immigrant, was sentenced to life imprisonment for her role (which was never fully defined) in the murder of her employer Thomas Kinnear and his housekeeper Nancy Montgomery. Kinnear and Montgomery were having an affair, and many people have speculated that Marks, who was recently brought into the Kinnear household as a servant, was jealous. Montgomery, after all, was a maid, not the mistress of the house, and Marks resented Montgomery's airs of superiority. At least, that

Margaret Atwood

is one version of the story. Marks claimed various interpretations of her involvement in the murders, including one in which she states that she could not remember what happened on the day of the murders and another in which she claims to have been temporarily possessed by a dead girl-friend of hers. *Alias Grace* does not solve all the puzzles of this mystery, but it does present a patch-work story, details of which come from a variety of real sources as well as from Atwood's imagination, thus leaving readers to come to their own conclusions.

Alias Grace, Atwood's ninth novel, became a bestseller in North America, Europe, and in other countries around the world. The book helped win Atwood several literary prizes including the Premio Mondello, *Salon Magazine*'s best fiction of 1997, the Norwegian Order of Literary Merit, the Giller Prize, and the Canadian Booksellers Association's Author of the Year award.

Author Biography

Margaret Atwood is often referred to as Canada's greatest living writer. She was born on November 18, 1939, in Ottawa, Ontario. She wrote her first story when she was six. Atwood's father, Carl Edmund Atwood, is an entomologist and her mother, Margaret Dorothy Killam Atwood, is a di-etician. In 1945, her family moved to Toronto, where she graduated from high school and after-ward attended Victoria College. While there, she studied under Northrop Frye, another famous Canadian author and literary critic, and the poet Jay MacPherson. Upon graduating from college, Atwood won the first of many literary prizes. The E. J. Pratt Medal was awarded to her for her self-published book of poems, *Double Persephone*. She then went to the United States, where she earned her master's degree at Harvard.

In 1966, Atwood won another prestigious honor, The Governor General's Award, for yet another collection of poetry, *The Circle Game*. In 1967, Atwood married Jim Polk; they divorced in 1977. Atwood's first novel, *The Edible Woman*, was published in 1969. By the 1970s, Atwood's published works secured her a position as one of Canada's rising stars in both poetry and fiction.

To date, Atwood has written twelve books of poetry, four children's stories, four nonfiction books, and ten novels. *Alias Grace* was her ninth novel. Atwood has also written scripts for televi-sion and has edited several collections promoting Canadian writers. Many of her works have been translated into foreign languages and published in other countries, where she enjoys a wide readership. Two of her novels, *Surfacing* and *The Handmaid's Tale,* have been made into movies.

Atwood's ability to win awards began early in her career and has not diminished throughout her career. One of the most coveted was the Booker Prize, which she won for *Blind Assassin* in 2000.

Besides her writing and editing skills, Atwood has also taught at numerous universities: York University in Toronto, New York University, and the University of Alabama–Tuscaloosa. Atwood is also a rather humorous cartoonist, especially when based on the experience she has gathered while promoting her works on book tours. (See her website.) Atwood is also prone to travel all over the world, giving lectures on literary themes or on her experiences as a writer. She is active in several organizations, such as Amnesty International.

Atwood is married to Graeme Gibson, another Canadian writer. They have three grown children. In 2004, Atwood was living in Toronto.

Plot Summary

Chapter 1

Alias Grace begins with a recurrent dream that Grace Marks has. Grace narrates this chapter and states that it is 1851, she is twenty-four years old, and is in prison. She is a model prisoner, she claims, but it is difficult. The chapter ends with the conclusion of Grace's dream.

Chapter 2

A clip from the *Toronto Mirror* from November 23, 1843 and a statement from the *Punishment Book* from the Kingston Penitentiary start Chapter 2. The remaining text is a long poem written about Grace Marks and James McDermott. McDermott was hanged for the murders. Grace went to prison.

Chapter 3

Grace works at the governor of the penitentiary's home. She describes the governor's family. She mentions the scrapbook in which the governor's wife keeps stories of criminals. Grace reads the accounts of herself and says most of them are lies. Grace mentions her friend Mary Whitney. When a doctor enters the scene, Grace screams. She is afraid of him, but she does not tell the reader why.

Grace faints and is awakened and dragged back to the prison, still screaming. Later she describes her cell. She briefly relates her previous experiences at the "Asylum." It was in the asylum, Grace contends, that she stopped sharing her thoughts. "At last I stopped talking altogether, except very civilly. . . ." And because of this, Grace is allowed to go back to the penitentiary.

Dr. Simon Jordan enters Grace's cell and tries to quell her fears by stating he is not "the usual kind of doctor." Grace protects herself, carefully selecting her words. Dr. Jordan brings Grace an apple. When he asks, in his analytical way, what the apple makes Grace think of, Grace plays stupid, something her lawyer had told her would save her life. Jordan tries to gain her confidence. He tells her he wants to talk to her, and her answers will not cause her any harm.

Chapter 4

Three letters begin this chapter: one from a doctor friend of Jordan's explaining what Jordan is trying to do in talking to Grace; one from Jordan's mother; and the final one from Jordan to a friend, further explaining his project with Grace.

The narration then switches to third-person, describing portions of Jordan's life. Jordan is having

Media Adaptations

- A movie of *Alias Grace* is in the making and is scheduled to star Cate Blanchett. The movie will be directed by Dominic Savage, an award-winning young British talent. Casting for the movie is expected to be completed by the end of 2003.

- For more information on Atwood's life and career, connect to the Margaret Atwood Society's world wide web page at http://www.cariboo.bc.ca/atwood or to Atwood's personal web page at http://www.owtoad.com where you will find some of her speeches and cartoons.

second thoughts about his research on Grace. There follows a description of Jordan's room in a boarding house, as well as an account of a servant woman who unnerves Jordan.

The narration returns to Grace, who talks about daily routines in prison. Jordan visits Grace at the governor's house. Grace does not say much during their first meetings. To help begin a conversation, Jordan talks about himself. This approach seems to work as Grace opens up.

The third-person narration then returns as Jordan meets Reverend Verringer, who is fighting for Grace's release but needs someone of Jordan's stature to help. Jordan believes that the reverend might be in love with Grace. Jordan is invited to attend the Tuesday Discussion Circle. Miss Lydia, the governor's daughter, flirts with Jordan before the meeting begins. The chapter ends with Jordan trying again to get Grace to talk.

Chapter 5

Grace narrates. Jordan asks what she dreamt about the night before. Grace relates her dream to the reader but tells Jordan that she does not remember. Jordan asks about her confession, which she says was only what her lawyer told her to say. Then Grace tells Jordan about her life in Ireland and her trip to Canada. There were nine children in her family. Grace was the third oldest. Her mother died after giving birth on the voyage to

Canada. Her father was worthless, but found the children a cheap room at the back of Mrs. Burt's house. Mrs. Burt introduces Grace to Mrs. Honey, the housekeeper of Mrs. Alderman Parkinson. Grace lands her first job. The chapter ends with a letter Jordan writes to a friend, further relating his dealings with Grace.

Chapter 6

Mrs. Humphreys, Dr. Jordan's landlady, brings Jordan his breakfast and faints. Dora, the housekeeper, has left because Mrs. Humphreys could not pay her. Mrs. Humphreys's husband has abandoned her. Jordan buys food and cooks for her. He also gives her an advance on the rent.

Grace takes up the narration with Jordan visiting her again. She tells of her working at Mrs. Parkinson's and her relationship with Mary Whitney. Mary teaches Grace how to be a good housekeeper and offers practical wisdom about life. Jeremiah the Peddler, who befriends Grace, is introduced. At Christmastime, Mrs. Parkinson's son, Mr. George, falls sick and does not return to college. During the winter, Grace suspects that Mr. George and Mary are having an affair. Mary gets pregnant, and when Mr. George does not follow through on his marriage proposal, Mary has an abortion and dies.

Chapter 7

Dr. Jordan and Reverend Verringer discuss Susanne Moodie's account of Grace. Verringer concludes that Moodie tends to "[e]mbroider" her stories.

Grace continues. She leaves Mrs. Parkinson's and wanders from one job to another until she meets Nancy Montgomery, who offers Grace a job at Mr. Thomas Kinnear's, where Nancy is the housekeeper. Grace arrives at Kinnear's and describes the house and land. She meets James McDermott and Jamie Walsh. After a short period of time, Grace is disappointed with Nancy's treatment of her. Nancy is not as friendly as Grace had hoped and acts as if she is better than Grace. McDermott coarsely tries to seduce Grace.

Chapter 8

The next day, Grace tells Jordan that Nancy asks Grace to kill a chicken, which Grace cannot do. So Jamie Walsh kills the hen for her. Nancy invites Grace to go to church with her. At the church, Grace notices how coldly they are greeted. A few days later, Nancy, tired of McDermott's attitude, gives him his notice to leave. Later, McDermott tells Grace that Nancy is sleeping with Mr. Kinnear.

McDermott tells Grace that Kinnear and Nancy "deserved to be knocked on the head and thrown down into the cellar. . . ." Jordan interrupts Grace's narration and tells her that in his confession, McDermott stated that Grace had been the one to put him up to the murders. Grace denies this. She returns to her story and tells about spending her birthday afternoon with Jamie, who said he wanted to marry her. Jeremiah the Peddler shows up a few days later and suggests that Grace leave and come with him.

Tension grows between Grace and Nancy Montgomery. Nancy is showing signs of pregnancy and is jealous of Kinnear's attention to Grace. Grace overhears Nancy telling Kinnear that she might get rid of Grace.

Chapter 9

The story switches back to Dr. Jordan. He is becoming disoriented and unorganized. Mrs. Humphreys hangs around his room too much. Jordan is distracted when he goes to see Grace. One night, after he has gone to bed, Mrs. Humphreys comes to his room in her nightgown and gets into his bed.

Grace is concerned about coming to the end of her story, the actual murders. She tells herself she cannot remember all the details. She wonders what she should tell Dr. Jordan.

Dr. Jerome Dupont appears and asks Dr. Jordan if he might hypnotize Grace. When Grace sees Dr. Dupont, she realizes it is Jeremiah the Peddler.

Later, Dr. Jordan asks Grace about her relationship with Kinnear. Jordan drops the subject and asks for more details about the day of the murders. Grace says Nancy told her to leave. James McDermott tells Grace he is going to kill Thomas Kinnear and Nancy Montgomery. Grace thinks he is just bragging. She did not warn Nancy because Nancy would not believe her. Grace relates the same dream that was recounted at the beginning of the novel. She sees Nancy with blood on her face.

James McDermott goes to Nancy's room and kills her. McDermott threatens to harm Grace if she tells Mr. Kinnear, who has just come home. Later, when McDermott tells Grace to shoot Kinnear, she cannot. So McDermott does. Grace sees him throw Kinnear's body into the cellar. Jordan presses for more details, but Grace says she cannot remember.

Chapter 10

Grace faints when McDermott threatens her with a gun. She awakens in her bed, and McDermott is telling her she must keep her part of the bargain, implying she was to have sex with him. She fears for her life and keeps putting him off, hoping that will give her time to figure things out. She talks him into leaving the house. McDermott agrees, and they go to Toronto. They leave the next day by ferry. Grace plans to leave McDermott the following morning, but the two of them are caught.

Chapter 11

Dr. Jordan travels to Toronto to meet with Grace's lawyer and to visit the Kinnear house. In his absence, Grace continues her story to herself, relating the trial. Jordan reflects on the cumbersome relationship he has entered into with Mrs. Humphreys.

Chapter 12

Kenneth MacKenzie, Grace's lawyer, proclaims that Grace is "guilty as sin." After visiting the Kinnear house, the graves of Kinnear, Nancy, and Mary Whitney, Jordan whispers "[m]urderess, murderess" as he thinks about Grace on his trip home.

Chapter 13

Dr. Dupont hypnotizes Grace. Dr. Jordan asks if she had sex with James McDermott. Grace lashes out at him, accusing Jordan of desiring her. Grace says McDermott and Kinnear would do anything for her. When asked if she killed Nancy Montgomery, Grace replies, "The kerchief killed her. Hands held it." When the governor's wife calls Grace by name, Grace replies, "I am not Grace! Grace knew nothing about it!" Eventually the so-called spirit emanating from Grace says it is Mary Whitney. When Grace is brought out of her trance, she remembers nothing.

Jordan returns home, feeling oppressed about his involvement in Grace's case. He cannot continue. He also must break off his relationship with Mrs. Humphreys. He decides to leave town and return to Europe.

Chapter 14

A series of letters follows. Mrs. Humphreys writes to Dr. Jordan's mother. Dr. Jordan's mother responds, telling Mrs. Humphreys to leave her son alone. Grace writes to Jeremiah the Peddlar, also known as Dr. Jerome Dupont, who is now a part of a circus.

Chapter 15

Grace is pardoned. She is taken to New York where Jamie Walsh is waiting for her. He marries her.

Characters

Agnes

Agnes is the chambermaid at the Parkinson's home. She helps Grace after Mary dies. She cleans the room and defends Grace when Mrs. Honey and Mrs. Parkinson accuse her of not telling the truth about Mary.

Dr. Bannerling

Dr. Bannerling is the director of the asylum. He believes Grace pretends to be mentally incapacitated and that Grace is guilty of murder. He thwarts any attempt made to release her from prison.

Mrs. Burt

Mrs. Burt rents a cheap room at the back of her house to Grace's family when they first arrive in Toronto. She befriends Grace's father at first because she feels sorry for him. However, when she finds out that he wastes his day drinking instead of working, she grows tired of him. When Grace's father insists that Grace find a job, Mrs. Burt introduces her to Mrs. Parkinson's housekeeper.

Dr. Jerome Dupont

Dr. Jerome Dupont is a charlatan. He takes on several different disguises. He first appears in the story as Jeremiah the Peddler. He is somewhat infatuated with Grace but not to the point of getting married. He asks Grace to leave the Kinnear place and travel with him. He returns later as Dr. Jerome Dupont, a hypnotist. He tells Grace not to give him away. Then he puts her into a trance. Later, Grace sees a poster advertising a circus and recognizes his face.

Governor's Wife

The governor's wife employs Grace as a servant. She is fascinated with crime and criminals and keeps a scrapbook of newspaper clippings of crimes. She hosts discussion club meetings, bringing together people who support Grace's release. She does not fully trust Grace, however.

Mrs. Honey

Mrs. Honey is the head servant at Mrs. Parkinson's house. She is anything but sweet, Grace says. She is strict and quick to blame Grace.

Mrs. Rachel Humphreys

Rachel Humphreys rents out a room to Dr. Jordan. When her husband leaves her, Rachel is distraught. Jordan befriends her, paying for her food and consoling her. Later, Rachel slips into Jordan's bed and begins a more personal relationship with him. When Jordan leaves her, she writes letters to Jordan's mother in search of him.

Jeremiah the Peddler
See Dr. Jerome Dupont

Dr. Simon Jordan

Jordan takes an interest in Grace's case several years after she has been imprisoned. He is involved in the early studies of psychiatry and wants to pry as many details from Grace's mind as he can, trying to determine if she is lying or truly suffers from amnesia. He is fascinated with her and her story. But when she is hypnotized and speaks in a voice that is vile and accusatory, he cannot accept that she is possessed by the spirit of Mary Whitney, as some of the other spectators believe. Jordan eventually leaves without coming to any substantial conclusions. Instead, he runs away from Grace, from his landlady with whom he was having an affair, and from his mother who wants him to marry. He returns to Europe, where he finds life less burdensome. At the end of the book, he returns home and is involved in the Civil War.

Mr. Thomas Kinnear

Thomas Kinnear is a well-to-do, although somewhat socially stymied gentleman who lives outside of Toronto. He is a bachelor and a well-known womanizer. For this reason, respectable women tend to shun him. He is also suspected of having ties with a revolutionary political group, therefore making many men wary of him. Kinnear lives with his housemaid, Nancy Montgomery, with whom he is having an affair. When Grace Marks comes to work for him, he flirts with her, arousing Montgomery's jealousy. Although he sleeps with Montgomery, and she eats at the dinner table with him, Kinnear often reminds her that she is only his maid. He is found dead in his cellar, the victim of bullet wounds. It is suggested that James McDermott killed him.

Miss Lydia

Miss Lydia is the older of two daughters of the governor. She has a crush on Dr. Jordan and openly flirts with him. Although Dr. Jordan is flattered and even slightly aroused, he does not pursue her.

Kenneth MacKenzie

MacKenzie is Grace's court appointed lawyer. According to Grace, MacKenzie told her to lie and to pretend to be stupid in order to save her life. Later, when Dr. Jordan visits him, MacKenzie says that in his honest opinion, Grace is "guilty as sin."

Grace Marks

Grace's story dominates this novel. Grace is the sixteen-year-old who is accused of the murders of her employer, Mr. Kinnear, and his housekeeper, Nancy. Grace narrates much of the story, sometimes allowing the readers into her private thoughts and exposing some of the contradictions in her story. She is in prison at the time of the story and relates much of what has happened to her through her talks with Dr. Jordan. She maintains a somewhat innocent manner, turning over any vile remarks she makes to her friend Mary Whitney. When she is hypnotized and suggests that she killed Nancy, she talks in a very different voice, which many people believe is Mary Whitney. Grace has been told by her lawyer to maintain the demeanor of stupidity in order to save her life. She also learns, while at the asylum, that if she truly opens up her thoughts to anyone, she is accused of being crazy. If she acts out in prison, she is punished. So she learns to keep everything to herself. She chooses her words very carefully. When she is in doubt about the truth of something, she claims she does not remember. She also reverts to dreamlike sequences, in which only vague images prevail. In the end, her story is so incomplete no one knows for sure if she is guilty. She does win her pardon, though, and marries the once-young boy, Jamie, who had a crush on her in his youth.

James McDermott

James is a stable boy at the Kinnear household. He is very hostile most of the time. He talks back to Nancy, and she grows tired of him. He is given his notice to leave, which angers him further. He decides to kill Kinnear and Nancy. He supposedly tries to bring Grace into the act and later forces her to leave with him. He is caught, found guilty, and hanged.

Nancy Montgomery

Nancy is the only housemaid in Thomas Kinnear's home. When she meets Grace she tells her that she is looking for extra help. Grace finds Nancy friendly and decides to take the offer. When Grace arrives at Kinnear's, however, she finds Nancy to be less welcoming than Grace had hoped. Nancy is often harsh and puts on airs as if she were the mistress of the house. Nancy dresses very well, eats dinner with Mr. Kinnear, and as Grace finds out later, also sleeps with Kinnear. When Kinnear travels to Toronto for a day or two, however, Nancy warms up to Grace and even asks Grace to sleep with her. As soon as Kinnear returns, though, Nancy once again dismisses Grace. When Nancy discovers Kinnear flirting with Grace, she decides to fire Grace. Nancy is discovered, later, in the cellar. She has been strangled and her throat has been cut. It is unclear whether James McDermott or Grace has killed her.

Mrs. Alderman Parkinson

Mrs. Alderman Parkinson is the mistress of the house where Grace lands her first job. The Parkinson family is very rich, and the house is very elegant, employing many servants. It is here that Grace meets Mary Whitney and Jeremiah the Peddler.

Mr. George Parkinson

George is the son of Mrs. Parkinson. He comes home from college for Christmas and gets sick. After the holidays, he is too weak to return to school. While at home, he becomes involved with Mary Whitney and gets her pregnant. Then he refuses to marry her.

Aunt Pauline

Pauline is the sister of Grace's mother. She lives in Ireland and often gives money and food to her sister. When Pauline becomes pregnant, her husband, Roy, tells her that she can no longer support her sister. So Pauline gathers enough money to send Grace's family to Toronto, where she believes they have a better chance.

Mrs. Quennell

Mrs. Quennell is a famous spiritualist of the time. She tries to explain the voice that emanates from Grace while Grace is hypnotized. She believes it is someone else talking through Grace.

Uncle Roy

Roy is Grace's uncle. He is very generous toward Grace's family until his wife becomes pregnant. Then he puts his foot down and says he can no longer afford to help them.

Reverend Verringer

Reverend Verringer heads the committee that is trying to free Grace. He enlists Dr. Jordan's help. He also brings together other supporters, including Dr. Jerome Dupont. After many years, Verringer is successful.

Jamie Walsh

Jamie is a year younger than Grace. He develops a strong crush on her when she comes to the Kinnear household. He tells her that he wants to marry her when he grows up. At her trial, however, Jamie says he was surprised at how Grace looked and acted when he saw her immediately after the murders. His testimony helps to convict her. Later, Jamie is instrumental in her release. He promises to marry and take care of her.

Mary Whitney

Mary is the same age as Grace, but she has more experience both in her job and in the world in general. She teaches Mary about life. The two of them are very close until Mary begins her affair with Mr. George. Mary gets pregnant and is jilted. She has an abortion and dies from it. The spirit of Mary stays with Grace, and under hypnotism, the supposed spirit speaks out.

Themes

Sexuality

The topic of sexuality permeates this novel. Grace, for instance, is accused of using the promise of sexual favors to persuade James McDermott to kill Thomas Kinnear and Nancy Montgomery. It is also highly suspected that Grace and Jamie Walsh had a sexual encounter in the orchard, when in fact their meeting was quite innocent, at least in Grace's recounting of the event. There are social repercussions toward Nancy Montgomery when she enters the public realm. Most villagers assume that Montgomery and Kinnear are sleeping together, and they shun her and Grace when the two women show up at church one Sunday. Montgomery, like Mary Whitney, more than likely, offers herself to Kinnear in hopes of elevating her position, hoping to obtain a marriage contract.

Mary Whitney, the young girl who befriends Grace, becomes involved in a sexual encounter with her employer's son. Mary hopes for marriage, but Mr. George is obviously in the relationship only for the sex. Mary is abandoned once she becomes pregnant and dies because of a botched abortion.

Grace, while in prison, must constantly fend off the sexual overtures of the guards who transport her from the penitentiary to the governor's house. And Mrs. Humphreys, Dr. Jordan's landlady, seeks the comfort of a sexual relationship with the doctor in

Topics For Further Study

- Atwood used the word "alias" in the title of this work for a specific reason. Re-read the novel and pull out the different ways in which Grace hides behind or uses an alias. Although using Mary Whitney is the most obvious of Grace's aliases, there are also more subtle ones. Write a paper on how Grace's use of aliases either helps or hinders her.

- Dr. Simon Jordan was attempting to psychoanalyze Grace, prompting her to delve into her subconscious by using objects that he believed might enliven their discussions. List all the objects, such as the apple and the radish, that Dr. Jordan used, and write a short essay on each, describing what kind of metaphors Dr. Jordan was trying to employ. For example, the apple is often associated with Eve and the Garden of Eden. What might Dr. Jordan have been trying to suggest by using each object?

- Grace shares several dreams with the readers throughout the story. One of them is often repeated. Find these dreams and write your interpretations of what they might represent. Do not worry about being factual. Let the ideas flow from your first impressions, much as you might try to figure out what your own dreams might mean.

- Investigate modern techniques of criminology. Then pretend you are the leading investigative detective of the murders of Thomas Kinnear and Nancy Montgomery. Write a report of your findings. Do not hesitate to make them up, but base them on real technology of the present time. Gather enough information to prove Grace Marks was either innocent or guilty.

- Spiritualism was very popular in the 1800s and early 1900s. Research this practice. What did it entail? Who were some of its greatest followers? What effects did it have on popular culture? Do you see any remnants of spiritualism in modern culture?

- Gather news accounts of sensational murders in modern times, such as the O. J. Simpson case. Atwood demonstrates how journalists of Grace Marks's day exaggerated many of the details. Do you think this still happens today? If so, how? Bring in various versions of a single event, demonstrating discrepancies in the stories.

---

order to ease the financial and matrimonial trouble that faces her. Dr. Jordan's problems with his own sexuality, whether he is in bed with Mrs. Humphreys, or fantasizing about Miss Lydia, the governor's daughter, or Grace, his patient, presents the male side of the story.

In many ways sexuality drives this story and its characters. It is suggested that sexuality might have been the underlying cause behind the murders. James McDermott lusts for Grace. Grace lusts for Kinnear. And it is their opposite attractions that lead to the murders, at least according to some accounts. Sex ultimately brings about the death of Mary Whitney. Dr. Jordan all but cracks under the pressure brought about by his sexual involvement and by his sexual fantasies. Those characters who only flirt with sexuality, such as Jeremiah the Peddler and Jamie Walsh, are spared.

Interestingly, according to Grace's interior dialogue, her sexual feelings are all but fully oppressed. Grace acts embarrassed and shocked at Dr. Jordan's intimation that McDermott had sex with her. She proclaims at one point that her sexual relationship with McDermott is all that any one cares to hear about. She is appalled by McDermott's attempts to have sex with her, and leaves one of her jobs because the master of the house makes attempts to have sex with her. When under hypnosis, although she claims to be Mary Whitney, Grace decries Dr. Jordan for his sexual fantasies about her. She is also completely dismayed when McDermott, Kinnear, and Montgomery accuse her of having sex with Jamie Walsh in the orchard.

Feminism and Pre-Feminism

Atwood recounts the details and circumstances of women in the nineteenth century. She portrays these women through the eyes of her own experiences in the twentieth century, eyes that are attuned to the history of discrimination against women. Atwood has the advantage of hindsight and an education in feminism—things that the women in her novel were unaware of. So either wittingly or unconsciously, Atwood emphasizes the imbalance that is inherent in the patriarchal society of this earlier period of time, relating the events of this story with a somewhat accusing tone.

Atwood constructs the women in this story, for the most part, as either privileged women with soft hands and many layers of petticoats or as working-class women with chafed skin and tired faces. Neither group is composed of fully realized women. The privileged class is tightly entrapped in corsets and are dependent on men. An example is Mrs. Humphreys, who is devastated by her husband's departure, not so much because she has lost the great love of her life but because she envisions herself being thrown out onto the street, unable to take care of herself. On the other hand, the working-class women, according to Atwood's portrayal, have three options in life. They work as servants all their lives; they marry and are taken care of by a man; or they become prostitutes.

Ironically it is the nineteenth-century concept of femininity that may have saved Grace from hanging and from completing her life sentence in jail. It was believed, during those times, that women were frail, moral, and incapable of vicious crimes such as murder. Even though circumstantial evidence pointed to Grace's involvement in the murders, she avoids the death sentence and eventually wins an early release from the penitentiary. Would this have been true if she had been a man? The answer seems to lie in the fate of her accomplice, James McDermott. There appears to have been little discussion as to whether or not he was guilty and should be hanged. There also is the strange relationship between Grace and Jamie Walsh. Walsh developed a crush on Grace, but later he testified against her in court. It was his evidence that finally pinned the murders on her. Atwood suggests that Walsh may have done this because he was jealous of Grace's supposed relationship with McDermott. However, in the end, Walsh is instrumental in gaining Grace's early release. He

promises to marry her, to support her, to protect her. Grace's femininity, or at least the nineteenth-century definition of her femininity—one in which she once again becomes incapable of hurting anyone—convinces Walsh that he has betrayed her and must now rescue her.

Style

Point of View

Alias Grace is told through a variety of points of view. These points of view alternate, giving the reader, for example, a more personal testimony as related by Grace Marks throughout most of the novel and then switching to a more distant observation offered by the third-person account of Dr. Simon Jordan's circumstances. It should be pointed out that Grace's first-person point of view is often unreliable. Although Grace sometimes admits that she is not being fully honest with Dr. Jordan, there are other times when it is not clear if she is even being honest with herself. Other points of view include replications of newspaper accounts of the murders of Thomas Kinnear and Nancy Montgomery and the subsequent trials of Grace and McDermott. There are also lyrics of popular ballads concerning the murders, accounts quoted from Susanna Moodie's journals, and from letters to and from Dr. Jordan and other correspondents. By providing this collection of points of view, Atwood lays out different interpretations of the events, demonstrating the confusion that surrounded the real court case and the inability of either proving or disproving Grace Marks's innocence or guilt.

Metaphor

The main metaphor employed in this novel is that of the quilt. Atwood names each of her chapters after a specific quilt pattern. Graphic depictions of the patterns are also offered, showing the reader that these designs, much like the testimony of Grace Marks, can be construed in a variety of ways. For example, when one looks at the patterns, the pieces of the quilt arrange themselves in different ways, depending on how the eyes align them. The names of the patterns offer clues on how to look at them. These names include Jagged Edge, Rocky Road, Secret Drawer, and Pandora's Box. The quilt names each suggest the tone of the chapter that is to follow. The use of the quilt metaphor is appropriate because Grace's skill in sewing is mentioned quite often throughout the story. Also, while Grace relates the events of her past to Dr. Jordan, her hands are often kept busy with piecing together the scraps of material to make the cover of a quilt. As she creates the quilt, so too does she create her story. Overall, the quilt metaphor refers to the piecing together of information that has been gathered from different sources, which offer many different interpretations.

Reality and Fiction

Atwood offers a combination of real events mixed with her own imagination in an attempt to create a complete story. Although no solid conclusions can be drawn at the end of her novel with regard to Grace Marks, the novel does present a story with a beginning, middle, and an end. In order to glue all the real events together, Atwood had to invent fictionalized characters, such as Dr. Jordan. Jordan helps to fill in some of the widest holes in the recorded real events by acting as a vehicle through which Grace can retell her version of the circumstances. Of course, Grace's interior dialogue is a creation of Atwood's imagination, which provides an attitude that is probable even though it might not be true. By mixing real news accounts, lyrics of real songs, and parts of real journals, Atwood adds authenticity to her fictional work. By mixing the author's imagination to the reality of trial and murders, Atwood provides her readers with a more rounded version of the Grace Marks story.

Historical Context

Toronto's Kingston Penitentiary

The Kingston Penitentiary, which opened in 1835 (eight years before Grace Marks was sentenced), was the first so-called modern prison to be built in Canada. It was to take on a different approach to incarceration. Instead of being a place solely dedicated to punishment, the official program was based on reform. Today, it remains one of the oldest prisons in continuous use in the entire world. Across the street from the main penitentiary is the Kingston Prison for Women, which opened in 1934. Prior to the opening of the Prison for Women, females were jailed in the main building but segregated from the male population. The penitentiary, with its massive gray limestone walls, has the appearance of an ancient and imposing fortress. It is located right on the waterfront of Lake Ontario; and in 1976, the sailing events of the Olympics were held right outside the building. The

Kingston Pen, as it is referred to, houses Canada's most dangerous and notorious criminals. A riot occurred in 1971, during which much of the Kingston Pen was destroyed. Today, the prison accommodates up to four hundred inmates, all housed in separate cells.

Susanna Moodie

Susanna Moodie was born in England in 1803. After she married, she moved with her husband, in 1832, to the wilderness in Upper Canada. Susanna had been well educated by her father, and she and her sisters were accomplished writers. One of Moodie's most famous books was published in 1852. She called it *Roughing It in the Bush: Or Life in Canada*. In the book, Moodie offered sketches of her life and the cultural shock she experienced in moving from a lively city life in England to the challenging existence she encountered in the woods of Canada. Moodie visited Kingston Penitentiary, which many people did in the nineteenth century as part of a tour, and she asked to meet Grace Marks, who was the most notorious prisoner at that time. Moodie then went home and wrote about Grace. Later Moodie toured the Toronto Lunatic Asylum and again found Grace there. Moodie recalled that Grace was screaming continually during her visits, which lead Moodie to describe Grace as a wildly crazy woman. Moodie died in 1885.

Toronto's Lunatic Asylum

Not until the 1800s was there made any distinction, in Canada, between criminals and people with mental problems. Up until that time, criminals, the insane, and those who were in debt were all imprisoned together. This changed in 1841, when the first asylum for the insane was built in Toronto. Of the group of insane, the criminally insane were the most difficult to house. They disrupted the order and discipline of the penitentiary and required continual observation in the asylum. Females deemed criminally insane were even more difficult to deal with, since at the time, women were considered the gentle sex, so the definition of a criminally insane woman was a hard concept for the general public to accept. Consequently, female criminals exhibiting traits of insanity were often taken back and forth between the penitentiary and the asylum as doctors and prison officials tried desperately to define who and what these women were. The women themselves sometimes took advantage of this quandary. The asylum was more comfortable than the penitentiary. In fact, the asylum was one of the first buildings in Toronto to have running water (hot and cold), steam heat, and ventilation. Therefore, many female criminals were accused of faking their mental illness in order to remain housed in the asylum.

Irish Immigration to Canada

By 1867, almost one-quarter of the entire population of Canada was Irish; and in the earlier part of the nineteenth century, most of the Irish immigrants were Protestant. One of the most influential causes of this immigration was the promise of land, which in Ireland had become a distant dream of many of its poor inhabitants. Between the years of 1829 to 1859, it is estimated that over 600,000 Irish landed at Grosse Île, the major clearing port of immigrants coming to Canada by sea. In 1855, according to British records, more than two million people left Ireland. Most of them emigrated to North America, either to Canada or the United States.

Journeys across the Atlantic were far from easy. Most ships were overcrowded, and most people were not prepared for the length, or the hardships, of the journey. Many did not realize they would have to supply most of their own food, so by the end of the journey, most people were malnourished. Many others died during the journey. By 1847, these ships, overflowing with poor immigrants, were disrespectfully referred to as Coffin Ships because of the number of deaths that occurred during the trip. Once landed on Grosse Île, all immigrants were quarantined, much as was done in the United States at Ellis Island. The facilities at Grosse Île, however, were not equipped to handle the huge numbers of people who were arriving, and in 1847, five thousand immigrants died of an outbreak of typhus. Most of these victims were Irish.

Critical Overview

Alias Grace was a bestselling novel not only in North America but in other countries as well. The mystery of Grace Marks's involvement in the murders that take place in the novel, as well as in real life, plus Atwood's deep research into nineteenth-century Canadian life are two alluring factors that draw readers to this book. Or as Susan H. Woodcock, writing for the *School Library Journal*, found: "Atwood may be playing a game with her readers but it is one in which many will willingly participate for the fun and mystery while learning about life in colonial Canada." Woodcock's attraction to this novel was based on Atwood's ability to create

compelling characters who differ a lot from one another and are well developed. Barbara Mujica, writing for *Americas* also enjoyed Atwood's ninth novel for the author's well developed characters, but also for Atwood's extensive research into nineteenth-century Canada. "She brings to life not only the enigmatic and fascinating Grace Marks, but also an entire period in Canada's history." Mujica also points out the theme of quilts, which Atwood used throughout the work. Grace Marks was noted for her fine sewing skills, particularly quilting. Atwood uses a different quilting pattern for the title of each of her chapters to reflect Marks's skills and to set a theme for that section of the story. "The novel is structured like a quilt," Mujica writes, "in which each piece contributes to the total image, yet often the image changes form, depending on the angle from which it is viewed."

Another way to look at the novel might be through the observations of Mona Knapp, who wrote a review of the book for *World Literature Today*. Knapp focuses on the psychological aspects of the novel. She writes: "The novel's form is an elaborate exercise in fragmentation." Rather than looking at the metaphor of the quilt, Knapp sees the novel as a representation of Grace's mind, which is also fragmented. The story, Knapp writes, "is unsettled, perhaps in an effort to reflect the fact that [Grace's] story, like her personality, will never be wholly known." Knapp also points out how the fictional character of Dr. Jordan, unlike a quilter, who takes random pieces and sews them together to make a unified cover, becomes "unraveled" by Grace. He becomes so involved in Grace's fragments that he himself becomes disassociated.

The quilting theme also appealed to Melinda Bargreen, who reviewed the novel for the *Seattle Times*. However, Bargreen found, "[t]he strongest aspect of the novel is Atwood's use of detail, recalling vividly the scents of smoke and laundry, the shapes and textures of clothing, the state of medicine and fledgling psychology. . . ." For Mel Gussow, writing for the *New York Times*, it was Atwood's keen observation of her characters' psychology that drew him into the story. "With dry, ironic wit, a poetic sensibility and more than a hint of the Gothic, [Atwood] has uncompromisingly observed the psychology of the people in her society."

Most critics have praised Atwood for not trying to solve this mystery that will never be solved. As John Skow for *Time* stated it: "[Atwood] is scrupulous in not pretending to know the whole

Nineteenth-century illustration depicting prison laborers outside the Kingston Penitentiary, located in Toronto, Canada

truth of Grace Marks." The result, Skow concluded, is that "[t]he formidable and sometimes forbidding Margaret Atwood has turned a notorious Canadian murder case from the mid-nineteenth century into a shadowy, fascinating novel."

Criticism

Joyce Hart

Hart is a freelance writer and author of several books. In this essay, Hart examines Atwood's character, Grace Marks, as a symbol of the Victorian definition of woman.

Grace Marks, in Margaret Atwood's *Alias Grace*, is an extremely complex creature. Her complexities, however, are intensified for many reasons. Some of her personal traits are distorted because they are recorded by unreliable sources, such as newspapers accounts, popular ballads, and people who were swayed by ulterior motives. But there are other reasons for Grace's complexities. She was living at a time when women were defined by Victorian notions of femininity, which ranged from some of the highest ideals to some of the worst

evils. Women were often considered the receptacles of morality at the same time as they were seen as seducers and manipulators. *Alias Grace* is about a young woman who committed murder, but it is also about the conflicts that women, influenced by the Victorian Age, suffered.

The identity of Grace Marks is confusing because it is complicated by her either trying to protect her innocence or trying to hide her guilt. But Atwood's story about Grace goes beyond the question of whether Grace committed murder. And it goes beyond the question of whether she was confused or mad. The main issue of the novel focuses on Grace, but true to Atwood's feminist pursuit, the search for Grace's true identity is symbolically the search that all women living in a suppressed environment are involved in—the search for self. Although Grace embodies this search in Atwood's novel, the real question seems to be: Who was the Victorian Woman? Was she the frail, lesser member of the two sexes? Or was she an equal in stamina and intelligence? Was she the epitome of virtue? Was she violent and capable of vicious crimes? Or, did she encompass all of these traits, and more? To gain a better glimpse into the author's feminist attitude, readers have only to take a deeper look at Atwood's protagonist.

In the opening of *Alias Grace*, Grace describes herself as a woman who abides by the rules of her Victorian society. "I tuck my head down while I walk," she declares, as befits her station in life. She is a maid, symbolically declared by her "chapped" hands. She bows her head in humility, reflecting her lower status, both economic and that determined by her sex. And she walks in silence "inside the square made by the high stone walls." She is the essence of conformity. "These shoes fit me," she states, "better than any I've ever had before." She is, at the time of this statement, a prisoner of the state. But she is also, as were most women of her time, a prisoner of social laws. Women, whether they were the well-kept wives and daughters of the rich, or the poor uneducated daughters of the underclass, were held in their place by concrete walls—even if they could not see them.

"[T]he cellar walls are all around me," Grace continues, "and I know I will never get out." This quote also comes from the first chapter. With these words, Grace describes her feelings at the scene of the murders. But is it an honest depiction? After the above quote, Grace immediately says: "This is what I told Dr. Jordan, when we came to that part of the story." This sentence qualifies her previous statement, and, in the process, Grace provides a hint of her real feelings. Grace is not saying that her sense of imprisonment, "I know I will never get out," is an honest one. Rather, she is implying that it might merely be a version of a "story." She might be saying this because it is what she believes Dr. Jordan wants to hear, something she often admits to doing throughout her story. Using Grace as the speaker of her feminine contemporaries, one might ask, what is Atwood declaring with these words? Is she stating that the women of Grace's time might also have been playing roles, ones they believed the men in their lives wanted? In other words, does Grace truly feel confined? Is she really comfortable walking in those shoes? Or is she pretending, hoping that in playing out her role according to the rules, she will eventually win some small portion of freedom? After all, this could have been the way Victorian women found release. They might have performed, as Grace did, only what was expected of them so they could find peace within the four walls of their confinement.

Obviously Grace did not always act according to law. She was angry and jealous of Nancy Montgomery, so Grace got rid of her. In some limited and short-lived way, Montgomery's murder freed Grace. But Grace soon found out that acting upon her crudest emotions ultimately caused her

> "Women, whether they were the well-kept wives and daughters of the rich, or the poor uneducated daughters of the underclass, were held in their place by concrete walls—even if they could not see them."

imprisonment. Her confinement was compounded later when she also acted out her emotions inside the penitentiary. When she vocalized her frustrations and fears in loud screaming fits, she was defined as mad and thrown into the asylum. While there, she was constantly probed and no doubt further confined either in solitary loneliness or by other means of constriction such as straight jackets. It was while in the asylum that Grace learns to keep her thoughts to herself. Her emotions must be kept under control. She discovers that if she remains nonresponsive or at least if she answers questions with minimal and socially acceptable short statements, she is left alone and eventually is returned to the prison, where the stigma of madness somewhat disappears. If she has any dream of realizing her release from jail, it will be actualized through her practice of silence.

There are many stories of Victorian-influenced women being driven mad because their emotional lives are too heavily suppressed. Emotions are often looked upon as a sign of weakness and acting them out is a disturbance to the controlled notion of sanity. Many women, like Grace, learn that silence brings them more acceptance and favor. Other women take on a different mode of silence, such as feigning ignorance. Grace relates that her lawyer tells the court she is "next door to an idiot." Playing out this role, he tells her, is her "best chance." She "should not appear to be too intelligent." Not only were Victorian women being fed this line, many women, up until the late 1960s, not only pretended to be unintelligent, many of them often believed it. Education was for men. Women's motives for going to college were said to be only to find a husband. It was also believed that professional careers were too far removed from the home—the socially accepted domain of women. Once again, in playing the role of the less intelligent, women

What Do I Read Next?

- Alice Munro is a fellow Canadian author, who often writes about people who live in small, rural Canadian towns. The lives of the characters she writes about, however, are any thing but simple. Her collections of short stories are legendary. One of her more recent collections is *Dance of the Happy Shades and Other Stories* (1998). There are fifteen stories included, each of them depicting ordinary moments in life, but they are looked at through the eyes of someone who can decipher the underlying meaning.

- Carol Shields, an American who has adopted Canada as her home, wrote the Pulitzer Prize–winning *The Stone Diaries* (1993), her most famous work. Shields creates a fictional character and then writes the book as if it were her protagonist's autobiography. The story follows the life of Daisy Goodwill as she tries to make sense of her somewhat dull life. The introspective monologue is the strong point of this work.

- Angela Carter's works are often compared to Atwood's, or vice versa. Carter was known for taking fairy tales and twisting them to reflect her favorite feminist theories. *Bloody Chamber* (1990) is her most critically acclaimed collection of short stories. In this book, Carter retells the famous "Bluebeard Tale," turning it on its head so that women, rather than being the victims, are victorious in the end.

- *Surfacing* (1972) and *The Handmaid's Tale* (1985) are two of Atwood's most popular novels. In *Surfacing*, Atwood's female protagonist returns to her childhood home on a remote island to search for clues about her father's mysterious disappearance. The search brings more to the surface than the protagonist could have imagined. This story is often classified as a thriller. *The Handmaid's Tale* was a departure in writing for Atwood, as the story takes place in the future. Atwood's depiction of the future represents everything a feminist would never want to experience, one in which women are completely without freedom.

- For a male's perspective of life in prison, Ernest J. Gaines has written *A Lesson before Dying* (1993). It is a story set in the South in the 1940s, and its protagonist is a young black man who is asked to teach another young black man, waiting to be executed for murder, how to die. The prisoner insists he was wrongfully convicted, a condition not improbable in the South for black men during this time.

---

found, if not fulfillment, at least acceptance and a synthetic peace.

Another question that Atwood raises is that of women's sexuality. At one point in the story, Dr. Jordan notices that Grace is a bit prudish when it comes to discussing sex. He wants to know if Kinnear ever made advances to her, but Dr. Jordan doesn't know how to ask Grace. During his first visit with her, he offers Grace an apple. In biblical terms, the apple represents temptation. And it is Eve who offers it to Adam, an act that has forever identified Eve, in some interpretations, as the seductress and the source of Adam's fall. But Dr. Jordan's questions about sex are double-edged. He is, on one hand, trying to find out if Grace is guilty or innocent. But he also finds the discussion of sexuality titillating.

There are suggestions in the novel that Grace was not so prudish as she seems. In some accounts, Grace is said to have enticed James McDermott to commit the murders in exchange for having sex with her. On the other side, Atwood reveals Dr. Jordan's own sexual desires, which include not only the seduction of his landlady but also his sexual dreams as a young boy. He also is aroused by Miss Lydia's attention as well as by his contacts with Grace. In exploring Dr. Jordan's sexual desires, Atwood is setting up the dichotomy between the definition of women as innocent virgins and, at the other end of the spectrum, as whores, while men suffered no such labels and were able to enjoy socially acceptable sexual passion. Grace in her so-called normal state does sound like a prude, but when she is put in a trance, another side appears, one more crude but also more exacting. Once she is fully hypnotized, Dr. Jordan says: "Ask her . . . whether she ever had relations with James McDermott." Then the narrator explains: "He [Jordan] hasn't been intending to pose this question; certainly not at first, and never so directly. But isn't it—he sees it now—the one thing he most wants to know?"

Grace is momentarily released from her inhibitions, and she points an accusing finger. "Really, Doctor," Grace says, "you are such a hypocrite!" With this revelation, the tables are turned. Now Dr. Jordan feels as if he must suppress his emotions. "He's shaken, but must try not to show [it]." Grace has taken off her social mask and in doing so, she has seen Dr. Jordan more clearly. Grace says, "[w]hether I did what you'd like to with that little slut who's got hold of your hand?" And then Grace admits she allowed McDermott to do all the things, as she says, that Dr. Jordan wanted to do to her.

But Grace's awakening does not last. When pressed further, she cannot take credit for having seen things as they are, for expressing her inner feelings. Instead, she gives credit to Mary Whitney, her dead friend, whom she claims has possessed her. Grace has crawled back into her shell. If she had not, she would never have been released from jail. "I must have been asleep," she insists upon coming out of the trance. ". . . I must have been dreaming. I dreamt about my mother. She was floating in the sea. She was at peace." It is interesting to note that both Grace's strength and her peace come from women who are dead—her mother and Mary Whitney. Both of these women had passed to the other side. And in their passing, as Grace sees it, they have climbed over the four walls of their prison and found peace and freedom.

Source: Joyce Hart, Critical Essay on *Alias Grace*, in *Novels for Students*, Gale, 2004.

Patricia F. Goldblatt

In the following article, Goldblatt discusses Atwood's writings in the context of her life experiences.

TO CONSTRUCT: to build; to fabricate; to devise or invent.

TO RECONSTRUCT: to rebuild.

A weaver employs fragments from life, silk, raw yarns, wool, straw, perhaps even a few twigs,

> **" This is the artist's art: to reconstruct the familiar into new, fascinating, but often disturbing tableaux from which stories can unfold."**

stones, or feathers, and transforms them into a tapestry of color, shape, and form. An author's work is similar, for she selects individuals, locations, images, and ideas, rearranging them to create a believable picture. Each smacks of reality, but is not. This is the artist's art: to reconstruct the familiar into new, fascinating, but often disturbing tableaux from which stories can unfold.

Margaret Atwood weaves stories from her own life in the bush and cities of Canada. Intensely conscious of her political and social context, Atwood dispels the notion that caribou-clad Canadians remain perpetually locked in blizzards while simultaneously seeming to be a polite mass of gray faces, often indistinguishable from their American neighbors. Atwood has continually pondered the lack of an identifiable Canadian culture. For over thirty years her work has aided in fashioning a distinct Canadian literary identity. Her critical catalogue and analysis of Canadian Literature, *Survival*, offered "a political manifesto telling Canadians . . . [to] value their own" (Sullivan, 265). In an attempt to focus on Canadian experiences, Atwood has populated her stories with Canadian cities, conflicts, and contemporary people, conscious of a landscape whose borders have been permeated by the frost of Nature, her colonizers and her neighbors. Her examination of how an individual interacts, succeeds, or stagnates within her world speaks to an emerging a sense of self and often parallels the battles fought to establish self-determination.

In her novels, Margaret Atwood creates situations in which women, burdened by the rules and inequalities of their societies, discover that they must reconstruct braver, self-reliant personae in order to survive. Not too far from the Canadian blueprint of the voyageur faced with an inclement, hostile environment, these women struggle to overcome and to change systems that block and inhibit their security. Atwood's pragmatic women are drawn from women in the 1950s and 1960s: young women blissfully building their trousseaus and imagining a paradise of silver bells and picket fences.

Yet the author herself was neither encumbered nor restricted by the definition of contemporary female in her life as a child. Having grown up in the Canadian North, outside of societal propaganda, she could critically observe the behaviors that were indoctrinated into her urban peers who lacked diverse role models. As Atwood has noted, "Not even the artistic community offered you a viable choice as a woman" (Sullivan, 103). Her stories deal with the transformation of female characters from ingenues to insightful women. By examining her heroes, their predators, and how they cope in society, we will discover where Atwood believes the ability to reconstruct our lives lies.

WHO ARE THE VICTIMS? "But pathos as a literary mode simply demands that an innocent victim suffer." Unlike Shakespeare's hubris-laden kings or Jane Austen's pert and private aristocratic landowning families, Margaret Atwood relies on a collection of ordinary people to carry her tales: university students, museum workers, market researchers, writers, illustrators, and even house-maids. In her novels, almost all dwell on their childhood years in flashback or in the chronological telling of their stories. Many of her protagonists' early days are situated in a virtual Garden of Eden setting, replete with untamed natural environments. Exploring shorelines, gazing at stars, gathering rocks, and listening to waves, they are solitary solus, but not lonely individuals: innocent, curious, and affable creatures. Elaine Risley in *Cat's Eye* and an unnamed narrator in *Surfacing* are two women who recall idyllic days unfolded in a land of lakes, berries, and animals. Offred in *The Handmaid's Tale*, in her city landscape, also relates a tale of a happy childhood. She is a complacent and assured child, her mother a constant loving companion. In their comfortable milieus, these girls intuit no danger. However, other Atwood protagonists are not as fortunate. Their backgrounds suggest an unhealthy, weedy soil that causes their young plants to twist and permutate. *Lady Oracle*'s Joan is overweight. Her domineering, impatient mother and her weak father propel her to seek emotional satisfaction away from them. Lesje in *Life Before Man* is the offspring of dueling immigrant grandmothers who cannot agree on the child's proper upbringing. Not allowed to frequent the Ukrainian "golden church with its fairytale onion" (LBM, 93) of the one, or the synagogue of the other, Lesje is unable to develop self-confidence and focuses instead on the inanimate, the solid traditions of rocks and dinosaurs

as her progenitors. Similarly, the females in *The Robber Bride* reveal miserable childhoods united by parental abuse, absence, and disregard: Roz must perform as her mother's helper, a landlady cum cleaning woman; her father is absent, involved in shady dealings in "the old country." Charis, a second character in *The Robber Bride*, abandoned by her mother and deposited with Aunt Vi and Uncle Vern, is sexually violated by those who should have offered love and trust. Toni, the third of the trio, admits to loneliness and alienation in a well-educated, wealthy family. Marked by birth and poverty, Grace Marks, an Irish immigrant in the early 1800s in *Alias Grace*, loses her mother en route to Canada. Grace is almost drowned by the demands of her drunken father and clinging, needy siblings. These exiled little girls, from weak, absent, or cruel families, made vulnerable by their early situations, cling to the notion that their lives will be improved by the arrival of a kind stranger, most likely a handsome suitor. Rather than becoming recalcitrant and cynical, all sustain the golden illusion of the fairy-tale ending. In short, they hold to the belief, the myth perpetrated by society: marriage.

Atwood's women are cognizant of the nurturing omissions in their environments. They attempt to cultivate and cope. Charis in *The Robber Bride* decides to reinvent herself. She changes her name and focuses on what she considers her healing powers inherited from her chicken-raising grandmother. She, Roz, and Toni turn their faith to the power of friendship, a solid ring that lessens the painful lack of supportive families. In *Alias Grace* Grace's burden of an absent family is briefly alleviated by her friendship with another housemaid, Mary Whitney. Mary takes an adoring Grace under her wing and creates for Grace a fleeting vision of sisterly support. Unfortunately for Grace, Mary herself, another trusting young woman, is deceived by her employer's son and dies in a botched abortion, leaving Grace once again abandoned and friendless.

In an attempt to reestablish stable, satisfying homes, these women pursue a path, as have women throughout history, to marriage. They search for a male figure, imagining a refuge. Caught up in the romantic stereotypes that assign and perpetuate gender roles, each girl does not doubt that a man is the solution to her problems.

In *The Edible Woman* Marian and her co-workers at Seymour Surveys, "the office virgins," certainly do not question that marriage will provide fulfillment. In spite of the fact that Marian is suspended between two unappealing men, she does not deviate from the proper behavior. Marian's suitor,

Peter, with his well-chosen clothes and suave friends, his perfectly decorated apartment, and even Marian as the appropriate marriage choice, is rendered as no more than the wedding cake's blankly smiling ornament. If appearance is all, he should suffice. Peter is juxtaposed to the slovenly, self-centered graduate student, Duncan, whose main pleasure is watching his laundry whirl in the washing machine. Marian is merely a blank slate upon which each man can write or erase his concept of female.

The narrator and her friend Anna, in *Surfacing*, are also plagued by moody men who are not supportive of women's dreams. In one particularly horrifying scene, Anna's husband Dave orders her to strip off her clothes for the movie camera. Anna, humiliated by the request, nevertheless complies. She admits to nightly rapes but rationalizes his behavior: "He likes to make me cry because he can't do it himself" (Sf, 80). Similarly, when Joe, the narrator's boyfriend, proposes, "We should get married . . . we might as well" (56), he is dumbfounded and furious at her refusal. Men aware of the role they play accept their desirability as "catches." They believe that women desire lives of "babies and sewing" (LO, 159). These thoughts are parroted by Peter in *The Edible Woman* when he proclaims, "People who aren't married get funny in middle age" (EW, 102). Men uphold the values of the patriarchy and women conform, few trespassing into gardens of their own design.

In *Alias Grace* Grace's aspirations for a brighter future also dwell on finding the right man: "It was the custom for young girls in this country to hire themselves out, in order to earn the money for their dowries, and then they would marry . . . and one day . . . be mistress of a tidy farmhouse" (AG, 157–58). In the employment of Mr. Thomas Kinnear in Richmond Hill, Grace quickly ascertains that the handsome, dark-haired housekeeper, Nancy Montgomery, enjoys many privileges as the reward for being her master's mistress. Yet, although men may be the only way to elevate status, Grace learns that they cannot be trusted when their advances are rejected. Grace, on trial for the murders of Kinnear and Montgomery, is incredulous when she hears a former friend, Jamie Welsh, testify against her.

> Then I was hoping for some token of sympathy from him; but he gave me a stare filled with such reproach and sorrowful anger. He felt betrayed in love . . . I was transformed to a demon and he would do all in his power to destroy me. I had been counting on him to say a good word for me . . . for I valued his good opinion of me, and it was a grief to lose it.

Women, it seems, must be made malleable to men's desires, accepting their proposals, their advances. They must submit to their socially determined roles or be seen as "demons."

However, it is not only men but also women as agents of society who betray. In *The Robber Bride* Charis, Roz, and Toni are tricked in their friendship by Zenia, an acquaintance from their university days. Each succumbs to Zenia's web of deceit. Playing the part of a confidante and thoughtful listener, Zenia encourages the three women to divest themselves of their tales of their traumatic childhoods. She learns their tortured secrets and uses their confidences to spirit away the men each women believes to be the cornerstone in her life.

From little girls to sophisticated women, Atwood's protagonists have not yet discerned that trust can be perverted, that they can be reeled in, taken advantage of, constantly abused, if they are not careful of lurking predators in their landscapes. Joan in *Lady Oracle*, longing for friendship, endures the inventive torments of her Brownie friends: deadly ploys that tie little girls to trees with skipping ropes, exposing them to strange leering men under cavernous bridges. Her assassins jeer, "How do ya' like the club?" (LO, 59). Elaine Risley in *Cat's Eye*, like Joan, is a young girl when she discovers the power of betrayal by members of her own sex. For years she passively succumbs to their games. Perhaps, because she has grown up alone in the Canadian North with her parents and brother, Elaine seeks the warming society of girls. Only when Elaine is deserted, left to freeze in a disintegrating creek, does she recognize her peers' malevolence that almost leads to her death. Elaine knows that she is a defeated human, but rather than confronting her tormentors, she increases her own punishment nightly: she peels the skin off her feet and bites her lips.

Unable to turn outward in a society that perpetuates the ideal of a submissive female, these women turn inward to their bodies as shields or ploys. Each has learned that a woman is a commodity, valued only for her appearance. Therefore it comes as no surprise that Atwood's protagonists measure their worth in terms of body. Joan in *Lady Oracle* sees herself as "a huge shapeless cloud" (LO, 65); she drifts. However, her soft edges do not keep her from the bruising accusations of society. Although she loves to dance, Joan's bulging body is an affront to her mother and ballet teacher's sensibilities, and so at her ballet recital she is forced to perform as a mothball, not as a butterfly in tulle and spangles.

Joan certainly does not fit her mother's definition of femininity. Because her ungainly shape is rejected, Joan decides to hide her form in a mountain of fat, food serving as a constant to her mother's reproaches: "I was eating steadily, doggedly, stubbornly, anything I could get. The war between myself and my mother was on in earnest; the disputed territory was my body" (LO, 67). Interestingly, Joan's loving, supportive, and also fat aunt Louisa bequeaths to Joan an inheritance with the stipulation that she lose one hundred pounds. Atwood herself was fascinated by transformations in fairy stories: a person could not become a swan and depart the dreaded scene that mocked the tender aspirations of an awkward ingenue in real life; she could, however, don a new mask and trick those people who had previously proffered harm.

In *The Edible Woman* Marian's body is also a battlefield. Unable to cope with her impending marriage to Peter, Marian finds herself unable to ingest any food that was once alive. Repulsed by her society's attitude of consumerism, Marian concludes that her refusal to eat is ethical. However, her mind and body have split away from each other. Her mind's revulsion at a dog-eat-dog world holds her body hostage: captive territory when a woman disagrees with her world. Marian "tri[es] to reason with [her body], accus[ing] it of having frivolous whims." She coaxes and tempts, "but it was adamant" (EW, 177). Marian's mind expresses her disapproval on the only level on which she possesses control: ironically, herself. Her punishment is circular: first, as a victim susceptible because she is a woman subject to her society's values; and second, as a woman only able to command other women, namely herself. Her sphere is so small she becomes both victim and victimizer.

This view of a woman who connects and projects her image of self onto her body also extends to the functions of a female body: the ability to control life by giving birth. Sarah in the story "The Resplendent Quetzal" (1977) is drained of all vitality and desire when her baby dies at birth. Her concept of identity is entangled with her ability to produce a child. When this biological function fails, Sarah's being ebbs. Lesje in *Life Before Man* also observes that, without children, "officially she is nothing" (LBM, 267). Offred's identity and value as a childbearer as well, in *The Handmaid's Tale*, are proclaimed by her clothes in her totalitarian city of Gilead. She is "two viable ovaries" (HT, 135). She no longer owns a name; she is "Of Fred," the concubine named for the man who will impregnate her. Every step, every mouthful of food, every

move is observed, reported, circumvented, or approved for the sake of the child she might carry to term. Her only worth resides in her biological function. Her dreams and desires are unimportant. Her goal is survival.

The women described here do not lash out openly. Each who once trusted in family, marriage, and friendship discovers that treading societal paths does not result in happiness. These disillusioned women, with aborted expectations, turn their misery inward, accepting responsibility that not society and its expectations but they themselves are weak, unworthy, and have therefore failed.

WHO HAS LAID PREY AND WHY? "Sometimes fear of these obstacles becomes itself the obstacle." Atwood's girls are a vulnerable lot, manipulated, packaged, and devastated by the familiar faces in uncaring, dictatorial circles that reinforce societal imperatives. Those once free to roam and explore as children as well as those repressed from an early age are subject to the civilizing forces that customize young girls to the fate of females. Ironically, this process, for the most part, is performed by mothers.

Mothers, rather than alleviating their girls' distress, increase their children's alienation. When Elaine's mother in *Cat's Eye* ventures to discuss the cruelty of Elaine's friends, her words do not fortify Elaine; they admonish her: "Don't let them push you around. Don't be spineless. You have to have more backbone" (CE, 156). Fearing her weakness is comparable to the tiny crumbling bones of sardines, Elaine maligns herself: "What is happening is my own fault, for not having more backbone" (156). Joan's mother in *Lady Oracle* doesn't mince words: "You were stupid to let the other girls fool you like that" (LO, 61). Instead of offering support, the mothers blame their daughters, aligning themselves with the girls' accusers.

Mothers who themselves have not found acceptance, success, or ease in society persist in transmitting the old messages of conformity. Joan's mother in *Lady Oracle* is dumbfounded that "even though she'd done the right thing, ... devoted her life to us, ... made her family her career as she had been told to do," she had been burdened with "a sulky fat slob of a daughter and a husband who wouldn't talk to her" (LO, 179). Joan echoes her mother's complaints when she murmurs, "How destructive to me were the attitudes of society" (102).

Even the work women do conspires to maintain the subjection of their own kind. In her job, in *The Edible Woman*, Marian investigates what soups, laxatives, or drinks will please and be purchased. Sanctioned female activities also reinforce the imposition of correct values. In *Surfacing* and *Cat's Eye* little girls are engrossed in cutting up pictures from Eaton's catalogues that offer labor-saving devices along with fashionable clothes: children piece together a utopia of dollhouse dreams. So brainwashed are these girls that when asked to indicate a possible job or profession, they answer, "A lady" or "A mother" (CE, 91).

In *Cat's Eye* Elaine Risley's mother does not fit the stereotype. She wears pants, she ice skates, she "does not give a hoot" (CE, 214) about the rules that women are supposed to obey. Rendered impotent as a role model in her daughter's eyes because she does not abide by the Establishment's code of correct deportment, Elaine's mother is an outsider to a woman's world that captivates Elaine.

Instead of her own nonconforming mother, Elaine is most deeply affected by the indictments from her friend Grace Smeath's mother. Mrs. Smeath, spread out on the sofa and covered with afghans every afternoon to rest her bad heart, damns Elaine for being a heathen: there is something very wrong with Elaine's family, who ignore the protocol of proper women's wear, summer city vacations, and regular church attendance. Worse yet, Mrs. Smeath, aware of the cruel games inflicted on Elaine, does not intervene. Instead she invokes deserved suffering when she decrees, "It's God's punishment for the way the other children treat her [Elaine]. It serves her right" (CE, 180). With God on her side, Mrs. Smeath relies on the Bible as the oldest and surest way of prescribing a female identity and instilling fear.

In *The Handmaid's Tale* the Bible is likewise the chief source of female repression. Words are corrupted, perverted, or presented out of context to establish a man's holy vision of women: Sarah's use of her handmaid, Hagar, as a surrogate womb for an heir for Abraham becomes the legalizing basis for fornication with the handmaids. Acts of love are reduced to institutionalized rapes, and random acts of violence, banishment to slag heaps, public hangings, endorsed public killings, bribery, deceit, and pornography all persist under other names in order to maintain a pious hold on women endorsed by the Gilead Fathers.

In spite of the fact that Gilead is praised by its creators as a place where women need not fear, carefully chosen "aunts" persist in treachery that robs women of trust. To perpetuate the status quo, women are kept vulnerable and treated as children: girls must ask permission, dress in silly frocks, are allowed no money, play no part in their own self-determination. Yet Atwood's girls tire of their rigidly enforced placement that would preserve some outdated notion of female acceptability.

THE ESCAPE. "She feels the need for escape." (Sv, 131). After enduring, accepting, regurgitating, denying, and attempting to please and cope, Atwood's protagonists begin to take action and change their lives. Atwood herself, raised on *Grimms' Fairy Tales*, knew that "by using intelligence, cleverness and perseverance" (Sullivan, 36), magical powers could transform a forest into a garden. However, before realizing their possibilities, many of Atwood's protagonists hit rock bottom, some even contemplating death as an escape. In *Surfacing* the narrator, fed up with the superficiality of her companions, banishes them and submits to paranoia.

> Everything I can't break . . . I throw on the floor . . . I take off my clothes . . . I dip my head beneath the water . . . I leave my dung, droppings on the ground . . . I hollow a lair near the woodpile . . . I scramble on hands and knees . . . I could be anything, a tree, a deer skeleton, a rock. (Sf, 177–87) She descends to madness, stripping herself of all the trappings of civilized society.

Although often consumed with thoughts of suicide in *Cat's Eye* and *The Handmaid's Tale*, Atwood's heroines never succumb. Instead they consciously assassinate their former identities through ritual deaths by water. Joan in *Lady Oracle* orchestrates a baptism in Lake Ontario. Pretending to drown, she relinquishes her former life. With sunglasses and scarf, she believes herself reborn, free to begin anew in Italy. Elaine Risley, after her bone-chilling encounter in the icy ravine in *Cat's Eye*, is finally able to ignore the taunts of her friends. Resurrected after two days in bed, a stronger Elaine affirms that "she is happy as a clam, hard-shelled and firmly closed" (CE, 201) against those who would sabotage her; she announces, "I'm ready" (203). Fortified by a new body image with a tougher veneer and a protective mask, Elaine no longer heeds her former tormentors. She has sealed herself from further outrage and invasion.

Marian's revelation in *The Edible Woman* is experienced at the precipice of a ravine, where she comments, "In the snow you're as near as possible to nothing" (EW, 263). Perhaps the fear of becoming one with the ubiquitous whiteness of the landscape and forever losing herself motivates a stand. Similarly, Sarah in "The Resplendent Quetzal" forges a more determined persona after her trial by water. Instead of throwing herself into the sacrificial well in Mexico as her husband Edward fears, she hurls a plaster Christ child stolen from a crèche into the water. Believing the tribal folklore that young children take messages to the rain god and live forever in paradise at the bottom of the well, Sarah pins her hopes on a representative facsimile that she hopes will bring her peace for her lost child in the next world as well as rebirth, freeing herself from anxiety and guilt regarding the child's death.

Rather than resorting to the cool, cleansing agent of water, Grace Marks, the convicted murderess in *Alias Grace*, reconstructs her life through stories of her own invention. She fashions a creature always beyond the pale of her listeners' complete comprehension. As told to Dr. Simon Jordan, who has come to study Grace as a possible madwoman, her story ensnares him in a piteous romance. Grace appears outwardly as a humble servant girl always at peril from salacious employers; however, when Grace ruminates in her private thoughts, she reveals that she is worldly wise, knowing how to avoid bad impressions and the advances of salesmen. She is knowledgeable, stringing along Dr. Jordan: "I say something just to keep him happy . . . I do not give him a straight answer" (AG, 66, 98). After rambling from employ to employ in search of security, Grace constructs a home for herself in her stories. Her words, gossamer thin, have the power to erect a facade, a frame that holds her illusions together.

In an attempt to discover the missing parts and prove the veracity of Grace's story, her supporters encourage her to undergo a seance. Although she recognizes Dr. Jerome Dupont, the man who will orchestrate the event, as a former button peddler, she does not speak out. When a voice emerges from the hypnotized Grace, it proclaims, "I am not Grace" (403). As listeners, we ponder the speaker's authenticity. Just who our narrator might be, madwoman or manipulator, is cast into doubt. We can only be sure that the young innocent who arrived on Canada's shores penniless and motherless has been altered by the necessity to cope with a destructive hierarchical society unsympathetic to an immigrant girl. Rather than persist and be tossed forever at the whim of a wizened world, each saddened young girl moves to reconstruct her tarnished image of her self.

How? "One way of coming to terms, making sense of one's roots, is to become a creator" (. . .) Atwood's victims who take control of their lives discover the need to displace societal values, and they replace them with their own. In *Lady Oracle* Joan ponders the film *The Red Shoes,* in which the moral warns that if a woman chooses both family and career, tragedy ensues. Reflecting on

childbirth, the narrator in "Giving Birth" (1977) hopes for some vision: "After all she is risking her life . . . As for the vision, there wasn't one" (GB, 252; italics mine). Toni in *The Robber Bride* and Grace Marks in *Alias Grace* acknowledge that it is not necessary to procreate. Each is more than her body. A grown-up Elaine Risley in *Cat's Eye* and the narrator in *Surfacing* accept motherhood, but not as an outcome of their gender that will foreclose the possibilities of a creative job. In fact, Roz in *The Robber Bride* is quite able to combine motherhood and a successful career. Dissatisfied with traditional knowledge, Atwood's women again turn inward, now avoiding masochistic traps, fully able to deviate from society's dicta. Freed from constraining fears, they locate talents, wings that free them.

Rather than becoming cynical and devastated by society's visions and its perpetrators, Atwood's women forge on. Roz, Toni, and Charis in *The Robber Bride*, who have been betrayed by Zenia, put their faith back into friendship, allowing mutual support to sustain them. It is solid; it has been tested. They have turned to one another, cried and laughed, shared painful experiences, knowing that their friendship has endured in a labyrinth of twisted paths.

Offred in *The Handmaid's Tale* also begins to reshape her world. She envisions a better place in her thoughts, recording her words on tape. She has hope. Consciously, she reconstructs her present reality, knowing she is making an effort to project an optimistic picture. She says, "Here is a different story, a better one . . . This is what I'd like to tell" (HT, 234). She relates that her tryst with Nick the chauffeur, arranged by her commander's wife, is caring and loving, enhanced by memories from her earlier life in order to conjure an outcome of happiness. In the short story "Hair Jewellery" (1977) Atwood's narrator is an academic, a writer who warns, "Be careful . . . There is a future" (113). With the possibility of a new beginning, there is a chance that life can improve. In *Alias Grace* Grace's fabrications in her stories provide an escape hatch, a version of reality tailored to fit her needs. For both Offred and Grace, stories are ways of rebelling, of avoiding the tentacles of a society that would demean and remold them. Their stories are outward masks, behind which they frantically repair their damaged spirits. Each alters her world through language. Each woman speaks a reconstructed world into existence, herself the engineering god of her own fate. Offred confides that handmaids live in the spaces and the gaps between their stories, in their private silences: only alone in their imaginations are they free to control their own destinies.

However, Atwood's protagonists inhabit not only their minds in secret, but also their bodies in the outside world. Joan, after her disappearance from Toronto in *Lady Oracle*, decides that she must return home and support the friends who have aided her disguise. In the past, just as she had wielded her bulk as a weapon, so she has used her writing in order to resolve relationships. She has indulged in Gothic romances, positing scenarios; she has even played out roles with lovers in capes. In the end, she rejects her former craft of subterfuge: "I won't write any more Costume Gothics." Yet we must ponder her choice to "try some science fiction" (LO, 345).

Although it is difficult to extirpate behavior, women trust the methods that have helped them cope in the past in order to alter the future. In *The Edible Woman* the womanly art of baking provides Marian with a way to free herself: she bakes a cake that resembles herself. Offering a piece to Peter, she is controlling the tasty image of a woman, allowing him and, more importantly, herself to ingest and destory it. "It gave me a peculiar sense of satisfaction to see him eat," she says, adding, "I smiled comfortably at him" (EW, 281). Her pleasure in their consumption of her former self is symbolic of the death of the old Marian.

One might say that Marian's ingestion of her own image, Joan's adoption of science fiction, and both Offred's and Grace's stories "in the head" do not promise new fulfilling lives, only tactics of escape. However, their personal growth through conscious effort represents a means to wrest control of their lives from society and transform their destinies. These women become manipulators rather than allowing themselves to be manipulated.

In *Cat's Eye* Elaine Risley deals with the torment of her early life in her art by moving to Vancouver and exerting power in paint over the people who had condemned her. She creates surreal studies of Mrs. Smeath: "I paint Mrs. Smeath . . . like a dead fish . . . One picture of Mrs. Smeath leads to another. She multiplies on the walls like bacteria, standing, sitting, with clothes, without clothes" (CE, 338). Empowered by her success as an artist, Elaine returns to Toronto for a showing of her work, able to resist the pleas of her former tormentor, Cordelia, now a pitiful patient in a psychiatric facility. In a dream, Elaine surpasses her desire for revenge and offers Cordelia Christian charity: "I'm the stronger . . . I reach out my arms to her, bend down . . . It's all right, I say to her. You can go home" (CE, 419). Elaine is reinforced by the very words spoken to her in the vision that saved her life years before. Her work fosters her liberation. By projecting her rage outside of herself, she confronts her demons and exalts herself as a divine redeemer.

CONCLUSION. "You don't even have to concentrate on rejecting the role of victim because the role is no longer a temptation for you" (Sv. 39). The creative aspect that fortifies each woman enables her to control her life: it is the triumphant tool that resurrects each one. As artists, writers, friends, each ameliorates her situation and her world, positively metamorphosing reality in the process. In societies tailored to the submission of females, Atwood's protagonists refuse to be pinned down to the measurements of the perfect woman. Instead, they reconstruct their lives, imprinting their own designs in worlds of patterned fabric. Atwood has observed that all writing is political: "The writer simply by examining how the forces of society interact with the individual . . . seek[s] to change social structure" (Sullivan, 129).

Literature has always been the place where journeys have been sought, battles fought, insights gleaned. And authors have always dallied with the plight of women in society: young or old, body or mind, mother or worker, traveler or settler. The woman has been the divided or fragmented icon who, broken and downcast, has gazed back forlornly at us from the pages of her telling tale. Margaret Atwood has reconstructed this victim, proving to her and to us that we all possess the talent and the strength to revitalize our lives and reject society's well-trodden paths that suppress the human spirit. She has shown us that we can be vicariously empowered by our surrogate, who not only now smiles but winks back at us, daring us to reclaim our own female identities.

Source: Patricia F. Goldblatt, "Reconstructing Margaret Atwood's Protagonists," in *World Literature Today*, Vol. 73, No. 2, April 15, 1999, pp. 275–82.

Roberta Rubenstein

In the following article, Rubenstein discusses the structure of Atwood's novel Alias Grace *in the context of her other writings.*

Justifiably regarded as one of Canada's most distinguished writers, Margaret Atwood is equally accomplished as the author of fiction and poetry. In addition to a dozen volumes of poetry—several of which have been honored with prestigious literary awards—she has published nine novels and four volumes of short stories and prose pieces. Additionally, her critical study of major themes and ideas in Canadian literature, *Survival* (1972), though now

> *Alias Grace* is by turns a 'tales of Scheherazade,' a suspenseful courtroom drama, a reconstruction of Victorian manners and attitudes toward women, a slice of the history of Canadian settlement, and a meditation on the intersections of history, storytelling, and narrative."

dated, delineates the early years of a Canadian literary tradition that Atwood herself helped to establish.

As the daughter of an entomologist who conducted his research in the rural northern areas of Quebec and Ontario, Atwood did not attend formal schools until she reached adolescence; at home, she read widely and taught herself to write poetry, novels, stories, and plays. Her first volume of poetry was published in 1962, the year she graduated from the University of Toronto. After receiving an M.A. from Harvard in English literature, she taught English for a time, until the publication of her second novel in 1972 permitted her to pursue a full-time career as a writer.

What is always fascinating about Atwood's fiction is that, while certain preoccupations are present in virtually all of her longer fiction, these ideas achieve fresh and original expression in each narrative. In *The Edible Woman* (1969) and *Surfacing* (1972), Atwood explores the circumstances of female characters whose inner self-division also reflects the changing cultural forces and expectations shaping female experience. *Life before Man* (1979) and *The Handmaid's Tale* (1986) demonstrate the author's capabilities as an acerbic analyst of contemporary male-female relationships; the latter novel projects an imaginary dystopia: a future in which religious fundamentalism and declining fertility in the population converge to produce a political state based on female reproductive oppression.

In a lighter vein, Atwood enjoys playing with and revising traditional narrative forms, as in *Lady Oracle* (1976), in which she wittily revises the gothic romance form of contemporary popular culture. More seriously, in *Cat's Eye* (1988), she experiments with the conventions of biography; the novel is a richly textured portrait of the quintessential artist not as a young man but as a middle-aged woman. In *The Robber Bride* (1993), Atwood, winking at vampire stories and fairy tales, transforms her fictional fascination with the idea of victimization into a revisionist story of female self-discovery and female evil; the utterly amoral but irresistible Zenia, vampire of illusions, succeeds in turning inside out—but also redeeming—the lives of three women who were once her friends.

One of those women is Tony, a military historian through whose perspective Atwood ponders the slippery categories of history and fact, truth and invention. Near the end of *The Robber Bride*, Tony muses that

> "every sober-sided history is at least half sleight-of-hand: the right hand waving its poor snippets of fact, out in the open for all to verify, while the left hand busies itself with its own devious agendas, deep in its hidden pockets. Tony is daunted by the impossibility of accurate reconstruction."

With her newest novel (which was short-listed for the Booker Prize), Atwood, assumes the postmodern historian's equivocal role. *Alias Grace* is based on a celebrated murder in Canada in 1843, comparable in notoriety to the story of Lizzie Borden of Fall River, Massachusetts. The two victims, an unmarried landowner and his housekeeper/mistress, were presumably murdered by James McDermott, a stablehand, and Grace Marks, a sixteen-year-old serving maid. McDermott was found guilty by a court of law and hanged for his crime. Though Grace was also convicted of the murders, her death sentence was commuted at the last minute; her youth and inconsistencies in her testimony led to doubt about her role in the slayings. She spent several years in the Provincial Lunatic Asylum in Toronto, followed by a decades-long incarceration in the Kingston Penitentiary.

A Verbal Quilt

Each section of Atwood's textured exploration of Grace's life, and the circumstances of the murders in which she is implicated, is preceded by excerpts from actual documents of the period: trial testimony, official confessions of the suspects, newspaper stories covering the sensational story, and observations made by Susanna Moodie, the pioneer woman who interviewed Grace in prison. Excerpts from poems and other literary texts of the period capture the flavor of Victorian manners suggest ideas explored in the narrative proper.

These introductory artifacts establish an aura of authenticity and lend credibility to Atwood's invention of the details of Grace's story on which history itself remains silent or inconclusive. Atwood also brings to the particulars of the crime the postmodern awareness that, regardless of the "facts," the truth is elusive; despite the reports of witnesses and even the accused themselves, no one can absolutely establish what happened on the day of the murders. Even Grace is uncertain, having provided three different stories in which she protested her innocence and one in which she confessed her guilt.

Alias Grace is by turns a "tales of Scheherazade," a suspenseful courtroom drama, a reconstruction of Victorian manners and attitudes toward women, a slice of the history of Canadian settlement, and a meditation on the intersections of history, storytelling, and narrative. These diverse strands are imaginatively blended through the medley of distinct voices through which the tale unfolds. Indeed, the narrative itself might be said to form the verbal equivalent of a quilt of complex patterns: The title for each of the fifteen sections is the name of a quilt pattern, which is also rendered in an accompanying visual design. Grace herself is a skilled seamstress who stitches, among other things, quilts. Following her seven years in an asylum after the reprieve from hanging, she is moved to a penitentiary, where, as reward for her behavior as a "model prisoner," she is released during the daytime to sew for the penitentiary governor's wife and daughters.

Grace comes to the attention of a young American doctor, Simon Jordan, who hopes to advance his understanding of mental illness by probing Grace's buried memories of the traumatic events for which she is being punished. Quietly, as Grace stitches quilts in the governor's parlor, she tells her story to Jordan. Like the doctor who listens attentively to her narrative, the reader is offered a number of pieces of Grace's story, patches that he is only gradually able to incorporate into a larger design. The process is, like the fabrication of a quilt, methodical and leisurely, achieved by successive rearrangements of the parts and by crucial invisible stitches along the way.

Quilt is a particularly apt metaphor for the multiplicity of Grace's truths. As Grace points out, perception of a quilt pattern depends entirely upon "looking at the dark pieces, or else the light."

Moving figuratively between quilt and guilt, the narrative invites the reader to determine, on the basis of contradictory information, whether Grace is innocent or guilty, sane or insane, contrary or possessed, an unfortunate victim of circumstance or a manipulative actress. Through challenging us to determine Grace's guilt or innocence, the dark or light, Atwood dares us to question the nature of truth itself: What constitutes "proof" and how is it verified, given the intrinsic limitations of all facts and the biases of all perspectives, to say nothing of distortions introduced by the vagaries of memory?

Historical Authenticity

One of the many pleasures of Atwood's novel is the social commentary and sense of historical authenticity that frame and enliven Grace's story. From the excesses of Victorian fashions for upper-class women to the more literal excesses of mistreatment of their female servants, from the horrors of prison life to the emerging science of the study of the mind, she convincingly re-creates the social realities of the period. Through Grace's articulation of details of her troubled life, Atwood renders a vivid slice of the history of nineteenth-century immigration to Canada and its aftermath. The determination of innocence or guilt of the "celebrated murderess" also partakes of then-raging clashes between science and religion. To the Reverend Verringer, who leads a religious group dedicated to securing Grace's pardon, Dr. Jordan remarks, "It may be that much of what we are accustomed to describe as evil ... is instead an illness due to some lesion of the nervous system, and that the Devil himself is simply a malformation of the cerebrum."

Much of the narrative's tantalizing suspense arises from the manner in which the tale unfolds, an alternation between the first-person account— Grace's story as she articulates it to Dr. Jordan— and the third-person narrative that conveys the doctor's ruminations on Grace's story, as well as on what becomes his increasingly complicated personal life. Intermittently, letters exchanged between Jordan and others, including his mother and several doctors, add to the narrative's medley of perspectives. As we learn through Grace's own narrative, she was one of nine children of a poor Irish family; her father was a whiskey-loving stonemason, her mother his frequently abused wife. The journey to Canada, precipitated by her father's need to flee criminal activities in Ireland, involved a shipload of similar poor immigrants, packed into what Grace describes as "a sort of slum in motion, though without the gin shops"; her mother died on the foul journey and was buried at sea when Grace was twelve.

Virtually abandoned by her father once the rest of the family arrived in the New World, Grace found her early experiences in Canada equally traumatic. Her hard life as a servant girl led to the one true friendship of her life, with a laundry girl named Mary Whitney who treated her with kindness and introduced her to some of the ways of the world. Mary's own knowledge, however, was inadequate; her brief life and gruesome death offer a vivid object lesson illustrating the double standard of nineteenth-century life that is reiterated in various ways throughout the narrative: Men were dangerous, and unaccompanied women were at the mercy of any man who felt free to pursue his own pleasures, yet women were expected to remain virginal until marriage and ignorant of their own sexuality afterward. From doctors to prison guards, sexual abuses of women were so frequent as to be almost unremarkable. The impressionable Grace, already deeply distressed by her mother's sudden death and burial at sea, is further traumatized by her discovery of her friend Mary bleeding to death as a result of a doctor's carelessness in terminating an unwanted pregnancy.

Dr. Jordan, a would-be psychoanalyst several decades before Freud established the discipline, is fascinated by Grace's amnesia and attempts to understand the symptoms of what would only later come to be called hysteria. (Atwood, as part of her historical reconstruction of the period, incorporates contemporary speculations about the nature of mental life and the unconscious mind, including forays into mesmerism, hypnotism, spiritualism, and dream interpretation.) In their interviews Jordan attempts to jog Grace's memory through associations with the rather ludicrous props he brings to their meetings, and probe her dreams as pathways into repressed memories. Complicating his earnest efforts, however, are the gaps in her narrative, omissions that may or may not reflect her genuine uncertainty or ignorance about crucial events on the fatal day: Did she imagine them, dream them, or actually experience them?

A complication of another order is her desire, whether innocent or cunning, to tell the well-meaning doctor not simply what she knows but what she thinks he wants to know. At one point early in her meetings with him, she confides, to the reader only, "I have a good stupid look which I have practiced." In response to one of Jordan's questions about whether she has had any dreams she can describe to him, Grace remarks (again, to us but not to the doctor),

"As he was looking forlorn, and as it were at a loss, and as I suspected that not all was going well

with him, I did not say that I could not remember. Instead I said that I had indeed had a dream. And what was it about, said he, brightening up considerably, and fiddling with his pencil. I told him I'd dreamt about flowers; and he wrote that down busily, and asked what sort of flowers. I said that they were red flowers, and quite large, with glossy leaves like a peony. But I did not say that they were made of cloth, nor did I say when I had seen them last; nor did I say that they were not a dream."

More poignantly, some of Grace's asides to the reader reflect philosophical insights painfully acquired through harsh experience. As she phrases it, Dr. Jordan "doesn't understand yet that guilt comes to you not from the things you've done, but from the things that others have done to you."

Grace's Voice

Thus, a central delight of *Alias Grace* is the voice of Grace Marks herself. So successfully does Atwood create her idiom and tone and sustain her unique perspective that the reader finds himself present in the room with Dr. Jordan, listening intently to Grace as she speaks and enjoying access to some (but hardly all) of her innermost thoughts. Though not educated, Grace is a shrewd observer of what transpires around her. At one point, she attends church with Nancy Montgomery, the housekeeper with whose murder she is later charged. Because Nancy is believed to be Mr. Kinnear's mistress, the churchgoers avoid her. Grace sees their hypocrisy, observing,

"These are cold and proud people, and not good neighbours. They are hypocrites, they think the church is a cage to keep God in, so he will stay locked up there and not wandering about the earth during the week, poking his nose into their business, and looking into the depths and darkness and doubleness of their hearts, and their lack of true charity; and they believe they need only be bothered about him on Sunday when they have their best clothes on and their faces straight, and their hands washed and their gloves on, and their stories all prepared. But God is everywhere, and cannot be caged in, as men can."

Grace's enigmatic qualities thus emerge from a mingling of earnestness, evasiveness, and self-censorship. Neither Dr. Jordan nor the reader (nor, at times, Grace herself) can be certain whether the details of her story correspond accurately to the true circumstances of the murders and her life. As Grace explains,

"When you are in the middle of a story it isn't a story at all, but only a confusion; a dark roaring, a blindness, a wreckage of shattered glass and splintered wood; like a house in a whirlwind, or also a boat crushed by icebergs or swept over the rapids, and all aboard powerless to stop it. It's only afterwards that it becomes anything like a story at all. When you are telling it, to yourself or to someone else."

Through such passages, Atwood reminds us that every story, no matter how apparently true, is artifice; there is never an altogether "reliable" narrator. Depending on the circumstances and the audience, every teller controls the terms of her story, selectively imposing (both deliberately and unintentionally) order, emphasis, and other elements that transform the raw material or experience into a story—in other words, into fiction. As Dr. Jordan comes to understand, "What he wants is what she refuses to tell; what she chooses perhaps not even to know."

Several other characters in *Alias Grace* might also be said to have an alias or hidden self, not least Dr. Jordan himself. Drawn to Grace and charmed by her apparent guilelessness but also troubled by his inability to decide whether she can be trusted, Jordan becomes obsessed with her. The more she discloses, the more he wants to know—and, at the same time, not to know—whether she was actually an accessory to the abhorrent crime for which she has been incarcerated. Additionally, Jordan finds it increasingly difficult to manage his own inconvenient double life; beneath his urbane and rational medical facade hides a lustful man who relishes, even as he resists, the furtive advances of his landlady. In another twist in this elusive narrative, an itinerant friend of Grace's doubles as a hypnotist who may—or may not—succeed in tapping the deeper levels of memory and consciousness that Dr. Jordan so industriously but unsuccessfully pursues.

An occasional detail and a few plot twists seem a bit contrived; it may be that these are the elements that Atwood has taken from the historical record rather than invented herself. As *Alias Grace* compels us to consider, truth may not be simply stranger than fiction but utterly inseparable from it. Such is Atwood's brilliant accomplishment that, in this spellbinding and skillfully crafted narrative, the concealed seams / "seems" that join the materials of history and invention, the fabrics of quilt and guilt, can scarcely be discerned.

Source: Roberta Rubenstein, "Quilt and Guilt," in *The World & I*, Vol. 12, No. 2, February 1, 1997, pp. 262–67.

Sources

Bargreen, Melinda, "Hidden Grace—A Cunning, Brutal Killer or a Terrorized Victim? Atwood's Creation Offers Few Answers," in the *Seattle Times*, January 5, 1997, p. M.2.

Beauchesne, Mitt, Review of *Alias Grace*, in the *National Review*, Vol. 49, No. 2, February 10, 1997, p. 58.

Gussow, Mel, "Atwood Adds Dazzling Twists and Turns to Her First Work of Historical Fiction," in the *New York Times*, January 3, 1997, p. 17.

Knapp, Mona, Review of *Alias Grace*, in *World Literature Today*, Vol. 71, No. 3, Summer 1997, p. 587.

Mujica, Barbara, Review of *Alias Grace*, in *Americas*, Vol. 49, No. 6, November/December 1997, pp. 61–62.

Skow, John, "In Very Confused Blood," in *Time*, Vol. 148, No. 27, December 16, 1996, p. 76.

Woodcock, Susan H., Review of *Alias Grace*, in the *School Library Journal*, Vol. 43, No. 6, June 1997, p. 151.

Further Reading

Cooke, Nathalie, *Margaret Atwood: A Biography*, ECW Press, 1998.
There are many critical works about Atwood's writing but little if anything about the author's private life. This is the first full-length biography of the Canadian author.

Gray, Charlotte, *Sisters in the Wilderness: The Lives of Susanna Moodie and Catherine Parr Traill*, Duckworth Publishing, 2001.
Gray gives a detailed glimpse into the life of Susanna Moodie, an early pioneer in Canada, recounting the hardships that Moodie and other immigrants had to face. Moodie came to Canada filled with hope, but in the end she wrote back home, trying to dissuade anyone from following her to the North American wilderness.

Hartman, Mary S., *Victorian Murderesses: A True History of Thirteen Respectable French and English Women Accused of Unspeakable Crimes*, Robson Book, 1995.
The period covered here is much earlier than Grace Marks's time, but this book provides very interesting reading. Hartman takes the reader back in time and provides a detailed recounting of women's lives in prison.

Shorter, Edward, *A History of Psychiatry: From the Era of the Asylum to the Age of Prozac*, John Wiley and Sons, 1998.
Shorter is a medical historian at the University of Toronto. In his book, he writes about the earliest treatments of madness, which were often considered satanic possession. Shorter also examines the long history of hiding people away in asylums. The book follows treatments to contemporary times, in which a variety of pills are administered to counter many mental illnesses. Critics praise Shorter's storytelling skills used in this book.

Vanspanckeren, Kathryn, and Jan Garden Castro, *Margaret Atwood: Vision and Forms*, Ad Feminam: Women and Literature series, Southern Illinois University Press, 1988.
This is one of the more accessible of the critical studies of Atwood's work.

Babbitt

Sinclair Lewis

1922

Lewis won the Nobel Prize for Literature in 1930 on the strength of a number of significant works, including *Arrowsmith* (1925), *Elmer Gantry* (1927), and *Babbitt*, a satire of the prosperous and conservative business class of 1920s America. Published in New York in 1922, Lewis's novel follows two years of realtor George F. Babbitt's life, during which Babbitt goes from a lifestyle of complete conformity with the business world, to a period of rebellion including heavy drinking and adultery, and back again to conformity. Throughout this journey, Lewis skillfully highlights the lack of culture in medium-sized American cities during the Prohibition Era, the hypocrisy and corruption of pro-business organizations, and the emptiness in typical businessmen's lives.

Babbitt is more than an embodiment of what is wrong with America, however. He is a vivid and lifelike character searching for meaning in a life dominated by conformity and loneliness. Babbitt tries to rebel in every way he knows until a conservative organization threatens his business because of his new liberal ideas, at which point he falls back into the lifestyle of what Lewis called a "Standardized Citizen." In a society that, today, retains many of the basic values that Lewis attacks, Babbitt's struggle continues to engage readers and expose some of the deepest and most longstanding infirmities of American culture.

Author Biography

On February 7, 1885, Lewis was born in the prairie town of Sauk Centre, Minnesota, where he spent a childhood biographers have described as awkward and lonely. He did not find much social success at Yale University either, but he began to develop his talents as a poet and short story writer, and he took time away from the college to travel to England and Panama. After he graduated in 1908, Lewis worked as a journalist and an editor in California, Washington D.C., and New York. In addition, he traveled more extensively throughout Europe and America.

In 1914, Lewis married Grace Livingstone Hegger, and they had a son, Wells Lewis, who would eventually die in World War II. In 1928, he divorced Grace and shortly thereafter married journalist Dorothy Thompson. They had one son named Michael.

By the end of World War I, Lewis was regularly selling short stories and had published his first novel. In the 1920s he became a prolific novelist. *Main Street* (1920) was his first widely successful satire, followed by *Babbitt* (1922), *Arrowsmith* (1925), *Elmer Gantry* (1927), and *Dodsworth* (1929), all of which satirize American culture. In 1926, Lewis was the first writer ever to decline the Pulitzer Prize, citing the award's emphasis on the "wholesome atmosphere of American life," although he did not turn down the Nobel Prize for Literature in 1930.

Ironically, the Nobel Prize marked the turning point of Lewis's critical and popular success. He continued to write novels through the 1930s and 1940s, including one of his more successful portrayals of interpersonal relationships, *Cass Timberlane: A Novel of Husbands and Wives* (1945). None of these were as successful as his previous efforts, partly because of an alcohol problem and increasing fatigue. Meanwhile, Lewis began an affair with a young actress in 1939 and divorced his second wife in 1942. He then lived in Duluth, Minnesota for two years before moving to Massachusetts. In 1950 he moved to Italy, where he died of heart troubles on January 10, 1951.

Sinclair Lewis

Plot Summary

Chapters 1–7

The first seven chapters of *Babbitt* follow one day in the life of its title character, beginning with his process of waking up, talking to his wife, and squabbling at breakfast with his three children. Babbitt starts his car and drives to work, stopping to chat with his neighbor Howard Littlefield, and to pick up a man waiting for the trolley, before he parks outside his real estate office. After a morning of dictation, taking advantage of a grocer looking to expand his shop, and smoking cigars—which he promises himself he will quit—Babbitt meets his best friend Paul Riesling at their club for lunch.

The Athletic Club is chiefly a meeting place for Republican businessmen, and Paul does not fit in there very well, as he talks to Babbitt about his marital problems and complains about their meaningless lifestyle. Babbitt and Paul plan to take a trip to Maine without their wives, and Babbitt goes to pick up his partner and father-in-law Henry T. Thompson. After Babbitt denies his salesman Stanley Graff a raise at the office, Babbitt goes home, has a talk with his son about college, takes a long bath, and falls asleep. Chapter 7 reveals glimpses of the intrigue in other parts of Zenith while Babbitt slumbers.

Chapters 8–14

Time moves forward more rapidly after chapter 7, and the major event of the spring is the Babbitts' dinner party, for which Babbitt makes bootleg cocktails. The dinner party seems to go well despite its commonplace conversation. But Babbitt is anxious for his guests to leave, and when they do he explodes to his wife, "I'm sick of everything and everybody!" He tells her he wants to go to Maine alone with Paul. The Babbitts visit the Rieslings in their apartment and, after Paul's wife has a fit and Babbitt yells at her, she agrees to let the men spend some time alone.

Babbit and Paul have a nice and peaceful time fishing, sleeping, and playing poker before their wives come to meet them, although Babbitt is just beginning to feel "calm, and interested in life" when it is time to go home. Chapter 12 describes Babbitt's leisure time. In chapter 13, Babbitt attends the annual State Association of Real Estate Boards conference, followed by a trip to a brothel. The speech he gives at the conference is the first step in Babbitt's social climbing, and he follows it with political talks against the liberal lawyer Seneca Doane's candidacy in the local election, as well as a long speech about "sound business" values to the Zenith Real Estate Board.

Chapters 15–21

Trying to ingratiate himself with his wealthy and powerful classmate Charley McKelvey, Babbitt chats to him at their class reunion and has him and his wife to dinner. This is not a success, but Babbitt has more luck with the banker William Eathorne during their campaign to improve the Presbyterian Sunday school. Babbitt pays the young reporter Kenneth Escott to give the Sunday school favorable press, and Kenneth begins a friendship with Babbitt's daughter Verona. Babbitt's son Ted, meanwhile, is beginning a relationship with their neighbor Eunice Littlefield, and her father Howard is angry to find them dancing together at Ted's high school party.

At work, Babbitt makes a corrupt deal with a loan off the books from Eathorne, fires his salesman Stanley Graff, and then takes a business trip to Chicago with his son. After Ted goes back to Zenith, Babbitt happens to meet the Englishman Sir Gerald Doak, who had been a guest of Charles McKelvey while in Zenith, and entertains him thoroughly. Then Babbitt sees Paul Riesling with a suspicious woman and waits for him in his hotel room. Paul tells him that he can't stand his marriage anymore, and Babbitt tells him he will make an excuse to Paul's wife, Zilla. After Babbitt is elected vice-president of the Boosters, he finds out that Paul has been arrested for shooting his wife. Paul's lawyer will not allow Babbitt to testify on his behalf, and Paul is given a three-year prison sentence.

Chapters 22–29

Paul's imprisonment deeply affects Babbitt, and it inspires a series of increasingly rebellious activities. He goes to the movies during work hours, flirts with three women including a client named Tanis Judique and a young girl from the barbershop, whom he takes out to dinner. Babbitt goes to Maine by himself but fails to stop thinking about all of his problems in Zenith or to be satisfied by the "woodsman" life. On his way back to Zenith, Babbitt meets Seneca Doane, who inspires him to hold increasingly liberal opinions and even take the side of the strikers in the big walkout. This earns Babbitt the suspicion and contempt of his conservative friends at the Boosters.

Babbitt then begins a love affair with Tanis, after he goes to her apartment ostensibly to fix a leak. He makes no protest when his wife says she is going to visit her sister, and after she leaves he sees Tanis frequently, meets her socialite friends called the "Bunch," and becomes a heavy drinker and party-goer. His liberal sympathies increase, and when Vergil Gunch, the president of the Boosters, asks him to join the conservative "Good Citizens' League," Babbitt says he has to think it over.

Chapters 30–34

Babbitt finally writes to his wife that he misses her, and she is somewhat suspicious on her return. But Babbitt spends time with her and takes her to a spiritualist talk she wants to hear before he goes back to Tanis. Dissatisfied with this relationship as well, he breaks it off and assures himself that he's going to "keep free" and "run my own life!" After he takes a stand against the prominent citizens asking him again to join the Good Citizens' League, he begins to lose business; even his stenographer goes to a competing firm.

But Babbitt's wife's appendicitis and his devotion to her during and after the operation, cause him to return to his old ways, and he accepts when he is once again invited to join the conservative Good Citizens' League. Returning to his prominent conformist role, Babbitt's business prospers (through corruption), and he even partially confesses his sins to the uninterested Presbyterian priest. Verona marries Kenneth Escott and the Babbitts find, to their shock, that Ted has eloped with Eunice Littlefield. Although the rest of the family are very critical, Babbitt takes his son aside and tells him he has his support because, as Babbitt could never do, he has ignored what others think and done what he really wants.

Characters

George Follansbee Babbitt

The oblivious and conforming, yet inwardly restless, character of George Babbitt has penetrated American culture and become a pervasive cultural symbol. An unthinking, cultureless, greedy, and corrupt businessman can still be called a "Babbitt" and reactionary, selfish, absurd, and conservative behavior can still be called "Babbittry" with wide recognition. Babbit has come to represent the absurd and corrupt aspects of the American business world that Lewis was so effective at satirizing.

In many ways, Babbitt has been created to be the perfect target; he holds none of his own opinions, has no genuine passions, and rarely even manages to be a good or dependable husband and father. Yet there is an unmistakable inner life in Babbitt that fascinates readers and makes them sympathetic to his vivid character even if they finds all of his opinions and beliefs detestable. Chubby, pink-skinned, and wrinkled, with thinning hair and thick glasses, Babbitt makes an unlikely hero, yet he inevitably draws the reader into his struggle and his hollow life. Despite all of his falseness and emptiness, he is an unmistakably real character.

In the course of the novel, Babbitt undergoes the only major rebellion against the meaninglessness of his life that he will ever have. This is sparked by the imprisonment of his friend Paul Riesling, and it extends from a search for the calm outdoor life to debauchery and adultery. Afterwards, Babbitt once again becomes the corrupt, ignorant businessman content to oppress the poor and the standardized, dutiful husband who does not love his wife.

Myra Thompson Babbitt

Paul Riesling's second cousin, Myra is a "nice" and "gentle" person who does not have many opinions except for a desire to be a social climber and an interest in hokey spiritualism, but her own struggles and thoughts in the novel are undeveloped. She began to spend time with Babbitt while he was studying to go to law school and Paul was falling for Zilla. Babbitt did not love Myra then, but merely grew used to her after she assumed (without his proposal) that they were engaged, and he never really loves her during their marriage except with a bland sort of affection. Myra's feelings for her husband are not so clearly stated. She is upset, however, when he is having an affair with Tanis, and he fails to show her the expected level of devotion.

Ted Babbitt

Babbitt's slightly pert son, named after Theodore Roosevelt, graduates from high school, begins college, and elopes with Eunice Littlefield in the course of the novel. His two main interests are Eunice and cars, and he does not want to study anything except mechanical engineering, but Babbitt does not allow him to transfer colleges. Nevertheless, Ted has an increasingly close relationship with his father, and Babbitt is the only one to support his elopement at the end of the novel.

Tinka Babbitt

Tinka is Babbitt's youngest daughter, with "radiant red hair and a thin skin which hinted of too much candy and too many ice cream sodas." Despite his fondness for her, Babbitt does not seem to spend much time with his daughter, and Tinka does not play an important role in the novel.

Verona Babbitt

A "dumpy brown-haired girl of twenty-two," Verona is Babbitt's socially conscious child. She talks earnestly about all kinds of liberal social issues with her friend and eventual husband Kenneth, and the rest of the family often makes fun of this. She has graduated from college and works as a secretary, although she would like to work for a charity of some kind.

Dr. A. I. Dilling

Dr. Dilling is a prominent member of the Good Citizens' League and the surgeon who operates on Babbitt's wife. He is a chief influence in the group that warns Babbitt he must join the league and then ostracizes him from the community until he turns back to conservative conformity.

Sir Gerald Doak

Charles McKelvey's guest when he visits Zenith, "Sir Gerald" is something of a celebrity and considered to embody the stereotypes of the old English gentry. However, as Babbitt finds out when he makes friends with him in Chicago, Doak is an uncultured conservative businessman much like Babbitt.

Seneca Doane

Doane is Zenith's most radical lawyer and politician, as well as Babbitt's former college peer. He loses the mayoral election to a corrupt Republican but remains committed to social change through the strike. He even briefly draws Babbitt into his liberal thinking.

Sam Doppelbrau

Babbitt's neighbor and the "secretary of an excellent firm of bathroom-fixture jobbers," Sam and his wife throw wild parties and go for late-night car rides.

Dr. John Jennison Drew

Dr. Drew is the reverend of Babbitt's Presbyterian church, but he is much less interested in religion than in conservative politics. He uses his sermons as a platform for Republican ideas including anti-labor sentiments. Drew fails to pay any attention to Babbitt when the confirmed rebel tries to confess his sins.

Captain Clarence Drum

The leader of the force to suppress the strikers during Zenith's major walkout, Drum wishes he could use violence to solve labor conflicts.

William Washington Eathorne

Eathorne is the president of the First State Bank and a prominent member of Zenith's old-fashioned rich and powerful folk. He is also a member of Reverend Drew's Presbyterian church, and he befriends Babbitt during the drive to make a better Sunday school. Because Eathorne approves of Babbitt, he later allows him to take loans off the books for Babbitt's corrupt real estate ventures.

Kenneth Escott

The reporter that Babbitt hires to publicize the Presbyterian Sunday school, Kenneth is a young liberal writer at the newspaper. He begins a relationship with Babbitt's daughter Verona that eventually leads to marriage.

Sidney Finkelstein

The buyer for a department store, Sidney is a loyal Booster and Elk.

T. Cholmondeley Frink

"Chum" is the Booster and a good friend of Babbitt's that writes poetry and advertisements for a living. He is one of those disturbed by Babbitt's rebellion. Lewis uses his character to satirize the ridiculous platitudes of popular newspaper and magazine poetry.

Stanley Graff

Graff is the outside salesman of the real estate office until Babbitt fires him for tricking a tenant. Graff takes much of the abuse for Babbitt and Thomson's corrupt practices. He resorts to trickery because Babbitt has denied him a much-needed raise.

Vergil Gunch

Vergil is the President of the Boosters, a model for the conservative businessman, and a good friend of Babbitt's, except when Babbitt refuses to join the Good Citizens' League.

Orville Jones

Orville Jones is in the Babbitts' dinner party circle, although Myra does not want to invite him to their dinner party because he owns a common laundry shop.

Tanis Judique

Tanis is a lonely widow of forty or forty-two who has an affair with Babbitt. Babbitt meets her because she rents one of the office's apartments. She is a "slender woman" that Babbitt sometimes finds very attractive in one of her black frocks, although he is generally more interested in hearing her praise him than in her physical affection. Part of a "Bunch" of socialites and "Midnight People" that drink and party through the night, Tanis and her friends prove to be no more substantial, and their lives no more meaningful, than those lived by the conservative business types. Tanis eventually fails to excite Babbitt, and he leaves her, realizing that she is old and lonely.

Eunice Littlefield

The daughter of Babbitt's neighbor and Ted's eventual wife, Eunice is obsessed with the movies. Babbitt, who like his son is charmed by her short skirts and bobbed hair, suspects her of smoking. In this sense, she represents some of the typical characteristics of the "flappers," women of the 1920s who defied traditional roles.

Dr. Howard Littlefield

Howard Littlefield, father of Eunice, is Babbitt's neighbor and close friend. Full of trivia and obscure facts supporting conservative politics, Howard is a welcome accessory to the Babbitts' dinner parties, and Babbitt considers him extremely knowledgeable. In fact, Littlefield is full of nonsense, which Babbitt only begins to suspect during his rebellious phase. Otherwise, their only conflict comes over Eunice's relationship with Ted Babbitt.

Miss McGoun

Babbitt's able and efficient stenographer, Miss McGoun is much better at letter-writing than her employer and does a good deal of his work. This is why, in addition to his attraction to her despite her consistent refusal to so much as have a conversation with him, Babbitt is so upset when she briefly goes to a competing firm.

Charles McKelvey

McKelvey is one of the most rich and powerful men in Zenith, and Babbitt and his wife aspire to his social position. During their college reunion, Babbitt convinces McKelvey and his wife to come to dinner, but the party is a failure. Afterwards the McKelveys do not return the invitation.

Mrs. Opal Emerson Mudge

A pudgy, ridiculous lecturer that Myra enjoys, Mrs. Opal Emerson Mudge is a satire of trendy spiritualists.

Ed Overbrook

Like Babbitt's relationship with Charles McKelvey, Ed wants to ingratiate himself with a college classmate who is higher on the social ladder. The Babbitts ignore him after they go to his failure of a dinner party.

Joe Paradise

Half Native American, Joe is Babbitt's guide for both of his trips to Maine. Although Babbitt thinks of him as the perfect outdoorsman, Joe would rather set up a shoe store if he had enough money.

Professor Joseph K. Pumphrey

Owner of the "Riteway Business College," Professor Pumphrey is a fellow Booster.

Ida Putiak

Ida is the "small, swift, black-haired" young girl that works in Babbitt's barber shop. Babbitt asks her out to dinner while he is getting a manicure, and she agrees mostly for a free meal and a joke at Babbitt's expense.

Paul Riesling

Babbitt's best friend and the only person around whom he feels calm and happy, Paul Riesling is a misfit and an outcast in Zenith. Because of his sensitivity and his lack of business skills, the conservative and standardized society simply does not accept him. After his wife, Zilla, nearly drives him insane, he spends a period with another woman. Paul then shoots his wife and is imprisoned for three years, which completely breaks his spirit. At this point Paul disappears from the story

and is "dead" to Babbitt. Although, during his rebellious phase, Babbitt imagines that Paul is in Maine with him at the front of a canoe. Since his role is to bring out the genuine aspects of Babbitt's character, Paul has no place in the novel as it becomes more and more clear that Babbitt and Zenith are empty and false.

Zilla Riesling

Paul Riesling's wife, Zilla is characterized by her vanity, her moodiness, and her constant nagging of her husband. After Paul shoots her, she becomes fanatically religious and bitter. As Babbitt's wife understands, however, Zilla justifiably feels locked-in and unappreciated during her life with Paul, and as she says, if she did not nag Paul he would not motivate himself to do anything.

Sheldon Smeeth

Smeeth is the educational director of the Y.M.C.A. and is active in the Presbyterian church, where he conducts the musical program.

Louetta Swanson

Louetta, who lives across the street from the Babbitts with her husband Eddie, is a "pretty and pliant" woman full of excitement and flirtatiousness. The Swansons and the Babbitts attend each other's dinner parties, and Louetta is the first woman Babbitt tries (unsuccessfully) to seduce.

Henry T. Thompson

Babbitt's father-in-law and partner in the real estate business, Thompson is made to represent the "traditional, stage type of American business man." He is an "old-fashioned, lean Yankee," and he lacks the "subtlety" of the modern businessman. This is why, for example, Thompson is more willing to be outwardly corrupt while Babbitt prefers to lie even to himself when bending the law.

Themes

American Business

Babbitt has chiefly been understood as a satire of the prosperous, conservative business class of which Babbitt is a prominent member and a perfect example. At a point in the political and social climate where, Lewis felt, private enterprise and the economic interests of the business and ruling classes were valued above cultural endeavors or basic ethics, the novel struck an important critical tone.

Topics
For Further
Study

- The critic David Pugh has suggested that Lewis's satire is no longer powerful or applicable to young Americans today. Do you agree? Discuss the implications of *Babbitt* in contemporary American culture. What would Lewis say about today's government and today's business world? How would you describe a modern-day Babbitt and how would he or she differ from the original? Which lessons from the novel remain important and which remain poignant?

- *Babbitt* is full of references to the political and cultural life of 1920s America. Do some research on the era and discuss whether the novel is a justified and accurate portrayal of life in medium-sized American cities in the late 1910s and early 1920s. Is the fictional Zenith grounded in research and fact? How much, if any, of the satire is an unfair exaggeration?

- Read another of Lewis's novels from the 1920s, such as *Dodsworth* or *Main Street*. How does the novel you have chosen compare with *Babbitt*? Does Lewis use similar methods to satirize other aspects of American society? Are the plot and the melodrama of the novel more or less effective and engaging?

- Writers have approached the business world in many different ways. What makes *Babbitt* unique? Why has it been so influential? Does its approach have anything in common with other famous works that take American business as their theme, such as Arthur Miller's *Death of a Salesman* (1945) or David Mamet's *Glengary Glen Ross* (1984)? How is *Babbitt* suited to its era?

The novel has a host of targets for its business satire, and most of them are institutions of which Babbitt is a member or a co-conspirator: the Boosters, the Elks, the Chamber of Commerce, the Good Citizens' League, the fraudulent financial powers of big cities such as William Eathorne's bank, and underhand political interests like the Street Traction Company. Lewis stresses that these institutions create a greedy and corrupt business atmosphere in Zenith. They ruin anyone who seems to go against their agenda (as they begin to ruin Babbitt before Myra becomes ill), they are only interested in cultural endeavors like a symphony orchestra if it brings money to the city, and, as becomes clear during the suppressed telephone-workers' strike, they ruthlessly exploit the working classes.

Lewis also penetrates the deep hypocrisy of conservative American businessmen (that they say one thing and do another). The men of Babbitt's organizations preach the value of free competition and then ostracize all those who do not hold the same religious and social values, they support Prohibition but frequently drink themselves, they cheat on their wives, they suppress labor unions but organize into pro-business action groups, and they support religious groups like the Young Men's Christian Association (Y.M.C.A.) without holding any real Christian convictions.

One of the most condemning features of the American business class as portrayed in *Babbitt*, however, is its lack of any culture, imagination, or conviction. Babbitt's beliefs and those of his fellow Boosters and Elks are simply a conglomeration of the day's presiding commonplaces, and their only reason for holding an opinion is to fit in with their peers. Babbitt seems briefly to encounter some of his actual feelings in the course of the novel, but these "liberal" sentiments come more from a general discontentment he doesn't understand than from any genuine conviction. Presenting a culturally destitute society controlled by an insensitive and unthinking business class, Lewis launches a biting attack against the predominant American ideology of the 1920s.

Religion, Marriage, and Social Life in the Prohibition Era

Lewis's satire is not confined to the business world; he exposes many of the contradictions and absurdities in American private life during the era of Prohibition, focusing on family and social life in medium-sized cities such as the fictional Zenith. Ridiculing Babbitt's passionless marriage, his uninteresting social clubs, and even his depraved yet ultimately unexciting period of rebellion and adultery, Lewis highlights the emptiness of this social world. It is taken for granted that men do not love their wives, that couples rarely enjoy their dinner parties except as a chore, and that parents show a minimum of care or attention to their children. The alternative, emblematized by Tanis Judique and her "Bunch," is shown to be equally tiresome.

Religion and spirituality in Zenith are also absurd and unfulfilling. Babbitt has no conviction whatsoever in the Presbyterian Church, and when he tries to partially confess he meets with nothing but an uninterested reverend fitting in his prayer before a political meeting. Reverend Drew uses his sermons to make Republican political statements, and religion seems to have no more meaning than Mrs. Opal Emerson Mudge's ridiculous spiritualism. Lewis incorporates the emptiness of religious and social pursuits into the discontentment of the business world to more effectively satirize the American lifestyle in cities like Zenith.

Midlife Crisis

Babbitt is forty-six at the beginning of the novel and forty-eight by its end. In these two years, triggered by the imprisonment of his one real friend, he has undergone the major rebellion of his life. The various aspects of this crisis, from his trip to the movies during office hours and his developing liberal convictions, to his adulterous love affair and his drinking bout, represent his only departure from conformity. Babbitt had some liberal ideas in college but these do not represent serious, earnest, or original ideas. He stresses that he wants to stop all of his dirty dealing before he retires in twelve years.

Babbitt's one revolt, then, however much it is merely a tame and ineffectual attempt at escapism, is extremely important to Lewis's ambitions in the novel. *Babbitt* is more than a simplistic satire; it is the study of a character trying to escape from the standardized culture of which he is so prominent a member. And it is not simply that Babbitt cannot escape the business culture because he is fundamentally a conformist; his livelihood is severely threatened by his mildly liberal ideas when he sees his business start to disappear after failing to join the Good Citizens' League. Lewis is exploring the

fears and doubts that result from half a lifetime in the American system, the dissatisfaction that can result from conformity, and the futility of outward rebellion at such a late stage.

Style

Satire

Lewis's insightful exposure and condemnation of American values and institutions in the 1920s is effective and compelling mainly because he is such an adept satirist. He understands the conventions of humor, mockery, and social commentary, and he is able to draw a full and compelling portrait of an insecure and doubtful businessman in order to draw his readers into his way of thinking. By weaving his satirical points and attacks on American society into the various characters and dilemmas in Babbitt's life, Lewis establishes a convincing argument and wins over his readers.

Lewis is also effective because he so thoroughly understands the elements of American society he wishes to attack. One of the author's particular talents is in satirizing characters, ideas, and organizations by exposing their hypocrisy. Sometimes he forms the observation into a joke, as in Babbitt's thoughts about the Chamber of Commerce:

> No one ought to be forced to belong to a union, however. All labor agitators who try to force men to join a union should be hanged . . . In union there is strength. So any selfish hog who doesn't join the Chamber of Commerce ought to be forced to.

Other times, particularly towards the end of the novel when Babbitt joins the Good Citizens' League and the fraudulence of his business endeavors become less silly and more contemptible, Lewis engages in more earnest social commentary. When the Good Citizens' League burns down the Zenith Socialist Headquarters, throws their desks out the window, and beats their office staff, it is a significantly less funny instance of hypocrisy. In fact, Lewis is here using a classic satirical device, which is to make the audience laugh and later reveal the brutal reality behind the joke, implicating the audience in the problem.

Plot

Lewis balances his satire with the building action of Babbitt's social rise and midlife crisis. His novel develops Babbitt's struggle to reconcile his vibrant inner life with the meaninglessness around him into a plot with rising action of his dissatis-faction, the climax of his rebellion, and the de-nouement (resolution) of his renewed conformity. But one of the principal criticisms of the novel has been that its plot is poorly managed, and it lacks a compelling struggle against the corruption and standardization in Zenith. For critics such as Mark Schorer, in his afterward to the 1961 edition of *Babbitt*, the details of Babbitt's life and Lewis's episodes of parody and satire do not provide the convincing dramatic action of a finely crafted plot.

Historical Context

The Roaring Twenties

After World War I, American politics and so-cial life became increasingly conservative. Republi-can Warren G. Harding defeated Woodrow Wilson in the 1920 presidential election on a very conserv-ative platform claiming to be a "return to normalcy." Cutting government expenditures, vetoing bonuses for World War I veterans, and lowering income taxes for the wealthy, Harding vigorously supported private enterprise and suppressed labor unions. Harding's conservative administration also, in some ways, set the stage for a decade that enjoyed un-precedented prosperity, at least for the middle and upper classes. As was notoriously exposed after his death in 1923, however, his administration was in-volved in a great deal of corruption and bribery.

The social conservatism of the 1920s was evi-denced most notably by the prohibition of alcohol. Supported by claims that alcohol is bad for health and productivity, as well as by religious groups and post-war racist sentiments towards the German Americans who owned much of the alcohol trade, the Eighteenth Amendment went into effect in January of 1920 and persisted until 1933. Prohibition was, ultimately, a failure; it increased health risks because of unsafe bootleg alcohol and led to a sharp rise in organized crime since illegal brothels and saloons were so popular. But it was also a policy in line with a puritanical and conservative culture that frowned upon socialism, organized labor, and devi-ations from convention. The decade saw a major rise in the activities of the Ku Klux Klan, a sharp decrease in the immigration allowance, and the raiding and suppression of suspected "radicals."

There was, however, an active counterculture to the mainstream, although it was not always much more socially conscious. The decade showed considerable progress in women's rights, however, as the Nineteenth Amendment to the Constitution allowing women to vote was passed by Congress in 1919 and ratified in 1920. This was the era of "flappers," or women who defied domestic social constraints and were often associated with smok-ing and short hair. Jazz music was becoming in-creasingly popular, the film industry was thriving, and America was becoming increasingly inundated with technological advances such as cars and household appliances.

Late American Realism and Social Comedy

Nineteenth-century authors such as Mark Twain and William D. Howells, though committed to the "realist" goals of accurate representation by detailed description, were often involved in social satire. Like Lewis's chief English influences, Charles Dickens and H. G. Wells, Twain wrote comedic novels that attacked and parodied unjust social and governmental institutions. Howells's novels, like those of Henry James, were less comedic and more staunchly realist, but they also raised questions about social institutions such as marriage and business.

Realism began to split into a variety of fac-tions in the late nineteenth century, however. Among the chief new influences on writers such as Edith Wharton was the "naturalist" movement, which concentrated on the inevitable helpless rise and fall of an individual character's fortunes. Also, novelists including Stephen Crane were deeply in-fluenced by symbolist and romantic tendencies, while later expatriate American writers such as T. S. Eliot and Ezra Pound turned to the develop-ing influence of European modernism.

There remained a strand of writers, however, that were chiefly interested in social comedy and satire that posed as American realism. Upton Sinclair's "muckraking" books and pamphlets, written to expose social injustice, and with a spe-cific political agenda, were one aspect of this strand, although they were perhaps less concerned with strict realism than with propaganda. Never-theless, Sinclair was very influential over one of the most famous and bestselling realist satirists of the early twentieth century: Sinclair Lewis. Creat-ing his own brand of late American realism with a heavy emphasis on comedic satire, Lewis was the chief writer to bring the convention of American realism and social comedy through the 1920s.

Compare & Contrast

- **1920s:** Prohibition is in effect throughout the United States, making it illegal to manufacture or consume alcohol. Although supporters of Prohibition argue that it increases health and safety, organized crime has skyrocketed and over four times as many people will die of alcohol-related causes, due largely to unregulated bootleg liquor.

  Today: The legal drinking age in the United States is twenty-one, and the major alcohol-related health concerns are injuries and deaths from drinking and driving.

- **1920s:** The conservative culture of the early 1920s is characterized by conformity, pro-business politics, Puritanism, and a desire to return to normalcy after World War I.

Today: The election of George W. Bush's Republican administration and the terrorist attacks of September 11, 2001 have marked a shift in American culture. Legislation such as the Patriot Act, the attempt to outlaw certain types of late-term abortion, and the pro-business shift in environmental policy suggest an increasing promotion of conservative agendas and values.

- **1920s:** Upper middle-class businessmen and their families continue to live near the center of medium-sized American cities, although the decade will see the development of the first automobile suburbs.

  Today: Families of the Babbitts' class typically live outside of congested urban areas, in the suburbs. This trend exploded in the 1950s and continues to dominate American demographics.

Critical Overview

In his introduction to *Critical Essays on Sinclair Lewis*, Martin Bucco writes that the literary community reviewed *Babbitt* very positively and saw it as an improvement on *Main Street* (1920) despite the fact that: "Reviews in business and club magazines naturally remonstrated against Lewis's bestselling raillery of a 'standardized' American businessman discontented amid zippy fellow Rotarians, Realtors, and Boosters." H. L. Mencken and Rebecca West were among the most influential early critics to praise *Babbitt*. West wrote in the *New Statesman* that the novel "has that something extra, over and above, which makes the work of art."

In 1930, Lewis won the Nobel Prize, and this award secured the place of the novel as a classic in American and international literature. Afterwards, however, Lewis suffered a major decline in reputation from which he never fully recovered. He was possibly less successful during the 1930s because America was no longer enjoying the prosperity of the 1920s; critics have suggested that the privileged

circumstances of the 1920s caused people to be more receptive to Lewis's satirical talents. Interest in Lewis revived after his death in 1951, but critics continued their skeptical reevaluation of all of his novels, including *Babbitt*.

Critics have most often treated *Babbitt* as a satire of the American business world, although topics have ranged from Clare Virginia Eby writing on the influence of social critic Thorstein Veblen over the novel, to Stephen Conroy writing on the popular-culture trend in Lewis's work. David Pugh discusses whether the novel is applicable to the modern world in his 1975 essay "Baedekers, Babbittry, and Baudelaire," and he continues the debate about Lewis's critical appraisal by asking: "Babbitt: alive, readable? . . . or cold, boring, and very dead?" This question of whether *Babbitt* and Lewis's other works will stand the test of time continues. John Updike observes in a 1993 article in *The New Yorker* that, "Sinclair Lewis is at last fading from the bookshops." However, in his lengthy biography *Sinclair Lewis: Rebel from Main Street*, published in 2002, Richard Lingeman highlights "the apparent consensus among scholars and general readers that it was time for a fresh look at Lewis."

Criticism

Scott Trudell

Trudell is a freelance writer with a bachelor's degree in English literature. In the following essay, Trudell discusses the role that Babbitt's homoerotic relationship with Paul Riesling plays in Lewis's novel.

Babbitt is primarily a satire that exposes the emptiness and discontent in the life of its main character, but it is not always clear that Babbitt's life has no value or meaning. From his occasional pleasant drive to his self-satisfaction with his rise in the social hierarchy, Babbitt sometimes revels in and enjoys his conformity. He has moments of bonding with his children, particularly with Ted, although the children can seldom hold his interest. Although he finds his wife distasteful, he sometimes feels a passionless affection for her. And the various aspects of his rebellion, such as his relationship with Tanis, are initially very exciting until they are revealed to be nothing more than unsuccessful attempts at escapism.

All other relationships fade, however, in comparison to Babbitt's one worthwhile relationship, with the one person around whom Babbitt feels truly and consistently happy. Paul Riesling is not only Babbitt's best friend; he represents all that is genuine and valuable in Babbitt's life, a fact that Babbitt himself acknowledges after Paul is given a three-year prison sentence: "Babbitt returned to his office to realize that he faced a world which, without Paul, was meaningless." With Paul "dead" to him, Babbitt loses the only person around whom he can express his real thoughts and be silent and calm, and he can no longer face his family or the business world. Babbitt is willing to perjure himself for Paul, ignoring the effect this would have on his career and social status. Paul's imprisonment sparks a major mid-life rebellion in which Babbitt overturns nearly all of his beliefs and habits to escape his now "meaningless" existence.

Lewis is careful to emphasize that Paul is a misfit whose sensitivity, lack of business acumen, and inability to endure his wife are incompatible with the standardized business world of Zenith. Indeed, the satirist seems eager to stress that Paul represents the genuine side of Babbitt that cannot conform to

his outward life. Just as Zilla is a foil (a character whose purpose is to reveal something about another character) that emphasizes the vain, insecure, and nagging aspects of Myra that repel her husband and do not fit into Zenith domestic life, Paul is a foil for his best friend. Lewis makes this point most overtly after Babbitt's visit to Paul in prison:

> Babbitt knew that in this place of death Paul was already dead. And as he pondered on the train home something in his own self seemed to have died: a loyal and vigorous faith in the goodness of the world, a fear of public disfavor, a pride in success.

Paul does not embody these characteristics, but he has always been the one to reveal them in Babbitt. So, in order to drive the plot and test Babbitt's character, Lewis imprisons him and removes him from Babbitt's struggle. Paul is an expendable device in Lewis's satire, which needs to demonstrate that Zenith has no place for him, that Paul's genuineness, his "moodiness, his love of music," and his inability to conform are incompatible with Lewis's satirical vision. The author seems intent on refuting the possibility of a meaningful relationship for someone like Babbitt, although this is initially a realistic possibility. As D. J. Dooley observes in his book *The Art of Sinclair Lewis*, it is after Paul's imprisonment that this possibility is extinguished, the plot begins to fail, and the storyline loses its vitality:

> But in the melodramatic story of how Babbitt, now a hero, battles his former friends, now villains, the characters are simple and unreal, the plot is full of improbabilities, and Lewis does not come close to pulling it off.

This is because Lewis has abandoned Babbitt's central hope and purpose, turning the struggle of his main character into a desperate but ultimately futile attempt at escapism. The futility of the plot becomes particularly clear when Babbitt fails to enjoy his time in Maine; whereas before the outdoors had been his only truly calm and completely happy moment, without Paul: "He was lonelier than he had ever been in his life."

As is clear from Babbitt's pursuit of women around the same time, this loneliness is for both a friend and a lover. Babbitt's wife sometimes makes him feel less lonely, but he has never loved her and finds her completely repulsive sexually. Tanis also makes a brief dent in Babbitt's loneliness, but their affair is (like her) superficial and desperate, and it is shortly extinguished. Indeed, Babbitt never seems to be genuinely attracted to women; even his "fairy child" is a completely unconvincing fantasy, as Virginia Woolf notes in her 1947 essay, "American

Fiction." With Paul, on the other hand, he feels "a proud and credulous love passing the love of women," and their relationship is far more erotically charged than any of Babbitt's encounters with women.

There are a number of hints of this homoerotic aspect of Paul and Babbitt's relationship. During their trip to Maine, for example, where they need to abandon their wives and "just loaf by ourselves and smoke and cuss and be natural," this idea of the "natural" comes to a climax with the reaction one might expect from a taboo erotic encounter: "The shame of emotion overpowered them." And, when Babbitt returns to Maine, he has a desire for male affection, to "be a regular man, with he-men like Joe Paradise—gosh!" that culminates in a vision of Paul playing his violin at the end of Babbitt's canoe. Perhaps the most convincing example, however, comes as Babbitt is considering Paul at the only moment in which he considers the carnal and sexual aspects of his otherwise quite frigid fairy girl:

> But he did know that he wanted the presence of Paul Riesling; and from that he stumbled into the admission that he wanted the fairy girl—in the flesh. If there had been a woman whom he loved, he would have fled to her, humbled his forehead on her knees.

There is no woman Babbitt loves; his only true love is a man in prison. The end of chapter 6 reveals that even the passionless and insubstantial love of Babbitt's marriage is an extension of his romantic feelings for Paul. Myra became a replacement for Paul's companionship while Paul was "bespelled by Zilla Colbeck," and Myra's role of ineffectively substituting for Paul is underscored by the fact that she is Paul's second cousin. Lewis is (wittingly or unwittingly) emphasizing that his novel is describing a homoerotic love story.

Unfortunately for Babbitt, this story comes to an abrupt end in chapter 21. It is at this point that, in the novelist's struggle between his satirical goals and his desire to develop the dramatic conflicts of his characters, the love story is sacrificed to the demands of Lewis's satire. Genuine homoerotic love is the central aspect of Babbitt's search for meaning, but it is certainly not something that Lewis is willing to accept into his satirical agenda. Just as Paul is a misfit who has no place in the cultureless and standardized Zenith, Babbitt and Paul's love must be eradicated from a city that does not tolerate deviations from passionless and duty-bound marriage.

There is seldom any love at all in Zenith, either among the married Boosters and Realtors who cheat on their wives and pay no attention to them, or among Tanis's escapist and insincere "Bunch." The only

> "With Paul, on the other hand, he feels 'a proud and credulous love passing the love of women,' and their relationship is far more erotically charged than any of Babbitt's encounters with women."

instances of passion, aside from that of Babbitt and Paul, are the relationships of Babbitt's children, particularly of Ted and Eunice Littlefield. So it is no coincidence that Ted's bonding with his father and the escalation of his relationship with Eunice begin to develop just before Paul shoots Zilla. Lewis requires the developing dramatic energy of Paul and Babbitt's relationship to move along his reader and power his satire, but it is too vivid and taboo to follow to its natural destination. Not only is a homoerotic relationship unacceptable in Zenith, it is unacceptable to Lewis and to his readers. It is as if, recognizing that the course of Paul and Babbitt's relationship as the central dramatic energy of the novel was becoming too dangerous and developing too fully, Lewis forcefully steers the plot towards the safer Ted.

Ted is not too safe; his dislike of college and his elopement are edgy enough to create a potential dramatic conflict against the empty, satirical Zenith. And Babbitt is shown to enjoy a sort of genuine, though compromised, passion by proxy at the end of the novel: he allows Ted to follow his dreams although he cannot follow his own. Despite the fact that it does not ring true or genuinely address Babbitt's struggle, Lewis manages to power his satire to the end of the novel with this secondary dramatic action.

After Lewis abandons the central conflict of the novel and imprisons its only real solution, however, his novel loses steam. As discussed above, the plot flattens and dies after Paul's imprisonment, and Babbitt's relationship with Ted fails to convince or even interest many readers and critics. Lewis has crafted a thorough and compelling satire, but his suppression and abandonment of the main love story leaves his famous main character unhappy, unchanged, and undeveloped. It sucks the life out of the novel and leaves the reader wondering whether, had Lewis not succumbed to a cheap plot trick, Babbitt might have fought a successful battle for meaning.

Source: Scott Trudell, Critical Essay on *Babbitt*, in *Novels for Students*, Gale, 2004.

Clare Virginia Eby

In the following essay, Eby explores parallels between Babbitt *and the ideas of social critic Thorstein Veblen, focusing specifically on Veblen's critique of manliness.*

> "The well-worn paths are easy to follow and lead into good company."
> —Thorstein Veblen, *The Place of Science in Modern Civilization*

The significance of Thorstein Veblen to American literary realism and, more widely, to the early twentieth century intellectual climate has been often noted. The "dean" of American realism, William Dean Howells, wrote one of the reviews of *The Theory of the Leisure Class* (1899) which launched Veblen's reputation, significantly titled "An Opportunity for American Fiction." Veblen scholars have also noted his importance to literary history. His biographer Joseph Dorfman claims "the book [*Leisure Class*] or at least its language relatively early made its appearance on the stage and in novels." Veblen's message and style were especially welcome to antagonists of the status quo. As Max Lerner puts it, "Veblen was more than a thinker" for his generation; he was "a symbol by which men measured their rejection of the values of the established order." So pervasive was Veblen's social critique that Maxwell Anderson wrote in 1918 in *The Dial*, "I once asked a friend if he had read *The Theory of the Leisure Class*. 'Why no,' he retorted, 'why should I? All my friends have read it. It permeates the atmosphere in which I live.'"

Yet in the case of Sinclair Lewis one need not rely on claims of Veblen-by-osmosis, for these two Midwesterners (Lewis was born in Minnesota, where Veblen moved at age eight) and Yale graduates were familiar enough with each other's work to cite some details. The "pariah," Red Swede in *Main Street* (1920), is not only Veblenian in his iconoclasm, in his failure to "'decently envy the rich,'" in his analyses of "'your leisure class'"; he also has a book of Veblen's on his shelf. Indeed, according to Mark Schorer, "in some ways the major contribution of Lewis's novels was their continuation (or, at least, popularization) of certain leading ideas of Veblen, especially as to the leisure class and business enterprise." More surprising

given Veblen's tendency to avoid citing authorities other than himself is his allusion in *Absentee Ownership and Business Enterprise in Recent Times* (1923) to *Main Street*. He opens his chapter on the country town by invoking "the perfect flower of self-help and cupidity ... Its name may be Spoon River or Gopher Prairie, or it may be Emporia or Centralia or Columbia."

Noting the parallels between Veblen and Lewis can help to clear up what has seemed a problem to many readers of *Babbitt* (1922). Many have complained that in this novel Lewis' method of characterization seems at war with itself. The title character splits into "two Babbitts," a boosting conformist and a rebel wannabe, which coexist uncomfortably. Lewis' insistence that George F. Babbitt is not a type—a claim which sits uneasily with most readers—has only contributed to the devaluation of his art. The author, it is said, must be as confused as his character, for he cannot choose between satire and sociology, or between romance and the novel. The result, claim many critics, is disappointingly static, a museum piece or a portrait done in a morgue. Lewis was indeed torn between individualizing a sympathetic Babbitt and satirizing a member of a herd, but the criticisms seem to me to miss the point. Lewis provides a valuable chapter of cultural history by tracing Babbitt's rebellion against "the duty of being manly": a duty to manifest boosterism, clannishness, chauvinism, and anti-intellectualism.

This definition of white, middle class, middle America manliness and Lewis' understanding of the damage it causes the autonomous self point to the author's correspondence with Veblen's works, which, in turn, provides a theoretical explanation for the perceived gap perceived between the "two Babbitts." The typical and often stereotypical qualities of Babbitt and his friends conform to the broad strokes of Veblen's critique of manliness. In contrast, the reader sympathizes with Babbitt only insofar as the realtor casts off his "He-Man" role that his cohorts rightly perceive as a challenge to the status quo. The horror of the novel's closed circle, the meaning of Babbitt's aborted rebellion, lie not in revealing a static life but in illustrating Veblen's theory of how an unruffled surface is maintained by institutional coercion.

The works of Lewis and Veblen exist within a wider field of concerns, one of which historians have identified as the American "crisis of masculinity." Although the crisis has been variously defined and dated, its broad outlines can be traced.

The nineteenth century witnessed an extraordinary rigidity in gender roles that increasingly strikes analysts as compensatory. With the process of industrialization came a "new uncertainty about what it took to be a man" and, as traditional ways of proving individualistic manhood become increasingly difficult to sustain, sex roles became dichotomous. Add to these technological and industrial challenges the ferment for women's rights in the latter half of the century, particularly the "New Woman" movement of the 1890's and the result is manhood beseiged, a "paradigmatic revolution in self-perception [for males] during the nineteenth and twentieth centuries." One of the responses to the masculinity crisis was hypermasculine behavior, such as that seen in *Babbitt*. Peter N. Stearns sums up this state when he writes: "As it became harder to be a man ... it became vital to prove one's manhood, especially to oneself."

The relevance of this crisis in the male paradigm to *Babbitt* becomes clearer as we move into the 1920s. Women's suffrage, achieved in 1920, seemed apocalyptic to those bewailing the erosion of masculine privilege. After 1920, as males lost even the illusion of remaining in control which had sustained them in the previous century, there was a "shift in ... masculinity-validating criteria" from active to reactive behaviors. The decade of the 1920s, according to several historians, marks a new period of American men's history. Elizabeth and Joseph Pleck's categorizations are useful: the Strenuous Life Period characterized by substantial male bonds (1861–1919) gave way to more interdependence between men and women during the Period of Companionate Providing (1920–1965). But, as Veblen was fond of noting, most people can't keep up with historical change; institutional lag keeps us hanging on to "imbecile" models of behavior. *Babbitt* reveals the anxieties of this transition from macho to domesticated man: George Babbitt runs from (and, ultimately, back to) women in a frenzied search for a separate men's culture that would help him to prove his manhood. Babbitt's behaviors respond unconsciously to the marked decline in beliefs about distinctive "male" and "female" traits that was characteristic of the 1920s.

Little wonder that Veblen would write in the same year *Babbitt* was published of the "Dementia Praecox" (precocious dementia) afflicting so many American males, which reduced their behavior to adolescent hysteria. Well known for deconstructing "woman's sphere" as conspicuous consumer, Veblen joined many other social scientists in reassessing early twentieth-century masculinity. In

> **Veblen's unique approach to the masculinity crisis is especially akin to Lewis' in *Babbitt*; both combine two unlikely poses, as satirists and as anthropologists of everyday life."**

this time when the male gender became suddenly visible, Veblen argued for the social construction of masculinity—or, more precisely, for the social coercion of masculinity. While other social scientific analogies might well be drawn, Veblen's unique approach to the masculinity crisis is especially akin to Lewis' in *Babbitt*; both combine two unlikely poses, as satirists and as anthropologists of everyday life.

Readers who dispute the effectiveness of Lewis' novel can nevertheless agree on its satiric target: the monotonously ugly faces of standardization. Veblen foresaw in 1904 this "standardization . . . of the details of everyday life," even of "conduct and knowledge." A prescient observer of turn-of-the-century capitalism, Veblen accused it of breeding standardization not only in commodities but in consumers themselves—an insight fundamental to *Babbitt*. (*Business*, 7, *Instinct*, 313). Babbitt's rebellion against the pull of standardization provides the key which unlocks the satire and his critique of manliness.

Lewis examines several possible interpretations of this monotonous world. The unwary reader can follow Babbitt, who thinks he is in revolt against the pressures imposed by women: in the first chapter he "resent[s] . . . return from this fine, bold man-world to a restricted region of wives and stenographers, and of suggestions not to smoke so much," and toward the end, his fling with Tanis Judique leaves him again "want[ing] to flee out to a hard, sure, unemotional man-world." But Babbitt incorrectly identifies the source of the pressures on him to function like a standardized product. As Nina Baym explains,

> we all ... experience social conventions and responsibilities and obligations first in the persons of women, since women are entrusted by society with the task of rearing young children ... Thus, although

women are not the source of social power, they are experienced as such.

Joe Dubbert's distinction between women's *influence* and men's *power* is also useful here. Babbitt is actually rebelling against social power—against, that is, regulation manliness.

In Zenith, which prides itself on producing "manly men and womanly women," males are the true conformists. The narrator makes this point while providing two levels of commentary on the Babbitts' dinner party:

> there were six wives, more or less—it was hard to tell so early in the evening, as at first glance they all looked alike, and as they all said, "Oh *isn't* this nice!" in the same tone of determined liveliness. To the eye, the men were less similar . . . and the strange thing is that the longer one knew the women, the less alike they seemed; while the longer one knew the men, the more alike their bold patterns appeared.

The comparison is certainly, as Veblen might say, invidious. Lewis distinguishes not only between surface (women's) and deep (men's) conformity here, but also between levels of observation: only those able to see beneath the surface will recognize the true agents of conformity. Babbitt is too myopic to see that his revolt against standardization enlists him in a battle against manliness.

According to Veblen, who relished the "masculinity crisis," the contemporary American model of manliness rests on the foundation of business enterprise. His paradigm begins with the premise that modern business derives from primitive humans' distinction between "industry" (the "effort that goes in to create a new thing") and "exploit" (the conversion to [one's] own ends of energies previously directed to some other end"). Productive industry, diminished in status as it comes to be aligned with drudgery, falls to women, while the honorific and counterproductive exploits are valorized into men's sphere (*Leisure*, 12–13; also see *Business*). Hence business, evolved from exploit, is predatory, competitive, and destructive. These same traits, Veblen contends, define American male prowess: business *is* manly, and manliness is businesslike.

Lewis employs the Veblenian sexual division of labor while equating manliness with business and exploit in *Babbitt*. Zenith cautiously segregates men's from women's spheres; "the realms of offices and of kitchens had no alliances." The Floral Heights matrons with "nothing to do" illustrate Veblen's theory that contemporary women's work includes conspicuous leisure. Against this backdrop, Babbitt fights the "manly battle" of business. Driven by his need to feel heroic, Babbitt's mock

epic behaviors illustrate Veblen's conflation of business with predation: his "preparations for leaving the office to its feeble self . . . were somewhat less elaborate than the plans for a general European war." The iconoclastic Paul Riesling translates the point into colloquial terms: "'All we do is cut each other's throats and make the public pay for it!'"

Veblen's analysis of businessmen finds them as dazzlingly inept at making things as they are skilled at making money. Producers "only by a euphemistic metaphor," businessmen profit from "the higgling of the market" (*Place of Science* 294). A realtor who knows nothing about architecture, Babbitt personifies the Veblenian businessman as do few characters in American literature. As Lewis says, Babbitt "made nothing in particular, neither butter nor shoes nor poetry, but he was nimble in the calling of selling houses for more than people could afford to pay." This description of the parasitic businessman follows Veblen's explanation that

> To "do well" in modern phrase means to engross something appreciably more of the community's wealth than falls to the common run . . . Men are conceived to serve the common good somewhat in proportion as they are able to induce the community to pay more for their services than they are worth. (*Instinct*, 349–50)

Veblen considers it ironic that Americans venerate business, for the worshipping attitude permits the rapacious individual to profit at communal expense (*Business*, 291).

What Veblen says about "the types of manhood which the life of sport fosters" characterizes as well his view of business: "the reason for the current approval and admiration of these manly qualities, as well as for their being called manly, is the same as the reason for their usefulness to the individual" (*Leisure*, 263). Manliness, in other words, is divisive, self-serving, and counter-productive. Lewis evidently agrees about the host willingly supporting the parasite, for the self-interest and smug complacency of Babbitt and his friends are unthinkable without their culture's approval of business. Babbitt illustrates the point: "He serenely believed that the one purpose of the real-estate business was to make money for George F. Babbitt." Why the serenity? Veblen pins down what is ultimately at stake here: pecuniary success constitutes "the final test of manhood" (*Higher Learning*, 82). So ingrained are pecuniary criteria that "when we say that a man is 'worth' so many dollars, the expression does not convey that moral or other personal excellence is to be measured in terms of money, but it does very distinctly convey the idea that the fact of his possessing

What Do I Read Next?

- F. Scott Fitzgerald's *The Great Gatsby* (1925) uses techniques associated with European modernism to display the empty and hollow undercurrent in American life in the years following World War I. It is one of the most influential masterpieces of the era.

- *Main Street* (1920), Lewis's novel written just before *Babbitt*, is a satirical portrait of small-town American life based on Lewis's home town of Sauk Center, Minnesota.

- A famous muckraking novel about the working conditions in a slaughterhouse, Upton Sinclair's *The Jungle* (1906) is one of the enduring satires of the early twentieth century. It greatly influenced Lewis's work.

- Arthur Miller's play *Death of a Salesman* (1949) centers on the tragedy of Willy Loman, a salesman whose life becomes meaningless except for his love of his sons. It focuses on a very different kind of family. The play employs distinct melodramatic methods in order to examine family and business culture after more than two decades of vast social and economic change, but it sharply resonates with Babbitt's struggle.

- Charles Dickens's *Hard Times* (1854) tells the story of a hardware merchant with firm beliefs in rationality and fact coming into conflict with the world of imagination and culture. The novel, by the famous and influential satirist of English culture, is one of Dickens's shorter and more readable works.

- John Dean's new biography *Warren G. Harding* (2004) examines the controversy and scandal behind Harding's presidency and illustrates the political environment of the early 1920s.

---

many dollars is very much to his credit" (*Place of Science*, 393).

But Veblen's successful male does not live by individual and invidious business success alone. As much modern research into male identity formation has demonstrated, manhood demands a more public form of testing than that expected for women. According to anthropologist David Gilmore, "true manhood is a precious and elusive status beyond mere maleness, a horatory image that men and boys aspire to and that their culture demands of them as a measure of belonging." This is certainly the case in Veblen's writings, as in *Babbitt*. Veblen concluded that manhood is sustained by group affiliation. Indeed, since he repeatedly contrasts ceremonial with functional behaviors to the detriment of the former, men's public, competitive, and ritualistic behaviors only make the social construction of masculinity an even easier satiric target for him to hit. Veblen considers the back-slapping, herding tendency fundamentally masculine, and traces it from the "instinct of sportsmanship" in *The Theory of the Leisure Class* (1899)

to patriotism in his war writings. By *The Nature of Peace and the Terms of its Perpetuation* (1917) he is defining patriotism as "the prime attribute of manhood" (40). Clannish acts, whether in war or in sport, share the competitive spirit of business enterprise, but they differ in being collective endeavors, forcefully binding the individual man to his habitat. Hence the American male's "sentiment[al] . . . approval" of patriotism along with property necessitates an unsteady psychic balance between "servitude" and "predation" (*Business*, 290). Veblen's brilliantly homely metaphor which explains patriotic behavior nicely characterizes his view of all manly clannishness:

> The analogy of the clam . . . may at least serve to suggest what may be the share played by habituation in the matter of national attachment. The young clam, after having passed the free-swimming phase of his life, as well as the period of attachment to the person of a carp or similar fish, drops to the bottom and attaches himself loosely in the place and station in life to which he has been led; and he loyally sticks to his particular patch of oose and sand through good fortune and evil. It is, under Providence, something of a fortuitous matter where the given clam shall find

a resting place for the sole of his feet, but it is also, after all, "his own, his native land" etc. It lies in the nature of a clam to attach himself after this fashion, loosely, to the bottom where he finds a living, and he would not be a "good clam and true" if he failed to do so . . . [A]ll men of sound, or at least those of average, mind will necessarily be of a patriotic temper and be attached by ties of loyalty to some particular establishment. (*Nature of Peace*, 134–5)

Babbitt provides a veritable stew of such bivalves. The realtor knows well that being a He-Man is not only about looking out for Numero Uno. The compulsion to attach himself to the right groups in order to sustain his manhood is the downfall of the sympathetic side of Babbitt. A deep and insidious peer pressure influences his actions at the Realtors' Convention where he stirs himself into a state of "hysteric patriotism." Lewis aligns his views with Veblen's as he documents Babbitt's speech on, appropriately, manhood:

> "the ideal of American manhood and culture isn't a lot of cranks sitting around chewing the rag about their Rights and their Wrongs, but a God-fearing, hustling, successful, two-fisted Regular guy, who belongs to some church with pep and piety to it, who belongs to the Boosters or the Rotarians or the Kiwanis, to the Elks or Moose or Red Men or Knights of Columbus or any one of a score of organizations of good, jolly, kidding, laughing, sweating, upstanding, lend-a-handing Royal Good Fellows, who plays hard and works hard, and whose answer to his critics is a square-toed boot that'll teach the grouches and smart alecks to respect the He-man and get out and root for Uncle Samuel, U.S.A.!"

To adopt the phrase of Gilmore, Babbitt's speech confirms that masculinity is preeminently about "the need to establish and defend boundaries." This policing of boundaries may involve vehement defenses of "male" versus "female" territory, or, as it does here in Babbitt's speech, necessitate declaring a specific version of manhood as the norm, the natural, the right.

One of Lewis' most satirical deflations of the American businessman is surely this revelation that the "self-made man" is, in fact, group-made. John Remy's discussion of the "men's hut" illuminates this aspect of *Babbitt*. Distinguishing between patriarchy and fratriarchy, the latter, argues Remy, "is based simply on the self-interest of the association of men itself" rather than the needs of the family unit protected by the partriarch. Most of Babbitt's male bonding rituals are, likewise, fratriarchal—as Lewis depicts them, reactive measures to counter female influence and to prop up flaccid egos. Yet the seat of power in both patriarchal and fratriarchal societies is the "men's hut" which defines itself by setting up boundaries, excluding women as

well as any dissident males. Such is clearly the intent of Babbitt's speech at the Realtors' Convention which defines who are, and who are not, his cohorts.

It is fitting that Lewis lodges his satirical vision of "the ideal of American manhood" in Babbitt's oratorical triumph, its cliches and slogans revealing the grammar of standardization. Lewis discloses a frightening territory with this map showing how manliness sanctifies chauvinistic and violent response to dissidents. Babbitt's cliches lead us into the land of institutional coercion and, indeed, "Babbittry" has passed into general circulation to mean conformity of a most depressing sort. The contrast with Veblen's prose is, at first glance, striking. Far from following predictable paths, Veblen startles readers by using unfamiliar juxtapositions. He is remembered most often for the arcane rather than the familiar. While Lewis revels in documenting slogans and banalities as surely as Veblen resists using language like anyone else, I would like to resist the temptation to use the contrast to (invidiously) privilege one writer's discourse over the other's. Lewis and Veblen's contrasting prose styles illustrate how different methods can work toward a similar end. Lewis' deadening cliches, like Veblen's idiosyncratic phrases, make readers uncomfortably conscious of the prisonhouse of language. Raising our awareness of the extent to which language entraps its user is precisely their shared goal. Parroting contemporary platitudes, Lewis shows from the inside how langage restricts thought and, therefore, action. Situating his writing on the outside, Veblen illustrates the subversive possibilities of discourse that does not bow to received wisdom. Yet Veblen, too, invents cliches, however unwittingly—"conspicuous consumption" being only the most famous example. The "Man from Main Street" and "Man from Mars" both use language to illustrate the brilliantly transformed cliche which lies at the heart of Veblen's most famous work: "Whatever is, is wrong" (*Leisure*, 217).

Babbitt, however, prefers Whatever Is. The compulsion to belong to the right groups insinuates itself into all facets of his life. Babbitt's business ethics—"he followed the custom of his clan and cheated only as it was sanctified by precedent"—directly follow Veblen's characterization of American business as "a spirit of quietism, caution, compromise, collusion, and chicane." (Veblen illustrates the idea with another homely metaphor: "the silent hog eats the swill" [*Higher Learning*, 70–71].) Men's play follows the same pattern as their work.

Lewis uses the precise terms of Veblenian conflationary logic to describe Babbitt's enthusiasm for baseball: "the game was a custom of his clan, and it gave outlet for the homicidal and side-taking instincts which Babbitt called 'patriotism' and 'love of sport.'" Veblen could easily explain Lewis' odd comment that Babbitt "honestly believed . . . he loved baseball." According to Veblen, the "lower motive of unreflecting clannishness . . . stands out perhaps most baldly in the sentimental rivalry . . . shown at intercollegiate games and similar occasions of invidious comparison" (*Higher Learning*, 235). Even the rebelliousness of Babbitt's sexual play, his fling with Tanis Judique, is compromised by the need for acceptance by "The Bunch."

Although Babbitt's business ethics, sportsmanship, and general love of boosting provide targets for raucous satire, his inability to realize a sense of self apart from his clan identification is chilling. The compulsion to remain identifiably male prohibits self-realization. Existing beneath the back-slapping, mutually re-enforcing surface of Zenith's He-Men is a core of self-immolation. This is the dark center of American manhood percieved by Veblen, who finds the effacement of individual desires in the service of the clan's wishes characteristic of the masculine patriotic spirit (*Nature of Peace*, 46). What follows is that acceptable men, who recognize themselves only by their group identification, *cannot be* autonomous.

It follows as well that manliness can only be confirmed by other males. Myra Babbitt, for instance, is "too busy to be impressed by that moral indignation with which males rule the world" and ignores her husband's cries for kudos as Vice President elect of the Boosters Club. Once Babbitt's business contacts begin to erode and he faces retribution for "treachery to the clan," the ceremonial proofs of his identity vanish. This process again illustrates the breakdown of the traditional male role. As Peter Stearns says, the more difficult the process of "male self-definition," the more crucial becomes "proof before other men." Babbitt faces a frighteningly uncharted territory without the familiar signposts to confirm his masculinity and responds with hypermasculine behaviors.

Readers of scholarly journals hardly need reminders that American culture has a history of excluding intellectual work from the approved masculine realm—that the athlete need not share his laurels with the academic. Lewis' treatment of this scenario is Veblenian in spirit and in detail. He recognizes how the clannishness fundamental to middle class manliness would breed anti-intellectualism.

He makes the equation explicit when he comments that Paul, by "becom[ing] highbrow," "committed an offense against the holy law of the Clan of Good Fellows." Babbitt's son, Ted, must be herded away from such blasphemy. (Ted's full name, Theodore Roosevelt Babbitt, harkens back to a favored model of masculinity.) The father instructs the son about anti-intellectualism, illustrating again how men confirm each other's identity, and the faith:

> "Course I'd never admit it publicly—fellow like myself, a state U. graduate, it's only decent and patriotic for him to blow his horn and boost the Alma Mater— but smatter of fact, there's a whole lot of valuable time lost even at the U., studying poetry and French and subjects that never brought in anybody a cent."

This conflation of patriotism, boosting, and education illustrates Veblen's observation that "invidious patriotism has invaded [academia], too." It is manly to boost the local university, but effeminate to learn about culture. Recommending the study of Business English over Shakespeare, Babbitt pushes for a business degree—a specialization which Veblen drily describes as "thereby widening the candidate's field of ignorance." Babbitt's opposition to Ted's pursuit of an engineering degree fits the Veblenian pattern perfectly. In his most revolutionary work, *The Engineers and the Price System* (1921), Veblen argues that productivity would be increased by anywhere from three-thundred to twelve-hundred-percent were the engineers to overthrow businessmen and run industry themselves.

Lewis' satirical treatment of Babbitt's educational values also corresponds to Veblen's argument about the decline of *The Higher Learning in America* (1918). He finds that the bastion of manliness, business, has "infect[ed]" the university (*Higher Learning*, 62). The result is monstrous: "corporations of learning" run by "captains of erudition" and operated as if they were "business house[s] dealing in merchantable knowledge" (85). He warns against the confinement of knowledge to the "quantitative statement" or the "balance-sheet" (86). Lewis illustrates the effects of this contamination with Babbitt's speech about "'Those profs. . . . If we're going to pay them our good money, they've got to help us by selling efficiency and whooping it up for rational prosperity!'" The correspondence course advertisement, crowned by "an inspiring educational symbol—no antiquated lamp or torch or owl of Minerva, but a row of dollar signs," reiterates the point.

Lewis' characterization of the professional academic, Howard Littlefield, particularly shows the influence of Veblen's critique of the higher learning. Littlefield holds, appropriately, a Yale Ph.D. in Economics; Veblen a Yale Ph.D. in Philosophy. Veblen would appreciate Lewis' character's name, with its insinuation that his "field" is narrow, for he dedicated his career to railing against colleagues who upheld business as usual. Economists, says Veblen, "ten[d] to work out what the instructed common sense of the times accepts as the adequate or worthy end of human effort. . . . [They justify] a projection of the accepted ideal of conduct" (*Place of Science*, 65). The reigning "quasi-science" in economics "necessarily takes the current situation for granted as a permanent state of things . . . It is a 'science' of complaisant interpretations, apologies, and projected remedies" (*Higher Learning*, 187). Rather than pursue disinterested research, economists conform to the "homiletics and wool-gathering" that the common man mistakes for science: "the conclusive test of scientific competency and leadership, in the popular apprehension, is a serene and magniloquent return to the orthodox commonplaces" (*Higher Learning*, 182). In short, they specialize in "taxonom[izing] . . . credenda" (*Place of Science*, 21).

Lewis illustrates this co-optation of the academic economist through Littlefield, who,

> confirmed the business men in the faith. Where they knew only by passionate instinct that their system of industry and manners was perfect, Dr. Howard Littlefield proved it to them, out of history, economics, and the confessions of reformed radicals.

He is what Veblen describes as a "spokesman for the competitive system" (*Place of Science*, 189) and one of the queries put to him, to define the meaning of "sabotage," seems an unmistakable allusion to Veblen's lengthy discussion of the word in the first chapter of *Engineers*, which appeared in book form the year Lewis was working on *Babbitt*. Boosting business, justifying the clan's exploits, and curtailing dissident thought, Littlefield is the only sort of academic likely to seem manly in Zenith. He belongs, and rationalizes the belonging of others. Babbitt understandably admires him for "'put[ting] the con in economics!'" Littlefield illustrates Veblen's point that economists, like the patriotic clan, are "due to be the creatures of their heredity and environment" (*Essays in Our Changing*, 3).

Lewis' treatment of Zenith's anti-intellectualism draws strength from Veblen's fears that higher education had lost its integrity by serving the manly interests of boosting, conformity, and business. Veblen was horrified that the university should be the handmaid of business, considering these "two extreme terms of the modern cultural scheme"

antithetical and predicting that only the intelligentsia could save "the substantial code of Western civilization" after the great war (*Higher Learning*, 76, 52). He contends that "the two lines of interest—business and science—do not pull together; a competent scientist or scholar well endowed with business sense is as rare as a devout scientist—almost as rare as a white blackbird" (*Higher Learning*, 149–50). Clearly, the insistence that science serve business lies at the heart of Zenith's anti-intellectualism. He-Men fear any method of reckoning other than the pecuniary. Knowledge is acceptable to them only insofar as it furthers business as usual. Littlefield illustrates the point nicely.

But, according to Veblen, the true intellectual does not confirm the faith; he subverts it: "Intellectual initiative . . . [cannot] be reduced to any known terms of subordination, obedience, or authoritative direction" (*Higher Learning*, 86). He was well aware that this, his alternative model of manhood, did not correspond to "the current ideal of manhood" (*Place of Science*, 30). Veblen's description of the scientist suggests why Zenith cannot tolerate intellectual initiative: it would mean challenging "habitual convictions" and looking at,

> the nature of the conventions under which men live, the institutions of society,—customs, usages, traditions, conventions, canons of conduct, standards of life, of taste, of morality and religion, law and order . . . Skepticism is the beginning of science. (*Higher Learning*, 180, 181).

Rather than policing established boundaries, Veblen's model of manhood would trespass them. His skepticism is devoutly to be feared by the custodians of convention.

Veblen names this skeptical spirit of inquiry "idle curiosity." We who read Veblen—much less, scholarship on Veblen—manifest this trait. Idle curiosity is Veblen's construct to explain—and to celebrate—the academic's devaluation in an anti-intellectual culture. Although the "most substantial cultural achievement of the race" (*Instinct*, 86), idle curiosity is not pragmatic. Indeed, idle curiosity has no "ulterior purpose"; it is wholly "fortuitous" when the fruit of scientific investigation is turned to useful ends (*Place of Science*, 18, 16). Because the spirit of free inquiry threatens to unmask what passes as practical knowledge—and "'practical' in this connection means useful for private gain; it need imply nothing in the way of serviceability to the common good" (*Higher Learning*, 193)—it must be co-opted or suppressed.

Littlefield, as much a police of the status quo as Vergil Gunch, illustrates the process of co-optation. Babbitt's retribalization illustrates the suppression. Early in the novel, Babbitt patrols his own thought and self-censors any opportunity for idle curiosity. For instance, he tells his son, "'what's the use of a lot of supposing? Supposing never gets you anywhere. No sense supposing when there's a lot of real facts.'" Strategically, Babbitt's rebellion consists of a lot of supposing: suppose he sat at a different table at the club? suppose he went on a trip alone? suppose Paul were right? suppose he cross the line of acceptable flirtation? Lewis describes Babbitt's moment of crisis as the glimmering of an intellectual awakening: "he was thinking . . . perhaps all life as he knew it and vigorously practiced it was futile . . . What was it all about? What did he want?" He senses how his known "world . . ., once doubted, became absurd." As Babbitt grows intoxicated with the heady freedom of supposing, he manifests such independent behaviors as "enjoy[ing] the right to be alone" and declaring to Myra, "'I know what the League stands for . . . the suppression of free speech and free thought.'" These rebellious suppositions illustrate Veblen's point that idle curiosity, by definition, breaks the rules. Babbitt's rebellion lets him peer beyond the sportsmanlike clannishness and anti-intellectualism of Zenith men into the subversive territory of independent thought.

But Babbitt, of course, is no Arrowsmith, the scientist whose idealistic and intellectual principles lead him to renounce civilization. The realtor's story is about the inexorable pull of the status quo. Veblen's theory of institutional coercion accounts for the failure of the realtor's rebellion and the triumph of the status quo. Babbitt succumbs to what Veblen, in an unusually paranoid moment, describes as "those massive interests that move obscurely in the background." Babbitt had long parroted what Veblen calls the Vested Interests. His words and thoughts have always been those of the advertisers, the press, ultimately of the Republican Party and big business. Veblen comments upon this phenomenon: "farmers, workmen, consumers, the common lot, are still animated by the fancy that they themselves have something to say" (*Vested*, 175). Babbitt illustrates how "bias of loyalty" and "civic duty" allow the Vested Interests to control duped citizens (*Nature of Peace*, p. 10). So strong are the ties that bind that Veblen prophecies in *The Engineers and the Price System* the inevitable failure of revolution in America:

> By settled habit, the American population are quite unable to see their way to entrust any appreciable responsibility to any other than business men . . .This sentimental deference of the American people to the

sagacity of its business men is massive, profound, and alert.

Babbitt, finally unable to let go of this valued cultural identification of power, respect, and manliness, illustrates Veblen's point. As he succumbs to the pressure of the aptly named Good Citizens' League he affirms, "'I'm a business man, first, last, and all the time!'" With these words he returns to the men's hut.

Internal pressures such as habits of thought play as large a role in Veblen's theory of institutional coercion as do the external pressures exerted by the Vested Interests. All customs "exercise a selective surveillance" over mankind: partly a "coercive, educational adaptation" (as we see in the case of Babbitt); partly "a selective elimination of the unfit" (as the instance of Paul Riesling illustrates) (*Leisure Class*, 212). Habits of thought, "sanctioned by social convention, . . . become right and proper and give rise to principles" (*Instinct*, 7). On this observation rests Veblen's brilliant theory of institutional lag, according to which any innovation comes to be seen as "bad form" (*Leisure Class*, 200). Babbitt's aborted rebellion illustrates the ingrained oppositions to change: he discovers "that he could never run away from Zenith and family and office, because in his own brain he bore the office and the family and every street and disquiet and illusion of Zenith" (242). Veblen explains the point nicely: "The most tenacious factor in any civilization is a settled popular frame of mind" (*Vested*, 147).

Veblen means "popular" in two senses: widespread and favored. Perhaps most chilling about his theory of institutional coercion is the part that the duped common man plays in sustaining the status quo. The common man,

> beset with the picturesque hallucination that any unearned income which goes to those Vested Interests whose central office is in New Jersey is paid to himself in some underhand way, while the gains of those Vested Interests that are domiciled in Canada are obviously a grievous net loss to him,

is in fact *indispensible* to the maintenance of the status quo (*Vested*, 133, 16). This is the ultimate purpose served by clannishness. Men pride themselves on their affiliation with the expensive, the impressive, the large—with the Vested Interests. Babbitt, like Zenith's other He-Men, sustains the status quo by "respec[ting] bigness in anything; in mountains, jewels, muscles, wealth or words," by feeling "clever and solid . . . to bank with so marbled an establishment" as The Miners' and Drovers' National Bank. Lewis puns in his description of another bank to emphasize Veblen's point: "the tower [was] a temple-spire of the religion of business, a faith passionate, exalted, *surpassing common men*" (emphasis added). The common man, says Veblen, "pays the cost [for the Vested Interests] and swells with pride" (*Vested*, 137). This is why even so petty a character as Babbitt must be reclaimed: he is part of the skeleton to which the muscle of the Vested Interest attaches.

Reading *Babbit* as a Veblenian critique of manliness sheds light on the problem of the "two Babbitts": one a stereotype and the object of Lewis' satire; the other an appealing, if failed, individual. The alleged conflict vanishes once we recognize a sustained treatment of the crisis of American masculinity. The end of the novel depicts Babbitt reaffirming his manliness at the expense of his individuality. He returns to the sanctuary of "facile masculine advice" and "true masculine wiles." The status quo of Zenith is restored, and Lewis has demonstrated the pressure and even coercion needed to maintain the unruffled surface. He-men marshal the battle to uphold the established order, receiving in return the confirmation of their manliness. All this so that the Vested Interests can continue business as usual—which, says Veblen, "means working at cross-purposes as usual, waste of work and materials as usual, restriction of output as usual, unemployment as usual, labor quarrels as usual, competitive selling as usual, mendacious advertising as usual, waste of superfluities as usual by the kept classes, and privation as usual for the common man" (*Vested*, 140–1). Babbitt's aborted rebellion against business as usual illustrates Veblen's ironic truism: "history records more frequent . . . instances of the triumph of imbecile institutions over life and culture than of peoples who have by force of instinctive insight saved themselves" (*Instinct*, 25).

Reading Babbitt in this way may also help to rejuvenate the decidedly old-fashioned reputation Lewis has in most quarters. Recent findings in "Men's Studies" suggest the currency of Lewis' Veblenian views on male identity formation. Part of the "ubiquitous" pattern located by anthropologist David Gilmore is that "the manhood ideal is not purely psychogenetic in origin but is also a culturally imposed ideal to which men must conform whether or not they find it psychologically congenial." Sociologist Michael Kimmel extends this troubling insight further: "The constitution of men's power over women is simultaneously the power of one version of masculinity over multiple masculinities. Women are subordinated by men in

different but parallel mechanisms by which non-normative men are marginalized from the hegemonic construction." Veblen and Lewis were early subscribers to this belief that masculinity coerces men as well as women. If, as Joe Dubbert says, American males are "trapped by a masculine mystique," dating from a "crisis of the male paradigm" threatening men in the last two decades of the nineteenth century with "urbanization, civilization, and feminization," it is little wonder that the next generation would all the more belligerently assert their manhood. In an ingenious new reading of literary naturalism, Mark Seltzer speaks of the "statistical persons" which abound in early twentieth century texts and cautions, "This is not, however, to replace individuality with standards . . . but to make the achievement of the standard the measure of individuality." *Babbitt* and the writings of Veblen document a concern that coercive standards for masculinity were strangling the autonomy of individual males. They disclose the operations of the imbecile institution of white, middle class, middle American manliness in the early decades of this century.

Source: Clare Virginia Eby, "*Babbitt* as Veblenian Critique of Manliness," in *American Studies*, Vol. 34, No. 2, Fall 1993, pp. 5–24.

Sources

Bucco, Martin, "Introduction," in *Critical Essays on Sinclair Lewis*, G. K. Hall, 1986, pp. 4–5.

Dooley, D. J., *The Art of Sinclair Lewis*, University of Nebraska Press, 1967, pp. 82–95.

Lewis, Sinclair, *Babbitt*, New American Library of World Literature, 1961; originally published by Harcourt Brace Jovanovich, 1922.

Lingeman, Richard, *Sinclair Lewis: Rebel from Main Street*, Random House, 2002, p. xii.

Pugh, David G., "Baedekers, Babbittry, and Baudelaire," in *Critical Essays on Sinclair Lewis*, edited by Martin Bucco, G. K. Hall, 1986, pp. 204–13; originally published in *The Twenties: Fiction, Poetry, Drama*, edited by Warren French, Everett Edwards Press, 1975.

Updike, John, "Exile on Main Street," in the *New Yorker*, Vol. 69, No. 13, pp. 91–97.

West, Rebecca, "*Babbitt*," in *Sinclair Lewis: A Collection of Critical Essays*, edited by Mark Schorer, Prentice-Hall, 1962, pp. 23–26; originally published in *New Statesman*, No. 23, October 1922.

Woolf, Virginia, "American Fiction," in *The Moment, and Other Essays*, Hogarth Press, 1947, pp. 99–100.

Further Reading

Allen, Frederick Lewis, *Only Yesterday: An Informal History of the 1920s*, John Wiley & Sons, 1997; originally published by Harper & Row, 1931.

> This book, written with the atmosphere of the 1920s fresh in the author's mind, provides a useful glimpse into the politics and intrigue of the era.

Hutchisson, James M., *The Rise of Sinclair Lewis: 1920–1930*, Pennsylvania State University Press, 1996.

> Hutchisson's book offers a further critical perspective on Lewis's years of critical and popular success.

Lewis, Sinclair, *If I Were Boss: The Early Business Stories of Sinclair Lewis*, edited by Anthony Di Renzo, Southern Illinois University Press, 1997.

> These stories, which Lewis wrote during his early career as a short story writer, are important examples of his developing ideas about American business, and they expand upon some of the key themes in *Babbitt*.

Love, Glen A., *Babbitt: An American Life*, Twayne Publishers, 1993.

> Love's study follows the influence of the "Babbitt type" throughout the literature of the twentieth century. It is a very useful source in determining Lewis's influence over the American literary scene.

Schorer, Mark, *Sinclair Lewis: An American Life*, McGraw-Hill, 1961.

> Schorer is perhaps Lewis's most famous biographer, and this work was instrumental in re-evaluating Lewis's reputation in the latter half of the twentieth century.

The Count of Monte Cristo

Alexandre Dumas

1844–1845

The Count of Monte Cristo (Paris, 1844–45), by French novelist and playwright Alexandre Dumas, is one of the most popular novels ever written. Set in Marseilles, Rome and Paris in the nineteenth century, it tells the story of Edmond Dantès, a young sailor who is falsely accused of treason and imprisoned in a dungeon for fourteen years. A fellow prisoner tells him where to find treasure buried on a Mediterranean island called Monte Cristo. On Dantès's escape, he acquires the treasure, gives himself the name Count of Monte Cristo, and ruthlessly goes about the slow destruction of his enemies.

Dumas got the idea for *The Count of Monte Cristo* from a true story, which he found in a memoir written by a man named Jacques Peuchet. Peuchet related the story of a shoemaker named Francois Picaud, who was living in Paris in 1807. Picaud was engaged to marry a rich woman, but four jealous friends falsely accused him of being a spy for England. He was imprisoned for seven years. During his imprisonment a dying fellow prisoner bequeathed him a treasure hidden in Milan. When Picaud was released in 1814, he took possession of the treasure, returned under another name to Paris and spent ten years plotting his successful revenge against his former friends.

Generations of readers have responded to Dumas's riveting, romantic tale of revenge by a man who believes he acts as the agent of Providence. The story has adventure, intrigue and romance in full measure, and also presents a vivid portrait of France from the end of the Napoleonic years to the early 1840s.

Author Biography

One of the most prolific writers of all time, Alexandre Dumas was born on July 24, 1802, in Villers-Cotterêts in France. He was the third child of Thomas-Alexandre Dumas, a general in the French revolutionary army, and Marie-Louise-Elisabeth Labouret Dumas. Dumas's father died in 1806, leaving the family poor. Dumas's schooling was therefore scanty, but he soon developed literary interests, stimulated by his friendship with Adolphe Ribbing de Leuven, a young Swedish nobleman whom he met in 1819. In 1823, Dumas moved to Paris and gained a position on the staff of the Duc d'Orleans. In collaboration with Leuven, Dumas wrote many melodramas. His historical play *Henri III et sa cour* (*Henry III and His Court*) was produced to great acclaim in 1829.

Dumas took part in the revolution in 1830 that placed the Duc d'Orleans on the French throne, as King Louis Philippe. During the 1830s, Dumas continued to write hugely successful plays, and his tours of Switzerland and Italy produced many travel books. In 1838, Dumas met Auguste Maquet, who became his collaborator on many works, although they were officially attributed solely to Dumas. During the 1840s, Dumas and Maquet began a series of romanticized historical novels, which were published in serial form: *Le Chevalier d'Harmental* (1842; translated as *The Chevalier d'Harmental*, 1846); *Les Trois Mousquetaires* (1844, translated as *The Three Musketeers*, 1864), and *Le Comte de Monte Cristo* (1844–45, translated as *The Count of Monte Cristo*, 1846). These books were enormously successful, turning Dumas into a worldwide literary celebrity.

His output remained prodigious. Among the works he published in the 1840s were *La Reine Margot* (1845; translated as *Marguerite de Valois*, 1846) the first of a sixteenth-century trilogy; *Vingt ans aprés* (1845; translated as *Twenty Years After*, 1846), a sequel to *The Three Musketeers*; *La Guerre des femmes* (1845–46; translated as *The War of Women*, 1895); *Le Chevalier de Maison-Rouge* (1846; translated as *Marie Antoinette; or, The Chevalier of the Red House*, 1846). Dumas adapted many of these books for the stage. His total literary output amounted to over three hundred volumes.

Dumas became wealthy from his writings. Always flamboyant, he built a mansion for himself called Château de Monte Cristo on the outskirts of Paris. He also built a theatre, the Théâtre Historique, specifically for the performance of his

Alexandre Dumas

own plays. These establishments were expensive to maintain, and Dumas, who spent money as quickly as he earned it, accumulated many debts. In 1851, he moved to Brussels to escape his creditors, remaining there for several years before returning to Paris. In 1860, he traveled to Italy, where he supported Garibaldi in the campaign for Italy's independence. He lived in Naples for four years before returning to France.

Dumas fathered two children by two different mistresses. His first child was Alexandre Dumas fils, who was to gain fame as a playwright. Dumas eventually married yet another mistress, though the marriage was short-lived.

Dumas continued to write prolifically well into the 1860s. He died of a stroke on December 5, 1870, at Puys, near Dieppe.

Plot Summary

Imprisonment and Escape

The Count of Monte Cristo begins with the arrival of a ship in Marseilles, France. One of the crew is a young sailor named Edmond Dantès. Dantès seems to be on the threshold of great happiness. Morrel, the shipowner, promotes him to captain, and

Media Adaptations

- *The Count of Monte Cristo* has often been adapted for film. The most recent version (2002) was directed by Kevin Reynolds and stars Jim Caviezel as Dantès, Guy Pearce as Fernand Mondego, Richard Harris as Abbé Faria, James Frain as Villefort, and Dagmara Dominczyk as Mercédès.

- A 1975 film version was directed by David Greene and starred Richard Chamberlain as Dantès.

he is about to marry a beautiful girl named Mercédès. However, at the feast before the wedding Dantès is arrested for treason. He is innocent, but has been entrapped by a plot hatched by Danglars, a fellow sailor who is jealous of Dantès's promotion, and Fernand, who was his rival for the love of Mercédès. The plot is aided by Villefort, a corrupt prosecutor, and Dantès is imprisoned in the Château d'If. He is not told why he is imprisoned. He remains in the Château d'If for fourteen years. During this time he meets the Abbé Faria, a fellow prisoner who has been digging what he hoped would be a tunnel to freedom, but which leads instead to Dantès's cell. The Abbé is a learned man, and he teaches Dantès everything he knows. He also tells Dantès the location of a secret treasure, which is buried on an uninhabited island called Monte Cristo, in the Mediterranean. When the Abbé dies, Dantès switches places with the corpse and is carried out of the prison for burial. He plans to escape from the grave. But instead of burying him, the jailers toss him into the sea. Even so, he manages to swim to safety. He makes his way to Monte Cristo and discovers the treasure.

Dedication to Revenge

Now a rich man, Dantès dedicates himself to gaining revenge on those who wronged him. Taking on the first of many disguises, as the Abbé Busoni, he tracks down Caderousse, a former untrustworthy neighbor who is now an impoverished innkeeper. Caderousse tells him the story of Dantès's arrest and what has happened since. Villefort, Danglars and Fernand are all now powerful men. Dantès rewards Caderousse and his wife with a valuable diamond. Based on what Caderousse told him, Dantès, now disguised as an Englishman, Lord Wilford, rewards the ship owner Morrel, who had tried many times to intercede with the authorities on Dantès' behalf. Morrel has suffered many losses at sea and is on the verge of bankruptcy. He is about to commit suicide when his daughter Julie brings proof that all his debts have been paid by a mysterious benefactor, who has also given Morrel a diamond for his daughter's dowry.

The scene switches to Rome, where two young Frenchmen, Baron Franz d'Espinay and Viscount Albert de Morcerf (Fernand's son) attend the carnival. They meet Dantès, who has given himself the name Count of Monte Cristo. Monte Cristo uses the influence his wealth buys to save a man named Peppino from execution. He then saves Albert, who has been kidnapped by bandits led by the notorious Luigi Vampa. In gratitude, Albert agrees to introduce Monte Cristo to his social circle in Paris. There Monte Cristo meets Lucien Debray, a diplomat, Beauchamp, a journalist, and Captain Maximilien Morrel, the son of Morrel. They are all fascinated by the remarkable count. Monte Cristo meets Fernand, who is now the Count of Morcef. Morcef is grateful to him for saving his son's life. Monte Cristo also meets Mercédès, who recognizes him but says nothing.

Monte Cristo buys a house at Auteuil, near Paris, which was the scene of a crime committed by Villefort, when he buried the infant child of his lover, Baroness Danglars. Monte Cristo knows this from his servant Bertuccio, who had a grudge against Villefort and tried to kill him at that house. Bertuccio saved the infant's life and raised him as Benedetto. Bertuccio also tells the count that he was a witness to a murder committed by Caderousse and his wife, who killed the jeweler who came to buy a diamond.

Monte Cristo next meets Danglars, who is now a rich banker. He discovers that the Danglars are unhappily married and that Danglars's wife is having an affair with Debray. Monte Cristo causes Danglars to lose a large amount of money when the banker acts on a rumor spread by Debray about political events in Spain. Danglars demands that his wife, whom he knows is having an affair with Debray, repay him for the loss. Monte Cristo then exploits the latent ill-feeling between Danglars and Morcerf by encouraging Danglars to investigate Morcerf's behavior many years ago in regard to a French ally, Ali Pasha, in Greece.

Monte Cristo gets into the favor of Villefort by saving his wife and son when their carriage goes out of control. Then he deliberately arouses Madame Villefort's interest in the medicinal use of poisons. Villefort and Madame Danglars are terrified when they guess that Monte Cristo knows the secret of their affair. They fear that their child may be alive.

Maximilien wants to marry Villefort's daughter, Valentine. But the Villefort family, except for Valentine's grandfather, Noirtier, want her to marry Franz d'Epinay. The marriage is called off after the paralyzed Noirtier, who many years before was a Bonapartist, communicates that it was he who killed Franz's father, a royalist general. Madame Villefort schemes to arrange an inheritance for her son Edouard by poisoning her father and mother-in-law, and attempting to poison Noirtier and Valentine. Noirtier and Valentine survive.

Enemies Vanquished

Caderousse escapes from the prison to which he was sent for aiding his wife in murder. He burgles Monte Cristo's house, but Monte Cristo, disguised as the Abbé Busoni, catches him in the act. Monte Cristo lets him go but Caderousse is then murdered by his accomplice, Andrea Cavalcanti. Andrea is in fact Benedetto, who has been given a fake identity as an Italian nobleman by Monte Cristo. As Caderousse dies, Monte Cristo reveals his real identity.

Morcerf is disgraced when it is revealed that many years ago, when he was in the French army, he betrayed his benefactor, Ali Pasha, and sold Ali Pasha's wife and daughter into slavery. The daughter, Haydée, was bought by Monte Cristo. Albert realizes that Monte Cristo arranged for his father's disgrace and challenges him to a duel. But Mercédès tells Albert the whole story of Dantès' betrayal by Fernand, and Albert apologizes to Monte Cristo before the duel begins. Mercédès leaves her disgraced husband for a life of poverty, while Albert renounces his name and fortune. Morcerf commits suicide.

Andrea, who was to be married to Eugénie Danglars, is arrested for murder. Eugénie, who never wanted to marry him, disguises herself as a man and runs off with her friend Louise d'Armilly. Andrea briefly escapes, but he is recaptured. At his trial, he explains that he is the son of Villefort, the man who is prosecuting him. Distraught, Villefort rushes home. There he finds that his wife has committed suicide. Villefort had discovered that it was she who was poisoning his family, and told her to kill herself or face trial and a death sentence. When

Villefort discovers that his wife has also killed their young son, Edouard, he goes insane, but not before Monte Cristo has revealed his real identity to him.

Monte Cristo arranges for Danglars to be ruined financially. Danglars leaves his wife and goes abroad, while Madame Danglars falls out with Debray. Danglars embezzles some money and goes to Rome, where he is kidnapped by bandits led by Luigi Vampa. They rob him of all his money, except for fifty thousand francs. Monte Cristo tells him he is now forgiven. Then he reveals to Danglars his true identity as Edmond Dantès. Danglars is completely broken by the loss of all his wealth.

With all his enemies vanquished, Monte Cristo arranges for Maximilien, who believed Valentine to be dead, to be reunited with her. Then he sails off in his yacht, having found love once more with Haydée.

Characters

Ali

Ali is Monte Cristo's mute valet. He is totally loyal to his master, who saved his life.

Beauchamp

Beauchamp is a radical journalist and a loyal friend of Albert de Morcerf. He is one of Albert's seconds in the duel with Monte Cristo.

Benedetto

Benedetto is the son of de Villefort and Madame Danglars. Villefort buried him at birth, believing he was dead. He was found by Bertuccio, who raised him. Benedetto grows up to be a scoundrel. Because of who Benedetto is, Monte Cristo uses him in his plot against Villefort, giving him a new identity as an Italian nobleman, Andrea Cavalcanti. Andrea becomes engaged to Eugénie Danglars, but he is then arrested for the murder of Caderousse. At his trial he identifies Villefort, who is prosecuting him, as his father, thus ruining Villefort.

Bertuccio

Bertuccio is a Corsican who swears a vendetta against Villefort because Villefort made no effort to find the murderer of Bertuccio's brother. Later, Bertuccio is wrongly arrested for the murder committed by Caderousse and his wife. Monte Cristo, in the guise of Abbé Busoni, manages to arrange his release. Bertuccio then enters the service of Monte Cristo.

Abbé Busoni
See Dantès

Gaspard Caderousse

Gaspard Caderousse is a greedy and untrustworthy neighbor of Dantès. He is present, and drunk, when Fernand writes the note accusing Dantès of treason. Caderousse knows Dantès is innocent but does nothing to help him. Many years later, when Caderousse is an innkeeper, Dantès visits him, disguised as the Abbé Busoni. Caderousse tells him the entire story of why Dantès was imprisoned and what has happened to the conspirators since. Busoni rewards him with a diamond. But after Busoni has gone, Caderousse and his wife murder a jeweler who offered to buy the diamond. Caderousse is arrested and sentenced to hard labor. He escapes but continues a life of crime. His end comes when he burgles Monte Cristo's house. Monte Cristo, in disguise as the Abbé Busoni, catches him red-handed, but then lets him go, guessing correctly that he will be immediately killed by his accomplice, Benedetto.

Andrea Cavalcanti
See Benedetto

Cloclès

Cloclès is a loyal elderly employee of Morrel.

Count of Monte Cristo
See Dantès

Doctor d'Avrigny

Doctor d'Avrigny is physician to the Villefort family. He suspects that the mysterious deaths of several family members are murder, but he says nothing to the authorities.

Franz d'Epinay

Franz d'Epinay is a young nobleman who visits Rome with his friend Albert de Morcerf. Later, Franz engages to marry Valentine de Villefort, but he cancels the engagement when he discovers that Valentine's grandfather, Noirtier, was the man who killed his father, a royalist general, many years earlier.

Baron Danglars

As a young man, Danglars is a sailor on the *Pharaon*. He is envious of Dantès and writes a note falsely accusing him of being a Bonapartist conspirator, causing Dantès to be imprisoned. Using unscrupulous means, Danglars pursues a career as a banker. He becomes rich and marries an aristocrat. The marriage is an unhappy one, however. Monte Cristo arranges for Danglars's downfall by plotting a series of financial disasters for him. Danglars leaves his wife, and his daughter runs away from their home. Eventually, when Danglars has only fifty thousand francs left, Monte Cristo forgives him, but Danglars is completely shattered by his financial ruin and his hair turns white.

Eugénie Danglars

Eugénie Danglars is the daughter of the Danglars. She is horrified at the thought of marriage and is pleased when her fiancé, Andrea Cavalcanti, is arrested for murder. Deciding to live independently, she disguises herself as a man and runs away with her friend, Louise d'Armilly.

Madame Danglars

Madame Danglars comes from an ancient family and was married to a marquis. After his death, she married Danglars. However, the marriage is not a happy one, and the couple live largely separate lives. Madame Danglars takes lovers, including Villefort, with whom she has a child, and later Debray. After her husband leaves her, she is also abandoned by Debray.

Edmond Dantès

Edmond Dantès is a highly capable and good-hearted young man of nineteen who is on the brink of great success and happiness. He is about to be promoted to captain of a commercial trading ship and to marry the girl he loves. But the envy and treachery of Fernand, Danglars, Caderousse and Villefort result in his being falsely imprisoned for treason for fourteen years. On his escape, he vows to reward those who in his absence were kind to his father and punish those who conspired against him. Dantès acquires great wealth by finding the treasure that his fellow prisoner, the Abbé Faria, told him was buried on the island of Monte Cristo. Giving himself the title of Count of Monte Cristo, as well as several aliases, he then rewards his friends in the Morrel family and pursues his enemies with single-minded determination and great ingenuity. He sees himself as the agent of divine Providence. However, he comes to doubt this when his scheme against Villefort results in the death of the innocent boy, Edouard. He overcomes his doubts when he makes a trip to the chateau where he was imprisoned, which rekindles his memories of the injustice he suffered. He can then pursue his vengeance against his final enemy, Danglars.

Monsieur Dantès

Monsieur Dantès is Dantès's father. He lives in poverty, which worsens after his son's imprisonment. Mercédès and Morrel try to look after him, but eventually, overwhelmed by his misfortunes, he refuses to eat and starves himself to death.

Albert de Morcerf

Albert de Morcerf is the son of the Count and Countess de Morcerf. Unlike his father, Albert is a man of integrity and courage. His life is saved by Monte Cristo when he is kidnapped by bandits in Rome, and Monte Cristo comes to recognize Albert's essential goodness, even though they come close to fighting a duel. When Albert learns of his father's disgrace, he forgives Monte Cristo for his part in making his father's crimes public. He also renounces his name and fortune and vows to make a fresh start in life by joining the army.

Count de Morcerf

See Fernand Mondego

Countess de Morcerf

See Mercédès Herrera

Marquis de Saint-Méran

Marquis de Saint-Méran is a wealthy royalist in high favor with the court. His daughter Renée marries Villefort. He is later poisoned by Madame Héloïse de Villefort.

Marquise de Saint-Méran

Marquise de Saint-Méran is the wife of the Marquis de Saint-Méran. She and her husband are poisoned by Madame Héloïse de Villefort.

Renée de Saint-Méran

Renée de Saint-Méran becomes Villefort's first wife and the mother of Valentine. She dies young.

Edouard de Villefort

Edouard de Villefort is the Villeforts' young son. He is poisoned by his mother just before she commits suicide. His death causes Monte Cristo to reconsider whether his actions have been just.

Héloïse de Villefort

Héloïse de Villefort is Villefort's second wife, and the mother of Edouard. She poisons the Marquis and Marquise de Saint-Méran, and Valentine, as part of her plot to ensure an inheritance for her son. On being found out by her husband and told to commit suicide or face prosecution, she chooses suicide, and she also murders her son.

Monsieur de Villefort

Monsieur de Villefort is the twenty-seven-year-old deputy public prosecutor in Marseilles who sends Dantès to prison unjustly. Villefort knows Dantès is innocent, but he wants to protect his father, Noirtier, a Bonapartist, who was the addressee of the letter that Dantès had been asked to deliver from Elba. During Dantès's imprisonment, Villefort becomes the powerful Deputy Minister of France in Paris. However, Villefort is guilty of one secret crime. He had an affair with Madame Danglars, and he buried their baby alive. However, the baby was rescued and was raised as Benedetto. When as a young man, Benedetto is charged with murder, he exposes Villefort's crime in court. Villefort goes home and finds his wife has committed suicide and also killed their son Edouard. The shock of all these events drives him insane.

Valentine de Villefort

Valentine de Villefort is the daughter of Monsieur and Renée de Villefort. She is in love with Maximilien, but she falls victim to the poison plot of her stepmother, who wants Valentine's inheritance to end up with her son Edouard. Monte Cristo saves Valentine's life and arranges for her to be united with Maximilien.

Lucien Debray

Lucien Debray is the Secretary of the Minister of the Interior in Paris who carries on an affair with Madame Danglars. She eventually finds out that Debray is only interested in the money they are making from a profitable joint business venture which has drained the fortune of her husband.

Abbé Faria

Abbé Faria is a learned and resourceful priest imprisoned in the Château d'If. He and Dantès become close friends after Faria digs through to Dantès's cell. Faria teaches Dantès languages, science, culture and spirituality. He also tells him where to find buried treasure. Although Faria dies before the two of them can put their escape plan into action, it is Faria who equips Dantès with all he needs to successfully take on the identity of the Count of Monte Cristo.

Haydée

Haydée is the daughter of Ali Pasha, who was betrayed by de Morcef. As a young girl, Haydée was sold into slavery and purchased by Monte

Cristo, in whose service she remained. Haydée testifies against de Morcerf at his trial, which ensures his conviction.

Emmanuel Herbault

Emmanuel Herbault is a clerk who works for Morrel. He marries Julie Morrel.

Julie Morrel Herbault

Julie Morrel Herbault is the daughter of Morrel. Monte Cristo, calling himself Sinbad the Sailor, uses her as the channel through which he pays Morrel's debts and restores the family fortunes. She marries Emmanuel Herbault.

Mercédès Herrera

Mercédès Herrera is a beautiful young girl in Marseilles who is engaged to marry Dantès. After Dantès is imprisoned, she is grief-stricken. Eighteen months later, she agrees to marry Fernand, but she never ceases to love Dantès. Although she ascends to a high social position in Paris, her marriage is unhappy. Later, when Dantès as Monte Cristo visits her, she recognizes him immediately, but says nothing. At another meeting, she persuades him not to kill her son in a duel. When her husband commits suicide, Mercédès renounces her title and her husband's wealth. Helped by a monetary gift from Monte Cristo, she goes to live in the small house in Marseilles which was once owned by Dantès' father. She plans to spend the rest of her life in prayer.

Jacopo

Jacopo is a sailor who saves Dantès's life after Dantès has escaped from prison and is trying to swim to safety. Jacopo pulls him out of the water just as Dantès's strength gives out. He becomes a loyal friend of Dantès and stays devoted to him after Dantès becomes Monte Cristo. Monte Cristo rewards him by making him captain of his yacht.

Fernand Mondego

Fernand Mondego is a fisherman from Marseilles who is in love with Mercédès. When he learns that Mercédès is to marry Dantès, he mails the letter Danglars has written to the authorities accusing Dantès of being a Bonapartist conspirator. After Dantès is imprisoned, Fernand joins the army, and when he returns he marries Mercédès. Fernand rises in the world, accumulates wealth by dubious means, and takes the title of the Count of Morcerf. His wife and son are his pride and joy, but he loses them both when it is revealed that many years earlier he betrayed a French ally, Ali Pasha, and sold Pasha's wife and daughter into slavery. In disgrace, de Morcerf shoots himself.

Maximilien Morrel

Maximilien Morrel is the son of Morrel the shipowner. He is an upright young man who becomes a captain in the army. He falls in love with Valentine de Villefort, and after many twists and turns, Monte Cristo, who admires Morrel and befriends him, arranges for them to be together.

Monsieur Morrel

Monsieur Morrel is a shipowner in Marseilles. He promotes Dantès to captain of the *Pharaon*. After Dantès's arrest, he tries many times to intercede with the authorities on Dantès's behalf, even though is it politically dangerous for him to do so. Fourteen years later, after Dantès has escaped, Morrel has fallen on hard times. His ships are lost at sea and his creditors are pressing him for payment. He is about to commit suicide when Monte Cristo intervenes and pays off his debts.

Monsieur Noirtier

Monsieur Noirtier is Villefort's father. He and his son are on opposing sides politically. Noirtier is a prominent Bonapartist who kills a royalist general in a duel. As an old man he suffers a paralyzing stroke, but he still manages to save his beloved granddaughter Valentine from being compelled to marry Franz d'Epinay. He does this by producing an old journal that records his duel with the royalist general, who was Franz's father.

Signor Pastrini

Signor Pastrini is the owner of a hotel in Rome. He arranges the meeting between Monte Cristo and Albert de Morcerf.

Peppino

Peppino is a member of Luigi Vampa's gang of bandits. He owes his life to Monte Cristo, who used his wealth to buy a pardon for Peppino just before Peppino was due to be executed.

Sinbad the Sailor

See Dantès

Luigi Vampa

Luigi Vampa is a notorious bandit leader in Rome who is responsible for kidnapping Albert de Morcerf. He releases Albert on the instructions of Monte Cristo, to whom he owes friendship because the Count once declined to hand Vampa over to the

Topics For Further Study

- Research the role of DNA in freeing people who have been wrongly convicted. How many prisoners on death row have been freed by DNA evidence showing they could not have committed the crime? How can a man be compensated for spending ten years or more in prison for a crime he did not commit? How can such mistakes be avoided in the future?

- On the evidence of *The Count of Monte Cristo*, is there justice in the world? For everyone, or just for some? If there is such a thing as innocent suffering, how could that be reconciled with the existence of a God who is love as well as justice?

- Write a paragraph describing the wrongs committed by each of Monte Cristo's three main enemies. Who committed the worst crimes? Was the punishment each man received related to the nature of his crime? Were the punishments appropriate?

- Analyze the role Caderousse plays in the writing of the letter accusing Dantes, and Monte Cristo's visit to him after the prison escape. Does Monte Cristo give him the diamond in genuine appreciation, or is it to test him, knowing that Caderousse's greed will get the better of him?

---

authorities when he had the opportunity. Vampa's gang later kidnaps Danglars and again follows the instructions given by Monte Cristo.

Lord Wilford

See Edmond Dantès

Themes

The Limitations of Human Justice

When Dantès escapes from prison, he is obsessed with gaining revenge against those who betrayed him, as well as rewarding those who remained loyal to him. The revenge theme drives the entire narrative, and Dantès, as Monte Cristo, pursues it patiently and ruthlessly. He believes he is one of those "extraordinary beings" who act as agents of divine Providence. He brings punishment when it is deserved and when it is due. Monte Cristo states this quite explicitly to Villefort when they first meet in Paris and engage in a philosophical discussion (Chapter 48, "Ideology"). Monte Cristo takes Villefort to task for thinking about justice only in terms of human law and society. He, on the other hand, is aware of a more profound reality. He tells the astonished Villefort of an encounter he had with Satan, in which he declared that "the most beautiful, noblest,

most sublime thing in the world is to recompense and punish." Dantès requested that he become Providence itself. Satan told him that the most he could aspire to was to be an agent of Providence.

Eventually, Monte Cristo comes to see the limitations that attend a human being who seeks to appropriate to himself a function of the divine. Having previously used the Biblical notion that the sins of the father are visited on the children to justify the devastation he was prepared to wreak on whole families, he is brought up in shock at the death of the innocent nine-year-old Edouard. He realizes that even though Edouard is the son of Villefort, one of the guilty men, Edouard does not deserve the death he receives. For the first time, this supremely self-confident man doubts the wisdom of his mission of revenge. Monte Cristo feels he has gone too far and can no longer say, "God is for and with me." With unaccustomed humility, he acknowledges to Maximilien that the gods operate with a kind of infallibility that is not permissible to a mere man. He leaves Paris with many regrets, although he tries to reassure himself that he never misused the power he was given for any "personal good or to any useless cause." But he cannot shake off his misgivings: "Having reached the summit of his vengeance by a long and tortuous path, he saw an abyss of doubt on the other side of the mountain." Although a visit to the Château d'If rekindles his sense of righteousness about his mission, fortifying him for his final revenge on Danglars, he is still a changed man. He tells Danglars that he forgives him, because Monte Cristo himself is in need of forgiveness for what he has done.

Love is Stronger than Hatred

For all the years in which he plots and carries out his vengeance, Monte Cristo cuts himself off from the values of the heart. He does not permit himself to love, or to have normal human relations. Even though he rewards the Morrel family for their loyalty to him, he does not get emotionally close to them. He remains distant. After he has done his duty to the Morrels, he bids farewell to kindness and gratitude, and vengeance becomes his only goal. His state of mind can be seen in the cold manner in which he speaks about torture, justice and punishment to Albert and Franz before they witness the execution in Rome. Albert is so shocked by Monte Cristo's words and manner he almost faints.

However, Monte Cristo's heart is not quite dead. He does show compassion when he grants Mercédès's request not to kill Albert in the duel, and again when he visits her in Marseilles after he has left Paris, his revenge almost complete. He plans to give her half his fortune, and would have done so there and then had Mercédès not insisted that Albert must first approve of the arrangement.

A major step in Monte Cristo's recovery of his ability to love comes when he goes to great efforts to ensure that Valentine is united with Maximilien. He has realized that he does not have to hate Valentine just because she is Villefort's daughter. The sins of the father do not always have to be visited upon the children. But it is only when he allows himself to fall in love with Haydée that he recovers his full humanity. He can now enjoy life again in the present moment without having to dwell on the injustices of the past. As he explains to Maximilien, only those who have known great unhappiness can enjoy its opposite, ultimate bliss. After the grim execution of justice, the love of Maximilien and Valentine, and of Monte Cristo and Haydée, shows that love will triumph in the end.

Style

The Romantic Novel

The Count of Monte Cristo is an example of a romantic historical novel. In a romantic novel, the emphasis is on action, adventure, heroism and love. Characters are usually either good or bad, with few shades in between. There is always a happy ending. Good triumphs over evil.

The hero of a romantic novel is a larger-than-life, usually idealized character. He is a man of courage, integrity and daring. In *The Count of Monte Cristo*, Dantès's qualifications to be a romantic hero are clearly delineated in the opening few chapters. This, for example, is the very first description of him:

> He was a fine tall slim young fellow, with black eyes, and hair as dark as the raven's wing, and his whole appearance bespoke that calmness and resolution peculiar to men accustomed from their cradle to contend with danger.

The early chapters go on to show Dantès behaving with integrity and virtue in all areas of his life. His credentials as a romantic hero are established. Similarly, the bad characters, Danglars and Fernand, are given their envious, duplicitous natures right at the beginning. The reader then clearly knows what to expect from them. Once these simple character lines are put down, they do not change. Character development is not where the interest of the romantic novel lies.

The romantic novel is often considered escapist literature. It does not reflect events that could really happen. For example, Monte Cristo's prodigious ability to be at the right place at the right time and to manipulate events and people exactly as he pleases would strain credulity to the breaking point in a realistic novel, but in a romance, such things are willingly accepted by the reader.

Historical Context

Napoleon and the Restoration of the Bourbons

The year 1815, in which *The Count of Monte Cristo* begins, was a watershed year in European history. It brought to a conclusion over twenty years of war. The turbulence had begun in 1789, with the outbreak of the French Revolution. In 1792, France established itself as a republic, and King Louis XVI was beheaded on January 21, 1793. Revolutionary France alarmed the rest of Europe with its aggressive territorial ambitions, and within two months of the king's execution, a general European war broke out. It was during this war that Napoleon Bonaparte, who was born on the island of Corsica, rose to power within the French

Compare & Contrast

- **1840s:** France is ruled by King Louis Philippe until he is overthrown in the February Revolution in 1848. The monarchy is succeeded by the Second Republic, which lasts from 1848 to 1852.

  Today: As a long-established parliamentary democracy, France is a more stable society under the Fifth Republic, which began in 1958.

- **1840s:** The use of the recently invented electric telegraph makes communications much faster than ever before.

  Today: Electronic communication reaches new levels of sophistication with the invention of the Internet and the widespread use of electronic mail.

- **1840s:** Railway construction begins all over Europe. The French railway system is constructed with Paris at its center.

  Today: France has a high-speed rail network that is one of the most advanced in Europe. High-speed trains travel at top speeds of between 150 mph and 180 mph. The system is safe and there have been no fatal accidents in two decades of operations.

Army and transformed it into a formidable military force. In 1799, he seized control of France, and in 1804 declared himself emperor. Until 1812, Napoleon controlled most of Europe. But he overreached himself by invading Russia in 1812. After his army was forced to retreat from Moscow, Napoleon's power was on the wane.

In April, 1814, Napoleon abdicated as Emperor and was sent into exile on the island of Elba. The major European powers, Prussia, Austria and Britain, had declared him to be a destroyer of the peace of the world. Louis XVIII, brother of the executed Louis XVI, ascended to the French throne. This event, which put the Bourbon dynasty back in power, is known as the First Restoration. It is this political situation that existed in France when *The Count of Monte Cristo* begins.

The restored Bourbons had the support of the old aristocracy, who had been dispossessed of their lands by the revolution, but they did not have the allegiance of all the people. Many wanted the Emperor to return, and there were conflicts between royalists and Bonapartists. This is reflected in the early part of the novel. Villefort's father, Noirtier, is a Bonapartist and a former Girondin (the Girondins were a political faction during the French Revolution), whereas Villefort is content to serve whoever is in power, although he claims to be a royalist. It is this situation, in which a restored monarchy represses and persecutes the remaining Bonapartists, that Dantès gets caught up in.

Napoleon remained on Elba for only ten months. He escaped and landed with 1,100 men near Cannes on March 1, 1815. He crossed the Alps and marched on Paris, gathering support from peasants and soldiers alike. When he entered Paris, Louis XVIII realized the danger too late—he is presented in *The Count of Monte Cristo* as complacent—and fled. But another war soon broke out. Heavily outnumbered, Napoleon was defeated by the British general, Wellington, at the Battle of Waterloo in June, 1815. Napoleon returned to Paris and abdicated. His return had lasted only just over three months, the period known as the Hundred Days. He was again sent into exile, this time to the island of St. Helena, in the South Atlantic, where he died six years later. Louis XVIII returned to the French throne. It was then dangerous once more to be known as a Bonapartist (as Dantès finds out). In the south of France there was an outbreak of unrest in which many Bonapartists were killed, and the Chamber of Deputies, under Royalist control, demanded and took action against Bonapartists active during the Hundred Days, whom they called traitors.

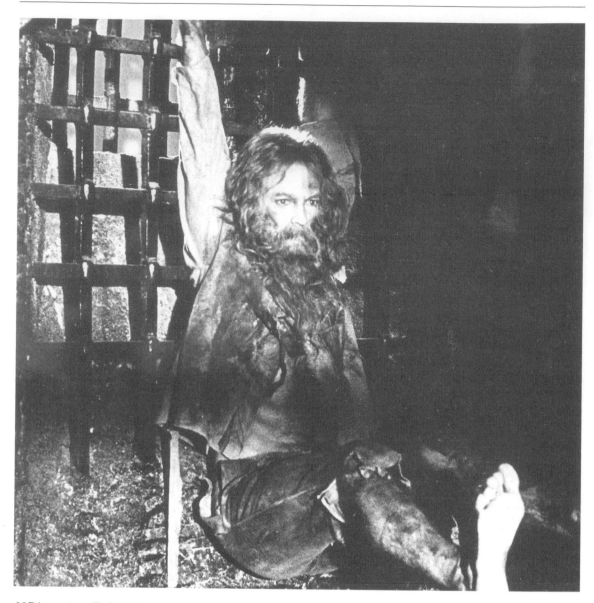

1974 movie still depicting a scene from The Count of Monte Cristo, *starring Richard Chamberlain as Edmond Dantès*

Critical Overview

The Count of Monte Cristo was originally published in serial form, and was a huge success. People would wait in long lines to buy the latest installment. Within a few months the novel was translated into ten languages. Dumas had also published another extremely successful novel, *The Three Musketeers*, in the same year. With the publication of *The Count of Monte Cristo*, Dumas became famous worldwide. In Europe, his literary reputation was higher than that of Charles Dickens or Victor Hugo.

The Count of Monte Cristo has remained popular with readers for over 150 years, and is often considered to be Dumas's masterpiece. Writing in 1902, H. A. Spurr (*The Life and Writings of Alexandre Dumas*) stated that the theme of the novel "is taught so effectively, so honestly, and on so great a scale, that the book has a moral value which should preserve it from oblivion for generations to come."

Spurr's prediction proved to be correct. In recent years, F. W. J. Hemmings, in *The King of Romance: A Portrait of Alexandre Dumas*, described the novel as "the greatest 'revenger's tragedy' in the whole history of the novel." And in 2003, Robert McCrum, literary editor of the British newspaper, *The Observer*, in his list of the 100 greatest novels of all time, placed *The Count of Monte Cristo* in fourteenth position, calling it "a masterpiece of adventure writing."

However, in spite of the novel's high standing amongst readers in every generation since its first publication, *The Count of Monte Cristo* has not generally received such high accolades from literary scholars. There is a perception that Dumas's novels fall short of the demands of serious literature. In fact, *The Count of Monte Cristo* has often been viewed as a well-plotted adventure novel, well suited to popular taste, but little more. In *Writers for Children*, Avriel H. Goldberger has tried to bridge this gap between popular acclaim and literary standing in the work of Dumas. She acknowledges that *The Count of Monte Cristo* ranks with the great revenge stories of all time, but states:

> This is not because *Monte Cristo* has equal merit as a work of art or as a probe of the psyche, but because it speaks so powerfully to our need to fantasize impossible victories of the individual against injustice.

Criticism

Bryan Aubrey

Aubrey holds a Ph.D. in English and has published many articles on nineteenth-century literature. In this essay Aubrey discusses The Count of Monte Cristo *in the context of its literary allusions to Byron and Shakespeare, with reference to some of the philosophical implications of Monte Cristo's beliefs about divine justice.*

The Count of Monte Cristo vicariously satisfies the fantasies of everyone who has ever dreamed of winning the lottery or who has idly plotted revenge against their enemies, knowing full well they will never act on their darkest desires. Monte Cristo is like a nineteenth century Superman. His miraculous, Houdini-like escape from prison, when he manages to escape drowning even though a cannon ball is tied to his feet, sets the tone for what follows. Everything goes right for the formidable Count, who seems like a lord in charge of his own destiny and that of others. Coincidences happen at the most opportune time for him; he seems to have eliminated from life the element of unpredictability and chance. He never makes a mistake, he seems

> " The problem of innocent suffering does not trouble Monte Cristo (at least not until the death of Edouard), even though his revenge wreaks devastation on whole families."

to know everything, he is always in full possession of himself, and he has an air of invincibility about him. Given his single-minded dedication to his mission, his extraordinary force of personality and his prodigious wealth, it is not surprising that others regard him with a kind of awe. Beauchamp, for example, when he witnesses Monte Cristo's utter certainty of victory in the duel with Albert, is not sure whether he is dealing with a mere braggart or a supernatural being. And Villefort, when he first meets Monte Cristo in Paris, has a similar thought, not knowing whether the man who thinks he is an agent of Providence is a mystic or a madman.

During the part of the novel that is set in Rome, to give his character some extra heft, Dumas hints that Monte Cristo is to be regarded as something of a Byronic hero. The English Romantic poet Lord Byron, a favorite of Dumas's youth, was revered throughout Europe as the incarnation of the rebellious Romantic spirit. He died a heroic death in 1824, fighting for the cause of Greek independence. During his lifetime, Byron's magnetic personality, his cultivation of the persona of an outsider, and the whiff of scandal that always seemed to surround him, made him one of the most talked about men of the age, the precursor of the modern celebrity. Women were drawn to him, and chaperones were anxious to steer their young charges away from him. When Byron visited Rome, one aristocratic English lady warned her daughter, when Byron was in the vicinity, "Don't look at him, he is dangerous to look at" (quoted in Phyliss Grosskurth's *Byron: The Flawed Angel*). Byron seemed to embody the same spirit that he breathed into his restless, tormented heroes. Like Edmond Dantès heroes, the heroes of Byron's dramatic poems have suffered great wrongs that set them apart from the rest of society, but they remain indomitable. This is the background against which

What Do I Read Next?

- Dumas's famous novel *The Three Musketeers* (1844) is an adventure and a romance set in seventeenth century France and features the four heroes, Athos, Porthos, Aramis and D'Artagnan.

- Although it is on a much smaller scale than *The Count of Monte Cristo*, Edgar Allan Poe's chilling short story "The Cask of Amontillado," first published in 1846, also features a protagonist whose sole focus is revenge on the man who has wronged him.

- Lord Byron's poem "The Prisoner of Chillon," first published in 1816, was inspired by the story of a sixteenth century priest who spent six years in solitary confinement in the Castle of Chillon in Switzerland. Byron's prisoner goes through despair and near delirium but eventually finds a kind of peace.

- *Culture and Society in France 1789–1848* (1987), by F. W. J. Hemmings, is a much-cited study that traces the continuities and discontinuities of French culture and society during this turbulent half-century.

Franz d'Epinay's observation of Monte Cristo can be understood:

> Franz could not ... even think of [Monte Cristo] without representing his stern head on the shoulders of Manfred or beneath the casque of Lara. His forehead was marked by the line that indicates the constant presence of a bitter thought. He had those fiery eyes that seem to penetrate to the heart, and the haughty and disdainful upper lip that gives to the words it utters a peculiar character that impresses them on the minds of those to whom they are addressed.

Manfred and Lara are both heroes in Byron's dramatic poems of those titles. These works are mentioned again by Albert de Morcerf, when he tries to explain to his mother who Monte Cristo is. Like his friend Franz, Albert regards Monte Cristo as a Byronic hero,

> whom Misery has marked with a fatal brand ... one of those wrecks, as it were, of some ancient family, who, disinherited of their patrimony, have achieved one by the force of their adventurous genius, which has placed them above the laws of society.

In spite of the direct references to Byron, however, the resemblances between Monte Cristo and the Byronic hero are largely superficial. The Byronic hero is a much more complex figure than Monte Cristo. He is usually guilty of some sin or transgression against society's laws, and searches for meaning in a universe that refuses to yield one. This is not Monte Cristo at all; Monte Cristo is confident of the moral order of the world and his role in upholding it. The truth is that Dumas tossed in the Byronic allusions simply because he wanted a few more ingredients to stir into his literary pot. They are Romantic seasonings to give the stew a popular flavor.

The same applies to the opinion of the Venetian lady, Countess G———, also in the Rome episodes, that Monte Cristo is a vampire. She is convinced of this because of the count's pale appearance: "seems to me as though he had just been dug up," she says to Franz. Vampire lore was in vogue at the time, and was often associated with Byron, whose heroes' obsession with darkness and the destructive aspects of love made them resemble the vampire figure. John William Polidori, Byron's personal physician, published the first vampire novel in 1819. *The Vampyre* was soon adapted to the French stage by Charles Nodier, so it would have been familiar to French readers and theatregoers. Dumas himself attended a performance of *Le Vampire* in 1823. Readers of *The Count of Monte Cristo* would certainly have recognized the Countess's description of Monte Cristo as the "new Lord Ruthven," since Lord Ruthven was the name of Polidori's vampire. Of course, there is just enough of a similarity between the vampire myth and Monte Cristo to make the allusion work. Like the vampire, Monte Cristo has returned (seemingly) from the tomb (the Château d'If) to destroy the lives of the living.

In addition to beefing up his main character with whatever literary bric-a-brac he could lay his hands on, Dumas also appears to have raided another of his favorite authors, William Shakespeare, for some help with plot devices. When Madame Villefort faints in order to divert suspicion from herself after her victim Valentine is discovered apparently dead, she is following the example of Lady Macbeth, who pulls a similar trick after the murder of Duncan in *Macbeth*. Shakespeareans may also recognize in the flight of Eugénie and her friend Louise, in which Eugénie disguises herself as a man, an echo of Rosalind and Celia fleeing to the forest of Arden in *As You Like It*.

A Shakespearean plot device hard for anyone to miss is when Valentine drinks the potion given to her by Monte Cristo. The potion will induce in her a sleep that resembles death, she will be buried by her mourning family, but will then awake and be reunited with her lover, Maximilien. This is of course exactly what is planned in *Romeo and Juliet*, except that the outcome in the Shakespearean play is tragic. A happy outcome of the fake death of a lover can be found in *Much Ado About Nothing*, where Claudio and Hero are separated by Hero's apparent death (which is a trick), only to be reunited at the end. Maximilien's intense grief at apparently losing Valentine is an echo of Claudio's suffering at the apparent loss of his love.

The Shakespearean play that looms largest over *The Count of Monte Cristo* is of course that other great revenge story, *Hamlet*. Although *Hamlet* should not in any way be considered a source of *The Count of Monte Cristo*, it is interesting to note some of the similarities and contrasts between the two. Like the count, Hamlet believes he has a mission from God to avenge a wrong. He has been appointed by heaven as "scourge and minister" (act 3, scene 4, line 175). But the reflective, vacillating Prince of Denmark does not go about his task with the same cold fixity of purpose that characterizes Monte Cristo. Although he eventually accomplishes his revenge, two entire families are wiped out in the process, not to mention the fate suffered by those two hapless courtiers, Rosencrantz and Guildenstern. Innocent suffering is embodied in the tragic figure of Ophelia, who is caught up in events that are not of her doing but which overwhelm her just the same.

The problem of innocent suffering does not trouble Monte Cristo (at least not until the death of Edouard), even though his revenge wreaks devastation on whole families. The reason he does not question his own actions is because he believes that suffering is a punishment by God for sins. He uses that argument to the dying Caderousse (although Caderousse is certainly not innocent). The count absolves himself from blame for not preventing Caderousse's murder by saying that he refuses to interfere with the workings of justice. He considers it sacrilege to oppose the will of Providence. Caderousse thinks he sees through that argument, saying, "If God were just, you know many would be punished who now escape." But this does not cut any ice with Monte Cristo. He uses the same argument for inaction when Madame de Villefort goes on her poisoning spree, which produces four innocent victims. He tells Maximilien that he is not at all concerned by the poisonings, which demonstrate only that the justice of God has entered the Villefort house. He advises Maximilien to let justice do its work.

The idea that everyone who suffers somehow deserves their own misery, and those who die untimely deaths are merely recipients of the justice of God, is not an argument that can stand much scrutiny. If Monte Cristo were to be consistent, he would also have to acknowledge that according to the beliefs he has adopted, his own father's suffering and death, the injustice of which he seeks to revenge, must also have been a part of the judgment of God. And what of his own sufferings during his fourteen-year imprisonment? Could not the same argument be applied in that instance? It is surely a weak, self-serving argument for a person to hold that someone else's suffering or death is sent by God for purposes of justice, whereas their own suffering, or that of the people they love, is the result of the evil actions of other people.

To his credit, Monte Cristo eventually comes to realize that he erred in believing himself to be equal to God. He acknowledges that God is the only source of wisdom and supreme power. Ironically, if he had taken more notice of his enemy Villefort, who commented at their first meeting in Paris that "you may be above others, but above you there is God," he might have learned it a lot sooner. But humility is usually the last of the virtues to be acquired. It comes to Monte Cristo in his final words to Maximilien, that the sum of all human wisdom is contained in the two words, "wait and hope." Indeed. But mere waiting and hoping would make for a very dull novel. Revenge by a man appointed as the agent of Providence produces a much more exciting read, as Dumas well knew, and none of his readers would have it otherwise.

Source: Bryan Aubrey, Critical Essay on *The Count of Monte Cristo*, in *Novels for Students*, Gale, 2004.

Robert Stowell

In the following essay, Stowell compares elements of The Count of Monte Cristo *to Emily Brontë's* Wuthering Heights, *and speculates on how the former may have influenced the latter.*

Since few of Emily Brontë's private papers survived her death in 1848, whilst those close to Charlotte preserved whatever they could of *her* written material when she died, there is a huge imbalance of evidence for the reading preferences of the two writers. Literary influences on Charlotte are therefore easy to confirm; those on Emily far less so. Moreover, the novel-styles of the two are very different: Charlotte's prose is full of allusion and quotation (whether acknowledged or unacknowledged), her imagery often derived from her own favourite books; the prose in *Wuthering Heights* is by contrast reference-free, figurative language infrequent and original. Yet both writers are indebted to their intense reading habits as children, and it is possible that Emily had before her, during the composition of her novel, the model of the irresistible tale that was then sweeping through Europe, *The Count of Monte Cristo*.

Most of the literary influences on Charlotte Brontë are helpfully provided by the writer herself in a letter to Ellen Nussey, a schoolfriend, in 1834:

> 'If you like poetry let it be first rate, Milton, Shakespeare, Thomson, Goldsmith, Pope (if you will though I don't admire him), Scott, Byron, Campbell, Wordsworth and Southey . . . Scott's sweet, wild, romantic Poetry can do you no harm nor can Wordsworth nor Campbell's nor Southey's . . . For fiction read Scott alone; all novels after his are worthless.'

This letter was written hurriedly (at the end she wrote, 'If you can read this scrawl it will be to the credit of your patience') and it has significant omissions. Of course, Charlotte does not mention her Bible reading—the foremost influence on her prose as it was upon her life. Neither does she mention books Ellen would already have known: *The Pilgrim's Progress*, *The Arabian Nights' Entertainments* or *Aesop's Fables*—the last two of which inspired many of her juvenile stories. Nor is there mention of Ossian, whom we know she had read, or of Cowper, whose poems impressed her deeply. Charlotte's writing was influenced by her reading of periodicals as a girl, particularly *Blackwood's Magazine* and *Fraser's*, even to the extent of

certain of her novels' images being traceable to particular stories.

Of the books in Haworth Parsonage during Charlotte and Emily's formative years, the children had particular favourites, and what Lucy Snowe says in *Villette* applies certainly to the authoress:

> 'I had great pleasure in reading a few books, but not many: preferring always those on whose style or sentiment the writer's individual nature was plainly stamped.'

Accordingly, the few books that the young Charlotte Brontë read and re-read were intensely absorbed by her.

The reading list for Ellen Nussey shows Charlotte Brontë's fervent admiration of Scott's works, particularly the novels. Further statements in her letters refer to Scott as the greatest of novelists and to *Kenilworth* as 'one of the most interesting works that ever emanated from the great Sir Walter's pen.' Mrs Gaskell tells us that Scott's works were in the Parsonage library (some editions are still preserved at Haworth) and on her visit to Scotland, after her rise to fame, she made the pilgrimage to Abbotsford.

In all of Charlotte Brontë's novels, quotation from Scott's poems is frequent. In *The Professor* Crimsworth overhears Frances reciting lines from *The Covenanter's Fate*, lines which the author undoubtedly knew by heart herself since there are four slight mistakes in wording. There are four quotations from *The Lay of the Last Minstrel* in *Jane Eyre* alone. There is also the rhetorical passage on poetry inspired by the gift of *Marmion* from Rivers to Jane. In *Shirley* we read that Parson Helstone, 'in a shovel hat, sitting erect on the back of a shaggy pony, "rode lightly in"' to the yard at Hollow's Mill to help in its defence against frame-breakers. The humorous effect of the quotation from Scott presupposes in the novel-reader acquaintance with a dramatic incident in *The Lay of the Last Minstrel*, where five hundred horsemen appear unexpectedly at a confrontation in canto IV stanza xii. The very surname of Shirley Keeldar is taken from Scott's novel *The Black Dwarf*. And there is a reference to a vivid scene in chapter 8 of *Old Mortality* in a passage describing Lucy Snowe's attitude to the 'lecture pieuse' which was a nightly feature of life at the pensionnat in *Villette*:

> 'No Mause Headrigg ever felt a stronger call to take up her testimony against Sergeant Bothwell, than I to speak my mind in this matter of the popish "lecture pieuse."'

The indebtedness to Scott's poetry and prose is undeniably great. Charlotte Brontë wrote with the expectation of her audience's having full acquaintance with the great man's romantic tales. They become a source of common reference. One wonders, however, if the writer herself realised the full extent of her borrowings; for Charlotte's fondness for *Ivanhoe* influenced her plotting of *Jane Eyre* and *Shirley*, as well as the prose-style of all her novels. (*Ivanhoe* also furnished the plot for her juvenile story *The Green Dwarf*.) Miss F. Ratchford briefly indicated the connection between the old Saxon woman Ulrica in Scott's novel and Rochester's mad wife Bertha Mason as long ago as 1941. However, Miss Ratchford did not emphasise the degree of indebtedness of Charlotte's borrowings from Scott as much as she might have (preferring to see Byron as the chief literary source for the Brontë family's writings). The parallels between the deaths of Ulrica and of Bertha Mason are worth examination. Scott writes:

> 'The fire was spreading rapidly through all parts of the castle, when Ulrica, who had first kindled it, appeared on a turret, in the guise of one of the ancient furies, yelling forth a warsong, such as was of yore raised on the field of battle by the scalds of the yet heathen Saxons. Her long dishevelled grey hair flew back from her uncovered head; the inebriating delight of gratified vengeance contended in her eyes with the fire of insanity; and she brandished the distaff which she held in her hand, as if she had been one of the Fatal Sisters, who spin and abridge the thread of human life . . . [she sings a "barbarous hymn"] . . . The towering flames had now surmounted every obstruction, and rose to the evening skies one huge and burning beacon, seen far and wide through the adjacent country. Tower after tower crashed down, with blazing roof and rafter . . . The maniac figure of the Saxon Ulrica was for a long time visible on the lofty stand she had chosen, tossing her arms abroad with wild exultation, as if she reigned empress of the conflagration which she had raised. At length, with a terrific crash, the whole turret gave way, and she perished in the flames which had consumed her tyrant.'

Bertha Mason, like Ulrica, kindles the fire which eventually destroys her; she is on the roof of Thornfield Hall:

> 'standing waving her arms, above the battlements, and shouting out till they could hear her a mile off . . . She was a big woman, and had long, black hair: we could see it streaming against the flames as she stood . . . We saw him [Rochester] approach her; and then, ma'am, she yelled, and gave a spring, and the next minute she lay smashed on the pavement.'

Visually, the two incidents are almost identical; it is almost plagiarism.

A scene in *Shirley* concerns the defence of Hollow's Mill by Robert Moore and a body

> *Of course, it is always possible that Dumas and Emily Brontë are both working from similar literary backgrounds, that the influence of Scott and Byron was operating independently on both writers, and that Emily had no knowledge of Dumas' work. Even so, the comparison produces interesting results.*"

of soldiers against a Luddite attack. The scene replicates the storming and defence of the castle in chapter 30 of *Ivanhoe*. At first sight the similarities could be coincidental: the organised attack; the capturing by the attackers of the outworks and their breaking down of these (in *Ivanhoe* an outer 'barrier,' in *Shirley* the mill-yard gates); their attack on the main building; the arousing of Moore's and Ivanhoe's 'fighting animal' (Charlotte Brontë's phrase); and Ivanhoe's longing to help but powerlessness because of his wounds, just like Caroline Helstone's longing and helplessness. These could easily be mere coincidence. But what is vital here is the method of narration of the attack in both cases. In *Ivanhoe* the first stages in the storming of the castle are recounted through the medium of Rebecca, who describes the scene to Ivanhoe, using her eyes and her sensibility to enhance the effect by at once narrating the battle and portraying the wonder, horror and anxiety of the girl. This is precisely what Charlotte Brontë does when she uses Caroline and Shirley to give us their narration of the Luddite attack. Just as Rebecca looks down on the siege from the tower, protected by a shield, Caroline and Shirley look down into the hollow from the hill, protected by darkness. There can be little doubt that *Ivanhoe* was in the author's mind when she wrote of the attack on Moore's mill. This is confirmed by imagery that *Shirley* uses in her attempt to dissuade Caroline from trying to intervene:

> 'How [would you help Moore]? By inspiring him with heroism? Pooh! These are not the days of chivalry: it is not a tilt at a tournament we are going to behold, but a struggle about money, and food, and

life … It is not for love or beauty, but for ledger and broadcloth, he is going to break a spear.'

Because the scene in *Ivanhoe* inspired the writing of the attack on the mill, such imagery comes almost inevitably into the dialogue. The merest thought of Scott's classic sets the mind thinking of heroism, chivalry, tiltings at tournaments, and breaking spears for love and beauty.

Disparate ingredients come together in Charlotte Brontë's writing: extreme emotion and Christian stoicism; the Gothic novel and the novel of Victorian domesticity. In a similar way, her writing is a fusion of all the reading that she avidly pursued in her early years. Above, I used the word 'plagiarism,' but this does not do justice to the authoress. The comment of G. H. Lewes, writing in the December issue of *Fraser's Magazine 1847*, is more apt. Of her prose he said:

'Although by no means a fine style, it has the capital point of all great styles in being *personal*, the written speech of an individual, not the artificial language made up from all sorts of books.'

In the same way that Chaucer used source material from Boccaccio, and Shakespeare took ideas from Chaucer, Charlotte Brontë borrowed from Scott. But she was also so much under his influence that her prose-style was affected by his evocative romances.

For a considerable time after the publication of *Wuthering Heights* readers accepted Charlotte Brontë's attribution of the power of that novel to Emily's remarkable untutored imagination. In the preface to the second edition of Emily's book she wrote that it was:

'hewn in a wild workshop, with simple tools, out of homely materials. The statuary found a granite block on the moor; gazing thereon, he saw how from the crag might be elicited a head, savage, swart, sinister; a form modelled with at least one element of grandeur power. He wrought with a rude chisel, and from no model but the vision of his meditations.'

More recently, scepticism has been voiced of Charlotte's romanticising of her sister's creative processes. The origins of *Wuthering Heights* have been detected in local folk-lore and ballads, transmitted particularly from the Brontës' servant Tabitha; Patrick Brontë's Irish stories of his father Hugh Prunty and an uncle called Welsh have been suggested by Edward Chitham as furnishing the basic plot; stories heard by Emily during a brief stay at Law Hill school near Halifax about a certain Jack Sharp are said to influence the novel. On the literary side, Hoffman's Romantic works are cited as a source; and a particular tale in *Blackwood's*, 'The

Bridegroom of Barna,' which concerns the love of the children of rival families and the hero and heroine of which are united only in death when they are buried in a single grave, seems very reminiscent of the Heathcliff and Cathy story. And, once again, Scott comes into the picture. Q. D. Leavis has shown how *Wuthering Heights'* conflict between a primitive society (the Heights) and a refined society (Thrushcross Grange) echoes Scott, whose 'own sympathies were with the wild rough border farmers … *The Black Dwarf* has long been known as the source for the surnames used in *Wuthering Heights*.' Most recently Rose Lovell-Smith has examined the structuring of some of the dramatic scenes of *Wuthering Heights* and pointed out similarities with the Waverley Novels.

So far, the literary detection of 'sources' falls way short of that performed for Charlotte's novels. Much recent criticism of *Wuthering Heights*, inasmuch as it concentrates on identifying sources at all, focuses on the 'Gothic' ingredients of the story, although two critics explore completely different areas: Patricia Thomson establishes an influence on the novel by George Sand, and David Musselwhite argues at length that Emily's reading in Brussels of French literature was a formative factor. Interestingly, this last study suggests that, as well as the childhood influence of Gothic and Romantic literature, reading by Emily in her adult years had a strong effect—a finding that marks a significant difference from Charlotte's development; for Emily was twenty-four when she went to study under M. Heger.

According to Mrs Gaskell, Emily was initially far more reluctant to bow to M. Heger's unorthodox teaching methods than was Charlotte. For the sisters he dispensed with the traditional grounding in grammar and vocabulary, and instead proposed to read to them some of the masterpieces of the most celebrated French authors. The master and pupils would then analyse the literature, concentrating upon a value-judgement. The follow-up exercise was for the pupils to 'catch the echo' of the French writer's style 'so reproducing their own thought in a somewhat similar manner.' Emily may have disagreed with the teaching method, but in the words of her sister worked 'like a horse.' It is from the hints in Mrs Gaskell's biography that Mr Musselwhite deduces the influence of such authors as Casimir de la Vigne, Bossuet, Hugo, and Guizot.

One wonders what the intellectual M. Heger made of the prolific output of Alexandre Dumas. A man of academic restraint, he may well not have had much taste for the robust ripping yarns of the creator of D'Artagnan and Edmond Dantès. Yet the European general public was captivated. Dumas had scored an enormous success with *Henry III and his Court* in 1829, a play which helped to inaugurate the new 'Romantic' drama, and he followed this up with *Kean* in 1836. Meanwhile he began reading history, with a view to making himself into the French Walter Scott. (Scott's influence was as strong in France as in England; so was Byron's.) By 1844 *The Three Musketeers* had been published and, taking advantage of the new fashion for running novels in serial form, Dumas' story of love and revenge *The Count of Monte Cristo* began to appear in *Le Journal des Débats* in August 1844 and ended in January 1846. According to David Coward, 'when the episodes were collected (as they at first were by opportunist Belgian publishers who paid no royalties) and sold in multi-volume sets, he became not merely France's best-known writer but also the most famous Frenchman of his day . . .'

Emily Brontë was back home in Haworth Parsonage by the end of 1842. However, *The Count of Monte Cristo* was rapidly translated into many languages. The first English versions were made in 1846 and were immediate best-sellers. And did Emily Brontë need to wait for a translation? She was fluent in French and German and may have had access to the pirated editions of the novel available from Belgium. Charlotte wrote to M. Heger on 18 May 1845 'I read all the French Books I can get.'

Just when Emily Brontë started to write *Wuthering Heights* is a matter of conjecture. Dates as far back as 1837 have been implausibly suggested. The actual writing of the novel is 'not likely to have started before October 1845' and the manuscript was in the publisher Newby's hands 'during the months of early summer of 1847.' That is, the novel was probably written largely during 1846, just when Monte Cristo fever was at its height.

The similarities in the plots of *The Count of Monte Cristo* and *Wuthering Heights* are immediately obvious. In both books the male protagonist of low birth is deeply in love with, though not married to, a young female. This love is not allowed to be consummated because of the machinations of people close to the protagonist who have taken an instinctive dislike to him and wish to see him thwarted. The protagonist then must suffer years of deprivation and exile, yet almost miraculously he returns, far wealthier and more refined than he was previously to find his loved one married. He insinuates himself back into the society from which he was expelled. His purpose is revenge. Methodically and irresistibly he puts himself into a position of

power over his enemies, but chiefly by exploiting the children of those enemies. All the while he is careful to remain within the law. However, at the precise point when he can culminate his vengeance upon the second generation of victims (the first generation safely dealt with), the vengeance is perceived as unfulfilling and the need for it evaporates.

There are, of course, differences between the careers of Heathcliff and Edmond Dantès: the latter is formally engaged to Mercedes and is a respected young seaman; the plotting against Dantès is much more conscious and organised; when Dantès returns as the Count of Monte Cristo, the reader knows where he has been and how he has acquired his *Arabian Nights* mystique and wealth; and Dantès' abandonment of revenge is his own decision, brought on by witnessing the suffering he has himself caused.

However, the general pattern of the story of *Wuthering Heights* certainly follows that of Dumas' novel. What Emily Brontë does, and this makes the pattern less obviously a borrowing, is to disturb the chronology of her story by using several narrators, a device which is alien to Dumas who was far less of a craftsman.

It is not merely in terms of plot that the two novels have similarities. Both the adult Heathcliff and the later Dantès have physical appearances which are striking and yet sinister—both are 'Byronic,' with a fascinating yet dangerous magnetism for the women they encounter. Beneath a veneer of culture both have a ruthlessness which dominates their existence and causes them single-mindedly to control the lives of others. Both are solitary figures, associated with the supernatural (Heathcliff has a relationship with Cathy which goes beyond the grave. Dantès is often nicknamed 'Lord Ruthven' by Parisian society; Ruthven is one of the earliest vampires in literature, the forerunner of Dracula). Both books have passages of sickening violence, and the progression of the books seems to be inexorably towards the bitter and pessimistic triumph of vengeance until, happily, unexpected optimism enters the stories and 'civilised values' prevail. Finally, the books both take melodramatic characters, the stuff of legend or myth, and root them in real life.

It is fashionable at the moment to use *Wuthering Heights* as a text on which to formulate critical theory, whether it be from a position of psychoanalysis, deconstruction, Marxism, feminism, or whatever. Academic readers may well be fascinated with the relationship between the 'core story' and the 'frame story,' with the book's 'layered narrative' of power-structures in Victorian England,

Illustration, circa nineteenth century, portraying Edmond Dantès and the Abbé Faria imprisoned in the Chateau d'If, as described in Dumas' The Count of Monte Cristo

with the book as a 'dialogic text' or as some kind of myth. However, the impact of the novel on most readers is due to its being an excellent story, convincingly told. If this story also concerns primitive and universal desires in conflict with acquired cultural values, then the text is certain to appeal strongly to a 'civilised' readership where the strict taboos associated with sexual love and revenge create a need for vicarious escape.

Of course, it is always possible that Dumas and Emily Brontë are both working from similar literary backgrounds, that the influence of Scott and Byron was operating independently on both writers, and that Emily had no knowledge of Dumas' work. Even so, the comparison produces interesting results. Yet it is fascinating to think that Emily Brontë, borrowing in a way far different from the way her sister borrowed, was putting into practice M. Heger's method of composition: observing the ways an acknowledged French 'masterpiece' achieved its success, and then going away to write her own piece, using the reading as a general stimulus. We must remember that the only formal training the two Brontës received in composition was at the hands of M. Heger. Dumas' irresistible tale of love and revenge is transmuted through Emily Brontë's experience and imagination and brought solidly close to home in West Yorkshire.

Source: Robert Stowell, "Brontë Borrowings: Charlotte Brontë and *Ivanhoe*, Emily Brontë and *The Count of Monte Cristo*," in *Brontë Society Transactions*, Vol. 21, No. 6, 1996, pp. 243–51.

Emily A. McDermott

In the following essay, McDermott examines specific classical allusions in The Count of Monte Cristo, *including references to the story of "Pyramus and Thisbe," and Virgil's "Dido."*

The pages of *The Count of Monte Cristo* are dotted with classical allusions, little markers of the regimen of voracious reading which the previously little-lettered Dumas had undertaken at the onset of his literary career. To cite only a sample of close to a hundred such allusions, reference is made at one time or another in the novel to aspects of Plutarch, Martial, Pliny, Caesar, Cornelius Nepos, Ennius, and Pindar. Gods, mythological figures, and figures from history or historical legend abound, from Jupiter to Hebe, from Tantalus, Icarus, and Omphale to Curtius, Nero, and Poppaea. Ships, horses, and characters are graced with Greek and Latin names: Pharaon, Eurus, Médéah, Haydée, Coclès. In the scene in which Dantès first uncovers his treasure on the Isle of Monte Cristo, the hero is compared serially to Hercules, Sisyphus (who, ironically or not, in *The Count of Monte Cristo* is pushing his rock *down*), and a Titan; the Isle itself is styled "cet autre Pélion." The briefly mentioned Hellenophobia of Albert de Morcerf is well overbalanced by the classicophilia of Louis XVIII, who, in a scene of delicious parody, scribbles cribbed notes in his text of Horace and answers his advisors of state with gnomic pronouncements drawn from Vergil and Horace. In fact, a less hardy critic than the present one might well have been abashed to undertake a study of Dumas's use of classical allusion after reading the cutting description of the king as litterateur:

"Attendez, mon cher, attendez, je tiens une note très heureuse sur le *Pastor quum traheret*; attendez, et vous continuerez après."

Il se fit un instant de silence, pendant lequel Louis XVIII inscrivit, d'une écriture qu'il faisait aussi menue que possible, une nouvelle note en marge de son Horace; puis, cette note inscrite:

"Continuez, mon cher duc," dit-il en se relevant de l'air satisfait d'un homme qui croit avoir eu une idée lorsqu'il a commenté l'idée d'un autre. "Continuez, je vous écoute."

> "... the parallelism between the present lovers and Ovid's earlier ones (like Shakespeare's) has served to accentuate the reader's tense uncertainty of the outcome to be presented by the author and so to color his or her judgment of the righteousness of the Count's vengeful course of action."

All the examples of classical allusions or groups of allusions cited thus far are, in a sense, casual; that is, they are self-contained and fall into no pattern. While their identification serves as a gloss on the author's erudition and, perhaps even more, on the educational and literary prescriptions of the times, it provides no particular insight into Dumas's artistry. On the other hand, an early reference to a Roman hero provides more meat for analysis. The epithet "Brutus" is applied to Villefort when he returns to his betrothal dinner after treacherously committing Edmond Dantès to the Château d'If: "'Eh bien! trancheur de têtes, soutien de l'État, Brutus royaliste!' s'écria l'un, 'qu'y a-t-il? voyons!'" While more than one Brutus might merit the title "soutien de l'État," the conjunction of the name with the earlier epithet "trancheur de têtes" makes it clear that the reference is to the traditional story (Liv. 2.5) of Lucius Junius Brutus, who as consul meted out a sentence of death by beheading to his own two seditious sons. The reference may thus by seen to contain—even more than the evident ironic comment by the author on Villefort's unjust treatment of Dantès—a neat prefiguring of the events at the end of the novel, when an agonized Villefort will be compelled to "sentence" his wife (and, through her, unwittingly, his son) to execution for her crimes. The chapter in which he ponders her punishment in fact picks up the beheading image of this early allusion to Brutus, as discussed below.

On the other hand, this critic at least has been at a loss to discover any meaningful connection between this first reference to Brutus in the novel and three which follow. In the next reference, Dantès himself, when he first arrives at the Isle of Monte Cristo, is likened to the same Lucius Brutus, who was said by the Romans to have become leader of Rome through his successful interpretation of a riddling oracle which bade him to kiss his mother (Liv. 4.56): "Dantès, malgré son empire ordinaire sur lui-même, ne put se contenir: il sauta le premier sur le rivage: s'il l'eût osé, comme Brutus, il eût baisé la terre." Toward the end of the novel, the Count in turn likens himself to the Late Republican Marcus Brutus (like Lucius called by Dumas simply by his cognomen, "Brutus"): like Brutus before Philippi, he says, he too—on the eve of his duel with Albert—has seen a "fantôme," in the form of Mercédès. In a fourth locus, Albert likens the Count of Monte Cristo ambiguously to one of these two Brutuses, saying: "Je pense que c'est un homme charmant, qui fait à merveille les honneurs de chez lui, qui a beaucoup vu, beaucoup étudié, beaucoup réfléchi, qui est, comme Brutus, de l'école stoïque, et . . . qui par-dessus tout cela possède d'excellents cigares." One may wonder if the incongruity of the collocation of Stoic philosophy with hedonistic pleasure in the honors of the table and fine cigars may be taken as an index of Albert's self-noted failure to profit by his classical education. But these three later recurrences of reference to the Roman hero appear to be simply separate casual allusions, somewhat awkward in the aimless repetition of allusion to the same historical name.

In three other cases, however, I suggest that classical references by Dumas are more complex and, once fully appreciated, add wit, texture, and depth to his narrative.

The fifty-first chapter of *The Count of Monte Cristo* appears under the heading "Pyrame et Thisbé." The story begun therein, that of the courtship of Maximilien and Valentine through a garden gate, is thus obviously glossed by the tale told by Ovid (*Met.* 4.55f.) of young lovers whose only avenue of communication is a chink in the wall that separates their yards. But while the chapter heading itself is the only explicit reference in the novel to Ovid's star-crossed lovers, one and perhaps two elements of the diction of Dumas's narrative implicitly reinforce the identification of the two pairs of lovers. Twice Dumas attributes to Maximilien a heightened perceptivity occasioned by love: at one point in the narrative, Maximilien comprehends the cause of a delay in his assignation with Valentine "avec cette rapidité d'intuition particulière aux amants"; later, "avec cet instinct particulier aux amants," he knows instantly that the death of Valentine's maternal grandfather bodes ill for their

relationship. While such references to a lover's instinctive perceptivity may be too commonplace to have any special significance, it is at least conceivable that there is a specific echo here of Ovid's parenthetical exclamation concerning the perspicacity of lovers: "quid non sentit amor?" (4.68).

There is a clearer and more intricate relation between Ovid's and Dumas's narratives in the incident in which Valentine gives her little finger to Maximilien to kiss. The crack in Pyramus and Thisbe's wall is so small that it affords a path for speech alone: "vocis fecistis iter" (4.69), says Ovid in an apostrophe to the lovers; and again, "inque vices fuerat captatus anhelitus oris" (4.72). Fate, in the form of Dumas, has provided Maximilien and Valentine with a larger opening through which to communicate. Yet, when Maximilien requests that Valentine extend her little finger through the grating for a kiss, she responds, somewhat scandalized: "Maximilien, nous avions dit que nous serions l'un pour l'autre deux voix, deux ombres!." It is as if she rebuked him for asking for more than their prototypes received—as if she had said, "Maximilien, we said we would be to each other as Pyramus and Thisbe, two voices only." But Maximilien is hurt at her refusal, and she relents. This ability to touch lips to little finger constitutes a clever "improvement" by Dumas on Pyramus and Thisbe's situation. In Ovid's narrative, the lovers berate the wall:

> invide dicebant paries, quid amantibus obstas?
> quantum erat, ut sineres toto nos corpore iungi,
> aut, hoc si nimium est, vel
> ad oscula danda
> pateres?
>
> (*Met.* 4.73–75, emphasis mine)

What Pyramus and Thisbe ask of the wall in their contrary-to-fact wish, Dumas has wittily granted to Maximilien and Valentine. Their wall lies open for the giving of kisses.

The identification of the pairs of lovers, Pyramus/Thisbe and Maximilien/Valentine, has a pervasive effect on the reader's experience of the events of the novel. The ancient lovers' story ends tragically. Thisbe, arriving first at their midnight assignation, is frightened by a mountain lion into hiding in a cave; in her haste she drops her shawl, which the lion tears with its bloodied jaws before retreating into the forest. When Pyramus arrives, he is deluded by this token into believing Thisbe dead. In sorrow and remorse at his late arrival he kills himself. Thisbe, upon finding him dying, in turn takes her own life. This succession of story elements—a false death followed by serial suicide, is reinforced by the more familiar Shakespearean version of the story.

The classically astute reader of Dumas's work, then, having been alerted by the chapter-heading, would be led to fear that the parallelism between the affairs would extend beyond the lovers' mode of communication and end with tragic death for both Maximilien and Valentine. When the Count of Monte Cristo stages Valentine's death and burial to ward off further attempts at her poisoning, her fictive death presents the reader with one more realized element in the foreshadowed correspondence between the romances; all that is wanted to complete the equation is Maximilien's suicide from grief at a death he believes to be real and, finally, Valentine's suicide to join him. Dumas's repeated allusion to Maximilien's suicidal intent purposefully heightens the tension which thus affects the reader. This tension reaches a climax when Mme. de Villefort's suicide unexpectedly results as well in the unwarranted death of little Édouard. The Count's shattered reaction to Édouard's murder, his realization that the events he has so carefully put into motion now have momentum of their own and can escape his control, make one fear all the more that the foreshadowed tragic ending may fall on Maximilien and Valentine despite the Count's "controlling" hand and will. When the Count returns home directly after Édouard's death and his own frantic attempt to revive the boy, he meets Maximilien, "qui errait dans l'hôtel des Champs-Élysées, silencieux comme une ombre qui attend le moment fixé par Dieu pour rentrer dans son tombeau." Maximilien quickly makes it clear that the only obstacles between him and his longed-for release are the pledges he has made to the Count to meet certain conditions before he may indulge his suicidal desires. The reader who may have found the Count's timing recklessly close in averting Maximilien's father's suicide years before, who has since witnessed Édouard's unplanned death, and who has as well appreciated the ominous foreshadowing contained in the Pyramus and Thisbe parallel may be pardoned if his faith in the Count's ability to assure a happy ending for his protégés falters, at least temporarily.

In fact, Maximilien and Valentine's love story is destined to end happily. But until that happy ending has finally been achieved, the parallelism between the present lovers and Ovid's earlier ones (like Shakespeare's) has served to accentuate the reader's tense uncertainty of the outcome to be presented by the author and so to color his or her judgment of the righteousness of the Count's vengeful course of action.

A second significant classical allusion introduces a pattern of imagery woven into the chapter headed "Le Juge," in which M. de Villefort arrives at his resolution to exact from his wife full penalty for her crimes. Villefort's painful deliberations are characterized by Dumas as follows:

> c'était dans un moment où le magistrat, harassé de fatigue, était descendu dans le jardin de son hôtel, et sombre, courbé sous une implacable pensée, pareil à Tarquin abattant avec sa badine les têtes des pavots les plus élevés, M. de Villefort abattait avec sa canne les longues et mourantes tiges des roses trémières qui se dressaient le long des allées comme les spectres de ces fleurs si brillantes dans la saison qui venait de s'écouler.

We have already recognized from Dumas's references (previously discussed) to Lucius Brutus that the author was familiar with the first books of Livy. In this passage, when Villefort slashes at flowers while steeling himself to bring his wife to justice, he is significantly compared to Tarquinius Superbus, who in Livy's narration (in turn derived from Herodotus 5.92.6) sends a covertly murderous response to his son Sextus' inquiry concerning the next step in their campaign against a foe:

> nihil voce responsum est; rex velut deliberandus in hortum aedium transit sequente nuntio filii; ibi inambulans tacitus summa papaverum capita dicitur baculo decussisse.
>
> (Liv. 1.54)

The messenger cannot figure out why Tarquin will speak no word of answer to him; but when he reports Tarquin's actions and inexplicable silence to Sextus, Sextus immediately understands that his father's symbolic answer was that he should eradicate the enemy forthwith. The parallels between the two passages are patent: a sentence of death is decided after the judge has "descendu dans le jardin" (cf. "in hortum aedium transit"); there, "courbé sous une implacable pensée" (cf. "tacitus"), he beheads flowers in a manner which betokens the summary judgment soon to fall upon his victims.

The metaphorical identification between Villefort's role as judge and the motif of cutting or slashing is continued in two further passages within the same chapter. When Villefort awakes the morning after the flower-decapitation incident (recall his address as "trancheur de têtes"), even the phenomena of morning meteorology suggest the necessity for his following through in fact on the course of action symbolized by his actions the day before in the garden:

> Il ouvrit sa fenêtre: une grande bande orangée traversait au loin le ciel et *coupait en deux les minces peupliers* qui se profilaient en noir sur l'horizon . . . L'air humide de l'aube inonda la tête de Villefort et rafraîchit sa mémoire. "Ce sera pour aujourd'hui, dit-il avec effort; aujourd'hui *l'homme qui va tenir le glaive de la justice doit frapper partout où sont les coupables.*" (emphasis mine)

And, finally, as Villefort prepares to deliver to his wife the ultimatum that she must commit suicide or face public trial and execution, the same motif infects the father's last meeting with his son, whom Mme. de Villefort will include, Medea-like, in her suicide. Villefort bids his son leave the adults alone:

> Édouard avait levé la tête, avait regardé sa mère; puis, voyant qu'elle ne confirmait point l'ordre de M. de Villefort, il s'était remis à couper la tête à ses soldats de plomb.

It is not necessary to strain to explain the transfer of the decapitator image from Villefort to his son: we may simply note that the very presence of this third repetition of cutting/beheading imagery contributes to and continues the grimly foreboding atmosphere surrounding the events which will lead to Villefort's family ruin. And, while the recurrent imagery itself might be noticeable without appreciation of the allusion to Livy, it is only in light of the Tarquin parallel that its import may be fully felt.

The final classical allusion to be discussed here occurs early in the novel, at the point when Mercédès approaches Villefort seeking news following Dantès's arrest. Discomfited by Mercédès's dignity and (we may infer) by his own awareness of wrong-doing, Villefort falls prey to a sense of role reversal: "il lui sembla que c'était lui l'accusé, et que c'était elle le juge." He responds brusquely and disengages himself:

> Et, gêné par ce regard fin et cette suppliante attitude, il repoussa Mercédès et rentra, refermant vivement la porte, comme pour laisser dehors cette douleur qu'on lui apportait.

> Mais la douleur ne se laisse pas repousser ainsi. Comme le trait mortel dont parle Virgile, l'homme blessé l'emporte avec lui. Villefort rentra, referma la porte, mais arrivé dans son salon les jambes lui manquèrent à son tour; il poussa un soupir qui ressemblait à un sanglot, et se laissa tomber dans un fauteuil.

"Comme le trait mortel dont parle Virgile, l'homme blessé l'emporte avec lui." What is the point of the comparision of a guilt-ridden Villefort to a wounded character in the *Aeneid*? The evident point of reference is that "douleur" follows its object behind closed doors as if it were a physical weapon stuck in a wound. If that is the sole point of correspondence between the two compared loci, the allusion is clearly of the class I have earlier labelled "casual." Such an explication, however—while it offers a suitable interpretation of the point of reference in the equation *Villefort/l'homme blessé*—does not do full justice to the organic effect of the allusion. Rather, I suggest, the effect of Dumas's evocation of the *Aeneid* here is to prefigure Villefort's ruin at

the end of the novel and to reveal a complexity which is not usually imputed to Dumas's work.

First I will submit that readers of Vergil, upon initially reading Dumas's line, may be a bit taken aback. Arrows left in wounds? There are several in the *Aeneid*, but attempts to pinpoint a single Vergilian locus as Dumas's archetype here encounter various difficulties.

At least one translator has assumed that primary reference is to book 12 of the *Aeneid*, where Aeneas is struck by an arrow (12.318–319) while trying to calm the armies in preparation for his single combat with Turnus; wounded, he is helped back into camp by his comrades, where they remove the arrow, treat his leg and send him back into battle (12.383f.). Several points, however, argue against this assumption. First, that location of the reference is complicated by the patent incongruity of Aeneas' god-aided recovery and Dumas's application of the epithet "mortel" to the offending arrow. Even beyond the simple inapplicability of the epithet, the substantive parallelism asserted by such an allusion—that festering grief or guilt is like an arrow left in a wound—would surely be skewed by the miraculously speedy and complete recovery of Villefort's classical counterpart. On the other hand, this locus is the only one of those to be discussed in which the setting of the arrow-in-a-wound trope is such that Dumas's application of the trope to "l'homme blessé" is fully appropriate: for the other loci present us, respectively, with a wounded lion, woman, and deer, never a man or hero.

A second conceivable location of the allusion is the *Aeneid* passage in which Turnus' wrath in battle is compared to that of a wounded lion (*Aen.* 12.4–8). But such a location is inhibited by a context and effect which are strikingly dissimilar to those of Dumas's passage: whereas the keynote of the arrow which strikes Villefort is the lingering, hidden damage it inflicts, the missile ("telum": an "arrow" is not specified) which the lion bites off in his wound enrages him and spurs him on to greater ferocity. The lion's fearless joy in combat ("gaudet" [12.6], "impavidus" [12.8]) is far removed from Villefort's sinking, sighing capitulation to uncertainty.

The two passages in Vergil which not only leap to mind immediately upon reading Dumas's allusion but also provide the most fitting parallels to Villefort's sufferings here are the two striking and thematically interconnected passages in which first Dido, then a tame deer are struck by arrows. In the former, Dido in love is likened to a deer pierced by a hunter's arrow:

> est mollis flamma medullas
> interea et *tacitum vivit sub pectore vulnus.*
> uritur infelix Dido totaque vagatur
> urbe furens, qualis coniecta cerva sagitta,
> quam procul incautam nemora inter Cresia fixit
> pastor agens telis *liquitque volatile ferrum*
> nescius: illa fuga silvas saltusque peragrat
> Dictaeos; *haeret lateri letalis harundo.*
> (*Aen.* 4.66–73 emphasis mine)

The specific description of Dido's wound ("vulnus") as festering "tacitum . . . sub pectore" is strikingly echoed by Dumas's further reflections on Villefort's "blessure" on the page following his Vergilian allusion; after describing Villefort as prey to "ce battement sourd . . . retentissant *au fond de son coeur et emplissant sa poitrine* de vagues appréhensions" (emphasis mine), Dumas continues:

> Mais la blessure qu'avait reçue Villefort était de celles qui ne se ferment pas, ou qui ne se ferment que pour se rouvrir plus sanglantes et plus douloureuses qu'auparavant.

The motif appears again in book 7, when war is incited between Italians and Trojans as a result of Ascanius' thoughtless killing of an Italian herder's pet deer. This deer, nurtured since its infancy by human hands, wears garlands in its horns, obeys human commands, and nightly returns home of its own accord to its master's table. Pierced by Ascanius' arrow "perque uterum . . . perque ilia," the wounded pet staggers home to die:

> saucius at quadripes nota intra tecta refugit
> successitque gemens stabulis, questuque cruentus
> atque imploranti similis tectum omne replebat.
> (*Aen.* 7.500–502)

Both the deer's attempt to solace itself by retreat to its own home and the human-like sobs and laments with which it fills the house ("gemens," "questu," "imploranti similis") are forerunners of Villefort's sighing and sobbing as he sinks into his chair.

These two Vergilian loci are elaborately worked out in Vergil's opus and significantly connected. The female Dido compromises her role as leader of Carthage by capitulating to her more "natural" feminine subjugation to emotion and masculine domination; the tame deer represents a Golden Age harmony between man and nature which obtains in Italy before the arrival of the Trojans. Both fall victim to Aeneas in his march toward the destiny whereby he will found a nation whose summum opus will be to "regere imperio populos" (*Aen.* 6.851). The clear significance of the arrow-in-a-wound motif in these passages ensures that Dumas's mention of that motif in

Vergil will bring them, willy-nilly, to the reader's mind, despite the initial incongruity of coupling the referent "l'homme blessé" with allusion to an animal and a woman. Villefort's mental suffering is thus likened—through evocation of a broad Vergilian context in which suffering victims carry arrows in their wounds—not only to Aeneas' physical pain in book 12, but also to the suffering of Dido and a deer. The effects of this comparison are complex. Let us look first at the Dido parallel.

The implied identification of Villefort with a woman pierced by love and destined to be forever abandoned by her lover constitutes, along the lines of a transferred epithet, a metaphor transferred to Villefort's guilt from a seemingly more appropriate object, Mercédès's wound of love. This transferral underscores the topsy-turvydom of Villefort's stated emotions at this moment: "il lui sembla que c'était lui l'accusé, et que c'était elle le juge." Villefort's encounter with Mercédès has temporarily deposed him from his lofty, stern and essentially extra-human role as judge. He submits instead to the emotions of the judged; he becomes vulnerable; and for a brief moment he feels his true mortal helplessness in the face of the universe:

> si la belle Mercédès fût entrée et lui eût dit: "*Au nom du Dieu qui nous regarde et qui nous juge, rendez-moi mon fiancé*," oui, ce front à moitié plié sous la nécessité s'y fût courbé tout à fait.

Concomitant to the reversal of Villefort's and Mercédès's role as judge and judged is a distinct gender-reversal. A long-traditional antinomy of male and female asserts that allegiances to abstractions, like Villefort's to Justice or Aeneas' to pietas, are "masculine," while by contrast emotionalism such as Mercédès's or Dido's subjection to human love is "feminine." Likewise, strength and domination over others are traditionally viewed as masculine; passivity and victimization as feminine. Thus, Villefort's reduction in this passage from Judge/decapitator to a victim prone to Clarissa-like sighs, sobs and sinkings betokens as well his assumption of a female/passive victim's role. The completion of the transferral to Villefort of a role which is more naturally Mercédès's is glossed by the fact that her involuntary "sob" upon hearing his callous words concerning her lover's fate is picked up and outdone by his own emotional breakdown behind closed doors.

The evocation of the Vergilian episode of Ascanius' deer-slaying compounds the same effects and adds a further dimension. The deer falls victim to Ascanius' ambition to achieve honor in the masculine world ("laudis succensus amore"

[7.496]). In Ascanius' world the joint means to this end were war and the hunt; in Villefort's society such honor was won more often by wealth and power—the sort of wealth and power for which Villefort compromises his judge's soul in condemning Dantès, "cet homme qu'il sacrifiait à son ambition." The predictable equation, then, would be of Ascanius with Villefort as hunter and of the deer with Mercédès/Dantès as the hunted. As with the Dido parallel, however, the reference is transferred so that Villefort is likened instead to the hunted and wounded animal.

Thus, an apparently casual reference to Vergil's *Aeneid* in the scene in which Mercédès confronts Villefort seeking news of her imprisoned lover brings a broader Vergilian context to bear on itself. Through these allusions, the reversal of Mercédès and Villefort's roles as culprit and judge, which is stated by Dumas explicitly but briefly, is accentuated to such a point that Villefort's temporary failure of nerve provides a true prefiguring of his final peripeteia at the end of the novel—for in the end it will be readily apparent that Villefort will be the victim, the hunted one, while Dantès/the Count will have become the hunter.

In summary, then, it may be said that, although the majority of classical allusions in *The Count of Monte Cristo* are casual, aimed at display of authorial learning and replication of the kind of wittily erudite conversation which, one must assume, was de rigueur among the French upper class of Dumas's time, others are used in subtler and more thematically significant ways. The comparison of Villefort's executionary ruminations to those of Tarquinius Superbus colors the chapter in which several protagonists' doom is prepared, heightening the reader's sense of the disaster to come. Two early allusions (the first Brutus analogy and the reference to the *Aeneid*) prefigure Villefort's peripeteia from the heights of control and success to the nadir of defeated insanity. Conversely, the apparent prefiguring contained within the Pyramus/Thisbe analogy—which proves to be false, in that the foreshadowed doom does not actually befall Maximilien and Valentine—serves not only to heighten the suspense felt by the reader in anticipation of the outcome of events, but also subtly to call into question the moral premise upon which the Count's course of vengeance is based. All in all, Dumas's use of classical allusion suggests that, beyond being no mean reader of the classics, he exhibits in his writing an artful knack for turning the old to new and interesting use.

Source: Emily A. McDermott, "Classical Allusion in *The Count of Monte Cristo*," in *Classical and Modern Literature: A Quarterly*, Vol. 8, No. 2, Winter 1988, pp. 93–103.

Sources

Dumas, Alexandre, *The Count of Monte Cristo*, Grosset & Dunlap, 1946.

Goldberger, Avriel H., "Alexandre Dumas," in *Writers for Children*, Charles Scribner's Sons, 1988, pp. 209–13.

Grosskurth, Phyliss, *Byron: The Flawed Angel*, Houghton Mifflin, 1997, p. 311.

Hemmings, F. W. J., *The King of Romance: A Portrait of Alexandre Dumas*, Hamish Hamilton, 1979, p. 125.

McCrum, Robert, "The 100 Greatest Novels of All Time," in the *Observer*, October 12, 2003, located online at http://observer.guardian.co.uk/review/story/0,6903,1061037,00.html (2003).

Shakespeare, William, *Hamlet*, Cambridge University Press, 1980, p. 88.

Spurr, H. A., *The Life and Writings of Alexandre Dumas*, new ed., Haskell House, 1973, p. 183.

Further Reading

Maurois, André, *Alexandre Dumas: A Great Life in Brief*, Knopf, 1966.
> This concise biography presents a Dumas who resembles a hero out of one of his own novels.

Ross, Michael, *Alexandre Dumas*, David & Charles, 1981.
> This is an engaging and sympathetic biography that presents Dumas as a man of great charm and good nature, not as the charlatan that his detractors accused him of being. Ross places more emphasis on Dumas's life than on his works.

Schopp, Claude, *Alexandre Dumas: Genius of Life*, translated by A. J. Koch, Franklin Watts, 1988.
> This was first published in France in 1986 and is the most recent biography of Dumas to appear in English. It presents a panoramic view of Dumas's life in all its colorful detail.

Stowe, Richard S., *Alexandre Dumas (père)*, Twayne World Authors Series, No. 388, Twayne, 1976.
> This is the best and most concise guide to Dumas's work in English. It includes an analysis of Dumas's major works, a chronological table, and an annotated bibliography.

Darkness at Noon

Arthur Koestler
1940

Arthur Koestler's *Darkness at Noon* (1940, France) is one of the twentieth century's most famous "political novels," or fictional accounts of a historical reality. Written by a former member of the Communist Party, it is a unique glimpse into the volatile political situation under the government of the Union of Soviet Socialist Republics (USSR) in the late 1930s. Its main character Rubashov combines characteristics of key Soviet politicians and intellectual leaders from the Bolshevik Revolution, and the story of his imprisonment and confession explains and develops the topical political themes of totalitarianism, socialism, communism, and individualism.

Part of the reason for the novel's wide success is the fact that Koestler, who was influenced by Sigmund Freud, was able to weave his political and philosophical themes into a compelling psychological narrative. With the use of rationalistic argument and religious symbolism, Koestler is able to consider politics together with psychology and individualism. Despite the loss of the original German text, Daphne Hardy's English translation of the novel, published in London in 1940, has become an international classic and has profoundly affected how history remembers the Moscow Show Trials.

Author Biography

Koestler was born September 5, 1905, in Budapest, Hungary. His father owned a textile business, until

Arthur Koestler

it failed during World War I, at which time Koestler and his family moved to Vienna, Austria. While studying physics and engineering at the University of Vienna, Koestler became interested in the Zionist movement, which stresses that Jews should rule Palestine (modern day Israel). He moved to a Jewish settlement in Palestine in 1926 and began a career in journalism, but after three years he lost his faith in Zionism and transferred to Paris and then to Berlin, where he became a member of the Communist Party in 1932.

In 1932 and 1933, while working for a newspaper, Koestler traveled through the USSR, where he witnessed extreme poverty and met famous politicians Karl Radek and Nicolai Bukharin. These former intellectuals of the Bolshevik Revolution, who were later executed by the Soviet government, made a deep impression on Koestler and formed the basis for the main character of his 1940 novel *Darkness at Noon*, his most famous book. In 1936 Koestler traveled to Spain to cover the Spanish civil war, during which time he was arrested as a spy and sentenced to death until British officials successfully lobbied for his release. In England, Koestler wrote *The Spanish Testament* (1937), and after Bukharin and Radek were executed (in 1938 and 1939, respectively), Koestler resigned from the Communist Party.

Koestler was briefly imprisoned during the German occupation of France, but was released in 1940 and eventually made his way to Britain. After the war he began to be celebrated as a novelist, and he revived his interest in Zionism, campaigning for the creation of a Jewish state. He also was involved with the opposition to the Communist Party and campaigned against the death penalty.

Koestler continued to write political novels and journalism, as well as to participate in European and American leftist intellectual debate, until the mid-1950s, when his interests turned to science and spiritualism. He wrote and spoke about the social and physical sciences during the 1960s and 1970s, although he was increasingly influenced by theological ideas, and published popular books such as *The Act of Creation* (1962), which is a study of the creative process. In 1977 Koestler was diagnosed with Parkinson's disease, and he and his third wife committed joint suicide March 3, 1983, in London.

Plot Summary

The First Hearing

Darkness at Noon begins with its main character Rubashov being locked in his solitary prison cell, "No. 404," where he falls asleep, dreaming of his arrest, until the seven A.M. bugle call. When he wakes, Rubashov meditates on whether he will be shot, saying to himself, "the old guard is dead.... We are the last" and rubbing his "pince-nez" (eyeglasses that stay on the nose with a spring). After a "big man in uniform," later revealed to be examiner Gletkin, tells him he gets no breakfast because he has a toothache, Rubashov begins a conversation with the occupant of cell 402 by tapping out the letters of the alphabet to him.

Rubashov then has a flashback to one of his foreign missions to southern Germany, where the satellite communist group aided by the USSR Communist Party was falling apart. Since Richard, the leader of the group, had questioned and altered the party's propaganda, Rubashov told him he was no longer a member of the party and left him to his (very bleak) fate.

Looking out the window of his cell, Rubashov notices a man with a thin upper lip staring at him from the prison grounds, and finds out from No. 402 that this man was tortured yesterday. Rubashov then has a flashback to another of his foreign missions, when he met a long-standing party member named Little Loewy in a Belgian seaport. He had to tell Little Loewy and the dock workers to break the strike they have loyally followed for many years and allow Russian-made weapons into fascist Italy.

The next day Rubashov is taken to the examining magistrate, who turns out to be Rubashov's old friend Ivanov, whom Rubashov convinced not to commit suicide during the civil war (the Bolshevik Revolution). Ivanov develops a logical argument about Rubashov's involvement in the oppositional movement and states that he has evidence Rubashov planned an attempt on No. 1's life. Rubashov is scornful of the "idiocy" of the charges, but Ivanov gives him two weeks to consider partially confessing, which will get him out of prison in five years.

The Second Hearing

This section begins with an extract from Rubashov's diary discussing moral objectivity, followed by a scene between Ivanov and Gletkin, his more brutal subordinate. Gletkin is an officer of the "new type," and advocates keeping prisoners without sleep in order to obtain their confessions, but Ivanov orders that Rubashov be left in peace.

Rubashov passes his time trying to follow his thoughts to their logical conclusion in the old party habit, but he finds for the first time that his individuality, which he calls the "silent partner" of his thoughts or the "grammatical fiction," has begun to appear, often coinciding with a daydream or an ache in his tooth. He daydreams on the seventh day of his imprisonment, for example, about his secretary during his job at the Trade Delegation and his relationship with her.

Soon cell number 406 is occupied by an old peasant who continually taps the Biblical phrase "Arise ye wretched of the earth," misspelling the first word. Rubashov meets this old communist on his walks through the prison grounds, but their only communication is when the old foreigner draws a picture of Russia with the Soviet flag in its center and explains that he must not have arrived in this country.

The last night of Rubashov's two weeks of contemplation, Gletkin arranges for him to witness one of his close friends, Bogrov, led to execution. Ivanov explains the next morning that this was not his choice, and he continues his logical argument for Rubashov to follow the plan of partial confession in order for him to stay in the party and follow his lifelong convictions. By the time Ivanov leaves, Rubashov admits to himself that he has "half-surrendered."

Media Adaptations

- *Darkness at Noon* was produced on Broadway in 1951, with a stage adaptation by Sidney Kingsley.

The Third Hearing

The diary entry that begins that third section of the novel contains Rubashov's ideas about the "relative maturity of the masses," a theory he considers pursuing after his capitulation to the authorities. After he hands the warden a letter of partial surrender and tells No. 402 that he is giving in, Rubashov is confused that he is not immediately taken to see Ivanov. Finally, after two days, at two in the morning, Rubashov is taken from his bed by guards and brought before Gletkin, who says he will be the commissar in Ivanov's absence. As Gletkin later reveals, Ivanov has been arrested and executed as a traitor.

Gletkin begins a series of inquiries that blend for Rubashov into a single nightmare. Since he is not allowed to sleep, he cannot distinguish between episodes or remember much about the specific questions Gletkin asks him. Rubashov begins by firmly denying the criminal charges against him, confessing only to a "counterrevolutionary" attitude, but Gletkin tells him that he will not get off so easily. From here begin a series of arguments that eventually convince Rubashov he is a criminal, since the actions of which he is accused follow directly from his thoughts.

Confronting him with "Hare-lip," who turns out to be the son of Rubashov's old friend Professor Kieffer (himself executed as a traitor), Gletkin coaches the witness into describing how he made an attempt on No. 1's life, on Rubashov's orders. Although Rubashov, at most, vaguely suggested something related to the idea of assassination, he signs a statement of admission to the charges and returns to his cell. He also admits to having counterrevolutionary motives and to working for a foreign power; the only charge he denies, and which is dropped, is that he sabotaged the aluminum trust.

After signing the necessary statements, Rubashov is finally allowed to sleep.

The Grammatical Fiction

Koestler presents Rubashov's trial—in which Rubashov pleads guilty and is sentenced to death—in the form of a newspaper account that the daughter of Rubashov's former porter Wassilij reads to her father. Wassilij is bitter and cynical upon hearing it, but is afraid he will be sent to jail and signs a petition against "traitors" like Rubashov.

It is while waiting to be executed that Rubashov begins to have some of his most serious doubts about the party and its objective morality. Rubashov feels more strongly than ever before the presence of the "grammatical fiction" that represents his individuality, and he ponders whether there is any purpose in life, failing just before he dies to see any paradise in sight for the USSR. After he watches Hare-lip walk to his execution and listens to No. 402 console him by tapping his farewell, Rubashov is led down the spiral staircase and executed.

Characters

Arlova

A "heavy, shapely" woman with a sleepy voice, Arlova is Rubashov's secretary during his job at the Trade Delegation. They have an affair, and Arlova tells Rubashov, "You will always be able to do what you like with me" before the Stalinist purges begin, and she receives a warning in her new post as librarian to restock the books of opposition leaders. Shortly afterwards, Rubashov stops his little jokes with her, and she stops going to his room. Soon she is condemned as a traitor and sentenced to death.

Michael Bogrov

Bogrov is Rubashov's old friend. Rubashov befriended Bogrov when Bogrov taught him to read while they were roommates in exile. As Rubashov taps to his prison-cell neighbor, Bogrov was a "former sailor on Battleship Potemkin, Commander of the eastern fleet, and bearer of the First Revolutionary Order," which signifies Bogrov was a prominent member of the "old guard," since the Potemkin was the site of the first rebellion against the tsarist regime. Rubashov is forced to watch as Bogrov is led to execution. Bogrov is executed because of his advocacy of long-range submarines

to pursue the worldwide revolution, which goes against the Stalinist policy.

Elder Official

The older of the two officials who originally arrest Rubashov is slightly kinder than his younger counterpart, and more sympathetic and respectful to Rubashov than his counterpart.

Gletkin

Rubashov's examining magistrate after Ivanov is arrested, Gletkin embodies the new generation of Soviet officials. A civil war veteran with "expressionless eyes" and a shaven head with a large scar, he forces Rubashov to stay awake under blinding lights and ceaseless antagonism until, days later, the prisoner confesses to the specific charges against him. Gletkin has much to gain by "bringing down" Rubashov, and it is clear that party members with Gletkin's convictions and ruthless methods will be promoted and rewarded by No. 1.

The one time Gletkin reveals anything about his personal life coincides with Rubashov's one triumph during his examination—the withdrawal of industrial sabotage charges. Gletkin describes the first time he was posted to watch over the peasantry, using it as an example of the necessity of force to get the Soviet industrial economy in functional order. As Rubashov recognizes, Gletkin and other "Neanderthalers" have no humanity because they have lived entirely under a system that eradicates individuality. Rubashov comes to believe that this is the logical extension of the basic Bolshevik principles of the party, and that the "Gletkins" are the inevitable result of the Rubashovs.

Ivanov

Rubashov's old friend and his examining magistrate for the first two hearings, Ivanov is a former battalion commander with a wooden leg and, like Rubashov, a thinker of the old guard. Rubashov was present when Ivanov's leg was amputated during the war, at which time Rubashov argued with him for an entire afternoon, finally convincing him not to commit suicide. In the prison, Ivanov engages in two long arguments with his friend about rationality and usefulness to the party in order to convince him to partially confess. Recognizing that Rubashov will capitulate if allowed to follow his thoughts to their logical conclusion, Ivanov allows Rubashov two weeks for reflection. Although Rubashov does confess to a general oppositional tendency when his two weeks expire, it is because of Ivanov's handling of Rubashov's case that Ivanov is arrested and promptly executed.

Hare-lip Kieffer

Hare-lip is revealed to be the son of Rubashov's old friend Professor Kieffer, who had been previously condemned as a traitor and executed. Hare-lip is seemingly the party's only evidence of the specific charges against Rubashov. Gletkin tortured Hare-lip to obtain the false confession that Rubashov incited him to assassinate No. 1, and Rubashov admits to this act despite the fact that he and Hare-lip never met to plan an assassination. In his exhausted state, Rubashov finds himself guilty because he had a dissenting political conversation with Professor Kieffer that Hare-lip overheard.

Having undergone severe torture, Hare-lip is a "human-wreck" with a chalky white and yellow face, and he continually looks to Rubashov for sympathy or salvation. Rubashov ignores him, however, and Hare-lip goes to his execution without having spoken to his supposed collaborator.

Little Loewy

Little Loewy is Rubashov's contact for his mission for the party in a Belgian seaport. Born in southern Germany with a deformed shoulder, Little Loewy learned to be a carpenter and was involved lecturing to his revolutionary youth club until a daring mission stealing weapons for the Communist Party made it necessary for him to leave his town. The party abandoned him at this point, and left him wandering and in prison between Belgium and France for many years, in desperate circumstances, until he finally met an ex-wrestler named Paul who helped reinstate him in a section of the Belgian Party dominated by dockworkers. Rubashov's demand that the dockworkers allow Russian-made weapons into Italy, however, finally breaks Little Loewy, and after he refuses to follow orders, he is denounced by the party and hangs himself out of disgrace and disillusionment.

No. 1

The fictional representation of USSR leader Joseph Stalin, No. 1 plays an important role in the novel although he is entirely behind the scenes. He is the successor to the grand old leader, Vladimir Lenin, and he has eliminated all opposition to his reign. The dictator of the new, totalitarian party, No. 1 is immensely powerful, yet his alternate name implies that he is imprisoned like the other former leaders, perhaps by his own brutal policy that allows no deviation from the party's goals.

No. 402

Rubashov's neighbor in prison with whom he taps conversations through the wall, No. 402 is a "conformist" loyal to the tsar and a veteran of the civil war. He has eighteen years of his sentence left to complete, and although he briefly resents Rubashov for his communist beliefs, No. 402 is more interested in stories about women and sex. Rubashov finds No. 402 quite important to his time in prison; he envisions a variety of ways that No. 402 might look based on his personality traits, and he tells No. 402 just before he dies that their friendship helped him a lot. The individual human connection of their friendship, which is not based in politics, also gives No. 402 an important role as a representation of the novel's theme of individuality.

No. 406

Also called Rip Van Winkle, No. 406 is an old peasant who walks next to Rubashov during his outings in the prison gardens. After fighting for the communists in one of the small-scale civil wars that broke out across Europe during the Russian Revolution, he was arrested and imprisoned for twenty years. When he was finally released, he made his way to the USSR, the country of the revolution, only to be arrested by the Soviets fourteen days after his arrival. Rubashov speculates that he might have mentioned one of former Bolshevik heroes, having no idea that these "heroes" were now branded as "traitors."

While walking next to Rubashov, No. 406 draws two pictures of the USSR, one without looking, and tells Rubashov that he must have been sent to the wrong country. In this way, Koestler uses No. 406 to emphasize the disparity between the government of the 1930s and the original goals of the Revolution.

Reactionary Peasant

The unnamed peasant who walks next to Rubashov at the beginning of the novel's "The Third Hearing" section refused, like many peasants, to comply with government regulations for mass immunization. He and his family burned government supplies because of superstition and traditional values, and a month later they were arrested as "reactionaries."

Richard

The leader of a communist group in southern Germany, Richard has a nervous stutter, deep concerns about his pregnant wife's imprisonment, and has been disillusioned about the support of communist leaders in Moscow. After Rubashov informs Richard that he is no longer a member of the party, Richard begs him not to "throw me to the wolves, c-comrade," referring to the Nazi Secret Police.

Nicolas Salmanovitch Rubashov

Ex-Commissar of the People, Rubashov is the principal character in the novel and the person through whose mind almost all of the story unfolds. Arrested on charges of conspiracy to assassinate No. 1, industrial sabotage, espionage, and general oppositional tendencies, Rubashov is examined by two magistrates and denied sleep by the second until he confesses to the specific charges. He goes to public trial, and is executed by being shot twice in the back of the head.

Rubashov is an intelligent and important thinker who for all of his life has held a conviction in rationality and a belief in communist ideology. He was a military and intellectual hero of the Bolshevik Revolution, worked abroad for many years to sponsor international communist goals, and remained loyal to the party while being tortured in foreign prisons. He worked closely with No. 1, was paraded and championed upon his return to Russia after his major imprisonment (although he immediately left on another mission abroad despite a leg injury), and held a high position in the Soviet Trade Delegation.

A combination of major personalities of the Moscow Show Trials, Rubashov's personal appearance has been likened to Leon Trotsky, whom Stalin and others drove out of the party and into exile until one of Stalin's henchmen eventually murdered him abroad. Rubashov's political and personal history is perhaps closest to that of Nicolai Bukharin, the former head of the Comintern (the international organization intended to spread the communist revolution) who was tried and executed in 1938. However, Rubashov's admission of specific conspiratorial charges is closer to that of the former Bolshevik heroes like the head of Soviet propaganda, Karl Radek. In any case, Rubashov is intended to generally represent the dying "old guard."

As becomes immediately clear in the novel, however, Rubashov is a unique and psychologically profound character whose outlook develops a great deal through the course of his imprisonment and trial. He is quite shaken just after his imprisonment, but comes to the rational conclusions of the Ivanovs and many of the intellectuals on whom his character is based. In the course of his sleepless examination by Gletkin, however, Rubashov descends into a unique sort of irrational logic, a

paradox of thinking that causes him to admit to specific charges because of his belief he is guilty of oppositional thinking and the fact that a confession to "blacken the Wrong" is a service to the party. But by the end of the novel Rubashov has questioned the fundamental assumptions of this thinking and discredited the philosophy that the "ends justify the means."

Vassilij

Rubashov's thin old porter before the arrest, Vassilij has a large neck scar from the civil war, in which he fought in Rubashov's partisan regiment. Vassilij reappears in the novel's "The Grammatical Fiction" section to hear his daughter read the newspaper account of Rubashov's trial, although his name is here changed to "Wassilij." He is a religious man, although his daughter has taken away his Bible, and he fondly remembers Rubashov's eloquent ability to speak in phrases that seem to him divine. Worried that he is too old to go to prison, however, he signs a petition condemning traitors and allows his daughter to throw away Rubashov's portrait.

Wassilij

See Vassilij

Young Official

The younger of the officials who arrest Rubashov is an impetuous and aggressive soldier of the new type.

Themes

Political Philosophy

Darkness at Noon is concerned with the some of the most important controversies in twentieth-century political thought. In addition to a topical exploration of the political theory behind the Communist Party in Moscow, the novel engages in a wider debate on morality, justice, and philosophy in modern political systems. It considers the fundamental elements of revolutionary ideology and social morality, using a particular political atrocity to evaluate the set of values at its core.

The values under question are not, principally, Marxism or socialism, although Koestler is interested in questions of social justice, the distribution of resources, and how to adapt a socialist political theory to the demands of an actual society. Rubashov's philosophical crisis is better understood

Topics For Further Study

- Rubashov has been compared to Soviet political leaders Karl Radek, Nicolai Bukharin, and Christian Rakovsky, as well as to Koestler himself. Research the lives of these figures and determine which of them you believe influenced Rubashov's character, and how. Is Rubashov a fair representation of the leaders tried from 1936 to 1938? Did he have the same motivation for confessing?

- Koestler was an active Zionist (a believer that Jews should have a homeland in Palestine) during his youth, he supported the creation of an Israeli state after World War II, and later in his life he became very interested in spirituality. What are the religious undertones in *Darkness at Noon*? What is the nature of Koestler's allusions to Christianity and Judaism? How does the political ideology in the novel deal with religion?

- Discuss the treatment of women in *Darkness at Noon*. Could the novel be considered sexist? Research the treatment of women in the USSR during the 1930s, and compare it to the treatment of women in the United States during the same time period.

- Read a biography of Joseph Stalin such as Edvard Radzinsky's 1997 study. Was Stalin solely responsible for the Moscow Show Trials, or do you think they reflect the inevitable tendency of the Bolsheviks? How did the trials fit into Stalin's career and dictatorship? Did Koestler's novel affect Stalin's growing reputation as a tyrant? If so, how?

---

in terms of the debate on the basic tenets of revolution and the justification behind an authoritative totalitarian regime (a state of which the head is a dictator that forcefully suppresses dissenters), or, as Rubashov puts it, whether the "ends justify the means." Rubashov's conflict is whether an ultimate utopian goal such as a socialist state justifies brutal and totalitarian methods.

As becomes clear in the novel, Communist Party theory is only concerned with the objective. Morality is determined by the ultimate result of logic and rationality; intent, psychology, and individual desire are unimportant and merely serve to distract from what is important. One of Koestler's most successful efforts in his novel is to follow this very same method of rational thinking to the absurd result of Rubashov's confession. Koestler throws into question the philosophical basis for Stalinist policy and attacks the fundamental assumptions of a totalitarian government, skeptical that authoritative means can or ever will be justified.

By the end of the novel, Koestler is at his most doubtful about the end—"wherever [Rubashov's] eye looked, he saw nothing but desert and the darkness of night"—and he has highlighted the bleakest possible means. Under Koestler's analysis, it appears unlikely that an authoritative revolutionary model for a totalitarian system can result in a just state, and this statement is all the more poignant coming from an author who understands communist philosophy so thoroughly and presents it so convincingly.

Individualism

Rubashov is a lifelong supporter of the Communist Party; he believes individualism is a "petty bourgeois" notion and a "grammatical fiction" that is insignificant compared to the well-being of the masses. He views himself as an instrument of the party and, like many communists, is willing to sacrifice himself for the good of the country. Yet he undergoes a profound change during the course of the novel, and by the last chapter, the grammatical fiction is a prominent part of his character.

The most revealing sign of Rubashov's developing individuality is his relationship with No. 402, the neighbor with whom he communicates by tapping out ideas in a primitive fashion. No. 402's preoccupation with anecdotes, jokes, and stories about sex instead of political matters signals his connection to individualism. Also, No. 402's importance to Rubashov's developing individuality is emphasized by the fact that No. 402 is a conformist from an earlier ideological era, that their first words to each other are "WHO," and that their friendship, which becomes very important to each of them, has nothing to do with ideology but solely with human connection.

Individualism is not confined to Rubashov's sense of self; it invades his philosophizing and becomes vital to the political analysis of the novel. Just before he is taken to be executed, Rubashov's vision of a potential political future is dominated by what he calls the "oceanic feeling" and what psychologists would call an expression of the limitless sense of self associated with individuality. This political vision, with its religious cult of followers in "monks' cowls," is probably not posed as a viable alternative to communism, however. In fact, it appears to be an irony on the glorification of individualism that would be the opposite of the communist position and suggests that Koestler is by no means advocating any kind of unbounded individualism in politics. Nevertheless, the book refutes the idea that individualism should always be repressed and highlights a case where its repression has a dreadful result.

Psychological Limits

Along with political explorations of a totalitarian and authoritarian state, Koestler provides a focused portrait of a character undergoing a kind of psychological tyranny. The novel examines the results of the complete mental exhaustion of a character extremely firm in his rationality and accustomed to all kinds of physical torture. In what Gletkin calls "a matter of constitution," Rubashov is denied any sleep or mental rest, and is brought through a nightmare of questioning and humiliation until he arrives at what is, in a perverse way, the extreme conclusion of his rational thoughts. This study of the human capacity to be an instrument of logic without comfort or individuality is an important theme of the text and is one of the defining distinctions between what Rubashov considers the "old guard" and the "Neanderthal" new type of communist.

Style

Rational Arguments

In order to convincingly evaluate the communist emphasis on the furthest extent of rationality and the objective compulsion to action, Koestler employs the stylistic device of extremely thorough rational thinking. In other words, he uses the party's own game in order to attack its policy. Rubashov is such an effective voice for the argument of the novel because he follows rationality to its extreme, finds it to be absurd, and is left only with the irrational "grammatical fiction."

In this way, the first two hearings can be understood as an exhaustion of the calm and composed rational process with results, in the form of Rubashov's confession, that seem to make sense. But, as Gletkin and his methods reveal, Rubashov has not gone far enough. Rational thinking leads him directly into the next hearing, which becomes increasingly absurd in its conclusions but nevertheless perfectly in line with the previous logical argumentative style. Ultimately, Koestler's insistence on rationality in prose arrives at a point where rational argument itself is not a sufficient moral "ballast," a point that is only clear after such an impressive argumentative chain.

Religious Symbolism

Rubashov is an atheist and the Communist Party is forcefully secular, but there is religious symbolism throughout the text that serves to underscore Koestler's political and psychological themes. Rubashov's patronymic, or name derived from his father's, is the Jewish "Salmanovitch," and Judaic identity seems to become important before his execution, when he makes two references to Moses and the "Promised Land." But the most consistent symbolism throughout the book is Christian, and Rubashov is often identified with Christ. Rubashov remembers a Christian phrase as he is being arrested; his habit of rubbing his glasses on his sleeve is similar (according to Koestler) to praying with a rosary; the image of the outstretched hands of the Pietà dominates his dreams and ponderings; No. 406 insists on tapping Christian verse to him each morning; and in the sense that the accused is innocent of specific crimes but guilty of general opposition, Rubashov's trial and execution have an affinity with the trial and martyrdom of Christ.

These elements combine to place Rubashov in the position of a savior, but one without faith in his own religion. As Rubashov ponders shortly before his death, "But when he asked himself, For what are you actually dying? he found no answer." Koestler may be using religious symbolism as an ironic device to attack party policy, he may be emphasizing that Stalinism is very much like a religion, or both.

Historical Context

Leninism and the Bolsheviks

Between the first unsuccessful Russian Revolution of 1905 to 1907 and the beginning of the Russian Revolution of 1917, Vladimir Lenin and his Bolshevik faction gradually cut their ties with the Menshevik faction of the Communist Party. While the Mensheviks tended to support gradual reform and democracy, the Bolsheviks under Lenin favored revolution in order to achieve the goals of Marxism. In 1921, after the Bolsheviks had won the revolution, Lenin emerged as dictator of the party.

Before his first stroke in 1922, Lenin tried to support the extension of the communist revolution to other countries, and stressed that Marxist goals were to be achieved after a transitional period. Russia was in the midst of a severe economic crisis, however, and Lenin altered his policy to allow some forms of capitalism to coexist with communism until, he wrote, the country could grow into a purely socialist state. Meanwhile, he had eliminated opposition to the Bolshevik faction of the party, established dictatorial control, and set the precedent for an authoritarian regime, which Stalin would take to an extreme.

Stalin's Great Terror

After Lenin's death in 1924, Joseph Stalin earnestly began his quest for power, and within ten years he had all but eliminated the organized opposition to his dictatorship. In the early 1930s Stalin rapidly drove the USSR to a state of industrialization, but the immediate result of collectivization, which required farmers to live and work in government communes, was severe supply shortages and the deaths of many millions of peasants. Meanwhile, the hundreds of thousands of peasants who failed or refused to comply with Stalin's five-year plans were either murdered or sent to labor camps in Siberia.

The 1930s are also notorious for being a time of brutal oppression of suspected traitors and political undesirables in the USSR. After the murder of Stalin's underling Sergei Kirov in 1934 (which, historians have argued, Stalin may even have orchestrated himself), the political purges known as the "Great Terror" began. In the five years that followed, over a million suspected traitors, including most of the key intellectual leaders of the Russian Revolution, were arrested, imprisoned, sent to labor camps, or executed.

The important and lasting public demonstrations of the Great Terror were the "Moscow Show Trials" of 1936, and 1937 to 1938. Separate from the private hearings that internally disposed of political dissidents, the Show Trials were a forum for publicizing the confessions of prominent Soviet politicians in order to gain public support for the government. Although evidence suggests that most of the confessions were obtained by torture and intimidation (such as threatening the family of the accused), much of the Russian public and some members of the international press believed they were genuine. Koestler, himself a widely influential commentator on the trials, presents his own version of the circumstances of the confessions in *Darkness at Noon.*

The first of the Show Trials focused on three key Bolshevik leaders who pleaded guilty, with the exception of Ivan Smirnov, to conspiracy with the famous exile Leon Trotsky to assassinate Stalin. Smirnov pleaded guilty to charges of general opposition but refused to admit to specific charges, and the prosecution spent some time ridiculing his claim to have plotted but not acted. Convicted nevertheless, Smirnov was executed with his counterparts.

During the second trial, several more famous politicians were accused of plotting with Trotsky to sabotage the economy and spy for Germany and Japan. Among the accused was Karl Radek, the former head of propaganda for the USSR, whom Koestler had met during his tour of the country four years earlier. Again, the former leaders confessed, were given the death sentence, and received no pardon.

Finally, in 1938 the last of the trials convicted Bolshevik heroes such as Nicolai Bukharin on similar charges. Bukharin, perhaps the main model for Koestler's Rubashov along with Karl Radek, was a member of Lenin's original circle of power and had briefly led the USSR alongside Stalin. Despite the fact that he had a wife and small child under threat, during the trial Bukharin recanted his confession to specific crimes and maintained that he was innocent of them until, like the other former leaders, he was shot.

The Great Terror had lasting consequences for the regime of the USSR. It set a precedent for dictatorial and oppressive totalitarianism that, although later Soviet leaders did not approach the extremes of the late 1930s, failed to die with Stalin in 1953. In 1956 Nikita Khrushchev and other leaders accused Stalin of a reign of terror, but most of them had been active participants, and the

Compare
&
Contrast

- **1930s:** The USSR is the first communist state in the world, in the precursory stages to a half-century of Cold War with the United States.

  Today: Russia is now a capitalist democracy with a freely elected Federal Assembly. The Berlin Wall dividing communist East Germany from capitalist West Germany fell in 1989, and the USSR officially collapsed in 1991.

- **1930s:** The Russian economy has failed to recover from the revolution. There are shortages of almost every type of product, and widespread suffering.

  Today: In decline since the fall of communism, the Russian economy suffers from organized crime and the severe devaluation of the ruble.

- **1930s:** Famous political figures from the Bolshevik Revolution are tried and executed for industrial sabotage, among other conspiracy charges.

  Today: The Russian government is in the process of prosecuting a number of rich and powerful tycoons, all of whom tend to have political ambitions, for tax evasion and fraud.

- **1930s:** At one point during his purges, Stalin requires each of his generals to send him a list of a third of their officers to be promoted, a third to be sent to Siberia, and a third to be executed. Seventy percent of the army officer corps is arrested during the period.

  Today: The Russian military is underfunded and taxed by the war against rebels in Chechnya, but Russia has the second-most powerful nuclear arsenal in the world.

Stalinist infrastructure of secret police to stifle opposition remained in place.

The Comintern

In 1919 Communist Party leaders met in Moscow during the Bolshevik Revolution to form the "Communist International" or the "Comintern," a branch of the party with a mission to extend and foster a worldwide communist revolution. Funded and directed by the Soviet government, the Comintern soon became a method for the USSR to control the Communist Party in other countries, and leaders in Moscow actively pursued a worldwide agenda through most of the 1920s.

Under Stalin's control, however, the Comintern became less committed to sponsoring foreign revolutions, and the withdrawal of financial and advisory support to countries such as Germany and Spain led to severe consequences for party members in those countries. Nicolai Bukharin was the chairman of the Comintern from 1919 to 1929, but he abandoned this agenda by the 1930s as Stalin's priorities shifted to isolationism.

Critical Overview

George Orwell was the most influential initial critic of *Darkness at Noon*, which he called a "masterpiece" and explained in the *New Statesman*: "Brilliant as this book is as a novel, and a piece of prison literature, it is probably most valuable as an interpretation of the Moscow 'confessions' by someone with an inner knowledge of totalitarian methods." Orwell wrote that the book was not received well, but Koestler's biographers note that the book was indeed favorably reviewed. As David Cesarani writes in his biography *Arthur Koestler: The Homeless Mind*: "Praise for the novel flowed in from all quarters." Iain Hamilton points out in *Koestler: A Biography*: "Kingsley Martin, editor of the *New Statesman*, did a great deal to promote *Darkness at Noon* which he described (correctly) as 'One of the few books written in this epoch which will survive it.'"

Since its original reception the novel has become widely famous and influential, especially as a political tool during the Cold War. Cesarani writes: "The novel was regarded as a potent anti-Communist weapon from the 1940s to the 1970s when, alongside

Orwell's *Animal Farm* and *1984*, it was a set text in schools in the USA and Britain." It has been variously debated and attacked as a coherent philosophical work, believed and contested as a historical account of the Moscow Show Trials, and hated and loved by socialists and former socialists. Commentary on the novel, particularly on its influence over the debate about Communism, continues to be written.

Criticism

Scott Trudell

Trudell is a freelance writer with a bachelor's degree in English literature. In the following essay, Trudell argues that Darkness at Noon *advocates a socialist political philosophy similar to that of the Menshevik thinkers before the Russian Revolution.*

Most of the criticism of *Darkness at Noon* has concentrated on its convincing and insightful case against Stalin's totalitarian regime. Because he is so familiar with Party thinking, and because he is able to portray so compellingly the psychology of a former Communist hero losing his faith, Koestler has been uniquely influential in the twentieth-century debate about Soviet politics. His novel has been set as a classroom text in the United States and Britain and generally understood as a rebuttal of Communism or even as a vindication of capitalism. While it is true, however, that Koestler attacks Stalinist ideology at its roots, the political argument of his novel retains basic socialist beliefs.

This is not to say that Koestler confines his criticism to Stalin's dictatorship. *Darkness at Noon* is a thorough rebuttal of Bolshevik philosophy, which had always stressed the ends over the means and condoned violence in the name of the ultimate utopian goal. In his 1944 essay "Arthur Koestler," George Orwell paraphrases Koestler's argument: "all efforts to regenerate society *by violent means* lead to the cellars of the OGPU [the Soviet secret police], Lenin leads to Stalin, and would have come to resemble Stalin if he had happened to survive." Immoral and brutal totalitarianism is the necessary result of the Bolshevik doctrine that violent revolution, not gradual reform, is the way to achieve a Marxist economic system.

Koestler thoroughly establishes this point by connecting Rubashov's absurd final confessions to his Bolshevik beliefs. The third hearing and Rubashov's admission of specific crimes, which represent the furthest totalitarian extension of the

Communist theorist Leon Trotsky

original idea that he is guilty of "oppositional views," are obtained by Rubashov's own rationalistic logic, the same logic that justified his involvement in the civil war. In Koestler's analysis, Gletkin is merely a tool to help Rubashov think out everything to its logical conclusion, and Rubashov's physical exhaustion is an expression of the limits of human rationality, the inability for humans to actually see the final picture. This is why, in his final thoughts, Koestler emphasizes Rubashov's inability to see anything but "desert and the darkness of night," and this is why, with humans unable to see the end, the ends cannot possibly justify the means.

It is important to remember here that this is Koestler's unique view on the trials of the late 1930s; historians have come to the consensus that it does not reflect the reasoning behind the confessions on which the novel was based. As Stephen Cohen writes in his biography of Nicolai Bukharin, perhaps the principal influence on Rubashov's character:

> Owing to Koestler's powerful art, this image of Bukharin-Rubashov as repentant Bolshevik and morally bankrupt intellectual prevailed for two generations. In fact, however, as some understood at the time and others eventually came to see, Bukharin did not really confess to criminal charges at all.

Instead, Bukharin withdrew his confession (which was most likely given in hopes of saving

> It is at precisely this point in history, therefore, that Koestler aims his argument; Rubashov's logic stretches back to the break between Bolshevism and Menshevism."

his wife and child) and admitted only to general opposition to Stalin's regime. Although he may have believed that Rubashov's reasoning was a common cause of confession, Koestler was less interested in providing a historically accurate piece of political fiction than he was in emphasizing that the old Bolsheviks were responsible for the totalitarian trend of the USSR. He clearly sympathizes with the Rubashovs and Bukharins (having been a Party member himself), but his novel argues that socialists have been led astray ever since Lenin abandoned the idea of gradual reform and turned to violent revolutionary tactics.

It is at precisely this point in history, therefore, that Koestler aims his argument; Rubashov's logic stretches back to the break between Bolshevism and Menshevism. Lenin had always been in favor of actively, forcefully if necessary, guiding the population towards a Marxist society, but it was after the first major congress of Russian Marxists in 1903 that advocates of social democracy and institutional reform split to form a Menshevik ("smaller") faction. Meanwhile, Lenin led the Bolshevik ("larger") faction with increasing emphasis on a revolutionary program, and between the first Revolution of 1905 and the Revolution of 1917, he gradually separated from Menshevik leaders until the Bolsheviks were an independent party.

After the Revolution, Menshevik thinkers were isolated from the massive influence of the newly created Communist state and faded from influence. Appalled and dismayed by the results of the Bolshevik philosophy, however, Koestler subtly rehabilitates its alternative, which by Rubashov's logic would not have led to Stalinism. *Darkness at Noon* identifies that the key problem in Bolshevik thought is its inevitable tendency towards a dictatorship that ignores the will of the people, whereas this would not occur

in the "Social-Democracy" of Menshevism. As Solomon M. Schwarz writes in his book *The Russian Revolution of 1905: The Workers' Movement and the Formation of Bolshevism and Menshevism,* "Bolshevism logically developed dictatorial conceptions and practices; Menshevism remained thoroughly democratic."

One of the ways Koestler supports a Menshevik form of democracy is by introducing Rubashov's own ideas on the "relative maturity of the masses," which, as Rubashov writes in his diary, "lies in the capacity to recognize their own interests." Rubashov goes on to write that the masses are at a point of immaturity, unable to recognize what is good for them in economic terms, and he tries to justify a dictatorship until they advance. But Rubashov fails to recognize until after he has been condemned that a dictatorship is no more mature or ethical than the masses. Totalitarian dictators merely lead the population into "desert and the darkness of night," and the population's "immature" idea of self-interest is the only moral assurance available.

Koestler reinforces this idea at the end of the novel, when Rubashov realizes, "We have thrown overboard all conventions. . . . Perhaps it did not suit mankind to sail without [ethical] ballast." Despite their immaturity, the masses know what is good for them in the sense that they choose leaders to uphold the social conventions of morality, such as religion. Christian or Judaic morality fundamentally stress the means over the ends, and it is far better to follow these "immature" ethics than it is to be subjugated to a violent dictatorship that eradicates individuality. Koestler is thus able to imply that, if its leaders were democratically elected, the Communist Party might have been focused on the means rather than the ends enough to avoid the brutality of Stalin's purge trials.

Notice, however, that Koestler does not in any way connect capitalism to his democratic implications. *Darkness at Noon* denounces totalitarianism, but it provides no condemnation of a socialist economic system, and Koeslter seems to envision a democratic republic with a set socialist economic system. Again, examine Rubashov's idea of the maturity of the masses; Rubashov eventually discovers that the masses are able to recognize their own interests as far as the "ethical ballast" of conventional morality is concerned, but there is no hint that they can freely elect leaders that will make the correct economic decisions for their well being. This idea is underscored when, directly after his thoughts on the maturity of the masses, Rubashov meets a

What Do I Read Next?

- Aleksandr Solzhenitsyn won the Nobel Prize for literature in 1970 principally for his novel *One Day in the Life of Ivan Denisovich* (1962), which describes in stark and innovative language one man's experience in a Soviet "gulag" (labor camp) towards the end of Stalin's rule. The novel is based on Solzhenitsyn's own experience.

- George Orwell's *1984* (1949) is a striking and insightful glimpse of a possible totalitarian future. Orwell was Koestler's friend and a prominent critic. The novel has a powerful political argument and its vision of the future makes a number of predictions that have, even in modern democracies like the United States and Britain, come true.

- Koestler's *The Gladiators* (1939) is a retelling of Spartacus and the Roman slave revolt. As in *Darkness at Noon*, Koestler uses themes of revolution and "ends versus means" to discuss political ethics.

- Edvard Radzinsky's *Stalin: The First In-Depth Biography Based on Explosive New Documents from Russia's Secret Archives* (1997) stresses the extent of Stalin's brutality.

- One of the best and most readable histories of the Soviet Union is Robert Service's *A History of Twentieth Century Russia* (1997).

"reactionary" peasant who out of superstition has refused to have his family vaccinated, and who burned the government-supplied threshing machine. This is a classic example of the Marxist theory that the peasantry is a reactionary class, and it highlights Koestler's continued sympathy with socialist goals.

This sympathy is apparent throughout the novel; perhaps one of the most moving episodes is Rubashov's other encounter with a peasant on the prison grounds. Rip Van Winkle, the occupant of cell 406, is apparently a devout Christian since he taps out Biblical verse every morning. But along with this moral convention, he is so firm a socialist that he can draw a map of Russia with his eyes closed, despite the fact that he has been imprisoned for twenty years by the same Party for which he fought. Koestler uses Rip Van Winkle as a flashback to the noble form of socialism compatible with conventional morality, with which he deeply sympathizes.

Perhaps the most convincing example of Koestler's socialist tendencies, however, is his continued logical rebuttal of Stalinism and Bolshevism in the form of Gletkin's questioning. It is no coincidence that the one charge of which Rubashov is cleared, his one "triumph" with Gletkin, is the withdrawal of the charges of industrial sabotage.

As Rubashov maintains to Gletkin's persistent questioning, the problem with the Russian economy is not socialism at all:

> "If you hold sabotage for a mere fiction, what, in your opinion, are the real causes of the unsatisfactory state of our industries?"
>
> "Too low piece-work tariffs, slave-driving and barbaric disciplinary measures," said Rubashov.

Indeed, Koestler seems to agree with Rubashov on this point; socialism has not been refuted. Rubashov's other crimes all stem back to the fundamentals of Bolshevik dictatorial violence, and he admits to them despite their technical absurdities because, as far as Koestler is concerned, he is indeed guilty by rational extension. Espionage and assassination are the necessary results of Bolshevism, and this is why Stalin, as "No. 1," is attributed the first prison cell; he is also guilty of the Bolshevik ideology that leads to his dictatorship, and he is a prisoner of his own Party philosophy. But socialism, in the form of a socialist democracy that had been advocated by the Mensheviks since 1903, remains for Koestler an ethical, worthwhile, and functional system.

Source: Scott Trudell, Critical Essay on *Darkness at Noon*, in *Novels for Students*, Gale, 2004.

David Lewis Schaefer

In the following essay, Schaefer examines Koestler's criticism of Marxism in Darkness at Noon *and defends Koestler's use of the novel form for the story.*

Darkness at Noon, Arthur Koestler's novel of the Soviet purge trials, does not make good bedtime reading. Considered as a historical novel, moreover, it may be contended (as Irving Howe has done) that the book is "crucially flawed" both historically and artistically: Koestler's account of his protagonist's "gradual surrender to Stalinism" as the product of a purely "dialectical process within his own thought" seems "manifestly untrue to our sense of human behavior" and reduces "an enormously difficult and complex problem" to "abstract and ultimatistic moral terms." Despite these possible flaws, the book has been recognized, in the words of a recent interpreter, "both at the time of its original publication in 1941 and ever since, as one of the truly powerful works of twentieth-century political literature." It will be argued here that a great deal of the work's power is due to Koeslier's recognition not only that the evils of Stalinism are traceable to difficulties inherent in Marxism, but also that the latter in turn reflect the problematic orientation of modern political philosophy as a whole. It is for this reason, I believe, that *Darkness at Noon* still retains what Howe regards as its chief virtue: its immediate relevance to "the problems that most concern intelligent men." At the same time, I shall suggest, the novelistic form of the book is essential, not only rhetorically but intellectually, to the accomplishment of its author's purpose. The fundamental criticism Koestler wishes to make of Marxism and of modern political philosophy can best be brought home by embodying it in the workings of an individual psyche whose possessor faces the type of personal-political crisis that the novel depicts. It may be that criticisms of the book as history and as fiction are misdirected, inasmuch as they overlook the fundamental necessity for an author with Koestler's intention to construct the work as he has done. It is precisely the party-induced refusal to face the real meaning of man's mortality that Koestler will represent as the ultimate cause of the evils of twentieth-century totalitarianism.

In a 1973 postscript to the novel, Koestler emphasizes that even though it grew out of his own experiences as a member of and gradual defector from the Communist party during the 1930s, his central concern in writing it transcended the issue of communism itself:

> *Darkness at Noon* is the second novel of a trilogy which revolves around the central theme of revolutionary ethics, and of political ethics in general: the problem whether, or to what extent, a noble end justifies ignoble means, and the related conflict between morality and expediency. This may sound like an abstract conundrum, yet every politician is confronted with it at some stage of his career; and for the leaders of a revolutionary movement, from the slave revolt in the first century B.C. to the Old Bolsheviks of the nineteen-thirties and the radical New Left of the nineteen-seventies, the problem assumes a stark reality, which is both immediate and timeless. It was the realization of this timeless aspect of Stalin's regime of terror which made me write *Darkness at Noon* in the form of a parable—albeit thinly disguised—without explicitly naming persons or countries; and which made Orwell, in writing *Nineteen Eighty-Four,* adopt a similar technique.

The plot of *Darkness at Noon,* such as it is, concerns the imprisonment, interrogation, and execution of an erstwhile revolutionary leader whose efforts to institute a truly humane form of government bore fruit in the establishment of the terroristic, totalitarian regime by which he now stands condemned. As Koestler notes in the above quotation, despite his choice of fictional names for his characters and his avoidance of naming the country in which the events take place, the resemblance to real events in the Soviet Union is unmistakable. In the foreword to the novel, Koestler explicitly states that the life of its protagonist, N. S. Rubashov, "is a synthesis of the lives of a number of men who were victims of the so-called Moscow Trial," several of whom "were personally known to the author"; the book is dedicated to their memory. More specifically, we learn from a volume of Koestler's autobiography, Rubashov's "manner of thinking" was modeled on that of Nikolai Bukharin, an Old Bolshevik leader whom Lenin had described as "the darling of the entire party" and as "a most distinguished Party theoretician," albeit somewhat "scholastic" rather than "fully Marxist" in his thinking, and whose 1938 trial and execution constituted a culmination of the Soviet purges. Rubashov's "personality and physical appearance" ("short, stocky, with a pointed goatee" and a pince-nez) were "a synthesis of Leon Trotsky and Karl Radek." Rubashov's final speech at his trial as Koestler constructs it paraphrases parts of Bukharin's final statement at his trial.

One of the points for which *Darkness at Noon* has been widely criticized is that, by representing Rubashov's confession as primarily the result of his own reasoning process, rather than of torture or threats against his family, it distorts the real causes of the confessions at the Moscow trials. In his autobiography Koestler argues that while many of the confessors "were merely trying to save their necks, like Radek; . . . were mentally broken like Zinoviev; or trying to shield their families like Kameniev . . . there still remained a hard core of men like Bukharin . . . and at least a score of others" with a long "revolutionary past" and a history of enduring "Czarist prisons and Siberian exile, whose total and gleeful self-abasement" at the trials "remained inexplicable." Rubashov, he explains, was intended to represent "this 'hard-core.'" In support of his interpretation of these men's motivation, he cites an account of the trials given by General Walter Krivitsky, the head of Soviet Military Intelligence for Western Europe prior to his defection in 1937, which he reports not having read until several years after completing *Darkness at Noon*: Krivitsky's account of why some revolutionary leaders confessed to the phony accusations against them is strikingly similar to what Koestler represents as the motivation of Rubashov's confession. At the same time Koestler emphasizes that "of the three prisoners that appear in the novel, Rubashov alone confesses in self-sacrificing devotion to the Party"; the confessions of the other two result respectively from torture and ignorant obedience to authority, while allusion is made elsewhere in the novel to "physical fear" or the hope of self-preservation as the cause of other confessions.

In the case of Bukharin, at least, it appears from more recently published sources that Koestler's explanation was incorrect; the chief reason Bukharin succumbed to Stalin's demand for a public confession (albeit while arguing against specific charges), it is now believed, was his concern to save the lives of his exiled wife and son. But in the light of Koestler's purpose in writing the novel, as described in the 1973 postscript, I suggest that this issue is largely beside the point. The true subject of *Darkness at Noon* is not the historical issue of why some victims of the purge trials confessed, but the politico-philosophical question of why a movement dedicated to the regeneration of mankind should issue in its enslavement, *and* of why such a movement, long after its failure has been made manifest, should retain its appeal for many thinking men. The persistent popularity of Marxism as a doctrine among well-intentioned Western intellectuals—who will bend logic in all directions to demonstrate that the flaws of Communist regimes result from accidental distortions of the doctrine, rather than flowing directly (as Koestler teaches) from the doctrine itself—indicates

> "The lack of serious reflection in the previous life of this party leader belies the claim of the revolutionary elite to be 'militant philosophers,' who bridged the gap between theory and practice by putting the 'dreams' of theory into practice: dreamers they may have been; philosophers they were not."

that we continue to stand in need of enlightenment in this regard. For this purpose it was a brilliant stroke on Koestler's part to present the protagonist-victim of his novel as one who still believes in Marxist doctrine at the time of his arrest, despite his recognition of the flaws of the existing regime; who argues mightily to convince himself that the evils he has witnessed and experienced do not refute the doctrine in the name of which they are justified; and who is only gradually forced—against his will, as it were—to perceive "through a glass darkly" what is wrong with the doctrine itself. It is striking that in a work that has been denounced by neo-Marxist critics for exhibiting the "irrational emotionalism" of the ex-Communist, the bulk of the explicit theoretical argument constitutes a case *for* Marxism, one no less plausible than many authentically Marxist writings. As one critic reports, some readers of *Darkness at Noon* come away "with the feeling that, in the end," the arguments Koestler presents on behalf of Marxism "are so irrefutable that Koestler has acted a kind of devil's advocate who has succeeded in making the bad cause appear the good." That such a reaction to the book is at least comprehensible would seem to contradict Howe's claim that, despite Koestler's counterideological intention, his writing "is suffused with ideology." It suggests that—despite the contrary claims of Marxist critics—Koestler was able to resist the temptation, which he himself acknowledged, for an ex-Communist "to go over to the opposite political extreme" and become a simplistic anti-Communist zealot. Koestler attributed his ability to maintain his "intellectual and emotional balance" in the period just after his emotionally traumatic break with the party, when he began working on *Darkness at Noon*, to his discovery that writing could be "a purpose in itself" for him. The fundamental "mission" of the novelist as Koestler understands it "is not to solve but to expose"; his accomplishment of this aim requires that he maintain "a totally open window" towards the world, rather than covering it with ideological shades. Let us consider how Koestler achieves this mission in *Darkness at Noon*.

The English title of *Darkness at Noon* may be understood in several ways. Koeslier attributes the idea for it to his translator, to whom it was suggested by a phrase uttered by the imprisoned Samson in Milton's *Samson Agonistes*: "O dark, dark, dark, amid the blaze of noon, / Irrecoverably dark, total Eclipse / Without all hope of day!" Literally, Samson's words accurately describe the situation of Rubashov, for whom there is no escape from the darkness of prison but the deeper night of death. At the same time, those words describe the situation of Rubashov's fellow citizens: at the moment that was to constitute their "noon"—their liberation from enslavement under the old regime and their elevation under a government ostensibly dedicated to their welfare—they find themselves the inhabitants of a mass prison, ruled by a most ruthless dictator, with no evident ground for hope of an improvement in their condition. (Hence, in the moment before his death, Rubashov compares his people's plight to that of the Jews wandering for forty years in the desert, but sees no sign of "the Promised Land"; "wherever his eye looked, he saw nothing but desert and the darkness of night.") On the other hand, the ultimate success of Samson in destroying his Philistine captors (albeit at the cost of his own life) suggests that from Koestler's point of view, if not from Rubashov's, there remains hope for the liberation of the people from their enslavement.

Beyond its Miltonian connotations, Koestler's title must also be taken as a reference to the hour of the Crucifixion. As such, it is one of many allusions in the novel by which Rubashov is represented as a latter-day Christ: a "scapegoat" or sacrificial lamb executed to atone for the sins of mankind. From the party's point of view, such scapegoats are a useful means for absolving the party itself of guilt in the eyes of the common people; from the point of view to which Rubashov ultimately ascends, their necessity reflects a fundamental aspect of the human condition, the neglect of which is the root of the party's decay.

Structurally, *Darkness at Noon* is fairly simple. The titles of the first three chapters—"The First Hearing," "The Second Hearing," "The Third Hearing"—refer to the successive interrogations of Rubashov: the first two by his erstwhile friend and revolutionary compatriot Ivanov; the last by Ivanov's more brutal successor Gletkin, who may be taken to represent the reality of the heralded "new Soviet man." The greater part of the first two chapters, however, consists of Rubashov's own self-reflections, during the days of solitude in his cell, by which he reconsiders the meaning of the cause to which he has heretofore dedicated his life, in the light of his imprisonment. The course of his reflections is further stimulated by exchanges with several other prisoners and by the recollection of his previous official dealings with three subordinate members of the party. The final chapter, entitled "The Grammatical Fiction," opens with a summary account of Rubashov-Bukharin's confession at his trial, read from the newspaper by a woman as her father mumbles Biblical passages describing the Crucifixion; the remainder of the chapter records Rubashov's ultimate recognition of the significance of his life, up to the actual moment of his execution.

By locating the novel in a solitary cell and the interrogation room of a prison, Koestler obviously forecloses the possibility of significant action (except in the form of flashbacks). The resultant focus of the novel on thought rather than action is integral to Koestler's intention, inasmuch as he represents Rubashov's former life as one in which fundamental questions that ought to have been squarely faced at the outset were set aside in favor of action grounded in blind faith that its effects would be salutary for mankind. The lack of serious reflection in the previous life of this party leader belies the claim of the revolutionary elite to be "militant philosophers," who bridged the gap between theory and practice by putting the "dreams" of theory into practice: dreamers they may have been; philosophers they were not. Not only the fact of his imprisonment but, more importantly, the suddenly imminent prospect of his own death wonderfully concentrates—as the well-known Johnsonian aphorism puts it—Rubashov's mind. It is precisely the party-induced refusal to face the real meaning of man's mortality that Koestler will represent as the ultimate cause of the evils of twentieth-century totalitarianism.

As was indicated by the previously quoted passage from Koestler's 1973 postscript, the central theme of *Darkness at Noon* concerns the extent to which "ignoble means" may be justified by "a noble end," as well as the connected issue of the relation between morality and expediency. The former issue is brought to the fore almost at the beginning of the novel, where Rubashov is awakened in his apartment from a recurrent dream in which he recalls his arrest by "the Praetorian guards of the German Dictatorship," only to be arrested in the present by the police of his own country's dictatorship. The means practiced by the latter and its putative ideological opponent are formally identical, so that at the moment of his second arrest, Rubashov suspects "that this awakening was the real dream." Only by the difference in the ends for which they arbitrarily arrest their subjects, if at all, can the two tyrannies be distinguished. But can ends and means so neatly be separated?

From the outset of his imprisonment, Rubashov's reflections on the meaning of that event vacillate between two poles: the individual and the ideological. Upon awakening on his first morning in jail, recognizing the inevitability of his execution, he indulges in "a warm wave of sympathy for his own body, for which usually he had no liking," and experiences "that peculiar state of excitement familiar to him from former experiences of the nearness of death," despite recognizing "that this condition was reprehensible and, from a certain point of view, impermissible." As the last surviving member of the "old guard" of revolutionary leaders, he briefly recollects the personal traits of a couple of his previously executed colleagues and doubts that "history" can be trusted to "rehabilitate" them (the revolutionary equivalent of Resurrection), because history is indifferent to the characteristics of individuals. Nonetheless, Rubashov "could not bring himself to hate No. 1 [the present dictator] as he ought," in view of the horrifying "possibility that he was in the right," when judged in terms of the ultimate historical consequences of his actions. "There was no certainty; only the appeal to that mocking oracle they called History, who gave her sentence only when the jaws of the appealer had long since fallen to dust." But at this stage of his life Rubashov still looks forward to the possibility that an enhanced knowledge of the workings of the human brain could someday transform historical explanation from oracle to science and thus make politics itself truly scientific.

The critical counterpoint to Rubashov's historical reflections at this moment is supplied not by any sort of argument he can formulate, but by a physical pain and an at first dim recollection, the significance of which will deepen as the book proceeds. The toothache of which Rubashov complains to a guard on the first morning of his imprisonment constitutes precisely the sort of private concern to which the party's doctrine denies significance; more importantly, it will come to represent Rubashov's conscience, a phenomenon to which the party also denies legitimacy, and will reappear and recede throughout the novel according to Rubashov's cognizance of having fulfilled his individual moral obligations. The troubling recollection—first suggested to Rubashov by the sight of another prisoner's bare, thin arms and his "palms . . . turned upwards, curved in the shape of a bowl" to receive bread—is of a drawing of the Pietà by an unnamed German master, in which "the Madonna's thin hands" were similarly "curved upwards" and "hollowed to the shape of a bowl." Rubashov had seen a part of that drawing six years earlier in the art museum of a south German town, while conversing with an innocent and idealistic young party member, Richard, whom he proceeded to expel from the party—and, apparently, caused to be denounced to the German authorities who arrested him—for deviating from party directives. In the course of expelling Richard, Rubashov had remarked that the party's strength depended on its "unbroken will" and consequently required the renunciation of anyone who "goes soft and weak," whatever his motives. Rubashov's position hinged on the claim that the party, as "the embodiment of the revolutionary idea in history," could "never be mistaken"; to serve her required that one have "absolute faith in History" and be free from any scruples about obeying the directives of her spokesmen, the leaders of the party hierarchy. As he spoke to Richard, the latter's head partly hid the Pietà from Rubashov's view; he forgot to look at it before leaving the room. Rubashov's failure to examine the drawing—and his disturbing recollection of it when in prison—indicate what has been lacking in his thought up to the time of his imprisonment, as is also suggested by a quotation from Dostoyevsky with which Koestler prefaces the novel: "Man, man, one cannot live quite without pity." It is significant that Koestler represents pity in its Christian form of *pietà* (and by the figure of the Madonna); thus he recalls the original link between pity and piety. He thereby appears to suggest the inadequacy or insubstantiality of the "secularized" pity of which various ideologies of the contemporary Left claim to be the embodiment: pity for man cannot be adequately or reliably grounded unless the individual human being is seen as linked to a truth that is both supra-individual and supra-historical. Contrariwise, the ultimate test of a theoretical or theological doctrine of human benefaction is whether it inspires its adherents to concrete acts of compassion and beneficence towards their fellow men. The party, while taking over from the Catholic Church the principle of the infallibility of its leaders (the revolutionary founder, Lenin, "was revered as God-the-Father, and No. 1 as the Son") and the demand for "absolute faith" and obedience towards the leader on the part of the masses, and while claiming to be the people's true benefactor, has liberated its functionaries from any operative sense of duty towards other human beings grounded in a recognition of their essential dignity as individuals. Thus, it has discarded the invaluable core of truth in the Biblical teaching.

A second incident recollected by Rubashov in the first chapter makes it clear how the claim of the party leadership to represent the sole authentic will of "history" and its consequent self-liberation from any fixed set of moral principles gives rise to consequences indistinguishable from hypocrisy. In a second mission abroad, Rubashov was called upon to demand that longshoremen belonging to the party assist in delivering petrol from the homeland of the Revolution to a "hungry dictatorship in the south of Europe" (Mussolini's Italy) for use in its "war of plunder and conquest in Africa." The refusal of the longshoremen to carry out this demand, given its direct contradiction of the principle of workingmen's solidarity against fascist aggression, led Rubashov to order the expulsion of their union leader, Little Loewy, from the party and thence to the latter's suicide. Reflecting on this incident, Rubashov observes that despite the putative rightness of the party's principles, "our results were wrong," inasmuch as they made the party "odious and detested" by the people, who should have had cause to love it; while Little Loewy, despite his deviation from party discipline, "was not odious and detestable." The contrast between the theoretical beauty of the party's principles and the ugliness of their results inspires in Rubashov the thought that "if the Party embodied the will of history, then history itself was defective." But it does not yet induce him consciously to seek a nonhistorical standard for judging political action. While increasingly burdened by a sense of personal guilt towards those he betrayed in the service of the party's "higher" morality—he repeatedly cites the need to pay his "fare" to Richard and Little Loewy, *i.e.*, atone with his own life—Rubashov remains unable to bridge the gap between individual and political ethics. It is Rubashov's inability, at this point, to transcend the "historical" standard of political morality that renders him vulnerable to the arguments of his interrogator Ivanov at the conclusion of the first

chapter—and that will ultimately prepare him to grant the authorities the confession to spurious "crimes" that they demand. Initially Rubashov challenges Ivanov by charging that the people's disaffection with the party undermines its claim to represent their will: "Other usurpers in Europe pretend the same thing with as much right as you . . ." Ivanov sidesteps this issue, but nonetheless begins to sap Rubashov's resistance by reviewing Rubashov's career, reminding him of how many individuals the latter had previously sacrificed in order, presumably, "to continue your work for your own ideas," and suggesting that under the circumstances it would be mere "petty bourgeois romanticism" for Rubashov now to refuse to confess and, thus, to bring an end to his career as well as his life, rather than cooperating with Ivanov so as to secure the chance that the latter promises (whether or not disingenuously) to achieve his freedom in "two or three years" and a consequent opportunity subsequently to "be back in the ring again." Although Rubashov's immediate response is to reject Ivanov's proposition, Ivanov foresees that their conversation will have a delayed effect and grants the prisoner a fortnight for reflection.

The tension which we have already noted between the ideological and the personal poles of Rubashov's reflections becomes manifest, from this point on, in the contrast between the diary which he now begins to keep and the less "logically" expressible thoughts to which he continues to be driven by his recollections and by his encounters with other prisoners. The diary is intended to reconcile Rubashov's Marxist belief with his awareness of the present evils of his country's regime by reformulating Marxist doctrine in a way that remains faithful to its overall spirit. In an excerpt from the diary at the beginning of the second chapter of the novel, Rubashov focuses attention directly on the problem of the relation of ends and means, and emphasizes the "Machiavellian" foundation of the party's view of this problem. The party's doctrine teaches that while "the nineteenth century's liberal ethics of 'fair play'" may be practicable in the relatively tranquil "breathing spaces of history," at the "critical turning points" of history "there is no other rule possible than the old one, that the end justifies the means." While the party's "neo-Machiavellian" policies have indeed been "clumsily imitated" by "the counter-revolutionary dictatorships," the distinguishing "greatness" of the former consists in their serving the ends of "universal reason" rather than "national romanticism," and consequently justifying their practitioners' hope of being "absolved by history" in the end. Prior to the end of history, however, the party is "thinking and acting on credit" in the sense that it must claim, without being able strictly to prove, that its actions will have the ultimately redemptive outcome it claims. To judge the legitimacy of policies purely in terms of their ultimate outcome or "consequent logic" (*i.e.*, the logic of consequences) means, moreover, that the party must disregard issues of "the subjective good faith" of a man's actions: assuming that No. 1 is right in his judgment of the best kind of agricultural fertilizer, he is entirely justified in having those who maintained a contrary opinion executed, regardless of the beneficence of their intentions. From the perspective of history, "virtue does not matter" and errors are far more significant than crimes. But since it cannot be proved that the party's reading of future history is correct, political leadership ultimately depends on "faith . . . axiomatic faith in the rightness of one's own reasoning." It is for no longer believing in his own infallibility that Rubashov now regards himself as "lost."

The specific consequences and the rationale of the party's understanding of history are worked out more extensively in the second and third chapters by Ivanov and his assistant Gletkin. In a conversation between them immediately following the excerpt from Rubashov's diary cited above, Gletkin exhibits the degree to which that view of history enables its exponents to employ a utopian view of the future as the justification for an unmitigated brutality in the present. For Gletkin the "patriarchal mental paralysis" of the peasantry prevents them from listening to reason (*e.g.*, by going along with the policy of collectivizing agriculture) and consequently necessitates the widespread use of torture against them to prevent the Revolution from "foundering." At the same time he promises that the present crushing of the "criminal's" mind and body will pave the way, a hundred years hence, for the reign of reason and mercy: the "abolition of punishment and of retaliation for crime; sanatoriums with flower gardens for the a-social elements." Gletkin still retains the "faith" in "the logical necessity" of the party's policies that Rubashov has lost; it is this that distinguishes him, he thinks, from a "cynic."

The other side of Gletkin's reflections—how the policies he favors appear from the perspective of those against whom they are applied rather than those who administer them—which Rubashov's recollections of Richard and Little Loewy had forced him to consider in chapter 1, Rubashov is again compelled to face in chapter 2 by the memory of his executed lover Arlova, the significance

of which is deepened by an event that takes place in the prison. Remarkably for the sole "love interest" of the protagonist in a novel, Arlova appears to be devoid of any substantive personality or character. Coolly efficient as Rubashov's secretary, she accepts his advances, as he remarks, as if she "were still taking down dictation" and responds, "'You will ways be able to do what you like with me.'" Arlova, it appears, is the perfect raw material to serve as the instrument of the Revolution; she is pure passivity, adaptable—unlike the recalcitrant peasantry—to whatever form her superiors should choose to impose on her. In her case, at least, the party's view of the masses as inherently "formless" and "anonymous" seems to he vindicated. But how can it be maintained that the process of issuing unquestioned orders to individuals like Arlova— and of breaking down the people by Gletkin's methods, so that they will all resemble her—will gradually "wean them from the habit of being ruled," as the party claims?

Despite her passivity, Arlova—owing to her brother's having married a foreigner—ran afoul of the regime; when she called on Rubashov at her trial as the chief witness of her innocence, he disavowed her. Never doubting "the logical rightness" of his behavior in the matter, since it was the only means of preserving his own career and hence advancing the goals of the party, Rubashov was able to avoid suffering pangs of personal guilt by regarding the death of an individual, in accordance with the party's doctrine, as a mere "abstraction." That is, the "individual" perspective is of a lower grade of reality than the intersubjective and hence "objective" course of history: in the "logical equation" of history, Arlova was "a small factor compared to what was at stake." What shakes Rubashov's confidence in that equation, however, is the execution of an erstwhile disciple of his and hero of the Revolution, Michael Bogrov, while Rubashov is imprisoned: by calling out Rubashov's name just before his death, Bogrov makes the previously "unimportant factor" of the individual appear concrete to him and hence "absolute."

Rubashov's confrontation with the reality of death at the time of Bogrov's execution may be regarded—along with his previous recollection of the Pietà—as one of the central "epiphanies" of *Darkness at Noon*. But just as in the first chapter, he is prevented from following out its implications by his inability to refute the contrary "logic" of Ivanov. What renders Rubashov vulnerable to Ivanov's persuasion, as Ivanov remarks to him, is that the latter's "way of thinking and of arguing" is identical with that to which he himself has subscribed throughout his career; Rubashov is unable to formulate an alternative logic by which to express the reservations arising from the realm of what the party dismisses as "the 'grammatical fiction,'" the individual. Ivanov at least half-persuades Rubashov that the scruples he has been experiencing are themselves a form of moral self-indulgence, a succumbing to the "temptation" of "Salvation Army" ethics. Machiavelli and Marx, rather than Gandhi and Tolstoi, he argues, constitute the true guides towards human benefaction, inasmuch as they squarely face the "amoral" nature of history itself. To follow the ethics of Gandhi and Tolstoi "means to leave everything as it is"; while salving the conscience of the individual, it allows mass suffering to remain the eternal lot of the race. Ivanov insists that there is no mean possible between the "Christian and humane" ethic which "declares the individual to be sacrosanct, and asserts that the rules of arithmetic are not to be applied to human units," and the opposite perspective which "starts from the basic principle that a collective aim justifies all means, and not only allows, but demands, that the individual should in every way be subordinated and sacrificed to the community—which may dispose of it as an experimentation rabbit or a sacrificial lamb." While a private individual may choose between these two ethics, "whoever is burdened with power and responsibility" cannot: the necessities of political life will inevitably compel him "to defer to another time the putting into practice of humanism." The strength of the party's doctrine lies in its self-conscious recognition of this fact and in the consequent opportunity it provides for enlightened rulers to "experiment" with humanity on a historically unrivaled level for the sake of elevating the future condition of the race: slaughtering men "in order to abolish slaughtering" and whipping them "so that they may learn not to let themselves be whipped." By this means "we are tearing the old skin off mankind and giving it a new one." To argue against this process on behalf of particular individuals is as irrational as to contend "that a battalion commander may not sacrifice a patrolling party to save the regiment" or to oppose the kind of experimentation on animals that spawned the development of serums against cholera, typhoid, and diptheria.

Once again Ivanov's arguments impel Rubashov to work on the theoretical elaboration of the party's doctrine in such a manner as to excuse the party's present crimes and overcome his own reservations. In another excerpt from his diary, at the beginning of chapter 3, Rubashov propounds a

"law of relative maturity" of the masses, according to which "the level of mass-consciousness" rises in a series of interrupted stages, like the water in a chain of canal locks, rather than, as "socialist theory" had formerly held, in a constant and steady sequence. According to this law, "the maturity of the masses lies in the capacity to recognize their own interests," which in turn "pre-supposes a certain understanding of the process of production and distribution of goods." Since "every technical improvement creates a new complication to the economic apparatus . . . which the masses cannot penetrate for a time," each "jump of technical progress leaves the relative intellectual development of the masses a step behind, and this causes a fall in the political-maturity thermometer." It follows that political institutions, instead of following a steady progress, must exhibit "a pendulum movement in history, swinging from absolutism to democracy" and back, depending on whether the masses at a given moment possess the degree of understanding necessary for self-government. In a complete capitulation to Ivanov's reasoning, Rubashov excuses "all the horror, hypocrisy, and degradation" of the present regime as "merely the visible and inevitable expression" of this law; only "the fool and the aesthete" would attach any absolute significance to them. For anyone who opposes the policies of the regime in such a situation where only a demagogue would appeal to the judgment of the immature masses, the sole truly honorable course is "the public disavowal of one's conviction in order to remain in the Party's ranks."

Two encounters with other prisoners immediately following his recording of these meditations give Rubashov the opportunity, respectively, to confirm his newly discovered "law" and to affirm its moral implication regarding his own situation. When taken for exercise in the prison yard, Rubashov converses with a peasant who has been imprisoned for "reactionary" activities: refusing to allow his children to be vaccinated, destroying new farm machinery, and burning up pieces of government propaganda. According to the peasant's understanding, as he later expresses it, the government has punished him "because the old days when we were happy must not come back." To Rubashov, who doubts the accuracy of the peasant's recollection of past happiness, the case is reminiscent of something "he had once read about the natives of New Guinea, who were intellectually on a level with this peasant, yet lived in complete social harmony and possessed surprisingly developed democratic institutions. They had reached the highest level of a lower back basin."

In an exchange of messages tapped through the common wall of their cells, Rubashov communicates his decision to capitulate to his monarchist neighbor, No. 402, who responds, "HAVE YOU NO SPARK OF HONOUR LEFT?" The subsequent exchange summarizes the opposition between "revolutionary" ethics and the moral code of the old aristocracy: No 402: "HONOUR IS TO LIVE AND DIE FOR ONE'S BELIEF;" Rubashov: "HONOUR IS TO BE USEFUL WITHOUT VANITY;" No, 402: "HONOUR IS DECENCY—NOT USEFULNESS;" Rubashov: "WE HAVE REPLACED DECENCY BY REASON."

There will be no going back on Rubashov's decision to capitulate by giving his interrogators the confession they demand. But his subsequent reflections, to be considered in the second installment of this study, will compel him to reconsider this antinomy between reason and honor or decency and thus to call into question the adequacy of the "revolutionary" ethics of utility.

Source: David Lewis Schaefer, "The Limits of Ideology: Koestler's *Darkness at Noon*," in *Modern Age*, Vol. 29, No. 4, Fall 1985, pp. 319–28.

Sources

Cesarani, David, *Arthur Koestler: The Homeless Mind*, William Heinemann, 1998.

Cohen, Stephen, *Bukharin and the Bolshevik Revolution: A Political Biography, 1888–1938*, Wildwood House, 1974, pp. 372–80.

Hamilton, Iain, *Koestler: A Biography*, Martin Secker & Warburg, 1982, pp. 68–71.

Koestler, Arthur, *Darkness at Noon*, translated by Daphne Hardy, 1940, reprint, 1965.

Orwell, George, "Arthur Koestler," in *Arthur Koestler: A Collection of Critical Essays*, edited by Murray A. Sperber, Prentice-Hall, 1977, pp. 13–24; originally published in 1944.

————, Review of *Darkness at Noon*, in *Koestler: A Biography*, edited by Iain Hamilton, Martin Secker & Warburg, 1982, p. 69; originally published in *New Statesman*.

Schwarz, Solomon M., *The Russian Revolution of 1905: The Workers' Movement and the Formation of Bolshevism and Menshevism*, University of Chicago Press, 1967, p. 29.

Further Reading

Berdyaev, Nicolas, *The Origin of Russian Communism*, translated by R. M. French, Robert Maclehose, 1937.
Berdyaev explains the beginnings of the Communist Party and the background to Stalin's dictatorship.

Calder, Jenni, *Chronicles of Conscience: A Study of George Orwell and Arthur Koestler*, University of Pittsburgh Press, 1968.
Calder compares two of the most influential twentieth-century writers on totalitarianism.

Levene, Mark, *Arthur Koestler*, Frederick Ungar Publishing, 1984.
Levene's literary biography of Koestler places *Darkness at Noon* in the context of the author's life and the political climate at the time.

Pearson, Sidney A., *Aruthur Koestler*, G. K. Hall, 1978.
Chapter four of Pearson's book provides a concise and helpful breakdown of the major themes and structural elements of Koestler's novel.

Tucker, Robert C., and Stephen F. Cohen, eds., *The Great Purge Trial*, Grosset & Dunlap, 1965.
Based on the transcript of the Moscow Show Trials, this book is a valuable resource for determining what actually went on during the 1938 trial.

Death Comes for the Archbishop

Willa Cather

1927

Published in 1927 in New York, Willa Cather's *Death Comes for the Archbishop* is based on the actual lives of Archbishop Lamy, the first bishop of New Mexico, and his vicar, Father Joseph Machebeuf. Both men were from France. When Cather came across Father Joseph Howlett's biography of Machebeuf (published in 1908), she was inspired by the thoughts, feelings, and experiences of pioneer priests and missionaries in New Mexico. Howlett's biography included letters Machebeuf wrote home to his sister, a nun. In *Death Comes for the Archbishop*, Lamy becomes Bishop Jean Marie Latour, and Machebeuf becomes Father Joseph Vaillant. Although the novel is based on historical figures and information, the bulk of the book is fictionalized. Without the factual information and the insights of Machebeuf's biography, however, Cather may not have been inspired to write the book, nor would she likely have been able to construct such believable, complex characters.

Set in the second half of the nineteenth century, *Death Comes for the Archbishop* spans almost forty years in the life of Bishop Latour. It is an episodic narrative that shows how the French priest gradually wins the trust and respect of the natives, and brings order to the Catholic Church in the Southwest. The novel is peopled with numerous minor characters who function to represent and relate the culture, folklore, history, and belief systems of the Mexican and Indian people in New Mexico. The novel is also known for its rich

descriptions of landscape and its role in the lives of the people who live among it.

Author Biography

Wilella ("Willa") Cather was born December 7, 1873, in Back Creek Valley, Virginia, the eldest of seven children. She spent much of her early childhood on her grandfather's sheep farm, where her energy and imagination found outlets in her rural surroundings. Her grandmother took an active role in her education, teaching her to read and appreciate language. Cather's fascination with stories drew her to gatherings of local men and women, who kept alive a rich oral tradition.

In 1883, the sheep farm burned down, and Cather's family moved to Nebraska. Surrounded by the vast landscape, Cather first reacted with fear and discomfort. According to many biographers, this move proved to be a defining experience in Cather's life. After a year of homesteading, Cather's father moved the family to the small town of Red Cloud and opened a loan and mortgage business.

As a teenager Cather rejected traditional femininity. She cut her hair short, wore boys' clothes, and indulged her interest in medicine by performing experiments and dissections. These unusual behaviors were neither understood nor accepted by the community of Red Cloud, and when Cather graduated in 1890, she immediately left for Lincoln to attend the University of Nebraska.

In college Cather discovered her love of journalism. She contributed columns and theater reviews to local papers to support herself so she could stay in school despite an economic downturn. She graduated in 1895. Her experience as a journalist took her to Pittsburgh, where she edited and wrote for *Home Monthly*. When new owners bought the magazine, she resigned but continued writing drama reviews for a local newspaper. In 1903 Cather met Edith Lewis, who became Cather's lifetime companion. Cather accepted a position with *McClure's* in New York so she could be with Lewis. While on assignment in Boston for *McClure's*, Cather met the novelist Sarah Orne Jewett, who became her literary mentor. After the shock of Jewett's death in 1909, Cather continued to work for *McClure's* as she honed her fiction. In 1911 Cather left the magazine and committed herself to a new career as a novelist and short-story writer, at the age of thirty-seven.

Willa Cather

In 1912 Cather accompanied her brother to the American Southwest. She was taken by the canyons, sweeping sky, folklore, and Native American ruins. The following year, *O Pioneers!* was published, the second of her novel-length works. Its critical success was followed by other novels such as *My Ántonia* (1918), *A Lost Lady* (1923), and *Death Comes for the Archbishop* (1927), all of which are still widely read today. In 1923 Cather won the Pulitzer Prize for fiction for *One of Ours* (1922). Although scholars find it difficult to categorize Cather's work, her unique voice, sense of setting, and complex characterization explain her continued popularity among readers and academics alike.

While sleeping on the afternoon of April 24, 1947, Cather suffered a cerebral hemorrhage that took her life. She is buried in Jeffrey, New Hampshire, where her tombstone features a quote from *My Ántonia*: "That is happiness; to be dissolved into something complete and great."

Plot Summary

Prologue

Death Comes for the Archbishop opens in 1848 in Rome, where three cardinals and a missionary bishop from America are discussing the situation of the Catholic Church in America. The missionary describes the neglect in New Mexico and the need for a young, strong, devoted priest to take charge and bring order to the region. They decide to send Father Jean Marie Latour, a thirty-five-year-old priest currently serving in Ontario, Canada.

Book 1: The Vicar Apostolic

It is now 1851 and Latour is making his way across the New Mexican terrain. He is exhausted, thirsty, and lost, but stops to pray before a tree in the shape of a cross. Soon he finds water, and a Mexican girl leads him to a nearby town. Latour performs long-overdue marriages and baptisms and continues on his way. He is returning to Santa Fe from Durango, Mexico, where he obtained proof of his church authority. As the apostolic vicar of New Mexico, Latour's seat is to be in Santa Fe, but when he and his lifelong friend Father Joseph Vaillant arrive, they are dismissed. Now, with proof from the bishop in Durango, Latour is prepared to assume authority. Arriving in Santa Fe, Latour discovers that in his absence the ugly yet lovable Vaillant has not only won the trust of the people, but has arranged for the previous priest to return to Mexico.

Book 2: Missionary Journeys

Father Vaillant is returning from a journey to Albuquerque and stops at a large ranch owned by Manuel Lujon. Lujon welcomes Vaillant, who performs the sacraments of marriage and baptism for his workers. Before leaving, Vaillant manages to talk Lujon out of his two beautiful cream-colored mules, one for himself and one for Latour.

On a trip to Mora, Latour and Vaillant stop at a rundown home to spend the night. They sense something evil about Buck Scales, the man who lives there, and when his meek Mexican wife warns them that Scales will kill them, they leave in haste and make it to Mora. They fear for the life of the woman who saved them. The next morning, they find that she escaped and got to Mora safely. Her name is Magdalena Valdez. She says that Scales has killed four other travelers and all three of their children. He is captured, jailed, and later hanged. Latour has befriended Kit Carson, a well-known scout. Carson takes Magdalena to his home, where his wife can care for her. She later goes to help a small group of nuns start a school for girls.

Book 3: The Mass at Ácoma

Determined to know his diocese better, Latour enlists a young Indian guide, Jacinto, to take him to the surrounding Indian missions. When they arrive in Albuquerque, Latour finds that the scandalous rumors about the priest, Father Gallegos, are true. He decides that Gallegos must be replaced.

Latour and Jacinto continue their journey, visiting small missions where Latour performs sacraments and holds Mass. Along the way, Latour visits various missions and pueblos, learning more about the people and their past.

Book 4: Snake Root

Vaillant replaces Father Gallegos in Albuquerque. When Vaillant does not return from a long journey, a messenger informs Latour that Vaillant has black measles. Latour and Jacinto set out at once. They encounter a terrible snowstorm, and Jacinto leads them to a secret Indian cave. Jacinto entreats Latour never to mention this place to anyone. Latour wonders if this is the cave significant to Jacinto's people's snake worship. The men sleep safely through the night and continue their trip. Delighted, Latour finds that Vaillant has recovered.

Book 5: Padre Martinez

Latour and Jacinto go to Taos to meet the notorious Father Martinez, who has a reputation as being selfish, materialistic, tyrannical, and cruel. Upon entering his home, Latour meets Trinidad, a young monk who is studying to be a priest. Trinidad is lazy, dull, and gluttonous. Latour and Martinez debate the authority of the church in New Mexico, Martinez claiming that in the new world, Rome has little relevance or power, while Latour heartily disagrees. Martinez threatens that if dismissed, he will take his numerous loyal followers and start his own church.

Latour has been called to Rome, and when he returns, he brings back new missionary priests. One, Father Taladrid, replaces Martinez, although Martinez retains minor duties. After a power struggle, Martinez and his longtime crony Father Lucero start their own church. Martinez and Lucero have a rocky past, but they are equally irreverent toward the church.

Latour sends Vaillant to deliver letters of excommunication to Martinez and Lucero, and Martinez dies shortly thereafter. Lucero's heath declines, and when he kills a burglar in his home, he never recovers from the trauma. Vaillant goes to Lucero's deathbed and delivers last rites to the repentant Lucero, but not before the dying priest tells him of a buried hoard. After Lucero's death, the hoard is recovered, and totals more than twenty thousand dollars.

Book 6: Dona Isabella

Latour decides to build a cathedral, and finds patrons in the wealthy Don Antonio Olivares and his young wife Isabella. When Olivares dies later in the year, his brothers set out to take the inheritance. They make the argument that Isabella is not old enough to be the mother of Olivares's daughter. Isabella would rather forfeit the entire inheritance than admit her true age. Latour and Vaillant plead with her to tell the truth and enjoy a comfortable future. She finally agrees and is granted the inheritance.

Book 7: The Great Diocese

After a journey and a long illness, Vaillant recovers in Santa Fe. Although Latour invites Vaillant to extend his stay, Vaillant is anxious to get back to his people.

Latour goes to visit Eusabio, an important man in the Navajo community who has lost his son. When Jacinto is sent to ask Vaillant to visit Santa Fe, Eusabio accompanies Latour back home. The two men enjoy traveling together and find that they have much in common.

Book 8: Gold Under Pike's Peak

With Vaillant in Santa Fe, Latour shows him a nearby golden mountainside where they will get the stone for the cathedral. Latour also wants a French builder so the style will be magnificent. Vaillant believes the cathedral is worthwhile, but does not share his friend's insistence on grand style.

Latour receives a letter about a gold rush in Colorado. Because so many people have come to the area, there is a need for priests. This area will fall under his jurisdiction, so Latour decides to send Vaillant. Vaillant prepares for his mission, and the parting is bittersweet. Latour fears he may not see his dear friend again, but he encourages him in his calling.

Over the years, Vaillant returns to New Mexico to visit and to see Latour made archbishop. Vaillant's travels and work in Colorado are arduous and demanding, but he is dedicated and perseveres.

Book 9: Death Comes for the Archbishop

In his old age, Latour retires to a home outside Santa Fe. He often meets with new priests to educate them on language and customs. In 1885 a young man named Bernard Ducrot comes to care for Latour.

After a busy December in 1888, Latour is caught in a January rainstorm and falls ill. He sends word to the new archbishop in Santa Fe that he would like to return there to die. Although Ducrot dismisses the idea that the man could die of a cold, Latour has made up his mind.

In his final days Latour recalls memories of his years in New Mexico. He remembers legends, people, and Vaillant, who has already passed away. As he grows weaker, he sleeps more and eats less, and his final thoughts are of Vaillant. The next morning, his body is laid before the altar in his cathedral.

Characters

Bernard Ducrot

Bernard Ducrot is a young priest who comes to Latour's aid in his old age. Ducrot is an admirer of Latour's work in the Southwest, and Latour becomes a fatherly figure to him. Ducrot accompanies Latour when he makes his final trip to Santa Fe to die.

Father Gallegos

Father Gallegos is the priest in Albuquerque when Latour arrives in New Mexico. Latour hears of his scandalous behavior, all of which is confirmed. Gallegos is robust and lively, favoring parties over serious religious observance. He enjoys dancing all night, playing cards, and accepting the patronage of a local widow. He makes no effort to minister to his people's spiritual lives, nor does he go out to neighboring villages to attend to ceremonial duties for those people. When Latour visits, he pretends to have an injury to his foot, even though he spent all night dancing. He does this so that Latour will not expect his company as he travels to the neighboring villages. Gallegos is the first priest Latour replaces as he sets about "cleaning house" in his diocese. Father Vaillant takes his place.

Jacinto

Jacinto is a young Pecos Indian guide who accompanies Latour on his journeys to the missions and pueblos of New Mexico. He has a wife and a sick baby at home, but he is highly attentive to his duties as Latour's guide. Jacinto knows the area very well, and his skills and companionship are important to Latour's outings. The two men do not share all the same religious views, but they respect each other for their devotion to their beliefs. Jacinto's affection for Latour is evident when he takes him to a secret Indian cave unknown to anyone outside the tribe. Because Latour understands the importance of the secret, he honors Jacinto's request never to mention it to anyone.

Jean Marie Latour

While working in Canada, Father Jean Marie Latour is appointed the new vicar apostolic of New Mexico, although he eventually ascends to the title of archbishop. His mantle is heavy, as it is his responsibility to bring order to the Catholic Church's presence in the American Southwest. When he arrives, some of the most influential priests are corrupt and irreverent. Gradually, Latour succeeds in replacing them with more suitable but equally strong priests.

Latour misses his home of France, and is often reminded of home by the landscape of New Mexico. He is refined and educated, but humble. He enjoys the arts, but does not resent missing such pleasures of home. Instead, he embraces the beauty and culture of his new home. He seeks to win over the people of New Mexico not by force, but by patience, sincerity, and faith. Latour is a servant at heart, first to the church and then to his people. He is kind, dedicated, serious, strong, and deeply devoted.

Throughout the novel, Cather depicts Latour as a very compassionate man. He is sensitive to Magdalena's terror that her husband will kill her, pained to have forced Isabella to reveal her age, and hurt by Eusabio's loss of his son. And when Vaillant is torn between duty and friendship before leaving for Colorado, Latour gives him the encouragement he needs to follow his calling in good faith.

Latour finds that among the differences between his faith and that of the native people, there are important similarities. The Indians, he finds, have a deep respect for tradition and ceremony. They also believe wholeheartedly in their religious views and are stubborn in compromising them. He finds them honorable and reverent, qualities he respects. As for the Mexicans in his diocese, he finds them mainly in need of good leadership. They are faithful, but many have been without respectable priests to guide them in their spiritual walks.

Just as Latour appreciates art and culture, he is very interested in history. He seeks reliable information about the history of the region that is his new home, and he becomes part of changing it for the better (as when he helps the Navajos regain their land). As much as he despises Father Martinez's ways, he admires his knowledge of the history of Taos. In his final days, Latour recites much of the history he has learned to Ducrot, so future generations will benefit from it. A man of balance, Latour also has an eye toward the future. From the time of his arrival in New Mexico, he takes steps to make the future of the land and the church better, and he makes his dream of building a cathedral a reality.

Antonio Jose Martinez

Father Martinez is the priest in Taos. He is very powerful and influential, and despite his tyrannical ways, has a faithful following. He is indulgent, materialistic, and very disrespectful of the church's authority. He has children in town and claims that celibacy is not a necessity for the priesthood. Martinez allows a young monk named Trinidad to live with him as he ostensibly studies to become a priest. Trinidad is lazy and gluttonous, but Martinez makes no effort to shape the young man's character. Martinez also has a reputation for being cruel to the Indians, even swindling seven of them out of their land before he lets them hang for his own crime.

Martinez tells Latour that if he tries to replace him, he will simply start his own church and take all the people of Taos with him. When this in fact happens, Latour is forced to excommunicate Martinez and his cohort. Martinez dies not long after, but he never repents of his wicked ways. His death, however, enables the new priest to assume full control.

Joseph Vaillant

Father Joseph Vaillant is Latour's longtime friend and supporter. Together they go to New Mexico to begin the hard work of bringing order to the region. Their friendship is the most important personal relationship in their lives, and Vaillant proves to be selfless, loyal, encouraging, and wise. He can also be impulsive, as when he gets in financial trouble for the church and must go to Rome to explain himself.

Vaillant is an ugly man who readily makes friends with his congenial personality. People are drawn to him and trust him, which makes him effective as a priest. When Latour assigns Vaillant to become the new priest in Albuquerque and later to the miners in Colorado, Vaillant is enthusiastic about the challenges. In both cases, his dedication, magnetism, and faith contribute to his success.

Latour admires Vaillant for his humility and willingness to do whatever is necessary to benefit the church. He begs when necessary and cajoles when necessary, but always seems to get what he needs. His lack of pride, however, prevents him from feeling compassion for Isabella when she resists revealing her real age to the court. He judges

Topics For Further Study

- Research the structure and hierarchy of the Catholic Church. For example, what are dioceses? And what are bishops, vicars, and cardinals? How do religious orders fit into the structure? Create an easy-to-follow chart that explains the distribution of authority and functions within the church. Include a brief write-up of how this chart sheds light on at least one issue in the novel.

- Choose one southwestern Native American tribe, and research its belief system. Prepare a presentation in which you explain the tribe's religious views, and compare and contrast them with Catholicism. In which areas would you expect Latour and Vaillant to have the least trouble making converts? In which areas would you expect the most resistance?

- Artists such as Georgia O'Keeffe, Rhonda Angel, Ritch Gaiti, Gary Myers, and Albert Dreher have found inspiration in the land and culture of the Southwest. Choose six works (by the same or different artists) that somehow illustrate *Death Comes for the Archbishop*. Create a museum guide as if these works were on display specifically to complement the novel. Write explanations (ideally with some quoted material from the novel) to help museum-goers appreciate the exhibit.

- Kit Carson is a good friend to Latour in the novel. Read about this real-life legend and write five journal entries as if he were writing about Latour and Vaillant. Include a brief biographical profile as an introduction to your work.

---

her as vain, while Latour has compassion for the woman's sense of privacy. Still, Vaillant is warm-hearted and accepting, even when he does not agree or understand someone's motives.

Themes

Faith

Because the novel relates the stories of Latour's missionary journeys throughout New Mexico, the theme of faith is significant. Without the motivation of his personal faith, Latour would lack the drive to endure the physical difficulties and rejection he must overcome to fulfill his mission. Latour is deeply devoted to his faith, making certain to pray, read, and reflect every day. When his thoughts have wandered from religious matters for too long, he feels urgency to pray or meditate. Never does the reader find that Latour wavers from his "calling" to the priesthood. He does not wonder what it would be like to have any other life, and he does not discuss his life prior to joining the priesthood. He gladly sacrifices comfort, family, wealth, and social opportunities for his vocation.

As a counterpoint to Latour's faith is that of the Native Americans in the area. Their beliefs vary from pueblo to pueblo, but they are marked by superstition and the worship of animals and deities. Their faith in their belief systems is at times as strong as Latour's is to his Catholicism. Zeb Orchard, a trader well acquainted with the natives and their beliefs, tells Latour that he "might make good Catholics among the Indians, but he would never separate them from their own beliefs." Still, what Latour and the Indians have in common is a strong tradition and solid faith.

Trust

In order for Latour to be a meaningful Catholic presence in New Mexico, he must not only earn the trust of the Mexicans, Americans, and Indians living there, but he must also earn the trust of the existing church leaders. He soon finds that earning this trust, especially that of the native people, will not be easy. They have endured a brutal and unjust past with Europeans, and their distrust is as firm as it is well grounded. Latour regards this challenge as a matter of showing himself to be a man of integrity and sincerity. He ministers to the people and remains humble in public and private. He does not develop elaborate social or political strategies to win them over, but instead relies on his faith and his own character. Although there are many people whose trust he never fully earns, he succeeds in winning the respect of many people, including Eusabio, Kit Carson, the slave girl, and Jacinto.

Similarly, if Latour is to assimilate to life and culture in New Mexico, he has to learn to trust its people and land. If he fails to embrace the ways of the American Southwest—its food, landscape, housing, customs, etc.—he will be too foreign to be effective. He is in an interesting predicament; he is there to assimilate the New Mexicans to his ways, but he must also assimilate to their ways. To pursue this is an act of faith because his future takes an unknown shape. He has to have faith that such a blend of the European Catholic ways and the New Mexico culture will be viable and meaningful.

The issue of trust is also important to Latour on a personal level, as his friendship with Vaillant demonstrates. As is evident throughout the book and in Latour's final thoughts, his bond with Vaillant is among the greatest treasures of his life. Their friendship is based on a long history together that is sustained by openness, encouragement, mutual respect, and deep trust. Latour knows that Vaillant is reliable and can be counted on to provide the support he needs. He is not at all surprised that, upon returning to Santa Fe from Durango, Vaillant has won the confidence of the people there and selflessly prepared for Latour's arrival. Latour's first major challenge as bishop of New Mexico is replacing Gallegos in Albuquerque, so he gives the position to Vaillant. He trusts that Vaillant, with the strength of his personality and integrity, will be able to restore the city's faith community to its proper reverence. Later Latour must decide how to address the need for Catholic leadership in the masses of people in Colorado for the gold rush. A truly challenging mission, he knows that Vaillant is suited to meet the needs of the area and that he will do so willingly. The trust Latour and Vaillant share comes from their hearts and their shared faith.

Style

Landscape

Throughout *Death Comes for the Archbishop*, Cather presents lavish descriptions of the southwestern landscape. With color and texture, she paints pictures of the mountains, deserts, mesas, plants, and vast skies of the region. She early on establishes the importance of the landscape, devoting the majority of the first, lengthy paragraph to describing the features of the land in which Latour finds himself. The color red is everywhere, a telling insight into the perception of the devout Catholic Latour. Red is the color of passion and suffering, and even in this foreign land, Latour finds the heart of the faith that has brought him there. When, in the next paragraph, he discovers a juniper tree in the shape of a cross, the reader begins to understand how the landscape will play a role in Latour's experience and how he will project himself onto it. Latour is a serene and resilient man, and that tone come across in his landscape descriptions.

As unlikely as it seems, Latour is frequently reminded of the French landscape as he explores New Mexico. Sometimes it is a sweeping view that takes his memory back, and sometimes it is a small detail. This tendency tells the reader two things. It reveals that Latour is drawn to landscape and natural wonders, wherever he is. He notices it and interprets it, usually at an emotional level. It also reveals that Latour is gradually accepting New Mexico as home. Because he sees in New Mexico much of what he loves about his own native land, he is opening himself up to recognizing it as his new home.

The landscape does not just reflect Latour's character and feelings. The Native American culture is very connected to its natural surroundings, and they learn it and build it into their lives. The Mexican people share a similar history of building a lifestyle around the offerings and hardships of the environment. Latour understands the link between the native people and their surroundings, which he observes when he visits Taos. Upon arrival, he and the local priest go to the church, where many people have gathered to kneel and greet them. Women toss down their shawls for Latour to walk on, and other men and women reach for his hand to kiss his ring. Cather writes, "In his own country all this would have been highly distasteful to Jean Marie Latour. Here, these demonstrations seemed a part of the high colour that was in the landscape and gardens, in the flaming cactus and the gaudily decorated altars." Latour accepts their behavior not out of pride or vanity, but out of understanding that the people are consistent with the landscape that surrounds them.

Narrative Structure

The plot structure of *Death Comes for the Archbishop* is episodic, stringing together a series of experiences, encounters, and mini-adventures that build on each other in that they develop Latour's character and give the reader a broad view of the region's people and culture. The novel begins with the decision to send Latour to New Mexico to bring order to the church presence and convert native people, then a lengthy middle follows relating Latour's and Vaillant's efforts, and the story ends with Latour dying after making significant progress over a forty-one-year time span. Cather relies on human interest and characterization to keep the reader invested in the story, rather than exciting plot twists or great conflicts.

Historical Novel

Death Comes for the Archbishop is considered a historical novel because it is a fictional story that includes historical people and events. While much of the story is fictionalized, it includes such historical figures as Kit Carson and Father Martinez, and the two main characters are based on actual missionary priests in New Mexico. In addition, references to such historical events as the Bent massacre and the Pueblo Revolt of 1680 contribute to the historic elements of the novel. Cather brings authenticity to her novel by incorporating the region's actual past.

The novel can also be considered a work of historical fiction, which is distinct from the historical novel. Historical fiction refers to a novel set in a different time period than the one in which it was written. Because *Death Comes for the Archbishop* takes place in the nineteenth century but was written in the twentieth century, it falls into the category.

Historical Context

America in the 1920s

Known as the "Jazz Age," the 1920s in America is remembered as a time of prosperity and high times. It was, in many ways, a period of excess. Flappers personified the carefree attitude of the youthful generations, enjoying all-night parties with drinking and dancing. Women in general enjoyed new social freedoms as they were allowed to vote, pursue education, and dress more to individual tastes. American big business was generally successful, but with consequences. Sinclair Lewis published his cautionary tale *Babbitt*, in which fictional American tycoon George F. Babbitt acquires wealth at the expense of his own humanity.

The 1920s also represented an introspective period for Americans. Having endured World War I, Americans were more inclined to attend to domestic needs rather than worry about Europe's postwar struggles. While the postwar years were an economic boon to many Americans, to others they were years of hardship. Miners and farmers, for example, struggled to make ends meet, and many were forced into other occupations altogether. The postwar years were also characterized by cynicism, as prohibition (making alcohol illegal) was found to be unenforceable and most Americans regarded the Bolsheviks involved in the Russian Revolution as either threatening or naïve.

In literature America saw the Harlem Renaissance and the Southern Renaissance play out in the 1920s. These movements signaled that America was opening itself up to new perspectives and experiences. The Harlem Renaissance represented the black experience in America and included such writers as Langston Hughes, Zora Neale Hurston, and Jean Toomer. The Southern Renaissance represented a retrospective view of prewar America. Originating in Virginia, the movement supported southern writers such as William Faulkner, DuBose Heyward, and Pulitzer Prize–winning Julia Peterkin. In both movements, women's voices were an important component of the collective voice.

History of New Mexico

According to artifacts found in a cave near Albuquerque, the state of New Mexico has been inhabited for about 20,000 years. The earliest people were nomadic, and later farmers settled in the area. A group of seminomadic people known as the Basket Makers became the Anasazi cliff dwellers. They were the ancestors of the Pueblo Indians of recent past and today. The Pueblo Indians mainly lived along the Rio Grande River, and the Navajo Indians became farmers and sheepherders in the northwestern region of the state. The two tribes did not always coexist peacefully. The nomadic Apache Indians arrived in the thirteenth century (about the time the Navajo arrived) and seriously threatened Europeans and Mexicans who came to New Mexico in later years.

The first European exploration of New Mexico was in 1540 by Francisco Vasquez de Coronado. Subsequent expeditions were made by other Spanish explorers, who gradually built settlements until the 1800s. When Mexico gained its independence from Spain in 1821, New Mexico became a Mexican land. The next three decades were tumultuous, with revolts and resistance to the Mexican government. Eventually New Mexico became an American holding in 1850 (the year before Father Latour arrives

Compare
&
Contrast

- **1850s:** The population of New Mexico is almost exclusively Native American and Mexican. It becomes a U.S. state in 1851, but Anglos are not accepted until close to the end of the century.

  1920s: The Native American population in New Mexico is 19,500. This number is more than double what it was in 1890.

  Today: The Native American population in New Mexico is estimated at 169,000, an increase of more than 30,000 since 1990.

- **1850s:** Immigration numbers begin to swell in the U.S., particularly from Ireland, Germany, and Sweden.

  1920s: This decade marks the beginning of an upswell of "nativist" sentiment. A Federal program is initiated to "repatriate" an estimated half million Mexicans and Mexican Americans living in the U.S. in order to free up jobs for "American" workers (i.e., people of non-Mexican descent). This campaign of forced immigration uproots people (many of whom are American citizens) in various states throughout the U.S.

  Today: Movements are being initiated to set up Federal investigation committees on the issue of forced repatriation, lawsuits for redress are beginning to emerge in state and national courts, and information and personal stories about this buried chapter of history are beginning to emerge.

- **1850s:** There are very few female authors in American literature. The major writers of the day are Ralph Waldo Emerson, Henry David Thoreau, Walt Whitman, Nathaniel Hawthorne, Herman Melville, and Edgar Allan Poe. A few women such as Kate Chopin and Harriet Beecher Stowe enjoy success, but the overall feminine presence is lacking.

  1920s: Although the literature of the era is largely associated with authors such as William Faulkner, F. Scott Fitzgerald, and Ernest Hemingway, women are becoming more respected as a literary presence.

  Today: Female authors are as common as male authors. Many of the bestselling and most respected authors are women, including Barbara Kingsolver, J. K. Rowling, Patricia Cornwell, and Anne Rice.

---

in *Death Comes for the Archbishop*). Little changed for those living in New Mexico; there were ongoing territorial disputes and struggles with authority. As Americans began to arrive in New Mexico to establish new homes, cultures clashed.

In 1879 the railroad came to New Mexico, bringing economic opportunities for its inhabitants. As the century neared to a close, the American Indians and the Anglo-Americans were finally learning to coexist. In 1912 New Mexico officially became a state.

The twentieth century saw great change in New Mexico. Natural resources were discovered and mined or drilled, and tourism brought Americans to visit the new state. The manufacturing and defense industries also found homes in New Mexico. In the twentieth century the state is thoroughly modern.

Critical Overview

When *Death Comes for the Archbishop* was published in 1927, readers and critics alike embraced the novel. Cather's love of the Southwest and its inhabitants was clear, and readers came to share her affection for the region. In *American Writers, Volume 1*, Dorothy Van Ghent observes, "Most of the episodes evoke the virtue of place, textures of earth and weather that are the basis of all sense of reality, and the relationships of human generations silently handing down their wisdom of place." Brad Hooper in *Booklist* remarks that *Death Comes for the Archbishop* is a story told "in a beautifully lyrical style." Cather's captivating language was intentional and hard-earned, according to Van Ghent, who notes that every day after writing, Cather went alone into the woods to read it aloud for sound and rhythm.

Cather's characters and their struggles are another topic of critical commentary. In *American Heritage*, Alexander O. Boulton writes, "Willa Cather's picture of the Southwest and its early inhabitants isn't easy to shake off, even today. She saw a racial contest where modern ideas struggled against ancient fears and superstitions." Van Ghent comments, "the people in the book, the 'strong people of the old deep days of life,' not only have each their legends but have become their own legends."

Statue of Archbishop Jean-Baptiste Lamy, whom Cather based the novel's main character, Bishop Jean Marie Latour, upon

Criticism

Jennifer Bussey

Bussey holds a master's degree in interdisciplinary studies and a bachelor's degree in English literature, and is an independent writer specializing in literature. In the following essay Bussey explores the specific challenges faced by Bishop Jean Marie Latour when he arrives in New Mexico, and how he gradually overcomes these issues.

When Father Jean Marie Latour arrives in New Mexico as its new bishop, he quickly realizes that there are significant barriers awaiting him. His purpose is to bring order to the Catholic Church in the American Southwest and to win converts among the non-Catholics. The people of New Mexico, however, are not all anxious to embrace the changes he sees as necessary. In order to fulfill his mission and become a respected church authority, he must overcome enormous obstacles. Latour must not only win the trust and respect of the American Indians who have been grossly mistreated by former Europeans and missionaries, he must also overcome the corrupt leadership of some of the current priests. He discovers that he faces the daunting task of overcoming the distant and recent past for the sake of New Mexico's future.

Latour is anxious to know the diverse people of his diocese, so he enlists the help of Jacinto, a young Indian guide who can take him to the area missions and pueblos. Although some groups of people welcome him and respect his authority, others have learned from the past that Europeans cannot be trusted. The cultural, economic, and emotional damage done to these people is almost incomprehensible to Latour, who is a very compassionate man. He understands the Indians' mistrust, but he does not give up trying to prove to them that true men of God are not selfish, cruel, and materialistic. Because Latour has a particular appreciation for history, he is able to take the stories of the past and interpret them as they relate to the present. The more he learns about the violent and unjust past of the Indians in his region, the more he comprehends their deep sadness.

In addition to the mistreatment doled out by European explorers and settlers, past missionaries and priests have been guilty of cruelty to the Indians. This is especially difficult for Latour because not only must he differentiate himself from those who wore the same vestments as he, but he must also come to terms with the fact that his own church's past is responsible for the Indians' plight. Perhaps this is why he is so resolute in working with the U.S. government to restore the Navajos to their rightful land. Although he assumes no personal guilt for past crimes, he may feel a bit of collective guilt that motivates him to right a wrong. Interestingly, some of the Indians generalize the actions of past missionaries and hold tight to their distrust, while

> " Latour must not only win the trust and respect of the American Indians who have been grossly mistreated by former Europeans and missionaries, he must also overcome the corrupt leadership of some of the current priests."

others judge each priest individually. Latour hears the story of Father Baltazar, who was a priest among the cliff dwellers in the 1700s. He was overbearing, materialistic, impulsive, and gluttonous. He used Indians to tend to his house, animals, and garden. Over the years, he wielded his power more harshly, but the Indians were afraid to revolt because they did not understand the priest's powers. One night, however, when Baltazar accidentally killed an Indian servant boy in a fit of rage, the tribe gathered for revenge. They tied him up and threw him off the cliff. Despite the years of suffering under his unjust rule, the Indians did not reject the next priest sent to them. That some of the Indians are willing to give each man a chance is a source of hope to a man as kind and honorable as Latour.

The final obstacle Latour faces is that of corruption among his contemporaries. As he learns about the native priests, he learns that two of the most powerful and influential priests, Father Gallegos of Albuquerque and Father Martinez of Taos, are embarrassments to the Catholic Church. The behavior and attitudes of Gallegos and Martinez grossly misrepresent the church, and their irreverence toward its authority and their vows is deeply troubling to Latour. To establish the dignity of his role as bishop of New Mexico, Latour knows he will have to replace these stubborn and powerful men. Again, this challenge is painful to Latour because it is essentially coming from within his own ranks. His love of the church is very deep, and to see it disrespected is difficult for him. In addition, he understands that he must undo the damage inflicted by these wayward priests.

Father Gallegos is a materialistic man who enjoys gambling and dancing. He also has a

questionable relationship with a local widow. He has no interest in serving the people of Albuquerque or the surrounding pueblos, as he is too busy hosting and attending festivals completely lacking in religious reverence. Luckily, Latour's decision to replace him with Latour's own friend Father Joseph Vaillant goes unchallenged. Vaillant is able to bring a stop to the parties and initiate serious religious observances.

Father Martinez proves to be a more difficult case. The priest in Taos, Martinez is a tyrannical, materialistic, cruel man with a strange magnetism that compels his followers to obey him. According to local legend, Martinez sent Indians on a massacre. When the Indians were captured, Martinez promised to help them if they would give him their land. Once he had their land, he let them hang. Upon meeting Martinez in person, Latour finds that Martinez is a renegade priest who makes his own rules. He dismisses the notions of celibacy and trying to live as sin-free as possible. Even more astonishing to Latour is Martinez's idea that the church in Rome has no relevance to the way things are in America. When Latour eventually replaces Martinez, Martinez and another renegade priest start their own church and face excommunication. The power struggle is hard-fought by both sides, but Latour eventually wins. In doing so, he overcomes the damage done by Martinez and proves to himself that he is capable of overcoming the scandalous past of his own church. He learns a critical lesson, that he *can* bring order out of chaos for the sake of his church's future.

In the face of such overwhelming obstacles, how does Latour begin to knock them down? He does it in two seemingly simple ways: he treats the Indians as they should be treated instead of how they have been treated, and he proves to everyone that he is not like past corrupt priests. In these two ways, he eventually wins the trust and respect of many Indians and Mexicans who initially rejected him and his authority. Of course, there remain people in his diocese who are unable to give him the trust he deserves, but the progress he makes is remarkable.

First, he treats the Indians with respect and dignity. He comes to them to serve them, not to lord over them. He never tries to use his position to coerce them to his way, but instead attends to their needs. He strives to understand them, not to control them. In book 4, chapter 2, Cather reveals that Latour "was already convinced that neither the white men nor the Mexicans in Santa Fé understood anything about Indian beliefs or the workings of the

What Do I Read Next?

- Dee Brown's 1970 book *Bury My Heart at Wounded Knee: An Indian History of the American West* is read by students, scholars, and history enthusiasts as one of the foremost treatments of the nineteenth-century American Indian experience. Although this book only covers 1860 to 1890, it will give students a better understanding of the early Anglo approach to Native American civilizations in America.

- Cather's *My Ántonia* (1918) is set in Nebraska and told from a male point of view. It is the story of Ántonia, a pioneer woman struggling against the challenges of her surroundings in a time when women enjoyed less freedom that they do

today. Considered a classic, this novel is one of Cather's most widely read works.

- *Willa Cather: Stories, Poems, and Other Writings* (1992) contains samples of Cather's short fiction, poetry, and literary commentary. Her subject matter is wide-ranging, and students find that Cather is much more than the voice of the American frontier.

- Translated by Ruth Butler, *Journal of Paul Du Ru, February 1 to May 8, 1700* (1997) relates the experiences of a Jesuit missionary in Louisiana in very early America. In addition to his missionary duties, Du Ru helped explore the area for possible French settlement.

Indian mind." This attitude motivates him to try to get to know the Indians on their own terms. Jacinto recognizes this and respects Latour for it. In book 3, chapter 2, Cather writes,

> The truth was, Jacinto liked the Bishop's way of meeting people. . . . In his experience, white people, when they addressed Indians, always put on a false face. . . . The Bishop put on none at all. He stood straight and turned to the Governor of Laguna, and his face underwent no change. Jacinto thought this remarkable.

When he hears that the influential Navajo Eusabio has lost his only son, Latour's heart breaks for this man. He goes to minister to him in his time of great need, and the two men come to like and respect each other. When Jacinto takes Latour to surrounding missions and pueblos, the priest comes to perform mass and offer sacraments. He never demands changes or gifts; his purpose is to attend to their spiritual needs.

Second, Latour differentiates himself from the corrupt priests of the past (and present). He is humble and kind, asking for little when he is a guest in a home or a pueblo. He knows that in the past some missionaries have expected the best food, clothing, and shelter from their hosts, but Latour is not that kind of man. He also proves he is different by

bringing his love for his homeland of France *to* New Mexico instead of trying to change New Mexico into France. Father Baltazar demonstrated his disdain for New Mexico when he all but enslaved the Indians to create a European setting for himself, complete with gardens that required precious water. The Indians knew Baltazar considered the people and land of New Mexico to be inferior, and they resented it. As soon as they had cause, they stoically bound him and threw him off the cliff to his death. In contrast, Latour embraces the similarities he finds between France and New Mexico, and he develops a deep and genuine love of the Southwest in its own right. He, like the Indians, makes New Mexico his true home.

The challenges in New Mexico are daunting to the young Latour, but he is equal to the tasks. By the time of his death, he has brought peaceful and respectable order to a region overrun with chaos and scandal. Amazingly, he manages to overcome some of the awful past of the early Europeans and missionaries in the area, and he does it by strength of character and resolve. Just as impressive as his accomplishments is how he handles them. He never brags or seeks any glory for himself, but instead gives it all to his church and God. The cathedral he builds is a testament not to his own great works, but to the drive and courage supplied through his faith, and the future he is committed to creating for the church is fulfilled.

Source: Jennifer Bussey, Critical Essay on *Death Comes to the Archbishop*, in *Novels for Students*, Gale, 2004.

Pam Fox Kuhlken

In the following essay, Kuhlken explores the symbolic meaning of landscape—specifically the Sangre de Cristo mountains—in Death Comes for the Archbishop.

Two fleeting glimpses of the Sangre de Cristo mountain range in Willa Cather's *Death Comes for the Archbishop* have eluded the critical attention of scholars. The first of these two epiphanies appears three-quarters of the way into the narrative, so we too will proceed to this revelation as though traipsing on mules with Cather during one of her pivotal visits to the Southwest. To begin, we will consider why the land is central to the novel's meaning and see how the text's mood is determined by the desert landscape. To appreciate Cather's art is to understand the sanctified nature of the land, which illuminates our own nature at the same time. The novel presents sangre de Cristo as a fact, as the ubiquitous undercurrent of existence. The land, like our nature, may have fallen, yet it has not been conquered but redeemed.

The critical range of relevant scholarship encompasses both secular and religious readings, even secularized religious readings. Many critics argue that Cather's vision is purely secular, with origins and finality in the material realm. Sally Peltier Harvey identifies Cather's use of distinctive garden imagery in *Death Comes for the Archbishop* as symbolic of a healthy community, yet Harvey mentions this symbol only to supplement her sociopolitical reading of the novel as a text that shows how to establish a happy balance between personal and public needs. It "redefines self-fulfillment in terms of service to and identification with community." In her definition of self-fulfillment—the American Dream—Harvey uses the land as a symbol but omits reference to visions of a landscape imbued with sanctity, and consequently she fails to integrate the landscape into her model of a viable community. For Harvey the land is not spiritually transcendent but a humanist's symbol—the color of vibrant cultural identity—or epic stage for a questing hero.

Other critics ask religious questions and find secular answers. In *After Eden: The Secularization of American Space in the Fiction of Willa Cather and Theodore Dreiser*, Conrad Eugene Ostwalt, Jr. analyzes how the influx of ideas from Charles Darwin, Karl Marx, and G. W. F. Hegel, among others, shaped American culture as it entered the twentieth century. Once promising face-to-face encounters with the divine, America, like Eden, had fallen from grace, shifting from sacred to secular, and thus faced the need to redefine its spatial orientation to all that was lost: relationship with the land, relationship with the divine.

Ostwalt argues that in Cather's fiction the frontier embodied otherness. Once this other was apprehended, it lost its ability to disclose the transcendent and sacred. When America became industrialized, the New World became profane: "Secularization of American natural space occurs when characters attempt to reduce the otherness of nature and to control the natural world." In place of a religious other, Ostwalt continues, the land in Cather's fiction embodies divine attributes of mystery, awesome power, beneficence, and ample providence that make human relationships possible. Depleted of transcendence, the land provides a forum for community. What became of religion? "In Cather's secular world, human relationships replace what one loses from the destruction of the sacred environment, namely a relationship with deity." Other people substitute for divine otherness.

Critics like Harvey and Ostwalt find Cather's religion—a relinking with a divine other—in human community. The land is merely the forum. In contrast to Ostwalt's view of a desacralized earth, this essay will argue that the land in Cather's novel, by virtue of creation, is sacred and could no more be profaned than it could lose its properties as earth or the Southwest its distinctively red tint. Previous analyses have shortchanged the novel by over-looking one essential, indestructible component—sangre de Cristo. *Death Comes for the Archbishop* presents the land as having an irrevocable, redemptive quality: instated at creation, tainted by Eden's die/dye, restained by sangre de Cristo, and sealed by the cross. . . .

Death Comes for the Archbishop is arguably less a novel than a performance. The role of the guide was first performed by the statue, then by Cather. Like Father Vaillant's letters to his sister, Mother Philomene, in Puy-de-Dome, France, the narrative may also be seen as a long letter to Cather's family back in Red Cloud, Nebraska, telling of "the country, the Indians, the pious Mexican women, the Spanish martyrs of old [, . . .] of those red deserts." Sharing Cather's adventures, relatives had a stake in her excitement and dread. Or perhaps the text is intended as fireside reading, to be recited by its audience as the French nuns read Vaillant's letters out loud. Either way, it compels more than a visit. It commands immersion, entry into its landscape; reading becomes travel, the experience of stepping through scenes as though on the stones of a path.

Death Comes for the Archbishop is pieced together with adobe bricks, or scenes, made from the clay of Lamy's life and Cather's own experiences. Stemming from her wagon trips, the result is indigenous to the Southwest—native to the adobe earth. Her awakening came when she could view the land as primordial, as though she were one of its first pioneers. One of the most "intelligent and inspiriting" people Cather met in the Southwest was a Belgian priest who told her about the country, the Indians, and their traditions. The breakthrough came as a kind of epiphany: "At last I found out what I wanted to know about how the country and the people of New Mexico seemed to those first missionary priests from France" ("On Death" 8). Cather visited the mission in Santa Fe, saw the statue of the missionary, found the history of Lamy in a 1908 biography, met the Belgian priest, and the rest is legend.

Overall, saintliness intrigued Cather more than any particular saint did. As she explained, "It is as though all human experiences, measured against one supreme spiritual experience, were of about the same importance. The essence of such writing is not to hold the note, not to use an incident for all there is in it—but to touch and pass on" ("On Death" 9). In contrast to the popular writing of the 1920s, in which, according to Cather, "situation" was all-important, and the general tendency was "to force things up" she undertook writing as a kind of discipline. Hardiness of spirit could not be captured by light prose. Cather cloaked her prose in another mood entirely—the frontier spirit "in which [pioneer priests] accepted the accidents and hardships of a desert country, the joyful energy that kept them going." The language was necessarily "a little stiff, a little formal," with some time-worn phrases. Trite phraseology of the frontier was used as "the note from the piano by which the violinist tunes his instrument"; the narrative's musical quality flows in tune to this analogy. The missionary's mood—heartiness of spirit and joyful energy—became Cather's lodestar: "mood is the thing—all the little figures and stories are mere improvisations that come out of it" ("On Death" 10). Perhaps the most appropriate way to appreciate this amalgam of the

> " The Sangre de Cristo mountains remind us of the once-and-for-all sacrificial death and the commission for disciples to spread the gospel, but *Death Comes for the Archbishop* does not indoctrinate."

Southwest in *Death Comes for the Archbishop* is through its mood, but Cather's elaborate result surpasses her stated intention.

With incongruous flashbacks to Latour's home in France, we exit linear time in the novel. Time liquefies, helping us to view the efficacious blood of Christ as ubiquitously present since Eden, implied in the moment of creation. In Eden, animals are killed to cover the shamed Adam and Eve; outside of Eden, Abel will be killed by his brother. A bloody battle ends history at Armageddon. Blood soaks the page from Genesis to Revelation. Red also infuses the world of *Death Comes for the Archbishop* with its scriptural bookends of a Roman garden (Eden) and a New World cathedral (the New Jerusalem).

Red in Cather's novel, however, is gentle and life-giving in its sanctity: there are no unhappy or unjust denouements to the work's nine books. As a sign, blood waters the New World and is the reason missionaries become exiles. It justifies the Christian faith and the Church's presence in the New Mexico territory. Without Christ's death Howlett's biography would be absurd. The blood of creation is sangre de Cristo—part of a holistic plan unfolding with a death as its crux. It is the signpost marking the entrance for Cather into the world of Southwestern missions within Lamy's diocese.

Blood's potency in *Death Comes for the Archbishop* transcends this New World, eluding cultural ruination as well as the Catholic Church's attempt to bridle the power of sangre through ritual, symbol, and text. Because of the vested blood, the land is exempt from conquest. It may change political hands, but it is not vanquished. While the land might be stained carnelian (the color of dried blood) rather than vermilion (the tint of living blood), this dry landscape is no less vital to understanding the mystery of the sacramental nature of sangre de Cristo. For this reason the untouchable, enduring "mood" of the blood is the most effective vehicle for a writer trying to "present the experiences and emotions of a group of people by the light of [her] own" ("On Death" 13). The characters and setting unite in a pervading bond of blood that culminates in two epiphanies of the Sangre de Cristo mountains. . . .

The pervasive color of the blazing sun on the clay desert tints the entire story red. We get the sense that the land has been red since creation, long before someone concocted the family recipe of Father Vaillant's cherished soup: from the Fall, to the murder of Abel, to the Flood, to the Crucifixion, the gospel story has been enacted in creation before the missionaries arrived. In Matthew 23:35 and Luke 11:51, Jesus catalogues seven woes to the scribes and Pharisees. The seventh and climactic woe curses the "brood of vipers" for killing prophets and shedding righteous blood from Abel to Zechariah. The shedding of Abel's blood is a pivotal moment, a sign of human depravity that will later be reversed by Jesus' culminating sacrifice.

The land is more than a metaphor for Christ; his name is not merely transferred to an object as a representative or symbol. Rather, the land metonymically denotes an attribute of Christ, his shed blood, and becomes the thing itself. While metaphors relate two disparate objects, metonyms are integrally linked, in this case identifying the Creator with creation and his death on earth with the Southwest's blood-dyed landscape. There is no explanation; the mountains are simply named Sangre de Cristo. This label seems permanent and indigenous, as though coined by Adam himself.

If the landscape in *Death Comes for the Archbishop* is to convey adequately the mood of the text, it needs a distinct language for its message. Its under-stated role communicates in part through the color red as the sun paints the land and sky, as fires and candles light dark scenes, and as sangre de Cristo incants the Passion. Two apparently marginalized treatments of the Sangre de Cristo mountains stain the text with the power of this color, event, and name. In these epiphanies all events culminate in the transfigured landscape, and the climaxes suffice for powerful dramatic and thematic effect. The first mention of the mountains is three-quarters of the way through the narrative, almost as though it were a postscript clue justifying the reference to the Passion in the first chapter and the predominance of red throughout the novel. . . .

In the closing chapter of Book 9 titled "Death Comes for the Archbishop," Father Latour is near death. His consciousness slips through time, and he recalls the Italian architect building the cathedral on the one golden mountain surrounded by carnelian hills. As the saint's death is approaching, the redness of Christ's Passion is recalled in the persecutors' anger and in his bleeding wounds. The Archbishop's obsession with his cathedral is both an acceptance of and preparation for his burial. The cathedral is called his tomb, the site of his death.

[Rev. W. J.] Howlett's biography [of a real-life pioneer priest] chronicles the lives of deceased missionaries and murderous terrain, but for Cather the mountains are a range of life, the backdrop for her saints' lives. The Archbishop lives until the final paragraph, hallucinating and believing. In the final sentence he lies dead, but he is ultimately a builder: "The old Archbishop lay before the high altar in the church he had built." Like the Creator buried in his creation, the architect is laid to rest in his. Or is he? Where has the discourse placed his body? In the penultimate paragraph the narrative states:

> But in reality the Bishop was not there at all; he was standing [. . .] among his native mountains, and he was trying to give consolation to a young man who was being torn in two before his eyes by the desire to go and the necessity to stay. He was trying to forge a new Will in that devout and exhausted priest.

The reality for the Archbishop is that he is not at all present in either world. He is in a state of flux, of being "in between." As God and man, Christ is best known through the sacrament of communion; his body and soul are permanently torn between this world and heaven. The Archbishop's body and will are torn between the old and new worlds in his final vision or, rather, his reality.

In perfect dramatic sequence, as a storm rises over the hills, Latour envisions an "intense lavender," a color appearing for the first time in the novel. As the sky grows black, "the carnelian rocks became an intense lavender, all their pine trees strokes of dark purple." In Cather's Episcopal heritage red signifies the Holy Spirit during the Feast of Pentecost and is also used for any of the martyrs' days; during Lent red also replaces purple as the color worn by the bishop, who is the symbol of Christ. Then a voice out of the present calls Latour from his visionary memories. His attendant, Bernard, says: "A fine sunset, Father. See how red the mountains are growing; Sangre de Cristo." Father Latour does not respond, but the narrative voice concurs with Bernard in a mythical explanation, reflective of the overall legendary tone of the novel's fantastic spiritual adventures coupling miracles and the mundane:

> Yes, Sangre de Cristo; but no matter how scarlet the sunset, those red hills never became vermilion, but a more and more intense rose-carnelian; not the colour of living blood, the Bishop had often reflected, but the colour of the dried blood of saints and martyrs preserved in old churches in Rome, which liquefies upon occasion.

One is certain that the blood of the saints in *Death Comes for the Archbishop* includes that of un-Christianized Indians who have places "more sacred" than churches. The Archbishop is buried in the New World cathedral, under indigenous yellow rock, emphasizing that he is buried under Indian ground that is not profane but sacred. The red sky blesses all of creation, severely humbling any attempt to judge other religious beliefs, since Christ is the head of his Church; all who participate in his body, whether through the Church or the land, are dependent on this source rather than on their own creeds.

Amid this profusion of vermilion, the next chapter opens with the cathedral, his tomb, as an illumination of the heavenly city Father Latour will soon inhabit. With this abrupt juxtaposition, in the spirit of Cather's literary aesthetic, the golden cathedral becomes colored with the red mood of the narrative. In spite of the lush green gardens, lavender sunsets, and golden cathedral, sangre de Cristo persists. Its touch predominates.

Before the Archbishop imagines rather than speaks his last words (in a vision of a boy deliberating whether to stay at home or leave), the narrative includes a story set in the Navajos' sacred canyon between red sandstone walls. The indigenous people believed that it would never be conquered until Kit Carson defeated them. Navajo blood is shed on the red sandstone, a potent image of dust to dust, and also of sacrificial martyrdom for a holy cause—their sacred canyon. The narrative defends the Indians' plight; they simply want their land and their religion. Their gods dwell in the canyon, "just as the Padre's God was in his church"; however, the Indians' sacred place is more sacred "than churches, more sacred than any place is to the white man." The Navajo chief from the Canyon de Chelly told Father Latour of his hardship as an "outlawed chief" who, though impoverished, refused to be exiled with his people: "My mother and my gods are in the West, and I will never cross the Rio Grande." He did not care for his life; he loved the sacred land and would die with it. Reflecting on the remnant of the Navajos who returned to their chief and their sacred places

after five years of exile, the Archbishop murmurs: "I do not believe, as I once did, that the Indian will perish. I believe that God will preserve him." Latour's belief is life-affirming: though the Indians lacked the sacraments, God tabernacled nomadically with them.

In these passages we see how Cather takes the single citation of the Sangre de Cristo mountains from her source and expands it into two cameos. The mountain range appears in two epiphanies, or spiritual revelations of creation's undercurrent, yet through Cather's aesthetics of accentuating "mood" the rare metonym spills over the entire novel from just these two instances. As seen from the perspective of a bronze statue and a woman of faith, sangre de Cristo has saturated the physical world for the Church and the "heathen." With only two brief appearances, the Sangre de Cristo mountains (and the nature of epiphany) epitomize Cather's "touch and pass on" method. The words barely imprint the page before erasure, and in that fleeting impression the reader knows the mountains' prominent signature.

The cathedral and the hill are golden, but we cannot forget that upon occasion the dried blood of saints and martyrs in Rome and the New World liquefies and the color vermilion spills. The blood of New World martyrs may not come from the pages of the Bible, but it becomes a narrated life and land, fueling legend, art, fiction, and heroic acts unimaginable to Europeans: "Surely these [early Spanish missionaries] endured Hunger, Thirst, Cold, Nakedness, of a kind beyond any conception St. Paul and his brethren could have had [. . .] in that safe little Mediterranean world." A New Eden necessitates a recast Christ; following his model are the martyrs who died in the New World, both indigenous people and saints listed in the novel's obituaries and war chronicles. Rather than usurpation there is inheritance and coexistence. The narrative embraces compatibility between different faiths, yet revelation of eternal truth comes through a saving, supralinguistic knowledge of sangre de Cristo. Missionaries do not prune other visions of the divine but live among people in peace. The presence of saints and blood, not dogma, signifies sanctity.

Cather's vision of the land as sacred allows people to unify as a community and to honor the gift of this resource, paradoxically surpassing materialism through the material of earth given to a sacred purpose. A similar paradox is that the physical novel embodies creation's metaphysical cry of both praise and agony for its Creator. The Sangre

1870 photograph exhibiting the construction of the Cathedral of Saint Francis in Santa Fe, New Mexico, which was developed under the direction of Jean-Baptiste Lamy

de Cristo mountains remind us of the once-and-for-all sacrificial death and the commission for disciples to spread the gospel, but *Death Comes for the Archbishop* does not indoctrinate. Father Latour merely serves the people by performing such rites as baptizing babies and sanctioning marriages. . . .

All-pervasive in *Death Comes for the Archbishop* is the blood of saints' lives and the blood of the land where European, Mexican, and Indian saints have died. Do Cather's "saints" include all innocently killed Indians and Mexicans who revere creation as sacred, and not exclusively Catholics

who received their "last rites"? Her art is not overtly didactic, yet Cather shows a redeemed humanity—indigenous Mexicans and Indians, as well as self-exiled Europeans—on a redeemed, red earth. *Death Comes for the Archbishop* is nonpartisan because it treats ethics rather than dogma and because it never brands any religious sect "superstitious." The natives' beliefs are validated as much as those of the Catholic Church. Veneration for old customs, as viewed in the novel, is an admirable quality shared by Indians and Catholics alike. Humble, poor characters are sympathetically portrayed regardless of creed. When missionaries are near death in the desert and Mexican shepherds appear, the priests do not offer this family the sacraments but instead wonder whether their deliverers could be Mary, Joseph, and the baby Jesus.

Just as the rainbow symbolizes God's pledge that the earth will not be destroyed by water again, so the red land may be seen as a promise signifying that there has been enough killing—that there is no need for more slaughter after sangre de Cristo. If we live metonymically with the sanctified land, we will not reign in conquest but in awe at having become the embodiment of redemption. It may sound naive, but the intended audience of a promise receives it with a trusting child's heart.

Source: Pam Fox Kuhlken, "Hallowed Ground: Landscape as Hagiography in Willa Cather's *Death Comes for the Archbishop*," in *Christianity and Literature*, Vol. 52, No. 3, Spring 2003, pp. 367–86.

Deborah Lindsay Williams

In the following essay, Williams explores how Cather uses aural and visual tropes to connect the Old World with the New in Death Comes for the Archbishop.

In her 1927 letter to *Commonweal*, written to explain how she wrote *Death Comes for the Archbishop*, Willa Cather indirectly offered a possible interpretation for the novel itself: "I used to wish there were some written account of the old times when those churches were built; but I soon felt that no record of them could be as real as they are themselves. *They are their own story, and it is foolish convention that we must have everything interpreted for us in written language*" (emphasis mine). In *Death Comes for the Archbishop*, Cather attempts to bring readers beyond "written language," trying to create on the written page that which is usually intelligible only with sound or sight. To teach us how to read beyond written language Cather offers two models, one aural and one visual: the Angelus bell and the figure of the southwestern mesa. The novel thus offers a pedagogy of interpretation: when we understand the mesa and the bell as tropes with which to organize our understanding of the novel, we arrive at new ways of reading Cather. She deliberately does not provide us with means to "translate" her landscape into meaning; we can only "divine" meaning—Cather's word for how we are to understand the "inexplicable presence of the thing not named" (*On Writing* 41). When we try to name the thing, we limit the full range of associations and reverberations; we do

> "It is this perspective—in which there is no perspective, in which everything, Old World and New, Catholic and pagan, youth and age, is layered together—that the novel pushes us to maintain while we read."

not hear the entire Angelus, and we do not see the full scale of the mesa. The aural and visual landscapes of the novel teach us to read; what we come to understand is that, in *Death Comes for the Archbishop*, tropes and topos are one and the same.

The novel makes meaning in much the same way as does the tolling of the Angelus bell in the beginning of the novel: a series of echoing associations that come together to form a whole. The bell's notes are "Full, clear . . . each note floated through the air like a globe of silver," but until the last note joins the first in the air, the Angelus itself is not complete. When Latour first hears the Angelus bell, almost in his sleep, he has the "pleasing delusion that he was in Rome." As the bell continues to ring the nine strokes of the Angelus, its sound sends Latour on an inner journey: "Before the nine strokes were done Rome faded, and behind it he sensed something Eastern, with palm trees—Jerusalem perhaps, though he had never been there. . . . he cherished for a moment this sudden, pervasive sense of the East. Once before he had been carried out of the body thus to a place far away. It had happened on a street in New Orleans. . . . he [had been] overcome by a feeling of place, was dropped . . . into a garden in the south of France. . . . And now this silvery bell had carried him farther and faster than sound could travel." The bell's sound sets up a series of reactions in Latour's mind, bringing him to places that he has not physically seen but that the sound allows him to imagine. He travels to the Old World, to places of origin: Jerusalem, the holy city; Rome (and thus by implication the Vatican); New Orleans, one of the first cities in the United States; and the south of France, Latour's boyhood home. Although Latour's thoughts are linear—from distant to recent past—they are triggered by the sound of the bell all at once and experienced synchronously. This synchronous experience of time becomes central to the novel; the novel works to represent time and space, history and tradition, in nonlinear ways.

The story of the bell's provenance continues the movement from past to present, from Europe to America: "the inscription [on the bell] is in Spanish ... it must have been brought up from Mexico City in an ox-cart ... and the silver of the Spaniards was really Moorish, was it not.... The Spaniards knew nothing about working silver except as they learned it from the Moors.... The Spaniards handed on their skill to the Mexicans, and the Mexicans taught the Navajos to work silver; but it all came from the Moors." Thus the skill of "infidel" Europe becomes the artisanship of Catholic Spaniards, the trade of colonized Mexicans, and finally the art and craft of Native Americans, who are in effect being displaced by the carriers of the traditions they have embraced. The two French priests, Father Latour and his companion Father Vaillant, listen to their Spanish bell ringing the Catholic Angelus in an American territory occupied first by the Native Americans, then the Spanish, then by the French, and finally by Americans. The bell's provenance illustrates historical movement; the tradition of silversmithing becomes a way of tracing patterns of Old World imperialism and yet also suggests that, in Cather's mind, aesthetic traditions continue regardless of who is in power.

Cather's descriptions of landscape—the New Mexican mesa itself—provide the visual counterpart to the Angelus bell. The mesa offers another trope that we can use to help us read beyond language. Father Latour and Jacinto, riding through this landscape en route to Acoma, stop so that Jacinto can show Latour where they are going, "The Bishop following with his eye the straight, pointing Indian hand, saw, far away, two great mesas ... at this distance [they] seemed close together, though they were really some miles apart." Mesas are perceptible only at a distance although distance can blur the perception of depth. The distance alters our perspective on the subject to the point that the distance—perspective—becomes the subject. And because each layer of a mesa is a compression or distillation of the landscape at a particular point in time, seeing the entire mesa allows us to see all the different eras of history *at once:* chronological time can be seen synchronously.

The layers of the novel, which resemble the striations in a mesa, create a novel structured to collapse seeming oppositions, such as pagan and Christian, Europe and America, past and present,

into one another. In order to see the full range of these complexities, we need to learn to read the landscape. The mesa is the site of that lesson. Each term of the opposition becomes a striation of the novel, and by collapsing these seeming dialectics, Cather calls into question the idea that any one history, any one set of experiences, can define America. The mesalike structure of the novel incorporates Old World and New and finds the Old World *in* the New.

Latour's reactions to the mesa and to the sound of the bell are examples of how the novel attempts to layer Old World and New, but Latour himself also offers an example of the connection between old and new. Latour's name indicates the presence of this layering: the aesthetic ideals of Walter Pater, whose final novel was titled *Gaston Latour* (1888), about a Frenchman in the Middle Ages. This in turn is eerily echoed by Cather's last, unfinished novel: a story of two French boys from Avignon, set during the Middle Ages. Although Cather seems to have quoted Pater directly only once, in her 1925 preface to Sarah Orne Jewett's short stories, Bernice Slote suggests that Pater was one of those "great essayists ... whose beliefs and whose rich, incantatory, or elegant styles certainly touched [Cather's] own." Cather's early statement that "a novel requires not one flash of understanding, but a clear, steady flame and oil in one's flask beside" (qtd in Skaggs 11) resonates directly with what Pater wrote in the conclusion to *The Renaissance:* "to burn always with this hard, gemlike flame, to maintain this ecstasy, is success in life" (Bloom 60). Pater's "hard gemlike flame" and Cather's "clear, steady flame" are clearly similar fires. Pater's ideas pervade this novel to the extent that Latour becomes a sort of Pater on horseback. So, for instance, when Latour says to Joseph Vaillant that "I do not see you as you really are, Joseph; I see you through my affection for you" it rephrases Pater's dictum that one should "know one's own impression as it really is" (Bloom 17).

Latour's burning desire to build a cathedral worthy of the beautiful setting echoes a Paterian comment that Cather made to Mariel Gere in an 1896 letter, to the effect that there is no god but one god, and art is god's revealer. She said that was her creed and indicated her commitment to it (August 4, 1896, Cather papers, University Archives/Special Collections Department, UNL Libraries). Latour is the artist figure within the artistic creation of the novel. He is *not* a representation of Cather herself although they do share a similarly Paterian vision. Latour's position at the end of the novel embodies Pater's idea that life is a "drift of momentary acts of sight and passion and thought . . . to such a tremulous wisp constantly reforming itself on the stream, to a single sharp impression, with a sense in it, a relic more or less fleeting, of such moments gone by, what is real in our life fines itself down" (Bloom 59–60). In *Death Comes for the Archbishop*, Cather records specific incidents in the life of Latour and his friend, Father Vaillant, but fleetingly, with large gaps of time and space between episodes. Ultimately, however, the novel "fines itself down" to the moment of Latour's consciousness before he dies: a refined moment, a precise moment, but composed of a flood of memories. This refined moment in the flow is like one note heard in the midst of many or like one striation of earth in the totality of a mesa.

Latour, like Pater, is interested in the beautiful more than the sensual; when his parishioners want to please him they give him "something good for the eye." Latour is made uncomfortable by the physical, a distaste nowhere more clearly marked than in the cave scene about a third of the way through the novel. Latour and his guide, Jacinto, are caught in a snowstorm and take refuge in a cave Jacinto knows of. The cave is a "mouth-like opening. . . . two great stone lips, slightly parted and thrust outward." From the beginning, the cave signifies a kind of appetite and physicality that will be distasteful to the priest.

The cave is a place sacred to the Pecos tribe's rituals, which is another reason for Latour's discomfort—he is outside his parish, so to speak. Jacinto tells him the cave is "used by [his] people," which suggests that somewhere in the underground cavern (perhaps in the hole that Jacinto so carefully blocks off from the priest) is the snake holy to his tribe. In the cave it is Jacinto, not the priest, who tends the altar and sacred flame. Jacinto's religion is the New World's own "Old World"; the European traditions represented by Latour seem youthful in comparison. The cave is a labyrinth of holes, throatlike passages, mouths, and caverns, suggesting that the French priest seems to be at the opposite end of his Catholic church and its idea of heaven. It is not coincidence that the chapter is titled "Snake Root"; Latour is at the *root* of things, the base. The cave is the site where many of the novel's apparent oppositions are conflated. It also becomes a site wherein the New World of America reveals its significantly ancient roots.

There is something primitive about the cave: the strong, devouring femaleness of the cavities and orifices directly contrasts with the icons of "dolorous Virgins" above ground. This cave is the first of two feminized enclosures within which Latour will encounter something he cannot name or control, something akin to the sublime. This powerful force resides in the cave below the Sangre de Cristo mountains, which adds to the sense that its sacredness antedates the blood of Christ under which it hides. The "pagan" lies under the Christian surface implying the presence of an earth goddess whom Latour senses but cannot name. There are also other resonances and other beliefs in this cave and as a result Latour feels quite ill.

After Jacinto lights the fire, however, Latour—and the reader—encounter still other juxtapositions, other layers of meaning. The fire relaxes the priest, warms him to the point that he becomes aware of "an extraordinary vibration . . . it hummed like a hive of bees, like a heavy roll of distant drums." Jacinto, also hearing the thrumming noise, leads the priest through a tunnel. The two men go "along a tunnel . . . where the roof grew much lower. . . . Jacinto knelt down over a fissure in the stone floor, like a crack in china. . . . he put his ear on the opening. . . . Father Latour lay with his ear to this crack for a long time." We are not allowed to ignore the continuous penetration, deepening, revelation—the two men go from a low-roofed tunnel to a fissure, a crack, an opening, another crack. The priest and the Indian are moving toward the innermost *sancta sanctorum*. Finally, we are at the source of the vibration and Father Latour realizes: "he was listening to one of the oldest voices of the earth. What he heard was the sound of a great underground river, flowing through a resounding cavern. The water was far, far below, perhaps as deep as the foot of the mountain, a flood moving in utter blackness under ribs of antediluvian rock. It was not a rushing noise, but the sound of a great flood moving with great majesty and power." The priest has encountered the creative imagination via British Romanticism and Coleridge's "Kubla Khan" (1816). In Coleridge's poem, of course, the visionary poet sees and hears:

> Where Alph, the sacred river, ran
> Through caverns measureless to man
> Down to a sunless sea.
>
> . . .
>
> And from this chasm, with ceaseless turmoil seething,
> As if this earth in fast thick pants were breathing.

Coleridge's underground river is also a "mighty fountain," and its tumult causes Kubla Khan to hear "ancestral voices." What Cather gives us here is a site of disjunction, an implicit confrontation between

Old Worlds: the allusion to Coleridge suggests the Old World of Europe, but the cave encloses one of the "oldest voices of the earth." The force of the flood is such that both Latour's Paterian Catholicism and Jacinto's Native American mysticism are humbled before its ancient sound. The voice of the ancient river echoes the voice of the bell: both sounds transport the priest, although the river terrifies him because he cannot name what it is that he hears. Latour and Jacinto do not talk about what they have heard—the priest's only response is "[i]t is terrible"—they simply return to sit by the fire.

Evelyn Hively suggests that this cave scene provides "one of the strongest points of contrast in religions in the book," but I would suggest that we are not being asked to *contrast* religions. Instead, we are forced to question which set of beliefs is informing the other. Can either be privileged? We are presented not with a contrast but with a relationship that implies connection, a connection that makes Latour uncomfortable because it asks him to acknowledge beliefs other than his own. Thus when he and Jacinto return to the cave, the fire that Jacinto had kindled is "giving off a rich glow of light in that lofty Gothic chamber." Prior to the encounter with the underground river, the cavern was only *like* "a Gothic chapel" "of vague outline," but now, as if the encounter with the Romantic imagination has transfigured the cave, it is "*that* lofty Gothic chamber" (emphasis mine), a specific site, recognizable to the priest in a way the voices of the river are not. Only after the cave actually becomes a Gothic chamber can the priest fully relax, eat, and sleep. Nevertheless, this Gothic space is also sacred to Jacinto's tribe and contains a river that reverberates with the sounds of histories that make Latour's religion seem brand-new by comparison. The cave becomes a nexus of shifting, apparently contradictory meanings: the cave's stone lips will provide refuge, but the refuge's smell makes the priest ill; the fire burns away the odor, but the voice of the river makes him dizzy. The cave is a place for Indian rituals and the site of High Romantic imagination. It seems hollow, but it supports mountains and from it emerge landscapes.

This already complicated scene is further tangled by Jacinto's presence, which becomes another site of simultaneous meaning. The priest, thinking Jacinto asleep, moves closer to the hole Jacinto had walled up, wanting to examine it more closely. What he sees instead is Jacinto, transfixed by the "oldest voice," in a posture Christlike and mystical: "there against the wall was [Jacinto], standing on some invisible foothold, his arms outstretched against the

rock, his body flattened against it, his ear . . . listening; listening with supersensual ear, it seemed, and he looked to be supported against the rock by the intensity of his solicitude." Jacinto is simultaneously the Romantic poet, the figure of Christ, and a Native American mystic. Jacinto can hear the voice of the sublime, even be supported by it—the "invisible foothold"—while his body is in the position of one who has been crucified. The cave is a place of Indian ritual, Romantic tropology, and now Christian typology. The phrase "he looked to be supported against the rock," which seems simple enough on the surface, in fact adds ambiguities. The phrase could imply that Jacinto is "looking for support" from the so-called rock of the church. However, it is also possible that he is asking the river for the strength to resist—"against"—the church.

Father Latour's vertigo, or what he thinks is vertigo, is caused by hearing the underground river. But Cather creates a dizzying scene for the reader as well, pushing us ever deeper into the cave, layering histories, typologies, and mythologies, until we too, feel that it is unlike anything we have experienced. Jacinto is the type of Christ, arms outstretched, supported by an intense "solicitude," a curious word to use here because according to the *Oxford English Dictionary*, it means both "care" and "disquietude, uneasiness." But Jacinto is also the Spanish word for hyacinth flower, which calls to mind the myth of Hyacinth and Apollo. Apollo loved Hyacinth, but when a discus Apollo threw was blown off course by the jealous Zephyr, the West Wind, the discus struck Hyacinth on the head and killed him. From his lover's body Apollo created the hyacinth flower, giving his lover immortality of a sort. The figure of Jacinto blends two stories of immortality and transubstantiation, one Christian, the other pre-Christian and homoerotic.

The multiplicity created through the layers of meaning in Jacinto's name continues the layering we have seen in descriptions of the cave: it is a Gothic chamber and a devouring (feminine) mouth. The vibrations in the cave are pastoral, "like a hive of bees," and threatening, "like a heavy roll of distant drums." And although Father Latour is the priest, it is Jacinto who lights the purifying flame and leads the way to the source; Latour's rituals have no meaning below the earth. The cave and Jacinto suggest the difficulty of deciphering what exactly is "Old World": the Old World of the Americas before the European settlers or the Old World of Europe. These layers implicitly allow Cather to question whether terms such as "New World" and "Old World," "ancient" and "modern" can provide adequate definitions with which to interpret history. We have to move beyond such seemingly dichotomous relations into a mode of interpretation that does not privilege any one set of tropes over any other.

As we move out of the cave, histories appear before us like the striations in the mesas: the river flows "under ribs of antediluvian rock," and from this antediluvian space we move up and out, into the "tender morning" outside the cave's mouth. The morning landscape that greets the two men when they emerge from the cave is a "gleaming white world," covered with "virgin snow," a new world, a blank. The virgin snow appears to cancel out the ancient systems of belief: the European's Virgin obliterates the stone lips of Jacinto's cave. The branches outside the cave are "laden with soft, rose-coloured clouds of virgin snow," an almost paradisiacal image: the pearly gates to the New World. The landscape and the description of the morning move us to a consideration of history and the movement from an Old World to a New, a shift that seems at first to be a straightforward linear progression. But the entire mesa, including the cave that supports it, is created from layers of Old World and New; the layers support and enable one another. Cather attempts to move us beyond written language in our apprehension of these layers of meaning: what happens in the cave happens through our raft of associations with the brief words she gives us. The language is the tip; it is not the whole. We comprehend the whole only when we cease to focus on singular, particular images.

Within the cave we begin to understand how the novel's layers complicate easy understandings of religion and history; the landscape outside the cave presents a visual correlation for that lesson. Latour's encounter with Sada, the Mexican slave, rewrites the cave scene in order to stress this visual lesson even as it presents another example of the complicated structures underlying the apparently simple surface of the novel. Their meeting, chronicled in the chapter called "December Night," begins with Father Latour's dark night of the soul and seems to be an overt paean to Catholicism and its salutatory powers. Once we see all the layers of this scene, however, we also see Latour's position as a Paterian observer and notice that what is at work in Latour's church is something much older than Catholicism. What happens between Latour and Sada reinforces the importance of seeing the whole rather than focusing on the particular.

The encounter with Sada stresses sight, highlighting the importance of the visual over the verbal.

The courtyard between Latour's house and the church is covered with snow, an etching in black and silver: "the court was white with snow, and the shadows of walls and buildings stood out sharply in the faint light." This snow is different from the blizzard that obliterated the trail and forced Latour into the stone-lipped cave. Here in his own churchyard Latour is in control, able to observe. Unlike in the cave scene, no voices terrify him. There is almost no sound at all except for Sada's confession and prayers. The whole scene emphasizes the way light plays over surfaces: from the silhouette of the church tower against moonlit clouds and shadows on the snow to Latour's candle shining on Sada's "dark brown peon face" and the "red spark of the sanctuary lamp" in the pitch dark of the church.

Even Sada's prayers express themselves visually. Latour is moved by the belief he *sees* on her face when she tells him it has been 19 years since she has "*seen* the holy things of the altar" (emphasis-mine). Latour had never "*seen* such pure goodness shine out of a human's countenance" (emphasis mine). When Latour lets Sada into the church, to the Lady Chapel, he *sees* "the working of [Sada's] face. . . . the beautiful tremors [that] passed over it [and] tears of ecstasy." All this light and shadow suggests Cather's essay "Light on Adobe Walls," her unfinished fragment about the possibilities of artistic representation. The artist can paint not sunlight but "only the tricks that shadows play with it. . . . some emotion . . . that happens to give him personal delight . . . that makes one nerve in him thrill and tremble" (*On Writing 124*). Both Sada and Latour experience this "thrill," Sada by seeing the Lady Chapel, Latour by seeing Sada's belief.

The visible power of Sada's ecstasy allows Latour to share her emotion: "He was able to feel, kneeling beside her, the preciousness of the things of the altar . . . he received the miracle in her heart into his own, saw through her eyes." Earlier Latour had said miracles "rest upon our perceptions being made finer, so that for a moment our eyes can see and our ears can hear what is there about us always." Ironically, the miracle Latour experiences with Sada involves him seeing "through her eyes" rather than his own. These moments of fine perception, moments that imply a fleeting unity, are described in the conclusion to *The Renaissance*, in which Pater talks about those instants when we are able to distinguish from among a "flood of external objects" and receive a "single sharp impression" (Bloom 59). Latour's "miracle" and Pater's "single sharp impression" are similar, if not identical, moments of perception that produce almost identical results.

Sada becomes the site of a Paterian miracle: what Latour sees in Sada helps him, as Pater says, to "gather up what might otherwise pass unregarded" (Bloom 61). This gathering up of sensation brings Latour to a moment of fullness, of being at one with what is outside himself: "the peace without [the church] seemed all at one with the peace in his soul." This is a marked contrast to Latour's feeling at the beginning of the chapter, when "doubt . . . made him feel an alien. . . . his soul had become a barren field." Even at the moment of fullness, however, there is what Pater calls a "vanishing away" (Bloom 60) in the description of "the line of black footprints [Latour's] departing visitor had left in the wet scurf of the snow." The silvery beauty of the newly fallen snow is now "wet scurf"; the moment of seeming "all at one" vanishes into a line of departing footprints. The Paterian moment is fluid, not static: "those impressions of the individual mind . . . are in perpetual flight" (Bloom 60). Thus this entire scene becomes a kind of passion play about a moment of beauty moving us out of ourselves. We recognize and "fine down" an impression, but at the moment of fining down there is loss. Latour is joined with Sada and feels his inner peace merge with the peace of the external world. But the footsteps vanish, and the next chapter begins with the announcement of the death of Eusabio's son.

Latour comforts Sada by giving her not warm words but a "little silver medal, with a figure of the Virgin"—something to look at. He thinks this a good gift for Sada "for one who cannot read—or think—the Image, the physical form of Love!" He offers her not language but an image, something which her soul can "adore." Sada's ability to gain comfort from an image reveals to Latour the limitations of his intellectual—verbal—faith, "his prayers were empty words and brought him no refreshment." Vision seems more important than language, an idea that may explain the elision over the name Mary: the name is not as important to Sada as is the feeling she gets when she sees the altar in the Lady Chapel.

Latour sees the Lady Chapel only in terms of Catholicism, but Cather creates layers of meaning in this feminized enclosure as well, linking it to the stone-lipped cave in which Latour found such uncomfortable refuge. Cather's description of the spiritual presence in the Lady Chapel links the Virgin Mary with other, earlier goddesses who offer comfort to the wretched: Latour is able to "feel all it meant to [Sada] to know that there was a Kind Woman in Heaven. . . . [o]ld people, who have felt blows and toil and know the world's hard hand, need, even more than children do, a woman's tenderness. Only a Woman, divine, could know all that a woman can suffer." Latour's God is dismissed in lieu of this other divine force that can understand female pain. This is not only a rare expression of female solidarity on Cather's part but also a link between the Mariolatry of the Lady Chapel and the ancient snake-goddess in the cave.

The female divinity within the Lady Chapel finds further expression in the images of the transformative moonlight that bracket the scenes inside the chapel itself. When Latour wakes up in the night and decides to go to the church, he sees the "full moon . . . [that] threw a pale phosphorescent luminousness over the heavens." Afterward, as Sada slips off into the dark, "the full moon shone high in the blue vault, majestic, lonely, benign." The moon, of course, has long been considered a female symbol and suggests again that Latour's religion should be seen in the context of older religions that have not been supplanted as much as they have been subsumed. Marina Warner, in her study of the Virgin Mary, places the Virgin in a context similar to what Cather does here. Warner suggests the possibility of a "chain of descent from Hippolyte [queen of the Amazons] to Diana to the Virgin. . . . that the Amazon queen venerated in Cappodocia was subsumed into the fertility goddess Diana of Ephesus, and that the memories of her emblem . . . survived in the city where the Virgin Mary was proclaimed." Warner also points out that "Diana was associated with the moon . . . and the Virgin Mary is identified with the moon and the stars' influence as well as with the forces of fertility and generation." It seems no accident that the title of the chapter that follows the scene between Latour and Sada is titled "Spring in the Navajo Country." We go from "Woman, divine" to spring: the power of the goddess is still at work.

The moon shining down on Latour as he looks down at Sada's vanishing footprints suggests an older religion, one that Latour would not or could not recognize. The image of the moon and the image on the medal Latour gives Sada are two incarnations of this "Woman, divine": the two virgins—Diana and Mary—watch over the priest and the suffering woman. These female divinities connect the ancient goddess with the Catholic icon with the stone-lipped cave's snake: the chapel becomes an extension of the cave. Just as Mary and her chapel support the church and the cave supports the mountains—recesses that strengthen—so too the "space" or gap in the text where the word Mary might appear supports the presence of Diana or any "Woman, divine."

The final paragraph of this section shifts from Latour alone, locking "his church," to the moon alone in the arched "blue vault" of the heavens and then back to Latour, looking at Sada's footsteps in the snow. Latour has his church, the moon has hers (the blue vault of the heavens), although what Latour may briefly sense but does not understand is that the Lady Chapel, the moon, and the cave are all connected. The rapid shifts in focus—from church to moon to Latour—are another manifestation of the novel's layers, again creating a deeper structure than at first seems apparent. As with the notes of the Angelus bell, this scene is not complete until the final note, sounded by the presence of the moon, has been heard or seen.

Cather's layering process moves us out of a dichotomized "either/or" reading of the novel into a way of reading based on "both/and." Thus Jacinto embodies both Christian and pre-Christian identities as well as that of the Romantic poet, Sada worships at the altar of an ancient goddess who is also the Virgin Mary, and Latour's cathedral is an edifice built from, and out of, a variety of traditions. The cathedral is "worthy of a setting naturally beautiful" and it will be built in the style of the Midi Romanesque, which Latour says is "the right style for this country." After it is finished, the cathedral seems to be one with the southwestern landscape; it is both southwestern and French, organic and constructed: "the tawny church seemed to start directly out of those rose-coloured hills. . . . the towers rose clear into the blue air while the body of the church still lay against the mountain." The description of the church on the mountain is similar to Jacinto's position clinging to the wall of the cave—both church and man unify seeming opposites. Pater seems to have presciently described Latour's church in "Winckelmann," when he explains that "Christian art was still dependent of pagan examples, building the shafts of pagan temples into its churches" (Bloom 213). Although Latour may not have actually used the *shafts* of pagan temples, his church is supported by the cave wherein Jacinto's goddess-snake is enclosed.

Latour's cathedral becomes not a colonizer's monument but an example of what can happen when, as Pater described in his essay on Coleridge, "a mind concentrates itself, frees itself from the limitations of the particular, the individual, [and] attains a strange power of modifying and centralising what it receives from without, according to the pattern of an inward ideal" (Bloom 150). Latour's idea about what "his" cathedral should look like moves free from the particularities of convention and allows him to build a church that reminds him of

something "nearer Clermont" in the Santa Fe hills that he describes as the color of "the dried blood of saints and martyrs preserved in old churches in Rome." His inward ideals about the sacred and the beautiful guide him in designing his monument. Pater's idea seems an apt description, not just of what the cathedral represents within the text of the novel itself but of what the novel itself represents in terms of Cather's aesthetic project and as we will see, of what happens in Latour's mind before his death. The "particular" would seem to force a choice in interpretive modes but the "inward ideal" can be adapted to suggest a way of reading that allows multiples, takes us beyond the words on the page.

Before Latour dies, his caretakers think that "his mind was failing," but Latour does not care about their opinion. They do not realize that his mind "was only extraordinarily active in some other part of the great picture of his life." Latour ranges through time and space, drawing on all episodes of his life without highlighting any one in particular:

> He observed also that there was no longer any perspective to his memories. He remembered his winters with his cousins on the Mediterranean when he was a little boy, his student days in the Holy City, as clearly as he remembered the arrival of M. Molny and the building of his cathedral. He was soon to have done with calendared time, and it had already ceased to count for him. He sat in the middle of his own consciousness; none of his former states of mind were lost or outgrown. They were all within reach of his hand, and all comprehensible.

None of Latour's history is lost to him: it is all there, all comprehensible. He has "modified" and "centralized" his past; it becomes what one reader called "the tower of consciousness." Of course, Latour's very name indicates his position: he is in *la tour*, the tower. Latour's far-ranging memories and associations echo the pattern of associations set in motion by the silver bell ringing the Angelus much earlier in the novel. In both instances he moves free from the particular—there is "no perspective"—yet each memory is a specific moment and the moments form a flow. It is this perspective—in which there is no perspective, in which everything, Old World and New, Catholic and pagan, youth and age, is layered together—that the novel pushes us to maintain while we read. We are asked to read with a perspective that, like Latour's, loses nothing, comprehends everything.

Source: Deborah Lindsay Williams, "Losing Nothing, Comprehending Everything: Learning to Read Both the Old World and the New in *Death Comes for the Archbishop*," in *Cather Studies*, Vol. 4, No. 1, 1999, pp. 80–96.

Nicholas Birns

In the following essay, Birns explores how Cather's choice of setting and character in Death Comes for the Archbishop *countered a "restrictively nationalistic American identity" popular in the early twentieth century.*

From the day of its publication, *Death Comes for the Archbishop* has been one of Willa Cather's most popular novels. Critics, though, have chafed against the book's historical setting and its interpretation of American culture. Many readers, especially among Cather's original audience, were completely unfamiliar with the donnée of the novel, which concerns the career of the Roman Catholic Archbishop Lamy of Santa Fe in the mid-nineteenth century.

This was not a matter of mere ignorance, but a result of the fact that the conventional fable of American origins and identity was of a sort to exclude Archbishop Lamy and anything associated with him. In the 1920's, the essence of "American identity" was white and Protestant, as much or even more so than it had ever been (see Berman). The promotion of this essentialist identity was not just a product of the Ku Klux Klan (which flourished in this era) or of other nativist and extremist sentiments. It exercised a firm hold over more educated precincts, even among those sectors that would have seen themselves as "progressive." For these, the Protestantism of America was essential to its democracy, and its democracy essential to a secular modernity that would not be enslaved by myth and superstition. In a context in which the only viable tradition was a secular and evolutionist one, Cather's novel serves to disrupt these assumptions. Archbishop Lamy's presence on American soil was a rebuke to ideologies of progressive modernity. But Cather is several steps ahead of any would-be interpreters on this issue. For Cather, Archbishop Lamy, a French cleric ministering to a largely Hispanic flock (and the representative of a Roman Catholicism deemed inherently retrograde by an American identity premised upon Protestantism and progress), is not an aberration upon American soil. He is as pivotal an element of Cather's construction of America as had been the more thematically assimilable scenes of agrarian life on the Great Plains (see Peck). By focusing attention on this French prelate and his Hispanic parishioners, Cather goes behind the rhetorics of progress and modernization to dislodge the ethnocentric platitudes of American self-assertion.

Strangely, it is Cather's interest in strains of American identity other than the dominant Anglo-Saxon one that has caused the greatest disturbance among critics who claim an ideological opposition to what they term her "conservatism." The numerous ideologically inspired attacks on Cather from such Marxist-affiliated or influenced critics as Granville Hicks, Edmund Wilson, and Lionel Trilling severely diminished her critical reputation in the 1930's, just as her popularity among the general public was reaching its peak. These attacks were all based on what these critics termed her neglect of contemporary social realities, her retreat into a nostalgic past that forswore the complexity of modern life. It is no surprise that these readings flourished in the 1930's, when any literature not overtly concerned with explicitly proletarian issues or at least with a socially referential milieu that could be adduced as "relevant" was vulnerable to attack. Even after some of these critics had shed their self-styled radicalism, the ideological habits remained ("relevance" being resurrected as an Arnoldian ideal of cultural order). Thus so too did their hostility to Cather, whose works are too complicated to serve the ideological purposes of the Left, in either its radical or opportunistic modes (see Skaggs).

Yet the misreadings of Wilson, Trilling, and Hicks, all less than major critics (though the first two remain tremendously overrated), cannot be simply attributed to this kind of bias. Sharon O'Brien has written an important article which devastatingly details the mean-spiritedness and bigotry behind Cather's critical demotion in the 1930's. O'Brien suggests that the denunciations of Cather proceeded not only from the lack of radicalism and the love of the past of which the critics accused her, but in addition, from the critics' fundamental misogyny. As O'Brien puts it, "a subtext in the attacks on Cather suggests that gender may have been the dominant, if unacknowledged, variable in shaping the case against Willa Cather" (O'Brien "Becoming Noncanonical." 116). O'Brien, in her survey of Cather's de-canonization, brings to bear overwhelming evidence, most crucially regarding the association of Cather's womanhood with her interest in the past, the latter of which was constantly styled "soft" and "minor" by such shapers of mid-century middlebrow taste as Maxwell Geismar and Alfred Kazin (O'Brien, "Becoming Noncanonical" 117). O'Brien's diagnosis of misogyny on the part of all the above-mentioned critics is an accusation one is certainly ready to accept, because these critics' ideas of radicalism seldom extended beyond the white male identity. Just as Cather's identity as a woman, and probably also her lesbianism, enabled her to appreciate the position of ethnic minorities, so too was the mainstream critical denunciation of the works closely tied with the cultural preconceptions of her critics. (The popular reaction, more enthusiastic, was presumably less ideologically blinkered). Even as radical social change was demanded, Protestantism and progress remained at the core of these critics's views of American history.

But their misogyny may be a symptom as well as a cause, a symptom of the desire of these critics and the normative institutions they represented to spurn the socio-cultural diversity and historiographical complexity of Cather's texts. To reduce the conflict to its most crude common denominator, all of the above critics were Arnoldians tacitly, or, in Trilling's case, explicitly. They were concerned with a literature at once timeless and relevant to the here-and-now, and unconsciously based on a white, male Protestant consensus. Cather was interested less in the historical object in itself than in the modes of perception it accommodated, and thus inevitably constructed the relationship between the past and present in a mode at once more plural and more personal.

For Cather to write about a transparent American present with a monolithic identity would be at once to diminish both personal idiosyncrasy and cultural tolerance, both traits highly valued by Cather. Cather adamantly refused the canonical idea of America prevalent in her time, a view as enthusiastically accepted by leftist, or formerly leftist, polemicists like Wilson and Trilling as by right-wing nativists. This idea asserted a fundamental national difference between America and Europe, a difference undergirded by a notion of America that was almost exclusively Anglo-Saxon. The American left tended to develop an *echt* American straw man that, because it could be decisively differentiated from an equally univocal idea of the European, could then be tacitly deployed in invidious contrast with it. This literary nationalism was based on a cultural relativism—that each nation had its own distinctive identity—which in many ways is more dangerous than racial absolutism, because it is not subject of any sort of verification. As Walter Benn Michaels points out with respect to American ideas of culture in this era, "the extraordinary power of culture as a concept . . . is manufactured out of an insistence upon the discrepancy between social and biological criteria of identity but it is . . . hostile to any attempt to require a choice between the two sets of criteria" (see Michaels 220–41). This belief in an American culture independent of but not contradicting an inclination

> " Yet *Death Comes for the Archbishop* is not only conscious of what it opposes (the American secular-nationalist paradigm) but of what it might at first seem to advocate (a Catholic neo-traditionalism)."

towards Anglo-Saxon racialism was often linked, in the 1920's and 1930's, to what Eric Goldman terms "Reform Darwinism." Goldman describes this school of thought, which informed most American reform movements during the first half of the century, as seeking to "dissolve away conservatism's steel chain of ideas while leaving Darwinism itself intact . . ." What can be heard behind the ostensibly radical rhetoric of Cather's 1930's critics is a coalescence of cultural nationalism and Reform Darwinism, a belief in the unity of American identity. This national unity was posited as inexorably, though not mechanically, advancing towards a transparent revolutionary present that would provide the intuitive capstone to an equally transparent American national essence. Cather's awareness of how no historical moment is ever authoritatively disentangled from the past, a past which in itself can never be assigned a stable identity, threatened the viability of the critics' desired revolutionary present.

Thus Cather's setting in *Death Comes for the Archbishop* is not a product of accident or nostalgic whim. The setting is so structured as to dispute this assertion of a politically "progressive" but nonetheless restrictively nationalist American identity. Cather does not at all quarrel with the American annexation of the Southwest after the Mexican War, as is shown by the statement that it was annexed "to," rather than "by," the United States, the former preposition signifying a more natural accession, not an opportune land-grab. Cather thinks that New Mexico should have been part of the United States, and the New Mexicans become "good Americans"; indeed, she values New Mexico's Hispanic Catholic history for precisely this reason. In wanting to reinvigorate "the faith of their fathers" Bishop Ferrand sees New Mexican Catholicism as a check to the monolithic tendencies of "a progressive government," and the revival of this Catholicism as a check on a self-confident, secular modernity.

By setting the novel in nineteenth-century New Mexico, Cather does not so much attempt to contravene the modern world as to oppose the evolutionist historicism proffered by the ideologues of modernity. This evolutionist tendency was premised upon an affirmative belief in the benefits of American expansionism, justified by its achievement of social progress and secular enlightenment, its advance beyond such European traditions as Christianity. A novel that would adhere to this evolutionist ideal would have focused not on Latour but on Kit Carson, the more classic pioneer figure who is pictured affirmatively in Cather's novel, but deliberately marginalized with regard to the central characters and, in terms of his persecution of the Navajo, termed "misguided." This novel favors the priests' aesthetic and religious values over the expansionist ones epitomized in Carson and applauded by Cather's Darwinist critics, who are interested, unlike Cather, in a historical narrative with clear winners and losers. By showing an interest in religion, Cather is bound to antagonize a Darwinist historical relativism anxious to banish past absolutisms in order to establish its own present absolutisms. Cather is neither nostalgic nor conservative, because she does not attempt to flee back into the settings she describes. Instead, Cather's novel displays the multiplicity and fortitude of Christian imagination, and, in addition, show how religious artefacts such as Latour's cathedral exist as aesthetic objects without at all surrendering their spirituality.

Yet *Death Comes for the Archbishop* is not only conscious of what it opposes (the American secular-nationalist paradigm) but of what it might at first seem to advocate (a Catholic neo-traditionalism). A respectful, if not totally reverential, fictional biography of a Roman Catholic archbishop is bound to arouse, among some readers, suspicions of a conservative or sectarian tract. But Cather informs the knowledgeable reader otherwise from the first preliminary scene of the novel, in which Jean-Marie Latour, Cather's fictional equivalent of the historical Archbishop Lamy, is first chosen by the Catholic hierarchy to take over the new diocese ("Agathonica") necessitated by the United States's conquest of the present-day American Southwest in the Mexican War. Cardinal de Allande, part of the conclave which chooses the new Bishop (and which, importantly, is an informal and casual one, not a rite of studied ceremony) is explicitly dissociated from conservative

tendencies within Roman Catholicism. De Allande is spoken of as "the most influential man at the Vatican" in the reign of the previous Pope, Gregory XVI. The successor of Gregory XVI as Pope was Pius IX, who started out as a liberal reformist but ended up as the founder and prime exemplar of the notion of the Catholic Church as a bulwark against progressive modernity. His most notorious gesture in the latter regard was his proclamation of papal infallibility in 1870, which according to one historian marked "the apparent extinction of the liberal Catholics" (Johnson 394). Cardinal de Allande, a favorite with the previous Pope but marginalized in the new pontificate, is marked off from both the liberal reform with which Pius began his reign and the ideological ultra-orthodoxy with which he concluded it.

The Cardinal is neither a Reform Darwinist, yearning to adapt old institutions to the imperatives of modern European progress, nor a traditionalist, retreating desperately to religious orthodoxy in order to roll back this progress. De Allande also possesses traits which make him in miniature an index of Cather's posture towards Christianity that will be observed in larger measure in her portraits of Archbishop Latour and his colleague, Father Vaillant. The Cardinal is passionately fond of tennis, and is half-English. His religion thus does not exclude enjoyable leisure, nor is it an expression of a strictly defined ethnicity, as anti-Catholic stereotyping has led us to expect (e.g., in the form of proverbial "Spanish cardinals" who stand as perennial enemies of the Reform Darwinist staples of Protestantism and progress) (Bridgers 93). The fact that it is instead Father De Allande who is most influential in the choice of Latour illustrates the direction in which Cather will take her vision of Christianity in the novel.

The way in which de Allande is between nationalities is also indicative of the novel's representation of ethnic groups. Recently, *Death Comes for the Archbishop* has been attacked because it places allegedly insufficient emphasis on the Hispanic inhabitants of New Mexico, preferring to see them through the prism of the French Latour instead of the native-born New Mexican Father Martínez (see Mares). Cather, in this view, both ignores the fact that Roman Catholicism had been practiced in New Mexico since the first Spanish settlement there in 1610 (ten years before the Pilgrims settled in Plymouth—a handy note to rebuke Anglo complacency), and tends to reprimand this historical form of Catholicism for lapsing into popular superstition (as symbolized by the avarice of Father Lucero and the lust of Father Martínez).

This Hispanic superstition is, in the critics' redaction of Cather's intention, then clarified and made acceptably rigorous only by the firm French hands of Fathers Latour and Vaillant. These criticisms are true enough in that Cather knew less about Hispanic New Mexicans than she did, generally, about French people, and that in general she had more sympathy, as well as understanding, for the latter. One certainly would not want to take *Death Comes for the Archbishop* as a plausible historical account of Father Lamy's New Mexico. But this is not only for the reason that all historical accounts are in a way fictive fashionings. In this regard, Paul Horgan's biography of the real-life Lamy (inspired, in fact, by Cather's book), as well as Father W. J. Howlett's biography of Father Machebeuf, the real-life equivalent of Father Vaillant (Cather's main source for this novel), and Lynn Bridgers's 1997 biography of Machebeuf are as fictional as the openly fictional text which intervenes between them. The salient feature of the novel is not that it is providing a fictive historiographical account: every novel does this, and in the wake of the legion of academic applications of Hayden White's *Metahistory* this has become a rather jejune point. What is important about Cather's work is not that it is *a priori* fictive, and thus can deal with historical givens with a global *carte blanche*, but that it is fictive in a manner that shows that, although it does not palliate this inadequacy, Cather's shaping of her narrative demonstrates that she is aware of the inadequacy of her own position towards the Hispanic New Mexicans.

Cather's stance was very different from that of the nineteenth-century historian William Hickling Prescott, whose history of the Spanish conquest of Mexico was popular and required reading for American intellectuals into Cather's own lifetime. As Jenny Franchot points out, Prescott's viewpoint was laden with anti-Catholic and anti-Spanish prejudice, which was always at the base even of the many complex and multi-layered aspects of his work:

> The degenerative character of the Aztec is due finally, then, to the indigenous Catholicism that constitutes the interior of that character. Positing a superstitious interior to be investigated by an enlightened Protestant outsider, the Catholic-Protestant opposition shaped not only Prescott's vision of both America's western and southern population but also more general views of perception and interpretation. Nourished by "nature," the enlightened mind is spontaneously able to perceive intended meanings. The superstitious mind, by contrast, is imprisoned within a Poesque interior, baffled by its own distorted perceptions and unable to exert sufficient interpretive control. (Franchot 44)

Cather's position on the matter is far more self-aware. Again, the brief appearance of Cardinal de Allande at the beginning of the novel can serve as a representative anecdote. In talking to a cleric who has actually been to the United States, de Allande is corrected for asserting that the "Indians" of the Southwest live in wigwams. The Cardinal responds, "No matter, Father. I see your redskins through Fenimore Cooper, and I like them so." Da Allende's "Indians" are seen through the distorting prism of Fenimore Cooper's highly debatable representation of them, rather than "in themselves." And Cather, like de Allande, is perfectly willing to concede her bias, but she is unwilling to renounce it. This is partially because it is all the information she has. Cather is not asking the reader to block out the historical inadequacies of her account and revel in their fictive nature; she is allowing an openness in her narrative that suggests that what is excluded can be, in a flexible way, included in the reader's construction of her text, even if that inclusion lays bare the bias inherent in her narrative posture.

Thus, there are ironies in the criticism of Cather for focusing on the French rather than the Spanish role in the conversion of New Mexico, for privileging the European lacing over indigenous primacy. These ironies reveal that Cather's approach may have been sounder than any attempt on her part for a cathartic breakthrough into the "Hispanic reality" of New Mexico. Cather was a visitor to New Mexico, not a native or even a long-term resident. She had nothing near the in-depth knowledge of its history and terrain that is seen either in her depictions of Nebraska in her many novels set in her home state or in her last novel, *Sapphira and the Slave Girl*, with respect to the Virginia of her birth. To expect Cather to write of the New Mexican land and people with the depth and learning of a Mary Austin is unrealistic. Without such a familiarity with New Mexico, any attempt by Cather to write a novel purportedly from a Hispanic point of view would have been doomed to failure. This is all the more true considering the climate in the 1920's, which was near the height of Modernism's romantic appropriation of the so-called primitive and authentic, often represented by non-Northern European peoples, as recently anatomized by Marianna Torgovnick and other critics. Any novel written by a white person about Hispanic New Mexicans would have been bound to be touched by this primitivism, with its condescending portrayal of nonwhites as creatures of liberated instinct and unsullied innocence. This is not to say that any novel written by Cather would have been afflicted with the pretense, prolixity, and racism of D. H. Lawrence's disastrous book *The Plumed Serpent*. But a more Hispanic-centered attempt would at best have portrayed Hispanics as admirable though doomed to succumb to the Anglo tide, and at worst been infected with Lawrentian strains of racism that would now be seen as far more offensive than Cather's own somewhat limited and critical depiction of Hispanics in the novel (see Torgovnick).

Cather's "gestures of cultural reciprocity" (Lee, *Willa Cather* 284) do not explore the history of Hispanics in the United States with anything like the personal knowledge or the creative agility of later writers such as Sandra Cisneros or Rolando Hinojosa. But the novels of Hinojosa, in particular, can assist in rebutting the supposition that the proper way to treat Hispanic subject matter is through an appeal to a monolithic ethnic identity. Hinojosa, by going out of his way to supply names for his imaginary terrain such as "Klail" and "Belken," names that sound, in a Spanish-speaking context, jaggedly and exotically Anglo-Saxon, deploys the same aesthetic of cultural disruption that Cather does in her work, and shows his interest, very like Cather's, in cultural border-crossing. Unlike Lawrence, with his posturings towards vatic truth and cultural breakthrough, Cather, by admitting her own inadequacies, provides, along with Mary Austin, a precedent for writers like Hinojosa. The culturally disruptive "French" approach highlights Cather's own distance from the scene, and represents her own position as outsider and stranger. Cather's relation to New Mexico is no more intimate than Father Latour's is at the beginning of the novel. Like the Archbishop, Cather's attitude never becomes fully integrated into the landscape. A larger instance of this perspective is the French identity of Latour and Vaillant. (This was, strictly speaking, not Cather's choice in that the real-life Archbishop was also French, but presumably it was her choice to choose him as a model for a character.) Robert J. Nelson finds Cather's life-long interest in France to be one of the major sources and preoccupations of her fiction. Nelson posits a "Catherian troping towards France as a prime instance" of her search for origins (Nelson 17). As Nelson recognizes, though, the turning towards France can block access to this origin as much as it yearns towards a reunion with it. This is part of the function of the Frenchness of Latour and Vaillant in *Death Comes for the Archbishop.* Cather avoids an ethnocentric Americanism just as she avoids a fetishization of the Hispanic authentic. Instead of being either American or Hispanic, Cather's posture in this novel is "French." This posture, in a novel not

about France, is inherently fictive. The French element in the text keeps the novel's subject matter off-balance, prevents it from subsiding into either a mainstream pioneer saga or a dithyramb to the indigenous primitive. The French elements in the New Mexican landscape prevent the setting from being totally indigenous; it is permeable to external influences. In a way, the Archbishop's relationship with the landscape is so intimate that he almost needs the distance between his own native landscape, the mountains of Auvergne, and the far different mesas and adobes of New Mexico. Cather's smaller but similar distance as a Nebraskan born in Virginia (landscapes as different from New Mexico in topographical terms as is any place in France) provide a parallel between her and Latour, who can with little distortion be called her authorial surrogate. Because Cather is not herself French, nor is writing in obvious relation to a French agenda, the French elements in Cather's landscape function as an emblem of the sacred, a weave in the fabric of the world that prevents it from ever collapsing into settled definition.

In addition, France, in geographical, linguistic, and historical terms, is the means of access to Greece and Rome on the part of the English. France is that which, both in space and in time, stands between England and the European past from which it aspires to draw its cultural origins. This mediation is characteristic of Cather's own treatment of French themes. It also typifies her treatment of Christianity, so much of which is seen through its particularly French manifestations. The idea of the "French" serves Cather as a metaphor for her celebration of Christianity, the way in which the manifestation of Christianity in space and in time means that it is always in the middle of everything, never merely a source of "original" authority. Cather's Christianity is not anti-modern and does not conform to the stereotype of Christianity as anti-modern held by Left and Right alike. It is part of modernity, and indeed it underscores the way that the Christian message, with its departure from the given and the normative, has always been laden with modernity.

Cather's ecclesiastical position was probably not far from that described by Hugh Trevor-Roper (created Lord Dacre of Glanton in 1979) as "neither Papist nor Protestant, but Gallican" (Trevor Roper 100). Trevor-Roper's phrase is apt in implying how Cather was interested in mediation between different ethnic and confessional modes of Christianity, but not in consensus. Cather, as Hermione Lee says, imagines an America where "bridges between pluralisms are only half-crossed;

distinguishing factors between cultures are celebrated . . ." (Lee, "Cather's Bridge" 39). She achieves reconciliation between different groups and temperaments without congealing them all into an artificial consensus.

Cather's French or "Gallican" Christianity would have been even more graphically displayed in the novel Cather was completing at the time of her death and which was almost entirely destroyed on Cather's instructions. This novel, entitled *Hard Punishments*, was to have been set in the city of Avignon during the time when the Popes were resident there. This period of the early fourteenth century was the result of the French monarchy's attempt to gain an undisputed hegemony over the Papacy; it was an attempt to make Catholicism less the heir of an ecumenical Roman empire, a post-imperial *ecclesia*, and more a specifically national French institution. Even though Cather, after 1922, was a professed member of the Episcopal Church, the geographical heart of Cather's Christianity was in Avignon, not in Rome or England. But in Cather's time there had not been a Pope in Avignon for over five centuries. The entire episode was a historical footnote, not the dawn of the kind of ongoing, socially powerful institution of the sort so admired by twentieth-century intellectuals. Even more to the point, Cather was not French, did not live in France, and had no significant French ancestry. Her promotion of a uniquely French Christianity was a far more gratuitous matter than was the case for a Charles Péguy or a Charles Maurras. Being a "Gallican" Christian was, for Cather, a way of possessing an *anima naturaliter christiana*, her to celebrate the joy of Christian affirmation while at the same time undermining the deployment of Christianity as an agent of cultural domination that would use its identity as a worldly authority in the interests of a conservative establishment. In the strict historical sense, Gallicanism originated with the desire of the French kings to exercise "power of government equally over clergy and laity" (Morris 240) and to use their power to eclipse the spiritual/temporal power of the Pope. But in Cather's vision "Gallicanism" was more mediatory in function, more of an analogue to "Anglicanism," in the sense that Anglicanism is both Catholic and Protestant, liturgical and evangelical (see Collinson 242, also Evans and Wright). Trevor-Roper speaks of Anglicanism as "humane and civilized . . . free from the intolerance of Geneva or of Rome" (Trevor Roper 53). Cather's Gallican twist of Anglicanism adds an appealing note of foreignness while wrestling free from any upper-class, Anglophile associations and

thus of any idea of cultural domination or authority. Cather's hearkening to the French image of Christianity suggests that any unambiguous affirmations of faith must not subside into a consolidated human authority, political or ecclesiastical. By resorting to a non-obvious French incarnation of Christian worship with no remote claims to authority in the America of either the time of the novel's setting or that of its composition, Cather is removing her Christian vision from polemical disputes, and concentrating on spiritual beauties far too delicate to be fully "realized" in the world.

This focus on imaginative truth liberates Cather's novel from the routine constraints of plot and narrative. *Death Comes for the Archbishop* seems more like a saint's life or a series of scenes from a stained-glass window than a full-fledged, mimetic narrative (Woodress 402–07). In *Death Comes for the Archbishop* dramatic tensions contingent on simple moral oppositions are replaced by structural tensions. These tensions display how a difference in rhetorical posture may be as fictively interesting as tensions between affective values, which the novel, with its basically undiluted admiration for the Archbishop, tends to lack. The foremost of these structural tensions lies in the opposition-within-similarity between Archbishop Latour and his chief assistant, Father Vaillant. Latour and Vaillant are priestly colleagues and close friends. But Latour and Vaillant exemplify an opposition that E. R. Curtius has diagnosed as the topos of *sapientia* and *fortitudo*, in which two people embodying the collateral but utterly disparate virtues of wisdom and strength are seen in close apposition (Curtius 178).

The classic example is in the *Chanson de Roland*, in which the brave Roland is accompanied by his friend, the wise Oliver. Cather takes the (not unusual) step of making her *sapientia* figure (Latour) the more important one of the pair, even as she preserves impeccably the basic features of this opposition. Latour is the figure of power as such, and Vaillant the adjutant who is responsible for the actual exercise of that power. He is the Prime Minister to Latour's sovereign, the Chief of Staff to his President. Latour is stolid, serene, almost immobile, signifying the majesty of *de jure* and diocesan centrality. This is signified by the name of "Latour," with not only its obvious source in Walter Pater's uncompleted novel *Gaston de Latour* (much admired by Cather) but its overall symbolist connotations of an aesthetic posture of supremacy and grandeur so proud as to almost prompt immobility. "Vaillant" on the other hand, indicates, if not "valiant," at last an active process of "willing." Cather deploys the *sapientia-fortitudo* topos by having Latour, the representative of formal authority, be more of an aesthete, and having the practical Vaillant not just be more of a man of affairs but possess a more thoroughly grounded sense of vocation in the world. "During their Seminary years," Latour reflects at one point, "he had easily surpassed his friend in scholarship, but he always realized that Joseph excelled him in the fervor of his faith." Despite their substrate of priestly kinship, it is Vaillant's differences from his friend that fascinate Latour. This is seen at the end of Book I of the novel, in a renowned passage that shows the workings of the Latour-Vaillant relationship as well as of Latour's imaginative vision:

> Father Vaillant began restlessly pacing up and down as he spoke, and the Bishop watched him, musing. It was just this in his friend that was dear to him. "Where there is great love there is always miracles," he said at length. "One might almost say that an apparition is human vision corrected by divine love. I do not see you as you really are, Joseph; I see you through my affection for you. The Miracles of the Church seem to me to rest not so much upon faces or voices or healing power coming suddenly near to us from afar off, but upon our perceptions being made finer, so that for a moment or eyes can see and our ears can hear what is about us always.

Latour and Vaillant are Catholic structural complements, not the kind of ethical opposites that readers usually expect in a culturally Protestant novel, especially one set in the American West. The tension between protagonist and antagonist that animates most narratives is here replaced by a more unusual and subtle tension between two characters who are friends. The lack of dramatic tension between them, though, does not mean that all is smoothly harmonious. One interesting source of tension between them is that Vaillant's knightly activity not only renders him modally variant from Latour, it also makes him emotionally opaque to his colleague. Latour and Vaillant are removed from the interior of each other's emotions, but the differences between the two men's spiritual vocations and psychological make-up is also what binds them together. Further, all these differences actually heighten Latour's affection for his major lieutenant. As opposites, they at once exclude, attract, and, finally, complete each other. One particularly salient difference between them is that Latour's connection with the New Mexico landscape is less grounded than that of Vaillant, a reflection of the ambivalent relationship this spiritual man has with the material world. His dominating presence continually tries to impose its stamp on the material world around him, but he can only fully achieve this by building his cathedral, which is also his tomb. The symbol of his aesthetic triumph is also the symbol of his resignation from his earthly life.

Latour, the artist-figure, is a celebrant of creativity, a creativity not confined to the aesthetic mastery of Christian rite. An apostolic and liturgical Christian, Latour plays the two roles of archbishop and aesthete in a way that makes them one. It is a true aesthesis, a sheer aesthesis, a response of delight rather than of connoisseurship.

> Something soft and wild and free, something that whispered to the ear on the pillow, lightened the heart, softly, softly picked the lock, slid the bolts, and released the poisoned spirit of man into the wind, into the blue and gold, into the morning, into the morning!

Latour is here drawing us into the emotional core of Cather's Christianity. Cather's vision of the Archbishop's "Frenchness" once again comes into play, as the Archbishop's imaginative spirit dances between and beyond any constraining absolutes, ranging beyond the conventional ideas of what a man like him "must" be in the eyes of uncomprehending observers. His French identity acts as a spiritual free space that countervails the unquestioning trust, so prevalent in America at the time, in Protestantism and progress as leading to a self-sufficient secularism. Latour's sense of the miracle comes from an aesthetic heightening so implicated in its own beauty that it can never be distilled into a doctrinal truth, even as it participates in a vision of the world that Cather would see as inherently religious (see Winters 76).

As mentioned before, Cather became an Episcopalian (Anglican) in 1922. She had been exposed to Christianity as a child, largely, as *My Ántonia* and *Sapphira and The Slave Girl* make clear, of a low-church Protestant variety. Despite this, much of her later fiction was taken up with specifically Catholic settings, indeed so much so that as Hermione Lee states, this orientation "understandably led many readers to suppose she was a practitioner" (Lee 285). Cather, though, was not a practitioner of Catholicism, although she certainly found Catholic settings and characters far more appealing in literary terms than she did Episcopal ones! It is interesting to surmise that her interest in Catholicism was largely associated with places she had travelled. She wrote little about the Catholics of New York, for example. Patrick Allitt describes a parallel instance of a Jewish convert to Catholicism in the 1950's who went to live among "Hispanic Americans, whom he saw as exotic, instead of among the irksomely familiar Catholics of New York" (Allitt 320). So there is an element of exoticism here, as there is in Cather's evocation of New Mexico itself. As Franchot points out, Catholicism in the nineteenth century was fetishized as an "other" by antebellum Protestant discourse, a projection which continued through the later nineteenth century into the twentieth. As with New Mexico, Cather never fully understood Catholicism from the inside. When compared to twentieth-century Catholic convert writers such as Evelyn Waugh or Graham Greene, Cather remained an outsider to Catholicism; she was an admirer, but not an admirer from within. Conversion is not a theme in Cather's novel, as her two protagonists, as Auvergnats born in the early nineteenth century, were cradle Catholics, and their apostolic mission is not so much to convert as to reanimate their flock. Cather's spiritual journey, unlike, for instance, John Henry Newman's as chronicled in *Apologia Pro Vita Sua*, did not have a dramatic moment of conversion at its core.

This differentiates *Death Comes for the Archbishop* from much twentieth-century literature concerned with Catholic religiosity. Patrick Allitt, in his recent book on British and American Catholic convert writers of the past two centuries, contends that, for the most part, twentieth-century Catholic converts tended to be anguished, as with Greene, or countercultural in a right-wing sense, in the case of G. K. Chesterton and others. "The convert who is more punctilious in his new faith than the life-long communicant is a familiar figure in Catholic lore" (Allitt 9). Nineteenth-century converts such as Newman, Orestes Brownson, and Isaac Hecker, were, according to Allitt, more optimistic and transcendental in their faith. If Cather had to belong to either category, it would be the latter, although her insistence on seeing landscape as and for itself would preclude any full-fledged typological transcendentalism in the manner of Emerson. But Cather did not, to quote Allitt's subtitle, "turn to Rome"; indeed, she did not really turn to anywhere so specific. Neither New Mexico (or Québec, her setting for her later novel *Shadows on the Rock*) were places she lived for any extended period of time, and her adult in New York City was far from either where she was born or where she grew up. Even her beloved France, as Nelson is at pains to point out, is essentially a France of the mind. Even her accession to Anglicanism was much more of the *anima naturaliter christiana* variety. It certainly lacked the thunder of T. S. Eliot's slightly later conversion to Anglicanism, or at least his poetic account of it in "Ash Wednesday."

Cather, a High Anglican in her concern with liturgy and ceremony, is perhaps not quite so high as Eliot; Cather's faith has a less "churchy," more open-air atmosphere about it, as befits an author so concerned with the American West. Finally, it must be admitted, that for all her many strengths, Cather was not a theologian or a historian. She started out as a journalist for *McClure's Magazine*, and spent the latter half of her life as a practicing novelist. As limned by her biographers James Woodress and Hermione Lee, most of Cather's friends were musicians, artists, or writers, the latter as likely to be journalists as novelists. Cather could never have written a straight, non-fictional account of a historical religious figure, as Evelyn Waugh did in his book on Edmund Campion. Cather was interested in theology and history, and deployed them meaningfully and intelligently in her work, but finally as part of an aesthetic pattern. This is suggested by the manner in which Latour, at the end of his life, finds his mind has amalgamated various historical stages, if not necessarily entirely risen above them. "He sat in the middle of his own consciousness; none of his former states of mind were lost or outgrown. They were all within the reach of his hand, and all comprehensible."

This statement immediately precedes Latour's final meeting with his old Indian comrade, Eusabio the Navajo. This encounter may signify a reconciliation not only with the native population and with the New Mexican landscape (Eusabio had earlier been described as "the landscape made human") but, on a more abstract level, with death itself. But Latour's delight in beauty is not confined to his personal relations. It molds the entire shape of his public career as well. In the moving conclusion of the novel, the final book which gives its title to the work as a whole, Latour's construction of a cathedral for his flock is both an act of vanity and one of sacrifice. "But the Cathedral is not for us, Father Joseph," the Archbishop points out. "We build for the future—better not lay a stone unless we can do that." This building for the future is a concession, a recognition of the inevitability of his own death. There is something incongruous in titling a novel after the death of its protagonist when the text assumes an affirmative, almost hero-worshipping view of this protagonist, and is far more concerned with his life rather than his death. Yet the novel's titular emphasis on death is not at odds with its substantive emphasis on great deeds and fine perceptions. It is as if only with death can one truly judge a life. Although Latour is buried in his beautiful cathedral, Cather's aesthetic does not identify beauty with its endurance in the world—the archbishop, after all, is dead. Her vision of art accepts the inevitable obsolescence of all beauty in its earthly incarnation with a grace that possesses overtones of the plenary. Art, for Cather, has transcendental bearings. It is not located exclusively in the material world.

Latour, after his death, lies "before the high altar in the church he had built." We might assume that this is a kind of ceremonial entombment, a confirmation in death of the solidity of his achievement in life. But the cathedral is more than an external correlative for the Archbishop's creativity. Latour builds himself outward, into the outer world. His construction of the cathedral is not a hylomorphic imposition of his soul upon the land, a grandiose form that is invariably supreme over matter, an art that can easily subdue nature. It is a slow accumulation of his spirit into the cathedral itself, made of New Mexican stone—but with the presence of Latour, Cather has us understand that he is also introducing European spiritual symbols into an ostensibly alien American landscape. "Every time I come here, I like this stone better," Latour muses to Vaillant. "I could hardly have hoped that God would gratify my personal taste, my vanity, if you will, in this way. I tell you, Blanchet, I would rather have found that hill of yellow rock than have come into a fortune to spend in charity. The cathedral is near my heart, for many reasons. I hope you do not think me very worldly." Through his impulse to construct the cathedral, Latour renounces any personal egotism (inevitable in his diocesan role, whatever his personal sanctity) and resigns his identity into the created artefact. His death is synonymous with his achievement.

Throughout the book, his greatest recognition of beauty has come when Latour has acknowledged its heavenly distance, not its earthly presence. Latour's Christian aestheticism is not subject to temporal circumstances, even if its enunciation is inevitably elegiac. The Archbishop has in no way conquered the land, but he is now forever a part of it, or, more accurately, a part of the perceptions of those who observe it. Latour's culminating achievement is not to be found in a religious paradise on earth. It is to remind us of a tradition of the sacred, one centered in *Death Comes for the Archbishop* around ideas of "France" and "the aesthetic," but a tradition that ultimately has no earthly home. This tradition of the sacred may include but is not necessarily limited to any doctrinal version of Christianity, and is as likely to be found in the work

of the artist as in the conventional precincts of the politician or the cleric. This tradition is always going to be in danger of becoming obscure or of momentarily slipping away. But, as the perseverance of Latour's cathedral signifies, it is never to be eliminated from the landscape.

Source: Nicholas Birns, "Building the Cathedral: Imagination, Christianity, and Progress in Willa Cather's *Death Comes for the Archbishop*," in *Religion and the Arts*, Vol. 3, No. 1, March 1999, pp. 1–19.

Sources

Boulton, Alexander O., "The Padre's House," in *American Heritage*, Vol. 45, No. 1, February/March 1994, pp. 92–99.

Hooper, Brad, Review of *Death Comes for the Archbishop*, in *Booklist*, Vol. 96, No. 15, April 1, 2000, p. 1442.

Van Ghent, Dorothy, "Willa Cather," in *American Writers*, Vol. 1, Charles Scribner's Sons, 1974, pp. 312–34.

Further Reading

Bohlke, L. Brent, ed., *Willa Cather in Person: Interviews, Speeches and Letters*, University of Nebraska Press, 1986.
    Bohlke presents insightful interviews and letters, dating from 1897 to 1940. Collectively, these writings show Cather's growth as an author and a person, while shedding light on her literary views.

Cather, Willa, *Willa Cather on Writing: Critical Studies on Writing as an Art*, University of Nebraska Press, 1988.
    Cather discusses elements of her own writing, and she comments on other works with which her contemporaries were familiar.

Jenkins, Myra Ellen, and Albert H. Schroeder, *A Brief History of New Mexico*, University of New Mexico Press, 1974.
    Jenkins and Schroeder provide a readable overview of the historical events and people of New Mexico. The book includes pictures and maps to complement the text.

Plog, Stephen, *Ancient Peoples of the Southwest*, Thames and Hudson, 1998.
    In an easy-to-understand style, Plog presents the long and challenging history of the Southwest American Indians. He gives special attention to the ways they have adapted over the years to keep their tribes and customs alive.

Walker, Paul Robert, *The Southwest: Gold, God, and Grandeur*, National Geographic, 2001.
    In this book, Walker brings together the many histories (Anglo, Spanish, Mexican, and Native American) of the Southwest. The book is illustrated with photography of the southwestern landscape.

East of Eden

John Steinbeck
1952

East of Eden (1952, New York) by John Steinbeck tells the stories of three generations of the Trask and Hamilton families. It is mostly set in the Salinas Valley in California and spans a period of nearly sixty years, from about 1860 to 1918. The novel focuses on the theme of good against evil and makes prominent use of the biblical story of Cain and Abel, in which Cain murders his brother out of jealousy after God rejects his gift but accepts Abel's. In the novel, Steinbeck ascribes great significance to his translation of the Hebrew word *timshel* ("thou mayest") in the Cain and Abel story. He believes it demonstrates that humans have free will and can triumph over sin if they choose to do so.

Reviewers were quick to point out the flaws in structure and theme in this long novel, and later critics have in general not regarded it as the equal of Steinbeck's finest works. However, the story of the Trask family is a powerful, if melodramatic one, and the Hamilton chapters show Steinbeck's ability to create living characters and set them in motion is undiminished. The selection of *East of Eden* by Oprah Winfrey for her book club (2003) revived reader interest in this serious but entertaining novel that endeavors to lift up the human spirit in the face of everything that would destroy it. As a result of Oprah's selection, this book was reissued in a 2003 edition by Penguin publications.

John Steinbeck

Author Biography

John Ernst Steinbeck was born February 27, 1902, in Salinas, California, the son of John Ernst Steinbeck and Olive Hamilton Steinbeck. Steinbeck graduated from Salinas High School in 1919, and enrolled at Stanford University. He attended classes sporadically but left the university in 1925 without a degree. He moved to New York City to pursue a career as a writer but met with little success. Returning to California, he married Carol Henning in 1930.

Steinbeck supported himself by doing various odd jobs, including caretaker of an estate and fruit-picker. His first novel *Cup of Gold* (1929) went largely unnoticed and did not even recoup the very small advance the publisher gave him. Two subsequent novels *The Pastures of Heaven* (1932) and *To a God Unknown* (1933) fared no better. The first of Steinbeck's novels to attract attention was *Tortilla Flat* (1935), which received the Commonwealth Club of California's General Literature Gold Medal for best novel by a California author. The money Steinbeck made from the film rights to *Tortilla Flat* eased his financial problems. Steinbeck's novels *In Dubious Battle* (1936) and *Of Mice and Men* (1937) followed. The latter was his biggest success up to that point, and the play version of the novel won the New York Drama Critics Circle Award. After

The Long Valley (1938), a collection of short stories, Steinbeck wrote his masterpiece, *The Grapes of Wrath* (1939), a chronicle of the exodus of farm families from the Dust Bowl to California in the 1930s. The novel won the Pulitzer Prize and established Steinbeck's international reputation.

In 1940, Steinbeck traveled to Mexico to make the documentary film, *Forgotten Village*. During World War II he wrote *Bombs Away!* (1942), a propaganda novel, and in 1943 he traveled to Europe as a war correspondent for the *New York Herald Tribune*. He divorced his wife Carol in 1943 and married Gwyndolyn Conger the same year. They had two sons, Thom and John, but the marriage ended in 1948. Steinbeck married for the third time, to Elaine Scott, in 1950.

Steinbeck's next novels were *Cannery Row* (1945), *The Pearl* (1947), and *East of Eden* (1952). *East of Eden* was made into a film starring James Dean in 1954, the same year in which Steinbeck's *Sweet Thursday* was published. The Rodgers and Hammerstein musical *Pipe Dream* was based on *Sweet Thursday*. During these years of success, Steinbeck guarded his own privacy and avoided publicity as much as he could. The works of his later years included *The Short Reign of Pippin IV* (1957) and his last novel, *The Winter of Our Discontent* (1961).

Steinbeck was awarded the Nobel Prize for literature in 1962 and received the Presidential Medal of Freedom from President Lyndon B. Johnson in 1964. In 1965 Steinbeck began a series, "Letters to Alicia," which appeared in *Long Island Newsday*. In these later years he divided his time between California and New York, and took on many assignments as a reporter abroad, including a trip to Vietnam. Steinbeck died of a heart attack on December 20, 1968, in New York City.

Plot Summary

Part 1

East of Eden begins with the narrator's description of the Salinas Valley in California, where the story unfolds. The next chapter introduces the Hamilton family, beginning with the narrator's grandfather Samuel Hamilton, who during the 1860s came to California from Ireland with his wife Liza.

The focus then switches to the Trask family, living on a farm in Connecticut. Cyrus Trask is a Civil War veteran who becomes a powerful man in the War Department in Washington, D.C. Trask has two sons, Adam and Charles. During their boyhood, Cyrus rejects a birthday present from Charles but accepts the present given by Adam. This angers Charles, and he beats Adam severely. Cyrus forces Adam to join the army.

The narrative then switches to the Hamilton family, which is thriving, even though Samuel never makes much money. Samuel's four sons, George, Will, Tom, and Joe, are born.

The narrative then returns to the Trasks. Charles is lonely by himself on the farm, but when Adam is discharged from the army in 1885 he immediately reenlists instead of returning home. He also visits his father in Washington, D.C. After Adam is discharged a second time in 1890, he drifts through the South and is arrested in Florida for vagrancy and put on a road gang. He escapes from the road gang and reaches Georgia, where he steals some clothes and wires his brother to send money so he can return home. Adam returns to the farm to find that his father is dead and has left his sons a large inheritance.

Cathy Ames is then introduced into the story. The narrator refers to her as a monster. As a teenager she murders her parents and becomes a prostitute. Her pimp, Edwards, falls in love with her, but then nearly beats her to death when he finds out she murdered her parents. She crawls to the Trask farm, where Charles and Adam take her in, although Charles is reluctant to do so. Adam falls in love with Cathy and marries her. She betrays him by drugging his drink and sleeping with Charles.

Part 2

It is now the year 1900. Adam moves to California with his new wife, who is pregnant. He buys a farm and is full of plans to develop it into another Eden. He asks Samuel Hamilton to drill a well for him, and Samuel becomes acquainted with Adam's Chinese servant, Lee. He also has an intuition about Cathy's evil nature. Cathy, after having tried unsuccessfully to abort her baby, gives birth to twins, which are delivered by Samuel. Liza Hamilton comes to take care of them for a week, after which Cathy tells Adam she is leaving him and the babies. When Adam argues with her, she shoots him in the shoulder.

When rumors of the shooting reach Horace Quinn, the deputy sheriff of King City, he investigates. Quinn discovers that Cathy is living in Salinas and has become a prostitute in a brothel run by a woman named Faye. He consults with the sheriff in

Media Adaptations

- *East of Eden* was made into a film by Elia Kazan in 1954. It features James Dean as Caleb, in Dean's first starring role.

- In 1981 *East of Eden* was made into a miniseries starring Timothy Bottoms as Adam Trask, Jane Seymour as Cathy Ames, and Bruce Boxleitner as Charles Trask.

Salinas, and they agree to keep what they know secret. At the brothel, Cathy is known as Kate, and she ingratiates herself with Faye. Eventually she poisons Faye and inherits Faye's business. Meanwhile, Adam has recovered from his wound but has withdrawn into himself after the shock of Cathy's departure. He refuses even to name the twins. Samuel Hamilton makes him snap out of his funk, and helps him to name the twins Caleb and Aron.

Part 3

The varied fortunes of the Hamiltons take up the first chapter of part 3. Samuel's favorite daughter Una dies, but all the other children except Tom prosper. Tom still has to find his place in life. Samuel is broken by Una's death and suddenly becomes old. During Thanksgiving 1911 Samuel's children arrange for him to leave the farm he created and live a few months with each of them. Samuel knows this means he will have little to live for, and he soon dies. After attending Samuel's funeral in Salinas, Adam confronts Kate at the brothel. In an acrimonious scene, she hints that Adam's two sons may not be his, but may have been fathered by Charles.

Meanwhile Cal and Aron are growing up. When they are eleven years old they kill a rabbit with an arrow, and Cal manipulates Aron over who is to claim credit for the kill. The two boys have very different personalities, and Aron is always more popular than Cal. They give the rabbit to a girl named Abra, whom they have just met. Abra rejects the gift because of a trick by Cal, and this upsets Aron.

Lee tells Adam the tragic story of his own birth to Chinese parents forced to work on railroad construction in the mountains of northern California. In a comic episode, Adam buys a new Ford car. Drama returns when Adam learns that his brother Charles is dead, and has left $100,000 to be divided equally between Adam and Cathy (Kate). Adam informs Kate of the inheritance.

While in Salinas Adam calls on Samuel's daughter Olive and her husband Ernest Steinbeck. Little John Steinbeck, the future author, is shown peeking around the skirts of his mother. Another of Samuel's daughters, Dessie, returns to the family farm to live with Tom. But Dessie dies of an illness, and Tom, tortured by what he feels is his own responsibility for her death, commits suicide.

Part 4

Adam, Lee, and the boys move to Salinas. Lee moves to San Francisco to fulfill his dream of owning a bookstore, but he soon gets lonely and returns. The boys attend the local school, and Aron has a romance with Abra. In 1915 Adam takes a business risk when he transports lettuce to the East Coast. There are delays, the ice melts, and he loses most of his money. Cal learns about his mother, and asks Lee about her. Cal follows Kate for weeks, and finally speaks to her. But he does not tell Aron anything about what he knows.

A prostitute named Ethel, who has guessed that Kate murdered Faye, tries to blackmail Kate. As America enters World War I, Cal invests in beans with Will Hamilton. Cal wants to make money so he can give it to his father to compensate for Adam's loss. Aron goes to college at Stanford; his goal is to become a minister. Abra becomes very attached to Adam and Lee. Kate is troubled by arthritis pain, and worries about Ethel. She sends Joe Valery to find her. Joe finds out that Ethel is dead, but he does not tell Kate. Instead, he tries to trick her and extort money.

World War I makes its impact felt in Salinas, and Adam finds his position on the draft board a heavy responsibility. During Thanksgiving 1917 Cal gives Adam the money he has made from the bean investment. Adam angrily rejects it, because he refuses to profit from the war. Upset by this rejection, Cal takes Aron to see Kate. Aron is so horrified he enlists in the army, even though he is underage. He goes off to war. Kate commits suicide. Joe robs her, but is picked up by police following a tip Kate gave before her death. Joe tries to escape, but is shot dead. In May 1918 Aron is killed in the war. Upon hearing the news of Aron's death, Adam has a paralyzing stroke. Cal feels overwhelming guilt. With Lee's encouragement, Adam indicates that he forgives Cal, and that Cal may overcome the evil in his nature.

Characters

Cathy Ames

Cathy Ames is described by the narrator as a monster. She is consistently evil in her thoughts and actions, manipulating others for her own ends without a trace of conscience. Cold and callous, she seems to be without a single decent feeling. Cathy is the only daughter of a respectable family in Massachusetts. As a young girl she is different from the other children; she is a nonconformist and a liar. At the age of ten she gets two boys punished for indulging in sex play with her, which she initiated; at high school she drives her Latin teacher to suicide. At sixteen she murders her parents by burning down the family home. She then becomes a prostitute, but when she is beaten almost to death by Edwards, she crawls to the Trask farm, where Adam and Charles take her in. After Adam falls in love with her, they marry and move to California. Cathy gives birth to twins but then decides to leave. She shoots Adam in the shoulder and walks out. She becomes a prostitute in Salinas, where she eventually murders the owner, Faye, and inherits the business. She turns it into a nasty establishment, keeping incriminating photographs of her clients, many of whom are prominent citizens, in order to later disgrace them. Caleb makes himself known to her, and later brings Aron to see her as well. After this she deteriorates physically, and even seems to feel some pangs of conscience. She writes her will, leaving everything to Aron, and then commits suicide.

Kate Ames

See Cathy Ames

Abra Bacon

Abra Bacon is the daughter of a dishonest county supervisor in Salinas. In high school she becomes Aron's girlfriend, and they expect to marry. But Abra is disturbed by their relationship because she thinks Aron has too high an opinion of her purity and does not see her for who she really is. After Aron goes to college, she falls out of love with him and burns his letters. She shifts her affections to Caleb and also gets close to Adam and

Lee. Abra is a marked contrast to Cathy; she has goodness, strength, and wisdom.

Mr. Edwards

Mr. Edwards runs a prostitution business in Massachusetts and Connecticut, even though on the surface he lives a respectable life as a married man with two sons. He employs Cathy as a prostitute but then falls in love with her. When he discovers she murdered her parents, he turns on her and beats her almost to death.

Ethel

Ethel is an old prostitute who thinks she can prove that Kate murdered Faye. She tries to blackmail Kate over the matter, but she dies by drowning before she can profit from her plot.

Faye

Faye is the owner of a brothel in Salinas where Kate works. Faye takes a liking to Kate and wills her business to her. Kate slowly poisons Faye and then inherits the business when Faye dies.

Dessie Hamilton

Dessie Hamilton is the daughter of Samuel and Liza. Warm-hearted and full of laughter, she owns a dressmaker shop in Salinas. But she sells her business and moves back to the ranch to be with her brother Tom. Dessie dies of an illness, and Tom, guilt-stricken, commits suicide.

George Hamilton

George Hamilton is Samuel Hamilton's eldest son. He lives an exemplary life, but suffers from anemia.

Joe Hamilton

Joe Hamilton is the youngest son of Samuel and Liza, and the darling of the family. He shows little aptitude for any kind of practical work, so he is sent to college at Stanford. He goes into advertising and is a great success on the East Coast.

Liza Hamilton

Liza Hamilton is Samuel Hamilton's Irish wife. She keeps a clean house and is a good cook, and is respected in the neighborhood. She is also extremely pious, and hates idleness, card-playing, and drink. She is suspicious of fun and has no sense of humor. Whatever happens in life she does not complain, since she believes she will be rewarded by God after death. Later in her life she begins to take wine for medicinal purposes, and becomes more relaxed and happier.

Lizzy Hamilton

Lizzy Hamilton is the oldest of the Hamilton daughters. She marries young and goes away, after which time she is seen only at funerals.

Mollie Hamilton

Mollie Hamilton is the youngest and the prettiest of the Hamilton daughters. She marries and moves to San Francisco.

Olive Hamilton

Olive Hamilton is the third daughter of the Hamiltons, and the narrator's mother. She becomes a teacher and is a source of pride to the family. She marries and lives in Paso Robles, then King City, and finally Salinas.

Samuel Hamilton

Samuel Hamilton immigrates to California from Ireland with his wife Liza. He is an intelligent, self-educated man who has a genius for invention, but he is not very astute when it comes to money, which means that the family never becomes rich. He is handicapped by the dryness of his land; he drills wells for everyone else but cannot find water on his own property. Samuel is a visionary, and he dreams of how the Salinas Valley might look in the future when it is fully developed. Samuel is lively, exuberant, full of joy, and is a fine storyteller. He can also take charge in a crisis, as when he delivers Cathy's twins. He also brings Adam to his senses when Adam refuses to acknowledge his own sons. Samuel is youthful and energetic until the death of his daughter Una, which saddens him and makes him old.

Tom Hamilton

Tom Hamilton is the third son of Samuel and Liza, and the one who is most like his father. He has a talent for inventing and is even bolder than his father. Remaining a bachelor, he lives on the ranch when everyone else has left. He is delighted when Dessie comes back to live there, but is devastated when she succumbs to an illness. He blames himself for giving her the wrong medicine and commits suicide.

Una Hamilton

Una Hamilton is the Hamiltons' second eldest daughter. She is thoughtful, studious, and dark, and Samuel Hamilton's greatest joy. She marries and moves to Oregon but dies young. Her father Samuel is crushed by her death and ages considerably as a result.

Will Hamilton

Will Hamilton is Samuel Hamilton's second son. He possesses great energy but not much imagination. Lucky and with a talent for making money, he develops a business selling Ford automobiles and becomes a rich man. He gives Adam sound business advice, which Adam ignores, and also advises Cal, enabling Cal to make $15,000 by selling beans in wartime.

Lee

Lee is Adam's Chinese cook, housekeeper, and advisor. He is an educated, philosophical, level-headed man, much given to reflection and serious thought. In contrast to the impractical Adam, Lee runs the household efficiently and plays a large part in the upbringing of Aron and Caleb. Lee harbors ambitions to leave the farm and start a bookstore in San Francisco, but when he finally makes the move he quickly gets lonely and returns. It is Lee who first brings up the definition of the Hebrew word *timshel* that plays such a large part in the novel, and it is Lee who at the very end, pleads with Adam to forgive Caleb.

Horace Quinn

Horace Quinn is the deputy sheriff in King City. He investigates the shooting of Adam and discovers that Cathy has become a prostitute in Salinas.

Adam Trask

Adam Trask is the son of Cyrus Trask and the half-brother of Charles. He has a difficult relationship with his brother, who is jealous of him and beats him when they are boys. Adam joins the army and fights in the Indian wars. When he rejoins his brother at the family farm they quarrel frequently. Adam is honest, and more innocent and good-natured than his aggressive and brooding brother. He falls in love with Cathy and idealizes her. He has no intimation of her evil nature, which Lee, Samuel, and even Charles all sense. Adam is not a success in business, and it is only because he inherits a fortune from his father that he can lead the comfortable life he does. For practical matters he is greatly dependent on his servant Lee. Adam learns only painfully through experience. Eventually he has to accept that Cathy is a prostitute in Salinas, and he even goes to visit her. But he bears her no hatred and even makes excuses for her conduct. When Adam is in his fifties, he is weighed down by his responsibilities on the draft board, and his health deteriorates. He shows great interest in the word *timshel* ("thou mayest") from the Cain and Abel story, and after his stroke, this is the last word he speaks. It indicates he has forgiven his son Cal.

Alice Trask

Alice Trask is Cyrus's second wife, and the mother of Charles. She is a quiet woman who does her duty without complaint.

Aron Trask

Aron Trask is the son of Adam and Cathy, and the twin brother of Caleb. As in the relationship of Adam and Charles (his father and uncle), Aron is the innocent, good brother, in contrast to the aggressive, malicious Caleb. Aron is fair, while his brother is dark, and Aron is the more popular of the two. Aron is pure-minded, and he goes to college at Stanford, wanting to train as a minister. He does not wish to face up to anything dark or difficult, and he knows nothing of his mother's sordid life as a prostitute until Caleb takes him to see her. Aron is extremely shocked by the experience and decides to leave college and enlist in the army. He is killed during World War I.

Caleb Trask

Caleb Trask is the son of Adam and Cathy, and the twin brother of Aron. Caleb is dark, unlike the fair Aron, and he has inherited from Cathy some of the evil that is in her. When he and Aron are boys, he dishonestly tricks Abra into rejecting Aron's gift of a rabbit. He is jealous of Aron because Aron is more popular than he. However, Cal has enough self-awareness to know the evil he is capable of, and he tries to fight against it and choose a better path. He knows that his mother is a prostitute, for example, but at first he protects Aron by shielding him from this knowledge. But he does not always succeed in mastering his tendency toward malice. After his father rejects his gift of $15,000, Cal takes Aron to see Cathy, with tragic results. Cal feels deep guilt because of his actions, but his father forgives him.

Charles Trask

Charles Trask is the son of Cyrus Trask, and Adam's half-brother. He is more aggressive than Adam. As a boy he is jealous of the fact that their father seems to love Adam but not Charles. Charles beats Adam severely because of this jealousy. When Adam joins the army, Charles remains on the ranch but he misses his brother. When Adam returns, there is always tension between the two men, and they quarrel. Charles sleeps with Cathy without Adam's knowledge. After Adam and Cathy move to

California, Charles becomes a miser, accumulating money but doing nothing with it. When he dies he leaves half his money to Adam and the other half to Cathy.

Cyrus Trask

Cyrus Trask is the father of Adam and Charles. Rather wild in his youth, he loses a leg only thirty minutes into his first taste of combat in the Civil War. But he becomes an expert in military matters, and he also lies about the extent of his own role in the Civil War. He goes to Washington and holds important jobs in the army administration. An authoritarian figure and a hard taskmaster, he forces the unwilling Adam to join the army. On his death he leaves his sons a fortune, but Charles suspects that he came about it dishonestly.

Mrs. Trask

Mrs. Trask is the first wife of Cyrus, and the mother of Adam. She is an unhappy woman who commits suicide by drowning herself.

Joe Valery

Joe Valery is employed as a bouncer by Kate at her brothel. He is a petty criminal who will do anything for Kate as long as he is paid for it. He uses Kate's fear of Ethel to try to extort money from her, but she outwits him because she knows he escaped from a road gang when he was serving a five-year sentence for robbery. She betrays him to the police, and he is shot dead trying to escape with her money after her death.

Themes

Good versus Evil

The main theme is the perpetual battle between good and evil. This battle may be between a good and an evil person, or between good and evil impulses within one individual. God has given humans free will, and they are able to choose good over evil, if they so decide.

The framework for this theme is the Cain and Abel story in the biblical book of Genesis, chapter 4, verses 1 to 16. Cain and Abel are the first offspring of Adam and Eve. Cain cultivated the ground while Abel was a shepherd. When they made sacrifices to God, God rejected Cain's gift of agricultural produce and accepted Abel's gift of the firstlings of his flock. Cain was angry and murdered his brother. God then cursed him, telling him

he would be a wanderer on the face of the earth. Cain despaired because he feared he would be murdered. But God put a mark on him to protect him. Cain went to live in the land of Nod, east of Eden.

The Cain and Abel theme is carried forward in the novel through the initial letters of the characters. Charles and Adam Trask represent Cain and Abel, respectively. This is shown when their father Cyrus rejects Charles's gift of a knife but accepts Adam's gift of a puppy. Charles reacts just as Cain did. He is angry, and he beats his brother severely. He would have killed Adam had he been able to find him when he returned with a weapon. Charles also suffers a wound on his forehead that leaves a prominent scar—just as God left a mark on Cain.

The allegory is continued in the third generation of Trasks. Caleb has the legacy of Cain, whereas Aron possesses the innocence of Abel. Just as Charles was angry and would take revenge whenever Adam beat him in sports, so Caleb is angry at Aron's greater popularity. He always seeks a way of undermining Aron by playing some kind of trick on the person who likes Aron better, as he does with Abra when Aron gives her a dead rabbit.

The Cain and Abel pattern continues into the boys' teenage years. Caleb's gift of money to his father is rejected, but his father approves of Aron's scholastic achievements and his desire to go to college. Caleb is distressed by his father's rejection and then symbolically murders his brother by taking him to see Cathy, their mother, which so shocks Aron that he joins the army and is killed in battle.

The initial letter symbolism is notable also in the characters of Abra and Cathy, good and evil, respectively, and, to a lesser degree, in Cyrus and his wife Alice. Cathy, like Charles, has a scar on her forehead, a sign of her identification with the evil of Cain.

The use to which Steinbeck puts the Cain and Abel story is brought out when Lee explains his interpretation of the story to Samuel and Adam. The crux of the matter is in the interpretation of the Hebrew word *timshel*. The word occurs in the story where God promises Cain "thou shalt" (*timshel*) rule over sin. Another translation reads "Do thou" rather than "thou shalt." Lee is intrigued by the difference in the translations. "Thou shalt" is a promise that Cain would triumph over sin, which has not been borne out in his offspring. "Do thou," on the other hand, is an order. Lee consults a group of old Chinese scholars in San Francisco, who learn Hebrew especially for the purpose. They come up with a new translation of *timshel*: "thou mayest."

Topics For Further Study

- World War I is an important part of the background to the last part of the novel. Why did America enter World War I, and what contribution did it make in the war effort?

- Analyze the character of Charles Trask and the role he plays in the novel. What are some of the many parallels between Charles and the biblical figure of Cain?

- The theme of the novel is that humans can choose good over evil. Discuss this in the context of social problems in America today. Do all criminals, for example, freely choose to commit antisocial acts, or does the environment in which they are born and raised also contribute to their actions? Provide an example of a twentieth-century criminal you believe supports your answer.

- Steinbeck said that all the anecdotes of the Hamilton family were true. Read over several of these (Mary wanting to be a boy in chapter 23 and Olive in the airplane in chapter 14 are just two examples), as well as the way Steinbeck describes each member of the family when he first introduces them. Then write an anecdote about a member of your own family.

Lee feels this is full of significance. It means that humans have a choice in the matter. They can choose to overcome sin or choose not to do so. Nothing is predestined.

The novel then works out this theme mainly through the character of Caleb. As a teenager, Caleb is fully aware of the Cain legacy he inherited from Cathy, and he tries to fight against it, not always with success. Even as a young boy he prays to God to let him be like Aron: "Don't make me mean. I don't want to be." When he is several years older, Lee tries to convince him that just because he has inherited part of his mother's nature, he does not have to let it have control over him: "Of course you may have that in you. Everybody has. But you've got the other too." Lee means that Caleb also has good in him. Lee emphasizes that life is a matter of taking personal responsibility for one's actions: "Whatever you do, it will be you who do it—not your mother," he tells Caleb. Caleb takes Lee's advice to heart, and repeats it when he confronts his mother in chapter 39. Caleb sticks to his beliefs even when Cathy pours scorn on him.

But when Caleb reacts vindictively to his father's rejection of his gift, he shows just how strong the Cain element in him is. His actions lead indirectly to Aron's death. It is left to Adam, in the last word of the novel, to take up the theme. Whatever Caleb has done, the word *timshel*, "thou mayest," still applies. His choice lies in his own hands, not in his inherited genes.

Style

Symbolism

The battle between good and evil is foreshadowed in the third paragraph of the first chapter, in the description of the mountain ranges that lie on each side of the Salinas Valley. The Galiban Mountains to the east are associated with light, sun, and warmth. The narrator associates them with a mother's love. To the west are the Santa Lucia mountains, which are "dark and brooding—unfriendly and dangerous." In his childhood, the narrator says, he dreaded the west and loved the east. Thus the dualistic framework of the novel is established symbolically on the first page.

That symbolism is developed through many biblical allusions (an allusion is a reference to a famous historical event or person, or to a literary work—in this case, the Bible). In addition to the Cain and Abel story, biblical symbolism is associated with two of the major characters. The first of these is Adam. Although at first he represents Abel in the Cain and Abel story, when he moves to the Salinas Valley he becomes like Adam, the first man in Genesis. In his innocence, he wants to create the garden of Eden on his land. Unfortunately, he is married to Cathy, who in this aspect of the novel plays the role of Eve, who first brought sin into the world by yielding to the temptations of the devil, in the form of a serpent. In the physical descriptions of Cathy, the serpent imagery cannot be missed. She has wide-set eyes and her upper eyelids droop, giving her a mysterious sleepy appearance. Samuel comments that her eyes are not human. Cathy has tiny ears, no more than "thin flaps" pressed close to her head, and "Her feet were small and round and stubby, with fat insteps almost like little hoofs." The scar on Cathy's forehead following her beating by Edwards corresponds to the bruise on the head of the serpent recorded in Genesis, chapter 3. And when Cathy has to drag herself along the ground to the Trask farm, she resembles the cursed serpent that crawls on its belly, as Genesis relates.

Allegory

The theme of good against evil, and the biblical symbolism, all function within the context of an allegory. An allegory is like a metaphor in which characters in a narrative are equated with meanings or other characters that are not present in the narrative itself. In *East of Eden*, for example, many of the main characters are linked by way of allegory to the Cain and Abel story in the Bible. Thus Cathy becomes a personification of the abstract quality of evil, which is associated with Cain in the biblical story. In this way the actions of the characters in the novel gain significance and interest because they are linked to ideas that occur in interpretations of the Cain and Abel story.

Historical Context

The Development of California

California became the thirty-first state in 1850, when its population, boosted by the gold rush, numbered over 100,000. This population included many Chinese immigrants. In 1852, 10 percent of Californian residents were Chinese. After the Civil War, more settlers moved west, attracted by high wages and cheap land. The first transcontinental railroad system, begun in 1863 and finished in 1869, linked Sacramento to the Eastern states. Many Chinese laborers were brought in to work on the railroads (including Lee's parents in the novel). They built the railroad through the foothills and over the

high Sierra Nevada. The work was hard and dangerous, and many lives were lost. But there was prejudice against the Chinese. For example, Chinese children were banned from attending public schools, according to a California law passed in 1860.

By 1870 California's population had risen to 560,000. But an economic depression during the next decade produced high unemployment. The depression was caused by the influx of cheap manufactured goods from well established industries on the East Coast, with which California's newer manufacturing companies could not compete. The unemployment was exacerbated by the arrival by railroad of thousands of European immigrants from the East Coast. Some Californians blamed their unemployment on Chinese laborers, who were willing to work for low wages. There were anti-Chinese riots in Los Angeles in 1871, and anti-Chinese prejudice was written into law. Chinese people were denied U.S. citizenship, which meant they were not allowed to vote or hold government office. They were even disallowed from testifying in court against whites. A hint of the white prejudice against the Chinese occurs in *East of Eden* when Lee tells Samuel he always speaks in pidgin English to whites because that is what they expect. If he were to speak grammatical English that would show he was an educated man, and whites would not understand him.

Because the Chinese in California often faced discrimination, they took to setting up their own laundry businesses, where there was little competition from whites. (In *East of Eden* when Lee says he is going to move to San Francisco, Samuel's first thought is that Lee must want to start a laundry business.)

America's Industrial Growth

The period covered by the novel was a time of growth in all areas for the United States. The population of the country increased by 140 percent between 1860 and 1900. There was a huge expansion in the production of coal, petroleum, pig iron, and crude steel. A system of railroads that crisscrossed the country supported this industrial expansion and allowed westward movement for farmers and immigrants. By 1890 all large American cities were linked by rail. One-third of all railroad tracks in the world were in the United States. It was also an inventive period. Between 1860 and 1890, 440,400 patents were issued. In every field the old ways were giving way to the new. In Chicago, for example, Gustavus Swift shipped meat under refrigeration and built refrigerator cars (thus making possible what

Compare
&
Contrast

- **1860s:** The American Civil War is fought, and when it ends in 1865 there are 620,000 dead soldiers.

  1910s: World War I is fought. Between April 1917 and November 1918, 116,708 American servicemen die.

  Today: The United States fights wars against terrorism in Afghanistan and Iraq. The modern war involves more advanced tactics supported by advanced technology in the areas of weaponry and defense, and fewer American lives are lost as a result.

- **1860s:** The great railroads are built across the United States.

  1910s: The aviation era begins. In 1919 the first transatlantic flight takes place, from Newfoundland to Ireland. The flight takes sixteen hours and twenty-two minutes.

  Today: The commercial airplane is the way most people prefer to travel from city to city within the United States. Unlike Europe, which has a thriving rail network, the use of the railroad system in the United States is in decline.

- **1860s:** Large numbers of Chinese and French Canadian immigrants arrive in the United States during this decade.

  1910s: This decade marks the middle of peak U.S. immigration years. The pattern of immigration has changed over the past fifty years, and most new immigrants are from eastern and southern Europe. The first large wave of Mexicans arrives during this time period.

  Today: Immigration patterns change once more. The majority of immigrants now come not from Europe but from Asia and Latin America.

Adam in *East of Eden* tries, but fails, to do when he ships lettuce to the East Coast packed in ice).

The period between the 1870s and 1890s is often known as the Gilded Age, during which aggressive individualism and the spirit of optimism fueled national growth, producing industrial growth through the exploitation of natural resources. There was a belief in the inevitability of progress. However, the ruthlessness of the leading industrialists of the era gained them a reputation as "robber barons." These were men such as Andrew Carnegie (steel industry) and John D. Rockefeller (oil industry). Such men amassed huge fortunes, but the lot of the ordinary worker was often dire, toiling long hours for low wages. This was an unfortunate age for Native Americans as well, as they endured two decades of wars with whites, from 1864 to the mid-1880s (these are the wars in which Adam fights as a young man in *East of Eden*).

By the beginning of the century, America was becoming the foremost industrial power in the world, and for those who could afford it, there was an abundance of consumer goods available. One of the newest inventions was the automobile. In 1900 there were only about 8,000 automobiles in the entire country, and they were only for the wealthy, but in the following decade Henry Ford began to build affordable cars (like the one Adam buys in the novel sometime in the 1910s).

Critical Overview

Reviews of *East of Eden* have been decidedly mixed. Although there is plenty of praise, almost all reviewers note major flaws in the novel. Orville Prescott in the *New York Times* calls it clumsy in structure and too melodramatic and sensational, but nonetheless declares it to be "a serious and on the whole successful effort to grapple with a major theme." Prescott also argues that after some trivial works unworthy of his talent, Steinbeck "achieved a considered philosophy and it is a fine and generous

1955 film portrayal of Steinbeck's East of Eden *with (from left) Julie Harris as Abra, Richard Davalos as Aron Trask, and James Dean as Cal Trask*

one." Mark Schorer in the *New York Times Book Review* describes *East of Eden* as "probably the best" of Steinbeck's novels. But Leo Gurko in the *Nation* writes that the characters are mere abstractions and that the novel resembles an old medieval morality play. According to Gurko, the novel marks a major decline in Steinbeck's talent. Some critics feel that Steinbeck reduces the complexities of life to a simple story of good against evil. For example, in the *New Yorker*, Anthony West writes that the novel is the equivalent of "those nineteenth-century melodramas in which the villains could always be recognized

because they waxed their mustaches and in which the conflict between good and evil operated like a well-run series of professional tennis matches."

Later critics have tended to agree with the earlier reviewers, often finding more to blame than praise in the novel. The structure of the novel has been much criticized, the argument being that the two strands of the narrative, the stories of the Trasks and the Hamiltons, are not properly integrated. Complaint is also frequently made that Steinbeck applied his moral philosophy in a heavyhanded way. Critics have felt that the author's focus on the moral dimensions of the story had a detrimental effect on his writing, which at its best allowed moral meaning to emerge from the details rather than being imposed on them. In *The Novels of John Steinbeck: A Critical Study*, Howard Levant comments, "*East of Eden* is a strangely unblended novel, an impressive, greatly flawed work." It is testament, notes Levant, "to the author's enduring difficulty in fusing structure and materials into a harmonious whole."

Criticism

Bryan Aubrey

Aubrey holds a Ph.D. in English and has published many articles on twentieth-century literature. In this essay Aubrey discusses East of Eden *in the context of a series of letters Steinbeck wrote to his friend and editor Pascal Covici as he was writing the first draft of the novel.*

Steinbeck labored long and hard on *East of Eden*, declaring it to be the most difficult book he had undertaken. For a long time he had wanted to be able to write such a book and had carefully prepared himself for the task. During the writing of the first draft, he wrote a remarkable series of letters to his friend and editor Pascal Covici. The letters were published as *Journal of a Novel: The "East of Eden" Letters* in 1969, a year after Steinbeck's death.

Steinbeck wrote one letter early each day from January to November 1951 as a way of limbering up for the writing task that lay ahead. The letters give a close-up view of the ups and downs of a novelist at work, his successful days as well as the days when nothing went right. One day he wonders whether the novel will be interesting to anyone other than himself. On another occasion he wonders whether his "devilish playing with the verities" (his metaphysical ideas) will put people off in an age when readers of novels want plot and action. Often, however, his enthusiasm for his task bubbles over, and he conveys how it feels to be a writer when the full rush of creativity sweeps through him. It is a very physical feeling for Steinbeck: "The joy comes in the words going down and the rhythms crowding in the chest and pulsing to get out."

The *East of Eden* letters provide many fascinating details about the novel (all the anecdotes about the Hamilton family are true, for example) and leave no doubt about the primary significance Steinbeck attached to the Cain and Abel story. His first idea for the title of the novel was "Canable."

Then he thought of "Cain Sign" before settling on *East of Eden*, which is itself taken from the Cain and Abel story. Steinbeck thought the story of jealousy and strife between siblings lay at the basis of all neuroses, and he was thrilled by his interpretation of the Hebrew word *timshel* as "thou mayest." He went to great trouble to be certain that his etymology was at least possible. He felt sure it would interest scholars and psychiatrists and provoke great argument and scholarly discussion (it did not).

Perhaps the most important idea to emerge from Steinbeck's letters is his great affirmative vision of what the purpose of the writer should be. He comments on this in the context of his character Samuel Hamilton, a man of energy and vision who goes through life without being defeated. Steinbeck laments the fact that it has become fashionable amongst writers to show the destruction rather than the endurance of the human spirit. He argues that there have been a few men—he names Plato, Lao Tze, Buddha, Christ, and Paul—who were not destroyed by life, and these are the men the world lives by. They are remembered not for negation and denial, but for affirmation. Steinbeck goes on to argue that "It is the duty of the writer to lift up, to extend, to encourage." Great writing must give out strength, courage, and wisdom rather than dwell on the weakness and ugliness that is also part of the human condition. Steinbeck believed he had achieved this affirmative vision in his novel. "Although East of Eden is not Eden," he said in the same letter, "it is not insuperably far away."

How far away from Eden is it? Some readers may feel that there are so many cruelties, vices, and tragedies in this novel, culminating in Aron's unnecessary death and Adam's devastating stroke, that if it is "not insuperably far away" from Eden, it is not far away from hell either.

But that may be part of Steinbeck's point. It is unlikely that he conceived the condition of Eden as one of perpetual bliss, but rather one of perpetual striving, because wherever there is good, there is also evil. In the interaction between the two lies the possibility of human growth and freedom. Steinbeck said as much in the letter he wrote to Covici on January 29, 1951, before he had written a single word of the novel. He wrote that the opposites of good and evil, strength and weakness, love and hate, beauty and ugliness, are inseparable: "neither can exist without the other." Out of the interaction of these opposites, "creativeness is born."

This comment is the key to so much of what goes on in the novel. Although the idea that good and evil are mixed up together in most individuals is not an especially interesting or original one, there is a more subtle idea at work too: the fact that even those characters in the novel who are firmly in one or other of the opposing camps are drawn inexorably together. Each quality, good and evil, has a kind of gravitational pull for the other, which is beyond the control of either. So it is that the mysterious processes of life place Charles (a Cain character) in close proximity to Adam (an Abel character) and through their stormy interaction Adam is forced to seek his own destiny, away from his brother. But then in his turn, Adam cannot help but pull into his life Cathy, who has as little good in her as Adam has evil.

It is interesting to note that while Cathy is as close to pure evil as one is likely to get this side of hell, the "good" characters Adam and Aron share culpability for the bad things that happen to them. Their errors are failures of perception, knowledge, and imagination. They fail to understand that life must be grasped whole, that it is a mixed bag of good and evil. Adam, for example, never comes close to seeing Cathy as she really is. He idealizes her, projecting onto her an unreal image of sweetness that he never questions. When Cathy indicates that she does not want to move to California, Adam does not listen; he does not take her objections seriously. Nor does he notice her unhappiness in California. He is too busy creating his Eden in the Salinas Valley. But this manmade Eden is not built on solid foundations, so it is no surprise (except to Adam) when it crumbles. In a sense, he is just as much to blame as Cathy is for the bullet she fires into his shoulder.

It is the same with Aron. Steinbeck alerts his correspondent Covici to the importance of Aron, telling him to note the gradual, subtle development of Aron's character. During his childhood, Aron's simple goodness wins him the affection of everyone. As soon as he reaches adolescence, however, he starts to lose his innocence and his balance. He channels all his emerging passions into religion. Deciding to become a minister, he devotedly attends the Episcopal church and takes spiritual instruction from the clergyman. Of course, there is nothing wrong with this, but Aron takes it to excess. He desperately needs (or thinks he needs) to shut out anything that seems to him impure. He soon reaches "a point of passionate purity that made everyone else foul." When he learns from the clergyman that the owner of a brothel is starting to attend church services—he does not yet know this is his mother, Cathy—he tells Lee that he wants to go away, because Salinas is a "dirty" town. Lee tries to prod him into a more realistic view of life ("Try to believe that things are

> **It is a very physical feeling for Steinbeck: 'The joy comes in the words going down and the rhythms crowding in the chest and pulsing to get out.'"**

neither so good nor so bad as they seem to you now"), but Aron does not have the maturity to grasp it. And when he goes off to Stanford, he shuts himself off from the life around him.

Aron's biggest mistake is in his attitude to Abra, in which he replicates his father's idealization of Cathy. Abra is mature enough to notice this. She says to Lee, of Aron, "He doesn't think about me. He's made someone up, and it's like he put my skin on her. I'm not like that—not like the made-up one." Aron wants a girl who is absolutely pure, with not a single bad thing about her. Abra knows that she can never live up to such an ideal. "He doesn't know me," she says. "He doesn't even want to know me." Like father, like son, and the outcome is inevitable. Abra and Aron drift apart.

The consequences for Aron of his refusal to accept life in its wholeness—the ugliness as well as the beauty—are dire. He is so devastated by his discovery that his mother runs a brothel that he literally runs away as far as he can go—to the battlefields of Europe, where he is killed. The false world in which he tried to wall himself off from the real one cannot stand the light of real experience.

If Aron and Adam are examples of the inadequacy of a one-dimensional view of reality, Steinbeck also offers many moments of illumination, when wisdom about life shines through. He poured himself into this novel with a passion, writing to Covici that it had to contain everything in the world he knew. Whether it is in the practical wisdom of Samuel, or the studious reflections of Lee, there are many such moments to savor. Each reader will find his or her favorite. The scene near the end of the novel, when Abra talks with Cal on their way home from school (chapter 52, section 3), is as good an example as any. Abra is only in her mid-teens, but she expresses a wisdom that others spend a lifetime missing. Steinbeck alerted Covici to Abra's importance in the story (she is "the strong female principle of

What Do I Read Next?

- Steinbeck's *The Grapes of Wrath* (1939) is considered his finest work. It describes the plight of migrant workers in California in the 1930s through the story of one family that makes its way to California from Oklahoma.

- Like Steinbeck, English romantic poet Lord Byron was inspired by the story of Cain. His dramatic poem "Cain: A Dramatic Mystery in Three Acts" is an attack on Christianity as well as on political and social institutions in nineteenth century England. It can be found in the Oxford World's Classics series volume edited by Jerome J. McGann and titled *Lord Byron: The Major Works* (2000).

- *Americans and the California Dream, 1850–1915* (1986) by Kevin Starr describes the emergence of Californian culture in the second half of the nineteenth century. Starr discusses the California dream from a social, psychological, and symbolic point of view, as well as some of its fallacies and contradictions.

- *John Steinbeck: A Biography* (1994), by Jay Parini, is a thorough, sympathetic biography of the author. Parini conducted many interviews with people who knew Steinbeck, and he also made use of published and unpublished letters, diaries, and manuscripts.

---

good"), and in this scene Abra is explaining to Cal that Aron never grew up. He lived in a story-world that he made up, and he refused to accept any outcome different from the one he wanted. But Abra's attitude is different. Not only has she outgrown the story that she and Aron made up for themselves, she comments, "I don't want to know how it comes out. I only want to be there while it's going on." Abra's refusal to live in a fantasy world, her determination not to be trapped by fixed expectations, and her courageous desire to live fully in the present, without illusions, make her, like Lee and Samuel, a touchstone of how life can be lived truthfully and with integrity.

Source: Bryan Aubrey, Critical Essay on *East of Eden*, in *Novels for Students*, Gale, 2004.

Charles L. Etheridge, Jr.

In the following essay, Etheridge examines how "the perception of Steinbeck's naturalism has changed since the early 1970s," and how "these changes have affected the reevaluation of East of Eden.*"*

Until a few years ago, John Steinbeck's literary reputation depended upon how critics perceived his naturalism. As long as he wrote in what was perceived as a naturalistic vein, he received high praise. When his work became less overtly naturalistic, his reputation declined drastically. During the past fifteen years this pattern of criticism has changed as critics have begun to question whether or not Steinbeck was a naturalist.

No novel is a better barometer of how Steinbeck's reputation is faring than *East of Eden*. Upon its initial publication, it was considered a disaster; now some scholars call it Steinbeck's finest work. The purpose of this study is to survey how the perception of Steinbeck's naturalism has changed since the early 1970s, when scholars began to reevaluate Steinbeck's post–World War II fiction, and to speculate on how these changes have affected the reevaluation of *East of Eden*.

The Steinbeck Society Session at the 1974 Modern Language Association Convention marks the beginning of the reevaluation of Steinbeck's Naturalism. These papers were collected and published in a special issue of the *Steinbeck Quarterly* in 1976. In his "Introduction," Warren French divides Steinbeck's work into two distinctive categories: the "Naturalistic" works and the "Dramas of Consciousness," placing both *The Grapes of Wrath* and *East of Eden* in the latter category. That he grouped these two novels into the same category marks a departure from previously held views such as the one Leo Gurko stated in his 1952 review of *East of Eden*: "The Steinbeck who was as much the genius of the 30's as Sinclair Lewis was of the 20's is scarcely in evidence" (235).

French continued to explore what he felt was a change on the part of Steinbeck from naturalistic to other forms of writing in "John Steinbeck: A Usable Concept of Naturalism," originally published in 1975. French finds three distinctive stages in the novelist's naturalism. Steinbeck's first two works exhibited no naturalism, the works from *Pastures of Heaven* to Chapter 14 of *The Grapes of Wrath* are decidedly naturalistic, and everything from that chapter on is neither naturalistic nor post-naturalistic. French concludes that in 1938 Steinbeck "was shaken out of the pessimistic viewpoint undergirding [his naturalistic novels]" (78) and points to Lee's speech explaining the significance of the "thou mayest" translation of *timshel* to show that "Steinbeck's post–World War II novels . . . are not naturalistic."

Although it was probably not apparent in 1975, the concluding sentence of French's essay marks an important step forward both in Steinbeck criticism and in the reevaluation of *East of Eden*:

> Apparently from his observation during and after World War II, he reached the conclusion that man must take responsibility for his actions and that man is capable—however reluctantly—of taking this responsibility. (78)

Unlike critics who had previously written on *East of Eden*, French was not holding Steinbeck to a preconceived standard of what his work should have been like. By concluding that Steinbeck's apparent departure from naturalism was a result of a conscious artistic and philosophical choice, French anticipates a generation of critics who will begin to examine and appraise the artistic choices Steinbeck made and the changes he underwent, rather than making the *a priori* assumptions that the later works were different from the earlier and are therefore inferior.

One of the most damning comments made about *East of Eden* was that in it Steinbeck virtually abandoned naturalism. Yet in papers such as Peter Copek's "Steinbeck's 'Naturalism?,'" critics began to question an assumption which a critic writing two decades earlier would have thought self-evident and unquestionable: that John Steinbeck was a naturalist. While Copek does find strong evidence of naturalistic elements in Steinbeck's fiction, he concludes that such elements do not necessarily a naturalist

> **"** Whatever the critics ultimately conclude about it, the issue of what form of naturalism is present in Steinbeck's writing will appear again and again in criticism which seeks to reevaluate the work."

make; he does not find the author of *East of Eden* or *The Grapes of Wrath* a naturalist "in that this does not lead to a pessimistic vision, a cynical vision, or even one which I could comfortably describe as a fiction whose characters are 'at the mercy of' omnipotent determining forces" (10).

Copek then points to a passage from Steinbeck's own work which apparently refutes a conventionally naturalistic reading of his work: "whoever employs this type of [non-teleological] thinking with other than few close friends will be referred to as detached, hard hearted, or even cruel. Quite the opposite seems to be true. Non-teleological methods more than any other seem capable of great tenderness, of an all-embracingness which is rare otherwise" (*Log 147*). Copek continues, "such thinking-without-blaming becomes 'living into'" (11). Rather than seeing Nature as something which places people "at the mercy of omnipotent determining forces," Steinbeck finds an "almost spiritual" quality in nature. What critics call Steinbeck's naturalism should instead be referred to as "ecology" or "a spirit of ecstasy" (12). Copek affirms the label Woodburn Ross placed on Steinbeck in 1949: "Naturalism's High Priest" (206). But Copek is careful to emphasize a less often-quoted passage from Ross in which he notes that Steinbeck was "the first . . . to build a mystical religion upon a naturalistic base" (Ross 214). Copek stresses over and over that when the term "naturalism" is used in conjunction with the work of John Steinbeck, it should not be confused with the naturalism of a Stephen Crane or a Frank Norris or an Ernest Hemingway.

Donald Pizer, author of a number of books on naturalism, reinforces Copek's thesis when he says, "I am uncertain that calling John Steinbeck a naturalist offers a useful insight into the distinctive nature of his work or of his literary imagination" (12). Like Copek, Pizer believes that "the term is too encrusted with the clichés and polemics of past literary wars to serve as a guide to the complex individuality of either a major Steinbeck novel or Steinbeck's work as a whole." Clearly, both critics felt in 1974 that the term "naturalism" as it had come to be understood was "not particularly useful" when applied to Steinbeck.

Such comments show the beginning of a movement toward a reevaluation of Steinbeck's work, and they question previously held views. And it is not unreasonable that such a critical reexamination may ultimately rejuvenate Steinbeck's literary reputation. Pizer implies that perhaps Steinbeck's work has been read in a less than advantageous light when he says, "it would probably be disastrous to attempt a complete explication of a Steinbeck novel as a reflection of naturalistic themes and techniques" (12). Ultimately, Pizer concludes that the naturalistic elements in Steinbeck's writing bear stronger affinity to the naturalists of the nineteenth century than of the twentieth.

Although in their discussion of Steinbeck's naturalism critics such as Pizer, Copek, and French do not always consider *East of Eden*, the issue of Steinbeck's naturalism is nevertheless central to an understanding of how critics perceive the book. One of the most bitter criticisms leveled against the novel by its earliest reviewers was that in it Steinbeck "abandoned" his naturalism. It would be inaccurate to say that the naturalism they found missing had never been there, but it would not be incorrect to look at the comments of a Pizer or of a French and conclude that the naturalism Steinbeck displayed in *East of Eden* is not the naturalism the book's reviewers expected to see. Whatever the critics ultimately conclude about it, the issue of what form of naturalism is present in Steinbeck's writing will appear again and again in criticism which seeks to reevaluate the work.

John Ditsky sought to explain the apparent change in Steinbeck's style in the first chapter of his 1977 book *Essays on East of Eden*. Entitled "Toward a Narrational Self," Ditsky's essay deals mainly with biographical elements, showing passages from Steinbeck's works and letters in the 30s and 50s and using them as examples of how Steinbeck's work changed. For the Steinbeck of the 1930s, the role of the artist is to become "merely a recording consciousness, judging nothing, simply putting down the thing" (1); as a result the author

"developed the device of the objective and dispassionate narrational voice."

Later, as Steinbeck's interests changed, he became less concerned with the idea of "group-man," a semi-deterministic theory about the biological nature of man which is central to what is probably the most naturalistic of Steinbeck's novels, *In Dubious Battle*, and informs the earlier chapters of *The Grapes of Wrath*.

In a letter which bears a strong resemblance to Chapter 13 of *East of Eden*, Steinbeck recants much of his previous belief in group man:

> I think I believe one thing powerfully—that the only creative thing our species has is the individual, lonely mind. Two people can create a child but I know of no other thing created by a group. The group ungoverned by individual thinking is a horrible destructive principle. (Ditsky 4)

At this point, says Ditsky, "John Steinbeck has finally resolved the issue of the group-man by returning to something like the Christian idea of moral responsibility—and is ready to incorporate the changes in his attitudes, and in himself as a person, into the novel" (4).

Ditsky maintains, as does French in "A Usable Concept of Naturalism," that the break from naturalism apparent in *East of Eden* is a stage in Steinbeck's development as artist. Ditsky takes his case farther than do either French or Copek, and provides for the first time in print an overt denial of Steinbeck's naturalism, saying, "Throughout a lifetime of writing third-person fiction, John Steinbeck had resisted the temptation to moralize, but he had done so at the cost of sundering spirit and substance. The price of his apparent objectivity was a *mistaken reputation as a naturalist, however impressive the achievement*" (13, emphasis added). Ditsky's position is clear; he is dissatisfied with prevailing wisdom about Steinbeck and about *East of Eden* and, like French and other critics who question Steinbeck's naturalism, feels that aspects of Steinbeck's art are as yet unexplored. It is Ditsky who labels much Steinbeck criticism "cookie cutter" (ix).

The question of naturalism and other strong disagreements with previous Steinbeck criticism figure prominently in Karen J. Hopkins' "Steinbeck's *East of Eden*: A Defense." Hopkins echoes Ditsky's commentary about "cookie cutter criticism" when she notes "that most critics who read *East of Eden* expect it to live up to some standard they've set, either for the novel as a genre, or for Steinbeck in particular, especially the Steinbeck of *The Grapes of Wrath*" (63). Furthermore, "both points of view respond to conventions rather than to the individual work." Like Ditsky, Hopkins feels that commentary about *East of Eden* has been prescriptive rather than descriptive. Steinbeck irritated a generation of critics by violating these conventions, or, as Hopkins puts it, "there are certain things which can't be done in a novel, and Steinbeck does them, QED" (63).

Borrowing from Charles Child Walcutt's *American Literary Naturalism: A Divided Stream*, Hopkins notes that "American naturalism has refused to accept" that "the mind is merely a chemical reaction" (65). In other words, American literary naturalism has tended to be idealistic. In *East of Eden*, Steinbeck articulated this tension between naturalism and idealism by incorporating elements of both.

Many critics have considered this novel anti-naturalistic because of the Old Testament elements and the discussion of *timshel*. However, says Hopkins, "The problem with this . . . is that the universe of the novel is as fiercely deterministic as even the most determined naturalist could want, more deterministic and much less pleasant, in fact, than exterior nature in some of Steinbeck's other novels" (67).

Hopkins also says that the essential element in *East of Eden* is the way characters react to their universe; she divides the characters in the novel into two categories: "those who tend to fictionalize and those who tend to analyze" (68). Characters who hold too closely to their fictions—Cyrus, Aaron, Cathy—are often destroyed. Put another way, "Man, enjoying a narrow and therefore false security in his ability to decipher and understand his surroundings, is suddenly destroyed or nearly destroyed by the intrusion of facts that imagination has refused to acknowledge" (68). The world of this novel is naturalistic.

Hopkins' study is instructive for a variety of reasons. Obviously, this work is a landmark in that it is the first article in a critical collection or journal which openly praises *East of Eden*. Also, it is instructive to note the way in which Hopkins summarizes and appraises earlier criticism of the work; to her it is a book whose reputation has sunk low enough (and in her opinion, unfairly so) that she feels it needs defense. Her reasoning anticipates Steinbeck criticism in the 1980s which seeks to reevaluate Steinbeck's naturalism.

During the 80s, the view that Steinbeck never was a naturalist gathered momentum. Robert DeMott's view, which he himself labels "extremely revisionary," stems from the proposition that "we

have misread Steinbeck" who is "primarily a Romantic ironist, who experimented tirelessly with varying formal and technical elements in his fiction, and maintained an intense lifelong interest in psychology, myth, and the shaping processes of the creative imagination" ("The Interior Distances of John Steinbeck" 87–88). DeMott, who bases his case solely on Steinbeck's post-1945 fiction, notes that "in his later years, from 1945 on, he consciously moved toward fabulation . . . in order to explore the implication inherent in the structural and epistemological tradition of the Romantic expressive fictional line" (88). Most of DeMott's premise hinges upon his discussion of the "interior life" of certain characters *East of Eden* and *Winter of Our Discontent* (a more detailed analysis of this argument follows here in discussion of changing critical reactions toward Steinbeck's characters such as Kate/Cathy). DeMott concludes his discussion of Steinbeck's "Romanticism" with a quote from *Travels With Charley:* "I am happy to report that in the war between reality and romance, reality is not the stronger" (136). DeMott is not the first to find Romantic tendencies in Steinbeck, but he is among the first to view these tendencies positively.

DeMott backs away from his somewhat radical suggestion in the last sentence of his essay by saying, "It is time, I suggest, to recognize Steinbeck's adherence not only to the tradition of mimetic or empirical writing, but to the larger and infinitely more exciting tradition of Romantic fictionalizing" (99); apparently Steinbeck used not only naturalistic elements but other elements as well.

DeMott is not alone in suggesting that Steinbeck should be read as a Romantic rather than a Naturalist. In 1979, Daniel Buerger writes that "the hero of *East of Eden* is the Romantic 'I' narrator" (12). By 1980, Paul McCarthy can write of "Steinbeck's Realism" as a "necessary realignment" to aid in the reading of Steinbeck's post–World War II fiction: "romance provides . . . [the] influence and mode in *East of Eden*" (118) and "something romantic is perceptible in the general patterns of *East of Eden*" (119).

Although it is risky to use a term such as "consensus" in connection with any Steinbeck novel, one might say that two of the most recent and influential works concerning Steinbeck have reached some sort of consensus in Steinbeck's naturalism. The first is Jackson J. Benson's *The True Adventures of John Steinbeck, Writer*, a book which has rapidly become the "standard" biography of the writer. Benson contends that Steinbeck was a naturalist, but differed

Landscape view of Salinas Valley, California, the setting of East of Eden

from other American writers of this tradition: "he would become, to use a term more familiar to those involved in literature, the most thoroughgoing naturalist among modern writers" (236). What distinguishes Steinbeck's particular brand of naturalism was that "he was the only major writer within the American tradition of naturalism who reacted to science in a positive way, embraced a scientific perception of the universe with enthusiasm, and who knew something about science" (244). Furthermore, "Steinbeck's own lack of ego made it easier for him to accept the relative unimportance of man and turn instead to a calm and even joyful realization of man's interdependence with the whole of nature." The

works of other naturalistic writers constitute something of a lament; Steinbeck accepted this view of the universe.

Benson does not view *East of Eden* as a "departure" or an "abandonment" of naturalism. Rather, he feels that it was an "outgrowth" of Steinbeck's naturalism, a further formulation or refinement of an idea he had worked out in his previous novels:

> Basic to his philosophy and carried over into *East of Eden* are the beliefs that man is but a small part of a large whole that is nature and that this whole is only imperfectly understood by man and does not conform to his schemes or wishes. Furthermore, as a part of

nature, man often obscures his place and function and the true nature of his environment by putting on various kinds of blinders—whereas it is essential to both his happiness and his survival that he learn to see himself and his surroundings . . . In *East of Eden*, Steinbeck adds a further element, prompted by his own recent struggle to survive and his concern for the future of his sons: in this materialistic, mechanistic universe, is there any chance for the individual to affect his own destiny? (236–37)

Benson's view gains strength because he is the "authoritative" biographer of Steinbeck. His opinion, as well, anticipates the increasingly accepted stance that *East of Eden* is philosophically consistent with Steinbeck's previous fiction. This is as "revisionary" as DeMott's thesis that Steinbeck was never a naturalist. And although Benson does not suggest that *East of Eden* is Steinbeck's best novel (in fact, he finds it seriously flawed), neither does he suggest that the work is without merit or reflects a "decline" in the novelist's powers.

John Timmerman's view, put forth in his 1986 *John Steinbeck's Fiction: The Aesthetics of the Road Taken*, takes a synthetic view, somewhere between that of Benson, who called Steinbeck "the most thoroughgoing naturalist" in American letters, and DeMott, who denies that Steinbeck ever was a naturalist. Instead, Timmerman finds in Steinbeck a "supernatural naturalism" and "a world which God has departed, like the dissipation of other ancient myths" (15). Timmerman places this aspect of Steinbeck's naturalism "solidly within the framework of his literary precursors" such as Crane, Hart, or Dreiser (26).

However, Steinbeck is also outside the naturalist tradition; "the term 'naturalistic' simply will not do as a final description of Steinbeck's view of humankind" (29). Instead, he "finds a supernatural power and presence observable *in* the natural, in the flora and the fauna and earth itself, and in humankind" (29). Where Crane would find the cosmos indifferent or perhaps even hostile, Steinbeck would find something which is nurturing and generative. He "probes the supernatural with typology and symbolism" (30).

In *East of Eden*, says Timmerman, Steinbeck's conception was basically naturalistic:

Furthermore, its vastness was compelling to him. Instead of being a small slice of life like *Tortilla Flat*, *Cannery Row*, or *Sweet Thursday*, this work took on the whole life. It contained in practice the theory of *The Log from the Sea of Cortez*—that all life must be seen whole in its whole environment, in relation to the all. It would bring all the threads together for him. It is no accident that over and over in *Journal*

of a Novel he concludes a letter to Covici with this phrase: "I will get to my knitting." (211)

Although Timmerman's view is unique, it presents a plausible synthesis of other views.

The various attitudes towards Steinbeck's naturalism, particularly its relationship to the novel under discussion, indicate recent changes in critical perception. Certain assumptions are simply no longer held or clung to. The issue of whether or not Steinbeck "declined" is no longer argued and, while the question has never been resolved, it has been replaced by new and perhaps more productive studies which examine the wealth of the Steinbeck canon. Perhaps the clearest indication that *East of Eden* is finally being given a close reading and judged on its own merits is that many studies of the novel make no mention of *The Grapes of Wrath*. Perhaps Steinbeck critics have abandoned the "cookie cutter" John Ditsky complained of more than a decade ago.

Source: Charles L. Etheridge, Jr., "Changing Attitudes toward Steinbeck's Naturalism and the Changing Reputation of *East of Eden*: A Survey of the Criticism since 1974," in *The Steinbeck Question: New Essays in Criticism*, edited by Donald R. Noble, Whitston Publishing, 1993, pp. 250–59.

Barbara A. Heavilin

In the following essay, Heavilin focuses on Steinbeck's theme of humans being able to triumph over evil in East of Eden, *and explores how Steinbeck develops characters and scenes to communicate this.*

In the final scene of *East of Eden*, Steinbeck employs a cinematic device that he used in the ending of *The Grapes of Wrath*, where Rose of Sharon nurses a starving stranger, bringing to its epitome the theme of hospitality, or kindness to strangers, that has run throughout the novel. This scene has the effect of freezing characters in the enactment of theme. With similar effect, in the final scene of *East of Eden*, Adam lies paralyzed by a stroke. His friend Lee, his son Cal, and Abra, who will eventually marry Cal, stand around him. With Lee's admonition and encouragement, Adam summons the strength to speak one final word of forgiveness, instruction, and inspiration to Cal: the Hebrew word *Timshel*, translated as "Thou mayest," from God's assurance to Cain in Genesis that he has the power to triumph over evil.

This final grouping of characters, like that in *The Grapes of Wrath*, symbolizes and affirms the theme that has run throughout *East of Eden*—that human beings can triumph over evil. This grouping serves also, however, to define Steinbeck's own view of the nature of good and evil, a necessary

> Like *The Grapes of Wrath*, then, the final scene of *East of Eden* ascends into the realm of the mythic, of the mysterious, of faith and religious belief in the human power of transcendence. The final scene is an accolade to the human spirit and to the human experience."

and corollary theme, which has also run throughout the novel to reach its epitome in this final scene. The enormous wickedness of Cathy/Kate has not endured, for in Steinbeck's view, overwhelming as evil may seem sometimes, it ultimately proves empty and transitory. Like Cathy/Kate's life and suicide, evil lacks endurance and continuity. With his final word Adam has assured their son Cal that he is not bound by his mother's evil nature, that he has the power to choose what is good.

Since the enduring strength of goodness lies in connections and continuity, this scene shows these characteristics, or qualities, in action. Adam's Chinese friend, Lee, is by his side, faithful to the end. Concerned with both the peace of Adam's own soul and the future of his troubled son Cal, Lee reminds Adam that "Cal will marry and his children will be the only remnant left of you." Cal and his future wife Abra, therefore, show the continuity of generations. As Adam's loving word *Timshel* sets Cal free to choose the good, by implication he and Abra will pass on to their own children the same freedom and power of choice, of transcendence.

In conversation with Cal and Abra before they enter Adam's room, Lee reveals his own feeling of destitution when Samuel Hamilton died—"the world went out like a candle"—and his "stupidity" in thinking that "the good are destroyed while the evil survive and prosper." With the analogy that the "craftsman" never loses "his hunger to make the perfect cup—thin, strong, translucent," Lee affirms his belief that "whatever made us" never stops trying for perfection and that human beings have this same innate desire. They must, therefore,

either keep striving to achieve their goals or else end up on "the slag heap."

Like *The Grapes of Wrath*, then, the final scene of *East of Eden* ascends into the realm of the mythic, of the mysterious, of faith and religious belief in the human power of transcendence. The final scene is an accolade to the human spirit and to the human experience. Human beings need not be defeated by the evil they encounter, for there is greater strength in goodness than in evil. And they have the power of choice. These beliefs some critics label "Romantic," or "sentimental."

Steinbeck, however, is a kindred spirit of Viktor Frankl, whose work no responsible, thoughtful person would dare label sentimental. Frankl, a Jewish psychiatrist imprisoned in Auschwitz and other Nazi death camps during World War II, emerged from his experiences with an optimistic belief in the capacity of human beings to withstand evil even in the face of the most monstrous evils in human history. Out of his own experience and from his own observations, Frankl declares that human beings have the potential to behave like "saints" or "swine," that they have both potentials within themselves, but "which one is actualized depends on decisions but not on conditions." This power of choice, Frankl writes, is "the last of the human freedoms—to choose one's attitude in any given set of circumstances, to choose one's own way."

Enacting Steinbeck's similar belief in the human powers of choice and of transcendence, the dying Adam whispers to his son Cal, *"Timshel,"* thus assuring him that his own decisions—not genetic predetermination, not his monstrously wicked mother, Cathy/Kate—will determine his destiny.

As Frankl authenticates his pronouncement that human beings have the potential to behave like "saints" or "swine," or to choose good or evil, so by his own observation and experience, Steinbeck must authenticate his own belief that human beings can overcome evil, that not all are destroyed. In doing so, through the lives of his characters, the Hamiltons and the Trasks, he carefully delineates and defines the nature of good and evil. Closely allied to the *timshel* theme, "Thou mayest rule over sin," is this corollary and necessary metaphysical exploration that seeks to discover what goodness is and what evil is. This thematic exploration is closely allied to the novel's structure, running from the opening pages describing the Salinas Valley to its dramatic enactment in the final scene.

In *Journal of a Novel* Steinbeck has revealed a concern for wholeness—for "form," "design," "pace," "balance," "proportion," "necessity," and "purpose." About two months before the novel's completion, he wrote to Pascal Covici: "This book which seems to sprawl actually does not at all. It is almost as tight as a short story." A survey of his exploration of the nature of good and evil, a necessary corollary of the *timshel* theme, reveals that Steinbeck has an Aristotelian sense of wholeness in which the parts of the action fit together so that structure and theme in *East of Eden* melt into a unified, coherent whole.

In "Outside of Paradise: Men and the Land in *East of Eden*," John Ditsky points out the role of the opening setting in Stienbeck's exploration of good and evil:

> The dual possibilities of good and evil, life and death, which the Valley affords its onlookers, its potential settlers, are emphasized by the contrast of moods associated with the two opposed mountain ranges: the "light gay mountains" to the east, suggesting as they do a "brown grass love," a maternal welcome, birth, and morning; and the "dark and brooding" peaks to the west, which intimate the "unfriendly and dangerous" sentiments, death and night.

Against this backdrop, symbolic of the good and evil poles between which human beings gravitate, Steinbeck sets the history of "the long Salinas Valley," beginning with a nondescript tribe of Indians, then Spaniards who were greedy "for gold or God," and finally Americans, who were even "more greedy because there were more of them"—who "took the lands, remade the laws to make their titles good."

Into this valley Steinbeck's grandfather, Samuel Hamilton, brought his wife Liza. In chapter 2, depending "on hearsay, on old photographs, on stories told, and on memories which are hazy and mixed with fable," Steinbeck introduces the Hamiltons. In the second part of the chapter, he tells of the original settlers—some penniless and some wealthy, with Adam Trask among the latter. Steinbeck has thus set up two family strands that run through the novel to the end of Part 3, after which the Hamiltons are no longer present—at least not physically. Since Samuel has in a sense passed his patriarchal mantle of goodness on to Adam, however, this physical absence poses no structural problem—for both Lee and Adam are Samuel's spiritual sons. Their relationship to Samuel is what Steinbeck calls "the continuing thing that bridges lives and ties the whole thing together" (*JN*, p. 116). He further elucidates what he means by "the continuing thing" in the next day's letter: "I have the same reluctance you have to lose Samuel except that we won't lose him. That is one of the theses"

(*JN*, p. 117). Part of the power of goodness, then, lies in its continuity. Samuel has been a good man, he has lived a good life, and his goodness will survive. For both Adam and Lee take up his mantle:

> "Maybe both of us have got a piece of him," said Lee . . . "I seemed to come out of a sleep," said Adam. "In some strange way my eyes have cleared. A weight is off me." "You even use words that sound like Mr. Hamilton," said Lee.

Samuel's presence and influence are felt, then, in the final scene when Lee recalls Samuel's parting exultation—"like a bird song in the night"—in his affirmation that there are those "who like pillars of fire guide frightened men through the darkness." Remembering, Lee acknowledges the "stupidity" of his previous belief that "the good are destroyed while the evil survive and prosper." And Adam, also Samuel's spiritual heir, whispers *Timshel* to his son Cal—freeing him from his fears that he is genetically predisposed to evil, enabling him to choose his own way.

As in character, deed, and word, Samuel is one of those who define the nature of goodness through their lives, he is also one who shows that goodness in this world always has some alloy, some stain. The alloy in Samuel's goodness is a remembered love who comes to his mind

> "night after month after year, right to the very now. And I think I should have double-bolted my mind and sealed off my heart against her, but I did not. All of these years I've cheated Liza. I've given her an untruth, a counterfeit, and I've saved the best for those dark sweet hours,"

he tells Adam.

This stain of one sort or another—this mark of Cain—all human beings share. Others in the novel share as well in this awareness of stain. John H. Timmerman points out, for example, that Horace Quinn "knows the evil that stands just on the other side of goodness; his response is to hold it communally in the delicate balance that brings peace." Although goodness, then, has endurance and continuity and is not finally destroyed, at the same time it nevertheless has an alloy, or flaw—for nothing in this world achieves perfection. In this belief, as well as in his belief in the human power of transcendence, Steinbeck again reveals an affinity to Frankl. For, acknowledging his own stain, Frankl proclaims honestly of his Auschwitz experience that "the best of us"—those unwilling to sacrifice others to save themselves—did not come back.

Just as the continuing capacity of goodness is balanced by the diminishing quality of evil, so the alloy, or stain, inherent in all human goodness is balanced by at least a glimmer of a redeeming human quality even in the most wicked. Even Cathy/Kate, in the midst of plotting Ethel's murder—unaware that she is already dead—realizes that she does not want her son Aron "to know about her." Daydreaming, she imagines his visiting her in New York:

> He would think that she had always lived in an elegant little house on the East Side. She would take him to the theatre, to the opera, and people would see them together and wonder at their loveliness, and recognize that they were either brother and sister or mother and son. No one could fail to know.

Before committing suicide, she writes a note: "I leave everything I have to my son Aron Trask." This slight glimmer of maternal protection and pride provides a glimpse of what might have been—connections she might have made, and affection she might have shared with her sons.

Here Steinbeck's introduction of what to some has seemed contradictory and out of character stems from his observation that even the most evil may have a modicum of goodness. Steinbeck's observation in this instance is similar to the Quaker tenet that along with the breath of life, God imparts a light that shines in every human being. That is, however wicked, a person may have some redeeming quality—even the Cathy/Kates of this world.

Despite this tiny speck showing the possibility of goodness—she is daydreaming after all—as Robert DeMott has pointed out, Cathy "embodies evil," and she is written large purposefully in order to depict later the emptiness the nothingness, the void that is evil's true nature. Thus, as the embodiment of evil she stands alone, her eventual diminution balanced by the continuity of goodness represented in Samuel, the Hamilton women, and Abra, who also participates in the legacy of Samuel because his mantle of goodness has passed to Adam and his heirs. From youth Cathy has followed a life of perversion, violence, and prostitution, corrupting young boys, instigating her Latin teacher's suicide, burning her parents to death in their own home, shooting her husband Adam, forsaking her twin sons for a house of prostitution, and torturing and murdering Faye, the madam who loved her as a daughter and bequeathed her establishment to her.

The balance between the enormity of Cathy's wickedness, which finally diminishes into nothingness, and the goodness of the Hamilton women, which extends in a long, continuing line, is probably best illustrated in two contrasting scenes: one depicting Kate's house and her room and the other depicting the house of Olive, Steinbeck's own mother, and his grandmother Liza's room in that house. For the character of human beings and their attributes of good or evil may be discerned in their surroundings and their possessions.

Having learned from Samuel that Cathy is in Salinas and that she is now a madam notorious for wickedness, after Samuel's funeral Adam gathers the courage to encounter her for the first time since she shot him and deserted her family. He finds her house a picture of an anti-Eden. The path to the house is "overgrown." The porch is "dark," "sagging," and "dilapidated," and its steps "shaky." "The paint had long disappeared from the clapboard walls and no work had ever been done on the garden. . . . The stair treads seemed to crumple under his weight and the porch planks squealed as he crossed them." As the front door opens, he sees "a dim figure holding the knob." Images of darkness, decay, and the chaos of neglect provide a fitting backdrop for Cathy's own psyche.

Inside the house, however, Adam finds "richness and order," and "Kate's private room was comfort and efficiency":

> The walls were clad in saffron silk, and the drapes were apple green. It was a silken room—deep chairs with silk-upholstered cushions, lamps with silken shades, a broad bed at the far end of the room with a gleaming white satin cover on which were piled gigantic pillows. There was no picture on the wall, no photograph or personal thing of any kind. A dressing table near the bed had no bottle or vial on its ebony top, and its sheen was reflected in triple mirrors. The rug was old and deep and Chinese, an apple-green dragon on saffron.

Luxurious as a showroom in a furniture store or the bedroom in a house decorated for display, Kate's room mirrors the emptiness of her life—"no picture on the wall, no photograph or personal thing of any kind," "no bottle or vial" on the ebony top of her dressing table The "apple-green dragon" on the deep-piled, saffron Chinese rug symbolizes her only connection—probably intended here to be "the dragon, the serpent of old, who is the devil and Satan" described in the Revelation of the Apostle John.

On a later occasion when Adam goes to see Liza Hamilton "to pay [his] respects," he walks up "wide veranda steps" to the "high white house of Ernest [and Olive] Steinbeck"—Steinbeck's own parents. "It was an immaculate and friendly house, grand enough but not pretentious, and it sat inside its white fence, surrounded by its clipped lawn, and roses and catoneasters lapped against its white walls." When Olive opens the door, John and his sister, Mary, peek "around the edges of her." Images of whiteness, neatness, and cultivated vegetation connect this house and the continuation of the Hamilton family living there—Liza, Olive, and her children, John and Mary—to the Edenic vision of goodness.

Liza's "pleasant little bed-sitting room" is the polar opposite of Kate's luxurious room, which has neither photographs nor knick-knacks. It is "crowded with photographs, bottles of toilet water, lace pin-cushions, brushes and combs, and the china and silver bureau-knacks of many birthdays and Christmases." On the wall hangs "a huge tinted photograph of Samuel." With her pet, an irreverent Polly parrot, who, despite all her efforts, refuses to "substitute psalms for the picturesque vocabulary of his youth," Liza, who is new "old and old," faces the end of her life with "iron gallantry." Her room mirrors a life full of connections to loved ones, of affections and fulfillment, of celebrations and losses. She has been a fitting mate for Samuel. Her goodness matches his. Confident of her goodness and sure of her insights, when he and Lee have dreadful forebodings after the birth of Cathy's twins, Samuel cries:

> "I want my wife.... I want her here. They say miners take canaries into the pits to test the air. Liza has no truck with foolishness. And, Lee, if Liza sees a ghost, it's a ghost and not a fragment of a dream. If Liza feels trouble, we'll bar the doors."

Unlike Cathy, then, Liza is like the ideal woman portrayed in Proverbs 31, for the "heart of her husband" could safely trust in her. And as Samuel's portrait is Liza's counterpart to Cathy's satanic "apple-green dragon," so their lives have run opposing courses—Liza's as a giver and nurturer of life and Cathy's as a destroyer of lives.

In the voice of the narrator, Steinbeck broadens the scope of this exploration of the nature of good in the setting and in the two families, the Hamiltons and the Trasks, to include anecdotes and observations that further elucidate this theme. In one of these anecdotes, he tells at length about his own mother—briefly of her teaching experiences and marriage and then in great detail the events leading up to the United States Treasury Department's awarding her the prize of "a ride in an army airplane." Some critics of Steinbeck's structuring of *East of Eden* have found this particular incident a diversion from the main story line, unnecessary to the novel's thematic design. But, like her mother, Liza, Olive is one of those Hamilton women who, in the continuity of their goodness, serve to give balance to Cathy who, though written large, stands alone as an evil monstrosity.

Like Liza, Olive furnishes an antithesis to Cathy. As Olive is associated with the "light and beauty" that her son humorously describes her as forcing "down the throats of her reluctant pupils," so Kate is associated with the darkness and grayness with which she surrounds herself, claiming that "light hurts [her] eyes." As Olive has the "great courage" it takes "to raise children," so Kate has attempted to abort hers. As Olive spared no effort in trying to save her son John from death from pleural pneumonia when he was sixteen—asking for the prayers of the "Episcopalian minister" and the "Mother Superior and nuns," and the "thought" of a distant Christian Science relative, as well as seeking out "every incantation, magic, and herbal formula, . . . two good nurses and the town's best doctors"—so Kate has heartlessly shot her husband and abandoned hungry twin sons. As Olive is known for her love and courage, so Cathy is noted for her self-absorption and wickedness.

Olive's altruism and courage during the occasion leading up to her ride in the Army airplane further distances her from Cathy. Even though the anecdote is humorous, it nevertheless shows Olive's love and courage in action. Tongue in cheek, Steinbeck tells of his mother's reactions to the death of one of the neighborhood boys in Germany in World War I:

> If the Germans had known Olive and had been sensible they would have gone out of their way not to anger her. But they didn't know or they were stupid. When they killed Martin Hopps they lost the war because that made my mother mad and she took out after them. She had liked Martin Hopps. He had never hurt anyone. When they killed him Olive declared war on the German empire.

She devotes herself, therefore, to the sale of Liberty bonds even though "she had never sold anything in her life beyond an occasional angel cake for the Altar Guild in the basement of the Episcopal church." Whereas Olive, therefore, increases the size of her personal world to take on moral combat with the international enemy, Cathy's world shrinks finally to her suicide in "the gray room" where in the end she grows "smaller and smaller and then disappeared—and she had never been."

First awarded "a German Helmet," then "a bayonet" and "a jagged piece of shrapnel set on an ebony base," when Olive quadruples her sales record, she is "awarded the fairest prize of all—a ride in an army airplane." Although she is terrified, she is courageously courteous and considerate of the pilot as he "barrel-rolled, made Immelmann turns, inside and outside loops, and turned over and flew over the field upside down" because he thinks she has consented to a "stunt," a word which, distorted by his "goggled face and the slip stream," Liza has interpreted as meaning that the throttle is "stuck." Swallowing her terror because she believes that she must "encourage" him in a difficult situation, she keeps nodding and smiling brightly to "give him courage." In contrast, when she is in labor, Cathy savagely bites the hand of the gentle Samuel who is trying to help her. Thus, this anecdote in the narrator's voice is an essential part of the intricate "balance" for which Steinbeck expresses concern in *Journal of a Novel*. Furthermore, for Steinbeck's own two sons, it endorses their own proud, continuing heritage of familial goodness.

Besides anecdotes, the narrator's voice introduces also some of the personal observations that give authenticity to Steinbeck's exploration of the nature of good and evil. One such observation is that in which the narrator muses on the attributes and contributions of "the church and the whorehouse," which "arrived in the Far West simultaneously." Although the narrator ironically relates the two, asserting that both accomplish "a different facet of the same thing"—to take "a man out of his bleakness for a time," Steinbeck's overall view of churches and whorehouses is not this simplistic or reductive. Rather, in the fuller context of the novel, the comments on churches and whorehouses serve to corroborate his observations of the alloy in goodness and the glimmer of light, or goodness, in evil. For the churches brought with them

> the Scripture on which our ethics, our art and poetry, and our relationships are built. . . . And they brought music. . . . And they brought conscience, or, rather nudged the dozing conscience. They were not pure, but they had a potential of purity, like a soiled white shirt.

Though stained, the church has the potential for purity—its goodness flawed but not destroyed.

The brothels, "the sister evangelism," brought "release and joy for the body," and their "celebrated madams," who each combine "the brains of a businessman, the toughness of a prize fighter, the warmth of a companion, the humor of a tragedian," are remembered by customers as "philanthropist, medical authority, bouncer, and poetess of the bodily emotions without being involved with them." Despite this very male view of brothels, Steinbeck is not blind to the very dark, reductive, and destructive life of the whore, whose life lacks the sweet connections and continuity he associates with the life of the Hamilton women and Abra. To illustrate, in the narrator's guidelines for being a madam, he notes, "You have to keep suicide at an absolute minimum, and whores, particularly the

ones getting along in years, are flighty with a razor; and that gets your house a bad name."

And even a madam does not want her daughter to become a whore, for when Faye begins "to think of Kate as her daughter, . . . her natural morality took hold. She did not want her daughter to be a whore." In his reductive statement, "A whore is a whore," the sheriff denies their personhood—seeing them as objects to be used, not as human beings with intelligence, feelings, and potential for anything higher than prostitution. Connected with this view of whores as non-persons, Steinbeck portrays them also as being among the lost ones, the drug addicts, who find solace in oblivion, in escape from the reality of their surroundings. For instance, in a conversation with Kate, a whore named Eva becomes so jittery that "her mind went to the box in her dresser drawer where her hypodermic needle lay."

Although he recognizes the momentary "release and joy for the body" for the male frequenter of brothels, Steinbeck also faithfully portrays the isolation, loneliness, darkness, and sorrow of the life of the whore. No glimmer of light reduces the inevitability of her destruction—physically or psychically, or both. After all, even Kate herself, who glories in her brothel, is finally reduced to suicide and nothingness, as though "she had never been."

In the end Kate is notable only because Adam must set Cal free of his fear that he is like his mother, that because of her he may be genetically predisposed to evil. Choosing her own isolation, she has left both husband and son to exult in their freedom from her as Adam whispers his parting word, *Timshel*. The cinematic freezing of this final scene brings to a fitting finale Steinbeck's exploration of the nature of good and evil.

In Kate is also shown the possibility of goodness in her daydream of what life might be like with her son, Aron. And the continuity of goodness is portrayed in Adam and Lee, who carry the mantle of Samuel's goodness, to be passed on in continuity to Cal and Abra's children. The alloy of goodness, the impossibility of human perfection, has been illustrated in all of their lives. Representative of Steinbeck's optimistic belief in the human power of transcendence, Lee, Cal, and Abra surround the dying Adam.

The scene is not one of defeat, but rather of triumph. In Adam's courage to speak through his paralysis, in Lee's faithful encouragement and support, in Cal and Abra's love for each other and for Adam and Lee, the sting has been taken from death. For in this final scene Steinbeck once more shares a vision with the psychiatrist Frankl, who tells of its experience of communing with his wife during his imprisonment in the Nazi death camps, not knowing whether she was alive or dead:

> Had I known then that my wife was dead, I think that I would still have given myself, undisturbed by that knowledge, to the contemplation of her image, and that my mental conversation with her would have been just as vivid and just as satisfying. "Set me like a seal upon thy heart, love is as strong as death."

Love and goodness, for both Steinbeck and Frankl, are inexorably intertwined, and that goodness, that love, endures—"the continuing thing," "the thesis," of which Steinbeck writes also in *Journal of a Novel*. Adam, like Samuel, will continue.

Source: Barbara A. Heavilin, "Steinbeck's Exploration of Good and Evil: Structural and Thematic Unity in *East of Eden*," in *Steinbeck Quarterly*, Vol. 26, Nos. 3–4, Summer/Fall 1993, pp. 90–100.

Barbara McDaniel

In the following essay, McDaniel examines alienation as a psychological force in East of Eden.

"I think there is only one book to a man," said John Steinbeck as he wrote *East of Eden*. "This is the book I have always wanted and have worked and prayed to be able to write" (*JN*, p. 5). Though Steinbeck wrote *East of Eden*, his "big book" (*JN*, p. 33), with a strong sense of purpose, critics have found it formless; and though he recorded his ideas about it daily, critics have been vague about his theme. Steinbeck expected these problems, but the expectation was not the confession of guilt it has been taken for. "My carefully worked out method will be jumped on by the not too careful critic as slipshod" (*JN*, p. 31), he predicted. Critics have taken as support Steinbeck's occasional concern about whether he would be understood, discounting his dominating enthusiasm about the basic soundness of his plan. *East of Eden* should seem "ordinary" and "casual," he wrote, but "it is the most uncasual story in the world" (*JN*, p. 40). "As you will have discovered . . . the technique of this book is an apparent lack of technique and I assure you that it is not easy" (*JN*, p. 60).

About midway through *East of Eden* Steinbeck wrote, "My patterned book is clear to me now—right to the end. And I am pleased that I am able to follow the form I laid down so long ago. I hope the book will sound a little formless at first until it settles in the mind" (*JN*, p. 112). As he drew toward the end he said, "What seems kind of accidental is not. I don't think there is a single sentence

> *East of Eden* is not only less formless, it is less sentimental than it has been taken to be. Just as it is not loosely 'about good and evil,' it is not vaguely 'about morality.' It is about morality only in the sense that it looks at human behavior from established perspectives."

in this whole book that does not either develop character, carry on the story or provide necessary background" (*JN*, p. 153). Again anticipating critical response to his work Steinbeck mused, "Years after I have finished a book, someone discovers my design and ascribes it either to a theft or an accident" (*JN*, p. 134). The purpose of the following essay is to do half of this, that is, to compare the novel and the *East of Eden* journal to clarify understanding of the theme; but it should exonerate Steinbeck from a felony regarding form. It will charge him, instead, with misdemeanors in tone.

Steinbeck thought a chapter should "have design of tone, as well as of form. A chapter should be a perfect cell in the whole book and should almost be able to stand alone" (*JN*, p. 25). But a chapter standing too strongly alone in *East of Eden* has often controlled interpretations of the book. These are the suasive words in Chapter 34:

> Humans are caught—in their lives, in their thoughts, in their hungers and ambitions, in their avarice and cruelty, and in their kindness and generosity too—in a net of good and evil. I think this is the only story we have and that it occurs on all levels of feeling and intelligence.

Out of context Chapter 34 seems a forthright statement of a theme of good and evil. Within the context of the book, however, this short essay relates to a point in the narrative much as the intercalary chapters did in *The Grapes of Wrath*. In Chapter 34 Steinbeck is generalizing about death, good, and evil just after he has particularized feelings about these things as they affect one man, Tom Hamilton, in Chapter 33. These words do not state the major theme; they give only a hint of it in *caught* and *net*.

It is possible to suggest, then, that *East of Eden* is even more complex than *The Grapes of Wrath* because along with tracing three generations of a fictional family, the Trasks, Steinbeck intersperses chapters about the Hamiltons, his own maternal relatives; sometimes intertwines the Hamiltons and the Trasks; and still writes essay chapters. But the materials are carefully related, and not at all "sloppy" and "confused" as Peter Lisca claims.

Another connection to the main theme appears in Chapter 34: "In uncertainty I am certain that underneath their topmost layers of frailty men want to be good and want to be loved. Indeed, most of their vices are attempted short cuts to love." But the theme is stated specifically in the middle of the book, Chapter 22; Steinbeck corroborates this fact (*JN*, p. 104). Lee, the wise Chinese servant of Adam Trask makes the thematic statement for the author:

> I think this is the best-known story in the world because it is everybody's story. I think it is the symbol story of the human soul.... The greatest terror a child can have is that he is not loved, and rejection is the hell he fears. I think everyone in the world to a large or small extent has felt rejection. And with rejection comes anger, and with anger some kind of crime in revenge for the rejection, and with the crime guilt— and there is the story of mankind. I think that if rejection could be amputated, the human would not be what he is.... It is all there—the start, the beginning. One child, refused the love he craves, kicks the cat and hides his secret guilt; and another steals so that money will make him loved; and third conquers the world—and always the guilt and revenge and more guilt.... Therefore I think this old and terrible story is important because it is a chart of the soul—the secret, rejected, guilty soul.

Steinbeck's publicized account of his writing of the novel, *Journal of a Novel*, consists of unmailed letters Steinbeck wrote his Viking editor, Pascal Covici about *East of Eden*. Writing daily letters to warm up for his work, he thus left a unique and valuable record of the composition of the novel, as well as of his creative processes per se. But it takes thorough knowledge of the novel as well as knowledge about Steinbeck to plumb all the letters because Steinbeck did not have to explain to Covici what other readers may not know. There are also problems in correlating the books because the manuscript of *East of Eden* was cut and changed. Nevertheless, comparing the *Journal* and the published text can refine our understanding of the theme, for week by week Steinbeck commented on his theme and structure.

The most telling note appears June 11, 1951, when Steinbeck was writing the section containing the words of Lee quoted above: "if you wonder why I am spending so much time on this naming—you must know that I am stating my thesis and laying it out" (*JN*, p. 104). "This naming" refers to Adam Trask, Samuel Hamilton, and Lee naming Adam's twin sons. Calling the boys Caleb and Aaron (which he shortens to Cal and Aron), Steinbeck makes their initials match Cain's and Abel's. Steinbeck wants "the whole book illuminated by the discussion," which is not "just a discussion of Biblical lore," but uses "the Biblical story as a measure of ourselves" (*JN*, pp. 104–05). Rather than expressing the "theme of the individual's struggle between good and evil, for even "the importance of the individual human soul," the central chapters explain the causes of evil from a psychological point of view: evil comes from feelings of rejection. Believing that people follow patterns in their lives (*JN*, p. 151), Steinbeck wanted to show that to break out of destructive patterns begun by rejection, people must feel accepted by others. Simplified, the theme of *East of Eden* is alienation—the alienation that writes the history of evil in the world. Alienation in this respect means feelings of unwanted separation. Once this theme is understood, supposed flaws in Steinbeck's structure disappear; the author's confidence in his design makes sense; and some recent views defending the book get new support.

Because the violent Cains are easiest to understand in *East of Eden*, people often see the Abel characters as simply "good." Steinbeck shows their complexity in Adam. Abels are "good," in that by personality, they are not inclined to be aggressive, but they can still experience alienation. (In real life, Abels as well as Cains suffer from guilt, but *East of Eden* is complex enough without trying to prove this.) Abels handle rejection subtly—by isolation and withdrawal, for example; by compulsive behavior; or by submitting to manipulation. They may even commit suicide out of despair or guilt. When Robert DeMott notes that the relationship of major characters in *East of Eden* indicates their "psychological personalities," he makes an important observation in this regard. Commenting on the behavior of Adam Trask, DeMott says the young Adam "foreshadows the separateness and isolation which characterizes Adam throughout the book." DeMott's "revisionary thesis" (his term) urges greater attention to three interests of Steinbeck—psychology, myth, and the processes of the creative imagination. In a manner of speaking, all three shaped the theme and structure of *East of Eden*, as will be seen in Steinbeck's effort to explain the consequences of rejection with Cain and Abel as his frame.

It is interesting to note that Steinbeck considered giving his principal characters the family name of Canable (Cain-Abel). He limited the symbolism to first initials, instead, yet because he wanted a broad span of time and place to suggest the role of rejection in human history, he portrayed three generations of Trasks with such names. Cyrus Trask, the first, is married to Alice, the first Abel. In the next generation Cyrus has sons named Charles and Adam. Adam marries Cathy and has the sons Cal and Aron. The third generation characters are the most fully developed, so that they can show that the sins of the fathers are visited upon their sons, as the Bible has said. To examine the destructive cycle seems to have been Steinbeck's plan from the start. The chief new discovery made while writing the novel was the way to give humanity hope of changing the pattern. Lee expresses the challenge. " 'Couldn't a world be built around accepted truth? Couldn't some pains and insanities be rooted out if the causes were known?' " Almost overwhelmed with excitement, Samuel replies to Lee, " 'I don't know, damn you. You've taken a contentious game and made an answer of it. Let me alone—let me think!' " Not the kind of artist he called "hard boiled," Steinbeck believed there is one purpose in writing . . . beyond simply doing it interestingly. It is the duty of the writer to lift up, to extend, to encourage" (*JN*, p. 115). In the process of intently re-examining Genesis he suddenly discovered what he needed. "I have finally I think found a key to the story" (*JN*, p. 104). His key was the Hebrew word *timshel*.

The letters to Covici show Steinbeck then sought justification for introducing a new translation of *timshel* (Chapter Four, Verse Seven). In the King James version of the Bible God says to Cain, "thou shalt rule over" sin, making a promise. The American Standard Version reads "Do thou"—an order. But through Lee, Steinbeck presents a translation that sets man free—"thou mayest." This translation gives man a choice. At the same time that he saw this possibility in his materials, Steinbeck discovered a new and final title: "I think I have a title at last, a beautiful title, *East of Eden*. And read the sixteenth verse to find it. And the Salinas Valley is surely East of Eden. . . . What a strange story it is and how its haunts one. . . . I began to realize that without this story—or rather a sense of it—psychiatrists would have nothing to do. In other words this one story is the basis of all human neurosis. . . ." (*JN*, p. 104). Having abandoned the regional title *Salinas Valley*, the personal *My Valley*, and the narrow *Cain Sign*, Steinbeck found the title grew with him; but he worried that it might seem "a soft title" though "it is anything but soft. . . . I think the quotation 'And Cain etc.' should be at the bottom of the title page. . . . There should never be any doubt in the reader's mind what the title refers to" (*JN*, p. 107). And believing it an author's obligation to contribute "to our developing species and our half developed culture," he wanted to show, to "say so sharply and so memorably that it will not be forgotten," that "although East of Eden is not Eden, it is not insuperably far away" (*JN*, pp. 115–16).

With Chapter 1 almost complete Steinbeck had said, "the theme is beginning to emerge . . . It will emerge again and again . . . The gifts of Cain and Abel to their father and his rejection of one and acceptance of the other will I think mean a great deal to you but I wonder if it will be generally understood by other readers" (*JN*, p. 25). The painstaking deliberations about *timshel* show the same great concern with language and medieval texts he later demonstrated in *The Acts of King Arthur and His Noble Knights*. "One of the most important mistranslations in the Old Testament" surrounds *timshel*, he said. "This little story turns out to be one of the most profound in the world." Besides the possibility of free will in the story there is the "other thing," a question of the significance of "firstling" and "fat." "If firstling and fat are qualitative, then fruit of the earth without a qualitative might be some *key to the rejection*" (*JN*, p. 108; (my italics). Certainly Steinbeck was concerned about how all the parts of the story fit— especially the cause and the effect of Cain's rejection.

Though Steinbeck wondered whether he was getting his point across, he went on being intentionally subtle. As he finished the chapter establishing his thesis, a very difficult section to write, he said with relief, "I could have put it in a kind of an essay but I think it was better to let it come out of these three" [Adam, Lee, and Samuel] (*JN*, p. 105). Following subsequent letters laboring over questions about Cain's rejection and the meaning of God's words, Steinbeck concluded: "Now tomorrow I will have a final statement of my theme and it will never again be mentioned in the book" (*JN*, p. 113).

Steinbeck was preparing for Samuel Hamilton's death as he said this, and for Samuel's final meeting with Adam "packed with information both about the men and about the story" (*JN*, p. 114). Several times he said that after Samuel's death "the whole tempo and tone of the story is going to change. It will speed up and leap toward the future" (*JN*, p. 114). Having shown Adam's life after Samuel's death, Steinbeck confirmed "it is all down now. Its thesis is stated—all of it. Now we will see the thesis at work" (*JN*, p. 123).

In the section Steinbeck was talking about Samuel leads Adam out of the long depression that followed Adam's rejection by Cathy. Samuel gives Adam some final advice and a push toward living without him. Thus a father figure, Samuel frees his "son" from rejection. For the first time in his life, Adam can live independent of the control of another.

But being free is a passage to knowledge—it is not knowledge itself. In the second half of the book Adam must repeat the errors of his own rejecting father, Cyrus, before he learns to set Cal free. Lee introduces the freedom of choice; Samuel exercises this freedom by taking the risk that frees Adam; Adam will free Cal. Steinbeck wanted to show that fathers visit sins upon their sons by denying them free choice. Freedom is a gift of love. Adam's deathbed bequest to Cal is clear when he says *"Timshel!"*

Steinbeck laid out his vision of the cycle of rejection and alienation *vs.* reconciliation when he presented his thesis in Chapter 22, then illustrated it in 24. On June 21, 1951, anticipating the illustration he wrote, "I will take up the little flute melody, the continuing thing that bridges lives and ties the whole thing together, and I will end with a huge chord if I can do it" (*JN*, p. 116). Achieving his goal the next day he exulted, "I have never been more excited in my life about a chapter than I have been in this one which is just now concluding [the present Chapters 23 and 24]. . . . I know it needs lots of work but the form and the content of it seem right to me and right for the design of the book" (*JN*, p. 117). He had made Samuel confront Adam with the truth of Cathy's perversion; and Adam had proved his strength. The focus of the book then shifted to Cal.

Two weeks later Steinbeck's intentions remain firm; he says he has no sense of wandering from his purpose and he is about to reverse the "C-A theme" of the first section taking "the burden" from the Abel (Adam) and putting it on the Cain figure, Caleb, "my Cain principle." "Charles was a dark principle who remained dark. . . . Part 3 is Caleb's part—since he dominates and survives it. Thus we get no repetition but an extension of Part I" (*JN*, p. 128). In other words, in Part I, Charles, a Cain, did not struggle against evil, but Cal will; and because Lee intercedes for Cal, Adam will set Cal free to conquer "evil." In a letter to Covici, Steinbeck calls Cal Trask his "baby": "He is the Everyman, the battle ground between good and evil, the most human of all, the sorry man. In that battle the survivor is both" (*SLL*, p. 429). Cal is Steinbeck's "baby" because of his struggle; Cal shows that the rejected, angry man can gain control over the forces that are directing him.

In existential terms, alienation is a loss of freedom. In psychological terms, alienation is a force that can cause isolation, destruction, submission, or unnatural control. *East of Eden* can be read as a novel illustrating either that philosophical or that psychological view of humanity. Lee's thematic statement closely resembles the classic statement on alienation of philosopher/psychoanalyst Erich Fromm in *Escape from Freedom* (1941). Loneliness, explained Fromm, is a powerful force in man derived from the need of others for the sake of survival. People feel insignificant when alone because they need love. But they need to relate to the world without losing their individuality. Not possessive love, nor materialism, but love which affirms others as well as the self, is the sign of a healthy person. Someone who feels insecure, doubtful, or powerless not only perpetuates isolation, but may perform destructive acts or seek or submit to unhealthy controls. Fromm concludes:

> If human freedom is established as *freedom to*, if man can realize his self fully and uncompromisingly, the fundamental cause for his asocial drives will have disappeared and only a sick and abnormal individual will be dangerous. This freedom has never been realized in the history of mankind, yet it has been an ideal to which mankind has stuck even if it was often expressed in abstruse and irrational forms. There is no reason to wonder why the record of history shows so much cruelty and destructiveness. If there is anything to be surprised at—and encouraged by—I believe it is the fact that the human race, in spite of all that has happened to men, has retained—and actually developed—such qualities of dignity, courage, decency, and kindness as we find them throughout history and in countless individuals today.

East of Eden is not only less formless, it is less sentimental than it has been taken to be. Just as it is not loosely "about good and evil," it is not vaguely "about morality." It is about morality only in the sense that it looks at human behavior from established perspectives. Steinbeck saw the Cain and Abel story as embodying the basis of all neuroses: "if you take the fall along with it, you have the total of the psychic troubles that can happen to a human" (*JN*, p. 104). Here he brings up, separately, the Garden of Eden, the classic symbol for themes of good and evil; he had used the Cain story because his theme was different. Steinbeck might have pleased "the neurosis belt" (*JN*, p. 115) if he had offered mankind no hope, but if *timshel* weakens his art, it strengthens his value to more readers, which was more important to him. His worst offense was belaboring the words that "lift up . . . extend"

(*JN*, p. 154). Perhaps overstating his beliefs resulted from too much planning and from overwhelming intentions—hence the misdemeanors in tone. His basic structure is sound.

Source: Barbara McDaniel, "Alienation in *East of Eden*: The 'Chart of the Soul,'" in *Steinbeck Quarterly*, Vol. 14, No. 1–2, Winter/Spring 1981, pp. 32–39.

Sources

Gurko, Leo, "Steinbeck's Later Fiction," in *John Steinbeck: The Contemporary Reviews*, edited by Joseph R. McElrath Jr., Jesse S. Crisler, and Susan Shillinglaw, Cambridge University Press, 1996, pp. 385–86; originally published in *Nation*, September 20, 1952.

Levant, Howard, *The Novels of John Steinbeck: A Critical Study*, University of Missouri Press, 1974, pp. 234–58.

Prescott, Orville, "Books of the Times," in *John Steinbeck: The Contemporary Reviews*, edited by Joseph R. McElrath Jr., Jesse S. Crisler, and Susan Shillinglaw, Cambridge University Press, 1996, p. 383; originally published in *New York Times*, September 19, 1952.

Schorer, Mark, "A Dark and Violent Steinbeck Novel," in *John Steinbeck: The Contemporary Reviews*, edited by Joseph R. McElrath Jr., Jesse S. Crisler, and Susan Shillinglaw, Cambridge University Press, 1996, p. 391; originally published in *New York Times Book Review*, September 21, 1952.

Steinbeck, John, *Journal of a Novel: The "East of Eden" Letters*, Viking Press, 1969, pp. 4, 112, 115–16, 132, 146.

West, Anthony, "California Moonshine," in *John Steinbeck: The Contemporary Reviews*, edited by Joseph R. McElrath Jr., Jesse S. Crisler, and Susan Shillinglaw, Cambridge University Press, 1996, p. 389; originally published in *New Yorker*, September 20, 1952.

Further Reading

French, Warren, *John Steinbeck*, 2d ed., Twayne's United States Authors Series, No. 2, Twayne Publishers, 1975.
  French discusses the novel in terms of Steinbeck's attempt to write about the evolution of a higher consciousness. The author holds that Steinbeck was not successful in this attempt because he remained essentially a naturalistic writer.

Lisca, Peter, *John Steinbeck: Nature and Myth*, Thomas Y. Crowell, 1978.
  Lisca gives a generally negative assessment of the novel, describing it as deficient in characterization, invention, style, and discipline. Lisca also faults Steinbeck for contradictions in his theme of good and evil.

Owens, Louis, "*East of Eden*," in *A New Study Guide to Steinbeck's Major Works, with Critical Explications*, edited by Tetsumaro Hayashi, Scarecrow Press, 1993, pp. 66–89.
  This work contains a background section, a synopsis of the novel, and a critical explication in which Owens describes the novel as one of the most misunderstood of all Steinbeck's works, contending that the real subject is not the biblical allegory but the creative consciousness.

Timmerman, John H., *John Steinbeck's Fiction: The Aesthetics of the Road Taken*, University of Oklahoma Press, 1986.
  Timmerman examines Cathy's role as the structural and thematic center of the novel, including her relationship with several other characters (Horace Quinn, Charles, Caleb, Lee and Samuel Hamilton) on the issue of good and evil.

Far from the Madding Crowd

Thomas Hardy

1874

In December 1872, having already published several moderately successful novels, Thomas Hardy was approached by the editor of *Cornhill*, a respected literary magazine, to write a story to run in serial form. The resulting book, *Far from the Madding Crowd*, was a popular attraction for the magazine and Hardy's first critical success. It was first published in serial form in *Cornhill* between January and December 1874, and then published the same year in London in book form. Hardy had already published several novels, but this was the first of the five novels that would assure his place in the annals of literature.

The plot of *Far from the Madding Crowd* concerns a young woman, Bathsheba Everdene, and the three men in her life: one is a poor sheep farmer who loses his flock in a tragedy and ends up working as an employee on Bathsheba's farm; one is the respectable, boring owner of a neighboring farm who takes Bathsheba's flirtations too seriously; and the third is a dashing army sergeant who treats her like just another of his conquests. In chronicling their hopes, plans, and disappointments, Hardy presents to readers a clear example of Victorian romanticism. At the same time, his understanding of the lives of farmers and ranchers in rural England makes him a forerunner to the realistic tradition in literature.

Wessex, the location for *Far from the Madding Crowd*, is an imaginary English county that Hardy colored with fine details throughout the course of his writing career. It is similar to Dorset, where Hardy lived most of his life, but its fictitious nature gave the author freedom to describe the landscape

at will. Hardy wrote *Far from the Madding Crowd* in the same Dorset cottage in which he was born and which his grandfather had built in 1800. Though fictional, the residents of Wessex—farmers, land owners, laborers, servants, and the like—are considered true representations of people living at the time the novel was published.

Author Biography

Thomas Hardy was born June 2, 1840, in Higher Bockhampton, Dorset, England, and he died there eighty-eight years later. His major novels, including *Far from the Madding Crowd*, take place in an intricately imagined English county he called Wessex, which he patterned on Dorset.

The town where Hardy was born, Higher Bockhampton, was poor, but Hardy was born into a line of skilled laborers. His father was a master mason, as was his grandfather, and throughout his childhood it was assumed that Hardy would be a mason also. In 1856 he was apprenticed to an architect and went to live in Dorchester, the county seat, where he was to live for most of his life. After gaining full status as an architect, Hardy took up writing poetry, but was not successful in getting his works published, and so he turned to writing fiction. In all, he published fourteen novels between 1871 and 1895. His first novel, *Desperate Remedies*, was published in 1871. In 1872 he published *Under the Greenwood Tree* anonymously, and in 1873 he published *A Pair of Blue Eyes*. None of these initial works garnered much critical attention from the literary establishment.

Far from the Madding Crowd, published in 1874, is considered the first of Hardy's five important novels. The other four are: *The Return of the Native* (1878), *The Mayor of Casterbridge* (1886), *Tess of the D'Urbervilles* (1891), and *Jude the Obscure* (1895). While these five novels are considered important works in the canon of British literature, Hardy published numerous other novels, short stories, sketches, travel writings, and poetry that received less attention.

Hardy's novels are known for their frank portrayals of love and sexuality, and as a result he was subject to harsh social criticism in his time. After the publication of *Jude the Obscure*, he grew tired of being surrounded by controversy, and so he gave up writing fiction and focused on poetry. His distinguished poetry career lasted for more than thirty years, until his death on January 11, 1928. His body was buried in the Poet's Corner of Westminster

Thomas Hardy

Abbey, next to the remains of Charles Dickens. Before his interment, Hardy's heart was removed and buried in Dorset.

Plot Summary

Chapters 1–4

The first chapter of *Far from the Madding Crowd* introduces Gabriel Oak, a hardworking farmer. One day, tending his fields, he sees a wagon with a beautiful girl in it. When her driver goes to pick up something dropped on the road, the girl, thinking no one can see her, takes out a small mirror and examines her face. Oak later observes the same young woman and her aunt caring for a newborn calf through a cold night.

Oak finally talks to Bathsheba Everdene, returning a hat that she has lost. She is flirtatious. Oak, smitten, goes to call on her at her aunt's house to ask her to marry him. She refuses, explaining, "I want somebody to tame me; I am too independent; and you would never be able to, I know."

Chapters 5–10

One morning Oak hears that Bathsheba has left town. Not long after, he suffers a tragedy: an

Media Adaptations

- An abridged audio edition of *Far from the Madding Crowd* is available from Blackstone Audiobooks. Released in 1984, it was read by Jill Masters and is available on both cassette and compact disc.

- Another audiocassette version, read by Hugh Rose and Kate Young, was released in 1980 by Century Publishing of Houston, Texas.

- An unabridged audio version, in cassette and compact disc form, was released in 1998 by The Audio Partners. It is read by Stephen Thorne.

- A big-screen blockbuster adaptation of this book was made in 1967, with an all-star cast including Julie Christie, Alan Bates, Terence Stamp, and Peter Finch. It was directed by John Schlesinger. Produced by Warner, it is available on Warner Home Video.

- A more recent film version, done for public television's Masterpiece Theatre series, stars Paloma Baeza as Bathsheba Everdene, Nathaniel Parker as Gabriel Oak, and Jonathan Firth as Frank Troy. Directed by Nicholas Renton, it was released on videocassette by Anchor Bay Entertainment in 1998.

- An unusual adaptation of this novel of lust and passion was the one done by London's SNAP People's Theatre Trust, adjusting the story of Bathsheba Everdene for a children's audience. A videotape of this production was released by Globalstage in 1998. It is recommended for audiences aged 12 and up.

- Readers can find hundreds of online links to articles about this novel and about Hardy himself at the Web site of the Thomas Hardy Association (http://www.yale.edu/hardysoceaders).

inexperienced sheep dog chases his flock through a fence in a hill, and most of them fall over a cliff and die. Oak is forced to sell all he has in order to pay back money he borrowed, and he ends up homeless.

After several months, Oak is traveling, looking for work. He comes across a barn on fire and takes the lead in fighting it. The barn is located on the farm Bathsheba inherited from her uncle. At the suggestion of her workers, Bathsheba offers Oak work as a shepherd, and he accepts. Traveling to the malthouse to find lodging, Oak runs into a pale girl who is later identified as Fanny Robin, and he gives her money.

Chapters 11–19

Fanny Robin goes to a town where the military regiment that had been in Weatherbury has been sent, and summons Frank Troy to come to the window. She asks when he is going to marry her. He tells her soon.

Bathsheba notices William Boldwood, who owns the farm next to hers, in the market, and comments that he looks interesting. Her maid Liddy explains that he is a confirmed bachelor. On Valentine's Day Bathsheba and Liddy decide to write an anonymous valentine, and Bathsheba decides on a whim to send it to Boldwood. The wax seal with which she closes it says "Marry Me."

Oak receives a letter from Fanny Robin, repaying the money he gave her and mentioning that she is going to marry Sergeant Frank Troy. Boldwood, who has been thinking constantly about the anonymous valentine, has Oak identify the writing as Bathsheba's. Soon Boldwood asks Bathsheba to marry him. She explains that the valentine was a joke, but he swears his love and says he will ask her again.

Sergeant Troy waits at All Saints' Church to marry Fanny. She shows up an hour late, saying that she mistakenly went to All Souls' Church. Annoyed, Troy now refuses to marry Fanny.

Chapters 20–34

Boldwood's love for Bathsheba grows, although she is disinterested. She discusses Boldwood with Oak, who says she should consider marrying Boldwood after the trick she played on him. Because Oak criticizes her behavior, Bathsheba fires him.

With Oak gone, no one feeds the sheep. The sheep break the fence and get into a field of clover, which makes them sick. The only person around who can heal them is Oak. Bathsheba sends him a note begging him to come back, saying, "Do not desert me, Gabriel."

Boldwood asks Bathsheba to accept his proposal when he returns from his trip. That night, walking home, Bathsheba meets Sergeant Troy, who is back on furlough from his regiment. He flirts with her in the dark. A few days later she finds him helping her workers tend her farm. In private, he demonstrates his swordsmanship and then steals a kiss. Oak later warns Bathsheba that Troy seems dishonest.

When Boldwood returns, Bathsheba declares her love for Troy. She leaves for Bath, where Troy has gone on vacation. When Boldwood next sees Troy, he offers him money to marry Fanny. Troy indicates that he and Bathsheba have already been intimate, so Boldwood offers him even more money to marry Bathsheba and make an honest woman of her. Troy takes the money and then announces that they are already married.

Chapters 35–40

Having used Bathsheba's money to buy his way out of the army, Troy establishes himself as the head of the farm. After the harvest, he provides hard liquor to all of the farm hands. Oak, meanwhile, senses a storm rolling in that could ruin the crops. When he goes to the barn, everyone is passed out and no one is available to help him save Bathsheba's harvest except Bathsheba herself. Oak races to cover the stacks while the storm rages. The next day he meets Boldwood, who has allowed his own harvest to be ruined.

Weeks later, Bathsheba and Troy run into Fanny Robin. Troy does not introduce the women to each other, but, seeing Fanny dressed in tatters, gives Fanny all of the money he has and promises her more if she will meet him the next day. Chapter 40 details Fanny's trek by foot through the dead of night to the poor house in Casterbridge.

Chapters 41–47

Bathsheba and Troy fight when he asks her for money, and he leaves. Liddy brings news that Fanny Robin has died, and Bathsheba sends one of the farm hands to bring back her body.

On Fanny's coffin, the people at the poor house have written the contents in chalk. Oak finds the man who was sent to retrieve the coffin at the malthouse. Oak notices the casket says "Fanny Robin and child," and erases the mention of the child, to protect Bathsheba.

Bathsheba, however, becomes suspicious. She goes to where the casket is and opens it with a screwdriver, finding the corpse of an infant child with Fanny's. Troy comes in and sees it too. He declares that Fanny was the love of his life, that Bathsheba means nothing to him. He runs away, and she locks herself in her room. After erecting an expensive tombstone for Fanny, Troy flees town. Swimming at the shore, a currant pulls him out to sea, where a boat picks him up.

Chapters 48–51

Word soon comes that Troy has drowned. Oak becomes the bailiff of Bathsheba's farm and also of Boldwood's. Months later Boldwood learns from Liddy that Bathsheba will not consider marrying again for seven years after Troy's disappearance, and so Boldwood counts the days.

At a fair late in the summer, Troy, who has been traveling with a carnival, notices Bathsheba and disguises himself. Boldwood, taking Bathsheba home from the fair, begs her to promise to marry him after six more years; when she stalls, he gets her to promise to announce her decision by Christmas.

Chapters 52–57

Boldwood throws a festive Christmas Eve party. He makes it clear he expects Bathsheba to agree to marry him in six years and offers her an ornate diamond ring. Troy enters the party and insists that Bathsheba leave with him. Boldwood shoots Troy and tries to shoot himself before the farm hands stop him.

While Boldwood is imprisoned and sentenced to die, facts come out about his mental state. In his house are found packages of women's clothes with the name "Bathsheba Boldwood" on them. In the end, he is not sentenced to death.

At the grave where Bathsheba has had Troy buried with Fanny, she runs into Oak, with whom she has not talked in months. He explains he stayed away because he was afraid people would gossip that he had designs on marrying her himself, and she encourages the idea. The novel ends with the marriage of Oak to Bathsheba.

Characters

Cainy Ball

Cainy is the boy who is appointed assistant shepherd to Gabriel. His mother named him Cain because she was confused about the story of Genesis, and thought it was Abel who killed his brother.

William Boldwood

Boldwood is a bachelor, about forty years old, who owns the farm next to the Everdene farm. He takes responsibility for Fanny Robin when her parents die. Bathsheba Everdene first becomes aware of Boldwood when he comes to visit soon after she takes over her uncle's farm. Her maid explains that Boldwood is a confirmed bachelor and shows no interest in women, which spurs Bathsheba to send him an anonymous valentine.

The valentine starts Boldwood thinking about women. He becomes convinced that he is in love with Bathsheba. Because he is used to business interactions and not personal ones, he pressures her to marry him and is confused when she is reluctant. When she marries Troy, Boldwood feels she has been stolen from him and lets his farm go to ruin. After Troy is thought dead, Boldwood interprets the fact that she will not remarry for seven years to mean that at the end of that time, she will marry him. When she says she will give him an answer at Christmas, he prepares a lavish party, assuming she will become his fiancée.

When Boldwood is jailed for killing Troy, the extent of Boldwood's delusions becomes apparent. Locked closets are found in his house, full of dresses, furs, and jewelry, all inscribed to "Bathsheba Boldwood," with a date seven years in advance, when he expects her to marry him. Because he is clearly insane, Boldwood is not hanged for Troy's murder.

Jan Coggan

Coggan is introduced as a man who often stands witness to weddings and baptisms in the county. When Oak arrives at Weatherbury, he takes a room at Coggan's house. Coggan becomes a confidante who knows the truth about Oak's past relationship with Bathsheba.

Bathsheba Everdene

Bathsheba is the central figure of the novel. At the beginning of the novel she is around twenty years old and poor, helping to tend her aunt's farm. She is vain. The first time Oak sees her she takes out a mirror and examines her face, unaware that anyone is looking. She flirts with Oak but does not accept his proposal of marriage because she does not believe he can put up with a strong-headed woman like herself.

When an uncle dies and leaves her his farm, Bathsheba takes control. She fires the bailiff for stealing, and instead of hiring another bailiff, she takes on the duty of managing the farm herself. She still has the flirtatious girl in her, though, and on Valentine's Day she sends an anonymous valentine to the stuffy bachelor who lives next door. When he takes this claim of love seriously, she feels guilty and finds herself unable to refuse him outright.

Bathsheba is a conscientious employer. She gives her workers bonuses when work is going well. When news arrives that Fanny Robin, who worked for her uncle, has died, Bathsheba arranges for the body to be brought back to Weatherbury, to be buried in the local cemetery.

When she meets the dashing Sergeant Troy, she falls for his extravagant flattery, falls in love with him, and ends up marrying him. He spends her money, ignores her, and almost ruins her farm. Throughout these difficult times, she relies on Oak, both for help in managing her farm and as a sympathetic ear to listen to her troubles.

Bathsheba becomes a colder, more pragmatic person after Troy leaves. She is hesitant to give Boldwood any hope of marrying her, because she is concerned about the way she hurt his feelings in the past. She focuses on business and tries to forget about men.

In the end, when Boldwood is in jail and Troy is dead, Bathsheba rekindles the same playful, flirtatious relationship with Oak that she had at the beginning of the novel. She recognizes his loyalty through all that has happened and realizes she has loved him all along.

Henry Frey

Frey is one of the workers on the Everdene farm. He always signs his name "Henery" and is often called that by the other workers.

George

George is the sheepdog who helps Gabriel Oak tend his flocks, and he is later brought to Weatherbury to help Oak with Bathsheba's sheep.

Matthew Moon

Moon is one of the workers on Bathsheba Everdene's farm.

Gabriel Oak

Oak is one of the novel's most important characters. In the beginning, he is a farmer. Though his farm is not a large one, it is secure. When he meets Bathsheba Everdene, he asks her to marry him. Soon his flock of sheep is wiped out in an accident, and he has to sell his farm to pay his bills. When he cannot find work as a bailiff, or foreman, of a farm, he looks for a job as a shepherd. He is hired at the farm Bathsheba has recently inherited.

Hardy presents Oak as a conscientious and intelligent worker, who intuitively understands the problems of grain and livestock. Oak is completely devoted to Bathsheba, watching after her farm so that she will profit from it. Unlike Boldwood, who is never able to get over the idea of Bathsheba's rejecting his offer of marriage, Oak goes for years without mentioning the feelings that he once had for her. He does not forget about his love, but instead channels it into labor on her farm. Oak takes on a brotherly role for Bathsheba in her romantic entanglements with Boldwood and Troy. She goes to him for advice about men, even though they are both aware of their romantic past.

Oak becomes Boldwood's friend. Boldwood recognizes and admires the way Oak is able to control his love for Bathsheba and also admires Oak's skill as a farmer. When Boldwood devotes his time to pursuing Bathsheba, he hires Oak to watch over his farm as well as hers. A less confident man than Oak would have refused to help another man court the woman he loves.

In the end Oak tells Bathsheba he plans to go to California. This decision, like other decisions in his life, is not made for his own benefit, but because he does not want people to gossip about Bathsheba, since they all know he is in love with her. Her decision to marry him in the end stems from her clear understanding of how much he means to her.

Pennyways

Pennyways is the bailiff of the Everdene farm. Soon after Bathsheba takes over the farm, she catches Pennyways sneaking out of the barn with half a bushel of barley, and she fires him. He later turns up at the Greenhill Fair, where he recognizes Troy as one of the performers. His attempt to point out Troy's presence to Bathsheba does not work, and he then becomes Troy's accomplice in Troy's drive to reestablish himself at the farm.

Joseph Poorgrass

Joseph is a very shy man, and the other farm workers kid him about it. He has a weakness for alcohol. When he is supposed to bring Fanny Robin's body back to the Everdene farm, he stops at the Boar's Head along the way and stays so late drinking that he cannot make it back in time for the funeral.

Fanny Robin

Fanny is a tragic young woman who is used by the womanizing Sergeant Troy and then abandoned. She ends up malnourished and pregnant. Fanny worked on the Everdene farm for years and leaves a few days after Bathsheba's arrival because Troy's company was relocated. She goes to the new barracks to ask when Troy will marry her. After she is late to the wedding ceremony because she went to the wrong church, Troy refuses to marry her. Troy runs into her after he is married to Bathsheba. Fanny is destitute. Troy wants to help her, but she dies before he can get money to her.

Oak tries to keep secret the fact that Fanny dies unmarried and with a child. When Troy finds out about it, though, he shows that he is truly sad. Instead of his beautiful wealthy wife Bathsheba, he declares that Fanny was his only true love.

Jacob Smallbury

The son of "the maltster," who owns the tavern in the village, Jacob is around sixty-five years old.

Liddy Smallbury

Liddy is the daughter of William Smallbury and the handmaid of Bathsheba Everdene. She is about the same age as Bathsheba and serves as a confidant from time to time.

William Smallbury

Son of Jacob Smallbury, William is about forty years old and is described as having "a cheerful soul in a gloomy body."

Laban Tall

Tall has recently, in middle age, married for the first time. He is bossed around by his strong-willed wife, Susan. Hardy describes him as "a young married man, who having no individuality worth mentioning was known as 'Susan Tall's husband.'"

Susan Tall

The new wife of Laban Tall is presented as a domineering woman who makes all of the decisions for the couple.

Frank Troy

Sergeant Troy is presented as a contradiction. Throughout the novel, his actions show him to be an opportunist and a womanizer. He is first introduced as responding to Fanny Robin, who has walked miles in winter to the town to which his battalion has moved. Fanny asks Troy when he is going to marry her, but Troy says he cannot come out and see her. Then there is laughter inside the barracks, as if he is mocking her. He does agree to marry her, though, but when she shows up late to the wedding he uses it as an excuse to call off the wedding. In courting Bathsheba Everdene, Troy shows himself to be skillful and witty.

In his marriage to Bathsheba, Troy exhibits confidence. He swindles Boldwood out of money Boldwood offers Troy to make Bathsheba an honest woman, taking the money although he and Bathsheba are already married. Troy spends Bathsheba's money on liquor for the farm hands, who are not used to hard liquor, and as a result almost ruins a year's work. He also loses heavily at the horse races.

On the other hand, he is, at heart, a romantic. When he hears of Fanny's death, he is truly grieved, to such an extent that he is willing to lose his comfortable position as Bathsheba's husband. He tells Bathsheba she means nothing to him, that Fanny was his true love. He erects a tombstone to Fanny that says he was the one to put it up, despite the scandal that could ensue. He then runs away, eventually joining a traveling show, in order to forget his one true love.

In the end Troy returns to being a scoundrel. He is dragging Bathsheba out of the Christmas party, saying she should obey him, when he is shot by Boldwood and killed.

Themes

Unrequited Love

Much of the plot of *Far from the Madding Crowd* depends on unrequited love—love by one person for another that is not mutual in that the other person does not feel love in return. The novel is driven, from the first few chapters, by Gabriel Oak's love for Bathsheba. Once he has lost his farm, he is free to wander anywhere in search of work, but he heads to Weatherbury because it is in the direction that Bathsheba has gone. This move leads to Oak's employment at Bathsheba's farm, where he patiently consoles her in her troubles and supports her in tending the farm, with no sign he will ever have his love returned.

Oak's feelings for Bathsheba parallel Boldwood's feelings for Bathsheba. Given the fact that Bathsheba sends Boldwood a provocative valentine, sealed with the strong message "Marry Me," Boldwood has good reason to believe she might love him. On the other hand, she tries to extinguish any such belief, telling Boldwood repeatedly she will not marry him. Unlike Oak, who is willing to take Bathsheba at her word, Boldwood looks for the slightest sign in what she says that there may be a chance she may change her mind. Since she is not strong or direct in her refusal of him, there is always room for him to believe that she is softening.

Bathsheba herself suffers a similar unrequited love for Sergeant Troy. She feels he is mistreating her once they are married, but she cannot help herself because she loves him so much. He, on the other hand, is not capable of a stable love relationship. When they argue over the fact that he is lying about the trip he plans to take to see Fanny, and Bathsheba regrets how much she used to love him, Troy can only mutter, "I can't help how things fall out ... upon my heart, women will be the death of me." When he is thought to have drowned, though, Bathsheba still thinks enough of him to go on waiting, to see if he will come back.

Catastrophe

This novel focuses on the way that catastrophe can occur at any time, threatening to change lives. The most obvious example occurs when Oak's flock of sheep is destroyed by an unlikely confluence of circumstances, including an inexperienced sheep dog, a rotted rail, and a chalk pit that happens to have been dug adjacent to his land. In one night, Oak's future as an independent farmer is destroyed, and he ends up begging just to secure the diminished position of a shepherd.

Potential catastrophe occurs throughout the novel, but Oak, having suffered already, uses skill and diligence to avert it. For instance, Bathsheba's flock is almost ruined as swiftly and thoroughly as Oak's flock is, on the day that Bathsheba dismisses Oak from her farm. It is only because Oak returns to his post, after forcing Bathsheba to ask him back, that most of the sheep survive. Then a thunderstorm arrives the day the harvest is complete. The rain could ruin the barley, corn, and wheat, destroying Bathsheba financially, if the grain is not covered. This catastrophe is averted because Oak works through the night in the rain to protect the harvest. Sergeant Troy, who is supposed to be the master

Topics For Further Study

- Research modern methods of raising sheep and make a chart comparing them to the practices described in the novel.

- Find a recording of pastoral flute music, like the music that Gabriel Oak might have played, and present it to your class with an explanation of its history.

- Hardy eventually quit writing novels because of public criticism of the sexuality displayed in his books. Try to imagine how this story would have gone if Fanny Robin had not been carrying Sergeant Troy's baby when she died. Would Troy have been able to stay with Bathsheba after Fanny's death, and if so, where would their relationship have gone? Write a short play featuring their dialog after Fanny's funeral.

- Some readers are surprised to find that people sent valentines to each other in the 1870s. Research the history of Valentine's Day, and present the different customs associated with it throughout the ages.

---

of the farm, sleeps off the hard liquor that has rendered him and all of his farm hands useless. With these episodes, Hardy shows that catastrophe can cause ruin, but it can also sometimes be avoided when care is taken.

Social Hierarchy

This novel offers modern readers a clear picture of how important social position was in England in the nineteenth century and of the opportunities that existed to change class, in either direction. In the beginning, Oak and Bathsheba are social equals: he is an independent farmer who rents his land, and she lives on her aunt's farm next door to his, which is presumably similar in value. The only thing that keeps her from accepting his proposal of marriage is the fact that she just does not want to be married yet. After Oak loses his farm and Bathsheba inherits her uncle's farm, there is little question of whether they can marry—their social positions are too different. She is more socially compatible with Boldwood, who owns the farm next to hers and is in a similar social position.

Unlike societies in which the social hierarchy is rigid, the situation in rural nineteenth-century England did offer opportunity to those in the lower positions to move up. With hard work, Oak works his way up to bailiff of both Bathsheba's and Boldwood's farms. Earning more money, he also has the social status that comes from being trusted with such a unique position. Still, at the end of the book he does not think that he has risen socially high enough to marry Bathsheba, as indicated by the fact that he offers to leave the country, rather than give anyone the idea he might think himself worthy of her. He has risen enough socially by this time to have their marriage accepted, however, and the rest of society has nothing but good will for them.

Style

Realism and Romanticism

Far from the Madding Crowd is considered by some to be a solid example of realism, a literary style that arose in Europe in the last half of the nineteenth century. The early half of the century was dominated by romanticism, which encouraged writers to emphasize their imaginations. Romantic writers, as a rule, focused on individual expression, and thus produced works that often featured elements of the supernatural and almost always showed the world as a projection of the individual's emotions. In response to the excesses of romanticism, which some writers felt took literary works too far from the way that most people actually experience the world, realistic fiction began in the 1840s in works by writers such as Gustav Flaubert and George Eliot. Because romantic writers often presented the world as being changeable by sheer willpower and, therefore, were inclined toward happy endings, realistic writers tended to show the harsher aspects of life. In *Far from the Madding Crowd*, the realistic world view is represented most clearly in the way Oak's flock of sheep die, suddenly and senselessly. It is also presented in the way that Hardy exposes the social standards of his time by making Fanny Robin not only a jilted woman but also pregnant out of wedlock. On the other hand, there are many romantic elements in the book. The way that the thunderstorm in chapter 37 mirrors the emotional turmoil of Gabriel and Bathsheba is a standard romantic idiom. The book's many strained coincidences constitute romantic device (such as the fact that a boat picks up Troy before he drowns and Troy subsequently encounters Bathsheba at the Greenhill Fair, to name two examples). The book's happy ending, with the longtime acquaintances finally free to admit their mutual love and marry one another, is a sign that, for all its realistic elements, this novel is basically a romantic novel.

Denoument

The word *denoument* comes from the French, and literally means "the unraveling" or "the untying." It is used in literature to describe the part of a novel that comes after the climax, when the excitement has peaked and readers gain an understanding of what life will hold in the future for the surviving characters. In this novel, the climax comes at the Christmas party when Boldwood kills Troy. This climax carries on into the next chapter, "After the Shock," in which Bathsheba dresses her husband's body and finally cures herself of his hold on her. The *denoument* occurs the following March, when Oak and Bathsheba, having had time to accept the shocking developments that removed the main obstacles from their way, find themselves able to playfully admit their love. For readers, it is clear that the shock of Troy's sudden return and just as sudden murder will not negatively affect Bathsheba. The future of the novel's two main characters is just as clear: they will live happily ever after.

Historical Context

Wessex

Critics often point out that Hardy created Wessex, the imaginary setting of many of his novels and poems, to resemble Dorset, located along the southern coast of England. His use of the word "Wessex" first appears in *Far from the Madding Crowd*.

There actually was a historical use of the word "Wessex": it was a kingdom in southern England, dating back to the invasion of the Saxons in 494 A.D. Though it underwent changes over the course of centuries, its most permanent configuration approximated that of the modern counties of Hampshire, Dorset, Wiltshire, and Somerset. It was in this place that King Arthur held domain over the Knights of the Roundtable, giving the area an important historical distinction. By 927, though, this kingdom had been absorbed into the greater polity of England.

By the nineteenth century the name "Wessex" had receded far into history. The use of this word for the area serves as a reference to the ancient myths and customs still practiced in rural municipalities across southern England in Hardy's time, but it is also an indicator that Hardy was not writing an exact history of any particular location. Still, the similarities between Dorchester and Wessex are so pronounced that whole books have been written tracing the connections of the fictitious county to specific locations in the Southwest England.

Urbanization

In the late nineteenth century, country life in England was under attack from many sides. For one thing, industrialization was on the rise. In part this was the effect of the Industrial Revolution, which had started in England in the previous century and by Hardy's time had spread across western Europe. Factories, clustered in the cities, offered wages beyond anything workers could hope to gain if they stayed in the farm towns of their parents and ancestors, so many workers moved to urban areas, which led to the overcrowding and pollution that has been recorded so graphically in Charles Dickens's novels about London in the 1830s and 1840s.

In addition, English farms lost a great deal of profitability when the Corn Laws were repealed in 1846. The Corn Laws, which had been in effect in various forms for over 400 years, were controversial throughout the nineteenth century. Supporters said the laws protected English farmers from market fluctuations by assuring them of a high price for what they grew; opponents felt they hampered industry by paying tax money to subsidize farm-owning landowners. When the Corn Laws were repealed, farm wages plummeted. The result was that many people whose families had been farmers for generations, if not centuries, found themselves relocating to urban areas.

To some degree, then, Hardy's stories of Wessex offered displaced farmers an outlet for the

Compare & Contrast

- **1870s:** England begins its shift from a farming economy to an industrial economy, as foreign imported meat and produce drive down farm wages. Over the next few decades, the population shifts from rural to urban settings at an unprecedented rate.

  Today: Britain has one of the world's most sophisticated industrial economies. Only about two-fifths of the land is usable for farming, and the country is only about 4 percent forested.

- **1870s:** A woman carrying a child out of wedlock would be shamed into traveling on her own in poverty rather than returning to her own town and facing disgrace before her friends and neighbors.

  Today: The social stigma against unmarried women is greatly diminished as the practice has become more common throughout the past three decades.

- **1870s:** It is considered highly unusual for a lone woman like Bathsheba to run a farm by herself. Most women who have come by farms through inheritance rely on bailiffs to tend to day-to-day operations.

  Today: A lone woman running a farm would be notable today primarily because a majority of farms are owned and run by corporations.

- **1870s:** A piano in the house is the mark of affluence for a woman living on a farm. Gabriel Oak promises Bathsheba that, if she marries him, she will have one "in a year or two."

  Today: Full-sized pianos are again a sign of luxury; electric keyboards, however, can produce similar sound quality for a fraction of the price.

- **1870s:** News is spread by word of mouth, most often at a public gathering place like Warren's Malthouse in the novel. Shepherds rely on natural signs to predict coming changes in the weather.

  Today: Even the most remote locations have access to twenty-four-hour-a-day news and weather channels, as well as Internet access for up-to-the-minute information.

---

nostalgia they felt when they looked back to the land on which their families had worked for generations. Hardy's rustic characters are not necessarily kind or wise, but they always have the characteristics that one would identify with country people: folk wisdom, tradition, and a sense of community, which are all absent from city life. In addition, Hardy is credited with capturing the nuances of workers in the rural south of England better than any other writer.

Critical Overview

Far from the Madding Crowd was Hardy's breakthrough novel. He had published three books before it, which generally left critics unimpressed. As Dale Kramer notes in *Critical Essays on Thomas Hardy: The Novels*, reviewers of Hardy's early works

> were struck by the seemingly uncoordinated, coincidence-laden plots, and also by the rural settings where the sense of time was that of an idyll, by fantastic implausibilities mixed with poetic revelation of inner identities, and by the folklore of "Wessex" that resisted the importunities of modern existence.

Kramer later continues,

> By the time of *Far from the Madding Crowd* even critical reviewers realized they were dealing with substantial works calling for judgment not in relation to popular writers of the day, but in relation to recognized masters.

Once Hardy's literary importance was established, critics were still divided in their analysis of his work. He faced tremendous pressure from his Victorian audiences for his frank portrayal of

Terence Stamp as Sergeant Troy and Julie Christie as Bathsheba, in the 1967 film depiction of Far from the Madding Crowd

sexuality, such as an unmarried woman like Fanny Robin being buried with her infant child, yet still loved by her neighbors and the man who had impregnated her. Hardy stopped writing fiction in 1895, after his novels had been attacked by critics who had called his fiction "vulgar" and "disagreeable." Still, there had been many positive reviews from critics who recognized him as one of England's finest writers. Hardy turned to writing poetry at age fifty-six. Because he was already a major literary figure, it was difficult to dismiss his poetry, though critics tended to pay less heed to it than to his fiction.

Throughout the twentieth century, Hardy's work held its place at the forefront of world literature. Still, the contradictions in his work afford new readers ample room for formulating contrasting opinions. Richard C. Carpenter explains the wide range of feelings readers have had about Hardy's novels this way:

> If he *is* great, he is bound to be problematic, showing new sides to new generations, demanding that we wrestle with him as with an angel and take a few falls before we realize what sort of man he is.

Criticism

David Kelly

Kelly is an instructor of creative writing and literature. In this essay Kelly argues that questions about Hardy's artistry in the novel are wrongly founded on whether the characters are too flexible to be believed.

Bathsheba Everdene, of Thomas Hardy's 1874 novel *Far from the Madding Crowd*, has been known to readers over the generations for her fiery beauty. The book details her romantic involvements with the three most sought-after bachelors in her county: Gabriel Oak, William Boldwood, and Sergeant Frank Troy. One reason for the book's enduring popularity is certainly the fact that it has two conclusions. First, Bathsheba ends up as a classic tragic heroine, able to have whatever she wants until her own success thrusts her into misery. After that, the book reverses order, and Bathsheba is presented as a romantic, almost comic heroine, who, despite the suffering that the world inflicts on her, is able to find happiness in the end.

Since the novel's first publication, critics have faulted Hardy for this ambiguity, just as audiences have found it very satisfactory to see a strong-headed and beautiful woman brought low and then redeemed within the same story. Novels can be satisfactory without being artistically honest. The strength of Hardy's plot line as true to life depends on how well he controls the main characters. If they are true to their characterizations, then the novel can ride them through the high points and low points to offer an honest look at the fictional world he presents. If, on the other hand, he allows them to change their basic personalities for his convenience in spinning a crowd-pleasing plot, then *Far from the Madding Crowd* can be considered just well-written and popular, but not necessarily a work of literature. This distinction, true of most books, requires even closer examination in this one because Hardy pummels his characters with such intense circumstances that it is not always easy to tell if they remain consistent.

Readers first encounter Bathsheba when Oak does. She is seated regally atop a wagon filled with her possessions, attended by a Norcombe commoner, and, when she thinks no one is watching, she sneaks a glance at herself in a mirror. That glance says that she is vain, but what is not made clear is exactly who she thinks her beauty is for. If she is concerned about how she looks to the driver, then it could be said that she values the admiration of everyone, no matter how lowly in status, no matter how unlikely a suitor. It could also be argued, though, that the secret glance in the mirror has more metaphysical implications: Bathsheba is not all that concerned with how her looks impress others, but is even more self-centered than that, and is concerned only with impressing herself. The fact that a mirror necessarily concerns outside appearances seems to indicate that this scene is about the face that she presents to the outside world; however, in her actions further in the book, with the workers at the farm she inherits, Bathsheba shows no desire to attract working men.

Her action is important because it is the first thing that attracts Oak to her, and Oak's judgment in all other things seems pretty good. As Peter J. Casagrande wrote in his essay "A New View of Bathsheba Everdene": Oak shows an "ability to observe the defects of non-human nature (the loss of his flock, the fire, the storm, the bloated sheep)" which allows him the flexibility he needs to make adjustments

> to observe, minister to, and finally to marry the faulty Bathsheba. The novel thus associates the imperfect nature of its heroine with defective non-human nature and offers in Oak an example of how to cope with the unregenerateness of things.

In other words, Casagrande assumes that what he elsewhere calls Bathsheba's "aggressive coquetry" is a flaw in her that places her in a category beyond human nature, instead of viewing it as the awareness of "self" that in fact defines human nature. That Oak understands Bathsheba better than she understands herself can hardly be argued, which leads readers to the frustrating conclusion that Bathsheba would be much happier throughout the book if she would only listen to Oak. What can be argued, however, is why, if she grows as a person throughout the book and becomes more human, that makes her a good match for farmer/shepherd Oak at the end.

Oak does in fact have the sort of understanding of nature that one expects from someone who spends his time observing the land, the skies, and animals, but he spends little time in the presence of other people. The novel mentions several times how useless his watch is to him, and how much more reliable his reading is of the alignment of the stars and planets. In this context, the love-at-first-sight that stirs in him when he sees Bathsheba staring at herself does not fit into an easy interpretation. It is not clearly the condescension of a man determined to redeem a woman from the sin of vanity. If Oak is attracted to her precisely because of her

> " Aside from trifling, though, the effect of Troy's story has little in common with Bathsheba's. While her flirtation with Boldwood seems to be a way of killing time, his is a more pathological diversion from his true self."

interest in herself, not in spite of it, then the novel's message would be that narcissism is as natural to humans as growing wool is to sheep. Bathsheba's interest in her self, then, would not be the flaw that critics tend to associate with her, but a benign part of her nature.

The ways in which Bathsheba interacts with the other men, though, certainly seem to indicate a tragic flaw as, after their involvement with Bathsheba, one ends up dead and the other goes to prison for having murdered him. Here too, though, there is room for seeing Bathsheba either as an instigator or as a victim of her own nature. The greatest sin she appears to perpetrate in the book comes when she attracts farmer Boldwood. It comes on an idle Valentine's Day, when she feels isolated. With nobody to send a card to, she decides to send one to the farmer who once tried to stop at her house for a social call, though she told the servants to send him away because she did not feel presentable enough. Here, too, Bathsheba's motives can be interpreted in different ways, ranging from childlike to cunning. Hardy explains her rationale for sending the valentine as a lark, an act of playfulness, down to her affixing a seal that says, "Marry Me." Hardy does, though, have it follow two incidents, at the sheep wash and at the Corn Market, where Boldwood fails to take any notice of her, raising the question of whether Bathsheba's flirtation is not as innocent as is presented, but is rather intended, subconsciously or not, to punish Boldwood for failing to give her the attention she desires.

Her attention changes Boldwood completely, from a man who is disinterested in women to one who is willing to devote his life to one, from there to the delusional extreme of buying clothes and

What Do I Read Next?

- *Far from the Madding Crowd* was the first of Hardy's Wessex novels to draw serious critical attention. While similarities exist throughout all of his novels, readers who like Bathsheba Everdene will probably appreciate Eustacia Vye, the heroine of Hardy's next novel *The Return of the Native* (1878).

- When *Far from the Madding Crowd* was first published, it was rumored to be the work of George Eliot (pseudonym for Mary Ann Evans). Eliot's novel *Middlemarch*, first published in 1872, is considered by many to be her masterpiece.

- Emphasis is often placed on the connection between Hardy's characters and the setting of his novels. One scholarly work that examines the subject closely is Noorul Hasan's *Thomas Hardy: The Sociological Imagination* (1982). Hasan's work has enough depth to dedicate an entire chapter to *Far from the Madding Crowd* and point out nuances that a modern reader might not at first appreciate.

- One of the best and most detailed biographies of Thomas Hardy is Martin Seymour-Smith's *Hardy* (1994), considered by many to be the most authoritative book on the author's life.

---

presents as gifts with which to shower Bathsheba seven years later. This "new" Boldwood is perfectly consistent with the dour loner he is when he enters the book. He is a mystery throughout, and the only difference from beginning to end is that he starts out a respected but aloof member of the community. He is pitied when people realize that Bathsheba has rejected him; and, as he tries to regain respect, his desperation is fueled by his own awareness of how apparent his desperation is. Boldwood's tragedy might be viewed, as it often has been, as his victimization by a vain woman, but his self-professed love for Bathsheba is so impersonal, so removed from the facts of the situation, that it is clear he is bound to have his self-esteem damaged by someone, somewhere.

Bathsheba's humbling marriage to Troy, who turns out to have not only fathered Fanny Robin's child but to care more for Fanny after her death than for his wife, is often referred to as the converse of the Boldwood situation, because Troy courts Bathsheba lightly, with no clear interest in her once he has won her love. Aside from trifling, though, the effect of Troy's story has little in common with Bathsheba's. While her flirtation with Boldwood seems to be a way of killing time, his is a more pathological diversion from his true self. It is clear that his love for Fanny is true, even though he does not realize it while it is in his power to act. He avoids her when she visits his barracks, and he takes the slightest excuse to back out of marriage, and he marries Bathsheba instead, but when Fanny is dead he thinks nothing of throwing away his comfortable lifestyle as a landed gentleman as he releases his heartfelt grief. Bathsheba flirts with Boldwood when she has nothing else to do, nothing to lose; Troy flirts with Bathsheba at the expense of the one true love of his life. This can be seen as a sign that she is a temptress, a distraction, except for the fact that their relationship is initiated by Troy and advanced at every step of the way by him. The only way to presume that Bathsheba is responsible for taking Troy away from Fanny is to see him as somehow not responsible for his own actions—being driven by his social-climbing, woman-chasing nature—while at the same time thinking that Bathsheba should be accountable for hers.

After the series of tragedies that mark Bathsheba's life, the novel comes to a happy ending because of Gabriel Oak's patience. Throughout the story, he offers Bathsheba a shoulder to cry on and some sound advice (which she takes sometimes, but often does not). After Boldwood goes mad, Troy returns, and the two of them come to tragic ends, Bathsheba becomes available again. Now somewhat wealthy, Oak is close enough to being her social peer that a marriage would not be unreasonable. And the personal characteristics that may once have made him seem lacking are nothing compared to the competition. If Oak once seemed impetuous in asking Bathsheba to marry her, she has Troy's hotheaded behavior to compare it to. If he seemed too awkward around a woman, he is positively graceful when compared to Boldwood.

In the end, the question of whether this is an honest novel comes back to whether readers can accept the fact that Gabriel Oak waits so long for Bathsheba Everdene. It does strain credulity that he would be such a good sport as to watch the world implode around her and then step up with a new offer of marriage once the dust has settled. If Oak views her as a pretty woman he can love in spite of her vanity, then it would be right to question whether Hardy has painted Oak as too angelic to be true. But there is plenty of evidence in the novel that Oak is more than just a smitten shepherd, that he knows exactly what he is getting with Bathsheba. And there is also enough to this story to believe that Bathsheba may be beautiful, and she may be interested in herself, but that the events that ruin some of the men who encounter her spring from their own characters and not from some sort of spell cast on them by her vanity.

Source: David Kelly, Critical Essay on *Far from the Madding Crowd*, in *Novels for Students*, Gale, 2004.

Roy Morrell

In the following essay, Morrell explores the distinction Hardy draws between romance and reality in Far from the Madding Crowd.

This novel is more typical of Hardy than a casual reading and a simplifying memory might indicate. The end, for example, is emphatically not a romantic happy-ever-after affair. We need not take Joseph Poorgrass's final "it might have been worse" at quite its long-face value; and we can see the title of the final chapter ("A Foggy Night and Morning") as perhaps Hardy's way of touching wood: there is, indeed, a suppressed and sober, but none the less noticeable, elation about the tone of the end; but the fact remains that Gabriel is no Prince Charming for a girl of three- or four-and-twenty. Ahead of Gabriel and Bathsheba is no romance, but a reality that Hardy represents as more valuable, a reality of hard and good work on the two farms:

> He accompanied her up the hill, explaining to her the details of his forthcoming tenure of the other farm. They spoke very little of their mutual feelings; pretty phrases and warm expressions being probably unnecessary between such tried friends. Theirs was

> *Hardy is disparaging romance, the dream and the dreamer. He is suggesting, instead, that one should live—not in accordance with nature—but in accordance with reality."*

that substantial affection which arises (if any arises at all) when the two who are thrown together begin first by knowing the rougher sides of each other's character, and not the best till further on, the romance growing up in the interstices of a mass of hard prosaic reality . . .

The trend of thought should by this time be familiar enough; but the passage also illustrates Hardy's "hard prosaic"—sometimes awkward—way of thinking and writing, born of a conviction that the truth must be told, even if it cannot always be told attractively.

The distinction Hardy draws between romance and reality does not appear only at the end of the book; it is worked into the scheme of the whole. In contrast to Gabriel Oak, the two other main male characters, Troy and Boldwood, one actively and the other passively, represent aspects of romantic unreality. Boldwood is the dreamer himself, and the unreality is in the way he approaches Bathsheba, seeing in her not a woman of flesh and blood, but a romantic dream. Troy, on the other hand, approaches Bathsheba realistically enough; but he is approached romantically *by her*: he seems to her a romantic figure, and initially, an escape from a dilemma into which the circumstances of her real everyday life have thrown her. Boldwood, for Bathsheba, has represented a certain social goal: propriety and respectability. For a short time, while he seems inaccessible, these things seem attractive to her; and it is these values that he tries to insist upon: the formal rightness of her keeping her "promise," her duty to reciprocate the love she has aroused in him. There is cruelty in Boldwood's romanticism, in the way he insists that she shall adhere to his idea of her (as there is cruelty in Angel's romanticism, and Knight's and Clym's); but Boldwood suffers more than he makes Bathsheba suffer, and the wildness and unhappiness of his love is conditioned by his dream and his distance from reality: "The great aids to idealization in love were present here: occasional observation of her from a distance, and the absence of social intercourse with her . . . the pettinesses that enter so largely into all earthy living and doing were disguised by the accident of lover and loved-one not being on visiting terms; and there was hardly awakened a thought in Boldwood that sorry household realities appertained to her . . ." But Boldwood remains just as blind to realities when he gets to know her. After the disappearance of Troy, he again nourishes his love, but "almost shunned the contemplation of it in earnest, lest facts should reveal the wildness of the dream" It is a "fond madness": and the anticlimax is the discovery (while Boldwood is in prison, awaiting trial) of all the jewellery and clothing labelled "Bathsheba Boldwood," bought for a woman who had never promised to marry him.

Hardy is disparaging romance, the dream and the dreamer. He is suggesting, instead, that one should live—not in accordance with nature—but in accordance with reality. And this point is made clearly by the three choices open to Bathsheba: Oak, Boldwood, and Troy. Boldwood, of course, ceases to attract her as soon as he forces his attentions on her: and there is a gentle irony in the fact that she sees in Troy, who has taken her away from Boldwood, something of what Boldwood has seen in her: a figure of romance, someone from another world. But it is not only Troy's glamour: it is also that "arch-dissembler" Nature that prompts Bathsheba to love Troy. She goes to meet him, hesitates, and then surrenders her heart, in the chapter called "The Hollow amid the Ferns." The scene is one of great natural beauty, of lush growth:

> . . . tall thickets of brake fern, plump and diaphanous from recent rapid growth, and radiant in hues of clear and untainted green.

> At eight o'clock this midsummer evening, whilst the bristling ball of gold in the west still swept the tips of the ferns with its long, luxuriant rays, a soft brushing-by of garments might have been heard among them, and Bathsheba appeared in their midst, their soft, feathery arms caressing her up to her shoulders. She paused, turned, went back . . .

But again she changes her mind, and goes on to the meeting place, a hollow where the fern "grew nearly to the bottom of the slope and then abruptly ceased. The middle within the belt of verdure was floored with a thick flossy carpet of moss and grass intermingled, so yielding that the foot was half-buried within it." Nature is softly inviting and reassuring her. She surrenders to Nature as much as to her lover,—to her own natural womanliness

which, Hardy tells us, she normally had too much sense to be quite governed by. The treatment of this theme is more subtle, perhaps, and certainly more extended, in *Tess;* but it is effective in *Far from the Madding Crowd*, all the same.

Bathsheba's third possibility is Oak; whose name at least cannot be made to suggest *compliance* with nature, but rather sturdy resistance, hard use and endurance. The distinction Hardy draws at the beginning of the novel between the intermingling sounds of one vast integrated body of Nature over Norcombe Hill, and the "clearness" and "sequence" of the "notes of Farmer Oak's flute," runs right through the book. Gabriel Oak is not a part of Nature. He may be a countryman, but he is always a human being, fully conscious of his human responsibility, always ready to modify, to deflect, to improve, Nature's workings; always, that is, after his first setback. A "natural" sequence of events destroys his sheep; but he does not see himself as a victim of fate—as Troy would have done, or Henchard ("I am to suffer, I perceive"). He realizes he is ruined, and that, not having insured his sheep, he himself is to blame. And his second thought is that things would be even worse if Bathsheba had married him: "Thank God I am not married: what would she have done in the poverty now coming upon me?" Thereafter he intervenes in the natural sequence of events in as timely a fashion as he can. He prevents the fire from spreading to the ricks and buildings of Bathsheba's farm; he cures the poisoned sheep; he saves Bathsheba's harvest from the storm; and he tries to intervene, but unsuccessfully, before Boldwood's optimistic dreams lead to disaster, and before Bathsheba gives way to her infatuation for Troy: ". . . But since we don't exactly know what he is, why not behave as if he *might* be bad, simply for your own safety? Don't trust him, mistress . . ."— Gabriel's version of Hardy's own advice to take "a full look at the Worst." But Oak's attitude towards Nature is best seen in the account of the storm, because here Nature appears in her two aspects: creator and destroyer. She is prepared, but for Gabriel, to destroy the harvest she has bounteously created; and it is Gabriel's appreciation of the bounty, his sense of its meaning in terms of human life and sustenance, that makes him put forth all this strength to save the bounty from the destruction and to pit himself against the whole scheme of things, the whole trend of circumstance at that time. He fights not only against elemental nature, but against "nature's" hold on the humanity around him: Troy's insidiously easy-going ways ("'Mr Troy says it will not rain, and he cannot stop to talk to you about such fidgets'"), the only too natural sleepiness and inertia of the drunken workfolk in the barn, and his own natural fears when the threat of the lightning becomes too great. The critics who suppose that Hardy shared and advocated the philosophic resignation of some of his rustics should read again the thirty-sixth and thirty-seventh chapters of *Far from the Madding Crowd:* if ever a man had the excuse of surrendering, of saying "It was to be," Oak has the excuse on the night of the storm. Instead, he fights.

Yet throughout his fight, there remains a sense in which Nature's opposition is "neutral"; nothing is purposely aimed against Oak. The changes mount against him; but they are still chances. And he seeks to keep ahead of them; he gets a lightning conductor improvised. Had there been any malicious purpose, an earlier flash of lightning would have struck him down. It is a fight between a man intelligently directing his efforts and "senseless circumstance." Oak persists; and he wins. He is not quite alone; in the latter part of the night he is helped by Bathsheba. The scene is one of many in the novels that vividly suggest the need of the human pair for each other, the individual's comparative—sometimes complete—helplessness alone.

There is another side to Gabriel's feeling for Nature: he fights her successfully because he understands and can sympathetically interpret the doings not only of his sheep, but also of Nature's smaller creatures—slug, spiders, and toad. He seeks to learn from Nature; for instance, from the sprig of ivy that has grown across the door of the church tower, proving that Troy has *not* been in the habit of entering here modestly and unobserved (as Bathsheba too readily believes), and that Troy is, therefore, a liar. Nature is one of Gabriel's resources; but he is never controlled by her, nor, in any Wordsworthian sense, does he ever trust her. The essential thing about Gabriel is not that he is in contact with Nature, but that he is in contact with reality. He neither evades it nor resigns himself to it; he makes something out of it.

This point is effectively made by a metaphor embodied in an incident early in the book, just at the turning point of Oak's fortunes, when he has proved he can survive even the worst that life has to offer and when his luck (if such a word can be used) is at last on the mend. He is drinking cider in the Malthouse, and has just endeared himself to the Weatherbury folk by refusing the luxury of a clean cup:

"And here's a mouthful of bread and bacon that mis-'ess have sent, shepherd. The cider will go down better with a bit of victuals. Don't ye chaw quite close, shepherd, for I let the bacon fall in the road outside as I was bringing it along, and may be 'tis rather gritty. There, 'tis clane dirt; and we all know what that is, as you say, and you bain't a particular man we see, shepherd."

"True, true—not at all," said the friendly Oak.

"Don't let your teeth quite meet, and you won't feel the sandiness at all. Ah! 'tis wonderful what can be done by contrivance!"

"My own mind exactly, neighbour."

The incident is a precise metaphor of what Oak has been doing in the wider sphere of his life: he has had his share of "unpalatable reality," but by contrivance he has managed to find life's grittiness not so "unpalatable" after all.

Hardy's attitudes and themes in this novel are, indeed, typical; what is not typical is the method: he is presenting his main theme—the value of pessimism as a practical policy ("...You cannot lose at it, you may gain...") through a pessimist, a central character who is successful. He is presenting it, that is, positively, instead of through the failure of a hero who is too optimistic or unrealistic. The total pattern, however, is not so different: there are unrealistic people (as we have seen) who are foils to Oak, just as in the other novels there are realists, like Farfrae, who are foils to the unsuccessful heroes. An advantage of *Far from the Madding Crowd* as an introduction to Hardy's novels is just that it *is* positive, and provides a basis for understanding the irony of most of the others.

Despite Meredith's advice that he should avoid the direct and positive method, Hardy has given us, in Gabriel Oak, as positive a model—after one or two initial overconfident slips—as Egbert Mayne. I see this as not without significance: Hardy wished, without doubt, to clarify the values for his readers. The fire in *Desperate Remedies* that seems to proceed haltingly, and to wait every now and then—but quite in vain—for some intelligent intervention, becomes the fire Oak sees at Weatherbury: it has already reached the stage of accelerated climax; but, even so, a man like Oak who can act promptly and courageously, is able to intervene, and to organize the firefighting, and he is just in time to prevent the spread of the flames to the farm buildings and to other ricks.

But the Weatherbury fire can serve as an illustration of Hardy's development in a more important respect. The point of the incident is not only to show how the courage and intelligence of a superior man can help the ordinary community when by itself that community is helpless; but also to show how that man gets a job. Oak has failed to get work at the hiring fair, and he is in desperate straits; but through the fire, and his ability to swallow his pride even when he discovers that the owner of the farm is Bathsheba, the woman who once rejected him, he gets the employment he needs. Hardy here embodies in action and incident what in *Desperate Remedies* had to be expressed in an explicit statement. What Edward Springrove reminds Cytherea, "... that the fame of Sir Christopher Wren himself depended upon the accident of a fire in Pudding Lane," is transposed from the key of the young architect to that of the countryman, and presented not in words, but in action. And there are other examples. We have already remarked that Hardy's note about the "figure" that "stands in our van with arm uplifted, to knock us back from any pleasant prospect we indulge in as probable" is paraphrased in *Desperate Remedies*, Hardy explaining that "a position which it was impossible to reach by any direct attempt was come to by a seeker's swerving from the path." Less than four years later, this does not have to be phrased at all. It becomes the sequence of events at the beginning of *Far from the Madding Crowd:* Gabriel, indulging in the "pleasant prospect" of success as a sheep-farmer, and even at one point accepting as "probable" his marriage with Bathsheba, is "knocked back." He is ruined. At Casterbridge hiring fair, subsequently, he fails to get a job as bailiff or even as shepherd. But then, "swerving from his path," he gradually contrives to reach all his original objectives, one by one: he becomes a shepherd, a bailiff, the owner of Boldwood's farm, and eventually Bathsheba's husband.

Let us now consider such of Hardy's favourite narrative devices as may be illustrated from *Far from the Madding Crowd*, beginning with two of the most important: the highly-charged expressionistic incidents that have been called "grotesques," and his contrasts. These ironical contrasts may be partly accounted for by Hardy's modest wish—expressed indeed at this very period of his life—to be considered a good hand at a serial." But this is certainly not the whole truth. Hardy's belief in the eternal possibility of change was something fundamental; and some of the contrasts he suggests are far more elaborate than anything required by the suspenses and sequels of a magazine serial story. In *Far from the Madding Crowd* it happens that one of the most extraordinary of Hardy's "grotesques" has an important place in one of his series of ironical contrasts; we shall therefore be able to discuss them together. But first a word about the "grotesques," since they have proved to be critical stumbling blocks: Hardy risked the

sleepwalking scene in *Tess*, and the trilobite and cliff rescue in *A Pair of Blue Eyes*, and other such scenes, because he saw their function as transcending their awkwardness and lack of realism. And they may fulfil their function not despite their awkwardness, but because of it. Read in their full contexts, they set chords vibrating through the whole novel. The sleepwalking scene, with its central incident of Angel carrying Tess precariously along the plank above the flooded waters of the Froom, reminds us of Tess's complete helplessness in Angel's care; and of Tess's responsibility too, since a false move on her part will be fatal; above all, the precariousness is a reminder that the happiness of both is in the balance; Angel's placing of Tess in the coffin powerfully suggests that he is killing his love for her; and, behind the mere fact of the sleepwalking, is the hint that Angel does not know where he is going. It is Tess, indeed, who finally takes control, leading Angel back to safety; this is an indication that the salvation may be in Tess's own hands. Through the very incident—if she tells Angel about it—she may help him to clarify his feelings. The cliff scene in *A Pair of Blue Eyes* is less complex; but this too might be taken primarily as an indication of the deep need of Elfride and Knight for each other, while subsidiary details suggest the completeness with which Elfride has renounced all thought of marrying Stephen. These are but suggestions; with the most interesting expressionistic scene in *Far from the Madding Crowd* I will try to give the implications a little more fully: it is the scene where the grotesque gurgoyle spouts water over Fanny's grave and undoes all that Troy's remorseful labour has accomplished.

The first irony is Troy's astonishment. He feels he has turned over a new leaf and made a virtuous show of remorse; but finds that "... Providence, far from helping him into a new course, or showing any wish that he might adopt one, actually jeered his first trembling and critical attempt in that kind ..." But Hardy, in the preceding chapter, "Troy's Romanticism," had shown Troy's activities in a different light. After a long and tiring day, in which he had walked to Casterbridge and back, arranged for a headstone to be inscribed and dispatched, and finally toiled at the grave late into the night, planting flowers by the light of a lantern, Troy had taken shelter in the church porch, and fallen asleep. "Troy," Hardy remarks, "had no perception that in the futility of these romantic doings, dictated by remorseful reaction from previous indifference, there was any element of absurdity." Here, then, is another and a greater irony: in the contrast between the immense trouble that Troy takes, to prove his love for Fanny now she is dead, and his neglect of her during her lifetime. Seen in this light, the gurgoyle's mockery is but a picturesque projection, an image, of Hardy's own feelings about Troy. But even if we share Troy's view that Fate cruelly prevents him from adequately displaying his remorse, we certainly cannot suppose it was Fate that had stopped him from marrying Fanny: it was injured pride. And is not this the explanation of his present defeat? His pride is hurt; the approving pat on the back that he expects from Providence has not come. If he had been thinking, not of the hurt to himself, but simply of what could be done to repair the damage, he could have done it; and with a quarter of the effort he had spent toiling by lantern-light the night before. Hardy pushes this point home, as there is no need to remind the reader, by showing Bathsheba doing simply and easily what Troy thinks it is useless to attempt: gathering up the flowers and replanting them, cleaning up the headstone, and arranging for the pipe in the gurgoyle's mouth to be deflected. For Troy such actions are impossible: "He slowly withdrew from the grave. He did not attempt to fill up the hole, replace the flowers, or do anything at all. He simply threw up his cards, and foreswore his game for that time and always. . . . Shortly afterwards he had gone from the village." He has no intention of returning to Bathsheba's farm; and surely the greatest irony of all is that in his remorse for the past, he is neglecting the present. He regrets having neglected Fanny when she was alive; but, repeating the same pattern, he is neglecting the woman—in every way Fanny's superior—whom he has actually married.

Indeed, as one contemplates the situation, the ironies seem to multiply. There is the fact that Troy, of all people, should not be surprised at what the rain can do: only a few weeks before, the storm he confidently predicted would not happen, did happen, and would have ruined him and Bathsheba but for Oak's courage. Then he had blamed the rain for all the money he had lost at the Budmouth races. And this reminds us that the money he spent on Fanny's grave, like that he lost on the horses, was not even his own; it was Bathsheba's. And again the realization is forced upon us that from the rain and the gurgoyle Troy had suffered no tangible harm; his ego was hurt, his gesture spoilt: nothing else. But the world of *Far from the Madding Crowd* is, after all, one where more is at stake, sometimes, than the success of a gesture; and beyond the ironies of what Troy had left undone, and still leaves undone, there is the further ironic contrast between the way Troy is immediately and utterly

defeated by the mere *appearance* of disaster and difficulty, and the way Oak has fought against what might have been a real disaster and at the real risk of his life. Many facets of Troy's character are recalled as we ponder over the incident; and in particular his weakness for display: a small point is the splendid impossibility of the lie about his modestly entering the church in such a way as to avoid being seen, and the blindness of Bathsheba in believing him.

The occasional importance of images in Hardy's narrative method is not likely to be overlooked. Discussion of these has proved easy, and sometimes uninformative. When Bathsheba first meets Troy, the gimp on her dress is caught in one of his spurs, and as Troy seeks to disentangle it, the lantern throws their shadows against the trees of the fir plantation so that "each dusky shape" becomes "distorted and mangled till it wasted to nothing." It is easy to see this as a "proleptic image," a hint of the trouble in store for them when their lives become entangled. But why "when"? Why not "*if* their lives become entangled"? Why should Bathsheba ignore a danger that almost everyone else in Weatherbury sees clearly? There is no need to repeat what I have already stressed: that far more striking images—such as those which predict death and disaster for Gabriel before the storm—indicate not a determined future, but undetermined possible dangers that can be averted.

But there is one image in *Far from the Madding Crowd* on which it is necessary to comment, since it has escaped the notice of other critics. Gabriel is investigating an unfamiliar light, and finds that it comes from a shed set into the hillside. He peers through a hole in the roof, and finds himself looking down upon a young woman whom he at first does not recognize, seeing her "in a bird's eye view, *as Milton's Satan first saw Paradise.*" There are ways of dealing with things as awkward as this: some critics may say that Hardy does not know what he is doing; that he is writing here without inner conviction; others may ridicule Hardy's attempt to display his book knowledge. But there is only one way of reading this in good faith: to assume that Hardy meant what he said. And Hardy is not parading his own book knowledge: *Paradise Lost* was one of Gabriel Oak's books, we discover later; and we are following *Gabriel's* eyes, *his* impressions, *his* slight feeling of guilt, as he peers into the hut. There is nothing satanic about Gabriel; and indeed there is something very unsatanic about his name; all the same, he would like to intrude, and does in fact later intrude, upon this girl's life. The function of the image is, indeed, clear: it strikingly raises the question whether the intruder is always evil, or whether he can be—as Gabriel turns out to be, by and large—a good angel.

It is through this image, in fact, that we approach the social theme of the book—in so far as it has one: the strengthening of a rather backward, pleasant, easy-going rural community by two newcomers, two intruders. The Weatherbury folk are too close to nature; ignorant, lazy, rather irresponsible, and superstitious: it is significant that when Bathsheba, against her better judgement and under Liddy's persuasion, consults the "Sortes Sanctorum," a rusty patch on the page indicates how often the Bible has been used before for this purpose. In all kinds of small ways the country people show that they are not adapting themselves for survival under new conditions of life, and weaknesses are creeping in. They need someone like Bathsheba, an unconventional woman, whose parents were townsfolk, to come and take a personal interest in the farm, to sack the dishonest bailiff, and take full responsibility herself. The workfolk are capable enough, but they are useless in an emergency: they get flustered or they are tipsy; and they have none of the new skills and scientific knowledge that enable Gabriel Oak to operate upon the sheep that have poisoned themselves in the young clover. But more than this, they need Oak's new conscientiousness, his firmness, his readiness, his refusal to let personal griefs affect his actions (he is contrasted strikingly in this respect with Boldwood, whose preoccupation with grief—as we learn when Gabriel meets him the morning after the storm—has caused him to neglect his harvest). Neither Oak's new skills nor the qualities of his character were learnt from the Weatherbury community; he brings them—as Bathsheba brings her vitality and unconventionality—from outside. They are strangers in a sense that even Troy is not; Troy slips only too readily into the easy-going country morality. Gabriel and Bathsheba have all the strength of newcomers, outsiders, who revitalize the old stock.

I have mentioned the fact that Bathsheba allows herself to be influenced by the irresponsible and romantic Liddy in the Sortes Sanctorum scene and the sending of the valentine. This does not contradict my argument: it is a lapse on Bathsheba's part, and she pays dearly for it. And every detail of the episode is interesting as revealing that Bathsheba is all the time aware of the more sensible course; for instance she reverses the conditions of the toss because she thinks the book is more likely to fall open: ". . . Open Boldwood—shut, Teddy.

No; it's more likely to fall open: Open, Teddy—shut, Boldwood." It falls shut. And Bathsheba, who knows perfectly well what she wants to do, and what she ought to do, acts instead as she is directed by chance. It is an interesting illustration of the fact that human beings who are capable enough of acting independently of chance, and more intelligently, sometimes choose to put themselves in chance's hands. The relevance of this point to incidents in the other novels (for instance, Elfride's decision that her horse shall choose her direction for her) needs no emphasis; nor need we stress the irony with which Hardy links Bathsheba's foolish and, indeed, disastrous action with the Sortes Sanctorum and tossing of a hymn book, and so, by ironic implication, with the workings of Providence.

So often is Hardy's attitude to change misunderstood, that it is perhaps worth adding that chances, in his books, are not always disastrous ones; and there is an instance in *Far from the Madding Crowd* of a singularly fortunate chance: Bathsheba happens to pass near Gabriel's hut and to notice that both ventilators are closed. Her chance discovery saves Gabriel's life.

"How did you find me?"

"I heard your dog howling and scratching at the door of the hut when I came to the milking (it was so lucky, Daisy's milking is almost over for the season, and I shall not come here after this week or the next). The dog saw me, and jumped over to me, and laid hold of my skirt. I came across and looked round the hut the very first thing to see if the slides were closed. My uncle has a hut like this one, and I have heard him tell his shepherd not to go to sleep without leaving a slide open . . ."

But there is more to it than the lucky chance of Daisy's milking not being quite over: the event is nearly a disaster; and the disaster is prevented only because the person happening to come by was—by Wessex standards—remarkably responsible, and intelligently alert to the worst contingencies.

A final point: Hardy was much interested in what one may call the psychology of the "object": the distress and sudden weakness felt by someone—often a woman—when she discovers she is being talked about, and has thus become an object in the eyes of others. Tess's "feminine loss of courage" at Emminster is caused by overhearing Angel's brothers talking about her; Sue cannot ignore the gossip she overhears about herself and Jude; Elfride is horrified to find that Knight is writing an article about her; even Ethelberta is disconcerted at overhearing some gossip about her own future; and, as we might expect, Hardy explicitly theorizes about this human weakness in *Desperate Remedies.* Bathsheba is vexed that Gabriel has seen her unconventional behaviour on horseback; and she is indignant at his tactlessness in letting her know. None the less, the fact that she knows he has seen her, and is critical of her conduct, makes her a little dependent on him; she finds herself sounding him as to what others are saying about her, and seeking Gabriel's good opinion. Her self-justifications and confidences are not just a narrative device: Hardy is doing more than conveying to us a few facts we should otherwise not know—Bathsheba's doings in Bath, for instance— he is showing her becoming more and more dependent upon Gabriel and Gabriel's approval. At the same time Gabriel himself is becoming more and more the controlling centre of all the activity on the two farms; and from looking *to* him, Bathsheba gradually finds herself looking *up* to him.

Romantic Westerners are sometimes a bit surprised that Bathsheba marries Oak; but between the man we meet in the opening pages, pleasant and unassuming but tactless and just a shade too confident, and the Gabriel Oak of the last chapters, there are many subtle differences; and perhaps her choice is not so surprising. In the East, feelings are reversed: surprise is sometimes felt that *he* could have brought himself to marry *her.* She had slighted him, as Japanese and Chinese readers point out, and she was not an easily controllable woman. Not many English people react in this way because, I suppose, we share Gabriel's liking for a woman who is exceptional. And also, surely, because we have learnt to understand his great merits; first, he leaves pride and pique to fools like Troy, and second, we feel he can cope even with Bathsheba: there has been nothing so far that he has failed to cope with. We have learnt to accept, as one of the greatest of qualities, Oak's adaptability; and, at the end of the book, we take Hardy's point that it is a special sort of goodness to arrange to go to California, if that seems best, and then to be able, equally easily, to cancel such plans when, at the last moment, the factors in the situation change, and he can marry Bathsheba after all.

Source: Roy Morrell, "*Far from the Madding Crowd* as an Introduction to Hardy's Novels," in *Critical Essays on Thomas Hardy: The Novels,* edited by Dale Kramer, with the assistance of Nancy Marck, G. K. Hall, 1990, pp. 123–33.

Richard Carpenter

In the following essay excerpt, Carpenter examines the features—"from the centrally tragic figure to the symbolic landscape to the rustic chorus"—that make Far from the Madding Crowd *"a kind of golden mean among the major works."*

> "
>
> Despite its occasional melodrama, the situations of *Far From the Madding Crowd* are more believable and more rooted in probabilities than those of any of the novels which preceded it. A good deal of this effect is due to the pervasive and richly developed rural setting.

Hardy's six major novels differ from the minor fiction principally in the increased creative energy and tension he brings to them. The plots are similarly complex but do not dominate the work to the enervation of character; the characters are enmeshed in situations compounded out their own weaknesses and the fell clutch of circumstance but retain their individuality and force; setting takes its proper place as symbolic and metaphoric of the lives of the characters; myth and symbol are integral to the total construction of the novel rather than being merely interesting for their own sake. In addition, the tragic themes which infuse the major novels give them a massiveness not to be found in Hardy's other fiction where he either essays the uncongenial mode of comedy or shilly-shallies between comedy and tragedy. Comedy, to be sure, does appear in the major novels (with the exception of *Jude the Obscure*); but it is complementary, a commentary on the principal theme rather than a rival. The major novels also have their undeniable weaknesses, usually of the same type as the lesser fiction. Yet it is clear, when one comes to any of the six great novels, that philosophical intrusions, unintegrated descriptions, stock characters, and artificialities cannot hide the work of genius. When Hardy gathers all his forces together to create a total effect, the flaws become insignificant. We know that we are encountering the work of a master who is striking the major chords on a rich and powerful instrument.

I Far From the Madding Crowd

The most representative and balanced of the Wessex novels is the fourth one Hardy wrote, following *A Pair of Blue Eyes. Far from the Madding*

Crowd (1874) combines the typical features of the other major novels without developing any one of them to an extreme: the vividly realized setting of field and farm without the overpowering grim majesty of Egdon Heath, a capricious heroine who does not demonstrate the neurosis of Eustacia Vye or of Sue Bridehead, and the influence of Chance and Time without the dominance they have in *Tess of the D'Urbervilles* or *The Mayor of Casterbridge*. *Far From the Madding Crowd* is not, however, a mere museum of Hardy qualities, but a significant novel in its own right—a kind of golden mean among the major works. Its balance may account for its great popular success in its own time, a success not without disadvantages for Hardy; for, in combination with *Under the Greenwood Tree*, *Far From the Madding Crowd* created an audience inclined toward the bucolic and one which was unable to fathom or appreciate his later, grimmer work.

The plot is one quality of this novel which is demonstrably superior to the minor works, for it grows principally out of character and natural situations. Bathsheba Everdene is a beautiful and willful young woman who spurns the earnest suit of Gabriel Oak from sheer caprice. Subsequently, Oak loses his flock of sheep and becomes an itinerant farmworker, while Bathsheba inherits a large farm. (Although this is coincidental, it is thoroughly embedded in the rural scene and does not seem gratuitous.) Oak saves her grain ricks from fire and is hired as her bailiff, his own motive being to look after Bathsheba and be near her; but though he may save her property, he cannot save her heart from disaster. Once again she overlooks the worthy man to become infatuated with the rakish Sergeant Troy and eventually to elope with him, neither of them being aware that Troy's former sweetheart, Fanny Robin, is pregnant and searching for him.

Bathsheba, too, has sown the seeds of later grief in her careless encouragement of Farmer Boldwood, a man who appears too solid and staid to lose his heart but who is actually a highly emotional and sensitive person. Fanny dies in childbirth in the workhouse; and Troy, distracted with remorse, tells Bathsheba that he really loved Fanny and not Bathsheba; then he disappears, to be reported later as drowned. Bathsheba is naturally crushed by all that has happened, but the way is eventually opened for Farmer Boldwood to renew his courtship. After much hesitation, Bathsheba agrees to become Mrs. Boldwood, only to have Troy reappear, quite alive and very sadistic. But he has not reckoned with Boldwood's emotional nature, and he is shot by the distracted farmer. Finally, after much suffering of

spirit and body, Bathsheba and Oak, who has remained loyally by her, are quietly married.

Despite its occasional melodrama, the situations of *Far From the Madding Crowd* are more believable and more rooted in probabilities than those of any of the novels which preceded it. A good deal of this effect is due to the pervasive and richly developed rural setting. From the very outset Hardy creates the essence of the countryside, with Oak moving through the accustomed round of his work as a shepherd while about him a dry, crisp December presents varied aspects of the landscape. He first sees Bathsheba atop a load of furniture arranged accordingly to the immemorial custom of peasants on moving day; he tells time by the stars, while around him on Norcombe Hill the wind touches the grass in "breezes of differing powers— one rubbing the blades heavily, another raking them piercingly, another brushing them like a soft broom." He cares for a new-born lamb and spies a cow shed where Bathsheba and her aunt are also looking after another newborn, a calf. This pastoral atmosphere is maintained throughout the novel, giving it a tone which is part not only of its charm but of its meaning.

The great thunderstorm, for example, provides an occasion to contrast the firmness and competence of Oak with the careless immorality of Troy; and, at the same time, it is a premonitory metaphor of the emotional tempest which will soon come crashing about Bathsheba. Hardy has some of his usual difficulty in "rendering," as Conrad would say, the feeling of the approaching storm; but he manages to convey the foreboding tension and the eerie stillness which are part of it. Gabriel feels sure that it will soon be on them, drenching the grain ricks; and he tries to arouse Troy and the drunken field hands to some action, without success. He feels "a hot breeze, as if breathed from the parted lips of some dragon about to swallow the globe . . . from the south, while directly opposite in the north rose a grim misshapen body of cloud, in the very teeth of the wind. So unnaturally did it rise that one could fancy it to be lifted by machinery from below." As Gabriel sets to work to cover the grain, Hardy says: "The night had a haggard look, like a sick thing; and there came finally an utter expiration of air from the whole heaven in the form of a slow breeze, which might have been likened to a death." And when the storm comes, it is similarly described, with its "mailed army" of lightning, as it springs like a "serpent," with "the shout of a fiend." Certainly Hardy is using such images with intent, even if intuitive intent, to create an impression of the forces of nature as malevolent and in some mystical way equivalent to the human forces which are gathering headway in the novel.

In contrast to this metaphoric use of setting we might instance one with a different import: the great barn, with its solidity and timelessness, where Gabriel and the men shear the sheep. It is "far nobler in design . . . than nine-tenths of our modern churches"; and with its "vast porches, lofty enough to admit a waggon laden to its highest point with corn in the sheaf," its stone arches and "striding buttresses," it has stood in this place for four centuries without any change in its purposes. "Today," says Hardy, "the large side doors were thrown open towards the sun to admit a bountiful light to the immediate spot of the shearers' operations, which was the wood threshing floor in the centre, formed of thick oak, black with age and polished by the beating of flails for many generations, till it had grown slippery and as rich in hue as the state-room floors of an Elizabethan mansion." Within this magnificent structure the rhythms of agricultural life have pulsed without change for hundreds of years, forming a bastion against the vicissitudes that overtake individual lives. Although the principal characters in the novel experience violent transformations—Fanny dies of neglect and Bathsheba suffers the pangs of bitter self-understanding; Boldwood is driven by his frustrated love from his secure position as a farmer to neurosis and murder; and Troy is agonized by futile regret and dies for his perverse egotism—the sheep washing and the sheep shearing go on. Against a background of timelessness Hardy poses human mutabilities. Thus through his setting Hardy intensifies and solidifies the themes which are conveyed by the misfortunes of his characters.

The physical setting is not the only means by which Hardy stresses the theme of Time, for the peasantry who make their appearance in this novel as a kind of rustic Greek chorus are also timeless and changeless. Their primary functions are to provide shrewd comment on the principal characters, to anticipate actions yet to occur, and to furnish comic relief; but they also are symbolic. No matter what happens to the principals, the rustics remain the same. Like the Mellstock Quire, to them things have always been the way they are and ought to stay that way.

We make our first extended acquaintance with them at Warren's Malthouse, where are gathered the ancient maltster, his sixty-five-year-old son, and his forty-year-old grandson, who speaks of his own grandchildren. The generations thus string out almost to infinity; this is, of course, standard country humor; but it also underlines the difference between the peasantry and the principals, none of whom is thus tied to his forebears. In addition to the maltster and his progeny are certain traditional types familiar in folk comedy, from Bottom and his crew in *A Midsummer Night's Dream* to L'il Abner. Henery Fay always insists on the middle *e* in his name, although it is an obvious mistake; Jan Coggan reminisces in a maudlin manner about the "lovely drunks" he and his companions have had; and Joseph Poorgrass is the archetypal timid soul who once answered an owl's "who-whoo" with "Joseph Poorgrass of Weatherbury, sir." Gabriel Oak, the sturdy and reliable yeoman of the principals, fits in well with this group since he alone among the main characters shares in the peasantry's perdurability. He agrees with the maltster that there's no harm in "clane dirt" and cheerfully eats the bacon which has been dropped in the road, following the old man's advice not to let his teeth quite meet.

Such a scene is mainly for comic relief—and is in fact the most effective kind of comedy in Hardy's work—besides helping to show the type of man Oak is. Beyond this, the rustics also serve the useful office of expositors, informing us about Bathsheba Everdene and her background. We learn that her father was "far from a common man" because he went bankrupt "for heaps of money, hundreds in gold and silver"; what sort of young lady Bathsheba is; and the troubles she has had with Bailiff Pennyways—this information in an early scene being a fair sample of what they provide in their quirky, penetrating countryman's way throughout the novel. They also add much by becoming involved in the action; unlike the chorus figures of the classical drama, they carry news, aid in the search for Bathsheba when she elopes, and transport Fanny's body. They form the substratum of the novel against which the fluctuating lives of the main characters are counterpointed, and without them *Far From the Madding Crowd* would be an almost meaningless title.

This group of peasants was one of Hardy's outstanding discoveries, one which he was to use to good effect in several future novels, and one which is a considerable advance in sophistication over the peasantry of *Under the Greenwood Tree*. His other important discovery was the character of Bathsheba Everdene, a logical development from Cytherea Graye who cannot make up her mind about the men she loves, the innocently vain village temptress seen in Fancy Day, and the emotionally motivated and irresponsible Elfride Swancourt. But Bathsheba is a more complex and a stronger character than any of her predecessors, having in addition some of Ethelberta's ambition and strength, and Eustacia's sexuality—a quality notably absent in the earlier heroines. Oak is her first suitor, the prototypal staunch and stable character to be seen in many other Hardy books—John Loveday and Giles Winterborne being the two outstanding examples. Only one thing can shake Oak—neither fire, storm, nor financial disaster—only the fair Bathsheba. In her hands he becomes easily disturbed and emotionally unsure, though never to the point where he loses his essential strength of character. When she first refuses to marry him for the totally feminine reason that he has agreed with her when she says she thinks it would not be practical, he meekly accepts her rejection. But he continues to put himself into her hands, and becomes her employee when she asks him for help in managing her farm. He sticks by her through the disaster of her marriage to Troy, until, following Troy's death, he receives the appropriate reward of long-suffering heroes and becomes her husband.

The root of many of Bathsheba's ills is her vanity, which could not allow her to accept the honesty of Gabriel and which throws her instead into the path of the raffish Troy. But she has sowed a more sinister seed of vanity with her treatment of Farmer Boldwood, the third man in her life. Piqued at his inattention to her, she indulges in the prank of sending him a valentine, little dreaming that the stable appearance of the middle-aged man is only a balance of great extremes, "enormous antagonistic forces—positives and negatives in fine adjustment," which once disturbed, bring him "into extremity at once." As a result of her heedless trick and subsequent unreflecting encouragement, Boldwood becomes hopelessly infatuated; but Bathsheba does not find it possible to love him; instead she allows herself the dubious satisfaction of the glamorous Sergeant Troy's flattery. She reaps the reward of this vanity when Troy shows his true self after their marriage: he squanders her inherited fortune, debauches her farmhands, and finally admits that he never loved her. She comes face to face with the truth when she sees Troy's remorse at the death of Fanny Robin and her bastard child; Troy's subsequent disappearance and reported death only *seem* to remedy the situation, for her engagement to Boldwood is shattered when Troy reappears to claim her as his lawful wife. Boldwood, finally driven to distraction by this final blow to his hopes, snatches a gun from the wall and shoots Troy, then tries unsuccessfully to commit suicide. Bathsheba's willfulness has reaped its ultimate reward in the death of one man and spiritual destruction of another. Eternal Eve has found the fruit of this tree bitter indeed.

Although Hardy allows us the questionable sop to our feelings of a marriage with Oak as a dénouement, the novel does not really end "happily." The vibrant and proud girl we see at the beginning has been as thoroughly destroyed as Troy and Boldwood. Never again, we are sure, will she burst forth in a fine blaze of fury, her black eyes snapping and her cheek flushed; nor will she blush as furiously with love or at her temerity. In subduing her to a mature and knowledgeable adult, Hardy has subdued our enjoyment of her as a character.

What is at work in this process is an implicit moral judgment, which becomes in later novels a metaphysical judgment as well: rebels against either the common sense of society or the inscrutable nature of the universe have their choice only of destruction or reform, and it is not always easy to decide which is preferable. Beyond this moral judgment, however, is another aspect to Hardy's analysis, one of which he may not have been entirely aware. Bathsheba, like other proud women, desires to be dominated by a sexually aggressive man; and, until that desire has been chastened, she cannot make a wife for Oak, who is essentially a passive lover, no matter how strong and good he is otherwise. On the discursive level Hardy informs us that it is Troy's ability as a flatterer and dissembler that enables him to capture Bathsheba; but on a deeper symbolic level Hardy brings out other characteristics of their interrelationship, in scenes which, in the words of Frederick Karl, "fulfill Hardy's genius, although they may well seem peripheral or incidental to the unsympathetic reader." Through such scenes Hardy manages to probe far beneath the realistic surface both of characters and events.

One of these is the scene in which Bathsheba first encounters Troy, as she is walking at night through a dense grove of firs on her farm. In the thick darkness she is unable to identify the figure who passes her on the path, but suddenly she feels herself caught somehow by her skirt. The stranger turns out to be a soldier whose spur has caught in her dress. He is revealed to her when he opens the shade of her dark lantern. She sees him, "brilliant in brass and scarlet," his appearance being "to the darkness what the sound of a trumpet is to silence." Hardy by this means objectifies Bathsheba's inclination toward the flamboyant. (She herself is dressed in scarlet in the first scene of the book where Oak gazes at her as she appreciatively smiles at herself in a mirror while seated atop the furniture on the wagon; scarlet is a symbolic motif of pride, passion, and death in the novel). Troy finds it difficult to disentangle his spur from the skirt, the rowel having "so wound itself among the gimp cord in those few moments, that separation was likely to be a matter of time." As both of them stoop over the bond that connects them, the rays from the dark lantern on the ground send "over half the plantation gigantic shadows of both man and woman, each dusky shape becoming distorted and mangled upon the tree-trunks until it wasted to nothing."

Obvious symbolism, of course. Hardy is making a Gothic device out of the shadows to forewarn us of what will happen to Troy and Bathsheba. At the same time, but less obviously, the spur—like the sword a traditional symbol of cruel male potency—is entangled inextricably with the soft tissues of the dress, which, as Hardy is fond of pointing out (accurately or not), is to a woman not merely a piece of clothing but an extension of her personality. Hardy is saying symbolically that Bathsheba will be connected with Troy through sex rather than through the romance or respect she could expect from her other lovers, and that she is to be dominated, phallically as D. H. Lawrence would say, by an aggressive male.

This symbolism is even more evident in a later scene, which has been dismissed as merely sensational, but which yields significant meanings when interpreted psychologically. In this episode Troy demonstrates to Bathsheba, in a lush hollow amid the ferns, his preternatural skill with the broadsword, using her as his mock victim. The setting is described with a wealth of feminine imagery that sets an erotic tone for the entire scene, while Bathsheba herself is passionately excited, "literally trembling and panting at this her temerity." The sword itself, even more patently phallic than the spur, gleams "a sort of greeting, like a living thing," while Troy demonstrates the "murderous and bloodthirsty" cuts of which it is capable. Bathsheba obeys Troy's request to stand still without flinching, while he flashes the sword around her in "beams of light . . . above, around, in front of her," enclosing her "in a firmament of light, and of sharp hisses, resembling a sky-full of meteors close at hand." As his final demonstration, Troy spits a caterpillar which has fallen from the ferns upon the bosom of her dress: "She saw the point glisten towards her bosom, and seemingly enter it," but of course she is unharmed.

Part of the meaning of this bizarre scene is in its characterization—of Bathsheba as a bold girl anxious for thrills and excitement, and of Troy as a devil-may-care adventurer with some

Mephistophelian overtones in his scarlet trappings and preternatural mastery of the sword. But, more than this, the scene represents seduction. Bathsheba knows for the first time, through this surrogate experience, the sense of the dominant male force that she really desires beneath her cloak of Victorian respectability. This is the clue to her perverse toying with men who are much better than Troy, and her refusal to take the advice of those who know him well. Hardy says that Bathsheba's goddess was Diana, the chaste huntress; but a curious commentary is that, as Frazer tells us, the King of the Wood, who prowled about the sacred grove of Nemi with a drawn sword, was a priest of Diana as a nature goddess, and that in one of his avatars was united with a priestess representing the goddess. Bathsheba wants at once to queen it over a man and to be dominated by him, a paradox which lies at the heart of Hardy's capricious heroines, as indeed it may lie at the heart of most women.

Bathsheba's problems do not arise alone from ambivalent desire; for, as with other protagonists, she is subjected to the influence of Chance and Time, which destroy the stable patterns of rural life and make breaches for character to exploit. *Far From the Madding Crowd* is not so dominated by these forces as is, say, *Tess of the D'Urbervilles*; nevertheless without them it could not take the course it does. Chance has its place in the prank of sending the valentine to Boldwood, because Bathsheba uses the ancient device of divination by Bible-and-key to decide what to do; chance acts in Fanny's mistaking the church where she is to marry Troy so that the wedding does not occur; it is operative in the encounter with Fanny on the road to the workhouse and in Bathsheba's seeing Fanny's hair in the back of Troy's watch; in the rain which washes away the flowers Troy has planted on Fanny's grave; in the current which sweeps Troy out to sea while swimming so that he is reported dead. While these are not the kinds of bizarre coincidences by which Hardy reminds us of the inscrutabilities of existence, they are yet frequent and crucial enough to make us feel that something malign lies at the root of things, ready to provide opportunities whereby weaknesses in character can bring about tragedy.

Inexorable Time does not function in cooperation with character in the novel so much as it is simply evident as a contrast to the mutability of human life. The shearing barn and the rustics, as we have mentioned, are permanent, or give an impression of permanence against which individuals are seen in their tragic finitude. Similarly, Hardy describes in such a way as to stress this finitude some features of the landscape, Norcombe Hill, for example, and such objects as the leering automation that marks the time while Troy awaits Fanny at the church, or the grinning gargoyle which has seemingly waited for four hundred years to pour a relentless torrent of rainwater on the flowers of Fanny's grave. Such images point up the fact that man struggles not only against himself but against the simple fact of change. If he could remain stable, if things were not subject to the hand of Time, then all would be well; but of course he cannot, especially if he has desire and intellect which inevitably lead to instability.

Far From the Madding Crowd is, then, Hardy's first undeniably assured venture into the realm where he was to have his greatest success. In it he developed some of his most characteristic and effective modes, from the centrally tragic figure to the symbolic landscape to the rustic chorus. In it, especially, we see in clear form for the first time the mythic and psychological patterns which he was to employ so effectively as he went on. In later novels he enriched and further developed each of these modes. . . .

Source: Richard Carpenter, "Fiction: The Major Chord," in *Thomas Hardy*, Twayne Publishers, 1964, pp. 80–91.

Sources

Carpenter, Richard, "Thomas Hardy Revisited," in *Thomas Hardy*, Twayne's English Author Series, No. 13, Twayne Publishers, 1964, pp. 15–16.

Casagrande, Peter J., "A New View of Bathsheba Everdene," in *Critical Approaches to the Fiction of Thomas Hardy*, edited by Dale Kramer, Barnes & Noble Books, 1979, pp. 51–53.

Kramer, Dale, "Thomas Hardy, Then to Now," in *Critical Essays on Thomas Hardy: The Novels*, edited by Dale Kramer, G. K. Hall, 1990, pp. 2–3.

Further Reading

Lock, Charles, "Hardy and the Nature of Fiction" in *Thomas Hardy*, St. Martin's Press, 1992, pp. 84–138.
This chapter of Lock's study of Hardy focuses on Hardy's artistic theory, drawn from his fiction and other writings.

Ray, Martin, *The Life and Work of Thomas Hardy: Allusions and Annotations*, Thomas Hardy Association, 2003, CD-ROM.
Hardy's works in general, and this novel in particular, are packed with references to folk songs and other writers. This work catalogs the exact sources for references to Shelley, Wordsworth, Milton, Tennyson, Swinburne, Byron, and Keats, along with Shakespeare and the Bible.

Stewart, J. I. M., *Thomas Hardy: A Critical Biography*, Longman, 1971.
Stewart gives detailed background information for each of the major novels.

Zabel, Morton Dauwen, "Hardy in Defense of His Art: The Aesthetic of Incongruity," in *Hardy: A Collection of Critical Essays*, edited by Albert J. Guerard, Prentice-Hall, 1963, pp. 24–45; originally published in *Craft and Character in Modern Fiction*, Viking Press, 1957.
This essay is thorough in its references to Hardy's writings about art and the critics who doubted him.

Farewell My Concubine

Lilian Lee

1992

Farewell My Concubine (1992, Hong Kong) has left an impressive mark in both the Eastern and Western worlds—at least, the film version of Lilian Lee's novel has done so. The novel itself has largely been overshadowed by the international success of the film adaptation. Although the book was first published in Chinese in 1992, the English translation did not reach the United States until 1993, the same year that the film—which is widely acknowledged as a revolutionary Chinese film—was released. Yet, even though the film dominates discussions about the story, the book stands on its own merits. Lee's novel takes readers deep inside the world of Peking opera during the twentieth century. The story, which centers on a love triangle involving two opera singers and a former prostitute, provides an emotionally charged lens through which to view the major historical events in China during the century, most notably the oppressive communist rule of Chairman Mao. Using the historical context of this time period to provide the novel's structure, Lee explores themes of survival, sex, and love. In the end Lee uses the transformation of Cheng Dieyi—a man who is effeminate as a boy and who, through specific opera training, is trained to think and act like a woman—to demonstrate the power and limitations of art in the real world. While Lee is a bestselling novelist in her native Hong Kong, *Farewell My Concubine* is the only major in-print English translation for which she is known.

It should be noted that names in China are arranged in reverse order from Western styling. In other words, the first name listed is the family

name, or surname, while the second name is the personal name, or first name as Western audiences understand it. In addition, many of the younger characters in the book are referred to by the term "Xiao," which means small and is an indication of childhood status.

Author Biography

Very little is known about the personal and professional life of Lilian Lee—at least in the Western world—including her birthdate. The few sources available still list Lee as alive in 2003. One possible reason for the lack of biographical information is Lee's many names. Lilian Lee is the English pen name for this Chinese author; some sources spell her name "Lillian" Lee. Her actual Chinese name is Li Pi-Hua, although she is also known as Li Pik-Wah.

Lee is a bestselling author in her native Hong Kong and has written more than thirty books. With the exception of *Farewell My Concubine* (1992) and *The Last Princess of Manchuria* (1992), Lee's books have not been translated into English, or at least are not widely available. Lee has co-written a number of screenplays, including one for the film version of *Farewell My Concubine*. The film was released in 1993 and became a worldwide sensation. Lee also co-wrote screenplays for *Rouge* (1988) and *Green Snake* (1993). In addition, Lee has acted in minor roles in some of these films.

Plot Summary

Chapter 1

Farewell My Concubine starts out with a brief discussion about prostitution and theater, and how both of these vocations are removed from reality. The reader is then introduced to the stage characters of the woman Yu Ji and the man General Xiang Yu, and learns that both roles are played by men and that one man is in love with the other. Following this short introduction, the narrative jumps back in time to winter 1929 to a marketplace in Peking, China.

Yanhong asks Master Guan, a noted Peking opera instructor, to take on her little boy, Xiao Douzi, as an apprentice. Guan refuses, until Yanhong chops off Douzi's extra finger—a birth defect—with a cleaver. Yanhong and Douzi sign a contract with Guan for a period of ten years,

during which time Douzi's life and earnings belong to Guan in exchange for opera training. Douzi finds it hard to fit in at first, but he soon befriends Xiao Shitou, the informal leader of the apprentices. The boys spend long days practicing their craft and Douzi and Shitou distinguish themselves as the ones with the most talent. When they are given their roles, which they will play for their entire lives, Douzi is chosen to be a *dan*, or female lead, and Shitou is chosen to be a *sheng*, or male lead.

Chapter 2

The apprentices stage a successful first performance at the Spring Blossom teahouse, which leads to many other performances. They give a birthday performance for Master Ni, a rich eunuch, who fondles Douzi after the show. During New Year's, Shitou spends his money on sweets, while Douzi spends his on handkerchiefs—the first pieces for his collection of opera clothes. They both see a magnificent sword and Douzi says he will buy it for Shitou someday. The apprentices and Guan take part in a group photo shoot. Ten years later, in 1939, the boys, who are now as close as brothers, graduate from Guan's school and enter professional careers.

Chapter 3

Douzi and Shitou join an opera company and are given new, adult names by the company's manager. Douzi becomes Cheng Dieyi and Shitou becomes Duan Xiaolou. Dieyi and Xiaolou gain fame for their performance of the opera *Farewell My Concubine*. During one show, Master Yuan Siye, a wealthy patron of the theater, notices Cheng Dieyi and is enraptured by him.

Chapter 4

After the show, Dieyi and Xiaolou get into an argument about the importance of opera, but they are interrupted by a backstage visit from Siye. While Dieyi is respectful, Xiaolou is not, and excuses himself to go see Miss Juxian, a prostitute at the House of Flowers, a local brothel. Xiaolou rescues her from a customer who is trying to force her to drink from his mouth. On the spur of the moment, Juxian asks Xiaolou to marry her, and he agrees. He quickly performs the engagement wine ceremony. The next day, Dieyi goes to a letter writer and dictates a letter to his mother, but then tears it up and throws it away. Juxian buys her freedom from prostitution.

Chapter 5

Juxian visits backstage with Xiaolou and Dieyi, and announces that she has bought her freedom from the House of Flowers to marry Xiaolou, who is dumbstruck since he was not serious about the marriage. He decides to go through with the wedding. Dieyi is shattered that he is losing Xiaolou to Juxian, and accepts Yuan Siye's invitation to come to his house, where Siye gets Dieyi drunk and rapes him. Dieyi leaves early that morning with the sword that he and Shitou saw in the marketplace ten years ago—a gift from Siye for Dieyi's sexual favors. Dieyi gives Xiaolou the sword as a wedding present. The Japanese cavalry arrives in Peking.

Dieyi becomes a famous *dan* without Xiaolou, who, after his marriage, no longer plays Dieyi's counterpart. Dieyi deals with his jealousy of Juxian by smoking opium. At the request of the Japanese military police, Dieyi and Xiaolou perform the opera *Farewell My Concubine* again, but Xiaolou refuses to continue after Japanese soldiers beat up Chinese patrons. Xiaolou is arrested and Juxian pleads with Dieyi to save him. Dieyi agrees if Juxian will leave Xiaolou. Dieyi performs opera for the Japanese official, winning Xiaolou's freedom, but Juxian breaks her promise and stays with Xiaolou.

Chapter 6

It is summer 1945 and Dieyi is deep in an opium addiction, while Xiaolou has given up opera to sell watermelons. Master Guan scolds them for fighting with each other and giving up opera, and sets a penance of putting on a show for him in one month. Guan dies before the month is through, and the two actors give a benefit concert at which they raise enough money to give Guan a proper funeral. The Japanese surrender, and the Chinese economy is thrown into turmoil as different factions vie for control. Xiaolou gets in a fight to protect Dieyi, and Juxian intervenes to protect Xiaolou. She is hit in the stomach, causing the miscarriage of their baby. Dieyi is arrested for treason, but earns his pardon by performing for a Chinese official. Dieyi and Xiaolou take their operas on the road, seeking an audience. Along the way, every part of China slowly falls under the control of the communist People's Liberation Army.

Chapter 7

It is 1949, and opera is in vogue once again. As time passes in the new People's Republic of China, however, the theaters are used for revolutionary activities. Xiaolou and Dieyi witness the trial of Dieyi's old lover, Yuan Siye, who is accused of being a counterrevolutionary and is sentenced to death. Xiao Si, Dieyi's old assistant, who Dieyi treated horribly, is elevated in the new Communist

Media Adaptations

- *Farewell My Concubine* was adapted as a feature film in 1993 by Beijing Film Studio. The English-subtitled film, directed by Kaige Chen and co-written by Lilian Lee and Wei Lu, features Leslie Cheung as Cheng Dieyi, Fengyi Zhang as Duan Xiaolou, and Li Gong as Juxian. It is available on DVD and VHS from Miramax Home Entertainment.

Party. As part of the party's directive, Dieyi and Xiaolou take literacy classes. By the mid-1960s, art is looked at as a tool to corrupt people by manipulating their emotions. Dieyi's and Xiaolou's social status is greatly reduced. In 1965 the party puts Dieyi and Xiaolou to work acting in formulaic propaganda plays. Xiaolou and Dieyi both destroy their old costumes before they can be used against them.

Chapter 8

Teenagers are assigned to be communist Red Guards, and are let out of school so that they can loot people's houses, searching for evidence of Western or traditional Chinese culture. One night, Red Guards make their nightly raid of Xiaolou's and Juxian's home, where they spot the sword from Dieyi, which Juxian had hung on the wall so that it is pointed toward the portrait of Chairman Mao—a potential sign that they want Mao dead. In an attempt to save both Juxian and Dieyi, Xiaolou takes credit for the sword.

The next night, Xiaolou and Dieyi are put on trial and told to confess their knowledge of each other's past wrongdoings. At first, the two tell harmless facts about each other's past, but as the guards threaten them, the actors get vicious, revealing incriminating aspects of each other's life. Worried that Juxian will be harmed, Xiaolou tells the guards that he wants to divorce her. She is mortified. Xiao Si breaks in and talks about Dieyi's homosexual activities, and Dieyi is arrested too. Dieyi tries and fails to kill himself while in custody. Xiaolou is sentenced to be reeducated through labor, and when he goes to his apartment to gather his things, he sees that

Juxian has hanged herself. The next day Xiaolou and Dieyi are put on separate trucks and taken to different work camps in remote areas of the country.

Chapter 9

Xiaolou works in a labor camp in Fuzhou for many years, thinking often of Dieyi, whom he has forgiven for his comments. Ten years pass, and in 1976 Chairman Mao dies. The Gang of Four—the nickname of Mao's political sect—is soon overthrown and put on trial for its crimes against the Chinese people. By this time, the 1980s, Xiaolou has escaped from his work camp and has fled to the island of Hong Kong. One day, while riding a tram, he notices an opera house that has Cheng Dieyi's name written on the marquee.

Chapter 10

Xiaolou meets with Dieyi, who is serving as the opera company's senior art advisor. Dieyi and Xiaolou spend a day together catching up. Dieyi pulls out the photograph from when they were apprentices at Master Guan's opera school. They talk about what happened to each of the boys in the photo, most of whom have died as a result of the various political campaigns in China. They go to a bathhouse, where they relax and talk about their current lives, including the fact that Dieyi now has a spouse. They apologize to each other for the harmful things they said and did to each other. Xiaolou and Dieyi get dressed up in their old makeup and costumes and perform the opera *Farewell My Concubine* again. During the performance, Dieyi imagines he actually kills himself as the heroine does, but it is just a daydream. Dieyi returns to mainland China, and Xiaolou stays in Hong Kong, where he loses his apartment.

Characters

Marshall Aoki

Marshall Aoki of the Kwantung Army is a Japanese official and opera aficionado from whom Dieyi win's Xiaolou's freedom by staging a private performance.

Cheng Dieyi

Cheng Dieyi is an opera singer who performs with his partner and childhood friend Duan Xiaolou, a man whom Dieyi loves. At the beginning of the book, Dieyi is known by the nickname of Xiao Douzi, or Little Bean. His mother Yanhong

is an unlicensed prostitute who cannot afford to raise him, so she enrolls him as an apprentice at Master Guan's opera school. Douzi and Xiao Shitou become friends shortly after Douzi arrives at the school, and Shitou often steps in to save his friend from teasing or punishment. Due in part to his delicate, girlish features, Douzi is assigned to the lifelong role of *dan*, or female lead, while Shitou is assigned to be his *sheng*, or male lead. This professional pairing makes the two grow even closer. When they graduate, Douzi is given the adult name of Cheng Dieyi by his opera company manager, while Shitou becomes Duan Xiaolou. Early in his career, as he is gaining fame for his singing—most notably in the role of Yu Ji in the opera *Farewell My Concubine*—Dieyi's life is changed when Xiaolou agrees to marry a prostitute, Juxian. Jealous that Juxian has taken Xiaolou away from him both professionally and personally, and hoping to get even with his friend, Dieyi allows himself to be seduced by a wealthy patron of the opera, Yuan Siye, who gets Dieyi drunk and rapes him. In exchange for sexual favors, Dieyi gets a sword from Siye—which he gives to Xiaolou as a wedding present.

Xiaolou's marriage affects Dieyi's theater career by forcing him to perform solo. Dieyi and Xiaolou grow apart, but reunite on stage at the request of the Japanese military. When Xiaolou is arrested by the military for offending them, Juxian comes to Dieyi, who agrees to intervene on Xiaolou's behalf if Juxian will divorce him. Dieyi sings for a Japanese official, who releases Xiaolou, but Juxian breaks her divorce promise. Worse, Xiaolou is upset that Dieyi groveled for the Japanese on his behalf. Dieyi is heartbroken, and retreats into an opium addiction to cope. Dieyi and Xiaolou eventually reunite and begin performing together again, and Dieyi is secretly pleased when Juxian has a miscarriage during an audience fight in the theater. Dieyi is arrested as a traitor—for the performance that he gave to the Japanese official to save Xiaolou. Dieyi wins his freedom through another performance, and he and Xiaolou perform together off and on for decades, as the political climate changes constantly and theater becomes a propaganda tool for the Communist Party. When Dieyi and Xiaolou are targeted as counterrevolutionaries, Dieyi tries to protect Xiaolou during their trial, but ends up revealing incriminating evidence about his friend. Dieyi is sent to a labor camp in Jiuquan. After the Gang of Four is overthrown, the new Chinese government rehabilitates him to remove the brainwashing of Chairman Mao's regime, and Dieyi resumes his stage career by acting as a senior art advisor. During a show in Hong Kong, Xiaolou comes to see him, and the two catch up on old times, apologize to each other, and put on their makeup and costumes one last time to perform the opera *Farewell My Concubine*.

Uncle Ding

Uncle Ding is an old violin player from the Peking opera who works with Master Guan and Master Shi to inspect Cheng Dieyi, Duan Xiaolou, and the other apprentices and help assign them their lifelong opera roles.

Duan Xiaolou

Duan Xiaolou is an opera singer who marries Juxian and who performs with his partner and childhood friend Cheng Dieyi. At the beginning of the book, when Xiaolou is an apprentice at Master Guan's school, he is known by the nickname of Xiao Shitou, or Little Rock, because he has such a hard head. Shitou and Xiao Douzi become friends shortly after the latter arrives at the school, and Shitou often steps in to save his friend from teasing or punishment. Shitou is assigned to the lifelong role of *sheng*, or male lead, while Dieyi is assigned to be his *dan*, or female lead. This professional pairing makes the two grow even closer. When they graduate, Shitou is given the adult name of Duan Xiaolou by his opera company manager, while Douzi becomes Cheng Dieyi. Early in his career, as Xiaolou is gaining fame for his singing—most notably the role of General Xiang Yu in the opera *Farewell My Concubine*—he steps in to save a prostitute, Juxian, from having to perform a distasteful act for a customer. When Juxian asks him to marry her, Xiaolou believes that she is just staging a performance so that she can deter the customer, and he agrees. He also defends her honor by fighting the customer. When Xiaolou realizes that Juxian is serious, he decides to keep his promise and marry her.

The marriage impacts Xiaolou's theater career, as he takes on less-demanding work so that he can spend more time with Juxian, which forces Dieyi to perform solo. Xiaolou's marriage also affects his friendship with Dieyi, who is extremely jealous of Juxian for taking Xiaolou away from him. Xiaolou and Dieyi reunite at the request of the Japanese military, but Xiaolou stops the performance when soldiers beat up some Chinese patrons. The military is offended and arrests Xiaolou. When Dieyi stages a private performance for a Japanese official, he wins Xiaolou's freedom, but Xiaolou is upset that

Dieyi has groveled for the Japanese, so he spits on Dieyi. The two meet up again much later, when Xiaolou has given up singing to become a watermelon vendor, and Xiaolou apologizes. Eventually, they begin acting together again. During one performance, the now-pregnant Juxian steps in to protect Xiaolou in an audience fight and gets hit in her stomach, which causes a miscarriage. Xiaolou and Dieyi perform together off and on for decades, as the political climate changes constantly and theater becomes a propaganda tool for the Communist Party. When Xiaolou and Dieyi are targeted as counterrevolutionaries, Xiaolou tries to protect Dieyi during their trial, but ends up revealing incriminating evidence about his friend. Xiaolou is sent to a labor camp in Fuzhou. He escapes and flees to Hong Kong, where he eventually runs into Dieyi. The two catch up on old times, apologize to each other, and put on their makeup and costumes one last time to perform the opera *Farewell My Concubine*.

Gang of Four

The Gang of Four is the nickname for Chairman Mao's communist political sect. Their policies caused massive strife in the lives of most Chinese people, including Cheng Dieyi and Duan Xiaolou. The Gang of Four is overthrown shortly after Mao's death, and the remaining members of the Gang of Four are put on trial for their crimes against the Chinese people.

Master Guan Jinfa

Master Guan Jinfa is an esteemed Peking opera instructor who accepts Xiao Douzi as an apprentice at his school for ten years. Master Guan is harsh on his apprentices, beating them often when they falter and rarely giving praise. This is the same way that he was educated in opera, and he knows from his own opera experience that the professional theater world demands this kind of perfectionist training. Master Guan notices Douzi's delicate features right away, and as he trains the boy in the basic techniques of opera, he realizes that the boy has a great singing voice too. With the help of Master Shi and Uncle Ding, Guan assigns Douzi to a lifelong role of *dan*, or female lead, while he assigns Xiao Shitou to be the *sheng*, or male lead. After Douzi and Shitou have graduated and become Cheng Dieyi and Duan Xiaolou, respectively, Guan agrees to let one of his new apprentices, Xiao Si, help the two actors during their shows. When Guan hears that Dieyi and Xiaolou have allowed their differences to separate them, and that Xiaolou has given up opera to sell watermelons, he is furious with both of them, and sets a penance of performing a special opera for him. Unfortunately Guan dies before they can perform, and his school is closed, forcing all of the current apprentices in his care to become orphans.

Miss Juxian

Miss Juxian is a prostitute at the House of Flowers brothel, who tricks Duan Xiaolou into marrying her, a relationship that drives a wedge between Xiaolou and Cheng Dieyi. Juxian meets Xiaolou when he and Dieyi are just making a name for themselves by performing the opera *Farewell My Concubine*. Juxian, whose name means "chrysanthemum," gives Xiaolou a teapot with chrysanthemums, which makes Dieyi jealous. When Xiaolou comes to visit Juxian at the brothel one night, he ends up rescuing her from a customer—who wants her to drink something from his mouth. She recognizes her chance, and asks Xiaolou if he wants to marry her. Thinking that they are just acting out a scene to save her from the insistent customer, Xiaolou readily agrees, and they perform an engagement wine ceremony. The next day, Juxian buys her freedom from the House of Flowers—and from prostitution—and goes to see Xiaolou, who is shocked when he realizes that Juxian was seriously asking him to marry her.

When Xiaolou decides to go through with it, Dieyi—who wants Xiaolou all to himself—becomes very spiteful toward Juxian. This animosity increases as Xiaolou gives up performing his duets with Dieyi. After Xiaolou's brash attitude offends the Japanese military and leads to his imprisonment, Juxian comes to Dieyi to ask him to intervene on her husband's behalf. Dieyi agrees, but only if Juxian will divorce Xiaolou, a promise that she breaks. Juxian becomes pregnant with the couple's first child, but the child miscarries when Juxian tries to protect Xiaolou in a fight—which starts when Xiaolou tries to protect Dieyi. This love triangle continues to create animosity between Juxian and Dieyi, although they both attend to the other when they are sick. Juxian's unfortunate placement of Xiaolou's sword—a wedding present from Dieyi—leads to the trial of Xiaolou, which in turn leads to the trial of the other two. Juxian refuses to follow the Communist Party's wishes by divorcing her husband, and is forced to get a yin-and-yang haircut—half of her head shaved—as a result. When Xiaolou tells the Red Guards he will divorce Juxian—his attempt to save her from any more punishment—she is heartbroken and commits suicide shortly thereafter.

Little Bean

See Cheng Dieyi

Little Rock

See Duan Xiaolou

Master Ni

Master Ni is a rich eunuch who wielded great power during the imperial days of the Qing dynasty, and who indulges in opera to try to remember those days. After Master Guan's apprentices perform for Ni's birthday, the old eunuch arranges a private meeting with Xiao Douzi, during which he first makes the boy urinate into a priceless jade bowl, then molests him. Later, when Douzi has become the adult Dieyi, he runs into Master Ni, who has lost his fortune and is reduced to selling tobacco and matches from a cart.

Red Guards

The Red Guards are teenagers enlisted by the Communist Party to seek out and punish suspected adult counterrevolutionaries. Although they wield power for a little while, in the end they are reduced to toiling in poverty like many other Chinese people. Duan Xiaolou realizes this when he catches one of the Red Guards—his former oppressors—trying to steal some yams out of his labor camp.

Master Shi

Master Shi is a representative from the Spring Blossom teahouse, where Master Guan's apprentices stage their first public opera. Shi works with Guan and Uncle Ding to inspect Cheng Dieyi, Duan Xiaolou, and the other apprentices and help assign them their lifelong opera roles.

Xiao Douzi

See Cheng Dieyi

Xiao Laizi

Xiao Laizi is a fellow apprentice with Xiao Douzi and Xiao Shitou; he constantly tries to run away from Master Guan's opera school and ultimately commits suicide.

Xiao Sanzi

Xiao Sanzi is a fellow apprentice with Xiao Douzi and Xiao Shitou, and tries to bully some of the other boys. When he picks on Douzi, Shitou comes to his friend's rescue. When Dieyi and Xiaolou review the old photo of their classmates at the end of the novel and discuss their various fates, Dieyi notes that Sanzi had both of his legs broken while being tortured, became an alcoholic, and died of hepatitis.

Xiao Shitou

See Duan Xiaolou

Xiao Si

Xiao Si is one of Master Guan's new apprentices after Cheng Dieyi and Duan Xiaolou graduate. Xiao Si is fascinated by the two actors, and makes an arrangement with Guan to help them out on the nights of their show. Xiao Si eventually becomes Dieyi's personal assistant and grows to hate Dieyi. Dieyi spends much of his time addicted to opium, and tells Xiao Si that the boy does not have the talent to sing opera. Xiao Si harbors a grudge for this treatment. As the communist revolution picks up speed and he gains some power, he acts on this grudge. He tells a group of Red Guards about Dieyi's illicit activities, which helps lead to Dieyi's sentencing to a labor camp. At the end of the novel, when Dieyi and Xiaolou discuss the various fates of people they have known, Dieyi notes that Xiao Si's suspected affiliation with the Gang of Four led to his being tortured in a water cell—a cell filled up with water to a person's shoulders—and that he heard Xiao Si went crazy as a result.

Yanhong

Yanhong is Cheng Dieyi's mother and an unlicensed prostitute. When Dieyi is nine years old and known by the childhood nickname of Xiao Douzi, his mother enrolls him as an apprentice in Master Guan's opera school, hoping that he can make a better life for himself than she can provide. Dieyi never sees Yanhong again.

Yuan Shiqing

See Yuan Siye

Yuan Siye

Yuan Siye is a wealthy opera patron who becomes infatuated with Cheng Dieyi after seeing the actor in his feminine Yu Ji costume and makeup. Siye invites Dieyi to his wealthy home, where he seduces and rapes Dieyi. In exchange for his sexual favors, Siye gives Dieyi a sword—which happens to be the same one that Dieyi and Xiaolou admired as children. After their first sexual encounter, Siye uses his power and influence to help nurture Dieyi's career. As the communist revolution gains speed, however, Dieyi and Xiaolou watch the trial of Siye, who is sentenced to death for using his power to take advantage of people in

the theater. The sword that Siye gives to Dieyi ultimately leads to the downfall of Dieyi, Xiaolou, and Juxian, after Juxian places it on a wall so that it is pointed in a disrespectful way at a portrait of Chairman Mao.

Themes

Survival

Survival is a key theme in *Farewell My Concubine*. In the beginning of the novel, many Chinese people have a hard time just trying to acquire the basic necessities of food and shelter. The marketplace scene in which Yanhong and Douzi are introduced is a good example of this harsh life. For example, one street urchin weaves his way through crowds, collecting cigarette butts before they can be trampled. "When he had gathered up enough discarded butts, he would take them all apart and salvage the tobacco. Then he would roll new cigarettes to sell on the street." This boy is most likely an orphan, and collecting the cigarettes is his only way to make money to try to pay for food and shelter. Yet, even those with adult caregivers are not much better off. When Douzi is introduced, his mother Yanhong is working in the only types of odd jobs she can find, "like rolling wax-coated pills in the back of some pharmacy during the influenza season, or washing other people's filthy clothes and fetid socks." And these types of activities do not earn enough money to provide adequate shelter for her and Douzi, especially during cold winter months when they have to huddle together "on a makeshift bed made out of a wooden board set up in the loft of a down-at-the-heel courtyard."

Faced with this grim reality, Yanhong signs Douzi's care over to Master Guan, hoping that her son will be able to have a better life. But Douzi must also struggle to survive at the school. He sleeps on a communal bed with several other boys, his clothes are rags, and his days are long and hard, filled with endless hours of physical training. They rarely wash, and they almost never have enough to eat. As Lee notes, "Their faces were never entirely clean, and their bellies were never completely full as they set out every morning behind Master Guan."

While basic survival necessities such as food and shelter remain a concern for most Chinese people throughout the novel, when the Communist Party takes over the Chinese government, people's physical survival is increasingly influenced by politics. People begin to exert extreme caution over

Topics For Further Study

- Read a first-person account from a Chinese man or woman who lived through the years of Mao's rule in China. Compare this person's experience with the experience of the main characters in *Farewell My Concubine*. Discuss what it must have been like to be alive in China during this time.

- Find another modern society from the past 100 years that experienced the same type of oppressive rule that citizens in China faced in the twentieth century. Research the particulars of this oppression, imagine that you are a citizen in this other society, and write a journal entry depicting what life is like during a typical day in your life.

- Research other art forms prevalent in China, specifically in Peking (modern day Beijing), during the time period when the book takes place. Choose an art form and a specific artist

within this genre. Write a biography about this person, noting any challenges the artist faced due to the social situation in China at the time.

- Research the interactions other countries had with China in the last half of the twentieth century. Choose five countries and plot them on a chart, including the country's name, political orientation, interactions with China, and reasons for these interactions. Discuss any common themes you find, and, if possible, pose a reason for these similarities.

- Watch the film version of *Farewell My Concubine* and compare it to the novel. Write a magazine-style review that includes your observations, including your opinion on whether the book deserves to receive less attention than the film, as has been the case thus far.

---

the things they say and do, for fear they may be singled out to be tortured or killed. As Lee notes about a time shortly after the Communist Party takeover: "But fear had become contagious, like a lingering flu nobody could shake. Politics was a matter of life and death, and people learned not to discuss certain subjects if they could help it." In this climate of extreme paranoia, nobody feels safe, even those who have power in the Communist Party. For example, during one scene, the party secretary in Peking is reciting a speech over a loudspeaker, and it is so loud it causes him to pause and think about the attention he is drawing to himself. "He looked up, a wary expression flickering across his eyes. He had only just begun to exercise some power himself, and already it seemed precarious. Anyone could become a victim, even he." In the end nobody is safe from the effects of communist politics. Those who are too traditional are labeled counterrevolutionaries and tortured, killed, or sent to work camps, as Dieyi and Xiaolou are. And those who embrace party politics often meet grisly fates after the Communist Party is overthrown. For example, at the end of the novel when the aged Dieyi

and Xiaolou are discussing what happened to Xiao Si, a young man who wielded some power in the Communist Party and who helped determine the sentence for the two actors, Dieyi notes that Xiao Si was accused of following the Gang of Four, was tortured until he went crazy, and is most likely dead. "It frightens me to think about it," Dieyi says. "You can't escape from politics—and it's always life or death, kill or be killed."

Sex and Love

Lee also explores the themes of sex and love in the novel. For some characters, sex becomes another tool for survival. In the beginning of the novel, Lee notes that Yanhong, Douzi's mother, worked as a prostitute for a while, because "it was the only way she could make enough money to support her child." For Yanhong, as with many other women in China at the time, her body was the only guaranteed means to make a living. The consequence of this is that prostitutes find it hard to love. As the author notes about Juxian, another prostitute, "Love at first sight and true love were things that existed for ordinary women, but not for women like her, not for prostitutes." For Juxian, selling sex and ignoring love has led to a comfortable life. By choosing to follow her heart and try to marry Xiaolou, she is taking a big leap. Even if he says yes, being his wife means living in the real world. As the author notes when Juxian is walking out of the House of Flowers, "Life outside the indolent precincts of the house of pleasure was harsh and grimy. She had lived a soft life, relying on her gentle charms. Now she was taking a big gamble."

Fortunately for Juxian, Xiaolou goes through with his promise to marry her. But their happiness is ultimately shattered by the Communist Party. Near the end of the novel, when they have been married for decades, the communist officials in Peking tell Juxian that she will be in serious trouble if she does not divorce her husband. Juxian refuses. "I won't divorce him, and I'm willing to accept the consequences. I am his true wife," Juxian says. When she holds by her decision at her trial, Juxian receives a crude yin and yang haircut. Xiaolou tries to prevent any further abuse of his wife by saying he will divorce her. Once a prostitute who thought that "If a girl allowed herself to be genuinely touched, she would only end up getting hurt," Juxian has since devoted herself completely to her husband, to the point where she is willing to be tortured or killed instead of divorcing him. When Xiaolou does not reciprocate this attitude, however, she is heartbroken and kills herself.

Dieyi also loves Xiaolou, a love that develops from the time when they are boys. As Lee notes in the beginning, "their story is not that simple. When one man loves another, it can't be simple." Dieyi's love begins with his fascination of the older boy, when he first sees him perform a play. "He had never seen anything like this before, nor had he ever seen a boy as brave as Xiao Shitou." As the boys get to know each other, they become good friends, and eventually get paired as stage partners. Throughout all of this, Shitou often comes to Douzi's rescue, "like a knight-errant saving a traveler from bandits." But while Shitou views their relationship as brothers, Douzi increasingly falls in love with Shitou in a romantic sense. Later, as adults, Dieyi still holds out hope that he can make Xiaolou love him in a romantic sense. When Xiaolou agrees to marry Juxian, however, Dieyi is shattered. "He knew how it felt to be an abandoned woman and remembered an old saying: A woman without a man is a vine with no stakes to support her."

In place of love, Dieyi turns to sex. Dieyi is introduced to sex as a little boy, when he sees his mother, the prostitute Yanhong, having sex with a customer. As the author notes, "she had seen him staring coldly at her and her customer through the door curtains." Dieyi's own initial experiences with sex are also negative. After the birthday performance for Master Ni, the old eunuch, enraptured by the little boy's penis—which, unlike Ni's, is still intact—performs oral sex on the boy. The experience leaves the boy feeling "bewildered and afraid." His next experience with sexual intercourse is also with a man, Yuan Siye, who gets Dieyi drunk and rapes him. Dieyi thinks of the experience in symbolically violent terms, associating Siye with the bat that Siye had killed and drained into their soup. "Dieyi had stumbled into a savage realm of purple, carmine, and black, where a bat darker than the depths of hell beat its wings and attacked." The experience leaves him "[f]illed with shame." At the same time, he notes, "It could not be undone; but he had no regrets. He had got back at Xiaolou."

In this way, Dieyi tries to use sex as a weapon, to make Xiaolou jealous. While this does not work, since Xiaolou is not interested in Dieyi in a romantic sense, Dieyi does learn a lesson about the power of sex. Given that his sexual experiences have all been negative, and the fact that the one person with whom he wants to have sex, Xiaolou, does not think of him in this way, Dieyi instead begins engaging in joyless sex to further his career, much as prostitutes like Yanhong and Juxian sold their bodies to try to make a better life for themselves.

Style

Setting

The setting, both in time and place, is very important to *Farewell My Concubine*. The story takes place during the twentieth century, from 1929 to the 1980s. While many nations underwent drastic changes during this time period, in China this period was marked by continuous change. As various political regimes gained or lost power in China, people's lives changed drastically. Throughout the novel, Lee chronicles this political change as Dieyi and Xiaolou grow older. When the narrative begins and Dieyi and Xiaolou are still boys, Lee notes, "Winter, 1929. The eighteenth year of the Republic of China." Shortly after this time period is introduced, the political situation is addressed. "A newspaper boy was calling out, 'Northeastern Army surrounded—Japs about to attack!'" The Japanese invasion of China is the first major political event that the Chinese people have to face in the story. Yet, since the two main characters spend much of their time in training at Master Guan's school, they do not see many signs of this threat.

Everything changes when the boys graduate from the school after completing ten years of training. Dieyi and Xiaolou go to a photographer to get professional publicity shots taken, but they are interrupted. "A group of student protesters had broken the plate-glass windows of the photo studio and were now zealously tearing up pictures of geishas and scattering them in the air." This attack, and another one that takes place shortly thereafter in the same scene, illustrate the animosity toward Japanese culture that existed in China at this time. Again, Lee includes a specific historical reference to the year that gives her readers a context for these events: "It was 1939, the twenty-eighth year of the Republic of China—the second year of the Japanese occupation."

As Dieyi and Xiaolou grow older and become public figures in the theater, they lose the shelter of anonymity that they had as young boys at the school, and the political climate increasingly impacts their lives. For example, Xiaolou is depicted as a brash, tough male from the time he is a child. From breaking bricks over his head as a boy to defending the honor of Juxian as a young adult, Xiaolou is depicted as a person who does what he wants and who rarely faces any drastic consequences for his behavior. But this changes when he exhibits his trademark stubbornness during a performance for the Japanese army, after they beat up some Chinese patrons. "I'm one man who won't sing for devils!' Xiaolou said adamantly." As a result, the Japanese army officers, offended at Xiaolou's disobedience, beat him unconscious, then lock him in prison until Dieyi saves Xiaolou by staging a private performance for a Japanese military official.

Though Dieyi saves his friend with this act, when the political tide turns again in 1945 after the Japanese surrender, the act comes back to haunt Dieyi. In a theater fight with some Chinese military veterans, Xiaolou attempts to protect Dieyi, but it is Dieyi who gets arrested when the police come. "The detainee was Dieyi. Cheng Dieyi, the actor who had sold his services to the Japanese, was being accused of treason." The police do not care about who started the theater fight, they are looking to punish those who collaborated with the Japanese oppressors during the occupation.

This attitude of condemnation increases as the Chinese nationalist government that accuses Dieyi of treason is in turn overthrown by a communist government. In this new political situation, art is once again in vogue, at least at first. "It was 1949, and theaters and opera houses all over Peking were thriving once more." But while this new government allows actors like Dieyi and Xiaolou to perform the old, pre-liberation operas, audiences are "discouraged from cheering and shouting." This attitude of separating emotion from art increasingly takes control in China, until, "By the mid-1960s, ideologues were saying that art was decadent and corrupt, and that it only existed to manipulate people's feelings." In this new political climate, in which Communist Party officials are searching for somebody to blame for China's troubles, paranoia becomes rampant, and those who represent anything traditional, such as art, are often accused of being counterrevolutionaries. These accusations lead many people, including Dieyi and Xiaolou, to be tortured or sent to work camps and contribute to the general paranoia of the times.

Imagery

In addition to the setting, Lee also makes use of many vivid images of violence, pain, and suffering to underscore the starkness of life in China during this time period. One of the most shocking images is of Yanhong chopping off Douzi's extra finger. Although Lee does not actually describe the act itself, she offers several vivid images that follow the act, which leave a strong visual impression in the reader's mind: "Drops of blood in the snow traced Xiao Douzi's path. He now crouched in a lonely corner of the compound, whimpering like a maimed animal." Without actually telling the reader that Douzi's finger has been cut off—something that Lee specifically notes later in the paragraph—the images of blood in the snow and Douzi whimpering in a corner let the reader know what has happened, and provide a powerful visual image.

Lee uses this type of vivid imagery throughout the novel to discuss the harsh training the boys undergo at the school; to describe the many beatings of Dieyi, Xiaolou, and the other characters; and to describe the various ways that characters meet horrible ends. For example, one of the most graphic deaths in the novel takes place when a woman jumps out of a window, trying to escape from a group of Red Guards:

> The impact had broken off one of her legs and sent it bouncing over to the base of a wall. Her head had cracked open, spreading brains across the pavement like bean curd. Blood and flesh were splattered everywhere. Something tiny had landed near Dieyi's foot, either a tooth or a finger; but he was too exhausted and numb to care.

Historical Context

When Lee wrote *Farewell My Concubine*, massive political changes were taking place in the world, many of which stemmed from events that took place after the end of World War II, in 1945. The dropping of atomic bombs on Japan ended the war, but it also ushered in the atomic age. After these demonstrations, several countries, including the Soviet Union, rushed to create and test their own atomic bombs. As tensions between the communist Soviet Union and the democratic United States increased, the American government began a policy of backing smaller foreign countries that were in danger of being overthrown by communism. The resulting tension between the Soviet Union and the United States—and between communism and democracy in general—was labeled the Cold War. Although much of the period was technically spent in peacetime, the pervasive feeling of suspicion and paranoia that was generated by this clash of superpowers made many feel that they were fighting a war. Although the peak years of the Cold War were over by the 1960s, America's fight against communism in foreign countries continued late into the twentieth century, and China, as a communist-ruled country, was viewed as one of the largest threats to democracy.

Yet, while China's communist policies during Chairman Mao's rule were destructive to many citizens, China's associations with the Soviet Union steadily degraded in the second half of the twentieth century, a split that weakened the strength of the communist bloc nations. In the late 1980s, a few years before Lee's book was published, the pro-democracy movement gained speed and a number of Eastern European nations such as Poland and Czechoslovakia established democratic governments. These developments took place with Soviet approval, largely due to the efforts of Soviet leader Mikhail S. Gorbachev, who worked throughout his rule to convert the Soviet political system to a democracy, a bold move for a leader who was part of the Soviet Union's Communist Party.

One of the most dramatic and symbolic events that signaled the weakening of communism and the rise of democracy was the fall of the Berlin Wall. The massive wall was first built to prevent East Germans from escaping to West Germany, an increasing trend that had threatened to weaken the East German state. By the 1980s this barrier, which had been hastily constructed in the beginning, had become a massive structure and a symbol of the divide between democracy and communism, West and East. In October 1989 East Germany's communist leadership was overthrown. The next month, the new East German leaders opened the barrier. The decline of communism quickly gained speed in the next few years, and in late 1991 the communist Soviet Union collapsed and was reformed into fifteen independent nations, including a democratic Russia.

While Russia had turned to democracy, however, China was still a communist country. As the book details, life under Chairman Mao's communist rule was harsh and unpredictable. Following his death and the subsequent overthrow of the Gang of Four in the late 1970s, the Communist Party in China resolved to clarify the political situation. While Mao was condemned for his dictator-like rule, the new party leaders still believed that Mao's social philosophies, known collectively as Mao Zedong Thought, should be followed. Under the rule of Deng Xiaoping, a leader who had been exiled during the Cultural Revolution, various aspects of communism and capitalism were combined in an effort to build China into a global economic power. Some of these steps, on the surface at least, gave hope to some that Deng Xiaoping was a new kind of leader and that China could eventually be a true democracy. Pro-democracy protests by students and others gained momentum, but were often quashed when the government arrested the activists. In 1989 these tensions came to a head in Tiananmen Square in Beijing (Peking). Following the death of Hu Yaobang, a party secretary whose sympathetic views of student protests had led to his dismissal, students renewed their protest efforts. After several weeks of demonstrations, during which the communist government debated how to handle the students, the military— as ordered by Deng Xiaoping—attacked the students with tanks and gunfire on June 4, killing several hundred students and instantly crushing the rebellion. The government, under criticism from the rest of the world—which had witnessed this highly publicized event—claimed that the students were not demonstrating, but were instead a highly organized and foreign-backed counterrevolutionary movement trying to overthrow the government.

Critical Overview

The novel *Farewell My Concubine* has lived in the shadow of its film adaptation, which earned a number of awards from prestigious institutions such the Cannes Film Festival, the Golden Globes, the Los Angeles Film Critics Association, and the

An audience of laborers in Wuhan, China enjoy an open theatre opera performance, circa 1959

New York Film Critics Circle, to name a few. In fact the movie was considered such a revolutionary piece of Chinese filmmaking that its director, Kaige Chen, is more readily associated with *Farewell My Concubine* than Lee, and film reviews only give casual mention of the book, if they even mention it at all. A *Publishers Weekly* review offers some insight as to why the novel has received less attention and praise than the film. The reviewer speculates that the film version of the novel might be more satisfying than the novel as the film has an "irresistible setting" and "smart plot" that overpowers the "wooden reactions" of the characters in the novel. The reviewer concludes: "[Lee] has tailored an intricate brocade gown, but has neglected to put a body inside it." The reader should bear in mind, however, that the critics are reviewing a translation of the original novel, so that some critical comments may in fact apply more to the translator's writing style and interpretation rather than to the original novel in its native language.

Criticism

Ryan D. Poquette

Poquette has a bachelor's degree in English and specializes in writing about literature. In the following essay Poquette discusses Lee's contrasting of art and reality in Farewell My Concubine.

From the first few paragraphs of the novel, Lee sets up a contrast between art and reality. The novel begins with a discussion of the acting that prostitutes must do to make their living, then moves on to talk about how professional actors also must remove themselves from reality and play a role for their customers. As Lee notes, "The stage is populated by brilliant young scholars and beautiful ladies whose exalted passions are more vivid than the drab colors of our workaday existence." From this overt expression of the contrast between art and reality, Lee goes on to include several other direct addresses to her readers about this contrast. "The actors bask in the admiration of hundreds of strangers, who are transported out of their small lives by the deep emotions enacted before them," Lee notes in another passage. While these heavy-handed ideological statements help to underscore her ideas in a plain fashion, Lee's most powerful tool is her transformation of the character of Cheng Dieyi. It is through this development that Lee makes the impact of the communist revolution seem that much more tragic.

When the story begins and Dieyi is the little boy known by the nickname of Xiao Douzi, Lee

What Do I Read Next?

- Lee is a bestselling novelist in modern China. She and her contemporaries draw from a long history of Chinese women's writing. *Women Writers of Traditional China: An Anthology of Poetry and Criticism* (2000), edited by Kang-i Sun Chang and Haun Saussy, includes a chronological selection of poetry and criticism from 222 to the early twentieth century, as well as helpful notes on the texts and biographical information on the authors.

- Richard Gunde's *Culture and Customs of China* (2002) examines what life is like for people in modern-day China. The book includes sections on every major aspect of Chinese life, including thought and religion; literature and art; food and clothing; architecture and housing; and family and gender.

- C. T. Hsia's *A History of Modern Chinese Fiction* (1999) provides a good introduction to Chinese fiction written from 1917 to the late 1990s. The book also covers many of the historical and political events that took place during this time period.

- In Michael David Kwan's *Things That Must Not Be Forgotten: A Childhood in Wartime China* (2000), the author, who is of mixed Chinese-Swiss descent, recalls his life growing up in China during the Japanese occupation, the nationalist-communist conflict, and the effects that these events, as well as his own mixed-race background, had on his life and the life of his family.

- Amy Tan's *The Joy Luck Club* (1989) is a collection of sixteen interlinked tales about the problems that Chinese-American women face when trying to reconcile their Chinese and American heritages. Set in San Francisco in the 1980s, the majority of the book is told in flashbacks, which include experiences in China during many of the same time periods examined in *Farewell My Concubine*. All the stories are narrated by either a Chinese-born mother or her American-born daughter.

- James and Ann Tyson, correspondents for the *Christian Science Monitor*, spent five years in modern China, seeking out life stories and opinions from a wide variety of Chinese people while avoiding government intervention in their project. The result of their research, *Chinese Awakenings: Life Stories from the Unofficial China* (1995), uses personal stories of modern Chinese people to chronicle the massive changes that the country has been undergoing in recent years.

---

starts planting little details, foreshadowing the character's transformation into a man who is more like a woman. When Yanhong, Douzi's mother, takes her son to Master Guan, Lee notes that Douzi's "features were surprisingly delicate. He was almost pretty." But in order to be a performer in the Chinese opera, Douzi must not have any features that make him stand out. He must be as perfect as possible to maintain the willing suspension of disbelief that audiences expect. Unfortunately, Douzi fails this test because he was born with an extra finger. Desperate to have her son accepted by Master Guan's studio, Yanhong uses a cleaver to chop off the extra finger. Satisfied that Douzi will

make a good opera student, Guan accepts him. It is at this point that Douzi's naturally effeminate looks and demeanor help to determine the course of his life and relationships. He is chosen as a *dan*, or female lead, while his friend Shitou is chosen to be his *sheng*, or male lead.

In Chinese opera at this time, these roles were meant to be played for life, so each actor received very specific training. In Douzi's case, "His once deformed hand became the embodiment of feminine beauty as his wrists circled elegantly, the posed fingers of his 'orchid hands' weaving through the air." Guan also teaches Douzi how to "play the coquette," flirting with Xiaolou's male

> " At the end of the novel, when they meet up again after several years apart, the transformation in Dieyi is complete. He no longer puts his faith in art to rescue him, because he has seen a harsh, communist reality that allows no place for art."

characters. As Lee notes later in the novel, "A *dan* has to be even more feminine than a woman." Douzi is taught how to be the ideal woman in a theatrical sense, and he relishes this task, preferring to live in this fantasy world. Later, as he enters his professional career as Dieyi, the lines between himself and Yu Ji—his character from the opera *Farewell My Concubine*—become even more blurred, and Dieyi attempts to live in this fantasy world all of the time. "The theater was a world of illusion, but it was the only world he knew. The rest of the world seemed to drift by him, no more substantial than a dream."

Others also fail to make the distinction between the actual man and the roles he plays. As the political situation gets darker and people seek comfort in the theater, each person finds what they need in Dieyi. As he notes after a fan tries to break into his dressing room, saying that she is his future wife, "It wasn't him they loved—it was the idea of him. Men loved him as a woman; women loved him as a man. Nobody knew who he really was." In fact, at this point, neither does Dieyi. He has been socialized, through his profession and his own choice, to be more of a woman than a man. One day when he is examining his soft hands, noting how they had never done a day's labor, he has the following thought: "It was as though they had been emasculated the day he cut off his extra finger."

But Dieyi's fingers are not the only thing that has been emasculated. His very essence has been castrated. Lee hints at this in the beginning by including the character of Master Ni, a eunuch who was physically castrated during the time of the old

empire, as this was a way to amass power. While Master Ni has been physically castrated, losing his male reproductive organs, through his training and upbringing, Dieyi has been emotionally and mentally castrated, and has all but turned into a woman. His self-identity becomes increasingly associated with the feminine. For example, at one point, the narrative says that Dieyi "practiced flirting in the mirror, too. His expressive eyes seemed to dance— he was beautiful. What man could resist him?" The answer, of course, is the one man he so earnestly desires, Xiaolou. But while Xiaolou enjoys his singing career, he does not base his identity on it as Dieyi does. For this reason, his general will always be just a character that he plays, and he will never love Dieyi, or the Yu Ji character that Dieyi plays, for more than the length of the performance. Dieyi, on the other hand, is so wrapped up in his opera identity that it means more to him than basic survival. When times are tough economically, he refuses to sell his costumes. "No matter how much difficulty he was in, Dieyi would not pawn his costumes. He would rather have gone hungry. He loved the opera with a passion few outsiders could have understood."

In addition to basing his entire identity on his feminine art, Dieyi also trusts in the power of art. As he enters his professional career and makes a name for himself, he thinks that he will always be able to hide behind his feminine charms, and that art will always transcend any situation. For a while, he is proven right. On two separate occasions, he sings first for a Japanese official, then a Chinese official, on both occasions using his talent to get Xiaolou and himself, respectively, out of jail. As the various factions take over control of China through successive political movements, Dieyi hardly notices, focusing only on his art. As a result, when he hears that the communists are going to be taking over, he does not worry about it. "'Let them come!' he whispered to himself. 'The Communists will want to see operas, too, won't they?'"

But Dieyi, like many others who had embraced traditional Chinese culture, gets a rude awakening during the Cultural Revolution. While art had been his way of escaping in the past, and he had used it to gain favor or save himself or his friends as necessary, art itself is attacked. The revolution is one that advocates extreme reality. In this type of climate, art itself comes under fire for distracting people from reality. Dieyi first begins to understand that communism might be different than all of the other political movements when he sees his former lover Yuan Siye put on trial and sentenced to death.

"What strange sort of show was this? And why had he given up the starring role to Xiao Si, who was such a poor actor? He began to wonder what the Party had in store for him." Still blurring the lines between art and reality, Dieyi views the trial, initially at least, as just one other show.

As with other realistic situations in the past, Dieyi fights the communist reality for a while too, resorting to dramatic acts to solve his problems. When he is commanded by party leaders to turn in his costumes, he instead chooses to cut them into pieces and burn them in a ritual cremation, a very dramatic act that could get him killed. "He felt he was killing off parts of himself, but this was far better than letting the authorities do it." Dieyi is willing to die for his art, or so he thinks. He wants so badly to be the Yu Ji character from the opera *Farewell My Concubine* that he puts himself in dangerous situations so that he can be the helpless heroine. For example, when Xiaolou rebukes him for rescuing him from prison, Dieyi retreats into an opium addiction. Yet, "There were times when Dieyi wondered if he hadn't started smoking just to arouse his friend's sympathy." Still trying to attract the attention of his general, Xiaolou, and get him to care for him, Dieyi resorts to self-destructive acts such as this.

Dieyi also believes he would never intentionally do anything to hurt Xiaolou. "Not only would a true friend never betray you, he would even accept punishment in your place, Dieyi thought as he gazed fondly at Xiaolou." Again, this idealism is shattered when Dieyi comes face-to-face with the harsh reality of the Cultural Revolution. Although he thought he would face death before giving up his art or compromising the relationship between he and Xiaolou, when he is threatened with death by the Red Guards at the trial, the two of them turn on each other, revealing salacious and incriminating details from each other's past. When they are led away to their respective temporary holding cells, Dieyi turns again to his art for an answer to his despair. "Like Yu Ji, he felt he had lost his mainstay. His General had been brought low—where could he turn? What was the point of living?" Dieyi tries, and fails, to kill himself. "He had failed where his heroine Yu Ji had succeeded. Life in the opera was more fulfilling, indeed."

Following their trial, the two men are sent to work camps in different remote areas of the country. For the next several years, they are both brainwashed with Mao Zedong Thought and are forced to face harsh realities. At the end of the novel, when they meet up again after several years apart, the transformation in Dieyi is complete. He no longer puts his faith in art to rescue him, because he has seen a harsh, communist reality that allows no place for art. Instead, he is faced with the facts. "His beauty had faded. He had no mother, no teacher, no brother. There was nobody left. Xiaolou was still talking, but Dieyi wasn't listening." Faced with the fact that he cannot live in the art world as completely as he has done before, Dieyi gets married—not out of love, but because it seemed the right thing to do for a stable life. As he tells Xiaolou, when he returned to Peking after rehabilitation, the new "Party leaders showed a great deal of concern for me and introduced me to my spouse. We could hardly refuse the kindness of the organization."

This is a far cry from the passion that Dieyi used to feel for Xiaolou. Still, Dieyi tries one more time to exit the world in a dramatic style, or at least he thinks he does. During one final performance of the opera *Farewell My Concubine* that he and Xiaolou put on for themselves, Dieyi begins daydreaming, thinking he is committing suicide once and for all. But Xiaolou nudges him out of this trance. "Dieyi returned to his senses. The glittering tragedy was over. It had all been a fake. He would not die for love." This is the last tie that Dieyi has to his imagined self, and when it is broken, he returns to Peking, presumably to end his life in a dispassionate relationship. The crushing reality of communism has beaten the artist out of him, and he is, as one student reporter notes, a skinny, dried-up old man.

Source: Ryan D. Poquette, Critical Essay on *Farewell My Concubine*, in *Novels for Students*, Gale, 2004.

Curt Guyette

Guyette received a bachelor's degree in English writing from the University of Pittsburgh and is a longtime journalist. In this essay, Guyette discusses how Lee is able to combine the story of a nontraditional romance with a sweeping historical backdrop to create a somber assessment of the dark side of love.

By any measure, the novel *Farewell My Concubine* by Lilian Lee is a nontraditional love story. Few mainstream novelists have dared to create a plot that revolves around a romance involving two men. Even today, homosexuality is still considered by many to be taboo subject. As Lee writes, "their story is not that simple. When one man loves another, it can't be simple." But, she could just as well have said the same thing about love in general. As this story shows, it is a complicated emotion

> The message: true love requires self-sacrifice, and the reward is heartache."

no matter who is involved. Certainly, it is much more complicated than the idealized, simplistic version often portrayed in popular culture, a portrayal that frequently seems to consist of little more than valentines and candy kisses. In the hands of a serious artist such as Lee, love is revealed to be something that can be destructive as well as uplifting. Self-sacrifice and jealousy and heartache are often inseparable from love. At the heart of this story is the somber idea that great love can lead to great tragedy.

The emotional hardships that can come from love are demonstrated from the outset of the novel when the mother of Xiao Douzi/Dieyi turns him over to Master Guan to be trained for a career in the opera. Mother and son inhabit a world of desperate poverty, one where their only protection from frigid winter nights is a pitifully thin blanket. Even worse than their deprivation is the fact that this little boy has seen his mother working as a prostitute, a job she performs because it is the only way to support her child. To spare him from the pain of watching his mother lead such a life, she decides to turn him over to Master Guan. It is a torturous decision for any mother to make, but she does it in the hope that "he might be able to make something out of himself" if he learns to be an actor. She cannot bear to look back as she leaves the child, because if she does, she will fail. The pain she experiences is immense, but she is willing to accept it. The message: true love requires self-sacrifice, and the reward is heartache.

That theme is emphasized later on when Dieyi, well into adulthood, is forced to learn to read. When one of Dieyi's classmates is asked to define what love is, the student, an old army general, says he cannot answer the question because he has never known love. "Besides," says the general, "I always get this character mixed up with the character for 'endure,' because they look so much alike." As the teacher turns to Dieyi, he too says he cannot tell the two characters apart. But it's not just the characters that are indistinguishable. His love for his friend and co-star in the opera has always remained unspoken,

creating a terrible longing that goes unfulfilled. This is a key passage in the novel because it so concisely sums up a theme that runs through this book. Lee makes certain that her point is not overlooked. The teacher wonders how anyone could confuse the two concepts, because endure means to "suffer hardship." But, that is exactly what Dieyi's love of Xiao Shitou/Xiaolou brings him. It also generates intense jealousy when Dieyi's love for Xiaolou went unrequited, meaning not returned.

The title of this book comes from the name of a Chinese opera that Dieyi and Xiaolou appear in many times over the course of their careers. That opera becomes a sort of parallel world. With Xiaolou repeatedly playing a courageous general and Dieyi his concubine Yu Ji, the two are cast in roles that reflect their true natures. It is an interesting, unusual plot device that Lee uses to help convey her ideas about love, as she compares the fate of the characters in the opera with that experienced by the novel's two protagonists. This device adds a level of psychological complexity to the story. At one point Lee writes:

Onstage, Yu Ji was able to tell her lover that just as a virtuous minister does not serve two princes, so a virtuous woman cannot marry twice; then she asks for his sword so that she can end her life in his presence. This was her way of demonstrating her love for him, and her acceptance of his boundless love for her. But in real life Dieyi's love was unrequited.

Because Dieyi's love is not returned, he becomes insanely jealous when Xiaolou falls in love with a prostitute and marries her. But using the opera as a way to make this tale richer is not the only devise Lee employs to make this a compelling novel. In a sense, the history of China during the twentieth century serves as a kind of character in this novel, because events taking place in the world around them have such significant impact on the relationship between Dieyi and Xiaolou. Other authors have done the same thing. *Gone With the Wind*, *Les Miserables*, and *Dr. Zhivago* are just a few examples of books where periods of tremendous political turmoil help generate unforgettable romances. Having characters thrust into situations where the world around them is undergoing drastic change creates the potential for high drama. *Farewell My Concubine* certainly fits in with that rich tradition. Lee's novel covers a particularly long time span, beginning in 1929 and concluding in the 1990s. The Nationalist revolution that overthrew an ancient feudal system is less than 20 years old when the story begins. As the lives of Dieyi and Xiaolou unfold, the story arcs across a span of history that includes the Japanese

Leslie Cheung portraying Cheng Dieyi in the 1993 film version of Farewell My Concubine

invasion of China, the civil war between Chinese Communists and Nationalists, up through the brutal Cultural Revolution conducted under Chairman Mao. As the character Xiaolou observes near the end of his life, "China had known too much suffering in this century." That pain is integral, or key, to the story, not just as a backdrop, but as an influence on the main characters, who have their love for each other tested by the turmoil and difficulty that surrounds them. The climax comes when Dieyi, Xiaolou, and his wife, Juxian, are all accused of committing a very serious crime by mounting a sword with its tip pointed toward a picture of

Chairman Mao during a period of terrible political repression in China known as the Cultural Revolution. It is a measure of their love that each attempts to take the blame. Again, true love, Lee is saying, means having the willingness to sacrifice one's self if it means saving a loved one.

Of all the pitfalls that can be found along the path of true love, jealousy is perhaps the most destructive. In this story, Dieyi is so jealous of Juxian he will do anything to see her marriage to Xiaolou ruined. Lee describes his state of mind by writing: "If the destructive force of the Cultural Revolution were to break up Xiaolou's marriage to

Juxian, then all of the violence and suffering would not have been wasted." He gets his wish when Xiaolou, in an attempt to save Juxian, announces he will divorce her. But she is unable to bear the thought of such separation and commits suicide. Her death, in turn, rips at Xiaolou's heart. Looking at his dead wife, he feels "like a drowning man watching the last life preserver slipping away from him." But Juxian's death brought no happiness to Dieyi. He and Xiaolou are forced to separate, and they see each other only once more as their lives are drawing to a close. And even then, there was no joy to be found in reuniting. "Seeing Xiaolou again was unbearably painful," explains Lee.

After separating from Dieyi for the final time, Xiaolou is left alone in the world. Throughout the book, he remained much like the character he was cast to play: brave, steadfast, and honorable. The wife he loved is long gone, and the man he loved as a brother leaves as well. Lee's concluding message is that, when it comes to love, even when one acts with the best of intentions, the results can be tragic. She uses thinly veiled symbolism to drive her bleak point home, pointing out that when he attempts to go to a public bath to seek some comfort, it's name has been changed from "BATHING IN VIRTUE POOL" to "FINLAND BATHS." "There wasn't even any refuge in virtue anymore," concludes Lee. The ending is a forlorn one. It reflects the kind of pain untold numbers of broken-hearted lovers have felt throughout the ages. The beauty of this book is that Lee is able to take that sorrow and transform it into a complex and compelling work of art.

Source: Curt Guyette, Critical Essay on *Farewell My Concubine*, in *Novels for Students*, Gale, 2004.

Benzi Zhang

In the following article, Zhang examines cultural violence and homophobia, as exemplified in Lee's novel.

This essay will examine the issue of cultural violence in relation to the homophobic discourse in Chinese culture, as exemplified by Chen Kaige's *Farewell My Concubine* (1993), a film that has widely been shown and reviewed in the United States. Cultural violence, in Foucauldian terminology, can be described as a "strategic field" of forces, where various discourses of power operate concurrently to generate a social body of repression in the name of normality and order. Deviance such as homosexuality has long been regarded in Chinese culture as a sign of "transgression" that demands a

different order of social normality. In China, homosexuality is never a pure "sexual" problem, but an issue that raises questions about the violent discourse in which the peremptory heterosexuality has been a pre-dominant force as the rule of normality. As Chen's *Farewell My Concubine* illustrates, homophobia is produced discursively as well as institutionally by a power that affirms and perpetuates a feudal, patriarchal and quasi-polygamous culture. It is important to understand that in *Farewell My Concubine*, the homophobic anxiety situates itself at a crisscrossing of discourses of historical and political violence, in which those detected to be traitors and counter-revolutionaries are en-gendered as alluring men who are both corrupted and corrupting. Artistically brilliant and ideologically profound, *Farewell My Concubine* bravely explores one of the most disturbing yet undisturbed fields in Chinese culture—homophobia as "second modality of violence," whose ideological mechanism and rhetoric of representation have not yet been fully recognized or explained.

As a fascinating drama, *Farewell My Concubine*, with the strongest storytelling power that the cinematic discourse can provide, presents an intricate story about the lives of two Peking opera stars, Chen Dieyi (nicknamed Xiao Douzi) and Duan Xiaolou (nicknamed Xiao Shitou), against a historical backdrop of the painful upheavals of China in the 20th century. The two met in a training school for opera performers when they were only little boys. Their friendship develops through a cruel training and hard life, in which violent and brutal punishments are only common treatments. The young Dieyi, a shy and slight boy, is trained to perform as a dan (female impersonator)—in a sense he is forced to "become" a woman—that requires him to sing and remember "I am by nature a girl, not a boy" throughout his life. Later on, he becomes well-known for his exquisite performance in the role of the "Concubine" in a famous opera, from which the film takes its name. His chunky, robust childhood friend, Xiaolou, is fitted to play the role of the masculine "King." For Dieyi, the bond between him and his "stage brother" is both emotional and professional; he attempts to carry his passion for the "King" over into real life. However, Xiaolou seems to be unaware of Dieyi's feeling and gives his heart to a prostitute named Juxian. Jealous, angry, distressed, frustrated, and confused, Dieyi starts to indulge himself in opium smoking. Their professional and personal bond, however, continues over next several decades of tribulations and violence until the moment when Dieyi, fully dressed up in Concubine's costume, cuts his throat in front of Xiaolou, the "King."

The death of Dieyi, which is prepared in the opening sequence and accomplished at the very end of this movie, provides a heart-rending frame for the tragic, intensive drama that spans five decades in China's most turbulent times. Dieyi's grace and elegance as an effeminate dan is presented against an extreme violent backdrop of tribulation and turbulence—as China moves from warlord era, through Japanese invasion, Communist regime, into Cultural Revolution. Dieyi survives numerous trials, torments, cruelties, and injustices to face his true self by death—finally, he chooses death to express himself and to assert his homosexual identity. Set in the whirlwind of historical, social and political violence, the film highlights the relationship between violence and homosexuality. Chinese culture places man at the center of social domain: he is the master—the source and end of social norms, moral meanings, and political order. In the "old society" of China, a man's masculinity as well as his social status is often indicated by the number of his concubines. A woman is defined absolutely in her relation to men. Different from Western culture, in which the woman is "the second sex" and "she is the Other" (de Beauvoir 16), Chinese culture treats women as "belonging" to/of men, and femininity has no independent status. The original Chinese story of "*Farewell, my Concubine*" is about Xiang Yu, a king in ancient China, who loses everything in a battle except his favorite concubine named Yu Ji. Surrounded by enemy troops, he waits for his doomed final moment, drinking and listening to his concubine's dreary chant: "Enemy troops surround us/Singing the songs of Chu, they mock us/My lord is doomed/ I have nowhere to turn." After her last chanting performance, the concubine cuts her throat and dies in the lap of the King.

Circulated in Chinese society as a "love story" for thousands of years, "Farewell, my Concubine" is transformed into a cultural discourse invested with male dominated values, which discriminate against not only women but also effeminate men. Phallogocentrism and Xiang-Yu-like masculinity, with all their institutionalized discursive practices, have been the dominant force of orthodoxy in Chinese culture. Any kind of dissidence or resistance to this masculine orthodoxy has been marginalized, denounced and persecuted throughout history. Parallel to political and social violence that is "out there" in the world, the oppression of homosexuality usually takes the form of the second

> In China, homosexuality is never a pure 'sexual' problem, but an issue that raises questions about the violent discourse in which the peremptory heterosexuality has been a predominant force as the rule of normality."

"modality of violence" which, as Armstrong and Tennenhouse have noted, is "excised through words upon things in the world, often by attributing violence upon them" (9). The discursive form of violence has put a seal of silence upon the discourse of homosexuality, which is ostracized and under-represented in Chinese literature and history. According to Jonathan Dollimore, the fact that the resistance to heterosexual orthodoxy and its "literature, histories, and subcultures" are "absent from current debates (literary, psychoanalytic, and cultural)" suggests the existence a violent force that suppresses the representation of "sexual dissidence" (21). The binary model of Xiang Yu (dominant masculinity)-Yu Ji (subservient femininity), which serves well the patriarchal, heterosexual orthodoxy, has been the dominating ideology in Chinese culture, which has an oppressive and suffocating consequences for homosexual discourse. In Chinese culture, homosexuality has a negative connotation of transgression that subverts the orthodox morality/normality.

"Sexual deviation," Dollimore notes, is often "thought to be a deviation from the truth; this is a truth embodied in, and really only accessible to, normality, with the result that, even if sexual deviants are to be tolerated, 'there is still something like an "error" involved in what they do ... a manner of acting that is not adequate to reality'" (69). Although homosexuality exists in social reality, the lack of its own "truthful" representation creates numerous misunderstandings that prevent the development of a positive homosexual sensibility in Chinese culture. Homophobia permeates every layer of China's "ideological apparatuses" (Althusser 171–72); the homosexual anxiety is silenced by the hegemony of a semifeudal, patriarchal and quasi-polygamous culture, which presses sexual deviation to self-negation and self-sacrifice. The lack of voice makes homosexual people, in Homi Bhabha's words, "become what Freud calls that 'haphazard member of the herd,' the Stranger, whose languageless presence evokes an archaic anxiety and aggressivity by impeding the search for narcissistic love-objects in which the subject can rediscover himself" (166). Bhabha's observation makes us aware of the discursive behavior of cultural hegemony that can act as a violent force both to marginalize difference and to constrain individual expression. The "languageless" silence, in the case of homosexual people in China, constricts the development of a speaking subjectivity and makes "failed speech" a pitiable mark of identity for this "muted group."

Farewell My Concubine tries to break the "languageless" silence in search of an appropriate voice to express homosexual experience and anxiety, which are situated in the most painful and violent period of Chinese history. From 1924 to 1977, although the dominating powers were constantly shifting in China, the discourse of peremptory heterosexuality and patriarchy has never been changed or challenged. Similar to the victims of rape, homosexual men meet the worst injustice and violence during that terrifying period of history. Dieyi's tormented fate as gay man is placed in the shadow of her mother, a prostitute who was raped by an old man. The film seems to indicate the connection between Dieyi's twisted sexuality and her mother's rape, which is intensified by the backdrop violence of wars and revolutions. Following Catherine MacKinnon, we can say, "taking rape [as well as homosexuality] from the realm of the 'sexual,' placing it in the realm of 'the violent,' allows one to be against it without raising any questions about the extent to which the institution of heterosexuality has defined force as a normal part" in sexual politics (219). The juxtaposition between rape and homosexuality in *Farewell My Concubine* suggests that both Dievi and her mother are violated by a culture that denies homosexuality and female sexuality. In Chinese culture, the representation of violence is particularly difficult and "often characterized by silence, elisions and ambiguities" (Rooney 92); rape and homosexuality are part of the "unspeakable" reality, which lacks concrete representation in cultural forms. "Excluded from representation by its very structure," to use Craig Owens's words, homosexuality and the victims of rape "return within it as a figure for—a representative of—the unrepresentable" (59).

For the most part of the film, Dieyi remains in female costume and concubine makeup. The transvestite stage of Peking opera seems to offer a place—an imaginative capaciousness—where Dieyi can both represent and masquerade his genuine sensibility. He seems to become a migrant between two worlds where masquerading becomes manifesting and misrepresentation displaces representation. He is (mis)taken for a woman on stage and "a woman's soul trapped in a man's body" off-stage, while he is actually a man—a gay man. "In all the culturally dominant forms of representation," as de Lauretis observes in The Practice of Love, "desire is predicated on sexual difference as gender, the difference of woman from man or femininity from masculinity, with all that those terms entail—and not as a difference between heterosexual and homosexual, or straight and gay sexuality" (110–11). The simple formulation of monological binarism of heterosexual patriarchy deprives Dieyi of the "third space." He is neither the prey of men's sexual desire nor a hunter of women's sexuality. Homosexuality, as Lee Edelman observes, has "been constructed as a threat to the logic of heterosexual, patriarchal representation" (xv). Refusing to be fixed and settled into an either/or trap, Dieyi becomes an enemy to the whole heterosexual structure, a "nomad" who refuses to "move from one fixed identity to another" (cf. Deleuze and Guattari). In a sense, Dieyi is turned into a woman and then crushed by the same phobic power in the name of normality or morality.

Dieyi is a female impersonator, or dan actor, which has a long tradition in Peking opera. "Originally these men were chosen for their looks and ability to appear feminine in women's clothes"; as Roger Baker has noted, "The use of men to play women's roles was the result . . . of a ban on women imposed by the authorities for moral reasons" (72). When discussing the transvestite theater in England, Stephen Orgel says, "The reason always given for the prohibition of women from the stage was that their chastity would thereby be compromised, which is understood to mean that they would become whores. Behind the outrage of public modesty is a real fear of women's sexuality" (26). Homophobia and the "fear of women's sexuality" derive from the same hegemonic values cultivated and reflected by the semi-feudal, patriarchal and quasi-polygamous culture which determines what is "normal" in Chinese society. Homophobia, as well as the "fear of women's sexuality," is violent and implicated in violence, because it often makes homosexuality and female sexuality convenient and pliable scapegoats for social, moral and even political problems. In popular literature and the political histories of China, sensual women and sexual dissidents are often presented as villainous, particularly when they are involved in politics; and they are victimized and also punished by the value system of normality which, ironically, treats polygamy and concubine customs as normal. In the "system that is male-supremacist," according to Andrea Dworkin, "women were defined as sexual chattel," and "systematically kept subservient to men"; "the sexuality of women has been stolen outright, appropriated by men—conquered, possessed, taken, violated; women have been systematically and absolutely denied the right to sexual self-determination and to sexual integrity" (239). In the "old society" of China, unfaithful concubines would be punished violently—death was the most common penalty, as illustrated by Zhang Yimou's film *Raise the Red Lantern*.

The problem of inequality between male and female sexuality is complicated by the issue of homosexuality which, crossing the assumed boundaries of the respective engendered domains of men and women, does not only suggest the repudiation of the masculine "kingdom," but also demands a "dominion" of a different kind of values, norms and powers, which challenge the binary structure that accommodates to hegemonic discourses such as homophobic patriarchy. In Chinese culture, there seems to be a clear demarcation line between female impersonation that appeals to male pleasure and homosexuality that threatens male normality. As a dan actor, Dieyi may remind us of Mei Lan-fang, one of the greatest female impersonators in China. Mei was admired for his ability to present convincing, impeccable femininity. As A. C. Scott opines, "Mei's stage technique was 'unsurpassed in its unity of gesture, expression, and exquisite grace and delicacy of line. His voice has purity and quality'" (cited in Baker 73). However, in China, Mei was always honored as a "man," who had two "Wives." Dieyi's case is different, because his gender-crossing involves more than just stage mannerisms. To use Marybeth Hamilton's words, Dieyi attempts to "display," not "perform," "his real, offstage self—as (in turn-of-the-century terms) a 'fairy,' a 'third sexer,' a being who straddled the gender divide" (115–16). In what Hamilton calls "a culture that demonized homosexuality," Dieyi's fate cannot be better than an unfaithful concubine. His defiant pertinacity, uncompromising personality, and refusal to give up the right to define his "real" identity and "proper" place, which have violently been disavowed by a phobic culture, eventually cost his life.

A homophobic culture often asserts "an exact equation between cross-gender behaviors and homosexual desire" (Sedgwick 59). In China, the violent force of power may also impose other "equations," by which those detected to be traitors and counter-revolutionaries, for instance, can be engendered as alluring men who are both corrupted and corrupting. "The interpretation of sexual deviance as political dissidence," as Katrin Sieg argues, can be considered as "communists' strategy of using the accusation of homosexuality in order to discredit the political enemy. It also reflected the specific, androcentric structure of a centralist state that expected its citizens to duplicate patriarchal relations in the domestic sphere as a sign of political loyalty" (94). What becomes significant, for example, in Dieyi's failed erotic adventures with Mr. Yuan, a wealthy admirer, is the refraction of a suppressive shadow of political violence. Later on, at a surprising turn, Mr. Yuan is identified as "a traitor and counter-revolutionary" and executed without a fair trial. While cross-dressing on stage is admired, cross-sexuality offstage is intolerable in both the "old" and "new" societies of China, in which sexual minorities, similar to other power minorities, are among the most susceptible to violence, because oversimplified labeling and "equation" make people learn to loathe homosexuality before they even understand it. The fear of the unknown generates violent suppression of any sign of transgression or deviation that might demand a different order of social/political normality.

It is widely observed that sexual discrimination in a patriarchal culture can provoke extreme violent acts. The issue of denouncing and persecuting homosexuality, therefore, should be examined in a large context of violent and phobic culture. Let us take a look at what Christina Gilmartin records in her essay about the violence in China: "Deeply imbedded in Chinese culture, this strong preference for boys has provoked both men and women to perpetrate the crime of infanticide. Even women who had not been pressured by their husbands or relatives to produce a son have been convicted of killing their infant daughters" (216). Infanticide and homophobia are provoked by the same system of cultural values which, in de Lauretis's words, "produces the human as man and everything else as, not even 'woman,' but non-man" (Alice 121). Such a mentalité produces a coercive force, a phobic hegemony that violently disavows the "concrete existence" of homosexuality as well as women's sexuality and their "actual weight in social relations" (cf. Armstrong and Tennenhouse 245).

Homophobic culture is a violent force that both marginalizes difference and constrains individual expression. Moreover, since it does not appear to be a historical and legal category, homophobia, as a "second modality of violence" that is different from the "out-there" crime of infanticide, takes an invisible privileged position from which phobic mentalité may continue to "demonize," "exclude" or "violate" the interests of women and "non-men." The issue of homosexuality, as Jill Campbell observes, has "open[ed] up the constellation of inter-related problems—sexual, political, and social" (62). However, beyond the sexual, political and social discourses that Campbell has envisioned from the perspective of a Western culture, homosexuality, as illustrated in Farewell My Concubine, has another dimension that is pregnant with symbolism; it represents an ultimate "absence" in Chinese culture, which is somewhat mysterious and unapproachable. Difference from the Western culture in which you can find the concrete existence or evidence of sexual, political and social discourses for homosexuality, Chinese culture only suggests a kind of anxiety for the "absence" or "non-being-ness" of homosexuality. It is not a sexual issue, and it is more than a political and social phenomenon or construction. It suggests a spiritual transcendence, a suppressed consciousness of "modernity." The issue of homosexuality is related to the suppressed consciousness of modernity that should have developed during the period of Chinese history the film covers—the period of China's modernization. However, what we are witnessing here is an ironic cultural permutation in which the sensibility of modernity, as well as that of homosexuality, remains "castrated" and "dismembered" as China moves into a "modern" society on its own terms.

Source: Benzi Zhang, "Figures of Violence and Tropes of Homophobia: Reading *Farewell My Concubine* between East and West," in *Journal of Popular Culture*, Vol. 33, No. 2, Fall 1999, pp. 101–109.

Sources

Lee, Lilian, *Farewell My Concubine*, translated by Andrea Lingenfelter, HarperPerennial, 1993.

Review of *Farewell My Concubine*, in *Publishers Weekly*, Vol. 240, No. 33, August 16, 1993, p. 88.

Further Reading

Cameron, Nigel, and Brian Brake, *Peking: A Tale of Three Cities*, Harper and Row, 1965.

This invaluable resource on the history of Peking includes a number of photos, illustrations, maps, and charts that increase the reader's understanding of the ancient city. In addition, the book includes a section on Peking opera.

Gudnason, Jessica Tan, *Chinese Opera*, Abbeville Press, 2001.

This coffee-table book explores the colorful world of Chinese opera in more than 100 full-page photographs by Gudnason. The photos, many of which are close-up portraits, offer a thorough examination of the types of costumes and makeup performers wear in Peking, Cantonese, and Yue opera. The book includes an introductory essay by Gong Li—the actress who played Juxian in the film version of *Farewell My Concubine*—which explains the various types of characters, costumes, and makeup involved in Chinese opera.

MacKerras, Colin, *Peking Opera*, Images of Asia series, Oxford University Press, 1997.

This illustrated introduction to Peking opera includes explanations of common character types, descriptions of sample operas, and a brief history of the art form and its cultural effect on modern China.

Roberts, J. A. G., *A Concise History of China*, Harvard University Press, 1999.

While the novel explores events in the twentieth century, reviewing China's history as a whole can offer additional insight into the causes behind the political events in the twentieth century. Roberts's book offers a brief but informative introduction to China, from prehistory to modern times. The book also includes chapter notes and tips for further reading about China's history.

Spence, Jonathan D., and Annping Chin, *The Chinese Opera: A Photographic History of the Last Hundred Years*, Random House, 1996.

This illustrated book chronicles the years from 1894 to 1996 in China. The narrative essays, which are arranged historically by major political developments such as the war with Japan and the communist Cultural Revolution, include striking photographs and informative captions that give a sense of life in each time period.

Memoirs of a
Geisha

Arthur Golden
1997

Memoirs of a Geisha is full of surprises, especially to Western readers unfamiliar with the mysterious Japanese geisha. Perhaps the biggest surprise, however, is the novel's author, an American man from Tennessee. Arthur Golden's fascination with Asian culture was sparked years before he began writing *Memoirs of a Geisha*, as he holds degrees in Japanese history and art history with a specialization in Japanese art. It was while learning and working abroad that he met Mineko Iwasaki, a retired geisha who agreed to numerous interviews with Golden in preparation for his novel. Iwasaki provided critical "inside" information that gives the novel both integrity and intrigue.

The rags-to-riches story of Sayuri, the novel's heroine, is a first-person account, as if she is relating her life story to an American professor. The novel addresses themes such as freedom, beauty, metamorphosis, and gender relationships. Upon publication in 1997, *Memoirs of a Geisha* quickly became a bestseller, an impressive showing for a first-time author. *Memoirs of a Geisha* has been translated into more than twenty languages and has sold more than four million copies in English. Critics and readers alike have embraced the novel, and in the first few years after publication, it was a popular book club selection.

Arthur Golden

Author Biography

Memoirs of a Geisha, published in 1997, is Arthur Golden's debut novel. The bestselling novel was a long time in the making; Golden spent more than ten years on the novel, throwing out the first two drafts before finding his "voice" in the first-person account that was a publishing success.

Golden was born in 1957 in Chattanooga, Tennessee, to a family of journalists. His parents, Ben and Ruth, published the *Chattanooga Times*, and in the early 2000s his cousin, Arthur Ochs Sulzberger, published the *New York Times*. Golden's parents divorced when he was eight, and his father died five years later. Golden relates this to his challenges with the Chairman's character as Sayuri's love interest. Because his father was absent for much of his childhood, Golden struggled to make the character and the relationship believable. Golden attended Harvard College (the school of fine arts at Harvard University), where he earned a degree in art history with a specialty in Japanese art. He then completed a master's degree in Japanese history (he also learned Mandarin Chinese) in 1980 from Columbia University. After a summer at Beijing University and a work stint for an English-language magazine in Tokyo from 1980 to 1982, Golden returned to the United States. He entered Boston University, where he

completed a master's degree in English in 1988. After his graduation, he worked as a writer and instructor in literature and writing.

In 1982, Golden married Trudy Legee, whom he met on a flight to Beijing. The couple has two children, a son named Hays and a daughter named Tess, and lives in Brookline, Massachusetts.

Plot Summary

Translator's Note and Chapters 1–3

The novel opens with a prefatory chapter written by a fictitious professor of Japanese history named Jakob Haarhuis. He explains that the book is the result of his interviews with a retired geisha named Sayuri.

Chapter 1 opens in the first-person voice of Sayuri, which will be sustained throughout the entire novel. She tells about her childhood in the small fishing village of Yoroido, where she (then called "Chiyo"), her older sister (Satsu), and her parents live a simple life. When Chiyo is nine and her sister is fifteen, their mother becomes deathly ill. On an errand, Chiyo falls and hurts herself. Tanaka Ichiro, the wealthy owner of the Japan Coastal Seafood Company that sustains the town, tends to her. He knows her family's difficult situation.

Tanaka visits Chiyo's father, and she is certain that he plans to adopt her and her sister after their mother dies. But instead, they go on a train to the faraway big city of Kyoto, where they are separated.

Chiyo's new home is a geisha house (called an "okiya"), whose resident geisha is Hatsumomo. She soon learns that Hatsumomo's beauty is equaled by her wickedness. Auntie, Mother, and Granny are the owners of the house. Chiyo also meets another girl, who is her age and who is currently working as a servant while she awaits geisha training. If Chiyo works hard, she may have the same opportunity.

Chapters 4–8

Hatsumomo tells Chiyo that Satsu had visited weeks before, and Chiyo is desperate to know where she is. Hatsumomo holds this information over her head, manipulating Chiyo to do her every bidding.

A month into her stay, Chiyo begins lessons at the demanding geisha school. One of Chiyo's duties at home is to wait up for Hatsumomo to return. One evening, Hatsumomo and a friend make Chiyo vandalize an expensive kimono that belongs to Hatsumomo's rival, Mameha. Chiyo is harshly punished and learns that she can never be free until she has repaid all of her expenses, including her purchase, schooling, medical expenses, food, and the replacement of the kimono.

Hatsumomo tells Chiyo where her sister is, and she sneaks out to find her at the brothel where Satsu works. They plan their escape. Chiyo, however, is caught, and Mother decides that she can no longer study to be a geisha; she will have to work as a maid instead. Months later, Chiyo receives word that her mother and father have both died and that her sister, having returned to Yoroido, has run off with the son of Tanaka's assistant.

Chapters 9–15

One afternoon, Chiyo sits sadly along one of the streets. A man called "The Chairman" shows compassion toward her, cheering her with kind words and money to buy a shaved ice. She goes to the temple to pray that somehow she can become a geisha so she can meet men like him.

Granny is electrocuted by a space heater and dies. Hatsumomo's rival, Mameha, comes to pay her respects. She notices Chiyo and asks her to meet privately. A few weeks later, Mameha visits Mother, and they strike a deal that Chiyo may return to her studies as a geisha with Mameha as her "older sister" (a very important mentor role), as long as Chiyo is able to repay all of her debts by the time she is twenty. If she does, Mameha will receive twice her fee; otherwise, she will receive only a fraction of her fee.

Hatsumomo takes Pumpkin as her "little sister." Pumpkin makes her debut as a geisha first, and Chiyo is envious. When Chiyo makes her debut and takes the geisha name Sayuri, Hatsumomo humiliates her publicly.

Chapters 16–24

Mameha takes Sayuri to a sumo match to meet a longtime client, Iwamura Ken and his friend and business partner, Nobu Toshikazu. To Sayuri's delight, Iwamura is the Chairman she has thought of for so many years. She sits next to Nobu, however, who is terribly scarred from burns received during a bombing.

Mameha devises a plan to get Nobu and another man, Dr. Crab, to bid up the price of Sayuri's *mizuage* (loss of virginity) to bring the young geisha acclaim. The Baron, her *danna* (a patron who pays a geisha to be his mistress), invites Sayuri to a party Mameha cannot attend. Mameha warns Sayuri to be careful to protect her virginity. Although Sayuri

Media Adaptations

- Audio adaptations of *Memoirs of a Geisha* have been released by Bantam Books-Audio, 1997 (cassette, abridged), 1998 (cassette, unabridged), and 1999 (CD, abridged).

---

tries to avoid being alone with the Baron, she fails. The Baron undresses her but does not take any liberties with her.

Back in Gion, Nobu gives Sayuri a ruby, which Mameha instructs her to give to Mother. A few days later, the bidding on Sayuri's *mizuage* begins between Nobu and Dr. Crab. Toward the end of the bidding, the competition was between Dr. Crab and the Baron, but Dr. Crab won by paying a record price. He and Sayuri perform the ceremonies and the event, and Sayuri is glad when it is done. For the price paid for her *mizuage*, Mother adopts Sayuri as the okiya's daughter. This means that her debts are clear and her future is secure. Hatsumomo is outraged.

Chapters 25–29

Mameha goes to collect on her deal with Mother. Sayuri is also about to have a *danna* of her own, almost unheard of for a geisha so young. Sayuri learns that Nobu has made the offer to be her *danna*, and she reveals her disappointment to Mameha. Although Mameha thinks she is being foolish, she shows Mother how General Tottori could benefit the okiya more as Sayuri's *danna* because of his position in the military. He is in charge of procurement and has access to resources not available to most civilians in this time of war. Tottori becomes Sayuri's *danna*, and Nobu all but disappears from her life.

When Sayuri gets Hatsumomo's large room, Hatsumomo's efforts to get Sayuri in trouble backfire. One night at a party, Mameha manages to make Hatsumomo so angry that she lashes out and attacks someone. She is removed from the party, and Mother kicks her out of the house. The last Sayuri hears of her, she is working as a prostitute.

With Tottori's help, Sayuri's okiya manages to survive the first years of World War II despite severe rationing. But his arrest changes everything. Things get worse in the Gion district, and finally the news arrives that the district is to close. Geisha scramble to contact men who can help them, as they have heard stories about women working in factories. Sayuri visits Tottori, but he is powerless. Then Sayuri encounters Nobu, who offers her a safe place to stay. She accepts his offer and stays with some of his friends. After the war, Nobu needs her help to get the company back on its feet. He and the Chairman need the support of a man called the Minister, although Nobu cannot stand him. Nobu needs her to help them entertain him while they pursue his help. She agrees and returns to Gion, which has recently reopened.

Chapters 30–34

Sayuri, Mameha, and Pumpkin entertain the crude and drunken Minister. The company recovers, and Nobu announces his intentions to become Sayuri's *danna*. While she is grateful to him, she knows that becoming his mistress means never becoming the Chairman's mistress. Sayuri devises a plan to destroy Nobu's affection for her. She knows how much he hates the Minister, so she asks Pumpkin to bring Nobu to "accidentally" discover her having sexual relations with him. Pumpkin, however, brings the Chairman because she knows Sayuri loves him. Pumpkin resents Sayuri's adoption at the okiya and has been seeking revenge. Sayuri resigns herself to being Nobu's mistress.

Back in Gion, Sayuri waits for Nobu at the teahouse where they will perform the *danna* ceremony. Instead, the Chairman arrives and confesses his long-standing feelings for her but explains that his friendship with Nobu prevented him from acting on them. He understands Sayuri's plan to rid herself of Nobu, so he told Nobu what happened with the Minister. Nobu could not forgive her, so the Chairman is now free to become her *danna*.

Chapter 35

Sayuri tells how pleasant life became after the Chairman became her *danna*: She visited the United States with him on several occasions and expressed her desire to live there and open a teahouse. She subtly revealed that she has a son by the Chairman, so rearing him in a distant country would be best for the Chairman's family-owned business. He agreed, and she took up residence at the Waldorf Towers in New York City. Since the Chairman's death, she has lived a self-sufficient and happy life for the first time.

Characters

The Chairman

Sayuri meets the Chairman years before she becomes a geisha, and his elegance and kindness inspire her to be a great geisha. She wants to be the kind of woman who spends time in the presence of such men. For years, she dreams about him and fantasizes about impressing him with her beauty and charm. When she meets him again years later, she finds that he is the head of Iwamura Electric, a prominent company. She is delighted that he is still the kind man she remembers.

The Chairman began working in his industry as a teenager and quickly progressed through the business ranks. When he invented a special socket that his company would not produce, he started his own business at the age of twenty-two. His business struggled for a few years until he collaborated with Nobu on a military base project, and the two became friends and business partners. The company grew tremendously because of their partnership.

The Chairman has secret feelings for Sayuri, which he does not reveal because of his loyalty to Nobu. But when Nobu rejects Sayuri, the Chairman becomes her *danna* (a man who pays a geisha to be his long-term mistress). He does not marry her (he already has a family), but he pays all of her expenses and allows her to move to New York to open her teahouse and rear their son. He takes care of Sayuri until his death.

Sakamoto Chiyo
See Sayuri

Dr. Crab

Dr. Crab is a physician in the Gion district. He is called "Dr. Crab" for the way he hunches his shoulders and sticks out his elbows. He is methodical in his practice and in his personal life. He has a particular interest in winning novice geishas' *mizuage*, or virginity. This arrangement is made with a geisha's okiya when both parties agree upon a sum of money. Mameha uses Dr. Crab's reputation as a "*mizuage* specialist" to drive up the price of Sayuri's *mizuage* to a record fee.

Hatsumomo

When Sayuri arrives at the okiya, Hatsumomo is the only working geisha in the house. Her great success brings in all the money for the house to function and support her profession. She is devastatingly beautiful but equally cruel. She can put on a charming disposition while entertaining, but in reality she is scheming, manipulative, and cold. Sayuri describes her this way: "She may have been as cruel as a spider, but she was more lovely chewing on her fingernail than most geisha looked posing for a photograph."

She sets her mind on destroying Sayuri's future as a geisha, and she begins early. Before Sayuri even enrolls in geisha school, Hatsumomo ridicules her and lies about her to Mother. When Sayuri becomes Mameha's apprentice, Hatsumomo takes on Pumpkin as hers. Hatsumomo thinks nothing of spreading lies about Sayuri in the teahouses to ruin her chances of achieving success. Her ambition is blinding, and she cannot tolerate competition or the thought of future competition. Ultimately, her selfishness and hate lead to her downfall, and she is removed from the okiya and reduced to prostitution. Sayuri imagines that she may have eventually drunk herself to death.

Tanaka Ichiro

Tanaka Ichiro is the wealthy owner of the Japan Coastal Seafood Company in Yoroido. He arranges the deal with Sayuri's father to broker her and her sister to businesses in Kyoto. Sayuri initially finds him very strong and kind, but she grows to hate him for orchestrating her fate. When Sayuri's parents die, Tanaka sends religious objects from their home to Sayuri, along with a letter meant to encourage the girl.

Nitta Kayoko

See Mother

Iwamura Ken

See The Chairman

Mameha

Mameha is one of the most successful geishas in Japan. She agrees to take Sayuri as her "little sister," an apprentice position. Mameha is not as beautiful as Hatsumomo, but she is kinder and wiser. She is very clever and knowledgeable about the social politics of Gion. She also makes more money than Hatsumomo because she has a *danna*. Mameha and Hatsumomo are rivals, so Mameha is happy to help Sayuri become more successful than Hatsumomo and end her reign of terror.

Sakamoto Minoru

Sakamoto is Sayuri's father, a fisherman. She says that he "was more at ease on the sea than anywhere else" and describes how his time at home was generally spent untangling nets. He had a prior wife and children, all of whom died, which may account for the deep creases in his face. As his wife is dying, he feels he has little choice but to accept Tanaka's offer to sell the two girls to have different lives elsewhere.

Mother

Mother is the head of the okiya, and her primary concern is money. Although she is younger than Auntie is, she is in charge at the okiya. She is strikingly ugly, described by Sayuri as a bulldog-looking woman with discolored features. Mother tries to be fair, as she knows that Hatsumomo is manipulative and conniving, but her main goal is to keep the finances in order. When Sayuri attempts to run away from the okiya, Mother stops paying for her geisha lessons until Mameha makes her see that there is serious money to be made. Later, when she adopts Sayuri as the daughter of the okiya, she continues to capitalize on any opportunity to make money from her.

Auntie Nitta

Auntie manages the staff and performs various functions around the okiya, run by her adoptive sister, Mother. Because her hip is malformed, she was destined early to the ranks of servitude in the geisha district. She interacts with Sayuri the most of the three women who own the house, and she is the most understanding. Still, she is harsh when she deems it necessary.

Granny Nitta

Granny is the adoptive mother of Mother and Auntie. She is a sour, mean-spirited old woman who complains constantly. In her younger years, she was a geisha, but she used a common face cream containing lead, and her skin is now ghastly as a result. Granny dies when a space heater in her room electrocutes her.

Toshikazu Nobu

Nobu is the Chairman's business partner and friend. As president of Iwamura Electric, he proves himself a perceptive and loyal businessman. Nobu's face and body have terrible burn scars from a bomb explosion during a military maneuver. His heroics also cost him his arm. For this reason, many people are afraid to get close to him, and his harsh demeanor does not make him any easier to approach. Those who know him well, however, find that he is a man of great character and loyalty, who has very human feelings hidden beneath his gruff exterior. He and Sayuri become friends, and he shows unusual affection in his treatment of her. Her ultimate rejection of him is deeply hurtful.

Pumpkin

Sayuri gives the other girl her age at the okiya the nickname "Pumpkin," and it stays with her even into her geisha years. Pumpkin begins working at the okiya as a servant until she is ready to begin geisha school. She is sweet natured, but not particularly intelligent. She has difficulty mastering the skills taught at geisha schools, and Hatsumomo has no trouble dominating her when she becomes her apprentice. Pumpkin and Sayuri are friends until their apprenticeships with rival geisha force them to compete with each other. The backlash of the rivalry generates bitterness in Pumpkin, who sabotages Sayuri's plan to alienate Nobu. Pumpkin seeks revenge because Mother makes Sayuri the okiya's adopted daughter after the position is promised to her.

Sakamoto Satsu

Satsu is Sayuri's sister. Although she is six years older than Sayuri (fifteen at the time she leaves home), she is brokered to a brothel to work as a lowly prostitute because of her plain features and chubby physique. At home, Satsu is a hard and conscientious worker who lacks the imagination of her younger sister. Later, in Kyoto, she cannot bear to live as a prostitute and plans to escape, taking Sayuri with her. Sayuri does not make it to their meeting place, but Satsu manages to escape successfully. She returns to Yoroido and runs away with Tanaka's assistant's son.

Sayuri

The novel's heroine, Sayuri (born "Chiyo") is born in the small fishing village of Yoroido. She lives with her older sister, Satsu, and her parents. Her unusual gray eyes distinguish her from other girls, and this feature plays a significant role in her success later as a geisha. She is clever, energetic, and imaginative. In childhood, her imagination shows her innocence as she dreams up fantasies about being adopted by Tanaka. As a woman, however, her imagination shows her maturity, as she is able to maneuver the complicated social and interpersonal workings of being a geisha.

Sayuri is adept at learning to socialize with men and manipulate them, although she does not use her skills for her own selfish pride. She learns to recognize good character, and she values friendship. This makes it harder when she must find a

way to avoid having Nobu as her *danna*. Sayuri is driven by feelings for the Chairman that she has been harboring since she was a young girl. This is what inspires her to be a great geisha, and it is what compels her to hurt Nobu. In the end, however, her years of longing are rewarded when the Chairman becomes her *danna* until his death.

Sayuri's voice is one that expresses quiet emotion and wisdom. She recalls her life through the perspective of retrospect, understanding more now than she did then. She sprinkles life lessons in her narrative but does not attempt to cover up her own foolishness. For all she has been through, she emerges gracious and kind.

General Tottori

General Tottori becomes Sayuri's *danna*. He is in charge of procurements in the military, so his connections make him an attractive *danna* prospect. It is wartime in Japan, and prices are rising while other items are being rationed. Tottori is able to provide things for the okiya that other men cannot. He is not affectionate or attentive, but he does provide for Sayuri and the okiya until his arrest.

Yukiyo

See Sakamoto Satso

Themes

Deception

From the time Tanaka brokers Sayuri and her sister away from their home, the theme of deception guides the course of events in the novel. While Tanaka's deception is indirect (after all, he never actually tells young Sayuri what her future holds), Hatsumomo's deception is overt. Hatsumomo not only lies about Sayuri, but she goes so far as to set her up to look guilty when she is innocent, as when she puts money into Sayuri's obi before telling Mother that Sayuri sold some of her jewelry. Hatsumomo also makes empty promises so she can manipulate and dominate the young apprentice geisha.

As much as Sayuri resents so much deception in her life, the irony is that she takes on the profession of a geisha, which relies on deception. As a geisha, Sayuri assumes an identity other than her true one, she laughs at jokes that are not funny, and she learns to make a certain kind of blank face that men can believe means whatever they like. Her success depends on her ability to appear not as herself but as whomever her clients want her to be.

Topics For Further Study

- Much is made of Sayuri's having a lot of water in her, as her mother did. Her father had a lot of wood in him. Research the meaning of the elements of water, wood, fire, metal, and earth in Japanese thought. How did they describe people, and were they used to describe anything else? Are they still used today? Finally, what insights into the characters and their fates do you gain from this research?

- Hatsumomo hates Sayuri from the moment she arrives at the okiya, but the reader is never told directly why. How do you explain her deep, malicious hate? Write an Afterword containing excerpts from Hatsumomo's memoirs that shed light on this issue.

- The dynamics between male and female power are unusual in the geisha-client relationship. What kind of power does each person hold? Research women's roles in modern Japan and prepare a binder in which you trace the history of women in Japanese society throughout the twentieth century. You may complement your text with drawings, charts, photographs, diagrams, or any other visuals that will enhance your research.

- Golden refers to the practice of Shinto in the okiya, but Sayuri is also aware of Buddhist practices. Read about these two traditional religions in Japan and compose a comparison of the two. Based on what you know about the okiya, its function, and the women in it, does it make sense that Shinto would be the religion of the house?

- To become a geisha, Sayuri works very hard to learn to play the shamisen, dance, sing, and perform tea ceremonies. Japanese arts are traditionally precise and expressive. Choose three forms of Japanese cultural expression or art, and prepare a presentation for westerners to help them understand and appreciate this culture. (You may choose a recording of shamisen music, an explanation of a tea ceremony, a video of a traditional dance, diagrams and examples of Japanese calligraphy, examples of art, a collection of haikus, etc.) To conclude your presentation, offer comments on how your work has affected your understanding of Sayuri's experience.

Deception is also depicted in the novel is in the way Sayuri outgrows her propensity for self-deception. As an innocent young girl in Yoroido, she absolutely convinces herself that Tanaka will adopt her, her sister, and her father after her mother dies. It is an idea she embraces and then persuades herself is the truth, which only makes the heartbreak worse when it is not true. In Kyoto, she convinces herself that her sister has been taken to another okiya and that they will reunite at geisha school and escape together. She does not consider any other possibility, which again makes the reality all the harder to endure. As she ages, however, Sayuri learns the cynical ways of Gion as she learns more about herself. Although her fantasies about the Chairman seem like a regression to her childish ways of thinking, in the end, her dream comes true.

Metamorphosis

There are two levels of Sayuri's metamorphosis depicted in *Memoirs of a Geisha*. The broader level is her journey from the fishing village of Yoroido to the heights of geisha success in Gion. Sayuri recalls, "I may have been no more than fourteen, but it seemed to me I'd lived two lives already. My new life was still beginning, though my old life had come to an end some time ago." She also remarks, "I've heard it said that the week in which a young girl prepares for her debut as an apprentice geisha is like when a caterpillar turns into a butterfly." Golden symbolizes her metamorphosis from the lowly fisherman's daughter to a glamorous geisha with the changing of her name from Chiyo to Sayuri. Among the most basic elements of a person's identity is her name, and to become a geisha, Chiyo must become Sayuri.

The narrower level is her daily transformation from an ordinary beautiful woman into a fully painted, tucked, and adorned geisha. The metamorphosis that she undergoes with makeup and kimonos is a sort of microcosm of the broader level of her complete transformation over the course of the book. Remembering the first time she saw herself in makeup, she says, "I knew that the person kneeling before the makeup stand was me, but so was the unfamiliar girl gazing back. I actually reached out to touch her." As she applies her makeup and has her obi tied, she also puts on her geisha self. In chapter 5, Sayuri explains, "Only when she sits before her mirror to apply her makeup with care does she become a geisha. And I don't mean that this is when she begins to look like one. This is when she begins to think like one too."

Beauty

As Sayuri slowly enters the world of the geisha, she becomes more and more aware of the role of beauty in her society. She realizes the importance of beauty immediately upon arriving in Gion, when she sees Hatsumomo at the okiya. Her beauty leaves Sayuri speechless, having never seen anything like her. Sayuri's lavish descriptions of the patterns and colors in kimonos attest to her appreciation of beauty, especially given the fact that she is recalling them from many years before. As she herself progresses through her studies and the levels of geisha standing, she is amazed at her own beauty when she is in full makeup and dressed in Mameha's kimonos. To others, Sayuri is beautiful, but she does not come to accept this as part of her identity until much later. She recalls as a child that Tanaka was the first to compliment her beauty, and she almost believed it was true.

Most pointed, however, is how Golden depicts beauty in Hatsumomo. In her character, he demonstrates the stark differences between superficial beauty and true beauty. As stunningly beautiful as Hatsumomo is in appearance, she is ugly in character. After she forces Sayuri to deface Mameha's kimono, Sayuri recalls, "Even then, amid all my fears, I couldn't help noticing how extraordinary Hatsumomo's beauty was." The more she is subject to Hatsumomo's cruelty, however, the less she is distracted by her beauty. While describing the tricks Hatsumomo used to undermine her apprenticeship, Sayuri recounts a time a military officer showed her his pistol:

> I remember being struck by its beauty. The metal had a dull gray sheen; its curves were perfect and smooth. The oiled wood handle was richly grained. But when

I thought of its real purpose as I listened to his stories, it ceased to be beautiful at all and became something monstrous instead.

This is exactly what happened to Hatsumomo in my eyes after she brought my debut to a standstill.

When Sayuri sees Hatsumomo among the men in teahouses and at parties, she wonders "if men were so blinded by beauty that they would feel privileged to live their lives with an actual demon, so long as it was a beautiful demon." As Sayuri's understanding of false and true beauty evolves, and as she sees how beauty can be as much a weapon as a comfort, the reader comes to understand the same truths.

Style

Imagery

Consistent with much Japanese art and literature, *Memoirs of a Geisha* includes a great deal of nature imagery. Traditionally, Japanese art features trees, insects, and bodies of water, just as poetry (most notably the haiku) often presents images from nature as metaphors for life's lessons. Golden's use of natural and Japanese imagery in *Memoirs of a Geisha* brings his fiction in line with this tradition and gives the novel a decidedly Japanese feel. Sayuri recalls a client who once mentioned her hometown of Yoroido, and she describes her feelings: "Well, I felt as a bird must feel when it has flown across the ocean and comes upon a creature that knows its nest." She also describes her mother's succumbing to her illness with a simile that seems fitting for a Japanese fisherman's daughter: "Just as seaweed is naturally soggy, you see, but turns brittle as it dries, my mother was giving up more and more of her essence." There are countless examples of Sayuri's use of natural or Japanese images in her descriptions of her experiences and feelings. That these are present in her memories of her early life as well as her more recent years indicates that this is a characteristic of her real self.

Fairy Tale

Memoirs of a Geisha fits the mold of a sort of fairy tale. Sayuri begins life in a poor fisherman's family. She is content until her mother's illness slowly and painfully takes its toll. Sayuri's father, unable to care for his two daughters, sells them to a broker. Although the older daughter, Satsu, goes to a brothel, Sayuri goes to train as a geisha. As an adult, she is refined, educated, and beautiful. She becomes, in the context of her world, a sort of princess after overcoming her humble beginnings.

Compare & Contrast

- **1930s:** After great difficulty, Japan is the first country to recover from the depression that affects so many nations worldwide. Economic growth is especially evident in manufacturing, which brings prosperity and modernity to Japan after many years of struggle.

  Today: Japan's economy is one of the strongest in the world. Rivaled only by the United States in gross national product (GNP), Japan is a major exporter in the international market. Particularly strong export industries are automobiles, electronics, and computers. Japan's imports are primarily raw materials, such as lumber, oil, and food items. Because Japan is such a technological giant, it is not surprising that agriculture only makes up about 2 percent of the GNP.

- **1930s:** Even into the early twentieth century, there are numerous geisha in various districts in Japan.

  Today: According to Jane Condon in her book *A Half Step Behind: Japanese Women Today*, in 1991, there were fewer than seventeen thousand geisha in all of Japan, down from eighty thousand before World War II. Today, the young women of Japan are more interested in modern careers than in carrying on old traditions that sharply delineate gender differences as dramatically as the geisha tradition does. Because of this, the number of geisha in Japan continues to decline, and the future of geisha is uncertain.

- **1930s:** The Japanese government is characterized by a heavy military presence. With it comes censorship, propaganda, and persecution of communists. Military personnel come to occupy most of the highest offices in government, including that of prime minister.

  Today: Japan's government is bicameral (having two legislative houses) and is parliamentary. Since its new constitution in 1947, Japan has transferred power from the emperor to the people, who now elect political leaders.

Sayuri's fairy tale is complete with a wicked stepmother (Granny), a conniving nemesis (Hatsumomo), a Prince Charming to rescue her at the end (the Chairman), and a castle (the Waldorf Towers in New York City).

Historical Fiction

Historical fiction is serious fiction that recreates an era other than that in which it is written. For *Memoirs of a Geisha*, Golden relied heavily on his own research and background in Japanese art and culture and on his extensive interviews with an actual retired geisha. He brings these historical details and truths to bear in a fictional account of a fictional person. Many historical novels depict cultures in conflict or cultures undergoing change, and this is certainly true of *Memoirs of a Geisha*. Interestingly, Golden also brings in another genre, the memoir. Although this memoir is fictional, it adheres to the traditional form of an actual memoir by using first person, concerning itself more with experiences and events than with deep introspection, and reflecting back over a long period of time.

Historical Context

Japanese Geisha

Prior to the mid to late 1700s, geisha (professional entertainers) were primarily men who sang, played music, told jokes, and performed dances and theatrical presentations. They first appeared around 1600 and became a staple of social functions. As women entered the profession, however, men who enjoyed the performances preferred the charms of women to the antics of men. Even in the eighteenth century, female geisha wore their hair in elaborate styles, applied distinctive makeup, wore beautiful silk kimonos and intricately tied obis, and followed certain rules of propriety.

A group of geisha girls receiving training from their teacher, circa 1955

Geisha live in houses owned by whoever purchased them and paid for their education. The geisha's education includes dancing, singing, playing music, performing tea ceremonies, conversation, etiquette, local dialect, and serving food and beverages. The house staff is responsible for managing a geisha's schedule, booking her appearances at parties, performances at teahouses and events, and private gatherings.

Today, the geisha is a dying vestige of a past society. The numbers of geisha have rapidly dwindled, and the inability to interest today's girls in such a profession means the future is dim. Young Japanese women today tend to be more interested in emerging opportunities than in carrying on the traditions of the past.

Critical Overview

A first-person account of a geisha's life written by a man from Tennessee seemed an unlikely success, but *Memoirs of a Geisha* proved a hit with readers and critics alike. Brad Hooper of *Booklist* describes the book as "sparkling" and commends Golden's "thorough research." *People Weekly* reviewer Lan N. Nguyen finds the novel "lyrical" and "evocative."

Nguyen adds that despite Golden's tendency to over-narrate and skim Sayuri's emotions, "his elegant language" and ability to transport the reader to such an unusual setting makes up for the book's flaws. Jeff Giles of *Newsweek* finds the book a "captivating, minutely imagined Cinderella story," adding, "A few reservations aside, Golden has written a novel that's full of cliffhangers great and small, a novel that is never out of one's possession, a novel that refuses to stay shut."

The novel's inside look at the mysterious life of a geisha inspired much critical commentary. Nancy Day and Alec Foege of *People Weekly* comment that "Golden's remarkable ability to imagine life in a highly secretive foreign subculture" results in a "powerful story." *Booklist* reviewer Joanne Wilkinson also appreciated the lavish setting, noting that Golden reveals "both the aesthetic delights and the unending cruelty that underlie the exotic world of the geisha." And a *Publishers Weekly* critic declares, "Golden splendidly renders the superficiality of geisha culture." In *Time International*, reviewer Hannah Beech deems the book "moving" and "evocative," noting that she was swept up until the very end. She writes, "Like a geisha who has mastered the art of illusion, Golden creates a cloistered floating world out of the engines of a modernizing Japan." At the end, however, as

Japan becomes more Westernized, "Golden's spell weakens, and the clarity of his narrative fades. And finally, as the edges of the floating world strain too much, we lose the grip of the illusion that kept us entranced for so long."

While numerous critics praised the novel, others found the book's characterization and tone flat. In *Library Journal*, R. Kent Rasmussen states, "Although often compelling, it is not always convincing," explaining that the characters "are mostly two-dimensional." While John David Morley of *New York Times Book Review* grants that Golden's first-person voice is "quite a daunting ventriloquist act to undertake in a first novel," he finds Sayuri "admirable but not terribly interesting." He explains that "she is not so much an individual as a faultless arrangement of feminine virtues." Morley suggests that focusing on the novel's "documentation rather than imagination" yields a better reading of the story, "filled as it is with colorful nuggets of information." Similarly, Gabriel Brownstein of the *New Leader* writes that Golden

> is more of a curator. He doesn't want to peek behind screens, he would rather examine their delicate woodwork. He is masterful at describing the teahouses, hairdressers' shops and alleyways of Gion. . . . His characters, however, fail to convey any emotional, psychological or historical complexities.

Brownstein evaluates Sayuri's characterization, noting that "throughout the book she remains elusive, her personality marked by a doelike innocence." The critic adds that Golden relies too heavily on distinctly Japanese references: "Disconcerting is the author's habit of limiting Sayuri to exclusively Japanese imagery. . . . The constant, heavy emphasis on Sayuri's Japaneseness ultimately serves to render it artificial."

In contrast to criticism of Golden's characterization of his heroine, reviewer Michiko Kakutani of *New York Times Book Review* finds Sayuri more interesting than the historical details of the novel. She writes, "What is striking about the novel is Mr. Golden's creation of an utterly convincing narrator, a woman who is, at once, a traditional product of Japan's archaic gender relations and a spirited picaresque heroine." Kakutani adds that her narrative voice engages readers: "Rather than contrive a stylized, period voice for Sayuri, Mr. Golden allows her to relate her story in chatty, colloquial terms that enable the reader to identify with her feelings of surprise, puzzlement and disgust at the rituals she must endure."

Despite the success of *Memoirs of a Geisha*, its most outspoken challenger of the book has been Mineko Iwasaki, the retired geisha who provided much-needed detail, background, and context. According to Galloway in *U.S. News & World Report*, Iwasaki went so far as to say that she regretted helping Golden, that he "did not get anything right," and that he "made a mockery of Japanese culture." In response, Golden stated that her reaction was not all that surprising because the closer a book is to the truth about something to which a person is loyal, the less that person is going to approve of it.

Criticism

Kate Covintree

Covintree is a graduate student and expository writing instructor at Emerson College. In this essay, Covintree explores Golden's novel in relation to classic fairy tale motif of Cinderella.

Fairy tales and folklore have contributed a great deal to the development of people and their understanding of their place in the world. As Maria Tatar points out in the preface to her book *The Hard Facts of the Grimm's Fairy Tales*, Jacob and Wilhelm Grimm "transformed the fables, yarns, and anecdotes of an oral storytelling tradition into literary texts destined to have a powerful influence on cultures the world over." The literary and critical community continue to return to their stories because the tales are filled with violence, sex, transformation, retribution, and redemption. The stories give readers a blueprint on how to read the world and the roles one can play in the world. Should one be the stepdaughter heroine, the enchanted beast, the witch, or the prince?

Fairy tale motifs can often be found throughout television shows, commercials, and films. Even contemporary novels return to the formulas of familiar fairy tales. According to the *New York Times*, *Memoirs of a Geisha* is "part fairy tale." Some elements of Golden's story seem to convolute some of *Cinderella*'s basic ideas. It is not until the fairy tale concepts in Golden's novel are read in conjunction with a tale-type index, with its variations made visible, that Golden's version of a *Cinderella* story becomes most clear.

Golden begins his novel with a "Translator's Note" introducing the reader to a false author of his tale. By giving over the story to Jakob Haarhuis, Golden plays the role of the Grimm Brothers, removing himself from the direct responsibility of the story. Since Haarhuis is not the actual author, but

> In an environment that looks down on love and romance by training geisha to remain detached from their emotions, Sayuri's motivations are based entirely on her desire for the Chairman."

the translator, Golden stresses the importance of storytelling even within the story he is telling. *Memoirs of a Geisha* is supposed to be Sayuri's story. But, like Haarhuis, she does not exist. she is merely a character who will travel through Golden's tale in search of what Golden believes will be her happily ever after.

In the mid twentieth century, Antti Aerne and Stith Thompson created an index that listed motifs, or common symbols and ideas, that classified all of the elements included in folk and fairy tales. The index is very detailed and specific by breaking down the aspects of each folk-tale. The *Cinderella* story and its variants are classified as Type 510. As Katherine Briggs (writing in *A Dictionary of British Folk-Tales in the English Language: Part A Folk Narratives*) explains in her breakdown of the tale *Ashpitel*, "this type of fairy tale includes the following: a cruel stepmother, . . . stepdaughter heroine, helpful animal reincarnation of parent, . . . Prince sees maiden at grave, and is enamored, . . . glass shoes, . . . and slipper test." Ashpitel's mother dies at the beginning of the tale. Similarly, Golden's main character, Sayuri, begins her tale in the fishing village of her childhood. Here, in Yoriodo, she is not called Sayuri, but Chiyo, and lives contentedly with her father, sister, and dying mother.

As in the beginning of *Cinderella*, this simple life soon dissolves. She and her sister are shipped to Kyoto and then separated. When Sayuri enters the Gion district, Kyoto's home for geisha training and entertaining, she is unhappy. She is brought to the Nitta okiya and must now call the matriarchs of this household "Mother," "Granny," and "Auntie." She also has two new sisters, Hatsumomo and Pumpkin. Everything about her new surrounding is unfamiliar, and she is out of place. She has a different

dialect than the other girls. She smells like fish. Her new "Mother" only cares about money, and her "Granny" constantly puts Sayuri to work with chores and errands. Even new privileges, like going to school, are made more unpleasant by the amount of work required when still at home. She is given little to eat and must stay up late into the night to wait on Hatsumomo. As Sayuri explains it in her tale, she believed she had been pulled from her family just to be a maid.

Sayuri's resistance to this new life only creates more problems for her. Hatsumomo views her as an enemy and falsely accuses her of stealing. Sayuri attempts to run away. These actions seem to remove whatever chances Sayuri has of moving out of her subservient state. Of course, as soon as she has lost her geisha training privilege, she discovers that she wants it. A letter from her home village confirms the death of both her parents and her sister's successful elopement. This new home in Gion is now all she has, and her place in it is fragile. By the time Sayuri desires to return to geisha training, Mother has given up on her. Her first encounter with the Chairman confirms her loss of status. The geisha that accompany him regard her with disdain. The Chairman favors Sayuri with a handkerchief. This is the motivation Sayuri needs for becoming a geisha, but still it would take a miracle for her to improve her life.

Granny's death brings such a miracle. It is then that the well-respected and seasoned geisha, Mameha, enters Chiyo's life. In many senses, Mameha acts as her fairy godmother. She helps Chiyo return to geisha training, dresses her in fine kimono, and takes her to social events. She even gives her the tools she needs to defeat her stepsister Hatsumomo by becoming the girl to be adopted into the Nitta okiya, and finally by becoming a successful geisha. Without Mameha's persistence and cleverness, it is most likely that Sayuri would have remained a maid.

With Mameha's help, Golden's main character raises her status and moves from the rags of her childhood to the riches and comforts that her new adoption can provide. Her debts are settled and her place in Gion is secure. Since she is now transformed from the Chiyo of her childhood into the geisha called Sayuri, suitors vie for her company. Dressed in kimono and adorned with jewels from admiring men, Sayuri should be able to live happily ever after.

Sayuri's motivations, however, are not just to become a successful geisha so that she can be

What Do I Read Next?

- *The Good Earth*, Pearl Buck's classic written in 1931 (and awarded the Pulitzer Prize in 1932), is an example of historical fiction set in Asia. Buck explores the lives of a family of hardworking peasants in China during the 1920s.

- Daniel Defoe's 1719 book *Robinson Crusoe* is an adventure story told in a manner similar to *Memoirs of a Geisha*. The story is of a sailor marooned on an island for several years, but it is related as if it were being told through another person.

- Translated by Kenneth Rexroth, *One Hundred Poems from the Japanese* (1956) spans time, form, and content in its presentation of Japanese poetry. The poems are generally very short, making it an accessible introduction to the seemingly simple tradition of poetry in Japan.

- George Bernard Shaw's play *Pygmalion* (written around 1914) is the story of a common flower girl transformed into a lady under the tutelage of two linguistics professionals. The story examines themes of metamorphosis, true self, and worth. It was the basis of the hit musical *My Fair Lady*.

---

financially successful. In an environment that looks down on love and romance by training geisha to remain detached from their emotions, Sayuri's motivations are based entirely on her desire for the Chairman. She carries his handkerchief around with her like a slipper, waiting for the right moment to expose herself to him. Now as a geisha, Sayuri is still not a fully realized princess, because her true prince, the Chairman, has not become her *danna*, or male sponsor. Without the Chairman, she is only another lady in waiting.

If the handkerchief is confirmation of the meeting between Sayuri and the Chairman, or encounter with her Prince, what is the glass slipper that he sends his footman in search of? It is her gray eyes. Her eyes, like the size of Cinderella's foot, are so unique and individual that only one woman can fulfill the requirement. Near the end of the book, Mameha's role of fairy godmother is brought even more to light as the Chairman explains that he wanted Mameha to search for the girl with the gray eyes. As he tells Sayuri at the end of the novel, he was "the one who asked Mameha to take you under her care. I told her about the beautiful young girl I'd met with startling gray eyes, and asked that she help you if she ever came upon you in Gion." Though Sayuri believed Mameha's decision to be her older sister was based on her rivalry with Hatsumomo, Mameha's actions toward Sayuri were also intended to aid the Chairman in his search for the girl with gray eyes.

But, like all good *Cinderella* stories, the union cannot be that easy. There are complications, the primary one being the Chairman's good friend Nobu. Nobu believes Sayuri is his destiny, but Sayuri evades intimacy with him as it could jeopardize a future with the Chairman. Nevertheless, Nobu's relationship to Sayuri is extremely important. Over and over, Sayuri and Nobu are put into situations where one can assist the other.

When the war comes to Japan and the Gion district, it is not Sayuri's danna who saves her, but Nobu. By sending her to work with a kimono maker, he places her in a life of poverty. Her hands become stained with fabric dye and she loses much of her physical beauty. Once again, Sayuri is a peasant. When Sayuri does return to the Gion district, it is through Nobu's insistence. He is the one who metaphorically welcomes her back into the castle. Of course, he has intentions to become Sayuri's new danna and to save his company, but Sayuri has other plans.

If the fairy tale motif Golden was following was that of an Animal Groom tale, then Nobu would be the perfect candidate for Sayuri's Prince Charming. Missing one arm and badly burned on

Traditional geisha, circa 1955, entertaining a group of men

his face and shoulders, he is nicknamed by some geisha as "Mr. Lizard." He is seen as unattractive and grotesque. His personality matches his rough exterior, and his affection for Sayuri is unique as he does not usually like geisha. He is a "Beast" waiting for a "Beauty" to reveal his true form. Sayuri is lucky to see Nobu's softer side. Because of his affection for her, he treats her with a kind of reverence atypical for his character. Even so, she continuously works to keep him from her.

It is not that Sayuri finds him repulsive as much as it is that Nobu is close friends with the Chairman. Sayuri's prince is not Nobu, and

building a relationship with Nobu jeopardizes her future with the Chairman. If it is not a beast tale then what role does Nobu play in this contemporary *Cinderella* retelling?

Nobu's character has relevance in the *Cinderella* storyline when a motif often found in variant form of the story (listed in the tale type index as 510B) is brought in. The story, *Thousandfurs*, is one example of this tale type. In it, the young girl leaves her home because of her own father's lust for her. After trying to remove herself from her father's affection, she is forced to escape her home in order to avoid an incestuous marriage. In Golden's novel, Nobu takes on the same role as this father. Though Nobu's affections are sexual in nature, they are also paternal. He saves her in wartime and chides her when she misbehaves. For Nobu, no other geisha compares to Sayuri. In the same way, the father in *Thousandfurs* is taken with his daughter because she is as beautiful as his first wife, his daughter's mother.

When Nobu is seen as a father figure, Sayuri's avoidance is understandable. To have a healthy relationship, Nobu must not be her danna. Their closeness may be one that destiny brings, but Nobu is a surrogate father, not lover. It is more acceptable to be lovers with her father's friend (in this case the Chairman) than the father himself (Nobu). As in *Thousdanfurs,* Sayuri takes her destiny into her own hands to keep herself out of Nobu's reach. In doing so, she knows she will destroy Nobu's affection for her, but she also knows this could open up the possibility to create a relationship with the Chairman.

Once Nobu is removed, Sayuri and the Chairman are free to share a life together. Finally, Sayuri, like the heroines of *Thousandfurs* and *Cinderella* before her, can move to her castle (for Sayuri it is in New York) and live happily ever after.

Source: Kate Covintree, Critical Essay on *Memoirs of a Geisha*, in *Novels for Students*, Gale, 2004.

Sources

Baughman, Ernest W., *Type and Motif Index of the Folktales of England and North America*, Indiana University Folklore Series No. 20, Mouton and Co., 1966.

Beech, Hannah, "A Tree Grows in Kyoto," in *Time International*, Vol. 150, No. 31, March 30, 1998, p. 49.

Briggs, Katharine M., "Ashpitel" in *A Dictionary of British Folk-Tales in the English Language: Part A Folk Narratives* Vol. 1, Routledge and Kegan Paul, 1970.

Brownstein, Gabriel, "Memoirs of a Geisha," in *New Leader*, Vol. 80, No. 17, November 3, 1997, pp. 18–19.

Day, Nancy, and Alec Foege, "Geisha Guy: Arthur Golden Isn't Japanese, and He Isn't A Woman. But He Does a Brilliant Impersonation in His Smash First Novel," in *People Weekly*, November 23, 1998, p. 89.

Galloway, Joseph L., "Protests of a Geisha," in *U.S. News & World Report*, Vol. 128, No. 10, March 13, 2000, p. 12.

Giles, Jeff, "Memoirs of a Geisha," in *Newsweek*, Vol. 130, No. 15, October 13, 1997, p. 76.

Golden, Arthur, *Memoirs of a Geisha*, Vintage, 1997.

Hooper, Brad, "Memoirs of a Geisha," in *Booklist*, Vol. 96, No. 15, April 1, 2000, p. 1442.

Kakutani, Michiko, "A Woman's Tale, Imagined by a Man," in *New York Times Book Review*, October 14, 1997, late edition, Section E, Column 1, p. 8.

Morley, John David, "Working Woman," in *New York Times Book Review*, October 5, 1997, late edition, Section 7, Column 2, p. 16.

Nguyen, Lan N., "Memoirs of a Geisha," in *People Weekly*, Vol. 48, No. 22, December 1, 1997, p. 49.

Rasmussen, R. Kent, "Memoirs of a Geisha," in *Library Journal*, Vol. 124, No. 3, February 15, 1999, p. 200.

Review, "Memoirs of a Geisha," in *Publishers Weekly*, Vol. 244, No. 30, July 28, 1997, p. 49.

Tatar, Maria, "Preface" in *The Hard Facts of the Grimm's Fairy Tales*, Princeton University Press, 1987, pp. xiii–xxxvi.

Wilkinson, Joanne, "Memoirs of a Geisha," in *Booklist*, Vol. 94, No. 1, September 1, 1997, p. 7.

Further Reading

Downer, Lesley, *Women of the Pleasure Quarters: The Secret History of the Geisha*, Broadway, 2001.
Written by a British journalist, this book is the result of extensive research about the highly secretive world of the geisha and its history. Downer wrote this book specifically with Western readers in mind.

Henshall, Kenneth G., *A History of Japan: From Stone Age to Superpower*, Palgrave Macmillan, 1999.
A professor of Japanese studies, Henshall offers a lively and accessible introduction to Japan's long history. The book is complemented by literary excerpts, diagrams, and chronologies.

Iwasaki, Mineko, and Rande Brown (translator), *Geisha of Gion: The Memoir of Mineko Iwasaki*, Simon & Schuster, 2003.
Written by the geisha interviewed by Golden for his novel, this memoir is an autobiographical account of an actual retired geisha.

Varley, Paul, *Japanese Culture*, University of Hawaii Press, 2000.
Often used as an undergraduate text, Varley's book covers religion, customs, art, and many other important aspects of Japanese culture.

The Portrait of a Lady

Henry James

1881

Henry James was an established author when *The Portrait of a Lady* was published. The novel was first published serially in 1880 and 1881, appearing in *Macmillan's Magazine* in England and in *Atlantic* in the United States. The first book edition was published in 1881.

The Portrait of a Lady was widely, and mostly favorably, reviewed. Some reviewers recognized it immediately as James's most important novel thus far, and a few called it a masterpiece. Both of these opinions have been affirmed as time has passed. Many scholars consider *The Portrait of a Lady* one of the greatest novels in modern literature. Its heroine, Isabel Archer, is widely considered one of James's most powerful characters.

The Portrait of a Lady is, above all, Isabel's story. Following the technique of Russian author Ivan Turgenev, James makes Isabel the axis around which the story revolves. All the story's events, and all the other characters, exist only to serve the purpose of revealing Isabel to the reader.

Author Biography

Henry James was born in New York City on April 15, 1843. His father, also named Henry, was a minister who had inherited wealth. His mother, Mary Robertson Walsh James, was devoted to her husband and five children. Henry was their second son. The first, William, became a Harvard professor and a philosopher whose best-known books, especially *Varieties of Religious Experience* (1902), are still read today. The younger children were Garth, Robertson, and Alice.

James's father took the family on an extended trip to Europe the year Henry was born. Henry's childhood was spent traveling between a family home in Cambridge, Massachusetts, and Europe, where the James's spent time in England, France, and Switzerland. In Cambridge and nearby Boston, young Henry came to know the American intellectual and literary stars of the time, including Ralph Waldo Emerson, Henry David Thoreau, and William Dean Howells. He was educated by private tutors at home and abroad until he enrolled at Harvard, where he studied only briefly. Howells, an influential magazine editor, helped James launch his literary career as a critic and writer for magazines including the *Nation* and the *Atlantic*.

In 1876, at the age of thirty-three, James moved permanently to England; he eventually became a British citizen. The meeting of American and European cultures is the predominant theme in his work. James is considered a master of the novel form and one of the leading practitioners of realism, the literary movement that arose at the end of the Civil War as a reaction against romanticism. James's work falls into the category known as psychological realism, in which the significant action in a work takes place inside the minds of the characters.

Although best known as a novelist, James was also a prolific and respected writer of short stories, plays (some were adaptations of his novels), criticism, and travel essays. As was common at the time, many of his novels were serialized in magazines before they were published as books. *The Portrait of a Lady*, first published in 1881, is widely considered the best of his early novels. Other lasting novels of this period include *The Europeans* (1878) and *The Bostonians* (1886). Well-known and still-popular later works include *The Wings of the Dove* (1902) and *The Ambassadors* (1903); James himself considered the latter his masterpiece. Two novellas, *Daisy Miller* (1878) and *The Turn of the Screw* (1898), appear in countless anthologies and remain popular.

Never successful as a student, James finally received honorary degrees from two of the most prestigious universities in the world: from Harvard, in 1911, and from Oxford, in 1912. He died in London on February 28, 1916, after a series of strokes. His ashes are buried in Cambridge, Massachusetts.

Henry James

Plot Summary

Chapters 1–9

The novel opens at Gardencourt, the English country home of the Touchetts. Mr. Touchett, his son Ralph, and their friend Lord Warburton are having tea. Mrs. Touchett arrives from America with her niece, Isabel Archer. Isabel is a young American woman of marriageable age. Her father has just died, her mother died some time previously, and her two older sisters are already married. Since Isabel is now alone, and since her aunt thinks well of her, Mrs. Touchett has brought Isabel to Europe so that she can become more sophisticated and therefore improve her prospects for a good marriage.

Just before Isabel appears, Lord Warburton tells Mr. Touchett and Ralph that he is bored with his life and will not get married unless he meets an especially interesting woman. When Warburton meets Isabel, he finds her interesting indeed, and he soon falls in love with her. He invites her to visit his home, and Isabel learns from her uncle that Warburton is very wealthy and highly placed socially. Isabel does visit Warburton's home, where she gets to know and like his two admiring sisters. She also finds that Warburton is kind and sensitive.

Media Adaptations

- A film version of *The Portrait of a Lady* was directed by Jane Campion and released in 1996. It stars Nicole Kidman as Isabel, John Malkovich as Gilbert, and Martin Donovan as Ralph. It is available on videocassette and DVD.

- A made for television movie adaptation was directed by James Cellan Jones and broadcast in 1968. Starring Suzanne Neve as Isabel, James Maxwell as Gilbert, and Richard Chamberlain as Ralph, this movie is available on videocassette and DVD.

- An abridged audiocassette recording of *The Portrait of a Lady*, with Gayle Hunnicutt as reader, was published by HighBridge in 1995. An unabridged version with Laural Merlington as reader was published by Brilliance Audio in 1998.

- An unabridged version of *The Portrait of a Lady*, with Laural Merlington as reader, was published by Brilliance Audio in 1998.

Chapters 10–14

Not long after her arrival at Gardencourt, Isabel receives a letter from Henrietta Stackpole, an American friend of hers who is in Europe working as a journalist. When Isabel mentions this to Ralph, he invites Henrietta to come stay at Gardencourt, which she does.

As soon as Henrietta settles in, Isabel receives another letter from another American friend, Caspar Goodwood. Caspar wants to marry Isabel and has followed her to England to press his case with her. Isabel, however, is irritated at Caspar for following her and refuses to answer his letter.

The same day that brings Caspar's letter also brings a visit from Warburton, who proposes to Isabel. She likes him but is not ready to settle down. An independent spirit, she wants to see the world and experience more adventure before she closes off her options in life. Although Warburton is both wealthy and kind, the idea of marrying him makes Isabel think only of her "diminished liberty." She gently but firmly rejects him via letter. Her aunt and uncle are baffled by this, as is Warburton, who comes to see her to ask for further explanation of her refusal. Isabel remains kind but firm toward him.

Chapters 15–21

Isabel, Henrietta, and Ralph travel to London together, since Isabel has not yet visited the capital. Ralph has become very fond of Isabel; her vigor and high spirits make her attractive to everyone she meets. Henrietta meets an old acquaintance of Ralph, Mr. Bantling, who quickly becomes her tour guide and companion. Caspar presents himself at Isabel's hotel and presses her to marry him. Isabel tells him, as she told Warburton, that she wants her freedom for the time being. She adds that, if Caspar still wants to marry her after two years, she will consider his proposal at that time.

Ralph receives a telegram telling him that his father is seriously ill. Ralph and Isabel return to Gardencourt, while Henrietta remains in London with Mr. Bantling. A friend of Mrs. Touchett, Madame Merle, is staying at Gardencourt and befriends Isabel. During this time, Ralph and Mrs. Touchett are preoccupied with Mr. Touchett, who is dying. Ralph persuades his father to leave half his estate to Isabel, so that she will be as independent financially as she is in spirit. Ralph is willing to have most of his inheritance go to Isabel because he, too, is ill, and he knows that he will only live a few more years. Mr. Touchett worries, rather prophetically, that having a large fortune could actually endanger Isabel, making her attractive to unsavory men who want her money. Ralph convinces his father that Isabel is too strong and independent to end up a victim.

Mr. Touchett dies, and Isabel receives her inheritance. Mrs. Touchett takes Isabel to Paris, while Ralph goes south to the Mediterranean, where the climate will be better for his health. In Paris, Isabel spends time with Henrietta and Mr. Bantling, whose travels have brought them to France.

When Mrs. Touchett and Isabel leave Paris, they visit Ralph on the Mediterranean shore. Isabel questions Ralph about his role in her inheritance and expresses concerns similar to those of her uncle that the money might not be altogether good for her. Ralph reassures her.

Chapters 22–35

Mrs. Touchett and Isabel go on to Florence, where Mrs. Touchett has a home. Here they again meet Madame Merle. Madame Merle arranges for Isabel to meet her friend Gilbert Osmond, an American-born man who has lived virtually his whole life in Europe. Madame Merle speaks highly of Gilbert to Isabel, and she has already told Gilbert about Isabel, as well—including the fact that Isabel is wealthy. Indeed, Madame Merle has told Gilbert that she wants him to marry Isabel.

At their first meeting, Gilbert invites Isabel to his home to see his art collection. There Isabel meets Gilbert's fifteen-year-old daughter, Pansy, and his sister, Countess Gemini. Through a conversation between the Countess and Madame Merle, readers learn that Madame Merle is orchestrating the marriage of Isabel and Gilbert so that Pansy will have money and will therefore be able to marry well. (Gilbert has little money but expensive tastes.) The Countess makes clear her objection to the trap that is being set for Isabel, but she does nothing about it.

Ralph has already let Isabel know that he does not like or trust Madame Merle and that Gilbert has no money. Now Mrs. Touchett begins to suspect Gilbert's motives in pursuing Isabel. She does not, though, suspect that her friend Madame Merle is working behind the scenes to bring the two together.

Isabel falls in love with Gilbert for the same reason she is impressed with Madame Merle: both have a very refined manner and are accomplished in all the social graces. They are the epitome of the sophistication that Isabel has been brought to Europe to acquire. Henrietta and Ralph make appearances in Florence to warn Isabel that Gilbert is a dilettante who is only interested in Isabel because she is wealthy and because she will impress his social circle. Isabel remains as independent-minded as ever, insisting that she loves Gilbert. She spends a year traveling, some of it with Madame Merle, and then returns to Italy. Caspar comes to see her, two years having passed, but Isabel rejects him again. Instead, she agrees to marry Gilbert. Mrs. Touchett

tells Isabel that Madame Merle has orchestrated the marriage for reasons of her own, but Isabel does not believe her aunt. Ralph also expresses his disappointment and misgivings—specifically that Gilbert will crush Isabel's independent spirit—but Isabel is determined to follow her heart.

Chapters 36–55

Four years have passed. Gilbert and Isabel are living in Rome. Isabel has realized that her friends and relatives were correct in their objections to Gilbert. He is selfish and controlling; he cares nothing for Isabel's ideas or her happiness but instead seeks to mold her into his idea of the perfect wife.

Isabel hears from Mrs. Touchett that Ralph is dying at Gardencourt and wants to see her. Gilbert tells Isabel that her place is with him, not with Ralph. Upset by this, Isabel talks with Countess Gemini. Gilbert's sister takes the occasion to tell Isabel about Gilbert's past: Pansy is not the daughter of Gilbert and his deceased first wife, as Gilbert has always told Isabel (and everyone else). In fact, Pansy is the daughter of Gilbert and Madame Merle. The two had a long affair, and Madame Merle has engineered Isabel's marriage for the benefit of her daughter, Pansy.

Isabel goes to England to see Ralph and admits to him that he was right about Gilbert's marrying her for money and crushing her independence. Ralph now believes that, indeed, the inheritance that he insisted his father give to Isabel has ruined her. Isabel is not bitter but instead seeks to understand what is the right solution for her predicament.

Ralph dies, and Isabel remains at Gardencourt for a time. Both of her former suitors, Lord Warburton and Caspar Goodwood, make final appearances and urge her to leave Gilbert. Isabel returns to her husband, though, because she believes that this is the right thing to do. She feels that if she does not keep her marriage vows, she would be the same kind of person as Madame Merle, whom she now realizes is profoundly corrupt. Isabel now understands that people like Madame Merle and Gilbert only have the appearance of refinement but are actually immoral. Isabel is not willing to be like them.

Characters

Isabel Archer

The novel's central character, Isabel is a young American woman who embodies all the best of what James depicts as American qualities, especially vitality, sincerity, and independence. As the novel opens, Isabel is arriving at the English home of her aunt and uncle. Her father has recently died. (Her mother died previously.) Her aunt, who traveled to the United States after Isabel's father's death, feels that Isabel has more potential than her circumstances in America will allow her to fulfill, and so she brings Isabel back to England with her.

Isabel wins the admiration of everyone she meets, including her cousin Ralph. Ralph talks his dying father into leaving half his estate to Isabel so that she can be free to do as she pleases. In addition to this benefactor, Isabel also has suitors. Caspar Goodwood travels from America to urge Isabel to marry him. Lord Warburton, a wealthy friend of the Touchett family, also wants to marry Isabel. But Isabel's independent nature leads her to reject both men. She finds Caspar boring and turns down Warburton partly because she is not ready to marry and partly because she fears life with him would be too easy. She longs for some adventure—even for some difficulty that will test her resourcefulness and mettle.

Isabel's independent spirit is the driving force in her personality, and it is what propels her into an unhappy marriage. When she falls in love with Gilbert Osmond, her friends and relatives almost unanimously warn her against him. But she refuses to take anyone's counsel but her own and learns too late that she completely misjudged her husband. Her failure to accurately judge Gilbert's character springs from an innocence that is characteristic of youth and also, in James's view, of Americans. Isabel's direct, trusting nature is contrasted to that of the book's European characters, who have secret pasts and ulterior motives for everything they do.

Although she makes a bad marriage, Isabel is not a tragic character. Once she realizes that she made a mistake in marrying Gilbert, she resolves to bring her strength of character to bear upon the circumstances that she has created by her own free choice. By refusing to leave her marriage, Isabel refuses to adopt the corrupt ways of her European circle. Instead, Isabel intends to graciously and courageously accept the consequences of her unwise decision and to make the best life she can.

Mr. Bantling

An old acquaintance of Ralph, Mr. Bantling meets Henrietta when she is in London with Ralph and Isabel. He becomes Henrietta's companion and guide as she travels around Europe as a journalist.

Countess Gemini

Countess Gemini is Gilbert Osmond's sister. She is well aware of Gilbert's true character and thus has no affection for him, but the two have a familial relationship in spite of this. The Countess catches on quickly to Madame Merle's scheme to get Isabel to marry Gilbert and voices her objection to it, but she doesn't actually do anything to prevent it. Four years after the marriage, at a time when Isabel is distraught over Gilbert's controlling nature, the Countess, out of sympathy, finally tells Isabel the truth about Gilbert's past.

Caspar Goodwood

Caspar is Isabel's American suitor. Having fallen in love with Isabel in the United States, he follows her to England to try to get her to agree to marry him. Isabel sees his persistence as aggression and is only irritated by it. However, the novel's one moment of passion takes place between Caspar and Isabel, when Caspar goes to see Isabel at Gardencourt one last time after Ralph's death. The couple's passionate kiss can be seen as Isabel's belated appreciation of the honesty and simplicity of character that Caspar personifies.

Madame Merle

Madame Merle is a friend of Mrs. Touchett. Isabel first meets her when both women are guests at Mrs. Touchett's home in England just before Mr. Touchett's death. Madame Merle is older than Isabel and very accomplished socially. She is charming and congenial and, as becomes clear only later, adept at manipulating people and events to serve her interests. Isabel is dazzled by Madame Merle's apparent refinement.

Gilbert Osmond

Gilbert Osmond was born in the United States but has lived virtually his entire life in Europe. He has the same qualities as Madame Merle, and Isabel is attracted to both of them for the same reason. Gilbert is an art collector, and he has an air of charm, sophistication, and refinement that greatly impresses Isabel. While all of her friends and relatives see Gilbert for the self-centered dilettante he is, Isabel is completely taken in and falls in love with him.

More than any other character, Gilbert is not what he appears to be. Although he has expensive tastes, he does not have money. Although he is charming and seductive, he does not really care about Isabel. And although he pretends that his daughter is the child of his deceased first wife, she is actually the product of an affair with Madame Merle.

Pansy Osmond

Pansy is Gilbert's daughter, and she is fifteen years old when Isabel meets Gilbert. Gilbert has always said that Pansy is the child of his first wife, who died giving birth to her, and Pansy was brought up in a convent. The nuns have reared her to be a completely obedient child, which pleases Gilbert.

Readers, along with Isabel, learn the truth about Pansy years after Isabel's marriage to Gilbert. Pansy is actually the product of a long affair between Madame Merle and Gilbert, whose first wife did die, but not in childbirth. Pansy does not know that Madame Merle is her mother but has an obvious dislike for the woman. Pansy likes Isabel and is very happy when she learns that Isabel is going to marry her father. Isabel's love for Pansy may be one reason why she returns to Gilbert at the end of the novel.

Henrietta Stackpole

Henrietta is an American journalist and a friend of Isabel. She is the quintessential "ugly American": loud, brassy, and boorish. Although Isabel sees Henrietta's faults, she is loyal to her friend, as Henrietta is to her. And, although Henrietta does not have Isabel's refinement, she is a better judge of people, and she warns Isabel not to marry Gilbert.

Mr. Touchett

Mr. Touchett is Isabel's wealthy uncle. Like most of the novel's characters, he was born in the United States, but at the time of the story, he has lived for many years in England. He comes to care deeply for Isabel and, when he hesitates to leave her half his fortune, it is only because he is afraid that the money will bring her harm rather than good. Mr. Touchett dies early in the novel after letting Ralph persuade him to leave Isabel a fortune.

Mrs. Touchett

Isabel's aunt, Mrs. Touchett, goes to New York after the death of her brother, from whom she was estranged, and decides to bring Isabel back to Europe with her. Mrs. Touchett is a well-meaning woman who shares some of Isabel's independence and, more surprisingly considering her age and her long time in Europe, her naiveté. Her independence is clear from the fact that she long ago set up her own home in Florence while her husband remained in England, since the two did not enjoy the same kind of life. The two crafted an amicable marriage out of visits to each other's homes. Mrs. Touchett's naiveté is clear in her unwarranted trust of Madame Merle. Like Isabel, Mrs. Touchett is impressed with Madame Merle's mastery of the social graces and

fails to see that she is corrupt until it is too late to save Isabel from her scheme. Mrs. Touchett does realize the truth before Isabel does, however.

Ralph Touchett

Ralph is Isabel's cousin. He becomes her admirer, friend, and confidant. Like Isabel, he is intelligent and good-hearted. Unlike her, though, he is physically frail. He is also much less naive than his cousin. He understands and condemns the conniving of Madame Merle and others like her.

Because Ralph cares for Isabel and sees her potential to blossom into a sophisticated woman, he wants to do what he can to give her an advantage in life. Ralph is ill and knows that he will not live long, and therefore he persuades his dying father to leave half his estate to Isabel.

Throughout the novel, until his death at the end of the story, Ralph remains Isabel's supporter, although Isabel's insistence on marrying Gilbert causes tension and even a brief rupture in their relationship. It is significant that when Ralph is near death and asks Isabel to travel to England to see him, she does so even over her husband's objections. Isabel also admits to Ralph that she made a terrible mistake when she married Gilbert. These two actions show the closeness and loyalty that Isabel feels toward Ralph.

For his part, Ralph dies feeling that, while he hoped to benefit Isabel by securing a fortune for her, he actually brought about her ruin.

Lord Warburton

Lord Warburton is a friend of the Touchetts who falls in love with Isabel almost as soon as he meets her. He proposes to Isabel, and when she rejects him, he asks for an explanation but then accepts her decision graciously. Since Warburton is not only extremely wealthy but also considerate and kind, Isabel's rejection of him stuns everyone. Isabel's choice of Gilbert over Warburton is a clear sign of her lack of judgment.

Like Caspar Goodwood, Warburton comes to see Isabel at Gardencourt at the end of the novel and, like Goodwood, he is rejected one final time.

Themes

American versus European Character

The contrast between the American character and the European character is a theme that appears

Topics For Further Study

- Do research to learn about Americans who lived in Europe in the last quarter of the nineteenth century. Why were they there? What were their lives like? How accurately did James portray these people and the times in which they lived?

- Discuss your opinion of Isabel's decision to return to Gilbert. What do you think were her motivations for doing this? Do you think the decision was a wise one, or not? Why or why not?

- Discuss James's ideas about Americans as depicted in the novel. According to James, what traits are distinctly American? To what extent do Americans today reflect these traits? What other traits would you consider to be characteristic of today's Americans?

- Ralph thought that a large inheritance would enable Isabel to fulfill her potential and have a good life. Many people today feel the same way—that having money is the key to happiness and fulfillment. What role did Isabel's inheritance play in her life? Would she have been better off without the money? What lessons can readers draw from her experience?

- Write an epilogue for the book, telling what the rest of Isabel's life is like. What happens to her independent spirit? How do her relationships with her husband and stepdaughter evolve? How much happiness does Isabel find?

---

throughout James's work. This is not surprising, since it is a contrast he observed throughout his life as an American who spent most of his adulthood in Europe. According to James, Americans tend to be naive, energetic, practical, sincere, direct, and spontaneous, and they value the individual above society. Conversely, Europeans are sophisticated, lethargic, formal, insincere, obtuse, and scheming, and they value society above the individual.

This theme is especially interesting in *The Portrait of a Lady* because most of its characters are Americans who have been living in Europe for varying periods of time. In general, the longer an American-born character has been in Europe, the more European traits he or she has. Gilbert has lived nearly his whole life on the Continent and is completely European in character. James uses him to personify the worst manifestations of European traits. At the other end of the spectrum is Isabel, who is just arriving in Europe as the novel opens. The things that make her distinctively American, such as her energy and independent attitude, are fresh and interesting to the European characters. They are also, however, the things that lead to her downfall. By refusing to take the counsel of those who care about her, Isabel falls prey to the more sophisticated Europeans who manipulate her for their own purposes.

James does make a moral judgment about which culture produces better people; he clearly portrays the Americans as having more integrity. But he also shows that, taken as individuals, most Americans and Europeans alike have both good and bad qualities. While Isabel is almost wholly admirable and Gilbert is almost wholly despicable, the other characters are drawn in shades of gray. Henrietta is an example of an American whom James portrays less positively. Her American qualities are exaggerated so that her directness is actually rudeness. Her lack of regard for society and convention is so extreme that she offends as routinely as Isabel enchants. Lord Warburton, on the other hand, exemplifies European qualities in their most positive form. He is sophisticated and conventional, but he is also courteous, sensitive, and gracious even in defeat. Ralph is also a positive European character, a physically weak man who is nevertheless morally strong.

Social and Emotional Maturation

Isabel's social and emotional development is thrown into high relief by James's contrast of American and European natures. Yet Isabel's experiences and the wisdom she gains from them are certainly not unique to American women coming of age in European society. Isabel's naiveté is common among young women in all cultures, which is one reason why the novel remains popular. It is almost a rule that young women make poor romantic choices. In fact, they often make exactly the mistake that Isabel makes: they choose a man who is charming and seductive, yet self-centered, over one who is less worldly but more substantial and caring. This oft-repeated error of youth has been the subject of many works of literature. Perhaps the best-known is Jane Austen's *Sense and Sensibility*, which contrasts the naive Marianne and her wiser sister, Elinor.

In *The Portrait of a Lady*, James uses one theme, the contrasts between Americans and Europeans, to intensify another, more universal theme of a woman's development from naive youth to mature wisdom as she suffers the consequences of a poor romantic choice.

Style

Psychological Realism

James is considered the foremost author of psychological realism, a subcategory of American realism.

The Realist period in American literature followed Romanticism, a movement that produced stories of idealized love and that elevated emotion above reason. The harsh realities of the Civil War suddenly made Romanticism irrelevant. The year of the war's end, 1865, marks the end of the Romantic period and the beginning of American realism.

Realism got its name from the fact that its stories depicted realistic characters in believable, life-like situations. Heroes and heroines were not larger than life; they were often "just plain folks" that readers could identify with. And these characters faced problems similar to those that real people faced—neither melodramatic and overblown nor magically solved by some unexpected and incredible twist of the plot. These stories were told in straightforward, objective prose that sought to engage readers' minds more than their emotions.

James was one of the leading authors of American realism, along with Mark Twain (who is sometimes classified as a regionalist) and William Dean Howells. Some critics complained that there was nothing realistic about James's stories, in which everyone was wealthy and refined. The simple

answer is that James never pretended to write about all elements of human society. He wrote about the wealthy because it was the wealthy and their problems that he was familiar with and interested in.

In addition to limiting his subject matter to the lives of the wealthy, James also built his stories on the psychology of his characters. The stories are about what goes on inside characters' minds, how they experience and think about the things that happen to them, and how these inner experiences change them as people. The events that happen in James's stories are included not primarily for their own importance but because they shed light on the minds and personalities of the characters. *The Portrait of a Lady* is the story of Isabel's mind and how it shapes her destiny and her character. For this and other masterful tales of human psychology, James is considered the father of psychological realism.

Point of View

Modern readers are unlikely to take special notice of point of view in *The Portrait of a Lady*, but James's contemporaries did. While the point of view that James uses is common today, it was an innovation in James's time. In fact, it was an innovation to which James was an important contributor.

In most novels published before this one, the author was a prominent narrator—almost a character. In addition to telling the story, the author-narrator often inserted asides directly addressing the reader, commenting on the characters' actions, and so on. This gives fiction an artificial quality; the reader never forgets that he or she is being told a story that has been invented and shaped by the author. To put it another way, the author is always "visible" as an intermediary between the characters and the reader.

This technique of storytelling was not suitable to realism, which strove to make the story seem lifelike rather than artificial. James wanted readers to observe his characters directly and to interpret characters' actions themselves, just as they would observe people around them in life. This meant that he had to get himself as author out of the picture. So, while *The Portrait of a Lady* does have a third-person narrator, that narrator is not James and does not intrude into the story. Instead of readers learning about Isabel through a narrator's comments and interpretations, readers learn about Isabel directly by observing Isabel's actions.

James was influenced by George Eliot, who was a pioneer in minimizing the author's role in the story, but he developed the new point of view into the form that is common today.

Compare & Contrast

- **Late 1800s:** England, France, and Italy are the cultural epicenters of the Western world. England produces the best literature and drama; Italy leads in art and architecture; and French style and society are considered the height of sophistication. The United States is viewed as a sort of cultural country cousin to Europe; its arts and culture are considered far inferior to those of the Continent.

  Today: The United States is the cultural pacesetter for the world. American movies, television, music, fashions, and lifestyles are in demand and emulated, not only in Europe but around the globe.

- **Late 1800s:** Most wealthy Americans made their money in industry during the Industrial Revolution of the early 1800s. Factory owners and railroad developers are among those who have amassed huge fortunes. Many of the wealth-producing ventures are family-owned and passed down from father to son. The gap between the rich and poor is growing, as the rich get richer and the poor struggle to maintain a decent lifestyle in an economy producing more and more expensive goods.

  Today: Many of the new wealthiest Americans made their money in the high-tech boom of the late 1990s and in other businesses, such as finance, that benefited from it. Most wealth-producing companies are publicly owned, and scandal erupts in 2001 when many of these companies suddenly fail, costing stockholders billions, while top executives continue to receive multi-million-dollar salaries.

- **Late 1800s:** Women do not have the right to vote in the United States or in England. In England, voting rights have long been limited to wealthy men, but they are gradually being extended to more men.

  Today: In both the United States and Great Britain, all men and women have the right to vote.

Historical Context

Although the period known as the Enlightenment took place a century before *The Portrait of a Lady* was written, the Enlightenment is the historical period that most influences the novel's characters and its story. Isabel, especially, is a product of Enlightenment ideas.

The Enlightenment was a philosophical, political, and literary movement that swept Europe and the United States throughout the 1700s. Its major feature was the elevation of reason and scientific observation above the mysticism and superstition of the Middle Ages. All traditions and conventions, from the religious to the political and social, were reevaluated. No idea or authority was to be accepted blindly or merely because it had been accepted in the past; only those ideas that could be supported by reason or proven scientifically were considered valid.

The idea of the superiority of the intellect led to the idea that human beings were essentially good and were capable of improving and even perfecting themselves. People did not need religious dogma or political authorities to tell them how to live; they had the ability, and therefore the right, to make their own decisions. It is easy to see how such thinking led directly to an emphasis on the political and social rights of individuals.

In *The Portrait of a Lady*, Isabel and the other American characters are products of the Enlightenment whose lives show how completely these ideas were adopted in the United States and how strong their influence still was a century later. It was the big ideas of the Enlightenment that fueled the American Revolution and forever shaped what it meant to be an American. Hence, Isabel takes for granted that she should be able to make her own decisions in life and to do what she feels is best, regardless of social conventions or other people's opinions.

Enlightenment ideas actually first took shape in Europe, but they never fully took hold in England, which is home to most of the novel's European characters. The French Revolution followed the American war of independence and represented the victory of Enlightenment ideas in France. But the English monarchy, Parliament, and ruling class defended themselves against the rising tide of democracy and individualism around them. England never had a revolution. Old ideas about authority and tradition were never swept cleanly away. In the late 1800s, when *The Portrait of a Lady* was written and takes place, England was still very much a society based on wealth, class, tradition, and the supremacy of society over the individual; and it was still consolidating its rule over a vast empire of subject peoples. In stark contrast to America, England saw democracy as a radical ideology and a threat.

Characters such as Ralph and Lord Warburton find Isabel's independence and individualism captivating because Isabel is a captivating young woman who clearly is not a threat. These men, although they reflect European ideas in their own lives, find Isabel's ways refreshing—as long as they are expressed by a lovely young woman and not by an angry mob. To the darker personalities of Madame Merle and Gilbert Osmond, on the other hand, Isabel's new and different ideas make her an adversary. She is not one of them—she does not value the same things or follow the same conventions—and therefore their impulse is to set themselves against her in some way, just as their government and their society has long set itself against the ideas she represents.

Critical Overview

When *The Portrait of a Lady* was published, James was a well-known and respected author whose story *Daisy Miller* was enjoying great popularity. *The Portrait of a Lady* was widely reviewed, and most reviews, including those in the leading American publications, were positive.

Horace E. Scudder reviewed *The Portrait of a Lady* for *Atlantic*, in which the novel was serialized before its book publication. Scudder's review focuses almost exclusively on what he calls the story's "consistency," by which he means that the novel's "characters, the situations, the incidents, are all true to the law of their own being." Scudder's single complaint is that he does not like the

novel's ending. Simply put, he objects to James's sending Isabel back to Gilbert. Isabel deserves better than this, Scudder insists, and when one reads of her return to the dastardly Gilbert, "one's indignation is moved."

An anonymous review for *Harper's*, the other leading American literary magazine of the day, calls *The Portrait of a Lady* a "long and fragmentary but profoundly interesting tale."

In the *Nation*, W. C. Brownell calls the novel "an important work, the most important Mr. James has thus far written" and "his masterpiece." Brownell, too, has one complaint, though he voices it hesitantly: he thinks the story lacks excitement. He writes:

> *The Portrait of a Lady* ... is not only outside of the category of the old romance of which *Tom Jones*, for example, may stand as the type, but also dispenses with the dramatic movement and passionate interest upon which the later novelists, from Thackeray to Thomas Hardy, have relied. In a sense, and to a certain extent, Turgeneff [Turgenev] may be said to be Mr. James's master, but even a sketch or a study by Turgeneff is turbulence itself beside the elaborate placidity of these 519 pages.

Brownell then calls his complaint "ungracious" and "hypercritical," and concludes that *The Portrait of a Lady* is the best piece of realistic fiction published to date.

A long, unhappy review in the British magazine *Blackwood's*, by Margaret Oliphant, is fascinating for its litany of political and cultural objections and its paucity of comment on the book's literary merit or lack thereof. Two brief excerpts from Oliphant's review sum up her attitude. Of James, she writes:

> This gentleman's work in the world seems to be a peculiar one. It is to record and set fully before us the predominance of the great American race, and the manner in which it has overrun and conquered the Old World.

This is an interesting view of an American who chose to live his life in Europe. But Oliphant is certain in it, and describes Isabel Archer as

> the young lady who suddenly appears in the doorway of an old English country-house, inhabited like most other desirable places by American tenants ... fresh from her native country, prepared to take instant possession of her birthright as explorer, discoverer, and conqueror of the old country,—and, in fact, reducing the gentlemen who meet her into instant subjection in the course of half an hour.

The Portrait of a Lady has grown in stature in the century and a quarter since its publication. It continues to be included among James's best novels, among the greatest novels written in English,

Nicole Kidman as Isabel Archer, from the film version of Henry James' The Portrait of a Lady

and even among the greatest works in all of world literature. George Perkins writes in his *Reference Guide to American Literature* article on James, "In *The Portrait of a Lady, The Wings of the Dove, The Ambassadors*, and *The Golden Bowl*, the theme of partial perspectives (which involves often the theme of too late awareness) merges with the international theme to provide the substance of James's most lasting achievement."

The chapter on *The Portrait of a Lady* in the Twayne's United States Authors Series volume *Henry James: The Early Novels* pays high tribute to the novel while acknowledging its impact on literature to come:

> *The Portrait of a Lady* shows James in the fullness of his powers. The sheer beauty, grace, and assurance of the writing, almost startling in the opening description of Gardencourt, and sustained for five-hundred pages, reveal James at a new level of achievement as a prose stylist; and the richness of his character portraits and intensity of his engagement with his subject are of a kind that belong to history-making novels. *The Portrait of a Lady* is history-making literally. The opening account of Gardencourt, in which a densely solid actuality has begun to dissolve into psychological atmosphere, shows literary impressionism at a high stage of development. And Isabel's chapter-length meditative vigil, projected in a long, dramatic interior monologue, lays the foundations of the

stream-of-consciousness novel of Joyce, Dorothy Richardson, and Virginia Woolf.

Criticism

Candyce Norvell

Norvell is an independent educational writer who specializes in English and literature. In this essay, Norvell discusses James's descriptions of the various houses in The Portrait of a Lady *and how these descriptions function in the story.*

Every novel can be said to have an architecture in the sense of having a structure. But *The Portrait of a Lady* has an entire neighborhood of architectures. It has a minutely planned, carefully executed structure that reflects the sensibilities of its designer every bit as clearly as a great building reflects those of its architect. But, in addition, James uses houses throughout the novel to create his settings, to establish moods, to illuminate the characters who occupy them, and to foreshadow what kinds of things will happen to his main character during the time she spends in each house.

Since the novel opens in England, Isabel's childhood home in Albany, New York, is described only as a memory—a dull memory to show that

Isabel's life and her prospects were dull compared to what Europe offers her. The house is described in minimalist terms as "the old house at Albany, a large, square, double house." The room in which Isabel met Mrs. Touchett on the latter's visit is pointedly described as "the most depressed" area of the house. The place is so shabby that, at least for Isabel, it cast a shadow even over the coming of spring. The narrator describes her sitting alone in the house on a (fittingly) rainy afternoon after her father's death and feeling that the promise of spring is only a "cosmic treachery."

In short, every piece of information that James gives about the house in Albany is designed to portray Isabel's life in the United States as little better than a prison that she was fortunate to escape.

The contrast between this and her aunt and uncle's English country house could not be greater—starting with the latter's name, Gardencourt. This beautiful old estate is where Isabel makes her first appearance in the novel, and to set the stage for his heroine's entry, James describes the estate at length. The first words about the place depict perfection: "the shadows on the perfect lawn were straight and angular." James continues that the house

> stood upon a low hill, above the river—the river being the Thames some forty miles from London. A long gabled front of red brick, with the complexion of which time and weather had played all sorts of pictorial tricks, only, however, to improve and refine it, presented to the lawn its patches of ivy, its clustered chimneys, its windows smothered in creepers. . . . Privacy here reigned supreme, and the wide carpet of turf that covered the level hilltop seemed but the extension of a luxurious interior. The great still oaks and beeches flung down a shade as dense as that of velvet curtains.

When Isabel makes her entrance into this scene a few pages later, James paints her as a pretty, gracious, enchanting young woman who belongs in just this kind of setting. The reader understands immediately that Gardencourt will be like a home to her; that this is a place where her fine qualities will be appreciated and where she will be loved and protected.

The next house Isabel visits belongs to the wealthy and noble Lord Warburton. James describes his house in just the way that Isabel will come to think of its owner; it has qualities that make it seem both chivalric and staid: "as they saw it from the gardens, a stout grey pile, of the softest, deepest, most weather-fretted hue, rising from a broad, still moat, it affected the young visitor as a castle in a legend." Warburton himself is the novel's most noble character, not only in title but in character, as gallant and strong as an old castle. But a moat is a

> **Having fled a moat, Isabel has been imprisoned in a fortress."**

symbol of isolation, and isolation is the last thing Isabel wants. Though she likes Warburton, Isabel sees him as "a stout grey pile" who would bore her at best and imprison her at worst, even if he did so with only the purest and best motives—those of protecting and providing for her.

The next house that James describes in detail is the villa in Florence, Italy, that belongs to Gilbert Osmond. As with Gardencourt, James describes it thoroughly before Isabel visits, so that once again he is setting the scene into which the heroine will step and planting clues about what will befall her there. If Isabel could have read James's description of the villa, it might have dissuaded her in a way that all of her friends and relatives could not:

> The villa was a long, rather blank-looking structure, with the far-projecting roof which Tuscany loves and which, on the hills that encircle Florence . . . make so harmonious a rectangle with the straight, dark, definite cypresses that usually rise in groups of three or four beside it. The house had a front upon a little grassy, empty, rural piazza which occupied a part of the hilltop; and this front . . . had a somewhat incommunicative character. It was the mask, not the face of the house. It had heavy lids, but no eyes. . . . The windows . . . seemed less to offer communication with the world than to defy the world to look in. They were massively cross-barred.

The house's occupant, of course, also wears a mask that prevents anyone from seeing what is really inside.

Four years later, Isabel has become Gilbert's wife, and the couple are living in a house in Rome. James describes it in much more explicit and forceful terms than he does Gilbert's house in Florence, signifying that Isabel's entrapment and ruin are complete. She lives with Gilbert in

> a dark and massive structure . . . a palace by Roman measure, but a dungeon to [an onlooker's] apprehensive mind . . . a kind of domestic fortress, a pile which bore a stern old Roman name, which smelt of historic deeds, of crime and craft and violence . . . which had a row of mutilated statues and dusty urns in the wide, nobly-arched loggia overhanging the damp court where a fountain gushed out of a mossy niche.

Having fled a moat, Isabel has been imprisoned in a fortress.

Though Isabel's fate is sealed in this house, her story does not end there. When the dying Ralph calls her to come to Gardencourt to see him, she temporarily flees her Roman prison and returns to the peaceful sanctuary on the Thames. It is her true home—the place where she is loved and safe. Ralph knows this and invites her to live there permanently. Her former suitors, Caspar Goodwood and Lord Warburton, return to her there as well, each offering her a second chance at real love.

Isabel refuses them both, though, and returns to the grotesque husband in the grotesque house in Rome. But it is significant that readers do not actually see her there again. Isabel's last appearance is at green, friendly Gardencourt, which confirms what James has already conveyed about Isabel: that she will not allow the tragic mistake she has made to destroy her good nature. Though it may seem on the surface that Isabel has traded a dingy house in Albany for a fabulous dungeon in Rome, it is clear that she will find some way to transplant a measure of Gardencourt's brightness to her home and her life in Rome. It may be only a small measure, but it will be enough to sustain her, as a single candle flickering in a dark window can enliven an entire house on a foreboding night.

Source: Candyce Norvell, Critical Essay on *The Portrait of a Lady*, in *Novels for Students*, Gale, 2004.

Ned Schantz

In the following essay, Schantz explores how James renders gossip to approach indirectly the development and definition of the female characters in The Portrait of a Lady.

> " . . . gossip is charming! History is merely gossip.
> But scandal is gossip made tedious by morality."
> —Oscar Wilde

Oscar Wilde could pack a lot into a one-liner. At a stroke he invokes all that a study of gossip must account for: pleasure, morality, and the status of discourse. But his language paradoxically enacts the very discursive confusion it describes, for if gossip is charming, it remains nonetheless a dirty word, a put down; it is itself a scandal with its reckless pleasures, its unaccountability, its status as the not-quite-domesticated discourse of women. For Wilde to say that history is *merely* gossip thus wields the power of gossip as a term of diminishment even as he enlarges its scope and frees it of hypocrisy. Wilde may not, as I do, have the concerns of feminism in mind, but his rhetoric shows

how feminism might navigate the hazards of gossip for itself. Such a critical practice might soften the stigma of gossip, emphasizing the value of discredited female discourse, while at the same time turning male discourse against itself. And while a feminist account of gossip must expand Wilde's categories of charm and tediousness, they may offer more of a starting point than first appears. For it is interest, to round off Wilde's discussion, that makes our pleasure something we actively pursue, and thus something with possible moral consequences. Indeed, if we pose the problem of the novel as the problem of taking an interest in the private lives of other people, the questions we can ask are morally—and politically—fundamental: In whom should we take an interest, and how should we show that interest? What is the difference between kind attention and cruel interference? Between mercy and neglect? What are the limits of human sympathy, identification, or generosity?

Far more than his brilliant contemporary, Henry James was to pursue these questions to vast artistic effect. Moreover, in light of his own extensive critical contributions, James represents an unusual opportunity for refining the study of gossip and the novel. Begun by critics such as Homer Brown and Patricia Spacks, and carried on most memorably in studies of Jane Austen, discussions of gossip at their best have emphasized its affinities with novelistic discourse itself, making gossip and its less-than-lofty concerns into the novel's own primary, if unofficial, business. But gossip is the business of criticism too, a point which becomes most clear when James blurs the roles of author and critic, particularly in his famous prefaces to the New York Edition of his works. Only with this in mind can we continue to develop what I see as James's most important legacy, a sustained commitment perhaps best described as a cultural politics of interest. What James and feminist criticism share most of all is simply a deep preoccupation with the risks and rewards of placing female characters at the center of attention.

Despite this shared concern, it would be a mistake to imagine James as too much of a feminist prophet. Clearly problems of interest proved so generative in his work precisely because he could not resolve them. Consider the unease James articulates in the preface to *The Portrait of a Lady:*

> By what process of logical accretion was this slight "personality," the mere slim shade of an intelligent but presumptuous girl, to find itself endowed with the high attributes of a Subject?—and indeed by what thinness, at the best, would such a subject not be

vitiated? Millions of presumptuous girls, intelligent or not intelligent, daily affront their destiny, and what is it open to their destiny to *be*, at the most, that we should make an ado about it? The novel is of its very nature an "ado," an ado about something, and the larger the form it takes the greater of course the ado.

Lingering over this passage, we catch a whiff of circular logic: that she is a subject because she is presumptuous seems clear—this is why James finds her interesting. But is she not also presumptuous because she is a subject? James calls his heroine presumptuous for "affronting her destiny," when both the presumption and the destiny are of his own design, then he worries about why this should interest us. His anxiety, I would suggest, turns on the definition of the novel as a great ado, as implicitly something that must rise above trivial gossip. Indeed, to trace the word gossip through *The Portrait of a Lady* is to find a consistently pejorative usage. Moreover, it is precisely the gender of his subject that produces the anxiety: he asks of young women "what is it open to their destiny to *be*?" as if the answer to that question were self-evident for young men.

Of course James does not balk at the question. After all, he did go on to write the book—indeed, for most of the preface he seems quite proud of it. As it turns out, what is "open" to Isabel Archer to be is a sensitive and expansive consciousness. James relocates the scene of interest to the inside of her head, as in the section he calls "obviously the best thing in the book," where Isabel stays late by the fire, meditating on what has happened to her: "It is a representation simply of her motionless *seeing*, and an attempt withal to make the mere still lucidity of her act as 'interesting' as the surprise of a caravan or the identification of a pirate." Regarding this statement, Peter Brooks points out that "The terms of reference in the adventure story are mocked; yet they remain the terms of reference: moral consciousness must be an adventure, its recognition must be the stuff of a heightened drama." Moreover, how are Gilbert Osmond and Madame Merle *not* pirates, given their financial and emotional plundering of Isabel? After all, Isabel's contemplation of the novel's criminal element is what makes her consciousness such an adventure—that and James's marked reserve about this very criminality, a reserve that makes the plot of consciousness an exotic plot indeed, and which bears a special relationship to gossip.

What feels most forbidden in Jamesian discourse is that basic dimension of gossip whereby acts are named and relationships spelled out. In its place is a tantalizing discretion that extends to the most unlikely characters, so that even a "vulgar" woman

> **"** What James and feminist criticism share most of all is simply a deep preoccupation with the risks and rewards of placing female characters at the center of attention."

like Osmond's sister, the Countess, waits a long time to make Isabel aware of Osmond and Merle's prior relationship, and then only through a minor triumph of indirection, announcing "My first sister-in-law had no children." In this light, Brooks's designation of James as a special example of what he famously calls "the melodramatic imagination" seems odd at first, for the definition of melodrama Brooks unfolds seems to belie such discretion:

> The desire to express all seems a fundamental characteristic of the melodramatic mode. Nothing is spared because nothing is left unsaid; the characters stand on stage and utter the unspeakable, give voice to their deepest feelings, dramatize through their heightened and polarized words and gestures the whole lesson of their relationship.

By conventional standards, of course, there is an enormous amount left unsaid in James. But perhaps only by resisting certain kinds of utterances can James avoid obstructing what he is really after, what Brooks calls a "metaphorical approach to what cannot be said." Obstruction is a concern because, perhaps even more than other systems of knowledge, gossip forces its subject into a narrative mold that smooths out particularity. The classic gossip's line, which the Countess avoids, would be something like "Merle slept with Osmond," a statement that disguises its violence in the apparent simplicity of its "truth," and that invokes a story as powerful as it is old. But *The Portrait of a Lady* makes it clear how violent such a statement would be, both in its traumatic impact on Isabel as a listener and in its distortion of the Merle/Osmond complex. Indeed, this bald declaration risks shutting off that complex forever behind a hard wall of fact. In James, gossip is not crude because it is intrusive (who is a more intrusive writer than James?), but because it is a primitive, blunt instrument that disfigures as it causes pain.

What Do I Read Next?

- James's *The Ambassadors* (1903) provides a counterpoint to *The Portrait of a Lady*. *The Ambassadors* is considered one of the finest works from the later period of his career and James himself considered it his masterpiece. Like the earlier work, *The Ambassadors* is a psychological novel that portrays Americans in Europe, but the later work clearly shows a shift in James's attitudes toward Americans.

- James was well known as a travel writer. In 1993, the Library of America published a two-volume collection of his travel essays: *Henry James: Collected Travel Writings; Great Britain and America* and *Henry James: Collected Travel Writings; The Continent.*

- American author Edith Wharton was a friend of Henry James, and the work of the two is often compared. Wharton's *The Age of Innocence* (1920) is often recommended as a paired reading

with *The Portrait of a Lady* because the novels deal with similar subject matter and are written in a similar style, yet Wharton's is written from a distinctly female point of view.

- Isabel in *The Portrait of a Lady* can be compared with Bathsheba Everdene, the heroine of *Far from the Madding Crowd*, written by Thomas Hardy and first published in 1874. Ranked as a Victorian classic, Hardy's story of a woman farmer and her three suitors is similar in subject matter to *The Portrait of a Lady* but is written in an earlier and very different style.

- George Eliot, an early master of psychological realism, was one of James's primary literary influences. Dorothea Brooke, protagonist of Eliot's masterpiece *Middlemarch* (1871), is another character who has often been compared to Isabel Archer. Like Isabel, Dorothea marries men her family and friends do not approve of.

What James desires and goes far in developing is a kind of supergossip, a discourse that will at once heighten gossip's potential while diminishing its violence. His work plays out a critical endgame in the long history of gossip and the novel by foregrounding gossip's double aspect, a dialectic of exclusion and intimacy. *The Portrait of a Lady* in particular draws us in with the threat of scandal even as its monumental restraint promises something finer. The point, then, is to articulate what is at stake in *our* seduction as readers into a novelistic narrative contract that requires our interest. I am calling this process seduction first to call attention to how interest is actively generated and second to put into play the issue of the reader's consent as a way of gauging what violence we are submitting to, or inflicting, when we read this or other novels. These complicities of narrative have been articulated with special emphasis by Laura Mulvey in a landmark essay of feminist film theory: "Sadism demands a story, depends on making something happen, forcing a change in another person, a battle of will and

strength, victory/defeat, all occurring in a linear time with a beginning and an end." To think of narrative in terms of sadism, then, is to think of it as a violent confrontation—one in which, to follow subsequent developments in film studies, the viewer or reader can be a guilty collaborator, a masochistic victim, or both, oscillating between the two positions. Sadism is a word more often used to perk people up in their seats than to specify precise behavior or attitudes; it diverges widely in its main usage from the best purchase we can obtain on Sade's own literature. But Mulvey's provocative formulation is worth pursuing nonetheless because its pejorative rhetorical force can give us pause, arresting the slide of narrative desire into violence in ways that free our attention for new possibilities—possibilities that include both new ways of defining our interest in the heroine and ultimately new ways of imagining where her best interests could lie.

Often lost among the major surprises and disappointments of *The Portrait of a Lady* is a sense of the strangeness of the process that launches our heroine's career as an interesting woman in the first place, as, indeed, a woman who is particularly worth writing or gossiping about. Once Isabel leaves the novel's opening scenes at Gardencourt, of course, the basic question of interest has already been established and taken for granted: Isabel is interesting, we understand, because she has refused Lord Warburton's excellent offer of marriage. Thus, as her cousin Ralph puts it, we will "have the thrill of seeing what a young lady does who won't marry Lord Warburton," a thrill Ralph literally, and tragically, invests in by insuring that Isabel inherits a large chunk of his fortune. In choosing to begin his novel at a place called Gardencourt, James of course alludes to Paradise and the Fall, but we might also consider the term garden in its mundane sense. A garden is a systematically cultivated—and fully domesticated—field of interest. Ralph's problem is that he cannot plant Isabel in a garden. She will move about, develop her own interests. His "seed money" will not bring him the return he expects. For the novel, however, Ralph's investment indeed yields compound interest, multiplying Isabel's attractions. By the time she succumbs to her fatal attraction to the reptilian Osmond, we have an intriguing picture of what René Girard calls mimetic desire, in which the beloved, the object of desire, is always identified by the interest of another. Working backwards through the plot: Osmond becomes interested in Isabel because Madame Merle suggests it, saying quite directly: "'I admire her. You'll do the same.'" Madame Merle is interested in her because Ralph fueled his interest with money, which Merle wants for her daughter Pansy, and Ralph is interested in Isabel, again, because she refused Lord Warburton. This mediation of desire filters nothing; on the contrary, instead of producing friction, mimesis tends toward a lethal inflation. Osmond ultimately thinks he has a triply-interesting bride: someone to admire, someone with money, and, to get back to the apparent source of interest, "a young lady who had qualified herself to figure in his collection of choice objects by declining so noble a hand" as Lord Warburton.

But why is everyone, including, presumably, the reader, content to accept Lord Warburton as the source of interest in Isabel? What does he find so attractive in this young American that he proposes to her after spending "about twenty-six hours in her company?" Looking over the scenes at Gardencourt, all we can really say is that he finds Isabel interesting because he has been prepared to find her interesting— that is to say, his desire is mimetic as well; he is not the source after all. James gives us the finishing

touches of Warburton's preparation for love in such suggestive remarks as Mr. Touchett's that "'The ladies will save us [. . .]. Make up to a good one and marry her, and your life will become much more interesting.'" But the implication is that Lord Warburton's education began long before, in his experience as a reader of novels. When he proposes to Isabel, he fails to recognize the role novels have played in his falling in love with her "at first sight." Instead of considering their possible role as a *source* of these feelings, he accepts their counsel as merely the wise echo of a desire he imagines was born within himself. As a symptom of this misrecognition, he reserves a special triple emphasis for precisely that aspect of his belief that is most unknowable: "'I don't go off easily, but when I'm touched, it's for life. It's for life, Miss Archer, it's for life.'" Knowing this about himself in advance can only mean that it's written elsewhere, that Lord Warburton recognizes himself, though only half-consciously, among the historic cast of novelistic characters who love properly— that is, at first sight and for life. What we may have to say then, following Roland Barthes, is simply that characters are slaves to the discourse in which they find themselves, and Warburton cannot forget that he is in a novel.

As readers, though, we get to have it both ways. Thriving on the consumption of interest, we are eager to believe we've found it, despite its unaccountable source. Indeed, our assent to Warburton's proposal, the fact that we find his love for Isabel credible, testifies loudly to our own training in novelistic discourse. We may in fact experience the opening of the novel as a sort of flattering allegory of reading:

> Under certain circumstances there are few hours in life more agreeable than the hour dedicated to the ceremony known as afternoon tea. There are circumstances in which, whether you partake of the tea or not—some people of course never do—the situation is in itself delightful. Those that I have in mind in beginning to unfold this simple history offered an admirable setting to an innocent pastime. The implements of the little feast had been disposed upon the lawn of an old English country house in what I should call the perfect middle of a splendid summer afternoon.

It seems quite natural to associate the "little feast" with the novel and the "innocent pastime" with reading. The scene is remarkably cozy, launching the reader straight into the comfort-zone, the "perfect middle," of novelistic subjectivity—a position all the more precious because it obtains only, we agree, "under certain circumstances." Indeed, glancing through the rest of the first paragraph, we see the key terms of reading take their cue: leisure, pleasure, privilege—especially privilege, since, like the gangsters in *Goodfellas*, we are making a side door entrance to the show: "The front of the house overlooking that portion of lawn with which we are concerned was not the entrance-front; this was in quite another quarter. Privacy here reigned supreme, and the wide carpet of turf that covered the level hill-top seemed but the extension of a luxurious interior." What we are looking at here is the scene of a seduction—ours, as James dangles a fantasy of luxurious interiority before us, the quintessential novelistic fantasy. All that is missing is the mood music, furnished later by Madame Merle on the piano.

What is the promise of this seduction? Most simply that James is going to tell us the right story, the story we want to read. My argument is that he does not do so, indeed, that he cannot. As in all seductions, there is a bait and switch: what is received is not exactly what is promised. What he does allow us—and perhaps this is the best he can do—is a lesson in how novelistic seduction works. A substantial part of this lesson covers the mimetic desire just discussed: we would do well not to neglect our own position as the final link of the mimetic chain, accumulating interest with every cue in regard to Isabel. Indeed, the problem of committing to this position is captured in the fact that, upon her entrance to the novel at Gardencourt, Isabel is noticed first, not by any of the characters loitering on the lawn, but by the dog, emblem both of the potential idiocy of desire and of our need to believe desire is something natural, something like instinct—and our best friend.

Our seduction, however, is actually well underway before Isabel appears on the scene. The first mention of her existence takes the form of the transparently paternal prohibition that her uncle gives Lord Warburton: "'you may fall in love with whomsoever you please; but you mustn't fall in love with my niece.'" When it comes to stimulating desire, of course, prohibition is the oldest trick in the book. James couples this alluring taboo with the attractions of novelty (we've never heard of her) and absence (she is not in the scene) to amplify our curiosity. Underscoring the sense of absence are the telegrams by which, as we learn momentarily, her uncle has learned of her imminent arrival from America. Ralph explains to Warburton:

"We hardly know more about her than you; my mother has not gone into details. She chiefly communicates with us by means of telegrams, and her telegrams are rather inscrutable. They say women don't know how to write them, but my mother has thoroughly mastered the art of condensation. 'Tired America, hot weather awful, return England with niece, first steamer decent cabin.' That's the sort of message we get from her—that was the last that came. But there had been another before, which I think contained the first mention of the niece. 'Changed hotel, very bad, impudent clerk, address here. Taken sister's girl, died last year, go to Europe, two sisters quite independent.' Over that my father and I have scarcely stopped puzzling; it seems to admit of so many interpretations."

As figured here, the telegram is the mortal enemy of the novel, upsetting an equilibrium that will be reimagined but never quite restored. It opposes novelistic expansion with a technology of such "'condensation,'" as Ralph says, that it achieves a syntax without subjects. Such a menace, however, only makes us seek the novel's warm embrace all the more. Indeed, Ralph shows us how to domesticate the telegram by subjecting it to the terms of novelistic interest, generating a hermeneutic problem that will govern our pursuit of Isabel throughout the novel:

"But who's 'quite independent,' and in what sense is the term used?—that point's not yet settled. Does the expression apply more particularly to the young lady my mother has adopted, or does it characterize her sisters equally?—and is it used in a moral or in a financial sense? Does it mean that they've been left well off, or that they wish to be under no obligations? or does it simply mean that they're fond of their own way?"

The table is set for a very interesting arrival.

The final lesson in James's course on seduction has to do with the perception of linear progress. When we actually encounter Isabel she is first "a person," then "a young lady." Three pages later we learn her last name; we wait five more for her first. This striptease of withheld knowledge yielding to gradual disclosure is one that James stages with characters and events throughout the novel. It reminds us of Mulvey's basic point about sustaining narrative interest: we must have a sense that we're getting somewhere, a sense of change through linear time. What is at stake is what counts as narrative progress, and what delays and detours we are willing to tolerate—for it is perhaps in the delays and detours that a novel has some chance of escaping subsumption into the conservatism of its own institution, of refusing simple obedience to the mimetic order. What demand scrutiny are moments where James says, in effect, "but I digress," cutting short our pursuit of other interests. To guide such scrutiny, we might follow Isabel's aunt, Lydia Touchett, who, in her impatience with digression, calls our attention to the irrelevant.

Of course Lydia hardly represents the voice of the author in this novel, but in one instance, she seems to represent precisely what is, if not quite James's idea of what counts as irrelevant, at least his view of the problem of irrelevance. Her comment occurs during Isabel's travels in the middle of the novel, and comes as a response to Isabel's apology for delaying a visit. Mrs. Touchett says that apologies are "no more use to her than bubbles" and describes the idea of considering, in a given circumstance, what might have been done *differently*, as belonging "to the sphere of the irrelevant, like the idea of a future life or of the origin of things." As it seems to function in Lydia's mind, the scope of this category is astonishing: what is irrelevant, apparently, is nothing less than the past, the future, and any alternate present. I have already suggested that to ignore the origin of things, the dubious sources of desire, is particularly hazardous, as it exposes one to endless seduction. But beyond that problem, in terms of narrative, what is intimidating is the way Lydia Touchett echoes the well-established principle of the "whole story." To call the past and future of a story irrelevant is to say that the story has given us exactly what we need to know, that it is sufficient and complete, and warrants no questions out of its temporal bounds; to call an alternate present irrelevant is to say the story got things exactly right, that other versions have no interest. We might sum up the problem of irrelevance, then, by saying that it always risks making the relevant—that is, anything worth narrating—look like the inevitable.

For James, one largely irrelevant detour is this same middle section of Isabel's travels, situated between Osmond's declaration of love and their eventual engagement. James moves through this chapter extremely quickly, claiming "it is not, however, during this interval that we are closely concerned with her." But the fact that Isabel's travels include an extended tour with Madame Merle makes this a striking assertion of irrelevance, particularly in light of a recent article by Melissa Solomon that rightly identifies Merle as the novel's not-so-secret erotic center—as the original "interesting woman." By denying our "close concern," James seems to want us to believe that nothing relevant is happening between Isabel and Merle, that in her travels all Isabel really does is orbit around Osmond. Indeed, it is just this sense of Osmond's almost hypnotic control that Jane Campion develops in her recent film adaptation. Despite its stylistic extravagance, Campion's treatment of Isabel's tour with Merle seems quite faithful—perhaps too faithful—to a conviction that the tour must be mere delay or detour, since during Isabel's travels we hear Osmond's voice repeating

his declaration of love and see his disembodied lips surrealistically multiplied on a plate. If there is a difference it seems mainly that Campion's revolting "little feast" brings the underbelly of seductive offerings to light, and prepares us more for the coming sadism (though of course we're already prepared because *The Portrait of a Lady* is such a famous story and because John Malkovich usually plays libertines and villains). But as striking as Campion's sequence is when James denies the importance of this section, we still have to register the denial as defensive, as betraying a certain doubt about what Merle and Isabel are doing together and a certain anxiety that the doubled interest of their combination could steal the whole show.

There are of course hints of what we miss in James's hasty summary of their travels, which upon reconstruction begin to look like a great tragic romance. In the first place they include nothing less than the "consummation" of Merle relating her own history (with, we know, key omissions) as well as a significantly heightened mood: "the girl had these days a thousand uses for her sense of the romantic, which was more active than it had ever been." But they also contain the final touches of the novel's central crime—Merle's transferral of Isabel's affections from herself to Osmond, and here James's reticent treatment of criminality becomes a serious issue, reduced as it is to a host of dark insinuations, such that Merle exhibits "a different morality," "an occasional flash of cruelty," and a "conception of human motives [that] might, in certain lights, have been acquired at the court of some kingdom in decadence." We should recall also that James presents the beginnings of this process, as Merle prepares Isabel to meet Osmond, in summary form: "Madame Merle [. . .] it must be observed parenthetically, did not deliver herself all at once of these reflections, which are presented in a cluster for the convenience of the reader." Given this representational strategy, it is no wonder that Merle seems such a shadowy figure, operating quite specifically "behind the scenes." But whatever effect James achieves with this enforced exile—an exile belatedly literalized in Merle's banishment to America by Isabel—must be weighed against its cost. Indeed, wherever characters stray into the category of the irrelevant is a potential site of violence, a violence I'm calling sadism in the hopes of checking our participation in the rampant inflation of mimetic desires that we may not want to have in the first place. Instead we could trust Solomon's reading, which declines to follow the mimetic chain as Isabel is handed-off from Merle to Osmond.

We might say that in this section the novel turns doubly sadistic, not only because it submits its heroine to the force of the villain's gravitational field, but because it does so by sacrificing in large part what may be its own most interesting relationship. As I see it, the novel never fully recovers from this unexplored detour, as it risks submitting Isabel to the kind of circulation among men—including a masculinized reader—that Eve Sedgwick has analyzed. No matter how many scenes of revelation James stages in the second half of the novel, Isabel remains firmly lodged in Osmond's orbit.

Or does she? *The Portrait of a Lady* features what has been called "arguably the most delicately understated ending in all Victorian fiction," an ending that surprises readers all the more because James has created expectations for something downright melodramatic. Recall that within a short space Isabel has defied Osmond to see the dying Ralph in England, Ralph has died, and her original American suitor, the relentless Caspar Goodwood, has demanded that she turn to him at last. It is only at this moment that the conclusion grows subtle, as the scene with Caspar ends with the following description of Isabel's mental state: "She had not known where to turn; but she knew now. There was a very straight path." The novel ends as Henrietta informs a bewildered Caspar that Isabel has left for Rome, supposedly to return to Osmond. In its extreme restraint, James's conclusion short-circuits the flow of gossipy narrative information, questioning the reader's "right to know" and denying the certainties sought by sadistic reading.

Historically, this ending has confused and troubled some readers—that is to say, some readers did not understand what happened, while others thought they understood but didn't like it. Over time though, and with a little help from James himself in a revision, both of these concerns have waned in favor of a general consensus not only that Isabel is certainly going back to Osmond, but also that she must, or should, do so. In other words, most readers now seem to agree both about what happens at the end and that this conclusion is appropriate, if not happy. The revision to the text that promotes this consensus came as a response to a contemporary reviewer, R. H. Hutton, who read Isabel's "straight path" at the end as leading to adultery with Caspar. Here is the new end of the novel, with the revised portion italicized:

> Henrietta had come out, closing the door behind her, and now she put out her hand and grasped his arm. "Look here, Mr. Goodwood," she said; "just you wait!"

> *On which he looked up at her—but only to guess, from her face, with a revulsion, that she simply meant he was young. She stood shining at him with that cheap comfort, and it added, on the spot, thirty years to his life. She walked him away with her, however, as if she had given him now the key to patience.*

All that is indicated by the few lines that James adds is that Caspar is, at least for now, out of luck. Yet in an odd leap of logic, this revision has been interpreted as evidence that James wants readers to believe that Isabel is returning to Osmond, as if eliminating one commitment implies another. What this assumption ignores is the possibility that James was not reacting to the content of Hutton's reading at all, but to the presumption of it, to the mere fact that Hutton assumed he knew what happened next for Isabel.

I submit that what James has tried to do above all as the novel ends is to keep Isabel away from us. It is no accident that we finish the novel in the position of Caspar, chasing an Isabel who won't be caught. In fact, whether we are fans of Caspar or not, whether we identify with him or hope he wins Isabel, the conclusion remains a disappointment, because structurally we are out of the loop. To find ourselves thus excluded is to find ourselves flung out of our comfy chairs into the vast loneliness outside of gossip. From this perspective, the critical consensus we have formed around the ending looks like a compensation, enabling readings that convert disappointment into satisfaction as they convert narrative silence into critical knowledge. But in restoring the comfort of gossip, the intimacy that consensus produces, we bear some complicity with the sadistic turn the novel takes. Leaping to a clear understanding of Isabel's "straight path," we succumb to the final seduction of the novelistic, the promise of full intelligibility and the completion of linear progress at the expense of other interesting possibilities.

A closer look at the rejection of Caspar, however, reinforces the limits of this intelligibility. I would suggest that, for the reader, Caspar has never felt like a real option for Isabel. For all the apparent passion of his own desire, he is not a strongly signifying part of the mimetic chain. It is not so much that we don't like him, though James is careful to indicate some faults, as that he is not positioned as a hero. If Isabel were to end up with Caspar we would have to feel a bit cheated, as though we had read the wrong novel, because if Isabel was actually in his orbit all along, the bulk of the plot becomes a detour, slipping suddenly into irrelevance. The reason Isabel cannot marry Caspar, like the reason

Lord Warburton must fall in love with her, stems more from a law of discourse than of character. We must feel that the narrative made a difference—forced a change, as Mulvey says. It won't do to thrust our interest back on Caspar's unaccountable love that predates the beginning of the story, for then our investment of time and labor will not have mattered. Isabel understands quite early that the reason Caspar won't figure into her plot is that he belongs to a different genre: "It pleased Isabel to believe that he might have ridden, on a plunging steed, the whirl-wind of a great war." As she sees it, the courtship novel is too banal for him, and he too overpowering for it: he would fit better in an epic. Caspar comes to stand for a principle of otherness, and his pro-posals are gestures beyond the confines of the novel.

With such gestures, I would argue, James has prepared us for another, more speculative kind of leap at the novel's end, one that he could not himself take. This would be a leap, not onto any straight path, but onto a perpetual detour, one that is also located, not coincidentally, in a connection between women. My fantasy of this detour is based on the unfounded guess that Henrietta could be *lying* at the end to Caspar. What if she has finally realized that Caspar is also wrong for Isabel, and she actually has our heroine stowed away somewhere, preparing for a daring break from *all* the possessive men in her life? Such sympathetic speculation is not just our right, but our job as critical readers. So, too, did James speculate at his best, as when he writes that Isabel "would be an easy victim of scientific criticism if she were not intended to awaken on the reader's part an impulse more tender and more purely expectant."

There is no doubt, however, that this alternate ending takes us beyond James's own commentary on the novel, for in his preface, James classes Henrietta among the characters who are "but wheels to the coach." This insistence on her non-essential status, however, cannot but make us wonder what the difference is, what it would mean to think of Henrietta as more than a mere reporter, more than a wheel that propels the plot. Moreover, James's very need to explain her, and the awkwardness of his attempt to do so, betrays a telling anxiety about her place in the novel: "I have suffered Henrietta (of whom we have indubitably too much) so officiously, so strangely, so almost inexplicably, to pervade." After a long detour into other issues, the only expla-nation James can provide for this supposed excess is that Henrietta was there to amuse the reader, that she corresponded to his "wonderful notion of the lively." But why should a character who can provide amusement not also generate real interest, and

become herself a source of plot? I would suggest that, at a deep level, James senses that Henrietta *is* somehow essential, but beyond his imaginative reach. All he can do is gesture toward this plot be-yond the plot, this unimaginable horizon, as when Ralph, perhaps the novel's most authoritative char-acter, says that "'Henrietta, however, does smell of the Future—it almost knocks one down!'"

Isabel's readiness for this future is suggested in her final encounter with Pansy, at the convent where Osmond has placed her. In this scene, Isabel proposes with breathtaking boldness that Pansy come away with her, and while the possibility is quickly shut down by Pansy's hopeless subjection to her father, it is worth noting that this other plot, the plot James can't or won't let happen, is again a plot between women. At the same time, the loss of this plot means that any fantasy of a future with Henrietta will likely feel incomplete if it leaves Pansy to her plight. But is this not the most insid-ious patriarchal ploy, to trap women in personal commitments, in the very emotional ties they have come to depend on? After all, one thing Osmond makes sure of is Isabel's interest in Pansy. In fact, this interest figures as the final touch of Isabel's seduction when, after their initial weeks together, Osmond has her visit Pansy on her way out of town. However sympathetic Pansy is, she is also the fi-nal iron link in Isabel's chains of mimetic desire. There is no easy way out of this dilemma, but the best advice James can provide may come from Osmond's sister, the Countess, who tells Isabel not to worry too much about Pansy: "'Don't try to be too good. Be a little easy and natural and nasty; feel a little wicked, for the comfort of it, once in your life!'" Strangely, to resist a sadistic reading may be to license a little sadism in others, partic-ularly in female characters, the regular victims of the masculine sadism Mulvey describes. Feminism can promote this resistance by insisting that read-ers learn to take a greater interest in a female char-acter's comfort—and freedom—than some image of the good, the necessary, or the appropriate that she is made to represent, one that somehow always seems to require her massive suffering.

Source: Ned Schantz, "Jamesian Gossip and the Seductive Politics of Interest," in *Henry James Review*, Vol. 22, No. 1, Winter 2001, pp. 10–23.

Jean Frantz Blackall

In the following essay, Blackall discusses how the elements of James' novel both embody classic Victorian ideals and set the stage for the classic elements of novels of the early twentieth century.

> " ... Isabel sits by the fire pondering what her husband has asked of her this evening, examining her marriage. ... Such a passage is nearer to the late James in point of view and figurative language, and anticipates the 20th-century psychological novel which his own subtler experimentation fostered at the turn of the century."

The Portrait of a Lady is the culminating work of Henry James's early period, a quintessential Victorian novel that yet adumbrates those particular qualities, architectonic and narrative, that James contributed to the development of the 20th-century novel.

The reader can perceive the older and newer impulses at work by comparing chapters 6 and 42. In chapter 6 a confidential narrator offers an analytic verbal portrait of Isabel Archer, enjoining the reader's indulgence and sympathy for a young heroine in whom theories may take the place of knowledge of the world, whose self-esteem may cause her to believe too much in her own opinion, and whose idealism and innocence may lead her into complexities she little anticipates. In short, "her errors and delusions were frequently such as a biographer interested in preserving the dignity of his subject must shrink from specifying." Not only the narrative manner in such a passage, but also James's theme, is Victorian, the marriage market and the relationship of money to marital options. Will money bring Isabel freedom of choice or make her an object of social predators? What effect has money upon her own imagination? In chapter 42, which James notes in his retrospective Preface as "obviously the best thing in the book," Isabel sits by the fire pondering what her husband has asked of her this evening, examining her marriage: "It was very well to undertake to give him a proof of loyalty; the real fact was that the knowledge of his expecting a thing raised a presumption against it. It was as if he had had the evil eye; as if his presence were a blight and his favor a misfortune. Was the fault in himself or only in the deep mistrust she had conceived for him? This mistrust was now the clearest result of their short married life; a gulf had opened between them over which they looked at each other with eyes that were on either side a declaration of the deception suffered." Here the action has moved inward, the point of view focused in the heroine's own consciousness, and the range of vision narrowed to what she herself can see and interpret. Question replaces answer, metaphor supersedes explicit statement, as Isabel searches for the similitude that will convey her intuitions and feelings. Such a passage is nearer to the late James in point of view and figurative language, and anticipates the 20th-century psychological novel which his own subtler experimentation fostered at the turn of the century.

The carefully crafted structure also looks to the later James. In his celebrated Preface to *The Portrait of a Lady*, written for the definitive New York Edition of his works, James has much to say about the architectonics of his novel, how he laid it brick by brick, building it outward from the initial perception of the character of Isabel Archer by devising those relations with other characters and those settings which would best reveal his heroine. "Such is the aspect that to-day *The Portrait* wears for me: a structure reared with an 'architectural' competence ... that makes it, to the author's own sense, the most proportioned of all my productions after *The Ambassadors*."

The Portrait of a Lady is also the crowning work, from his early period, in James's development of his theme of international contrast. Its plot is very simple and has been recognized as that of a fairy tale, in which the heroine must choose among three suitors; her fortunes must depend thereafter upon the wisdom of her choice. The first two suitors, Caspar Goodwood, an American businessman, and Lord Warburton, an English aristocrat, manifest national as well as personal characteristics, the dangers of ruthless self-assertiveness and of hereditary forms and obligations. Isabel's chosen suitor, Gilbert Osmond, is an American living abroad, who has absorbed effete and corrupt aspects of European civilization together with European aestheticism and sophistication. He becomes the principal foil for Isabel's new-world virtues of enthusiasm, innocence, and aspiration. Secondary characters, Mme. Merle, who betrays Isabel into this marriage, and Henrietta Stackpole, who remains her friend despite it, define similar polarities. Isabel's fate is left in the balance at the end. Having chosen wrongly, will she desert her husband or slavishly perpetuate the form of an empty marriage? Will she live by the memory of her deceased cousin Ralph Touchett, whom she now perceives as beloved? Or for the sake of her stepdaughter Pansy Osmond, to preclude a similar fate for her?

"The obvious criticism," James wrote in his *Notebooks*, "will be that it is not finished—that I have not seen the heroine to the end of her situation . . . . That is both true and false. The *whole* is never told; you can only take what groups together." Here again James analyzes his own salient qualities, his concern with form and the characteristic open-endedness of his fictions.

Source: Jean Frantz Blackall, "*The Portrait of a Lady*: Novel by Henry James, 1881," in *Reference Guide to American Literature*, 4th ed., edited by Thomas Riggs, St. James Press, 2000, pp. 1040–41.

Sources

Brownell, W. C., Review of *The Portrait of a Lady*, in the *Nation*, Vol. 34, February 2, 1882, pp. 102–03.

Gale, Robert L., "Henry James," in *Dictionary of Literary Biography*, Vol. 12, *American Realists and Naturalists*, Gale Research, 1982, pp. 297–326.

James, Henry, *The Portrait of a Lady*, edited by Robert D. Bamberg, W. W. Norton, 1975.

Oliphant, Margaret, Review of *The Portrait of a Lady*, in *Blackwood's Edinburgh Magazine*, Vol. 131, March 1882, pp. 374–83.

Perkins, George, "James, Henry," in *Reference Guide to American Literature*, 3d ed., edited by Jim Kamp, St. James Press, 1994.

"*The Portrait of a Lady*: The Caging of the Beautiful Striver," in *Henry James: The Early Novels*, Twayne's United States Authors Series, 1999.

Review of *The Portrait of a Lady*, in *Harper's*, Vol. 64, February 1882, p. 474.

Scudder, Horace E., Review of *The Portrait of a Lady*, in the *Atlantic Monthly*, Vol. 49, January 1882, pp. 127–28.

Further Reading

Anesko, Michael, ed., *Letters, Fictions, Lives: Henry James and William Dean Howells*, Oxford University Press, 1997.
    This selection of correspondence between James and Howells, two of the luminaries of American realism, provides insight into how both authors worked.

Bloom, Harold, ed., *Henry James's "The Portrait of a Lady"*, Chelsea House, 1987.
    Respected critic Bloom gathered criticism and essays from an array of James scholars for this volume.

Edel, Leon, "The Myth of America in *The Portrait of a Lady*," in the *Henry James Review*, Vol. 7, 1986, pp. 8–17.
    This scholarly journal is wholly devoted to James and his work, and volume seven contains several articles on *The Portrait of a Lady*. Edel, a James scholar, analyzes James's rendering of the United States in the novel.

James, Henry, *Henry James: Autobiography*, Criterion Books, 1956.
    This edition brings together all three volumes of James's autobiography: *A Small Boy and Others*, originally published in 1913; *Notes of a Son and Brother*, 1914; and *The Middle Years*, 1917.

Skrupskelis, Ignas K., and Elizabeth M. Berkeley, eds., *William and Henry James: Selected Letters*, University Press of Virginia, 1997.
    The editors have collected some of the private correspondence of the two famous brothers, William, the philosopher, and Henry, the writer.

Tender Is the Night

F. Scott Fitzgerald

1934

Published in 1934 by New York-based publisher Charles Scribner's Sons, *Tender Is the Night* is one of F. Scott Fitzgerald's last works. Although the novel was generally well received and has come to be regarded as one of Fitzgerald's most important works, it was less popular at its publication than his previous novels and was considered a commercial failure. More autobiographical than his other works, *Tender Is the Night* tells the story of American psychologist Dick Diver and his wife, the wealthy but psychologically unstable Nicole. Set largely in the small French coastal town of Tarmes between the years 1925 and 1935, the book portrays a cast of characters typical of Fitzgerald's fictional universe: wealthy, idle, sophisticated, and, in many ways, "troubled."

Tender Is the Night was written in a period of Fitzgerald's life when his wife, Zelda, was experiencing severe psychological problems, not unlike those of Nicole Diver. In the years following the book's publication, Fitzgerald's output diminished considerably due largely to his alcoholism. In 1940, with Zelda institutionalized, he died alone of a heart attack in Los Angeles, a death largely viewed in literary circles as a pitiful conclusion to what was once a promising life.

Like many of Fitzgerald's other books, *Tender Is the Night* focuses on the themes of wealth and the corruption it brings to people's lives. Set in Europe during the interwar years, the book also addresses themes particular to European history and politics, such as the effect wealthy Americans had on Europe

and the ascent of capitalism on the continent. Largely drawn on his own experiences with the mental health industry, *Tender Is the Night* also addresses issues of mental illness and psychiatry. Finally, with a cast of female characters who are largely portrayed as controlling, manipulative, and ultimately stifling to Diver's intellectual development, Fitzgerald may be remarking unfavorably on the role that women, particularly Zelda, had in his own life and career.

Author Biography

Francis Scott Key Fitzgerald, or F. Scott Fitzgerald, is considered one of the most important American writers of the twentieth century, particularly of the 1920s era known as the "Jazz Age." The debauchery of his characters' lives and their obsession with material wealth echoed the indulgent and tumultuous life he led with his wife, Zelda, and their group of expatriate friends.

Fitzgerald was born in St. Paul, Minnesota, on September 24, 1896, to Edward Fitzgerald and Mary McQuillan Fitzgerald, both of whom were middle-class Catholics. He attended various private schools and entered Princeton in 1913, where he neglected his studies and concentrated on extracurricular writing for various literary journals and theatrical groups.

After being put on academic probation in 1917, Fitzgerald left Princeton to join the army. In 1918, he was stationed in Montgomery, Alabama, where he met and fell in love with Zelda Sayre, daughter of a state supreme court judge and one of the most celebrated debutantes of the town, notorious for her fiery spirit and unpredictable escapades. The couple wed in 1920, the same year that his first novel, *This Side of Paradise*, was published by Charles Scribner's Sons to great financial success.

The Fitzgeralds moved to New York City, where Scott worked as a writer for various magazines, most notably the *Saturday Evening Post*. They quickly became known for their wild, indulgent lifestyle, spending money faster than they earned it in order to keep up the extravagance they quickly came to enjoy.

Fitzgerald completed his second novel, *The Beautiful and the Damned*, in 1921. Later that year their only daughter, Frances Scott, was born. After her birth, the family would constantly be on the move between various cities in the States and Europe.

Fitzgerald completed perhaps his most popular work, *The Great Gatsby*, in 1925, but his reputation

F. Scott Fitzgerald

for drinking and partying kept the literary establishment from taking his novel writing seriously. The couple's extravagant lifestyle, in both the United States and in Europe, also took its toll. He constantly interrupted his novels for the less serious but more financially rewarding popular short stories. Increasing tension with Zelda also affected his writing as well as their marriage. Quarrels were brought about by Fitzgerald's excessive drinking and were exacerbated by Zelda's penchant for theatrics and growing mental instability. Zelda had her first mental breakdown in 1930 and would be in and out of mental hospitals for the rest of her life.

Tender Is the Night, though today considered one of his most accomplished works, took several years to complete and was published in 1934 to what Fitzgerald considered commercial failure. Fitzgerald soon thereafter lapsed into a depression of drunkenness and increasing debt. In 1937, he moved to Hollywood, California, where he took a lucrative job as a scriptwriter. However, his skills in screenwriting proved inadequate. He died in Hollywood from a sudden heart attack on December 21, 1940. His uncompleted novel, *The Last Tycoon*, was published in 1941. Zelda was killed eight years later in a hospital fire.

Although at the time of his death Fitzgerald was not considered a major literary figure, a renewed interest in his work developed in the 1950s, which propelled him into a place among the most important American writers, a place he retains to the early 2000s.

Plot Summary

Book 1

Tender Is the Night opens in 1925 at the Gausse's Hotel in the French coastal town of Tarmes. Although narrated in the third person, the early chapters of the novel are told through the eyes of the seventeen-year-old actress Rosemary Hoyt. While visiting Tarmes with her mother, Mrs. Elsie Speers, she meets several Americans who are vacationing at the resort, including Dick Diver, a married man twice her age. She immediately falls in love with him and proclaims that love to her mother, who actively encourages her daughter to pursue Diver. Thus the stage is set for the affair that ultimately fuels the novel's tension.

Later that evening, Rosemary is invited to a party at the Divers.' During the party, Mrs. McKisco becomes privy to a scene in the bathroom between Dick and Nicole that hints at some kind of serious problem. After the party, a discussion between Albert McKisco and Tommy Barban about that incident turns ugly, with Barban defending the honor of the Divers, and the two men agree to a duel. Although the men do not harm one another, the duel highlights the passions they have for the Divers and the couple's status with their friends.

Rosemary joins the group as they venture to Paris the next day. While in Paris, Rosemary confesses her love to Dick. Although Rosemary begs Dick to have sex with her, Dick refuses, and their relationship remains largely platonic, though their feelings for one another continue to grow.

In Paris, Abe North gets particularly drunk during one evening, and the next morning, while the group is waiting for a train to take North out of the city, a woman whom Nicole knows shoots an Englishman, a foreshadowing of the violence that is about to enter into the Divers' lives.

On the morning following the shooting, Nicole is awakened by a man who is looking for North, and later she receives a call asking more questions about him. As far as Nicole knows, North is gone. However, unbeknownst to everyone, North has decided not to leave Paris and is spending the day drinking heavily in a bar. It turns out that North has been in-

volved in an exchange of money with a black man the night before, and as a result another black man has been wrongly accused of some related wrongdoing. North is too drunk to understand, so he returns to the Divers' hotel with Jules Peterson, one of the black men in question, to try to sort things out. Dick is in Rosemary's room making out with her when Abe knocks on the door. Dick takes North and Peterson back to his room and convinces North to leave for America right away to avoid problems. After Abe leaves, Rosemary returns to her room only to find Mr. Peterson lying dead on her bed, having just been shot.

Dick quickly removes all evidence of the dead man from Rosemary's room, thus ensuring that she will remain free of controversy, and as Book One closes, Rosemary becomes privy to a scene between Dick and his hysterical wife, and she understands what Mrs. McKisco has experienced back at the villa.

Book 2

Book Two opens by flashing back to 1917. Dick is a twenty-six-year-old practitioner of psychiatry who has come to Zurich to study with Dr. Franz Gregorovius. Shortly after arriving at Zurich, he is ordered to serve at a clinic in France where he engages in a correspondence with the young Nicole Warren, a patient in Zurich whom he has met briefly.

When the war ends, Diver returns to the Zurich clinic, and in the course of his discussions with Gregorovius, Nicole's story emerges.

Gregorovius has been approached by Devereax Warren, a wealthy American whose eighteen-year-old daughter, Nicole, has been experiencing bizarre "fits" and was having delusions about total strangers sexually abusing her. Nicole has just lost her mother and brother, and under closer scrutiny, Warren admits to having had sexual relationships with his daughter. Gregorovius agrees to treat the young woman as long as the father agrees to stay away from her for at least five years.

Although Gregorovius admits that Dick's letters to Nicole seem to have facilitated her recovery, he expresses his concerns to Dick about Dick's growing fondness for the patient. For several months thereafter, Dick remains distant from Nicole and invests his energies in a book he is writing. However, during a break in his writing, he visits the Alps where he runs into Nicole and her sister, Baby Warren. At a restaurant that night, Baby explains how she is planning to bring Nicole back to Chicago where she hopes to "buy" a doctor to marry and take care of Nicole. In the meantime, Nicole has wandered from the table, and when Dick finds her, Nicole kisses him. Dick is

Media Adaptations

- In 1955, *Tender Is the Night* was adapted as an hour-long television special, starring Mercedes McCambridge as Nicole Diver. In 1962, the novel was adapted as a Hollywood film by Henry King. Produced by Twentieth Century Fox Studios, the film stars Jennifer Jones, Jason Robards, Jr., Joan Fontaine, Tom Ewell, and Jill St. John and is available on video. A 1985 three-hour miniseries adaptation, starring Peter Strauss, Edward Asner, and Sean Young was directed by Robert Knight.

- A ten-cassette, unabridged reading of the novel was produced by Sterling Audio out of Thorndike, Maine.

- Of related interest, "Last Call: The Final Chapter of F. Scott Fitzgerald," starring Jeremy Irons and Sissy Spacek, was released as a Showtime Original Picture in 2003 and is available on video. This video depicts the last few months of Fiztgerald's life.

later cajoled into taking Nicole back to Zurich with him, and within a few months they are married.

The young couple quickly grows to enjoy the luxury of Nicole's money, and for awhile everything seems perfect. By now the book has moved forward to 1925 again. Through his burgeoning but still unconsummated relationship with Rosemary, Dick has come to realize that he no longer loves Nicole. He also realizes that since his marriage, he has spent little time on his writing or career.

Gregorovius arrives on the scene to tell Dick that there is a psychiatric clinic available in Zurich. Coincidentally, Baby and Nicole have just come into more than enough money for Dick to purchase the clinic. Despite his early protestations, Dick agrees to take Nicole's money and enters into practice with his former mentor.

Things quickly begin to go bad at the clinic, however. Dick feels owned by his wife and Baby, and Nicole, in return, feels deprived because Dick is spending so much time at work. A former patient accuses him of seducing her daughter, an accusation not entirely without merit. Nicole reacts angrily and makes a scene at a local fair where they have taken the children. On the way home from the fair, Nicole grabs the steering wheel, forcing the car off the road and nearly killing her family.

Dick takes time off from his marriage and the clinic and goes to Munich where he runs into Barban, who has just rescued a Russian prince. Barban informs Dick that Abe has just been beaten

to death in a speakeasy in New York. Saddened, Dick wanders to his hotel alone where he finds a telegram from Nicole informing him of his father's death in America. Guilt-ridden, Dick returns to Virginia to see his father buried.

On his return to Europe, Dick lands in Italy hoping to find Rosemary in Rome where she is at work on a new movie. After meeting her in her hotel room, they kiss passionately and make arrangements to meet again; at this second meeting, their relationship is finally consummated. Unfortunately, Dick does not feel the joy he thought the act would bring.

After meeting a few more times, Dick realizes that Rosemary no longer idolizes him and may in fact be in love with another man. Ignoring a note from Rosemary asking him to return to her room, Dick proceeds to get drunk with Collis Clay, a young Yale graduate and acquaintance of Rosemary. At a cabaret, Dick picks a fight with the orchestra leader and later fights with a cabdriver and is taken into police custody where he punches a man who turns out to be a detective. From prison, Dick must call Baby Warren to rescue him.

Bruised, battered, and well on his way to becoming a lonely drunk, Dick is sedated at the end of Book Two by a doctor as Baby smugly watches over him.

Book 3

When Dick returns to the clinic, he lies to Nicole about his bruises and quickly re-immerses himself in his work. He becomes attached to a woman painter who is struggling with a skin disease, and when she unexpectedly dies, he becomes so distraught that Gregorovius must send him away. He goes to Laussane to meet a prospective patient, and after interviewing the patient, Dick learns that Nicole's father is dying nearby of a liver failure caused by his drinking. Warren's doctor tells Dick that Warren wants to see his daughter one more time before he dies.

Through a series of botched communications, the news of her father's sickness mistakenly reaches Nicole, who immediately rushes to Laussane to be with her father. However, by the time Nicole arrives, the father has left the hospital on his own. The couple returns to the clinic, and soon thereafter a patient complains of liquor on Dick's breath. Dick and Gregorovius decide that it is best for Dick to leave the clinic, and Gregorovius makes arrangements to buy Dick out of his stake in the clinic.

Dick and his family travel through Europe and eventually return to the villa where several incidents take place that further highlight Dick's decline. For instance, Dick accuses a cook of stealing wine, but when the cook retaliates by calling him a drunk, the Divers must pay the woman off to get rid of her. On board T. F. Golding's yacht during a party to which Dick had invited himself and Nicole, he insults Lady Caroline Sibly-Biers, and the host of the party must step in to save the situation. On the deck of the yacht, Nicole tries to talk to Dick, but Dick interjects by accusing her of ruining him, and he grabs both of her wrists and suggests that they end it all right then and there by jumping overboard. This is the last straw for Nicole.

Later in the week, when Nicole and Dick go down to the beach together to look for their children, they notice Rosemary swimming. Dick swims out to show off for Rosemary, and in one of the book's most pathetic scenes, he tries several times to perform a stunt by lifting a man on his shoulders while waterskiing. Rosemary watches him make a fool of himself, an act that spells the definitive end of her infatuation with him. On the beach, an interaction with Rosemary forces Nicole to walk away from her husband definitively, and she sets off to seduce Barban, whom she had met again at the party on the yacht, with a letter.

The next day, while Dick is off following Rosemary to Provence, Nicole and Barban make love at a nearby hotel. The next day, Barban confronts Dick about Nicole, and the three of them go to a café where Barban declares that Nicole loves him and wants a divorce. Without arguing, Dick quietly agrees and simply walks away.

After spending a day with the children, Dick leaves Nicole a note, makes a final gesture of farewell to the beach, and leaves for America. He tries to settle down in upstate New York, near his boyhood home, but scandals and questionable situations shadow him wherever he goes. After moving from one small town to another, he quietly disappears.

Characters

Tommy Barban

Half-American, half-European, Tommy Barban is a mercenary soldier with few refined qualities. Without the social or cultural sophistication of the Divers or their other friends, Barban relies on his decisiveness and self-confidence to get by. Barban is introduced as one of Dick and Nicole Divers' devout friends. In fact, early on, Barban even fights a duel to defend the honor of the Divers. As the plot develops, however, it becomes clear that Barban loves Nicole, and by the end of novel he has successfully taken her away from Dick. He is portrayed by Fitzgerald as a man who knows what he wants, and when it comes time to take Nicole, he does so decisively and without qualms.

Luis Campion

Luis Campion is the effeminate friend of the McKiscos who informs Rosemary Hoyt, at 3 a.m., of the duel that is about to take place between Albert McKisco and Tommy Barbaran.

Prince Chillicheff

A character noted only in passing, Prince Chillicheff is the Russian prince whom Tommy Barban rescues from Russia.

Collis Clay

Collis Clay is a young graduate of Yale and an acquaintance of Rosemary. He tells Dick stories about Rosemary's past, which sends Dick into fits of sexual jealousy. Clay is also with Dick the night Dick gets drunk and ends up in prison.

Dick Diver

The protagonist of the novel, Dick Diver is a complex, handsome, and brilliant up-and-coming young psychiatrist when he is first introduced. A Rhodes scholar from America who is in Europe to study with the great psychiatrists of the time, he is introduced to Nicole Warren, a wealthy woman and one of the clinic's patients, by Dr. Dohmler, one of his colleagues at the Zurich clinic, which he has just joined. Dick treats Nicole, and when she shows signs of recovery, against the advice of Dohmler he marries her. It is the marriage of Dick and Nicole around which *Tender Is the Night* revolves. Although Dick must contend with Nicole's schizophrenia, for a while the Divers are happily married and gain a reputation for the parties they give and the social set that follows them around. Nicole's wealth affords the couple a luxury and comfort that Dick himself could never have attained. Over time, however, Dick begins to feel trapped in the relationship, and he becomes attracted to other women. In particular, he impetuously falls in love with the young and talented movie star Rosemary Hoyt. It is with Hoyt that Dick has a long-standing relationship that is fully consummated years after they meet. As one of the more complex characters of the novel, Dick allows his amours and his self-indulgence to get the better of him. Although he eventually comes to the realization that Rosemary is too young and immature for him, by this time alcohol has taken its toll, and Dick's career has been ruined and his marriage has been destroyed. Utterly alone, he returns to America and gradually disappears somewhere in upstate New York, far from the Europe that has indulged his fancy for years.

Although he is a psychiatrist and not a writer, Dick is seen as a fictional projection of Fitzgerald himself. Like Fitzgerald, Dick is a rising star in his field at a young age, and like Fitzgerald, who married the psychologically troubled Zelda Sayre, Dick marries the schizophrenically-inclined Nicole Driver. And finally, like his creator, Dick becomes a serious alcoholic and watches his vast talents waste away until he himself disappears.

Lanier Diver

Lanier Diver is Dick and Nicole's son. He plays a minor role in the novel.

Nicole Diver

Nicole Diver, born Nicole Warren, is the daughter of the wealthy Chicago magnate Devereux Warren. Barely eighteen years of age when she is introduced to Dick Diver, one of the clinic's new practitioners, she has been diagnosed at the Zurich clinic where she is a patient as "tending towards schizophrenic." One of the sources of her illness is the sexual abuse she experienced at the hands of her father shortly after her mother's death, a theme that

is played out throughout the novel. Despite her illness, she grows to fall in love with Dick, marries him, and has two children. It is with her wealth that she and Dick come to be regarded as one of Europe's most beautiful and sophisticated couples. Despite the air of cultural sophistication she projects, Nicole is portrayed as a weak and pathetic character. Throughout her life she has been at the complete mercy of other people. First it is her father, who sexually abuses her and sends her off to live in a European clinic; then Dr. Gregorovius and Dick, who treats her for her psychological problems; and throughout her recovery, her sister, Baby Warren, who controls her finances. At the end of the novel, when Dick's affairs and drinking have become too much for Nicole to live with, she is "rescued" by Tommy Barban, with whom she has an affair and marries.

In many ways, Nicole is the fictional representation of Zelda Sayre, Fitzgerald's wife. Sayre, the daughter of an Alabaman judge, suffered from years of psychological problems during her marriage to Fitzgerald, which is seen by many to be one of the causes of the writer's declining writing abilities, his financial problems, and his severe drinking.

Topsy Diver

Topsy is Dick and Nicole's daughter, about whom very little is written.

Dr. Dohmler

Dr. Dohmler is the psychologist who initially handles Nicole's case at the Zurich clinic that Dick first joins. It is Dohlmer who urges Dick to terminate his relationship with Nicole.

T. F. Golding

T. F. Golding owns a yacht that is moored near the Divers' villa. He is hosting the party on his yacht to which Dick invites himself and Nicole to shortly after their return from Zurich.

Dr. Franz Gregorovius

Dr. Gregory Gregorovius is a German psychologist and one of Dick's colleagues. With Nicole's money, Dick opens up a clinic with Gregorovius, but when Dick begins to lose control of his drinking and patients begin to complain, Gregorovius buys the clinic from him.

Rosemary Hoyt

Rosemary Hoyt is the successful seventeen-year-old film actress with whom Dick Diver has an affair. Only seventeen when she first meets the Divers, she is vacationing with her mother and taking a break from just having starred in the Hollywood hit *Daddy's Girl*. It is Rosemary who immediately falls for Dick, and it is her mother who urges her to follow through on her feelings. Although she maintains a cordial and even respectful relationship with Nicole during her affair with Dick, she is, in the end, the primary reason for the dissolution of Dick and Nicole's marriage.

Controlled by a domineering and amoral mother, Rosemary is portrayed as a polite, naïve young woman who is clearly a virgin when she first meets the Divers, but several years later, when Dick follows her to Italy during the shooting of a new film, it is clear that she has lost much of that innocence. It is in Italy that her relationship with Dick is willingly consummated. Dick eventually admits to himself that she is too young and immature for him, and Rosemary likewise realizes that she no longer has any interest in Dick.

Albert McKisco

Albert McKisco fancies himself as an American intellectual and writer, when the book opens. Following a duel with Tommy Barban, he actually grows to become a highly successful novelist in America.

Violet McKisco

Violet McKisco is the social-climbing, obnoxious wife of Albert McKisco. She is constantly described as clinging to her husband and praising his intellect and writing abilities.

Conte di Minghetti

Conte di Minghetti marries Mary North following Abe North's death.

Abe North

Abe North is a close friend of Dick Diver and is described as once having been a brilliant musician, although there is some disagreement among Diver's friends as to that description. A severe alcoholic, he often drinks himself into oblivion and finds himself immersed in troubles of his own doing. He is eventually killed in a fight in a speakeasy.

Mary North

Mary North is Abe North's wife, who helplessly watches Abe drink his life away. After Abe is killed in the bar fight, Mary marries the wealthy Conte di Minghetti.

Jules Peterson

Jules Peterson, a black man, is one of the victims of Abe North's drinking. Under mysterious circumstances, he is found dead in Rosemary's hotel room—a death that is attributed to events surrounding North's drinking the night before.

Lady Caroline Sibly-Biers

Lady Caroline is a thin, petite, good-looking British woman whom Dick meets on Golding's yacht and proceeds to insult. Later, Dick rescues Lady Caroline, along with Mary di Minghetti, from prison for picking up a woman while impersonating a man.

Mrs. Elsie Speers

Mrs. Elsie Speers is the mother and business agent of her daughter, Rosemary hoyt. After her second husband's death, she put all of her savings into Rosemary's career, and she sees herself not only as Rosemary's mother but also as her friend and business agent. It is she who prods Rosemary to pursue a relationship with the married Dick Driver. Speers's purpose in life is to provide her daughter with the support needed to become an emotionally and financially independent woman, experienced in the ways of the world—no matter the cost to the people around her.

Maria Wallis

Maria Wallis snubs Nicole at the train station just before she kills an American woman with a revolver.

Baby Warren

One of the more coldhearted and manipulative women in *Tender Is the Night* is Nicole Diver's older sister, Baby Warren. A spinster who lives in England, she is a true snob who makes it known at every available opportunity that she believes the English represent the finest the world has to offer. She is a woman who literally retreats from human touch. Baby Warren is in charge of her family's vast resources, and she uses that money to make certain that Nicole is taken care of. At one point she suggests to Dick Diver that she buy a Chicago doctor for Nicole to marry, and it is through her manipulation that Dick and Nicole travel alone together—a trip that leads to the couple's marriage. Baby Warren also knows that she holds the purse strings Dick needs to continue his lifestyle, and although she does not necessarily approve of Dick's marriage to Nicole, she ultimately wants what is best for her sister, and she is willing and very able to use Dick to those ends.

Devereux Warren

Devereux Warren is the wealthy Midwestern businessman who loses his wife and sexually abuses his daughter, Nicole. An alcoholic himself, he places Nicole into the Zurich mental clinic before returning to America. Fitzgerald portrays him as a weak and vile man.

Themes

Alcoholism

Alcohol came to play a leading role in F. Scott Fitzgerald's life. During his wife's emotional decline, he drank excessively, and though he technically died of a heart attack, there is no question that his lifestyle and his abuse of alcohol played a contributing role in his death. Likewise, alcohol came to rule and ruin Dick Diver. When we first meet Diver, he is a happy-go-lucky bon vivant, always reaching for a drink but never in excess. By the novel's conclusion, however, alcohol has helped to ruin his marriage and his career.

Dick Diver, however, is not the only character affected by drinking. Nearly everyone in the book drinks to varying degrees of excess, and Abe North is eventually killed because of his drinking. Fitzgerald is preoccupied in *Tender Is the Night* with the effects alcohol has on his characters and their careers.

Art

Although there are only a few characters who could be classified as artists in *Tender Is the Night*, Fitzgerald treats their characters with more respect than he does the others. Albert McKisco, for instance, is portrayed early on as an aspiring writer, but years later when Diver meets him on the ship coming back from America, he has emerged as a successful author and is a much more pleasant person to accompany. At the clinic that he runs with Dr. Gregorovius, Diver became intensely affected by the death of a woman painter—the one case he seems to have truly cared about.

European Capitalism

Following World War I, as Europe rebuilt its economy, there was great weight placed on attracting wealthy Americans to the continent. However, with that wealth came the stereotype of the "ugly American"—loud, brash, unsophisticated, and entirely self-centered.

Fitzgerald, who spent much of his adult life in Europe, saw the effects Americans had on European culture firsthand, and *Tender Is the Night* portrays some of those effects. In the process of courting money to help establish the burgeoning capitalist structures, Europeans were forced to compromise a great deal of their culture and in the process lost a fair amount of the identity that had always set them apart from America and the rest of the world.

Class Structure

Fitzgerald's world is a upper-class world, replete with servants, personal attendants, and all the formalities that great wealth affords. Nicole Diver, by virtue of her birth, has been given a handsome allowance by her sister, the executor of her family's money, and as a result she and Dick Diver are never without the luxurious decorations money brings. Their positions in society are never questioned, and discussions among friends often fall to the topic of pedigree. Baby Diver, for instance, interviews Dick on his family and wealth before he marries Nicole, and when she delivers Dick from jail, she continually reminds the police of who she and, by extension, Dick are. Abe North, in the oblivion of drink, falls to the depths of the lower classes where he dies, and even Dick Diver, once alcohol gets the best of him, falls into the oblivion of small-town America, far removed from the upper classes of his European life.

Family

Although Dick and Nicole Diver have two children, very little is made of them until problems in the marriage or other relationships occur. At the scene at the fair, following the disclosure that Dick was being accused of harassment by a patient, the children are left with a gypsy woman, and after the car accident, they are whisked off to the inn. In one of the few times a character directly addresses one of the children, Rosemary asks Topsy if she would like to be an actress, a question that causes Nicole to storm away. Only after he decides to leave Nicole, does Dick spend time with the children, but shortly following his exile to upstate New York, he stops corresponding even with them.

At the clinic, Dick is asked to interview a young man who is about to be disowned by his father because of his homosexuality. Nicole's family background involves incest. Even Rosemary and her mother, the other major example of a family in the book, are as much friends and business partners as they are mother and daughter to one another. Dick's relationship with his own father amounts to years of no communication and then, suddenly, news of the father's death.

In short, *Tender Is the Night* does not reflect well on the family structure; Fitzgerald has little to

Topics For Further Study

- F. Scott Fitzgerald was part of a group of writers known as the "Lost Generation." Research the origin of that term and the writers who were included. What did the writers have in common with one another? What made them "lost?"

- *Tender Is the Night* was published in 1934, nine years after Fitzgerald's previous book, *The Great Gatsby*, was published. Research some of the events that transpired in the United States and Europe in those nine years. What effects did those changes have on the critical reception of *Tender Is the Night*? Do you think readers would have responded to the book differently had it been published in 1928? What would have been the differences in their response?

- The title of *Tender Is the Night* comes from the John Keats poem "Ode to a Nightingale." Analyze Keats's poem, and explain why Fitzgerald quoted from this poem for his title. What does the title mean? Are there any thematic similarities between the Keats poem and *Tender Is the Night*?

- Many readers view *Tender Is the Night* as Fitzgerald's most autobiographical novel. Some see Dick and Nicole Diver as being Fitzgerald and his wife, Zelda, whereas others believe Fitzgerald intended Albert McKisco and his wife to represent himself and Zelda. Research the life of the Fitzgeralds. Who do you think are most representative of the Fitzgeralds in the book? Why?

---

say that is redeeming about families or their roles in any of the characters' lives.

Incest

Incest is a major theme in *Tender Is the Night*. Nicole is ruined emotionally and psychologically by the incestuous relationship her father inflicts upon her. That relationship colors every aspect of her and Dick's life; there is nothing that happens in *Tender Is the Night* that cannot be, in some way, attributed to Devereux Warren's sexual abuse of his daughter.

It is no accident that the movie Rosemary Hoyt has just starred in is called *Daddy's Girl*, and neither is it an accident that both Rosemary and Nicole fall for the much older Dick Diver who, in many ways, is as much a father to the women, especially Nicole, as he is a partner or lover. There is no question that Fitzgerald used the incest motif in his book consciously and to wide-ranging effect.

Psychiatry

Dick Diver is a brilliant, up-and-coming psychiatrist when he first meets Nicole. He is passionate about his studies and hopes to write a definitive text on psychiatry. However, the more he engages in

the practice, the more he sees psychiatry as a plaything for the very wealthy, for it is only the wealthy who can afford it. In Book Two, Dick engages in a conversation with Dr. Gregorovius about Gregorovius's youthful plans of opening "an up-to-date clinic for billionaires." Fitzgerald clearly portrays the field as more of a business than as an instrument for healing. Also, one of the few cases he actually shows passion about is with a woman artist who seems not to fit the stereotype of the rich, pampered client. When she dies, he is devastated, and he effectively moves to end his practice of psychiatry. And after years as a clinician, he seems so confused about his thoughts on psychiatry that he cannot even think clearly enough to properly title his book.

Fitzgerald, because of his years with his wife Zelda and her severe psychiatric problems, grew to know the industry and its practices intimately. *Tender Is the Night* does not paint a positive picture of the practice.

Violence

Just beneath the surface of the luxurious and idyllic life that the group of wealthy American expatriates lead, there exists a significant amount of violence. When Dick and Nicole are seeing Abe

North off at the train station, a woman shoots a man for no obvious reason. Much earlier in the novel, Tommy Barban and Albert McKisco engage in a duel. After his drunken spree, Dick assaults a band-leader, a taxicab driver, and a detective, and he him-self is then violently dealt with by the police. Abe North, who was the cause of the death of Jules Peterson, is last mentioned with respect to his vio-lent death at a New York speakeasy, and of course the entire novel is permeated by the violence inflicted upon Nicole by her father.

War

Although *Tender Is the Night* takes place dur-ing the interwar years, the echoes of the Great War, World War I, reverberate throughout the entire story. At the clinic, Dr. Gregorovius says that even though Diver lacks firsthand experience of war, that does not necessarily mean he has not been affected by it. Gregorovius tells Dick of "some shell-shocks who merely hear an air raid from a distance. We have a few who merely read newspapers." Much later Dick has a dream filled with war imagery, and he wakes up and notes, "Non-combatant's shell-shock." At the battlefields of Somme, standing with Abe North and Rosemary, Dick eulogizes at great length about what was lost during the war. "All my beautiful lovely safe world blew itself up here with a great gust of high explosive love," he says. World War I had destroyed much of what Europe had come to be known for, and with it, it had destroyed the lives of millions. Fitzgerald returns to this theme throughout *Tender Is the Night* and is pos-sibly making a connection between it and the vio-lence that underscores his characters' lives.

Wealth

First and foremost, Fitzgerald, in nearly all of his major works, addresses the theme of wealth and the effects it has on individuals and societies. In Fitzgerald's fictional universe, nearly everyone is rich or has access to the attendant luxuries of the very rich. Set in a time referred to as the "Jazz Age," *Tender Is the Night* explores how a small group of very rich Americans live and, eventually, die. None of the rich come off well under Fitzgerald's exam-ination. Baby Diver, as executor of her family's wealth, is portrayed as manipulative and control-ling; her father, the wealthy Chicago magnate, destroys Nicole's life through sexual abuse. And al-though Dick Diver himself is not rich, once he fully accepts Nicole's world, his own life and desires seep from him, and he slowly disappears into an alcoholic oblivion. Wealth seems to have no

redeeming value in Fitzgerald's eyes, other than its ability to allow for some exciting, but ultimately destructive, evenings.

Style

Title

The title comes from a line in John Keats's "Ode to a Nightingale": The poem, with its forlorn images of drinking, fits the character and tone of the book. As a young writer Fitzgerald was pro-foundly influenced by Keats. While in Italy, in chapter XXII of Book Two, on his way back to his hotel where a note from Rosemary is awaiting him, Dick feels his "spirits soared before the flower stalls and the house where Keats had died."

Three-Part Narrative Structure

Tender Is the Night is divided into three sec-tions, or Books. Although the novel is narrated in the third person, Book One opens from the per-spective of Rosemary Hoyt and focuses on the glit-tering surface of Dick and Nicole Divers' life. Just as Rosemary is seduced by the glamour and luxury of that life, so is the reader; though, as the per-spective evolves, there are hints that not all is well with Nicole and Dick and that the life they lead is not all glitz and glamour.

Book Two moves back in time to reveal what lies beneath the surface of the Divers' charm. It effectively unveils Nicole's case history for the reader just as it does the evolution of her relation-ship to Dick. Finally, in Book Three, Dick is shown trying to make sense of his life. The brilliant sheen of Book One has worn off, and the events told in Book Two have taken their toll, and now, in Book Three, it is time for Dick to move on.

Foreshadowing

The first sense that we have that something is not right with the Divers' marriage comes in Book One, when Mrs. McKisco comes upon a "scene" between Dick and Nicole in the bathroom during the party. The event foretells Nicole's emotional problems and is the first of many such "scenes."

Also in Book One, Tommy Barban meets Rosemary Hoyt for the first time and tells her that he is very fond of the Divers, "especially of Nicole." Barban eventually takes Nicole away from Dick and marries her.

A foreshadowing of the violence that is about to enter the Divers' lives takes place in the train station as Abe North is about to depart. A woman whom Nicole knows shoots an Englishman for no obvious reason. The next day, Jules Peterson is found dead on Rosemary's bed, and Dick must hide evidence to keep scandal from engulfing them.

The Symbolism of Names

Fitzgerald uses names and titles to add to the development of character and plot and to elaborate on the book's metaphors and themes. For instance, Rosemary Hoyt's film is called *Daddy's Girl*, an obvious reference to the incest theme that pervades the book. Nicole is a victim of sexual abuse by her father, and the allusion to the much older Dick being a father figure to Rosemary is obvious. Nicole is as much "daddy's girl" as is Rosemary; not only has she been sexually abused by her father, but Dick, an older man, assumes the father role in his treatment of his wife's psychological problems.

The name Dick Diver is suggestive of the dual role his character plays in the book. The vulgar associations of "Dick" and "Diver" fit well with his unabashed womanizing, and by the book's conclusion, his character has become something of a social "diver" as opposed to a social "climber."

Tommy Barban, a mercenary soldier who seems somewhat ill-fitting amongst the sophisticated crowds that surround the Divers, has a name that echoes "barbaric."

Flashbacks

Book Two employs flashback to reveal the history of Nicole's illness and her relationship with Dick. Fitzgerald was criticized for this structure when *Tender Is the Night* was first published, and following the book's publication, Fitzgerald began reconsidering the flashback sequence. In 1951, *Tender Is the Night* was reedited by Malcolm Cowley and published "With the Author's Final Revisions." Among those revisions was the placing of Nicole's case history, and much of Books Two and Three, at the start of the book and pushing the beach scene and most of Book One back. Cowley's revisions received tremendous criticism, and the original sequence of the book was eventually restored.

Historical Context

Set in Europe between 1925 and 1935, and with flashbacks that cover the years 1917 to 1925, *Tender Is the Night* describes a group of wealthy and idle American expatriates who, like their counterparts of the "Jazz Age" and the "Roaring Twenties," have little else to do but eat, drink, attend parties, and survive their personal crises.

When Dick Diver first arrives in Zurich, a war is raging across Europe. Although there are references to an earlier time when he was studying in Vienna and had a firsthand experience with the shelling and its resultant discomforts, Diver is largely unaffected on a personal level by the war. Europe, however, was recovering from the devastating effects of the war that was to have ended all wars. Millions of Europeans were killed, and entire cities were ruined. During the decade in which the book largely takes place, Europe as a whole was still working to rebuild its infrastructures.

Meanwhile, in America, the period known as the Roaring Twenties was well under way. With the stock market surging, a generation of "nouveau riche" Americans found their way to the European shores and cities with lots of money to spend. Desperate for the infusion of capital, Europe was forced to pander to these Americans, though not without some cultural conflicts. *Tender Is the Night* describes typical wealthy Americans who live idly off the European continent. Although the term "ugly American" would not be coined for many years, *Tender Is the Night* chronicles the early years of how that term may have evolved.

Fitzgerald himself was a member of what was called the Lost Generation of writers—a group of mostly young men that included Ernest Hemingway, among others. Coined by poet Gertrude Stein, the Lost Generation referred to writers who left their native America after World War I and settled in Europe, mostly France, where they wrote and claimed a rejection of the materialistic values that had engulfed America. Although Fitzgerald was immersed in the culture of the wealthy and was largely known as a chronicler of the "Jazz Age," his work can be seen as a serious indictment of the wealth that arose during those years.

Tender Is the Night, which had its genesis in letters and notes Fitzgerald wrote as early as 1925 shortly after *The Great Gatsby*, was not published until 1934. In that time, the great wealth that had come to define his subjects had suddenly disappeared in the crash of 1929. By the time the book was finally finished, America was in the midst of the Great Depression, and the country's literary tastes had shifted radically. The movement of social realism had begun to take hold, and Fitzgerald's work was suddenly seen by some as

Compare & Contrast

- **1920s:** Having just experienced the devastating effects of World War I, Europe is working to rebuild its economies and infrastructures.

  Today: After the fall of Communism in the 1990s, European countries form the European Union—an economic organization that brings European countries under a consistent monetary system and economic policies. The European Union today has the potential of becoming one of the strongest economic entities in the world.

- **1930s:** Many Americans who amassed fortunes in the stock market surges of the previous decade have lost everything because of the crash of 1929.

  Today: After the stock market decline of 2000 and the "dot com" crash, many of the young Americans who became rich with stock options in the 1990s have lost much of their wealth.

- **1930s:** Although many American blacks had relocated to France to avoid the discrimination in the United States, discrimination against blacks still exists, and blacks have a difficult time entering some businesses and public establishments.

  Today: Discrimination is illegal in France and is considered a human rights violation.

- **1930s:** By the time *Tender Is the Night* is published, many readers and critics have come to embrace the new movement of "social realism" in literature and the art.

  Today: Social realism is not a viable artistic movement, per se, although elements of the movement and working class themes abound in contemporary literature and art.

- **1920s–1930s:** F. Scott Fitzgerald's long-standing relationship with his editor at Scribners, Maxwell Perkins, is instrumental to his career. Perkins helps to guide virtually every aspect of Fitzgeralds' life, including his writing, finances, and health-related issues.

  Today: The role that editors in large publishing firms once held has been primarily replaced by agents. The "Maxwell Perkinses" of the past are mostly long gone.

---

anachronistic and petty. Although *Tender Is the Night* was deeply critical of the wealthy and the effects of their money, because it was not a "political" book, per se, it was not taken as seriously as it might have been had it been written before the crash.

With the greater perspective that the years have afforded, *Tender Is the Night* can now also be seen, on one level, as a chronicle of the effects the war had on an entire generation. While standing in the midst of what was recently a great battlefield where tens of thousands died, Dick Diver says:

> This land here cost twenty lives a foot that summer ... See that little stream—we could walk to it in two minutes. It took the British a month to walk it—a whole empire walking very slowly, dying in front and pushing forward behind. And another empire walked very slowly backward a few inches a day, leaving the dead like a million bloody rugs. No Europeans will ever do that again in this generation.

Tender Is the Night is also very much a critique of the burgeoning psychiatric industry to which the wealthy had access. When Dick Diver traveled to Zurich, Europe was being greatly affected by the psychoanalytic theories of Sigmund Freud and his contemporaries. Fitzgerald, because of his wife's long-standing psychiatric problems, became something of an expert on psychiatry and its various theories and cures. Although psychiatry was making huge theoretical and practical leaps during the time *Tender Is the Night* takes place, the fact is that it was very much a cure for the very wealthy, a point that Fitzgerald clearly recognizes and effectively criticizes throughout his work.

1961 film depiction of Tender is the Night *with Jason Robards as Dr. Dick Diver and Joan Fontaine as Baby Warren*

Critical Overview

When it was first published in 1934, reviewers and readers picked up *Tender Is the Night* with some trepidation. It had been nearly a decade since his masterpiece, *The Great Gatsby*, had been published, and there were rumors in literary circles that Fitzgerald was done for as a writer. Although the book did not sell nearly as well as his earlier books, reviewers were generally favorable in their response to Fitzgerald's new book. (*Tender Is the Night* sold about fifteen thousand copies in 1934, according to Matthew J.

Bruccoli, writing in his introduction to *Reader's Companion to F. Scott Fitzgerald's Tender Is the Night*, compared to the forty-one thousand copies *This Side of Paradise* sold in its first year of publication and the fifty thousand copies *The Beautiful and the Damned* sold in its first year.) Over the years, critics and scholars have come to regard *Tender Is the Night* not only as one of Fitzgerald's major works but one of American literature's most important novels of the twentieth century.

According to Bruccoli, of the twenty-four reviews published in "influential American periodicals, nine were favorable, six were unfavorable, and nine were mixed."

Writing in the *New York Times*, John Chamberlain called the rumors of Fitzgerald's demise "gossip," and he went on to write that from a technical viewpoint, although *Tender Is the Night* is not as perfect as *The Great Gatsby*, it is "an exciting and psychologically apt study in the disintegration of a marriage." In contrast, Horace Gregory, writing in the *New York Herald Tribune*, described the book as being "not all that it should have been. There is an air of dangerous fatality about it, as though the author were sharing the failure of his protagonist." Gregory, however, concluded his review by acknowledging that several isolated scenes in the book had "extraordinary power" and would "not be soon forgotten."

In a review titled "Fitzgerald's Novel a Masterpiece," Cameron Rogers, referring to the long period of time it had been since *The Great Gatsby* was published, wrote in the *San Francisco Chronicle* that "*Tender Is the Night* is so well worth [the wait] that Fitzgerald's silence … seems natural and explicable" and that "there is so much beauty, so much compassion and so much understanding [in the book] that it seems as though it could only have sprung from a mind left wisely fallow."

In a criticism of the book that continues to this day, Mary M. Colum, in her *Forum and Century* review, pointed to the weakness of Fitzgerald's characterizations, especially Nicole's. Colum calls passages describing Nicole "more like a case history from a textbook than a novelist's study of a real character." And in Fitzgerald's hometown paper, the *St. Paul Dispatch*, James Gray called the novel "a big, sprawling, undisciplined, badly coordinated book" and went on to call it "immature."

One of the issues that Fitzgerald faced was that in the nine years since he had last published, the cultural make-up of the United States had changed dramatically. In a short piece published in the *New York Times* a few days after his review of *Tender Is the Night* appeared, John Chamberlain encapsulated one of the effects this time lag had on the reception of the book. After reading the early reviews of the book, Chamberlain concluded that none of them were "alike; no two had the same tone." He noted that some critics thought "Fitzgerald was writing about his usual jazz age boys and girls; others that he had a 'timeless' problem on his hands."

Chamberlain's observations of the book's critical responses underscored the challenges Fitzgerald had with *Tender Is the Night*. In the nine years since

he had published *The Great Gatsby*, the American psyche and reading public had changed radically. Although *Tender Is the Night* was not the same type of book as was *The Great Gatsby*, it was not sufficiently different or enough reflective of society's changes to appease many of his critics or readers. The so-called "Jazz Age," a time noted for its extravagance and material excesses, and the period in which Fitzgerald's reputation had flowered, had been replaced by the severe austerity of the depression. As a result, the literary tastes of the society had changed radically; many reviewers and readers had little patience for books reminding them of the frivolous past, and the age of social realism had begun to emerge across all art forms. *Tender Is the Night*'s characterizations of the rich and idle seemed anachronistic to many readers and reviewers, and for many the book was not the type of literature the difficult times were calling for. As a result, the book's reception was not uniform in either its praise or its criticism; it would take years for critics to gain the distance necessary to understand the book's complexities and its relationship to Fitzgerald's other works.

Criticism

Mark White

White is the publisher of the Seattle-based Scala House Press. In this essay, White argues that the novel's structure is an integral part of Tender Is the Night *and helps to deepen the reader's understanding of the novel.*

One of the criticisms leveled at *Tender Is the Night* shortly following its publication concerned its structure. F. Scott Fitzgerald's use of flashback in Book Two, many critics felt, resulted in an unwieldy book. Writing in the *St. Paul Dispatch*, James Gray called the novel "big, sprawling, [and] badly coordinated" and went on to criticize the book for its "technical fault of poor organization." The issue of its organization plagued Fitzgerald so much in the years following the book's publication that he began to wonder if he should not have presented the story chronologically. A decade after Fitzgerald's death, Malcolm Cowley used the author's personal notes to justify the publication a new version of *Tender Is the Night*, which he subtitled "The Author's Final Version." In Cowley's revision, which was not well received by critics, the tragic story of Dick Diver is told chronologically; Cowley eliminated the book's flashback sequence by placing

> **"** Far from being a 'mistake,' the structure of *Tender Is the Night* works well to deliver the evolution of Rosemary's views of Dick, and without that structure, much of what Hemingway called the 'magic' of the book would have been lost completely."

much of Books Two and Three at the start of the novel, before Book One.

However, the three-part structure with the flashback sequence in Book Two is one of the novel's great strengths. Fitzgerald's decision to organize the book in this way allows the reader to experience the demise of Dick Diver, just as young and naïve Rosemary Hoyt experiences it. From what Fitzgerald reveals in Book One, who would not want to be, or be with, Dick Diver? He is rich, handsome, and the envy of his large circle of friends. Although there are hints of pending trouble in his life, his world is a wondrous one. However, as the *unwondrous* truths about his and Nicole's past emerge in Book Two, the stage is being set for his precipitous fall and ultimate disappearance in Book Three. The three-part structure of *Tender Is the Night* effectively mirrors the way Rosemary Hoyt views Dick Diver over time and helps to deepen the reader's understanding of his tragic story.

In the Introduction to *Reader's Companion to Tender Is the Night*, Fitzgerald scholar Matthew J. Bruccoli chronicles the genesis of what would eventually become "The Author's Final Version" of *Tender Is the Night*. Shortly after the book's publication, when it became apparent that it would not be the commercial success Fitzgerald hoped it would be, Fitzgerald questioned the novel's structure in letters to friends and in his own journals and notes. In 1938, he wrote his editor, Maxwell Perkins, asking him to consider republishing the novel with the middle section placed at the beginning. In the letter, Fitzgerald cited a "dozen reviewers" who had noticed the "mistake" of the book's structure.

Perkins declined Fitzgerald's suggestion, but Fitzgerald did not let the idea die. At the time of his death in 1940, he had in his possession an unbound copy of *Tender Is the Night* in which he had written, "This is the final version of the book as I would like it." Essentially, Fitzgerald's new version opens with Nicole Diver's case history, as told in Book Two, followed by necessary changes that would keep the rest of the story intact.

Tender Is the Night was the last novel Fitzgerald would see published in his lifetime. By the time the book was published, a combination of alcoholism and unmanageable debts had overwhelmed him. Not only was he desperate for income, he had also clearly lost much of his analytic abilities. Fitzgerald's hope that a new version of the book would breathe new commercial life into it blinded him to the aesthetic issues that such a revision would affect. As Matthew J. Bruccoli writes in the Introduction to his *Reader's Companion to F. Scott Fitzgerald's Tender Is the Night*, Ernest Hemingway, in a letter to Cowley years after Fitzgerald's death, wrote "I know you [revised the book] for Scott and it was what he wanted.... But I think if he had been completely sane I could have argued him out of it."

Far from being a "mistake," the structure of *Tender Is the Night* works well to deliver the evolution of Rosemary's views of Dick, and without that structure, much of what Hemingway called the "magic" of the book would have been lost completely. "It is just like takeing [sic] the wings off a butterfly and arrangeing [sic] them so he can fly straight as a bee flies and loseing [sic] all the dust that makes the colors that makes the butterfly magical in the process," Hemingway wrote in his letter to Cowley.

Tender Is the Night opens from the point of view of the virginal Rosemary Hoyt, the star of the recent Hollywood movie *Daddy's Girl*. Vacationing in France with her mother, Rosemary is immediately attracted to Dick Diver and his wife, Nicole.

"He looked at her and for a moment she lived in the bright blue worlds of his eyes, eagerly and confidently," Fitzgerald writes in the closing paragraph of the book's second chapter as Dick and Rosemary are standing together on the beach.

A bit later, Fitzgerald describes the moment Rosemary meets Nicole for the first time:

> She was about twenty-four, Rosemary guessed—her face could have been described in terms of conventional prettiness, but the effect was that it had been made first on the heroic scale with strong structure and marking, as if the features and vividness of brow and coloring, everything we associate with temperament and character had been molded with a Rodinesque

What Do I Read Next?

- *The Great Gatsby*, along with *Tender Is the Night*, is considered to be Fitzgerald's masterpiece. Published in 1925, at the height of the U.S. "Jazz Age," the book tells the tragic story of the rich and elusive Jay Gatsby and his love for Daisy Buchanan.

- *The Crack Up*, a collection of personal writings by Fitzgerald and his contemporaries, is the closest thing to an autobiography of Fitzgerald that exists. First published in 1945 and collected by Edmund Wilson shortly following Fitzgerald's death, the collection is named after a series of articles Fitzgerald had written for *Esquire*, offering insight into his own personal bankruptcy.

- *F. Scott Fitzgerald: In His Own Time* is a collection of miscellaneous writings by and about Fitzgerald. Edited by Fitzgerald scholars Matthew J. Bruccoli and Jackson R. Bryer, the book includes college writings and essays by Fitzgerald, as well as reviews of his works, interviews, and several obituaries that were published at his death.

- *A Life in Letters: F. Scott Fitzgerald*, edited by Matthew J. Bruccoli and written with the assistance of Judith S. Baughman, collects letters written by Fitzgerald between 1896 and 1940. Published in 1994, this book includes correspondence between Fitzgerald and his editor, Maxwell Perkins, and his many literary friends, and they offer insight into his own views on writing, his alcoholism and financial problems, and his wife's mental illness.

---

intention, and then chiseled away in the direction of prettiness to a point where a single slip would have irreparably diminished its force and quality.

Rosemary is clearly smitten by the couple, especially Dick. "I love him, Mother," she cries from her mother's lap. "I'm desperately in love with him—I never knew I could feel that way about anybody. And he's married and I like her too—it's just hopeless. Oh, I love him so."

In Book One, the reader is made to view Dick and his world essentially as Rosemary views them. More than simply being smitten sexually, Rosemary is also taken in by the whole of Dick Diver and his world: the lavish dinner parties and expeditions to Paris, Nicole's spending sprees, their circle of friends, and their obvious wealth. And just as a smitten young woman (or man) would not necessarily observe details that would contradict such an idealization, so too the reader may notice only in retrospect the foreshadowing of trouble that Fitzgerald sprinkles throughout Book One: the bathroom scene at the villa, the duel between Tommy Barban and Albert McKisco, and Abe North's drinking.

At the end of Book One, the Divers' world begins to unravel in Rosemary's eyes. North gets extremely drunk in Paris, and through a series of convoluted events, a black man, Jules Peterson, is discovered on Rosemary's bed shot dead. As if this is not enough, Nicole responds to these events by going into a state of hysterics in her hotel bathroom. "Rosemary, back in the salon, heard the bathroom door bang, and stood trembling: now she knew what Violet McKisco had seen in the bathroom at Villa Diana," Fitzgerald writes, suggesting that at least some of the brilliant sheen that had blinded Rosemary has now been dulled.

The main criticism of the flashback structure of Book Two was that it made for a confusing plot structure. Although it is true that placing the flashback sequence of Book Two at the beginning of the novel would have made for a clearer plot chronologically, the effect would have been both to take away from the naïve and idyllic worldview created in Book One, or the "magic," as Hemingway called it, and it would also have taken away from the effect the gradual realization of what the bathroom scenes in Book One signified. With a straightforward narrative, the mysteries of those scenes would have been eliminated entirely.

Book Two covers approximately an eleven-year period, from 1917, when Dick, an up-and-coming twenty-six-year-old psychiatrist, is studying at a Zurich clinic, to about 1928 when he consummates his relationship with Rosemary in Italy and proceeds to get arrested and beaten by Italian police after a night of excessive drinking.

It is true that there are some issues of plot structure in the way that Fitzgerald has managed Book Two. Rather than simply bringing the events back to where they were left off in Book One, there is some overlap and possibly some resulting confusion in the narration. More important, though, there is the "problem" of Rosemary Hoyt. After devoting an entire section of the novel to presenting the narration through her eyes, she disappears entirely through most of Book Two, and when she eventually does reappear, she is no longer the young, idealistic virgin Dick once knew.

Fitzgerald was on the receiving end of criticism on both of these accounts when *Tender Is the Night* was first published. But again, Fitzgerald's choice to present Book Two in flashback form, and to remove Rosemary from most of this section, makes perfect sense in light of Rosemary's newfound concerns at the end of Book One. With the drinking and the murder and the hysterics she has just been made privy to, Rosemary must be wondering whom she has gotten involved with. By using Book Two to provide the history behind those events, Fitzgerald effectively gives Rosemary, and the reader, the answer.

And Rosemary's "response" to that answer? She disappears from the Divers' circle, makes new movies, and, it is quite apparent, has affairs with other men. In short, she continues the process of growing up, but away from Dick. And when Dick returns from America and visits her in Rome, it is clear that she is no longer smitten by his worldliness and charm. She goes through the motions of consummating their relationship, just as Dick does, but the spark is no longer there for either of them.

More particularly for Rosemary, by the time the Divers' history has been recounted in Book Two, she has learned that the appearances of Book One were somewhat illusory and that the violence and hysterics that came to light were as much a part of Dick's life as were the attributes that she fell for in the first place. The effect of this realization, however, can only be made manifest with the structure that Fitzgerald has chosen. If Nicole's case history had preceded Rosemary's introduction to the Divers, neither she, nor the reader, would have been nearly

as smitten. The glamour of their lifestyle would clearly have been tarnished, and the effects of any new insights into the Divers, if there were any new insights at all, would be minimal.

To conclude Rosemary's relationship with Dick, Fitzgerald brings her back to the Divers' villa briefly in Book Three. After Dick's embarrassing flop with the water ski trick, Rosemary joins Dick and his family on the beach and engages in a telling moment of dialogue that essentially mirrors the structure of the book:

> 'The first drink I ever had was with you,' Rosemary said, and with a spurt of enthusiasm she added, 'Oh, I'm so glad to see you and *know* you're all right. I was worried—' Her sentence broke as she changed direction 'that maybe you wouldn't be.'
>
> 'Did you hear I'd gone into a process of deterioration?'
>
> 'Oh, no. I simply—just heard you'd changed. And I'm glad to see with my own eyes it isn't true.'
>
> 'It is true,' Dick answered, sitting down with them. 'The change came a long way back—but at first it didn't show. The manner remains intact for some time after the morale cracks.'

Just as Rosemary has gone from having her "first drink" with Dick in Book One through the knowledge of his past in Book Two, so has the reader. And so has the reader watched as Dick pathetically tries to remain "intact" in Book Three, despite the "crack" that events from years ago have caused. Without the structure that Fitzgerald provided *Tender Is the Night*, the reader would have learned the facts of Dick's demise as given forth in the novel's plot but would not have had the experience of coming to terms with that demise. Having the ability to tell a great story and being able to tell a great story while also finding the right structure for that story is what separates merely good writers from great ones. *Tender Is the Night* shows why F. Scott Fitzgerald is considered one of the twentieth-century's great writers.

Source: Mark White, Critical Essay on *Tender Is the Night*, in *Novels for Students*, Gale, 2004.

John F. Callahan

In the following excerpt, Callahan discusses the "pursuit of happiness" in Fitzgerald's novel.

"France was a land, England was a people, but America, having about it still that quality of the idea, was harder to utter." In this passage from "The Swimmers," a 1929 story later distilled into his *Notebooks*, Fitzgerald evokes the anguished intense patriotism he finds in American faces from Abraham Lincoln's to those of the "country boys dying in the Argonne for a phrase that was empty before their bodies withered" (*CU* 197). For Fitzgerald that American "quality of the idea" finds most worthy expression in the impulse to offer the best of yourself on behalf of someone or something greater than yourself. Directed toward the world, a "willingness of the heart" intensifies the individual's feelings and experience. In *Tender Is the Night* (*TITN*) as in *Gatsby*, the dream of love and accomplishment is distorted by the values of property and possession. Like Gatsby, Dick Diver has large ambitions: ". . . to be a good psychologist—maybe to be the greatest one that ever lived." Dick's colleague, the stolid Swiss, Franz Gregorovius, stops short hearing his friend's pronouncement, as did the aspiring American man of letters, Edmund Wilson, when the undergraduate Fitzgerald declared: "I want to be one of the greatest writers who have ever lived, don't you?" Like Fitzgerald, Diver mingles love with ambition, though passively, almost as an afterthought: "He wanted to be loved too, if he could fit it in."

Reminiscent of *Gatsby*, Diver's dream resides initially in a masculine world in which one man's ambition and achievement are measured against another's. But, as with Gatsby, experience changes the values implicit in Diver's equation. Stirred by professional curiosity, he meets Nicole Warren. Because of her youth and beauty, the patient becomes in Diver's eyes primarily a woman, though a woman imagined as "a scarcely saved waif of disaster bringing him the essence of a continent." To the inexperienced Diver—"only hot-cheeked girls in hot secret rooms"—Nicole is a figure for the romantic possibility of an America that, like the "fresh green breast of the new world" whose "vanished trees . . . had made way for Gatsby's house" (*TGG* 137) is, though violated and compromised, suggestive of innocence, vitality, and possibility, and above all, still worthy of love.

So Dick Diver gambles his "pursuit of happiness" on marriage to Nicole. But his desire to be loved—"I want to be extravagantly admired again," Fitzgerald said as he was writing *Tender*—seduces him away from his scholarly writing as a psychiatrist. Once diverted from his work, he does not find happiness as curator of the leisure-class expatriate American world he and Nicole create on the Riviera, or as psychiatrist in charge of the clinic bought with Warren money, or as Nicole's husband, or, finally, "wolf-like under his sheep's clothing" a pursuer of women more in mind than in actuality. For Diver, like Gatsby, the pursuit of happiness becomes personally hollow in love, and professionally

> Fitzgerald created his deepest, most realized novel out of his own predicament. His dissipation and need to write short stories for the *Saturday Evening Post* to sustain his and Zelda's standard of living seduced him away from his craft and to some extent his dream of love."

so in his work. Again, perhaps like Gatsby, only more so, Diver is more responsible than he knows for the dissolution of his dream of love and work.

For her part, Nicole, like Daisy, only more poignantly, veers between two selves. Cured, she embraces her heritage as her robber baron grandfather Warren's daughter; her white crook's eyes signify a proprietary attitude toward the world. More vividly and knowingly than before, she becomes the goddess of monopoly and dynasty described early in the novel. "For her sake trains began their run at Chicago and traversed the round belly of the continent to California." Nicole, "as the whole system swayed and thundered onward," is, in Europe, remote product and beneficiary of her family's multinational corporate interests. Like Daisy, Nicole "has too much money"; like Gatsby, Dick Diver "can't beat that."

Yet in *Tender is the Night*, the matter is not so simple. Marrying Nicole, Dick takes on a task demanding a heroic and perhaps a too stringent discipline and self-denial. After the most violent and threatening of Nicole's schizophrenic episodes, he realizes that "somehow [he] and Nicole had become one and equal, not opposite and complementary; she was Dick too, the drought in the marrow of his bones." Her personality reinforces rather than compensates for what is missing in him. Even more fatal for Diver's balance between husband and psychiatrist, "he could not watch her disintegrations without participating in them." Underneath the historical overtones of the American dream gone terribly, incestuously, wrong, Fitzgerald explores the strained and, finally, chilling intimacy of a marriage

F. Scott Fitzgerald with his wife Zelda, circa 1921

turned inward against the autonomy and independence of each person. With slow excruciating inevitability, Diver's "willingness of the heart," so catalytic to his imagination, charm, and discipline, deserts him.

> She went up to him and, putting her arm around his shoulder and touching their heads together, said:
>
> "Don't be sad."
>
> He looked at her coldly.
>
> "Don't touch me!" he said.

Diver has come so far from his former love for Nicole, "a wild submergence of soul, a dipping of all colors into an obscuring dye," that he now recoils from her touch. The Divers are no longer man and woman to each other. In truth, the conditions and pathology sustaining the marriage are played out. Nicole is rid of her incestuous dependence on Dick, and Dick seeks to recover the independence he sacrificed as Nicole's husband, doctor, and, above all, protector.

Discipline, spirit, and imagination attenuated if not broken, Diver returns to America a stranger. With Nicole now acting as Fitzgerald's chronicler, the last news of Diver tells of the "big stack of papers on his desk that are known to be an important treatise on some medical subject, almost in process

of completion." So much for his craft; as for the dream of love, he becomes "entangled with a girl who worked in a grocery store." Homeless in spirit, Diver drifts from one lovely, lonely Finger Lakes town to another, and whatever dreams he has, he dreams in oblivion without his former promise and intensity of feeling and action.

Fitzgerald created his deepest, most realized novel out of his own predicament. His dissipation and need to write short stories for the *Saturday Evening Post* to sustain his and Zelda's standard of living seduced him away from his craft and to some extent his dream of love. Still, Fitzgerald bled out *Tender Is the Night* at La Paix—"La Paix (My God!)"—in Rodgers Forge outside Baltimore. He brought his "big stack of papers" to completion. But when reviews were mixed and sales modest, also perhaps because, exhausted, he had no new novel taking shape in his mind, only the early medieval tale of Phillippe or *The Count of Darkness*, with its curiously anachronistic tilt toward Ernest Hemingway's modern code of courage, Fitzgerald sank deeper into drink and depression. Finally, as Scott Donaldson observes, Asheville, Tyron, and other North Carolina towns became suspiciously like the small towns of Diver's self-imposed exile at the end of *Tender Is the Night*.

Source: John F. Callahan, "F. Scott Fitzgerald's Evolving American Dream: The Pursuit of Happiness in *Gatsby*, *Tender Is the Night*, and *The Last Tycoon*," in *Twentieth Century Literature*, Vol. 42, No. 3, Fall 1996, pp. 374–86.

Robert Merrill

In the following excerpt, Merrill discusses Fitzgerald as a tragic novelist.

We do not think of Scott Fitzgerald as a tragic novelist, but Fitzgerald's novels are informed by what he once called "the wise and tragic sense of life." In his notes and correspondence Fitzgerald refers to *The Beautiful and Damned*, *Tender Is the Night*, and *The Last Tycoon* as formal tragedies (successful or otherwise). "Show me a hero," he once wrote, "and I will write you a tragedy." Using *Tender Is the Night* as my example, I would like to illustrate the difference it makes to approach Fitzgerald's novels as tragic actions . . .

I have chosen *Tender Is the Night* because it best represents Fitzgerald's practice as a tragedian.

II

Tragic theory often fails to square with tragic practice, but A. C. Bradley's later reflections on tragedy seem to me quite useful. Bradley believed that we are tragically moved by conflicts involving whatever we value highly and that any conflict involving spiritual waste is tragic. These remarks should remind us that tragedies from *Oedipus* to *The Heart of the Matter* have been shaped by rather basic principles. In any case, I think that *Tender Is the Night* is tragic precisely to the extent that it dramatizes the spiritual waste of people we value highly. Fitzgerald did not think that tragedy should be confined to the stage, but he did suppose that a truly spiritual suffering was necessary if his characters were to be valued properly. In this as in so many other ways, *Tender* is the work of a traditional tragedian, one who can be compared to Shakespeare himself. Indeed, Wayne Booth published an essay in the early 1950s in which he noticed several points of resemblance between *Macbeth* and Fitzgerald's novel. Booth's aim was to emphasize an aspect of Shakespearean dramaturgy, but the comparison can also be used to clarify the tragic structure of *Tender Is the Night*.

The most striking parallel between *Tender* and *Macbeth* is that each virtually begins with what Aristotle called "the tragic act." Unlike *Othello*, which builds toward one of the most devastating tragic acts ever conceived, *Macbeth* is a work in which the protagonist's fatal mistake is quickly accomplished. The resulting structure emphasizes the long process of reaction to this deed, including, of course, Macbeth's internal response. Booth suggests that the plot is therefore one of "degeneration," in which Shakespeare traces the tragic consequences (for Scotland, but especially for Macbeth) of the protagonist's initial, irredeemable action. In its revised version, *Tender Is the Night* is structured in much the same way. Like Shakespeare, Fitzgerald begins by introducing his hero as a man of great charm and ability, a man whose worth is rather more a matter of potential than Macbeth's but who is nonetheless an enviable model for his time. Then, again like Shakespeare, Fitzgerald has his hero commit himself to a course of action which cannot possibly succeed. At the end of Book I ("Case History"), when Dick looks at Nicole and supposes that "her problem was one they had together for good now," the attentive reader must find the moment as ominous in its own way as Macbeth's horrifying participation in the murder of Duncan.

There are obvious differences, of course. Whereas Macbeth indulges an unworthy ambition and commits a terrible act of violence, Dick acts from love and "commits" an act of faith in marrying Nicole. Indeed, it might be argued that Dick

"Dick has failed because of an initial, irrevocable mistake which derived from his own character, but also because the world of the 1920s was one in which talents such as his were misused or even abused."

does not so much resemble Macbeth, with his conspicuous tragic "flaw," as he recalls Aristotle's ideal tragic protagonist, "a man who is neither a paragon of virtue and justice nor undergoes the change to misfortune through any real badness or wickedness but because of some mistake." Nonetheless, Dick's "mistake" resembles Macbeth's in that each man consciously chooses his fate despite his basic soundness of character and his awareness that the chosen course is at best perilous. Macbeth's early soliloquies reveal that he *knows* the assassination of Duncan is both morally wrong and certain to end in his own destruction, for such an act cannot "trammel up the consequence." This clear-sighted perception of what he is about sets Macbeth apart from such tragic figures as Oedipus, Othello, and Lear. And Dick Diver is no less aware that his marriage to Nicole is likely to fail. He knows that Nicole's illness is probably permanent, for "the percentage of cures, even so-called social cures, is very low at [her] age." He knows that Doctor Dohmler is right to insist that it is absurd for a psychologist to marry his patient; indeed, he even *says* that Dohmler and Franz Gregorovius are right to counsel against such a marriage. Like Macbeth, however, Dick proceeds to ignore what he "knows," his perception that "the logic of his life tended away from the girl." No less than *Macbeth*, *Tender Is the Night* explores the tragic mystery of why a gifted man destroys himself while fully conscious of the dangers involved.

Though originally written as a flashback rather than as the opening section, Book I includes crucial details which initiate the tragic action. Dick Diver is introduced as a psychologist of great promise who is preparing to write his first book after training at Yale, Oxford, and Johns Hopkins. Yet he is burdened with certain misconceptions—"the illusions of eternal strength and health, and of the essential goodness of people ... the illusions of a nation, the lies of generations of frontier mothers who had to croon falsely that there were no wolves outside the cabin door." He is capable of saying to Franz, his friend and colleague, that his one real goal is to become the greatest psychologist who ever lived. A man with such confidence in his own ability may choose to believe that other psychiatrists should avoid marrying their patients, but he is different. Such a man may persuade himself that he can act on his "wish" that Nicole had no "background." Indeed, such a man may take the extraordinary step Dick takes at the end of Book I. Fitzgerald assures us that we are in the presence here of an Aristotelian "mistake," for Dick's optimistic assumptions are clearly labeled as *illusions*. Book I as a whole presents a man whose basic goodness is not in question but whose innocence leads him to act in a manner no less doubtful than that of the morally flawed Macbeth.

Book II ("Rosemary's Angle") is set six years later, on the soon-to-be-fashionable French Riviera, which the Divers have literally helped to create. This section of the novel, the original opening, is probably the least satisfactory in the revised version. As others have remarked, Rosemary's point of view on the Divers seems rather arbitrary, even coy, once we already know the nature of Nicole's problem. Moreover, Fitzgerald's use of Rosemary as the point of view character for over one hundred pages (most of Books II and III) requires him to elaborate on her affairs in ways which finally seem extraneous, as when we get a chapter recounting her first meeting with Earl Brady, a film director, or when her experience of the McKisco-Tommy Barban duel is treated in relatively fulsome detail. Rosemary is made to seem a more important character than she in fact turns out to be (a flaw in the original version as well).

Everything considered, however, this section of the book is still more effective in its revised position. It may make better sense to use Rosemary's perspective when there is a real mystery concerning the Divers, but the tragic significance of what she sees but fails to understand is much more affecting in the later edition. In the revised *Tender*, as Fitzgerald employs Rosemary to render the alluring dimensions of Dick Diver's "world," we are made acutely aware of what constitutes that "lack of innocence" which is said to underlie "the expensive simplicity of the Divers." Throughout Book II, in fact, our reactions must be distinctly ambivalent. We are made to feel, with Rosemary,

the immense charm of Dick's circle, as opposed to the vulgarity of the McKiscos, Mrs. Abrams, Dumphry, and Campion; and we are genuinely impressed by the beauty of the Divers' home, Villa Diana, which seems to Rosemary "the centre of the world." Book I behind us, however, we must also recognize what is *not* present in Dick's "world." Dick may have taught Nicole that "work is everything," but there seems to be no place for real work in the golden routine that we observe at the beach and Villa Diana. Because we know about Dick's promise as a psychiatrist, as well as his ambition to be the greatest of psychologists, the Divers' "absolute immobility" is ominous, even forbidding. Indeed, we must wonder if Dick Diver's shimmering "world" does not camouflage his own problems as well as his wife's mental condition.

The purpose of Book II is to create just this double effect. The elegance of life at Villa Diana confirms our initial sense of Dick's superior powers, his status as a kind of "superman" (Fitzgerald's description of his hero). Yet we are also made to feel that Dick's powers have been misdirected, so much so that they are on the verge of decline. Dick's lovely "world" is extremely fragile, as we see in the disastrous aftermath to his party in Book II. Dick is not directly involved in the duel between McKisco and Tommy Barban, but his inability to control such events is very much to the point. Although Book II offers an exquisite portrait of Dick's intelligence and taste, what it reveals most poignantly is the inadequacy of these resources. This is clearly suggested by Nicole's continuing illness, as we no doubt realize well before the stunning conclusion to Book III. It is most apparent, however, in the direction of Dick's life, the dubious road he has taken during the six years of marriage between Books I and II. Problems of narrative point of view aside, the achievement of Book II is to depict in vivid, suggestive images of social life the tragic vulnerability of Dick's beautiful but artificial "world."

Book III ("Casualties") continues the action of Book II, as the Divers and their entourage leave the Riviera to spend a week in Paris. Here Fitzgerald firmly establishes that sense of a fatalistic progression so crucial to his tragic conception. The events of Book III repeatedly confirm the ominous hints of Book II, until we are forced to see that the "casualties" referred to are the novel's principal characters, not the war victims Dick commemorates at the beginning of Book III. This section ends with a chilling revelation about Nicole's condition, but prior to that the solidity of Dick's "world" is exposed as an unsustaining fiction. The Divers and Rosemary have come to Paris to see Abe North off for New York, where Abe is planning to write music again. As everyone has noted, Abe is a foil for Dick, most obviously in his plan to rejuvenate his career and become once again what Franz would call a "serious" man. The complete collapse of this plan within the brief span of Book III is quite foreboding insofar as Abe and Dick are truly comparable. Abe's failure suggests the truth in Dick's piercing remark to Rosemary: "'Don't you know you can't do anything about people?'" It is ironic that Dick should say this—Dick, whose life has been devoted to the idea that everything can be done for people. Yet the events of Book III confirm Dick's pessimism. Abe's drunken antics are surrounded by the fatal shooting at the Gare Saint-Lazare, the unpleasant episode involving the three cobra women, the contretemps climaxed by Jules Peterson's death, and finally Nicole's hysteria. As disaster follows disaster, we are made to see that Dick's ability to create "graceful theatricals . . . out of life's daily ordinariness" is virtually anachronistic in the Paris of 1925.

By the close of Book III the novel's tragic pattern is unmistakable. In Book I Fitzgerald introduces a gifted hero who comes to make what is surely a terrible mistake in marrying Nicole. In Book II he presents the attractive but fragile results of Dick's attempt to make the best of his decision, suggesting all the while that this effort has misdirected Dick's energies and produced a social facade which can only temporarily protect Nicole. In Book III he confirms our worst expectations. This confirmation is all the more tragic because it occurs *despite* Dick's apparent mastery of the situation. Throughout Books II and III Dick is at his best, maneuvering various social engagements to their proper close and effectively minimizing the consequences of such messes as the Peterson murder. Yet his rewards are Nicole's hysterical relapse and the grim prospect of trying to put their world together again, the work of six years having disappeared in one week. If we need further proof that Dick is headed toward his own collapse, we have his reaction to Rosemary, in which "for a moment his usual grace, the tensile strength of his balance, was absent." It comes to seem inevitable that Dick's resistance will be less and less effective, that he will have fewer and fewer resources with which to combat his insoluble problem.

In Book IV ("Escape") Fitzgerald begins to trace Dick's agonizing downward arc, which will continue to the end of the novel. Here Fitzgerald faced a problem quite comparable to Shakespeare's in *Macbeth*. Plots of degeneration are inherently painful, requiring as they do the extended depiction of the hero's decline. While it is necessary that we share in his suffering, it is also important that we not be subjected to pointless repetition or allowed to reject this suffering as nothing more than deserved. Shakespeare handles this problem in a number of ways, notably by the use of soliloquies in which Macbeth contemplates with horror the series of self-destructive actions he has initiated with the murder of Duncan. These soliloquies offer relief from an otherwise dismal sequence of events, as Macbeth's sensitive reactions to his own crimes complicate and enrich the long process of disintegration which occupies most of Shakespeare's play. Conversely, Fitzgerald chooses not to reveal Dick's meditations upon his own condition, a decision I shall discuss shortly. Instead, he immerses us in the events which mark his hero's decline. Between Book III and the more crucial episodes of Book IV, four years pass in which Dick begins to drink more heavily, to experience uncontrollable fits of bad temper, and to feel strongly drawn to all attractive women except his wife. Then, in 1929, Dick undergoes his own great depression. Nicole suffers a relapse even more terrifying than the one in Paris; Abe North is beaten to death in a speakeasy; Dick's father dies; and Dick finds himself traveling to Rome to seek out Rosemary after not seeing her for four years. Dick's Roman experience is ghastly, as he engages Rosemary in an affair which means nothing to either of them, then stumbles into a drunken fight with local taxi drivers and police which leads to imprisonment and the ultimate humiliation of having to depend upon Nicole's rich and arrogant sister, Baby. After Rome, as most of Fitzgerald's critics have noticed, there is no turning back. Dick has "escaped" from his role as physician to a wealthy schizophrenic and the leisured class she represents. Unfortunately, he has abandoned his moral and professional standards as well.

Because Dick's flight to Rome is so obviously "the moral equivalent of leaping from a cliff," the novel's tragic drift from this point has been widely remarked. Fitzgerald's treatment has been questioned, however, especially on the crucial point of why Dick should decline so drastically. The views of Kent and Gretchen Kreuter represent a widespread, thoroughly human desire to understand this appalling sequence: "One wants to know why Diver meets his doom, why he has succumbed to the kinds of demands that his friends place upon him, and, above all, how this has happened to a man who knows himself as a man in Diver's profession must." I think there are two answers to these questions, though neither will satisfy a desire for unambiguous solutions. The answer emphasized by the revised text is that Dick meets his doom because he chooses to marry Nicole. The marriage is inevitably tragic because Dick is in a damned if he does, damned if he doesn't situation. Either he will manage to cure Nicole, in which case she will cease to depend upon his services and move on to a new life; or he will fail to effect a radical change in her condition, in which case he will remain tied to the unrelenting problems of keeping up that fragile "world" we observe in Book II. This is a game Dick cannot possibly win. His eventual unhappiness is no less certain than Macbeth's moral disintegration.

But why does Dick take on such an impossible task? Here the parallel with *Macbeth* is quite interesting. Norman Rabkin has recently suggested that Macbeth's announced motive for murdering Duncan—his "vaulting ambition" (I, vii, 27)—is simply inadequate. It is an explanation which does not explain; something else, a more mysterious force, appears to be at work. Similarly, Dick's love for Nicole is an important but insufficient motive for his decision. In addition to this wholly sympathetic emotion, we have what Fitzgerald called "the inner conflicts of the idealist." Dick is certainly an idealist, believing as he does in the illusions of eternal strength and health—especially his own—and the essential goodness of people. With such faith in his unlimited resources and the good will of others, he naturally underestimates the price he will be asked to pay for treating Nicole. But I think Fitzgerald meant to suggest something more ominous when he referred to the idealist's *conflicts*. The idealist's desire to assist others is real enough, but there is also the wish to impose his own strength, health, and goodness upon others, to make the world over in his own image. A man of superior powers is constantly tempted to ignore common sense because his ego tells him that what is impossible for others is quite possible for him. When he decides to marry Nicole, Dick indulges just this fatal sense of omnipotence.

Dick's own explanation for his collapse is that it is a mystery: "He had lost himself—he could not tell the hour when, or the day or the week, the month or the year. Once he had cut through things, solving the most complicated equations as the simplest problems of his simplest patients. Between the time he found Nicole flowering under a stone on the Zürichsee and the moment of his meeting with Rosemary the spear had been blunted." There is much to be said for this second "answer" to the question of why Dick collapses. Other solutions do suggest themselves. We might argue that Dick has placed too much faith in the healing powers of social forms and the personal charm required to maintain them. We might condemn his excessive desire to please others, at whatever cost to his professional goals. We might say that Dick has entertained contradictory images of himself, as social impresario and social scientist, thus ironically recalling Fitzgerald's famous definition of what marks a first-rate intelligence: "the ability to hold two opposed ideas in the mind at the same time, and still retain the ability to function." The point would then be that Dick's ability to balance these "opposed ideas" has eroded over the years. But how do these "explanations" significantly clarify the mystery to which Dick points? The ultimate question is why a first-rate intelligence should cease to function. Like the Kreuters, we want to answer such questions. We want to know why Dick meets his doom, why he has succumbed to the demands of others, why his resources are finally insufficient. But just as Shakespeare cannot tell us what cause in nature makes hard hearts, so Fitzgerald cannot say why we lack the capacity to do and be all things. What he can do is show us the inevitable fate of anyone who tries.

I suggested earlier that Fitzgerald revised his text to avoid the impression that Dick collapses precipitously. In point of fact, of course, Dick's collapse emerges in Books IV and V after a gestation period of no fewer than ten years. At the end, however, in Book V ("The Way Home"), Dick's condition is obviously terminal and its progress precipitous indeed. The novel's overall structure may remind us of *Macbeth*, but the contrast between the Dick Diver of Book II and the Doctor Diver of Book V is distinctly reminiscent of *Othello*. Just as Othello's elegant speech gives way to virtual inarticulateness, so Dick's wonderful manners are replaced by what Nicole calls "uncharacteristic bursts of temper": "he would suddenly unroll a long scroll of contempt for some person, race, class, way of life, way of thinking." Even the reader who has followed Dick through the painful stages of his decline may be surprised by the picture of him drunk, "belching now and then contentedly into the soft warm darkness." On the whole, however, such images are the stuff of Fitzgerald's uncompromising portrayal of Dick's fate. The real problems with Book V as tragic finale lie elsewhere.

I have already mentioned the first problem: Fitzgerald's decision to withdraw from Dick's thoughts during the final period of decline. This technique does emphasize the shocking external contrast between Dick's early elegance and later shabbiness, as well as lend an aura of objectivity to the portrait. But there are real losses as well. It is one thing to be forced to speculate about Jay Gatsby's inner life, but Dick's has been presented throughout as a source of his superiority. Moreover, we are forced to guess at matters of the first importance in our final estimate of Dick. The following is a representative but presumptuous account of Dick's character at the end: "Dick Diver is a man who because of his deep love for Nicole Warren makes a deliberate choice with full realization of the dilemma which it will eventually force upon him. And when the dilemma must be resolved, he chooses what is best for Nicole even though it brings heartbreak to him." The assumption here is that Dick *chooses* to divorce himself from Nicole. In other discussions this idea sometimes takes the form that Dick encourages Nicole's affair with Tommy Barban, thus hastening her withdrawal from his now unnecessary protection. In the text, however, we are only told that "from the episode of the camphorrub, Dick had anticipated everything." I take this to mean that Dick has expected Nicole to leave him for Tommy. If Dick has orchestrated the affair, we are not told how or why. Indeed, we are never even told what Dick *thinks* about the affair. Does he suppose that Nicole is now cured? Does he think she will be better off with Tommy? I fear that we have no reasonable way to answer these basic questions, let alone endorse the attractive but sentimental idea that Dick has heroically plotted the destruction of his own marriage in order to "free" Nicole from her doctor/husband—himself. I think we must question Fitzgerald's judgment in turning from Dick's point of view to Nicole in Book V.

Relating much of Book V from Nicole's perspective does allow us to witness what she is like after years of marriage, however, Regrettably, what Nicole is like—what she has always been—is rather less desirable than Othello's "pearl." As Fitzgerald's narrator remarks, "Nicole had been designed for change, for flight, with money as fins and wings." Echoes of Daisy Buchanan and her "low, thrilling" voice which even Gatsby recognizes to be "full of money"? Nicole's vanity has been apparent from the first; now, as she prepares to leave Dick, she is described as "a happy child," someone who has "fought [Dick] with her money and her faith that her sister disliked him and was behind her now ... [with] her unscrupulousness against his moralities." The problem here is suggested by Bradley's formulation of why tragic works are tragic. If we are tragically moved by conflicts involving what we value, it

follows that "the value must be sufficient—a moderate value will not serve." Othello's tragedy is immensely heightened because of the great value we attach to Desdemona, the pearl he so basely throws away. Lear's grief is so affecting because we have been made to share his final opinion of Cordelia. Nicole, on the other hand, never quite seems worth the exhaustion of Dick's resources. And in Book V, where we confront her point of view directly, she is presented as very much Tommy Barban's lover, essentially unworthy of Dick as he was. We are still affected by the loss of Dick's integrity, but the "loss" of Nicole is a mixed affair which compromises the effect of the conclusion.

I should not like to end on this note, however, for Fitzgerald's conclusion transcends the problems just noted. In fact, the novel's final pages are among its most brilliant, evoking as they do that "dignified and responsible" aspect to Dick which Fitzgerald wanted to capture. Whether these pages convey "the melodrama of unrealized life," as Maria DiBattista has argued, or conclude the genuine tragedy of an "homme epuisé," as Fitzgerald claimed, every reader must of course decide. Dick's composure in the final scene with Tommy and Nicole was no doubt in Fitzgerald's mind when he referred to Dick's dignified and responsible aspect, and Dick's competence in extricating Mary North and Lady Caroline Sibley-Biers from their disgraceful imprisonment is a touching reminder of his unquestioned gifts. These closing scenes remind us of what has been lost in the long course of Dick's attempt to realize the impossible. Here and in the final beach scene, Dick demonstrates precisely that "dignity under suffering" which Fitzgerald thought characteristic of the tragic hero. Dick has failed because of an initial, irrevocable mistake which derived from his own character, but also because the world of the 1920s was one in which talents such as his were misused or even abused. His story therefore does justice to Fitzgerald's belief that tragedy may derive from a combination of human error and circumstances. In any case, this story is one in which the tragic effect is achieved throughout the work, not at the end alone. Fitzgerald's final indications of Dick's fate derive their authority from his comprehensive portrait of great potential come to bitter failure—an unrealized life of more than moderate value, representing spiritual waste of very high order.

III

My analysis of *Tender Is the Night* was not intended as a complete reading. Indeed, my remarks have the weight of a sketch if compared to such readings as Milton Stern's. Instead, I have tried to illustrate the value of approaching Fitzgerald's novels from a certain point of view. To examine *Tender Is the Night* as a tragedy allows us to gauge the structural logic of Fitzgerald's revisions, to judge more accurately the advantages and disadvantages of employing Rosemary's point of view, to appreciate what I have called the double effect of Book II, to see how the first three books are informed by a foreboding pattern which emerges most clearly with the violent events in Paris, and to identify what is wrong with such crucial features as the withdrawal from Dick's point of view and the characterization of Nicole. It is a commonplace that *Tender Is the Night* is both deeply flawed and one of Fitzgerald's two most powerful works. To study the book as a formal tragedy is to see how both claims are true.

This approach also helps correct the understandable but misleading tendency to insist upon the cultural "significance" of a book such as *Tender*. In reaction against earlier readers who stressed Fitzgerald's ignorance and "popular" elements, recent critics have transformed the novelist into a kind of philosophical historian. Thus Alan Trachtenberg: "Fitzgerald's entire fiction is an extended meditation on America, its history and its notorious dreams." Thus Edwin S. Fussell: "Ultimately, Fitzgerald's literary stature derives from his ability to apply the sensibilities implied by the phrase 'romantic wonder' to American civilization, and to gain from the conjunction a moral critique of that civilization." Richard Foster tells us that the "true" subject of *Tender Is the Night* is "a 'mythic' interpretation of history," and even Milton Stern argues that "a philosophy of history" is projected in *Tender*. For these critics and many others, Fitzgerald's acquaintance with Spengler and Marx is a stepping-stone to the idea that he is a "serious" writer whose seriousness takes the form of historical meditations. The danger in this approach is that it is extremely abstract. It implies that the value of Fitzgerald's works lies in their historical insights, their "truth." No one who appreciates Fitzgerald would want to deny that his books are filled with observations, intuitions, and even ideas of a greater profundity than earlier critics were willing to grant. Yet I think the revisionists have obscured the fact that Fitzgerald's principal gift was for a certain kind of storytelling—tragic storytelling, I have argued—in which his ability to dramatize the fates of particular characters is what appeals to us. This is to suggest, of course, that Fitzgerald was a tragedian rather than a cultural historian.

Finally, I believe that to read Fitzgerald in this fashion permits us to make fairly fine discriminations among his novels. In the case of *Tender*, for instance, I would emphasize the book's deep affinities with traditional tragic models. Such critics as R. J. Kaufmann have argued that "significant" suffering—that is, tragic suffering—must be rooted in the conscious choices of the protagonist. Robert Heilman has extended this mode of thought into a more elaborate definition: "tragedy should be used only to describe the situation in which the divided human being faces basic conflicts, perhaps rationally insoluble, of obligations and passions; makes choices, for good or for evil; errs knowingly or involuntarily; accepts consequences; comes into a new, larger awareness; suffers or dies, yet with a larger wisdom." We might argue about whether Dick achieves a new, larger awareness. Otherwise, I think it is clear that Fitzgerald's novel is faithful to Kaufmann's and Heilman's rather traditional prescriptions. Unlike many of his contemporaries, Fitzgerald adopted conventional assumptions when he conceived the tragedy of Dick Diver. If we were to look closely at the tragic strategies of *The Beautiful and Damned* and *The Great Gatsby*, we would find rather different assumptions at work and would therefore be in a good position to define what is uniquely tragic about these earlier novels. If we were then to address *The Last Tycoon*, we would find Fitzgerald returning to many of the basic assumptions which underlie *Tender Is the Night*. Ultimately, we would be able to trace more precisely than before the fluctuations in Fitzgerald's career as a novelist—if I am right, his career as a tragic novelist.

Source: Robert Merrill, "*Tender Is the Night* as a Tragic Action," in *Texas Studies in Literature and Language*, Vol. 25, No. 4, 1983, pp. 597–615.

William F. Hall

In the following article, Hall discusses how the use of dialogue in Fitzgerald's novel provides the essential themes of the novel.

Fitzgerald's handling of dialogue in *Tender is the Night* has not so far received sufficient critical attention. In this article I intend to examine three quotations to demonstrate that it is, in fact, in the dialogue that the essential theme of the novel is most clearly revealed.

In the early part of the novel we witness the Divers' relationship through the innocent eyes of Rosemary, who "knew the Divers loved each other because it had been her primary assumption." The Divers have a party to which Dick invites Rosemary and her mother. There has been no indication before this point that Dick is interested in Rosemary, though she already loves him, and, to Rosemary, Nicole seems a cool self-possessed woman of the world. At the party Dick makes the following apparently empty remarks to Rosemary and her mother.

> "What a beautiful garden," Mrs. Speers exclaimed.
>
> "Nicole's garden," said Dick. "She won't let it alone. She nags it all the time, worries about its diseases. Any day now I expect to have her come down with Powdery Mildew or Fly Speck or Late Blight."
>
> He pointed his forefinger decisively at Rosemary, saying with a lightness seeming to conceal a paternal interest, "I'm going to save your reason—I'm going to give you a hat to wear on the beach."
>
> He turned them from the garden to the terrace, where he poured a cocktail. . .

Here, without any pursuit of the Freudian convolutions of the forefinger and the hat, Dick's unconscious preoccupations lie clear under the light, flippant, almost meaningless remarks. He stresses Nicole's ownership of the garden, revealing his own touchiness about the fact that they live on her money. His preoccupation with Nicole's disease is equally apparent and combined with his interest in Rosemary (*seeming* to conceal a paternal interest) expresses almost a wish that Nicole might become totally sick. Then his sudden leap to "I'm going to save your reason" (just as he consciously set out,, at the beginning of his relationship with Nicole, to save hers) reveals, as does the reference to paternal affection, that he is already thinking of Rosemary as he did of Nicole at the beginning of the novel. For, as I shall point out in more detail later, an integral part of the theme is that Dick's affair with Rosemary repeats for him every stage of his original feeling for Nicole.

The second quotation is taken from the final section of the book. Consciously, and this part of the novel is seen from Nicole's viewpoint, Nicole still respects Dick. She still regards herself as dependent on him, just as he still consciously maintains that he loves her and consciously ignores the possibility of an affair between her and Tommy Barban. But their true unconscious relationship, unrealised by either of them at this juncture, is clearly revealed to the reader in the exchange that takes place between them the morning after Dick has made a fool of himself on Golding's yacht. Nicole sits between Dick and Tommy, making a sketch of Tommy's head.

> "Hands never idle—distaff flying," Dick said lightly.
>
> How could he talk so trivially with the blood still drained down from his cheeks so that the auburn

> " ... it is clear that Fitzgerald reveals in his dialogue both what his characters consciously know and communicate to each other, and what lies buried beneath the surface of their own and others' conciousness where the truth about themselves and their relationships is to be found."

lather of beard showed red as his eyes? She turned to Tommy saying:

> "I can always do something. I used to have a nice active little Polynesian ape and juggle him around for hours till people began to make the most dismal rough jokes—"
>
> She kept her eyes resolutely away from Dick. Presently he excused himself and went inside.

Here Dick's suspicions are apparent to the reader in his opening remark, which ironically stresses their relationship as man and wife. But he speaks *lightly*, unaware of his own motive for saying it. And Nicole does not understand the unconscious barb any more than he does. To her he is talking *trivially*. Her own hidden contempt for Dick is even more obvious (though significantly not to either her or Dick or, we assume, Tommy) in her reference to the Polynesian ape after she has just noticed the red growth of beard on Dick's face and the redness of his eyes. Moreover what is further revealed by her remarks here—"I used to have a nice . . . ape and juggle him around"—is that at this point she is unconsciously viewing Dick as her sister has viewed him from the beginning; as bought with the Warren money, to serve the Warren purposes. She does not, as the action continues, persist in this view, but it brushes her mind, recorded only in the dialogue.

The third example occurs towards the end of the novel. At this point Nicole feels herself "so delicately balanced . . . between an old foothold that had always guaranteed her security, and the imminence of a leap from which she must alight changed in the very chemistry of blood and muscle, that she did not dare bring the matter into the true forefront of consciousness." Dick feels himself to have "gone into a process of deterioration." Rosemary, whom neither have seen for some time, comes to visit them at Antibes.

Just before the passage to be quoted here Rosemary has been surprised at Dick's bitterness about Mary North. She had "thought of him as all-forgiving, all-comprehending." Then the following scene takes place:

> . . .She [Nicole] guessed that Dick . . . would grow charming . . . make Rosemary respond to him. Sure enough, in a moment . . . he had said:
>
> "Mary's all right— . . .But it's hard to go on liking people who don't like you."
>
> Rosemary, falling into line, swayed toward Dick and crooned:
>
> "Oh, you're so nice. I can't imagine anybody not forgiving you anything, no matter what you did to them."

Rosemary then goes on to ask what they have thought of her latest pictures. Nicole says nothing but Dick goes on:

> ". . . Let's suppose that Nicole says to you that Lanier is ill. What do you do in life? What does anyone do? They *act*— . . . the face shows sorrow, the voice shows shock, the words show sympathy. . . ."
>
> "But in the theatre, no . . . all the best comediénnes have built up their reputations by burlesquing the correct emotional responses—fear and love and sympathy . . ."
>
> "The danger to an actress is in responding. Again let's suppose that somebody told you, 'Your lover is dead.' In life you'd probably go to pieces. But on the stage you're trying to entertain—the audience can do the 're-sponding' for themselves. First the actress has lines to follow, then she has to get the audience's attention back on herself. . . . So she must do something unexpected. If the audience thinks the character is hard she goes soft on them—if they think she's soft she goes hard. You go all *out* of character—you understand?" . . .
>
> "You do the unexpected thing until you've manouevred the audience back from the objective fact to yourself. *Then* you slide into character again."

This is clearly no answer at all to Rosemary's question about her pictures; yet everything Dick says is intensely relevant to his relationship with Rosemary, and with Nicole. That something of crucial importance has clearly been communicated to the two women, though not at the conscious level, is clear from their actions following the conversation. Rosemary turns to the Divers' daughter, Topsy, and asks her "Would you like to be an actress when you grow up?" indicating that a part of herself has understood that Dick has been discussing his own relationship with her and that the relationship has been,

at a certain level, that of father and daughter. Nicole, who has, we are told, consciously understood nothing immediately remarks, "in her grandfather's voice," "it's absolutely *out* to put such ideas in the heads of other people's children." She then leaves; and in the scene immediately following she has "a sense of being cured and in a new way. Her ego blooming like a great rich."

Dick begins by making an unconscious comment on Rosemary's reaction to the appeal of his "It's hard to go on liking people who don't like you." It is, as it were, dawning on him that she is burlesquing. She has "gone soft" to get the audience's (Dick's) attention "back on herself." He is acknowledging the truth about her. She is an actress in life. She does not "respond." Her audience does so. But this truth about Rosemary is a truth also about himself. In Paris Rosemary had "said her most sincere thing to him: 'Oh we're such *actors*—you and I.'" He had, he is suggesting, in his bitterness about Mary North, been doing the "unexpected thing," to get Rosemary's attention back on himself. He had done the unexpected in being bitter and unpleasant and is now "sliding into character again": the character of the charming, protective, essentially paternal figure. The sense that this is only a *role* and not his true nature is, I think, the main significance of this passage for Dick himself. And his apparently off-hand examples, "Let's suppose Nicole says to you that Lanier is ill," "Suppose that somebody told you, 'Your lover is dead'" indicate that at least a hint about the real truth of his own nature and of his relationship with Nicole is already afloat in his mind. This is a truth Nicole has begun to recognise a little earlier when in response to his wish to show his skill on the aquaplane "she indulged him as she might have indulged Lanier."

The passage reveals a dim awareness, then, on Dick's part, that no real relationship has ever existed between himself and Rosemary and that none can exist—because each of them is incapable of "responding." Unconsciously he also senses that the role he has maintained with Nicole is now slipping from him, that he is the child, the dependent and that she is sliding back "into character again." For Nicole the return to "character" is to be a return, as she tells Tommy Barban, to her "true self."

If my interpretation of these three examples is valid, it is clear that Fitzgerald reveals in his dialogue both what his characters consciously know and communicate to each other, and what lies buried beneath the surface of their own and others' conciousness where the truth about themselves and their relationships is to be found. And this buried knowledge is revealed only in the dialogue. Fitzgerald, as author, makes no explicit comment upon it and neither do any of the characters. "Here [in the world of the novel] there is no light" as the quotation from Keats on the title-page suggests there will not be.

Further this interpretation of the dialogue suggests that Dick Diver's tragedy is internal and not caused by the corrupting influence of Nicole's wealth. This is assuredly a contributing factor, since it affords Dick, as no other condition could, the opportunity to use to the full what is in fact his only talent (despite his own and others' misapprehensions about his brilliance); that is, his charm and great social ability. It is his final realization of the fact that this is all he in fact has, that destroys him. For in realising this, he realises also that despite his varied relationships, his apparent adult control of them, and his ability to arouse "a fascinating and uncritical love in others for himself," *he* is unable to love. He is capable not of responding, or of acting, but only of burlesquing.

Nicole's return to "her original self" results from a similar realisation of the hidden truth about herself. She understands that her dependence on Dick has been in fact her disease: a false on a false reality.

The true nature of their relationship with each other is forced upon them both by Dick's parallel relationship with Rosemary. The discussion of the 1st example on pages 2 and 3 above suggests that with both women, Dick plays the *role* of father. And it is clear that both Nicole and Rosemary attribute this *role* to him. Nicole, who was Rosemary's age when she first met Dick, leans on him for support as she might on an 'ideal' father until her return to health, when she abandons "her dry suckling at his lean chest." Her view of him as father is so complete that in her mad spells she sees him as the 'evil' father who seduced her.

And that this is Rosemary's view of him is made equally clear. He is to her "the beautiful cold image she had created," the idealized image of her dead father. Dick's refusal to take Rosemary when she offers herself in Paris confirms this image in her mind. When later Dick does make physical demands the result is to destroy whatever potential she may have had for real love. Her experience with him, in other words, parallels subtly and psychologically the brutal physical disillusion of Nicole as a child with her actual father.

The relationships are complicated by the fact that Dick, like the two women, has assumed that the thin layer of his "attentive seriousness" has concealed a deep fund of adult love and power. Whereas in fact, as the discussion of the third example indicates, he has been an actor burlesquing "the correct emotional responses." Incapable of loving, he has been beneath his *role*, a child seeking parental love—as he is in his final conversation with Mary North when "His eyes, for a moment clear as a child's, asked her sympathy." His "lesion of vitality," then, is rooted, as are Nicole's and Rosemary's, in a past family relationship; and the 'adult' relationships of all three are conditioned by this.

If this interpretation is accepted, it is clear *Tender is the Night* is not a fumbling attempt to reproduce again what Alfred Kazin describes as Fitzgerald's only theme, "the fitful glaring world of Jay Gatsby's dream and of Jay Gatsby's failure." The novel has its weaknesses, but these result, at least partly, from Fitzgerald's attempt to express a new theme. He is here concerned, as not before, with the hidden roots of adult relationships; and with the waste that results from the characters' misunderstanding of themselves and of each other. Throughout the novel this misunderstanding is the result of their mistaking *persona* for true self, even though in their communication with each other the preoccupations, motives, and desires of that true self are constantly revealed to the attentive reader.

Source: William F. Hall, "Dialogue and Theme in *Tender Is the Night*," in *Modern Language Notes*, Vol. 76, No. 7, November 1961, pp. 616–22.

Robert Stanton

In the following article, Stanton discusses the "major artistic devices" used in Fitzgerald's novel.

Francis Scott Fitzgerald has come a long way from the limbo into which some of his obituaries tried to thrust him in 1941; his return has been marked and encouraged by several important editions of his stories, novels, and articles, an outstanding biography, and a gradually increasing supply of critical articles. Fortunately, although the interest in his writing still stems largely from the excitement of the 1920's and the glamour and pathos of the author's life, his critics have become increasingly willing to view him—as they must, if his reputation is not to decline again—as an artist and craftsman.

The purpose of this article is to examine one of the major artistic devices used in *Tender Is the Night*. It will show that the novel contains a large number of "incest-motifs," which, properly understood, take on symbolic value and contribute to the thematic unity of the novel. The term "incest-motifs" may

> The term 'incest-motifs' may seem ill-chosen at first, since most of these passages allude, not to consanguineous lovers, but to a mature man's love for an immature girl."

seem ill-chosen at first, since most of these passages allude, not to consanguineous lovers, but to a mature man's love for an immature girl. I have used the term chiefly because the first of these passages concerns Devereux Warren's incestuous relation with his fifteen-year-old daughter Nicole, so that whenever Fitzgerald later associates a mature man with an immature girl, the reader's reaction is strongly conditioned by this earlier event. Devereux's act is the most obvious, and the only literal, example of incest in the novel. It is of basic importance to the plot, since it causes Nicole's schizophrenia and thus necessitates her treatment in Dr. Dohmler's clinic, where she meets Dick Diver. Nicole's love for Dick is in part a "transference" caused by her mental disorder; the character of their marriage is dictated largely by the requirements of her condition.

In spite of the importance of Devereux' act, the use of incest as *motif* is more evident in the fact that Dick, Nicole's husband and psychiatrist, falls in love with a young actress whose most famous film is entitled *Daddy's Girl*. As this coincidence suggests, Fitzgerald deliberately gives an incestuous overtone to the relationship between Dick Diver and Rosemary Hoyt. Like Rosemary's father, Dick is of Irish descent and has been an American army doctor, a captain. At his dinner-party on the Riviera, he speaks to Rosemary "with a lightness seeming to conceal a paternal interest." He calls her "a lovely child" just before kissing her for the first time, and in the Paris hotel he says, again with a "paternal attitude," "When you smile . . . I always think I'll see a gap where you've lost some baby teeth." Dick is thirty-four, twice Rosemary's age, and to emphasize this, Fitzgerald continually stresses Rosemary's immaturity. When she first appears in 1925, her cheeks suggest "the thrilling flush of children after their cold baths in the evening"; "her body hovered

delicately on the last edge of childhood—she was almost eighteen, nearly complete, but the dew was still on her." She and her mother are like "prize-winning school-children." Even Nicole pointedly refers to Rosemary as a child.

By the time of Abe North's departure, Dick admittedly loves Rosemary; now, "he wanted to . . . remove the whole affair from the nursery footing upon which Rosemary persistently established it"; but he realizes that Rosemary "had her hand on the lever more authoritatively than he." Helpless as is, he remains conscious—even over-conscious—of the incongruity of the situation; he tells Rosemary, "When a child can disturb a middle-aged gent—things get difficult." Finally he tells Nicole that Rosemary is "an infant . . . there's a persistent aroma of the nursery."

After Rosemary leaves the Riviera, Dick begins to exaggerate the immaturity of *other* women as well. He is uneasy when Nicole suggests that he dance with a teen-age girl at St. Moritz, and protests, "I don't like ickle durls. They smell of castile soap and peppermint. When I dance with them, I feel as if I'm pushing a baby carriage." He looks at a pretty woman, and thinks, "Strange children should smile at each other and say, 'Let's play.'" Gradually an obscure sense of guilt appears. When Nicole accuses him, falsely and irrationally, of seducing a patient's daughter—"a child," she says, "not more than fifteen"—he feels guilty. When he is being taken to court after the taxi-driver fight, a crowd boos him, mistaking him for a man who has raped and slain a five-year-old child; later that day Dick cries, "I want to make a speech. . . . I want to explain to these people how I raped a five-year-old girl. Maybe I did "

As his decline continues, Dick's attitude toward his own children, Topsy and Lanier, begins to change. In Rome, he decides that Rosemary "was young and magnetic, but so was Topsy." When Nicole realizes that his aquaplaning at the Riviera is inspired by Rosemary's "exciting youth," she remembers that "she had seen him draw the same inspiration from the new bodies of his children . . ." Earlier, Dick has exclaimed, "What do I care whether Topsy 'adores' me or not? I'm not bringing her up to be my wife," apparently assuming that the love of a child does not differ essentially from the love of an adult; he jokes with Lanier about "a new law in France that you can divorce a child." Finally, late in the novel Nicole notices his "almost unnatural interest in the children."

The presence of these incest-motifs may be explained in several ways. First, they may have been suggested, if only slightly and indirectly, by Fitzgerald's own ambivalent attitudes toward his mother and his daughter. He vacillated between being ashamed of his mother and devoted to her, one of the early titles for *Tender Is the Night* was *The Boy Who Killed His Mother*. According to his biographer, with his daughter Scottie, Fitzgerald was alternately "the severe father, the difficult alcoholic, and the man who loved his child intensely." But opposing this explanation is the fact that incest is not mentioned in his other works, and only "Babylon Revisited" and "The Baby Party" concern the love of father for daughter.

In any case, the incest-motifs may be fully accounted for by *Tender Is the Night* itself. Most of them grow logically out of Dick's relationship to Nicole. When Nicole first begins writing to Dick, she still pathologically mistrusts all men; her first letter to him speaks of his "attitude base and criminal and not even faintly what I had been taught to associate with the rôle of gentleman." Gradually Dick begins to take the place once occupied by her father, as a center of trust and security. As a psychiatrist, Dick realizes the value of this situation; he also realizes that Nicole must eventually build up her *own* world. After her psychotic attack at the Agiri fair, for example, he says, "You can help yourself most," and refuses to accept the father-role into which she tries to force him. But this sort of refusal costs him a difficult and not always successful effort of will. First, loving Nicole, "he could not watch her disintegrations without participating in them." Second, he is by nature a "spoiled priest," the father for all of his friends; he creates the moral universe in which they live. His nature and his love oppose his profession. It is therefore plausible, once his character begins to crumble, that he compensates for his long self-denial by falling in love with a girl literally young enough to be his daughter; that after the crowd has booed him for raping a five-year-old girl, he makes a mock-confession; and that when Nicole accuses him of seducing a patient's fifteen-year-old daughter, "He had a sense of guilt, as in one of those nightmares where we are accused of a crime which we recognize as something undeniably experienced, but which upon waking we realize we have not committed."

Ironically, although Dick's fascination with immaturity gives him an opportunity to be both lover and father, it also reveals his own fundamental immaturity. Like Nicole, who responds to Tommy Barban because she sees her own hardness and unscrupulousness reflected in his character, and like Rosemary, who responds to Dick at first because of his "self-control and . . . self-discipline, her own virtues," Dick is attracted to Rosemary's immaturity partly because of a corresponding quality within himself. Behind his facade of self-discipline, this central immaturity appears in the obsessive phrase, "Do you mind if I pull down the curtain?" Rosemary calls him "Youngster," "the youngest person in the world," and while he waits for Rosemary outside her studio, he circles the block "with the fatuousness of one of Tarkington's adolescents." When Abe North talks to Nicole in the railroad station, Fitszgerald says, "Often a man can play the helpless child in front of a woman, but he can almost never bring it off when he feels most like a helpless child" similarly, when Dick talks to Mary Minghetti just before leaving the Riviera, "his eyes, for the moment clear as a child's, asked her sympathy . . ."

The significance of the incest-motifs is not limited to Dick's personal disaster. After all, they do not all *issue* from him. It is not of Dick's doing that a patient accuses him of seducing her fifteen-year-old daughter or that a crowd boos him for raping a five-year-old girl. And except for Devereux Warren's act, the most conspicuous incest-motif in the novel is the motion picture for which Rosemary is famous, *Daddy's Girl*. Everyone, we are told, has seen it; and lest we miss the point of the title, we are given Dick's reaction to the final scene of the picture, "a lovely shot of Rosemary and her parent united at the last in a father complex so apparent that Dick winced for all psychologists at the vicious sentimentality." As the universal popularity of *Daddy's Girl* suggests, the incest-motifs symbolize a world-wide situation. In 1934, C. Hartley Grattan wrote of the relation between Nicole and her father, "Fitzgerald has tried to use this situation, this extreme (according to our tabus) example of decadence, to symbolize the rottenness of the society of which Nicole is a part." But the meaning of the repeated motif is both broader and more precise than this.

During the 1920's, the relationship between the prewar and postwar generations was curiously reversed. In Mark Sullivan's words,

> The Twenties, reversing age-old custom, Biblical precept and familiar adage, was a period in which, in many respects, youth was the model, age the imitator. On the dance-floor, in the beauty parlor, on the golf course; in clothes, manners, and many points of view, elders strove earnestly to look and act like their children, in many cases their grand children.

And Frederick Lewis Allen notes that "the women of this decade worshipped not merely youth, but unripened youth. . . ." That Fitzgerald agreed with this interpretation of the period is evident from a late essay in which he described the Jazz Age as "a children's party taken over by the elders. . . .By 1923 [the] elders, tired of watching the carnival with ill-concealed envy, had discovered that young liquor will take the place of young blood, and with a whoop the orgy began."

Here, on a world-scale, is Dick Diver's fascination with immaturity; and since the younger generation is the child of the elder, here is a situation to which the incest-motifs are relevant. Dick Diver's generation is older than Rosemary's, and he is the product of an older generation still, his minister-father's, with its stress upon "'good instincts,' honor, courtesy, and courage." Rosemary is the product of Hollywood, with its emphasis upon the future, and we are told that in *Daddy's Girl* she embodies "all the immaturity of the race." In embracing Rosemary, therefore, Dick Diver is a symbol of America and Europe turning from a disciplined and dedicated life to a life of self-indulgence, dissipation, and moral anarchy—a symbol of the parent generation infatuated with is own offspring. Dick's collapse, appropriately, occurs in 1929.

Even aside from Dick's relationship with Rosemary, there are many hints that he is gradually shifting allegiance from the past culture of his father to an unworthy future. In the beginning, he exhibits dignity and self-discipline, unfailing courtesy, and a firm (if unexpressed) moral code; before the novel is over, he has been beaten in a brawl with taxi-drivers, has insulted his friend Mary Minghetti, and, at the very end, has been forced to leave Lockport, New York, because he "became entangled with a girl who worked in a grocery store." To clarify this change, Fitzgerald underlines it in several passages. The most memorable example is Dick's remark at his father's grave, "Good-bye my father—good-bye, all my fathers"; later, as he enters the steamship to return to Europe, he is described as hurrying from the past into the future. But this is only his formal farewell to something he has long since left behind. Most of the allusions to the shift occur four years earlier, during the episode in which Dick falls in love with Rosemary. At the battlefield near Amiens, he tells Rosemary that the "whole-souled sentimental equipment" of the past generations was all spent in World War I. Next day, he takes her to the Cardinal de Metz's palace: the threshold of the palace connects the past without (the stone facade) to the future within (blue steel and mirrors), and crossing that threshold is an experience "perverted as a breakfast of oatmeal and hashish." Just after leaving the palace, Dick admits for the first time that he loves Rosemary. Next day, his attempt to visit Rosemary at her studio is explicitly labelled "an overthrowing of his past." And on the following day, in the hotel dining room, although Dick sees in the gold-star mothers "all the maturity of an older America," and remembers his father and his "old loyalties and devotions," he turns back to Rosemary and Nicole, the "whole new world in which he believed." It is worth noticing that at both the beginning and end of this episode, Fitzgerald emphasizes Rosemary's significance by placing her beside the memory of World War I.

One reason for the broad applicability of the incest-motif is its inherent complexity: it simultaneously represents a situation and expresses Fitzgerald's judgment of it. First, it suggests how appealing youth can be (whether as person or as quality) to the adult in whom the long-opposed edges of impulse and self-restraint have begun to dull. He longs not only for youth's vitality but for its innocence, which apparently confers moral freedom. In the first flush of love, Dick and Rosemary seem to share

an extraordinary innocence, as though a series of pure accidents had driven them together, so many accidents that at last they were forced to conclude that they were for each other. They had arrived with clean hands, or so it seemed, after no traffic with the merely curious and clandestine.

Similarly, most of the rebels of the Twenties sought not merely to discard the Victorian morality but to do so without any aftermath of guilt—to recapture the amorality of youth. But the incest-motif also suggests decadence and the violation of a universal taboo—particularly since in *Tender Is the Night* it appears first as the cause of Nicole's insanity—and thus indicates that the unconscious innocence of youth is forever lost to the adult, and that in searching for it he may find disaster: "that madness akin to the love of an aging man for a young girl."

The purpose of this study has been to give a glimpse of Fitzgerald's artistry by examining one of the major patterns in *Tender Is the Night*. The incest-motifs, as we have seen, help to unify the novel on several levels, as well as to show how those levels are interrelated. First, these motifs function literally as one result of Dick's relationship to Nicole; they are symptoms of his psychological disintegration. Second, they both exemplify and symbolize Dick's loss of allegiance to the moral code of his father. Finally, by including such details as *Daddy's Girl* as well as Dick's experience, they symbolize a social situation existing throughout Europe and America during the Twenties. Fitzgerald's ability to employ this sort of device shows clearly that he not only felt his experience intensely, but *understood* it as an artist, so that he could reproduce its central patterns within the forms and symbols of his work. His experience transcends the historical Fitzgerald who felt it and the historical Twenties in which it occurred, and emerges as art.

Source: Robert Stanton, "'Daddy's Girl': Symbol and Theme in *Tender Is the Night*," in *Modern Fiction Studies*, Vol. 4, No. 2, Summer 1958, pp. 136–42.

Sources

Bruccoli, Matthew Joseph, with Judith S. Baughman, "Introduction," in *Reader's Companion to F. Scott Fitzgerald's "Tender Is the Night,"* University of South Carolina Press, 1996, pp. 1–48.

Chamberlain, John, "Book of the Times," in *"Tender Is the Night": Essays in Criticism*, edited by Marvin LaHood, Indiana University Press, 1969, pp. 68–70; originally published in *New York Times*, April 13, 1934.

Colum, Mary M., "The Psychopathic Novel," in *"Tender Is the Night": Essays in Criticism*, edited by Marvin LaHood, Indiana University Press, 1969, pp. 59–62; originally published in *Forum and Century 91*, April 1934.

Gray, James, "Scott Fitzgerald Re-Enters, Leading Bewildered Giant," in *"Tender Is the Night": Essays in Criticism*, edited by Marvin LaHood, Indiana University Press, pp. 64–66; originally published in *St. Paul Dispatch*, April 12, 1934.

Gregory, Horace, "A Generation Riding to Romantic Death," in *"Tender Is the Night": Essays in Criticism*, edited by Marvin LaHood, Indiana University Press, pp. 72–74; originally published in *New York Herald Tribune*, April 15, 1934.

Rogers, Cameron, "Fitzgerald's Novel a Masterpiece," in *"Tender Is the Night": Essays in Criticism*, edited by Marvin LaHood, Indiana University Press, 1969, pp. 64–66; originally published in *San Francisco Chronicle*, April 15, 1934.

Further Reading

Allen, Frederick L., *Only Yesterday: An Informal History of the 1920's*, HarperCollins, 2000 (rev. ed.).

First published in 1931 and reissued in 2000, *Only Yesterday* is, as the book's subtitle suggests, an informal account of the decade that has come to be known as the "Roaring Twenties." The book has a special focus on the rising market and its subsequent crash and gives a good account of the atmosphere of the times in which Fitzgerald was writing.

Berg, A. Scott, *Max Perkins: Editor of Genius*, Riverhead Books, 1977.

Winner of the National Book Award, Berg's biography of Fitzgerald's editor reveals the profound influence Perkins had not only on Fitzgerald but also on Ernest Hemingway, Thomas Wolfe, and many of their contemporaries.

Bruccoli, Matthew J., *Some Sort of Epic Grandeur: The Life of F. Scott Fitzgerald*, University of South Carolina Press, 2002 (rev. ed.).

First published in 1981, Bruccoli's biography of Fitzgerald has long been considered the definitive work on the author. In the revised edition, Bruccoli adds new material from more recently discovered manuscripts and papers.

Bruccoli, Matthew J., ed., *Zelda Fitzgerald: The Collected Writings*, University of Alabama Press, 1997.

Although F. Scott Fitzgerald was the more well-known writer of the family, his wife Zelda wrote a novel, *Save Me the Waltz*, and many stories and poems, some of which were published during her life. Bruccoli's collection brings these writings together and helps to round out Zelda's character.

Milford, Nancy, *Zelda: A Biography*, HarperPerennial, 2001 (rev. ed.).

Based on the author's doctoral dissertation, the book offers the most complete picture of Zelda Fitzgerald from her youth as a southern belle through her tumultuous marriage to Fitzgerald, and to her death in a sanatorium fire.

Wheelock, John Hall, *Editor to Author: The Letters of Maxwell Perkins*, Charles Scribner's Sons, 1987.

Taken as a whole, the letters by Fitzgerald's editor, Maxwell Perkins, show the profound love and respect Perkins had not only for his writers but for literature in general. Perkins's relationship with Fitzgerald is revealed in dozens of letters he wrote to him, or about him, over the years.

White Fang

Jack London
1906

When *White Fang* was published in 1906, Jack London was the most widely read writer in the United States and was also popular in Europe, thanks to his second novel, *The Call of the Wild* (1903). (London had become, as well, the first millionaire American author.) The two novels are related in that while *The Call of the Wild* tells the story of a dog who becomes wild and leads a wolf pack, *White Fang* is the life story of a wolf who comes, after many hardships dealt him by both man and nature, to live a dog's life with a loving master. Both novels, along with scores of London's short stories, are set in the land the author called simply "The North"—the Yukon Territory to which he once traveled as a gold prospector.

Though not considered the literary equal of *The Call of the Wild*, *White Fang* was an immediate commercial success and continues to be popular a century after its initial publication. In its unblinking portrayals of nature's unforgiving harshness, of humankind's capacity for both shocking brutality and unconditional love, and of the struggle for survival that is common to all life, *White Fang* is classic London.

Author Biography

Jack London was born January 12, 1876, in San Francisco, California. His mother, Flora Wellman, was not married. It is generally believed that an astrologer named William Chaney was London's father. The year Jack was born, his mother married a widower named John London, who adopted Jack and moved the family to nearby Oakland.

Shunning formal education, London worked from a young age, first in a cannery and then as an oysterman in the San Francisco Bay. It was during his first sea voyage, in 1893, that London began writing. The following year, he traveled across the United States, a hobo journey that he wrote about in *Jack London on the Road* (1907).

In 1895, London finished high school in Oakland and then spent one semester at the University of California. During this time, he became interested in both literature and socialism. He was a member of the socialist party for the rest of his life.

London's next journey was as a gold prospector to the Yukon Territory during the Klondike gold rush, a trip he would also write about later. Failing to find gold, London went back to California and decided to make his living as a writer. His first published story was "To the Man on the Trail," (1899) published in *Overland Monthly* magazine. London's newspaper articles on politics earned him the nickname "Boy Socialist from Oakland." In 1900, London married Bessie Maddern and published his first collection of short stories, *Son of the Wolf.*

London's first novel was *A Daughter of the Snows* (1902). His second, *The Call of the Wild* (1903), made him famous around the world. The following year, his divorce added to his celebrity. He and his first wife had two daughters during their brief marriage.

London married Charmian Kittredge in 1905, the year before *White Fang* was published. The two made their home on a ranch in Glen Ellen, California. London continued to write both nonfiction and fiction, was in demand as a lecturer, and enjoyed sailing and working on the ranch.

In 1913, London published *John Barleycorn*, the story of his alcoholism, which became a bestseller. By 1915, London's health was in decline. He died November 22, 1916, in Glen Ellen, of an overdose of morphine. The drug had been prescribed for a gastrointestinal problem, and it is not known whether the overdose was an accident or a suicide.

Jack London

Plot Summary

Part 1—The Wild.
1: The Trail of Meat

Two men, Henry and Bill, are hiking through a spruce forest in the far North. It is deep winter. Snow covers the ground. The temperature is far below zero, and it is light only for a few hours each day. With the men is a team of six sled dogs. On the sled, along with equipment and supplies, is a coffin that holds the body of a man called Lord Alfred. Henry and Bill are taking the body to Fort McGurry. They constantly hear wolves howling, and they know that the nearly starved wolves are tracking them in hopes of killing them for food.

After the men make camp for the night, Bill feeds the dogs. He later tells Henry that seven dogs, not six, came to be fed. The men realize that one was a somewhat tame wolf. That night, one of their dogs disappears, lured away and eaten by the wolves.

2: The She-Wolf

The next morning, the men set off with the five remaining dogs. That evening, the tame wolf again comes to eat, but Bill sees her and drives her off. The following morning, another dog is missing.

Media Adaptations

- *White Fang* has been adapted to film at least eleven times in seven countries: the United States, France, Germany, Italy, the United Kingdom, Spain, and Australia. Among the most widely available versions are *White Fang*, made in the United States and released in 1991, directed by Randal Kleiser and starring Klaus Maria Brandauer and Ethan Hawke; and *White Fang II: Myth of the White Wolf*, another American film released in 1994, directed by Ken Olin and starring Scott Bairstow and Alfred Molina.

- There are at least two audio adaptations of *White Fang*. An unabridged version on cassette, read by William Hootkins, was released by Penguin Books Limited in 1998. An abridged version, read by the late actor John Ritter, was released by New Millennium Audio in 2002.

As the men camp the next evening, the wolves come closer. The men wish they could shoot at them to scare them away, but they have only three cartridges left. They decide that the tame wolf must actually be a dog. Bill tries to secure the dogs so that they cannot leave the camp, but that night a third dog disappears. Bill begins to be extremely anxious, convinced that the wolves will eventually kill all the dogs and then him and Henry. The She-Wolf, as the tame one is called, appears on the trail in daylight, and that night the wolf pack crowds closer than before to the camp.

3: The Hunger Cry

That night, no dogs are lost. But the next day, the sled overturns in an accident. While the men work to right the sled, the tame wolf lures one of the dogs away. Bill, unable to leave the dog to its fate, sets off with the gun to try to save it. Henry hears Bill fire all three shots and then hears sounds that tell him that the wolf pack has killed both the dog and Bill. After helping the two remaining dogs pull the sled briefly, Henry makes camp and a large fire. The wolves threaten him all night, and he is unable to sleep.

The next morning, Henry rigs a way to pull the coffin up into a tree so that the wolves cannot get it. Then he and the two dogs set off. Henry makes camp early and spends the night fighting off the hungry wolves with burning sticks. The next night, the wolves take the two remaining dogs, and Henry has to jump briefly into the fire to escape them. Just as an exhausted Henry is resigned to death, a group of men arrives with dogs and sleds. They drive away the wolves and ask where Lord Alfred is. Henry tells them that he is dead, his coffin in a tree for safety, before falling into a deep sleep as the men put him on a sled to take him to the fort.

Part 2—Born of the Wild.
1: The Battle of the Fangs

The novel follows the movement of the desperately hungry wolf pack after it leaves Henry. After running all day and night, the pack finds and kills a large moose—plenty of food for the forty wolves. The pack rests and then gradually splits into smaller and smaller groups. The She-Wolf, who had run at the head of the large pack, is left with three males. The oldest of the three, called One-Eye, kills the other two in a fight and becomes the She-Wolf's mate. They hunt together and learn to steal rabbits from snares set around an Indian camp.

2: The Lair

It is April. The She-Wolf finds a lair and has five cubs. The male hunts for himself and brings food to his mate.

3: The Gray Cub

Four of the cubs are reddish like their mother. One, the fiercest, is a gray male, like his father. After some weeks, One-Eye is unable to find food, and the She-Wolf can no longer provide milk for the cubs. Four of them die, but the gray cub survives until One-Eye brings food again. Then, One-Eye is killed by a lynx. The She-Wolf, who has resumed hunting while her cub stays in the lair, finds One-Eye's remains. She also finds the lynx's lair, where she knows that there are kittens.

4: The Wall of the World

One day, the cub's instinctive fear of leaving the lair is overcome by curiosity. The cub tumbles down the slope just outside the cave's entrance. Exploring, he finds a nest of small ptarmigan chicks and eats them. When the ptarmigan hen returns, he fights with her until she drives him away by pecking his nose. He finds a stream and is swept up in it but quickly begins to swim. Finally, he is attacked by a weasel and escapes death only because his mother hears the struggle and rescues him.

5: The Law of Meat

The cub begins to leave the lair daily and re-members all the lessons of his first outing. Then, for a time, neither the cub nor the She-Wolf finds food. In desperation, the She-Wolf raids the lynx's den, eating all but one kitten and taking it to her cub. Soon after, the lynx comes to the wolves' lair, and there is a terrible fight. The She-Wolf kills the lynx, but she is badly hurt, and the cub is wounded. Both recover, however. The cub begins to hunt with his mother and learns the law of meat: "EAT OR BE EATEN." The cub greatly enjoys hunting and eating, and also their rewards, the feeling of a full stomach and a nap in the sun.

Part 3—The Gods of the Wild.
1: The Makers of Fire

One day, the cub goes to the stream to drink and sees five Indians—the first humans he has seen. The men see the cub. One of them approaches the cub, whose instinctual awe of humans prevents him from running away. But when the man tries to pick him up, the cub bites. The man hits him, and the cub cries out, bringing the She-Wolf to his rescue.

One of the Indians, Gray Beaver, recognizes the She-Wolf as the former pet of his now-dead brother. He calls her Kiche and says that she is the offspring of a dog and a wolf and that she ran away to find food during a famine. Kiche lets Gray Beaver pet her, and Gray Beaver declares that Kiche is now his. He names the cub White Fang. Gray Beaver ties up Kiche, and White Fang stays close to her.

Soon, about forty more Indians and many dogs carrying packs arrive. Some of the dogs attack Kiche and White Fang, but the Indians rescue them. When the Indians move to another camp, a child keeps Kiche on a lead, and White Fang follows.

2: The Bondage

A puppy called Lip-Lip, larger and more used to fighting than White Fang, becomes his nemesis. Eventually, Gray Beaver knows that Kiche has become too tame to run away, so she is no longer tied. However, soon Gray Beaver gives Kiche to Three Eagles, who is leaving the rest of the group. White Fang swims after the canoe that is taking his mother away, and Gray Beaver comes after him and beats him severely. That night, when White Fang cries for his mother and wakes Gray Beaver, the man beats him even harder. White Fang longs to return to the wild, and he stays in camp only because he hopes his mother will return. Gray Beaver never pets White Fang but does not beat him as long as he obeys, and Gray Beaver also protects the pup from aggressive dogs and makes sure that he gets food. White Fang quickly learns that obedience prevents beatings.

3: The Outcast

Lip-Lip and other young dogs continually gang up on White Fang, possibly because they sense that he is three-quarters wolf. This makes White Fang mean and a good fighter. One day, he kills a dog. The tribe wants to kill White Fang, but Gray Beaver will not allow it. White Fang becomes an outcast; the other dogs will not allow him to be part of the pack, and the humans revile him.

4: The Trail of the Gods

In the fall, the Indians break camp. White Fang understands that they are leaving and that his mother will not return to him now. He hides in the woods until the Indians are gone, planning to return to the wild and ignoring Gray Beaver's calls. After a night alone, however, he longs for the companionship and food provided by humans. He runs for forty hours without stopping, following the Indians' trail. Exhausted, White Fang crawls to Gray Beaver, sure that he will be beaten. Instead, Gray Beaver gives him food and keeps the other dogs from taking it away. On this night, White Fang becomes tame.

5: The Covenant

It is December, and White Fang is eight months old. Gray Beaver, his wife, Kloo-Kooch, and his son, Mit-sah, take a trip. Gray Beaver drives a sled pulled by adult dogs, and Mit-sah has a small one pulled by White Fang and other pups, including Lip-Lip. White Fang remains solitary and fierce. His law is "to oppress the weak and obey the strong." White Fang feels no affection for Gray Beaver, and Gray Beaver shows none toward White Fang, but the two are companions who benefit each other.

6: The Famine

The following April, White Fang is one year old, and he returns with Gray Beaver and his family to the village. Now White Fang, because of his wolf heritage, is bigger and stronger than the young dogs that once bullied him. One day, White Fang meets Kiche in the village. He bounds toward her happily, but she does not remember him. She has a new litter, and she attacks White Fang, fearing that he may hurt her cubs. White Fang is confused but accepts the rebuff and withdraws.

When White Fang is three years old, a famine comes, and he leaves the tribe to hunt for food in the wild. He meets Kiche again, who has gone back to the lair where White Fang was born to give birth again. Because of the famine, once again only one of her cubs is alive. Soon after this, White Fang meets the famished Lip-Lip and kills him. Then he finds Gray Beaver's people, who have moved their village and now have plenty of food. Gray Beaver is not at his tent, but Kloo-Kooch welcomes White Fang happily.

Part 4—The Superior Gods.
1: The Enemy and His Kind

When White Fang is almost five years old, Gray Beaver takes him on a long trip to Fort Yukon. It is 1898, the time of the gold rush. Gray Beaver spends months trading at the fort. White Fang spends his time attacking and killing dogs that arrive on the steamboat that brings prospectors from the south. Some of the local men find it entertaining to watch these fights.

2: The Mad God

The fort's cook, a cruel man called Beauty Smith, loves to watch White Fang attack and kill the dogs from the steamboat. Beauty uses whisky to beguile a reluctant Gray Beaver into selling White Fang to him.

3: The Reign of Hate

Beauty Smith keeps White Fang chained up and teases him cruelly to make him as mean as possible. He does this both because he enjoys it and because he is preparing to use White Fang in staged dogfights, a favorite form of gambling and entertainment at the fort. White Fang kills every dog set against him—sometimes two at a time—but is sometimes wounded. Beauty Smith even forces White Fang to fight wild wolves and a lynx, which Indians trap for this purpose. White Fang's reputation for ferocity grows to the extent that Beauty Smith travels around with him in a cage, and people pay money just to watch Beauty enrage White Fang by poking him with sticks.

4: The Clinging Death

Finally, White Fang is forced to fight a bulldog. It is too short for White Fang to attack in his normal way. Eventually, the bulldog manages to lock its jaws into White Fang's neck and refuses to let go, working to chew through to White Fang's throat and kill him. After long minutes of flailing and trying to dislodge the bulldog, called Cherokee,

White Fang is on the verge of death. Beauty Smith is furious that he is about to lose money, so he enters the cage and savagely kicks White Fang.

Suddenly, two men arrive. One of them rushes into the cage and attacks Beauty Smith, hitting him so hard that he does not get up and screaming that all the men watching the dogfight are beasts. The two newcomers then try for several minutes before finally prying the bulldog's jaws from White Fang's neck. White Fang, his eyes glazed, is very close to death. Weedon Scott, the man who attacked Beauty Smith, gives Beauty one hundred and fifty dollars and says that he is buying White Fang. Beauty protests, but Scott threatens him and leaves with White Fang. Scott is a gold mining expert from California, and the man with him is Matt, his dog musher.

5: The Indomitable

Back at their cabin two weeks later, Weedon Scott and Matt have White Fang, who has somehow survived, on a chain. Matt tells Scott that White Fang is at least part dog and has been trained to pull a sled. They hope to rehabilitate White Fang, but when they unchain him, he immediately kills one of their dogs and bites both men. With deep regret, the men are about to shoot White Fang, feeling they have no choice. But White Fang's knowing fear of the gun and his quick dodge when he sees it convinces them that the wolf is smart enough to be rehabilitated.

6: The Love-Master

White Fang knows that the dog-killing and the man-biting that he has just done are serious crimes, and he expects to be savagely beaten but is beyond caring or running away. He is confused when Scott repeatedly comes outside the cabin, talks gently to him, and gives him meat. Eventually, White Fang takes meat from Scott's hand. When Scott first pets him, White Fang is sure that the man is going to hurt him. In time, though, White Fang comes to trust Scott and Matt. Scott becomes his master, and White Fang desires to please him, so he never attacks the sled dogs and in fact soon becomes the lead dog.

Part 5—The Tame.
1: The Long Trail

The time comes for Weedon Scott to return to California. He feels that he cannot take White Fang and plans to leave him with Matt, but White Fang cries pitifully. The men lock White Fang in the cabin as they leave for the steamboat, but when they arrive, they find White Fang on the boat's deck, bleeding from having crashed through the cabin's window. Scott takes White Fang home to California.

2: The Southland

Weedon Scott lives on a large country estate in the Santa Clara Valley with his extended family. As soon as White Fang arrives there, the family and their dogs, including a sheepdog named Collie, begin adjusting to him—and vice versa.

3: The God's Domain

Besides Weedon, the other residents of the estate are his father, Judge Scott (a retired judge), and his mother; his sisters, Beth and Mary; his wife, Alice; and his children, Weedon, four, and Maud, six.

4: The Call of Kind

White Fang lives a good life on the estate and comes to love Weedon Scott so much that he allows the man to wrestle and play with him. When his master is horseback riding and breaks his leg, White Fang runs home and alerts the family. After this, even the servants, who have been unable to overcome their fear and distrust of White Fang, accept him warmly. In the fall, Collie lures White Fang into the woods to mate.

5: The Sleeping Wolf

A murderer who was sentenced by Judge Scott, and who has threatened to kill the judge for revenge, escapes from prison and disappears. Weedon's wife, without letting anyone else know, begins to let White Fang into the house each night to sleep by the front door. When the convict, Jim Hall, sneaks into the house one night, White Fang attacks and kills him, but Hall shoots White Fang several times. The household awakes, and Judge Scott calls not a veterinarian but his own doctor for White Fang. The doctor works on White Fang for an hour and a half and says that his chances for survival are miniscule.

Out of love and gratitude, Judge Scott goes so far as to call a doctor from San Francisco, and the women of the house take care of White Fang as if he were their child. White Fang, wrapped in casts and bandages, lies immobilized for weeks and dreams of his past—many bad dreams, and some good ones of the wild—as he slowly regains life.

Finally, the day arrives to remove the last cast. With great effort, White Fang is able to walk a little, venturing out to the lawn and, after a rest, on to the stable entrance, where Collie is with her puppies. The puppies frolic and climb on White Fang, full of curiosity, and the old wolf rests.

Characters

Bill

Bill, along with Henry, appears in Part One of the novel. Bill and Henry are taking the body of Lord Alfred to Fort McGurry. When the two men are threatened by hungry wolves that kill some of their sled dogs, Bill becomes increasingly anxious and convinced that the wolves will eventually kill them. When the wolves lure one of the dogs away during the daytime, Bill rashly follows with the gun to try to save the dog even though it is extremely dangerous and almost certainly futile. The wolves kill both the dog and Bill.

Collie

Collie is a sheepdog who lives at Weedon Scott's estate in California. When White Fang first arrives there, she badgers him mercilessly, following her instinctual enmity against wolves. White Fang does not harm her, even when she attacks him, partly because he understands that Scott values her and partly because it is against his nature as a wolf to harm a female of his own kind (or, in this case, of a closely related kind).

After time has passed, though, Collie leads White Fang into the woods to mate with her. In the novel's last scene, when White Fang has finally recovered from his gunshot wounds enough to hobble outside, he sees Collie with their puppies and allows the puppies to clamber over him as he rests.

Dick

Dick is a deerhound and a pet of the Scott family. When White Fang first arrives at the Scott estate, Dick chases him, which White Fang, because of his experiences, interprets as a deadly attack. The only thing that prevents White Fang from killing Dick is Collie's intervention.

Jim Hall

Jim Hall is a murderer who was convicted in Judge Scott's court and who has vowed to take revenge on the old judge. When Hall escapes from prison, he goes to the Scotts' estate to take his revenge but is attacked and killed by White Fang. However, Hall manages to shoot White Fang several times, wounding him gravely.

Henry

Henry is Bill's companion on the trip to Fort McGurry with Lord Alfred's body. While Bill becomes unhinged by the threatening wolves, Henry remains calm and manages to survive until unexpected help arrives.

Kiche

Kiche is called the She-Wolf in the first part of the novel, when she is living in the wild with other wolves. Readers learn her name later when she rejoins the Indians with whom she had previously lived.

In Part One, Kiche is with the wolf pack that threatens Henry and Bill. She is somewhat tame and enters the camp to try to get food when Bill feeds the dogs. It is also Kiche who lures the dogs away from the camp at night so that the other wolves can kill and eat them.

After the pack is driven away from Henry and finally finds food, Kiche mates with an old wolf named One-Eye. All of her cubs except one die in a famine, and the one survivor is a gray male who will become known as White Fang. One day Kiche hears White Fang's cries and runs to rescue him, and she and the Indian Gray Beaver recognize each other. Kiche allows Gray Beaver to pet her and to tie her up until she has again become tame enough to stay with the Indians willingly.

Kiche is the offspring of a dog and a wolf, a mating arranged by Gray Beaver's now-dead brother, and therefore White Fang is one-quarter dog.

Kloo-Kooch

Kloo-Kooch is Gray Beaver's wife. She provides perhaps the only moment of affection that White Fang experiences among the Indians, when White Fang returns to the Indians after a famine and receives a warm welcome from her.

Lip-Lip

Lip-Lip is a puppy who lives with the Indians and who was born in the same year as White Fang. He is a bully and constantly picks fights with White Fang, which is the first step in White Fang's becoming a mean and solitary animal.

Matt

Matt is Weedon Scott's musher, who helps Scott rescue White Fang from the bulldog and then rehabilitate him. It is Matt who recognizes that White Fang is part dog and has been trained to pull a sled.

Mit-sah

Mit-sah is Gray Beaver's son. When White Fang is still a puppy, he helps pull Mit-sah's child-size sled when the family goes on a trip.

One-Eye

One-Eye is an old but smart male wolf who wins the right to mate with Kiche by killing his two rivals. White Fang is the sole surviving cub from this litter.

Salmon Tongue

Salmon Tongue is one of the Indians who is with Gray Beaver when they discover White Fang and Kiche.

Alice Scott

Alice is Weedon's wife. When she hears that Jim Hall has escaped from prison, she begins to let White Fang into the house each night after the rest of the family has gone to bed. This precaution saves the family's lives.

Beth Scott

Beth is one of Weedon's two sisters, who lives at the estate with the rest of the extended family. She lovingly helps care for White Fang after he saves the family from Jim Hall.

Judge Scott

Judge Scott is Weedon's father, a retired judge who lives at the estate with the rest of the extended family. He is hesitant to trust White Fang but willing to admit that he was wrong when White Fang proves himself. When White Fang saves the family from Jim Hall, the judge is so grateful that he calls the best doctors, rather than veterinarians, to care for White Fang.

Mary Scott

Mary is one of Weedon's two sisters, who lives at the estate with the rest of the extended family. She lovingly helps care for White Fang after he saves the family from Jim Hall.

Maud Scott

Weedon Scott's six-year-old daughter. White Fang understands how precious the children are to his master, and he learns to enjoy their petting.

Weedon Scott

Weedon Scott is a mining expert from California who comes to the Yukon for a short time. He comes upon the scene of the dogfight at which White Fang is about to be killed by a bulldog and is at the same time being brutally kicked by Beauty Smith. After rescuing White Fang, Scott asks his musher, Matt, how much an animal in White Fang's condition is worth. He then pays Beauty Smith the money and takes White Fang against Smith's wishes.

Scott rehabilitates White Fang through consistent gentleness, kindness, and affection, even though White Fang bites him the first time he has an opportunity. When he must correct White Fang, he does so with words, not blows, except on one or two occasions when the situation is extremely serious. White Fang becomes so attached to Scott that he crashes through a window to avoid being left behind when Scott returns to California. Scott relents and takes White Fang home with him, and he is rewarded when White Fang saves the family from a murderer.

Weedon Scott Jr.

Weedon is the elder Scott's four-year-old son.

She-Wolf

See Kiche

Beauty Smith

The cook at Fort Yukon, Beauty Smith is an ugly, cruel man. He goes to great lengths to persuade Gray Beaver to sell White Fang to him and then abuses White Fang to make him as fierce as possible. Beauty's goal is to win money by entering White Fang in dogfights, which he continues to do until Weedon Scott intervenes.

Three Eagles

Three Eagles is one of the Indians who is with Gray Beaver when they discover White Fang and Kiche. A short time later, Gray Beaver gives Kiche to Three Eagles, who takes her with him on a long trip.

Weedon Scott's Mother

Her name is not mentioned, but she lives with the rest of the extended family at the estate.

Themes

Nature versus Nurture

The overarching theme of the novel is that heredity and environment each contribute to White Fang's fate. London comes down on the side of nurture as being the more powerful force. White Fang's nature is malleable, and he adjusts to whatever conditions his environment presents in order to survive. Under the abuse of Beauty Smith, White Fang becomes a killer seething with hate; under the loving hand of Weedon Scott, he becomes a gentle pet.

While this theme is woven throughout the novel, it is stated explicitly in these lines:

> White Fang grew stronger, heavier, and more compact, while his character was developing along the

lines laid down by his heredity and his environment. His heredity was a life-stuff that may be likened to clay. It possessed many possibilities, was capable of being moulded into many different forms. Environment served to model the clay, to give it a particular form. Thus, had White Fang never come in to the fires of man, the Wild would have moulded him into a true wolf. But the gods had given him a different environment, and he was moulded into a dog that was rather wolfish, but that was a dog and not a wolf.

Survival of the Fittest

The novel portrays two worlds, the world of nature and the world of humans. In both these worlds, all life is subject to the law of the survival of the fittest. Famine is well known to both humans and animals, and when it comes, the weak, the sick, and the old die. When the Indians have no food to give the dogs, the dogs return to the wild and try to stay alive until the famine passes. If they succeed, and if they find their old masters again, they often return to human society. But when hardship comes, it is every man, woman, child, dog, wolf, and pup for himself or herself. Relationships are based on mutual benefit, not on affection.

In the last section of the novel, White Fang enters a kind of paradise where the law of survival of the fittest has been superseded by the law of love. Weeden Scott rescues him at the moment when the law says he should die, and from that moment on White Fang lives in a radically different kind of world. The world of love, however, is one that most creatures never experience and one that White Fang reaches only after much extreme suffering—only because a kind man happens to come along at just the right moment, only because he was born with enough intelligence to be rehabilitated, and, above all, only because he has been tough enough to survive until that moment.

Style

Omniscient Narrator

The narrator of *White Fang* is omniscient, which is a challenging choice for a writer and a fascinating one for a reader when the main characters are animals. Repeatedly, the narrator confidently describes the thoughts and feelings of dogs and wolves and explains how they experience the world. The best extended example of this comes when White Fang, as a small cub, leaves the lair for the first time. He has thought of the cave entrance as a strange wall that his parents have

Topics For Further Study

- *White Fang* tells the life story of the title character, but London chose a somewhat unexpected starting point and ending point for his story: The entire first section of the novel centers on the life of White Fang's mother before White Fang is born, and the story ends before White Fang dies. Discuss what reasons London might have had for these decisions and whether you think they are effective or not.

- In parts of western Canada and Alaska, dogsleds are still an important method of transportation. Do research to learn where dogsleds are still in use and what the lives of the dogs and the people who use them are like.

- The rights of animals—both domesticated and wild—and what constitutes acceptable treatment of them is an issue that is often debated today. The legal status of animals is changing as some lawmakers, attorneys, and activists push for increased protection of animals from human abuse, neglect, and exploitation. Discuss the issue of animal rights and humane treatment as it relates to the novel. Should laws protect animals from abuse such as that suffered by White Fang? If so, how should people who break these laws be punished? Should laws prohibit people from owning wild animals?

- Do research to learn about wolves and wolf-dog hybrids. Find out how accurate and realistic London's portrayal of White Fang was. Could an animal that is three-quarters wolf really become as tame as White Fang did?

- Using place names mentioned in the novel as your starting point, do research to learn more about the Native Americans mentioned in the novel. What tribe would they have been part of? What was their culture like? Do they still live in the area today?

- The novel is set just before and during the Yukon gold rush of 1898. Learn more about this event. How did it start, how long did it last, and how did it impact the settlement of the area?

---

the power to walk through. Then one day his curiosity outstrips his fear, and he approaches "the wall of the world." The narration of his first outing begins:

> Now the gray cub had lived all his days on a level floor. He had never experienced the hurt of a fall. He did not know what a fall was. So he stepped boldly out upon the air. His hind legs still rested on the cave-lip, so he fell forward head downward. The earth struck him a harsh blow on the nose that made him yelp. Then he began rolling down the slope, over and over. He was in a panic of terror. The unknown had caught him at last. It had gripped savagely hold of him.

The narrator goes on to describe in great detail how White Fang learns to distinguish what is alive from what is not alive, how he learns to interpret what his eyes are telling him about how far away things are, what he experiences when he steps into a stream and the current grabs him, and so on.

There is no way for readers to know how accurate these descriptions are, but it is clear that they are based on long, close observation of canines, and they succeed in making the novel's animals complex and compelling characters.

Figurative Language

London makes frequent use of several kinds of figurative language. The novel's first sentence contains an example of personification: "Dark spruce forest frowned on either side the frozen waterway."

> There was a hint in it of laughter, but of a laughter more terrible than any sadness—a laughter that was mirthless as the smile of the Sphinx, a laughter cold as the frost and partaking of the grimness of infallibility.

Such figurative language enriches the descriptions throughout the novel and makes the faraway

Compare & Contrast

- **Late 1890s–1900s:** In 1898, with the discovery of gold along the Klondike River, the Canadian government separates the Yukon district from the Northwest Territories, making it a separate territory. More than thirty thousand prospectors come north to search for gold.

  Today: The Yukon remains a territory of Canada. Mining (for lead, zinc, silver, copper, and gold) is its primary industry, followed by tourism. The entire population of the territory is less than the number who came hoping to find gold in the late 1890s, making it one of the least populated regions of North America.

- **Late 1890s–1900s:** Until the gold rush spurs the building of the first railroads in the Yukon, the only ways to travel are on foot, by dogsled, and by canoe. The White Pass and Yukon Railway are constructed to provide transportation for gold prospectors and the settlers who follow them.

  Today: The region's railroads have been shut down, replaced by air travel and the Alaska

Highway. Some residents of the Yukon still rely on dogsleds as a major form of transportation.

- **Late 1890s–1900s:** Life in the Yukon is extremely harsh, and famines affecting both humans and animals are common. Native Americans and animals alike depend on salmon and game for food, and in years when both are in short supply, only the strong survive. When people do not have food to feed their dogs, the dogs return to the wild and struggle to find enough food to stay alive.

  Today: Humans and animals in the Yukon still live in relative isolation and depend heavily on salmon and game. However, air travel and modern communications greatly reduce the threat of famine. In the late 1990s, when salmon and game were scarce and people in the region were unable to feed their sled dogs, word quickly reached the rest of the world. Pet food companies and others donated food, and private couriers flew it to the Yukon free of charge to prevent widespread starvation of sled dogs.

landscape and the special terrors of the North more real to readers by relating them to more familiar, universal realities.

One figure of speech that is especially prominent in the novel is antonomasia, in which the name of an office or role is substituted for a person's actual name. A common example of the technique is the use of "the Bard" to refer to Shakespeare. In *White Fang*, when the narrator speaks of men as they are viewed by dogs and wolves, he calls them "the gods." London writes several times that canines see humans in roughly the same way that humans see their gods. He even establishes a hierarchy of gods, making the claim that canines recognize white men as "superior gods" compared to Indians. This recognition is said to be based on the canines' comprehension that the white men in the story have more power than the Indians.

Historical Context

Naturalism

Jack London, along with Stephen Crane, Theodore Dreiser, Frank Norris, and others, is considered one of the premier writers of the naturalist style of American literature. Naturalism emerged in France in the last quarter of the nineteenth century and held sway in the United States between about 1900 and 1918, when World War I ended. It developed out of scientific ideas that were popular at the time, especially Charles Darwin's theory of evolution. Naturalist writers were interested in the closely related idea of determinism, which holds that the fate of an individual human or animal is determined by the interplay of heredity (nature) and the environment (nurture) in his or her life. These writers often created everyday characters and then subjected them to extreme circumstances to show how innate traits and life circumstances combined to create their destinies. In Crane's classic naturalist novel *The Red Badge of Courage* (1895), the extreme circumstances are provided by war. In *White Fang* and other fiction by London, they are provided by the harsh conditions of life in the far North. Several times in *White Fang*, London points out to readers that if a certain circumstance had been altered in a small way—for example, if the Indians who first tamed White Fang had camped across the river the night he ran to rejoin them, as they had first planned to—the wolf's fate would have been completely different.

London's naturalist fiction is especially interesting because many of his works feature animals as characters. This allows London to examine nature both in its wild state, untouched by human civilization and complications, and as it is affected by human intervention. In fact, *White Fang* portrays wolves both in the wild and relating to a range of different human cultures and temperaments, showing how each one affects the wolves. This, along with the novel's objective, detailed style, makes it an exemplar of naturalism.

Conservation

When *White Fang* was published, conservation of the wilderness was much on Americans' minds. Theodore Roosevelt, the most conservation-minded president the United States has ever had, was in the White House. He expanded the United States's national forests by more than 150 million acres. Roosevelt's friend John Muir, the founder of the Sierra Club and the United States's most famous conservationist, was publishing books about his visits to America's wild places and at the same time working for their protection. After centuries of expansion from the East Coast to the Pacific, Americans were for the first time realizing that although their nation was vast, its wilderness and resources were not unlimited and needed to be conserved and protected.

In addition, as more Americans moved to cities and as life became increasingly industrialized, the idea of the wilderness became more captivating. Americans and Europeans alike loved to read stories of adventures in wild places, and this undoubtedly contributed greatly to the popularity of London's fiction.

Critical Overview

The most noteworthy fact about criticism of *White Fang*—and of London's work in general—is the lack of it. In his day, London was considered a popular, not a literary, author. More recently, his novels have most often been classified as young-adult literature. As a result, literary publications and scholars have had little interest in London and his work. In addition, London's works featuring animals as main characters have received even less attention than others. *The Call of the Wild* has garnered some interest for the sheer power of its hold on the reading public and because it is the premier novel of its kind. *White Fang*, as a later and lesser novel, has largely been ignored.

Critic Maxwell Geismar does mention *White Fang* in his *Rebels and Ancestors: The American Novel, 1890–1915* but judges it inferior to *The Call of the Wild* because of what he views as a sentimental ending:

> It was only when White Fang was rescued from these extremes of cruelty and terror, to become "the blessed wolf" of a gracious California estate in the Southland, a perfect pet of an aristocratic gentry, that London succumbed to the sentiment which spoiled another beautiful little parable of the instinctual life.

Mary Allen, in her *Animals in American Literature*, seems to agree:

> What the author intends as the virtue of adaptation comes across instead as the case of a character who sells out, at least so it seems to the American reader. The case for civilization is apparently viewed differently in Europe, however, where *White Fang* outsells *The Call of the Wild*.

A comment in *The Cambridge History of English and American Literature*, published in multiple volumes during and shortly after London's life, sums up the literary establishment's view of London. In an entry on London's contemporary Richard Harding Davis, the editors declare that Davis "had what Jack London lacked utterly, literary traditions, poise, a certain patrician touch, and an innate love of the romantic." Clearly, the establishment was not ready to embrace London's style, which Allen calls "a realism that revolutionized popular fiction in the 1900s."

As if the disdain of literary critics were not enough, London even suffered a complaint from the White House. According to Allen, after reading *White Fang*, President Theodore Roosevelt, an outdoorsman and adventurer himself, claimed that an incident in which a lynx kills a wolf was a "gross falsifying of nature's records." London insisted on the authenticity of his account.

1991 film rendition of Jack London's White Fang *with Ethan Hawke as Jack*

Criticism

Candyce Norvell

Norvell is an independent educational writer who specializes in English and literature. In this essay, Norvell discusses character development in the novel's human characters.

The wolf is the hero of *White Fang*, and although his interactions with humans are an important part of his story, even in those interactions the animals remain at center stage. The humans are there to help Jack London demonstrate how the wolf's temperament and destiny are shaped by all the individuals and elements that enter into his sphere of existence. In this respect, the novel's human characters are equivalent to the rest of the supporting cast, from the pack of puppies who mark White Fang as an outcast to the harsh wilderness that challenges him throughout much of his life. Because the role of humans in the novel is peripheral and because London creates several human characters to show the full range of humanity's possible impacts on White Fang, it would not be surprising if each one were drawn very cursorily in two dimensions. If these characters had been stereotypes, many readers, attention riveted on White Fang by the author's design, would not have noticed. Those

alert readers who did notice would no doubt have excused the lapse, as they excuse similar lapses in a thousand other engaging stories. After all, even great artists give less attention to the figures in the backgrounds of complex paintings than they do to the central figures. And, if *White Fang*'s human characters had been stereotypes, it would have given critics who denied London the title of literary author something to sink their teeth into.

But, significantly (and with one exception), these characters are not two-dimensional or entirely predictable or stereotypical. Even though they are developed only as fully as their respective roles in the story demand, they are made complex and lifelike through small details and unexpected actions. Each human character is, indeed, a type who represents a broad slice of humanity. But each is also an individual who says and does things that strike the reader as being out of character, which is exactly what makes people—real people and fictional ones—authentic and memorable.

The first characters, human or animal, to appear in *White Fang* are Bill and Henry, who are trekking through a frozen forest with the mission of delivering the body of the mysterious Lord Alfred to Fort McCurry. Their distinct personalities soon emerge and predict their fates.

> "This makes Scott very much like people we have all known, people whom we think we know completely, who one day suddenly do something that makes us recoil and shrug our shoulders and add a question mark to what we have written in our hearts about them."

The hungry wolf pack is trailing Bill and Henry in the hope of making a meal of them. That much is acknowledged by both men. Bill is a talker and a worrier who expects the worst from the start. Henry is a stoic who speaks only to try to calm Bill and who seems to have no expectations at all. Whatever Henry actually thinks of their prospects, he keeps it to himself. He does not deny the facts— they are being hunted by a pack of forty famished wolves, and they have only three cartridges left for their shotgun—but he also does not allow them to touch his emotions. If he experiences fear, he refuses to give it any quarter or any expression. He knows that his best tool for survival is his mind, and he focuses all his energy there. He thinks, and then he does according to his thoughts. He thinks about when they should make camp in the evening and when they should set out in the morning, and he thinks about what would and would not be a good use of those three precious cartridges. Even when his own situation seems hopeless, he thinks about how to save Lord Alfred's noble corpse from the wolves. He has been charged with getting it to civilization, and his mind is on his mission, whether he lives to complete it himself or not. He is as detached and dispassionate as the spruce trees and the howling wind and the howling wolves. He devotes all his physical and mental resources to surviving and fulfilling his role for as long as he can, and when death seems certain, he does not whimper but accepts this as another fact. He understands all along the difference between what he can control and what he cannot; he controls what he can and ignores what he cannot. And in the end, his rationality and determination and focus keep him alive

just long enough for unexpected help to arrive. Henry survives.

Bill does not. As the wolves devour their dogs one by one and come ever closer to the men, Bill's mind becomes increasingly disordered. He lets fear destroy his ability to think clearly, and he is impatient. He cannot bear the suspense of not knowing whether he and Henry will survive. And when the She-Wolf lures one of their dogs to its inevitable death in broad daylight, Bill cannot bear to stand by and listen as the dog loses a desperate struggle for its life. He cannot accept life as it is, cannot put his survival above his feelings, and so he ignores Henry's warning, follows the doomed dog into the woods, fires all three remaining cartridges at the wolves, and is killed and eaten along with the dog.

Henry, of course, represents all individuals, human and animal, who have mastered the law of the survival of the fittest. He accepts that life is a struggle and that eventually he is bound to lose. He understands that his only choice is to struggle as intelligently and determinedly as he can and to surrender himself to fate at the appointed time. Henry lives by his wits, and Bill lives, and dies, by his emotions, which are as worthless and as impotent as Lord Alfred's noble title is in the wilderness.

But even as they play their parts in this two-man drama with universal applications, Henry and Bill are a couple of regular guys in a tight spot. They sit on the coffin lid to eat their meals, because it is a better seat than the ground. Bill rashly vows that if his latest effort to protect the dogs from the wolves fails, he will not allow himself a cup of coffee in the morning. When he insists, with equal rashness, on keeping that vow and denying himself the one warming pleasure in what could be his last day on Earth, Henry gently tries to make him drink the coffee. Henry knows that Bill's growing irrationality lessens his own chance of survival, but he accepts this just as he accepts the wolves, without complaint and without ill feeling. He tries to comfort Bill, to calm him, to prevent his final, suicidal mission; and when he fails, he thinks about what to do with Lord Alfred and how to help the dogs pull the sled, and he moves on.

As Henry and Bill are counterparts in the first part of the novel, Beauty Smith and Weedon Scott are counterparts in the last part. Beauty and Weedon represent the worst and the best in humanity, but they, too, are just a couple of guys. Beauty's behavior is evil and inexcusable, but London forces readers to see him as a human being nonetheless by describing the physical ugliness and deformity

What Do I Read Next?

- *The Call of the Wild* (1903) is London's most well-known novel. It was hugely popular when it was first published and remains a favorite today. It also is considered one of the leading novels of the naturalist period. *The Call of the Wild* has many similarities with *White Fang*. It is the story of a dog who suffers the cruelties and hardships of nature before being adopted by a kind man.

- *John Barleycorn* (1913) is London's painfully straightforward account of his alcoholism, published only a few years before his death. It is the only autobiographical work of substantial length that London wrote, and it includes descriptions of the writer's travels and adventures as well as of his struggles with alcohol.

- *My First Summer in the Sierra* (1911), by John Muir, is the most popular work of the famous conservationist. It is the diary of a summer that Muir had spent in the Sierra Nevada Mountains decades earlier, in 1869. This book and others by Muir were instrumental in bringing American tourists to wilderness areas and in expanding the national park system.

- *The Red Badge of Courage* (1895), by Stephen Crane, tells the story of a young soldier in the Civil War. Crane explores how the soldier's inborn traits and his environment combine to mold his character and his behavior. Like *White Fang*, *The Red Badge of Courage* has a long history as both a literary and a popular success and is considered an important work of American naturalism.

- *Winterdance: The Fine Madness of Winning the Iditarod* (1994), by Gary Paulsen, is the author's account of his 1983 running of the Iditarod, Alaska's famous, grueling dogsled race. Paulsen, who began the 1,150-mile, seventeen-day race by becoming lost, faced many of the same challenges described in London's fiction, including bone-chilling cold, exhaustion, attacks by wild animals, and dogfights.

---

that earned him not only the nickname Beauty but also a life as an outcast who has often been the victim of the kind of abuse he heaps on White Fang. There is no redemption for Beauty in the novel and no suggestion that readers should pity him. Yet the parallels between Beauty and White Fang cannot be ignored. White Fang is rehabilitated by love, which suggests that Beauty might be, too, given the opportunity. Beauty is three-dimensional because behind the length and breadth of his evil lies the same potential that lies within all creatures: the potential to be improved by improved circumstances. This is not, today, an inventive way to add depth to a character, but it was much fresher at the time it was written, and it is still credible.

Weedon Scott is, in London's term, "the love-master" to Beauty Smith's "mad god." The unique element of Scott's character is selflessness, the sacrifice of his own best interest for that of another. Henry was kind to Bill in spite of the fact that Bill's weakness threatened Henry's survival. But Henry had no choice, because he had no escape from Bill. Bill was a part of his environment that he had to accept, along with the wolves and the cold. Scott represents a greater good because he chooses to make White Fang his responsibility, and he chooses knowing that he is taking on a killer. After rushing into the middle of a dogfight—putting himself in danger not only from the dogs but from a furious Beauty Smith—and struggling to save White Fang, Scott then pays a small fortune for a wolf who is nearly dead. There is nothing in it for him. Two weeks later, the moment Scott unchains a recovering White Fang, the wolf kills one of his sled dogs and bites both Scott and his musher, Matt. Instead of anger, Scott feels deep regret at the thought of shooting White Fang as a hopeless case; he seizes on White Fang's next action, a knowing dodge when he sees the gun raised, as a reason to believe that the wolf is intelligent enough to be redeemed

---

after all. In coming days, Scott is willing to risk being attacked again to win White Fang's trust.

And yet, there is this: After Scott has taken White Fang back home to California, he sometimes takes him into town, where a trio of dogs harass White Fang mercilessly. White Fang has learned not to attack dogs, and so he soaks up their abuse for Scott's sake—until one day Weedon Scott, the icon of unconditional love, addresses this injustice, not by speaking to the dogs' owners or by taking some other civilized measure, but by giving White Fang permission to kill the dogs. White Fang does so with dispatch, and of course the townspeople henceforth make sure that their dogs do not bother him. Scott's solution is as effective as it is shocking to readers who thought they knew him. This makes Scott very much like people we have all known, people whom we think we know completely, who one day suddenly do something that makes us recoil and shrug our shoulders and add a question mark to what we have written in our hearts about them. Even people who make unconditional love a habit are not perfect.

There is one more human who is White Fang's master, the Indian Gray Beaver, and he is the one whom London fails to elevate above stereotype. Although he is not cruel, he is portrayed as being incapable of showing affection toward White Fang. The relationship between the two is strictly pragmatic: Gray Beaver provides food and protection and does not beat White Fang as long as he obeys; White Fang helps pull Gray Beaver's son's sled and guards his family and his property. The two have made a covenant, to use London's word, but after five years Gray Beaver breaks the covenant, and it is whiskey that makes him do it. He at first refuses to sell White Fang to Beauty Smith, but Beauty Smith, the least of all white men, finds it easy to manipulate Gray Beaver. He at first gives him whiskey and then sells him whiskey until the considerable amount that Gray Beaver has earned by trading at the fort is gone. By that time, Gray Beaver is addicted to alcohol and, drunk and broke, finally turns White Fang over to Beauty Smith in return for still more whiskey. He beats White Fang severely when the wolf tries to escape Beauty's tortures and return to him, and he leaves the fort, and the story, to return, ruined and shamed, to his village. Gray Beaver is a stock character, lacking individuality and vitality. London's portrayal of White Fang's Indian master is a distracting weakness in an otherwise strong supporting cast.

Source: Candyce Norvell, Critical Essay on *White Fang*, in *Novels for Students*, Gale, 2004.

Sophie Treadwell

In the following interview, Treadwell and London cover topics ranging from politics, literature, philosophy and social commentary.

"Magnifique, by gosh!"

One of the ranch men was driving me from the Glen Ellen station to Jack London's place in the hills. He was a French Swiss, who had lived in South America before coming to California; and he was giving polyglot expression to his love for the fields, the flowers, the trees, and Jack London. We had come to a crest in the road from whence we could see the startling ruins of the great brown stone pile London built for a home that was burned some months ago, just when it was done.

"Three years we work to build him and someone burn, What a tristesse for me! But Jack London say, 'Cheer Pierre, we build again.' 'Not for a life of you,' I tell to heem. 'There is not in me so bigness of heart for a work and a expense.' But already we cut the trees. One year to—what you call—season? Por Dios! Get up you lassie—Magnifique, by gosh!"

The Londons live in the sprawly old house of an ancient winery that was on the place. It is set in the midst of the quiet hills. Mrs. London has arranged it cleverly, and there is an air of comfort and happiness and work about it as well as sunshine and country calm.

At the end of a long hall running through the center of the house is a door bearing the legend in heavy black letters on a white card: "Hands Off!" Behind this mute but screaming protector the California author is secure until noon. One hundred dollars' worth of story writing is done there every morning—1000 words at 10 cents a word. This takes between one and two hours. Then the mail is gone through with, and about then a dull booming South Sea gong sounds. The midday meal is ready. The forbidding door opens, an attractive looking man with an adorable smile comes out—tramp, political economist, rancher, philosopher, author—and laugher.

Mr. London was late for lunch this day, but when he got there he made up for lost time—from the point of view of the interviewer—talking swiftly and to the point. I suppose he ate, too. That's what he was there for; so no doubt he did it. Action and directness seem to be two of his many middle names.

London answers every question one puts to him, quickly, directly and without hedging. Yet he is a very difficult man to interview. The very minute he came into the room, in spite of the blue eyes, in spite of the smile, in spite of a very charming expression, I knew that I was in for it. He has a steel-trap body and a steel-trap mind. He turns this battery on you, and lets it go at you, slam-bangs own success and self-confidence. And he laughs.

"Why have you come to ask me? Out with it! I know your paper didn't send you up here for nothing. Just to talk to Jack London? Here in California? I'm only interesting to interviewers away from home. All that the papers here can do for me is to misquote and belittle me! No? Say, I know what I'm talking about.

"So you know that when a university girl wandered into the hills in back of Berkeley and was attacked by a tramp the papers said it must have been Jack London? Don't know about that, eh? Well, do you know that when some Italians sought to play the badger game—do you know what the badger game is? All right! Well, these Italians tried to pull the badger game, and when the victim didn't come through with the money they cut him up in pieces and dumped him in the bay, or tried to, when they were interrupted. Do you know what the papers said then? That it must have been Jack London who did it. You don't believe that? Well, look it up in the files! How long have you been in the newspaper game? It was before your time. But it's the God's truth.

"Do you belong to the Woman's Press Club? No? Take a harp! Take two harps! Ever hear that story of Bierce's about the woman who had committed every sin in the book and went up to be questioned by Saint Peter? He told her to tell all and was just going to send her below, when she said she had been blackballed by the Woman's Press Club. 'Come in,' said Peter. 'Take a harp! Take two harps!' But they are no worse than the men's press club. Of all the flat-footed, bone-headed pinheads! Do you know that they knocked me consistently for twelve years; never as much as invited me to their club, and here the other day I got a letter asking me for $2000 for their clubhouse! Can you beat that?"

"My new novel? I think I'll call it *The Jacket*." It's a punch against prison conditions in California. What I have to say in it is just what is said by every well-known criminologist in the world. Everybody who thinks knows it, and they have been hiring little halls and telling it to each other.

"What's the use of people who all more or less, think the same, getting little halls, and agreeing with one another?"

"I'm trying to get some of these ideas over to fiction readers. Do you know that today it is possible to sentence a man to solitary confinement in

> "
> London answers every question one puts to him, quickly, directly and without hedging. Yet he is a very difficult man to interview."

California? That it is possible for us to hang a man for assault and battery? That, in fact, last year in 1913 we did hang a man for assault and battery? Jake Oppenheimer was hanged for assault and battery here in your own State, in California. The straitjacket still obtains in our prisons. Didn't you know that? "Do I put any constructive ideas for prison reform into this novel? No, I do not. I just draw the picture of conditions as they are now. Have I any constructive ideas along those lines? Of course I have. I would turn prisons into hospitals. My basic belief is one of pure determinism. Each person moves along a line of least resistance. We do what is easier for, us to do than not to do. We can't help doing what we do."

"If I'm short-sighted and bump into posts, I'm not to blame. It's because of my short sight. I ought to get glasses? Of course. That is just it! If I break our so-called laws, I can't help it. I do it because I am sick. There is something wrong with me, I'm a sick man. And I need doctors. I need all the skilled science of the twentieth century to investigate and see, and try if anything can be done for me to keep from doing what is hurtful to the whole body of my fellow-creatures. The whole school of scientific criminology is with me in this. It's only the fools who are not.

"Do I believe in capital punishment? No, I do not. It is too silly. I saw a man hanged because he killed another man. And he killed the other man over 25 cents. One said that the other owned the 25 cents. That one said he did not. They began to quarrel and finally, like two bulls in a pasture, they got to fighting; and in the fight one killed the other. So the state hanged him. Oh, the pomp and circumstances with which they stretched that man's body at the end of a rope! And when it was all over the warden said: 'Gentlemen, take your hats off!' It was then that I laughed."

"Am I still a Socialist? I'm in the same position that I've always been. Now they call it

Syndicalism. I'm a Syndicalist. I believe in taking over, by whatever means necessary, the existing forms of government. The Boston Tea Party was an expression of that kind of feeling. Revolution? What about it? Our Pinker-tons, our police, our soldiers— they are all organized for an allied purpose, the purpose of banging an offensive foreign substance into another man's body. But after all, Syndicalism is only a blind expression of personal feeling, of emotion."

"I have been interested in the Western Fuel case. And I'll tell you the point that got me, in that— the absolute horror and consternation of those men when one director was finally found guilty. Well, why not? They feel that they haven't done anything wrong. And they haven't. This is their society. The United States is their clubhouse. That same game is going on by gentlemen members all over the club-house. Why should these men go to jail?"

"Yet, other men are going to jail—thousands of them—every day. And some of them are going, denied the right of trial by jury, denied the right to plead guilty or not guilty. You don't believe that? But it is true. I myself have been sent to jail, denied the right of trial by jury; denied the right to plead guilty or not guilty. And my name is legion. What was I doing? Nothing. Absolutely nothing. Walking along the streets of a city, when a cop hauled me in."

"What was I booked for? -Vagrancy, yer Honor.' I tried to plead not guilty, to explain. The judge didn't even look at me. 'Thirty days. And I was yanked aside while the judge went down the line. You must have seen men sentenced like that, dozens of times, haven't you? Then why do you look at me as though you doubted when I told you men were sentenced to jail without the right to plead? You have heard too much Fourth of July oratory. Be more brass tacks! Lose some of your illusions!"

"It's your education that's to blame for your lack of brass tacks, not you. What a training we give to children! If I had a son I would not send him to school until he was ready for the last year of grammar school, and then only that he could get used to our form of democracy. No, I wouldn't give him a free choice of what he wanted to learn any more than I give a colt a free choice! I'd train him— freedom—but within limits. No, he would not go to a university; not unless he could run faster than I."

"The reason I quit the university was because I did not have money enough to get through and because I wasn't getting anything there that I wanted. Do you know what happened to me over there, in that State university at Berkeley, supported by the taxes of the people? I was called out before a whole regiment of students undergoing, as I was, enforced military drill, and I was publically humiliated by an officer of the regular army because my uniform was shabby, because I lacked $40 to buy a new one. My uniform was a second-hand one. I bought it from a fellow for five dollars, and he had bought it from one before him. It was handed down from one poor student to another, and no doubt it did lack style. But was that any reason why the poor boob who had to wear it because he couldn't get a better one should be humiliated?"

"Do you know who are the arbiters of American literature today? The failures of American literature! Men who could not get a half cent a word for a story of their own, dictate to men who get ten. When I was in New York this time a $6000 a year editor tried to tell me what to do. His magazine pays me $24,000 a year."

After luncheon Mr. London drove to the station. He drove a light team and handled it well; with all the firm ease one would expect of him. Conversation turned to farming. As the rig wheeled smartly down the country roads, Mr. London would wave the whip hand over the landscape."

"My land goes to the crest of those mountains there. We stretch the length of that valley. I have 500 acres in vines. These are my eucalypti. I put all these in. Got several hundred acres of them. This road isn't bad, is it, considering the rains we've had? This is my private road. Wait until you come to the county road—a fright. I always keep my own roads up—and my gates."

"Mr. London," I asked, widening my eyes to the breadth of valley and mountain that he calls "mine." "Is there such a thing as a Socialist capitalist?"

"I don't know," he answered easily. "When I was in New York I met a man who told me he was a bourgeois anarchist."

And I was just making a mental note about a clever hedge—when he burst out:

"You mean that for me. But I'm no capitalist. What is a capitalist?"

"One who has capital," I ventured weakly.

"No, a capitalist is one who lives off capital, who makes money earn money. I don't. I live off wage, the wages that I coin out of my Own brain. And you don't think this ranch earns me anything, do you? Why, if I'd die today you wouldn't believe it if I'd tell you how much in debt I'd be. But that's my way of getting ahead of the game. If I die owing $200,000 I'm just that much ahead of the game, am I not? If you die owing eight dollars, you'd be just eight

Gold prospectors trek the goldfields of the Yukon in Canada, circa 1896

dollars to the good, wouldn't you? Of course, one can take pride in always paying their bills and all that, but somehow that slide to eight bones as a possible debt capacity for me didn't thrill as it might."

"What are your ideas about marriage?" I asked. That's always a good way to change the subject.

"I believe in marriage. The march of civilization has proven out monogamy and shown it to be the best proposition along those lines for the human race. I insist that all the people that work for me be married. I'm not going to have any promiscuity around here."

"Nor celibacy?"

"I hope not."

I wanted to ask him if there is such a thing as a socialist dictator, but I knew he was laughing at me."

For there is something that I haven't been able to put into this interview, the undercurrent of laughter that is new in Jack London—that laughter that is born of vision and disillusion.

When I was on the train coming back the conductor came right away to punch. "Was that Jack London?" he asked. "That man in the sombrero at the station?"

"That was Mr. Aristophanes," I told him.

> " *That's why I am a pessimist. I see things in the light of history and the laws of nature."*

"Guess Jack London isn't back yet. Pretty smart fellow, all right." I thought of the words of the French-Swiss ranch-hand:

"Magnifique, by gosh."

Source: Sophie Treadwell, "Is Jack London a Capitalist? No! But Is Certainly 'Magnifique, by Gosh!'" in *Jack London Journal*, No. 3, 1996, pp. 199–203.

Emanuel Julius

In the following interview, Julius and London focus on London's politics and sense of pessimism with the political system.

Ten minutes after meeting Jack London, one is impressed by his grim pessimism. He is, confessedly, a pessimist. But, before viewing this phase of London, let us have some small talk about things that may prove interesting even though they may not be of great national importance.

To begin with, he looks much handsomer than his pictures, for the camera never gets his soft, gray eyes. Though 37 years old, he doesn't appear to be more than 30. He has a magnificent body—a fine form, with nothing pugilistic except his shoulders. He has a chin that doesn't appear to be of the son to invite dispute. When he laughs, his mouth looks like a Jewelry store window. Dressed simply, he wears a plain ready-made suit of clothes; a soft collared, white shirt and a black silk tie produce a striking effect. His hat is one of those abominable sombreros.

His conversation is decidedly colloquial, having neither the refinement of an over-cultured scholar nor the roughness of a stage westerner. It is just ordinary English, the kind one hears on city street cars and office building elevators. He is quite approachable, always willing to talk streaks just for the asking. His speech is interspersed with mild, harmless oaths. And, here let us give thanks, he doesn't carry himself with an air of dignity. In brief, he is an open, frank fellow, in appearance more of a good fellow than our common conception of a famous author.

When I saw him he was in the hands of a Los Angeles moving picture man, who was using him to pose before the camera. A company has contracted to have London appear in a number of films that will depict many of his famous stories. These films will begin with London sitting at a desk, pen in hand, cigarette at his elbow, writing one of his tales. Of course, if the moving picture man wanted to be realistic, he would have London seated before a typewriter, but that, it is generally agreed, would be lacking in romance. Authors, in pictures, should pen their stories, not typewrite them. He will scratch away for about 200 feet of film, when the scene will fade, soon to open with the action of the story. So says the manager.

After proper intervals, London will reappear on the screen. Then, it will close with a hundred or more feet of film showing the writer in the act of closing the story and inserting the manuscript in an envelope, intending doubtlessly to send it to the harsh, hard-hearted editor. A photoplay of "John Barleycorn," a serial that appeared in a popular weekly magazine, will be one instance, it is announced by the film managers, where London will actually take pan in the action. As this story is autobiographical, it will add much to have London himself in the cast. His famous trip in the Snark will be included. London's wife, Charmian, will also appear in this play, it is said.

"Of course," says London, "I never pretend to be an actor. I don't know a thing about the profession. I'll do whatever I'm told, for I am in the hands of my-friends."

"What, in your opinion, is the effect of the capitalist system on art?" London was asked.

"Awful! Absolutely killing! The editors are not interested in the truth; they don't want writers to tell the truth. A writer can't tell a story when it tells the truth, so why should he batter his head against a stone wall? He gives the editors what they want, for he knows that the stuff he believes in and loves to write will never be purchased."

"What a pleasant view you take!" I said.

"You may wonder why I am a pessimist," said Mr. London; "I often wonder myself. Here I have the most precious thing in the world—the love of a woman; I have beautiful children; I have lots and lots of money; I have fame as a writer; I have many men working for me; I have a beautiful ranch—and still, I am a pessimist. I look at things dispassionately, scientifically, and everything appears almost hopeless; after long years of labor and development, the people are as bad off as ever. There is a mighty ruling class that intends to hold fast to its possessions. I see years and years of bloodshed. I see the master class hiring armies of murderers to keep the workers in subjection, to beat them back should they attempt to dispossess the capitalists. That's why I am a pessimist. I see things in the light of history and the laws of nature.

"I became a Socialist when I was 17 years old. I am still a Socialist, but not of the refined, quietistic school of Socialism. The Socialists, the ghetto Socialists of the east, no longer believe in the strong, firm Socialism of the early days. Mention confiscation in the ghetto of New York and the leaders will throw up their hands in holy horror. I still believe that Socialism should strive to eliminate the capitalist class and wipe away the private ownership of mines, mills, factories, railroads and other social needs.

"I do not believe that Socialists should soften and yield, eventually becoming mere reformers whose greatest desire is economy in government and low taxes, and the like. They should take upon themselves the task of doing away with the robbing capitalist system, do away with the profit system and place the workers in possession of the industries."

"Are you opposed to political action?" Mr. London was asked.

"I believe there is much to be gained by entering political campaigns," he answered. "The real advantage, in my opinion, is the great opportunity to educate the workers to an understanding of the wrongs of the present system and the means of class consciousness."

"You think that a peaceful and legal change is impossible?"

"History shows that no master class is ever willing to let go without a quarrel. The capitalists own the governments, the armies and the militia. Don't you think the capitalists will use these institutions to keep themselves in power? I do."

"What do you intend to do, Mr. London?"

"I feel that I have done my part. Socialism has cost me hundreds of thousands of dollars. When the time comes I'm going to stay right on my ranch at Glen Ellen and let the revolution go to blazes. I've done my part." After a pause, he added: "That's the way I feel now. I suppose when the time comes I'll let my emotions get the best of my intellect and I'll come down from the mountain top and join the fray."

"What a grim, pessimistic view you have, Mr. London!"

"Well, I'm a pessimist; I admit."

As I rose to leave, I shook his hand and said: "Yes, and I think I know the cause of your pessimism."

"Tell me."

"I feel positive that your liver is out of order."

Source: Emanuel Julius, "The Pessimism of Jack London," in *Jack London Journal*, No. 3, 1996, pp. 189–91.

Sources

Allen, Mary, "The Wisdom of the Dogs: Jack London," in her *Animals in American Literature*, University of Illinois Press, 1983, pp. 77–96.

Geismar, Maxwell, "Jack London: The Short Cut," in his *Rebels and Ancestors: The American Novel, 1890–1915*, Houghton Mifflin, 1953, pp. 139–216.

Kasdin, Steven J., ed., *The Collected Jack London*, Barnes and Noble Books, 1992, pp. 217–329.

Ward, Adolphus William, Sir, Alfred Rayney Waller, William Peterfield Trent, John Erskine, Stuart Pratt Sherman, and Carl Van Doren, eds., *The Cambridge History of English and American Literature: An Encyclopedia in Eighteen Volumes*, Vol. XVI, Cambridge University Press and G. P. Putnam's Sons, 1907–1921.

Further Reading

Dutcher, James, Jamie Dutcher, and James Manfull, *Wolves at Our Door: The Extraordinary Story of the Couple Who Lived with Wolves*, Pocket Star, 2002.
    James Dutcher and his wife, Jamie, spent six years living in Idaho's Sawtooth Mountains with a wolf pack. The documentary film they made of their experiences, also entitled *Wolves at Our Door*, won an Emmy Award. This book details their experiences with the wolves, who lived in a twenty-acre enclosure with the Dutchers.

Kershaw, Alex, *Jack London: A Life*, Griffin, 1999.
    This engaging biography covers all aspects of London's life, including his politics and his love of the wilderness and of adventure as well as his writing.

Lawlor, Mary, *Recalling the Wild: Naturalism and the Closing of the American West*, Rutgers University Press, 2000.
    Lawlor discusses the various ways in which Americans have thought of the West throughout their history and examines how the literature of each period both influenced and reflected these ideas. Naturalism is a major focus of the book.

Pizer, Donald, ed., *The Cambridge Companion to American Realism and Naturalism: From Howells to London*, Cambridge University Press, 1995.
    Pizer discusses realism and naturalism as literary movements and then provides more in-depth analysis of ten representative works, including London's *The Call of the Wild*.

Wide Sargasso Sea

Jean Rhys

1966

Wide Sargasso Sea, published in 1966 toward the end of Jean Rhys's writing career, was the most successful of Rhys's literary works. The novel was well received when it was first published and has never been out of print. It also continues to draw the interest of academics and literary critics today. The popularity of *Wide Sargasso Sea* might be based on several factors. The general reader might enjoy this novel for the captivating story of a lonely young woman who is driven to near madness by her need to be loved. Literary theorists, on the other hand, find Rhys's novel rich in the portrayal of the damaging effects of colonization on a conquered people and the debilitating consequences of sexual exploitation of women. Another group of readers, those interested in multiculturalism, might be drawn to *Wide Sargasso Sea* for the insider's view that Rhys provides of nineteenth-century life and culture on a Caribbean island.

Wide Sargasso Sea was written as Rhys's attempt to explain the character of Bertha Mason in Charlotte Brontë's *Jane Eyre*. Rhys wanted to explore the reasons why Bertha Mason went mad. In doing so, Rhys fills her story with conflict. There is the clash between former slaves and their previous owners; the overall misunderstandings between the white and black races; the disparity in beliefs between the old white plantation owners and the new English immigrants who come to live on the island. There is also the battle between men and women as they try to satisfy their needs through their relationships with one another. And finally,

the ultimate conflict, the interior confusion the protagonist must face between her emotional and rational state of being.

Wide Sargasso Sea was honored with the prestigious W. H. Smith Award and the Heinemann Award of the Royal Society of Literature. The novel was also selected by Random House as one of the best one hundred books of fiction written in the English language during the twentieth century.

Author Biography

Jean Rhys was born in Roseau, Dominica, on August 24, 1890. Her father was a Welsh doctor. When she was sixteen years old, she was sent to England to live with an aunt and to attend the Perse School at Cambridge and later the Royal Academy of Dramatic Art. Although Dominica would influence her writing, Rhys would return to her birthplace only once, in 1936. When her father died, Rhys was forced to take on a variety of jobs in England, which included working as a chorus girl with a touring musical company, a mannequin, an artist's model, and a ghostwriter of a book about furniture.

In 1919, she moved to Paris with her husband, Jean Lenglet, a French-Dutch journalist and songwriter. In the same year, she gave birth to a son, who died when he was three weeks old. She later had a daughter. Around this same time, Rhys met Ford Madox Ford, with whom she had an affair while her husband was in jail for illegal financial transactions. Ford encouraged Rhys's writing and also wrote the introduction for Rhys's first book *The Left Bank* (1927), a collection of short stories. Rhys's marriage to Lenglet ended in divorce. Rhys would marry twice again. Each of these marriages left her a widow.

Rhys's first novel, published in the States as *Quartet* (1929) (originally published as *Postures* in Britain), was supposedly based on Rhys's affair with Ford. It was in this work that Rhys's sensitive, sexually attractive, vulnerable, and somewhat self-defeating heroine is first introduced, a figure that is often repeated in Rhys's later books. Subsequent works include *After Leaving Mr. Mackenzie* (1930); *Voyage in the Dark* (1934), reportedly Rhys's most autobiographical work; and *Good Morning Midnight* (1939).

For the next twenty years or so, Rhys disappeared from public view. Many people thought she had died. Then in 1958, Britain's BBC produced a drama based on Rhys's *Good Morning Midnight*.

Jean Rhys

In 1966, her *Wide Sargasso Sea* was published to critical acclaim.

Rhys did not receive much critical acclaim for her works during most of her lifetime, and when it finally arrived in her later years, Rhys stated that it came too late. Contemporary critics studying her work today believe that the reason for Rhys's going virtually unnoticed in the literary world was that she was ahead of her time. Feminist theorists, in particular, believe that Rhys's theme of women as exploited victims was not easily accepted in Rhys's day. After the publication of *Wide Sargasso Sea*, however, Rhys was made a CBE (Commander of the order of the British Empire, an honor bestowed by the queen) in 1978. She was also awarded the W. H. Smith Award for her last novel, as well as the Royal Society of Literature Award and an Arts Council Bursary. She died on May 14, 1979, in Exeter. Her unfinished autobiography was published posthumously under the title *Smile Please* (1979).

Plot Summary

Part 1

The first part of *Wide Sargasso Sea* is narrated by the female protagonist, Antoinette. She explains

Media Adaptations

- John Duigan directed a movie of *Wide Sargasso Sea* (1993). It starred Karina Lombard as Antoinette, Michael York as her father, Rachel Ward as her mother, Nathaniel Parker as her husband, and Claudia Robinson as Christophine. Although some critics believe that sexuality was favored over character development, the movie provides a relatively honest portrayal of two deteriorating marriages. It is currently available on DVD. Jan Louter, fascinated by the novel, made a documentary film about Rhys and her world in the Caribbean.

that she lives in isolation from the rest of the population of the small Caribbean island on which her family's plantation exists. The story opens in 1839 after the recent emancipation of slaves in the British Empire. The emancipation has not only caused her family to live in poverty but also to have to face the tension of freed slaves, as both the white and the black citizens of the island sort through their new relationships.

The picture that Rhys paints in part 1 is that of isolation. Of the main characters, Antoinette appears to feel the effects of that isolation the most. She lives with her mother, Annette Cosway, and her brother, Pierre, who suffers from some unnamed mental disability. Antoinette's mother spends most of her time mothering Pierre, at Antoinette's expense. Antoinette is forced to look for affection in other places. She tries to befriend the young black children who live in the nearby countryside, but she is made fun of and even threatened. So she turns to Christophine, the woman who cooks for the family and becomes a mother figure for Antoinette. Without Christophine, Antoinette says the family would have died. Christophine introduces Antoinette to the child of a friend. The girl's name is Tia. Antoinette and Tia spend several days together, swimming and eating. But one day, Antoinette becomes angry with Tia and calls her a "nigger." It is a name she herself had been called in the past: a "white nigger." The two young girls argue, and the friendship ends.

Around this same time, Antoinette's mother makes friends with a new family of white people, whom Christophine refers to as "[t]rouble." Antoinette's mother sells the last of her jewelry to buy material to make dresses for herself and Antoinette, to make themselves presentable. And shortly afterward, Antoinette's mother marries Mr. Mason.

With Mason's money, the family estate, Coulibri, is refurbished. However, Mason is careless in his attitude toward the black servants, and Antoinette's mother becomes filled with fear that something awful will happen. Antoinette, however, feels safe. Coulibri is the only place she feels secure. Fortune does not shine on the family, however. The local black people do not like Mr. Mason, and one night they burn down the family home. As the family attempts to escape, an angry mob awaits them outside. Only when the angry blacks see the Mason family parrot, with his feathers caught on fire, attempt to fly over their heads, do the blacks disperse. The burning parrot represents an evil omen to them. As the family makes its escape, Antoinette sees Tia and starts to run to her, believing that they are still friends. But Tia hurls a rock at Antoinette, which hits her on the head and knocks her unconscious. When Antoinette later awakens from a long illness, she discovers that her brother, Pierre, has died and her mother has been taken away. Antoinette is now living with her Aunt Cora. This section ends with a description of Antoinette's experiences at a convent school.

Part 2

The beginning of the second part of the story is narrated by the man who has married Antoinette. He remains unnamed throughout the story. However, since it has been acknowledged that Rhys has written *Wide Sargasso Sea* as a prequel to Brontë's *Jane Eyre* and because the details she offers about the male narrator match Brontë's male protagonist, it is easily assumed that this is Brontë's Edward Rochester.

Antoinette has left the convent school and has married Rochester. This marriage was arranged by Antoinette's stepbrother, Richard Mason. Antoinette cannot gain her inheritance unless she agrees to marry a man of Mason's choice. Rochester, the younger son of a British gentleman, has come to Jamaica for this precise reason.

The newlyweds have returned to the "little estate in the Windward Islands," as Rochester describes it in a letter to his father. The place is

Ganbois, property that Antoinette has inherited. Rochester is recovering from an illness, and he finds everything about the island too intense, from the colors of the landscape to the scent that Antoinette puts in her hair. Rochester does, however, promise Antoinette "peace, happiness, [and] safety," none of which he is ultimately able to give her. He is rather depressed about his marriage, wondering if he has sold his soul for money.

Forever swayed by doubt about his marriage and his wife, Rochester is easily influenced by a mysterious letter he receives from Daniel Cosway, who claims to be Antoinette's half brother. Cosway tells Rochester about Antoinette's mother's instability and suggests that Antoinette is not a virgin. In fact, Cosway names Antoinette's previous sexual partner as Sandi Cosway, her black cousin. Although prior to this letter Rochester seems to be trying to create a relationship with Antoinette, he now wants nothing to do with her. Rochester's narration ends with him reading a book about voodoo.

Antoinette now takes up the narration. She is miserable because Rochester will have nothing to do with her. She goes to Christophine and asks for a potion that will make Rochester want to make love to her. Although Christophine protests that "if the man don't love you, I can't make him love you," she gives Antoinette what she has asked for.

Rochester receives another note from Daniel, who demands that Rochester visit him, which he does. Daniel claims to be the illegitimate son of "old Cosway." Daniel is angry because Cosway never acknowledged him. Daniel also gives Rochester more details about Antoinette's affair with Sandi. When Rochester returns home, he questions Antoinette briefly but won't let her complete all her thoughts. She insists and fills him in on some of her background. In the midst of her telling, Rochester refers to Antoinette as Bertha, another reference to Brontë's *Jane Eyre*. Bertha, in Brontë's novel, was the mad woman who lived in the attic, Rochester's first wife.

The next morning, Rochester feels sick and recalls very little of what happened the previous night. He thinks he might have been poisoned. Later, when he is feeling better, he makes love to Amelie, a servant girl who comes with food to his room. When Antoinette confronts Rochester about his sexual encounter with Amelie, he confesses that he does not love Antoinette.

Christophine tries to help Antoinette, who is totally distraught. Rochester confronts Christophine and tells her to leave. Christophine does her best to stand up for Antoinette, asking Rochester to give back at least half of the money so Antoinette can have a new start on life. She tells him to leave Antoinette with her. But Rochester is a confused man. He looks for a sign that Antoinette loves him, but he does not find it. So he packs up all their belongings and plans to sell the house. He refers to Antoinette as his "lunatic," and he is taking her to England.

Part 3

Part three begins with a new narrator, Grace Poole, another character from Brontë's novel. Poole has been hired to take care of Antoinette. Rochester's father and brother have died, making Rochester a very rich man. He is not at the English estate but rather he is traveling. Grace finds Rochester's home "safe," and she accepts the job. Then the narration is turned over to Antoinette.

Antoinette's mind is obviously caught between dream and reality. She mixes memories up with the present time, so it is not clear what is really happening and what she is imagining. However, she mentions having made love to her cousin Sandi. And she talks about how cold and isolated she is, living in the attic of Rochester's estate. She talks about setting the house on fire and then wanders back to her memories of Coulibri in flames. As this short section of the story comes to an end, Antoinette takes a burning candle in hand. "Now at last I know why I was brought here and what I have to do," she says.

Characters

Amelie

Amelie is a servant girl at Ganbois, the house to which Rochester and Antoinette go after they are married. Rochester comments that Amelie reminds him of Antoinette. The day after Antoinette has secretly slipped a potion into his wine, Rochester has sex with Amelie. He then gives Amelie money so she can leave the island.

Baptiste

Baptiste is a manservant at Ganbois. Although not overtly supportive of Antoinette, he does sympathize with her, especially when Rochester forces Antoinette to leave Ganbois.

Bertha

Several times, Rochester refers to Antoinette as Bertha. He tells her that he likes that name and likes to think of her as Bertha. This is Rhys's reference to Brontë's story in which Bertha is Rochester's first wife.

Aunt Cora

Aunt Cora takes Antoinette into her home when Antoinette's mother is taken away. Aunt Cora does not approve of Antoinette's stepfather, Mr. Mason, nor of his son, Richard Mason. She also does not like the suitor Richard has arranged to marry Antoinette, Edward Rochester. Aunt Cora takes care of Antoinette after Coulibri burns down and Antoinette is knocked unconscious.

Annette Cosway

Annette Cosway is Antoinette's mother. Her first husband is dead when the story opens and Annette is depressed. She and her family are living in near poverty. She is the mother of two children and has little means of raising them. She leaves Antoinette on her own for most of the time. When she meets a group of rich people who befriend her, she eagerly jumps at the chance to be wed to Mr. Mason. She finds little happiness in her marriage, and with the destruction of Coulibri and the death of her son, she withdraws from reality.

Antoinette Cosway

The character of Antoinette is based on Charlotte Brontë's Bertha Mason in *Jane Eyre*. Bertha is the first wife of Brontë's protagonist Edward Rochester. In Brontë's story, Rochester kept Bertha locked up in the attic. Rhys wanted to tell the story from Bertha's point of view. So Antoinette is the younger version of Bertha, before she moved to England with her husband. Rhys's story demonstrates how Antoinette goes "mad."

Antoinette, the female protagonist, is a very young girl at the beginning of the story. Her childhood is difficult and marks her personality. Her father is dead. Her brother's dependence on her mother deprives Antoinette of motherly affection, and she is left to fend for herself. Her greatest support comes from Christophine, the woman who cooks for the family. Otherwise, Antoinette is very much on her own and is often lonely and scared.

Antoinette cannot find any place to fit in, except when she is alone. She is not as "white" as the well-to-do white plantation owners. She is also not as "black" as the freed slaves. Having Creole ancestors from the island of Martinique, she is considered an island outsider in Jamaica and Dominica. The closest she comes to a sense of security is while she is alone at Coulibri, which is burnt to the ground when she is still young. Later, when she returns to

the property, she accuses her husband of further destroying her security by cursing her family home with his bitterness and the great sadness he has caused her.

Although she has fallen helplessly in love with her husband, it is an unrequited love. Rochester's unfaithfulness tortures her further, and finally she, like her mother, withdraws into a world of her own.

Daniel Cosway

Daniel is the person who writes a letter to Rochester, telling him about the instability of Antoinette's mother and of Antoinette's supposed sexual encounter before she met Rochester. Daniel claims to be Antoinette's illegitimate half brother. Because of Daniel's accusations, Rochester becomes confused about his feelings for his wife and later decides that Antoinette is a "lunatic."

Pierre Cosway

Pierre is Antoinette's brother. He has a mental deficiency, but his specific problem is never disclosed. Antoinette's mother provides Pierre with constant care, while disallowing Antoinette any affection. When Coulibri is burnt, Pierre suffers and dies.

Sandi Cosway

Sandi is a distant cousin of Antoinette. He protects her in a brief scene when Antoinette is walking to school. Later, rumors are stirred about Antoinette and Sandi having been lovers, before Antoinette is married. Her liaison with Sandi, after Rochester forces Antoinette to leave Ganbois, enrages Rochester and is the stimulus for Rochester taking Antoinette to England. At the end of the book, Antoinette enjoys her memories of Sandi's last kiss. It may be the closest she ever comes to love.

Christophine Dubois

Christophine is a servant at Coulibri. She is also Antoinette's closest confidant. Her reputation as an obeah, or practitioner of voodoo, causes some people to fear her. Antoinette does not fear Christophine and often goes to her for counsel. Christophine is a mother figure for Antoinette, someone who notices her loneliness and tries to mend it. Christophine also admonishes Antoinette's mother for her lack of affection and care toward her daughter.

After she is married and her husband loses his desire for her, Antoinette asks Christophine to make a potion so her husband will love her and want her again. Christophine is wary of using voodoo in this way. When the potion fails, Christophine is the only person who understands the effects of Antoinette's broken heart, and she tries to help Antoinette, once again. Rochester finally sends Christophine away, threatening to turn her over to the police for her illegal voodoo practice.

Mr. Luttrell

Mr. Luttrell is the only friend that Antoinette's mother has in the space of time between her husband's death and her marrying Mr. Mason. Luttrell lived on the plantation next to Coulibri and one day "swam out to sea and was gone for always." He represents one of the old white families who suffered economically after the emancipation of slaves.

Mannie

Mannie is a manservant at Coulibri. He is one of the few black people who is loyal to Antoinette's family and who tries to extinguish the fire that destroys the house.

Annette Mason

See Annette Cosway

Mr. Mason

Mr. Mason (no first name is ever provided) is Antoinette's stepfather, the man whom her mother marries in the first part of the story. Mason has money but lacks affection, especially for the freed slaves. He does, however, use his money to refurbish Coulibri. Ironically, it is mostly due to his demeaning attitude toward the black community that the freed slaves rise against the family and burn the house to the ground. This and his lack of affection drive his wife mad. In his own way, he cares about Antoinette's future and tries to arrange a marriage for her before his death.

Richard Mason

Richard is Mr. Mason's son. It is Richard who brings Rochester to the islands and sees to the details of Antoinette's marriage to Rochester. His appearances in the story are brief, but he is partially responsible for setting Antoinette onto the path to madness. He gives Rochester the power over all of Antoinette's inheritance and thus the power over her life. He reappears at the end of the story, visiting Antoinette in England. She attacks him with a knife.

Myra

Myra is a servant at Coulibri. It is suggested that Myra reports all of Mr. Mason's derogatory comments to the other black people in the community. Myra is supposed to be taking care of Antoinette's brother on the night of the fire. She mysteriously disappears just as the flames begin in the brother's room.

Grace Poole

Grace narrates the first section of part 3. She has been hired to take care of Antoinette in England. She, like Antoinette, feels that the outside world is dangerous. She feels safe in the big house, and she receives extra money for taking special care of Antoinette, who sometimes frightens her.

Edward Rochester

Although he is never named in *Wide Sargasso Sea*, the male protagonist of this story is derived from *Jane Eyre*'s Edward Rochester. He is Antoinette's husband, and he narrates most of the second part of the story. Rochester comes to the islands in search of wealth but later feels he has sold his soul when he finds his money in Antoinette's inheritance. He is the second son of an English gentleman and therefore not entitled to an inheritance of his own. He is also somewhat sickly and weak of spirit and is easily persuaded that he has been deceived. The islands are very exotic to him and not in a way that he find pleasant. He completely misreads Antoinette's needs and her love and concludes that she is a "lunatic."

At first he is taken by her, at least on a physical level. It does not take long, however, for him to be repulsed by her scent and touch. When Antoinette tries to use a love potion on him, he seeks revenge by making love to one of the servants, within hearing distance of Antoinette. This truly drives her mad. He further punishes her by taking her away from her beloved family estate. Then, when he learns of a possible affair she has with a distant cousin, he forces her to go to England with him, where he locks her away in the attic. Although Antoinette's personality is never stable, it is Rochester who pushes her over the edge.

Tia

Tia is the closest that Antoinette comes to having a childhood friend. She is the daughter of one of Christophine's friends. Christophine introduces Antoinette to Tia in hopes that the relationship might cure some of Antoinette's loneliness. For a while, Tia and Antoinette are friends, swimming together and sharing their food. One day, when Tia tricks Antoinette out of a few pennies, Antoinette refers to Tia as a "nigger." This angers Tia, and she puts on Antoinette's dress after swimming, instead of her own. The two children do not see one another until the night of the fire at Coulibri. Antoinette runs to

Tia, hoping to embrace her. Tia, however, throws a rock and hits Antoinette on the head, knocking her out. Although they never see one another again, Antoinette imagines, at the end of the story as she is preparing to burn down Rochester's house in England, that Tia is waiting for her when it is all done.

Themes

Isolation

Antoinette lives on a small island throughout most of this novel. The island itself represents the sense of isolation that overwhelms Antoinette throughout this story. In the beginning of the story, Antoinette and her mother and brother live far away from even the small island towns. Furthering their isolation is the fact that her mother is from another island, thus making them, in the eyes of the local people, outsiders. But it is not just the island people who isolate Antoinette's family. The other white landowners, many of them recent immigrants, have little to do with Antoinette's family because they are extremely poor. And although a handful of former slaves remain faithful to the family, most of the black people who live around them want nothing to do with them and eventually force Antoinette's family to leave by burning down their home.

In many ways, Antoinette's feelings of isolation are mirrored in her mother. Annette Cosway is a widow trying to raise two children on her own. She has the extra burden of caring for a son who suffers from a mental disability. Annette is a woman who needs to be loved but who cannot find it. She is accused of using her sexuality, however, to find a second husband, one who has sufficient money to help take care of her family. Mr. Mason is not capable of love, however, so Annette withdraws further into herself. When her son is burned to death, her final link to reality is snapped, and she collapses into the dark isolation of her own inner world.

Antoinette also is starved for love. She tries to befriend the children her own age, but is turned away because she is white and they are black. Except for one brief encounter with Tia, a young black girl, Antoinette has no childhood friends. Antoinette is further isolated because her mother is consumed with two major challenges of her own: taking care of her disabled son and searching for love, or at least searching for someone who will help ease her financial burdens. Without the reassuring love of a mother, Antoinette finds herself living in a world that is dominated only by her own thoughts, fears, and needs.

When Antoinette is forced to live with her Aunt Cora, she is isolated in different ways. First, she is not allowed to see her mother. Then, the school that she attends is run by nuns who live behind tall, gated walls. This isolates Antoinette from the local children, who often threaten her. Antoinette is also unable to return to her childhood sanctuary, that of her family's estate. She has been cut off from the only place that she had previously known.

After Antoinette marries, her sense of isolation is momentarily relieved. She has found love and is returned to the land that she loves. However, this period is short-lived, as she soon discovers that her husband does not love her. When he makes love to another woman, even the relief of living on her ancestral land is stolen from her. The estate now makes Antoinette feel only unhappiness, and she begins to withdraw further into herself. By the end of the novel, Antoinette lives in an attic room in a large house in England. Now she finds herself in a completely foreign setting, one that is cold and dark. She no longer has the vibrant colors and the warmth of her island home. Her mother, brother, and father are dead. She has been removed from her aunt and from the mother figure of Christophine. Her husband stays completely away from her. Her only companion is a hired caretaker. It is here that Antoinette falls into the deepest isolation from the world. She is so far removed that she lives halfway between dream and reality.

Hunger

There are many different representations of hunger throughout this story. The story opens with Antoinette and her family living in poverty. So there is the obvious physical hunger caused by lack of food. But there is also the hunger for affection. Both mother and daughter, Annette and Antoinette, search for love. The mother tries to find that love in a man, whereas Antoinette looks for love from her mother. Later, Antoinette searches for affection from a friend, in the form of Tia. When Antoinette marries, her hungers are satisfied momentarily. The hunger for love, as well as for sexual expression, appears to be somewhat soothed. But this does not last long. As a matter of fact, in having felt love for the first time, when it is taken away from her, the hunger becomes even stronger. Her hunger to be loved eventually drives her mad.

Other hungers include the hunger for money, such as Rochester's, which makes him sell his soul in marrying Antoinette for her inheritance. There is also the hunger for land as white immigrants

Topics For Further Study

- *Wide Sargasso Sea* was inspired by Rhys's wanting to understand the character of Bertha Mason in Charlotte Brontë's *Jane Eyre*. Choose one of your favorite novels, and find a secondary character that is not well developed. Then write a short story about this character, filling out her history and giving her a stronger voice. In other words, write a story from this character's point of view.

- Antoinette enjoys very few moments of happiness in this novel. Find a passage in which she at least feels somewhat distracted from her sense of isolation, and write a song as if you were she, expressing your feelings about that moment.

- Antoinette mentions several dreams that she has. Pretend you are her analyst. What do you think her dreams mean? Do not worry about being accurate. Use your imagination, but try to base your conclusions on the details of Antoinette's life and what she must be feeling.

- Research slavery in the Caribbean. Then write a narrative as if you were a slave. Try to imagine what your life would be like. Choose a specific island, and decide the circumstances of your life. Are you someone who works in the fields, or someone who works in the house? Are you married? How old are you? From which African nation did you come?

- Research women and mental health. Are women's mental issues treated differently now than they were at the turn of the twentieth century? How do they differ? Then write a paper on how Antoinette might have been treated had she lived in the twenty-first century.

- The subject of voodoo is dealt with in this novel. What is voodoo? Research this topic, and find out if it is still practiced today. Find out if there are still laws prohibiting the practice of voodoo. How do Christianity and voodoo conflict? Where is voodoo still practiced?

- Look into the phenomena referred to as the Sargasso Sea. What is it, and what causes it? Then write a paper on why you think Rhys used this as the title of her book. Explore the Sargasso Sea as a metaphor. How does this fit into the overall themes of the book?

---

move to the island and establish large plantations on which to make a living. There is the hunger for freedom as ex-slaves fight for their rights and establish a new way of life. A hunger to be understood is played out between Antoinette and her husband, as mistrust builds between them. And on a more subtle level, there is Antoinette's hunger to feel safe, which is never fully realized.

Madness

Both Antoinette and her mother suffer mental breakdowns. They withdraw into their own private worlds, places deep inside of them where they are consumed by their thoughts so completely that they cannot distinguish between their fantasies and reality. They are forced there as a retreat from the circumstances of their lives. Annette's final link with reality is shattered when Coulibri burns down and her son dies. Antoinette's descent may have begun when she was a child, but it is the disintegration of her marriage and the move to England that finalize her fate. As Rhys presents it, both mother and daughter might have been saved from their collapse into madness had they received the affection and understanding that they so desperately needed.

Race Relations

Although not primary, the theme of race relations on the islands is woven throughout this story. The abolishment of slavery, although this happens before the story begins, affects the condition of life of Antoinette's family. Annette has no money to pay the freed slaves who used to work her family estate and this fact leads to her poverty. The anger between the white people and the black people, vestiges of the past, causes the destruction of Coulibri. At the other end of the spectrum, there is also the discussion of the mixed races, the children of white landowners and their female slaves. Antoinette's and Christophine's relationship demonstrates friendship between the races, one in which skin color might have affected the different ways both women were raised but also which shows how those differences can enhance their connection.

Style

Point of View

Rhys uses multiple points of view in this novel. She begins with the voice of her female protagonist, Antoinette. At the start of the novel, Antoinette is a young girl, so the reader gains the child's perspective on the lives of the characters from a child's advantage. Rhys continues with this narrator through the first part of the story. In using the child as narrator, Rhys gives the reader a personal account of isolation as only a child can relate it. This device pulls the reader into the story on an emotional basis, setting the tone for the remaining parts of the story. She then switches, in the second part, to the point of view of Edward Rochester, the male protagonist. By this time, Antoinette is a newly wed young woman, and she and her surroundings are portrayed through Rochester's eyes. Rochester is not at home on the island. As a matter of fact, he feels extraordinarily alienated from everything about the island, from the colors of its vegetation to its local customs. By hearing the story from Rochester's point of view, the sense of isolation, one of the main themes of this novel, is further enhanced. Readers are also privy to Rochester's fears and doubts about Antoinette's stability, which is more objectively recorded as Antoinette slips deeper into her madness.

Antoinette regains the role of narrator in the middle of part 2. By this point, she is distraught over Rochester's inability to love her. Rhys must switch point of view at this stage because she wants the reader to witness the relationship of Antoinette and Christophine, who plot to regain Rochester's love of Antoinette. But when Antoinette loses all hope of regaining Rochester's love, the point of view once again switches back to Rochester. He has, at this point, become master of Antoinette, demanding that she leave her ancestral home and go to England.

In part 3, Rochester is completely missing from the story. So Rhys uses Grace Poole, a hired

domestic, to fill in the gaps between the setting in the islands and the setting in England. Poole explains how she has been employed to take care of Antoinette who has become a rather wild and scary madwoman. After Poole's introduction to part 3, Antoinette once again gains control of the story as narrator. But her narration is distorted and unreliable. However, by this time, the story has unfolded as far as it is capable. The ending is inevitable. In using Antoinette's madness to close the story, Rhys leaves it to the imagination of the reader to fill in the blanks. Since she has based her story on Brontë's *Jane Eyre*, it can be assumed that Antoinette burns down the estate.

Setting

The story has several settings: Jamaica, Dominica, and England in the middle of the nineteenth century. Although Rhys does not spend a lot of time describing any of these settings, the tone of her writing changes. While her characters are in the Caribbean, there is mention of sun and light, warmth, and perfumed scents. Her characters are often outdoors, and they confront other minor characters. Even though there are many challenges for each of the characters, there is also hope of positive outcomes. There is death, but there is also marriage. There are parties and swimming and good food, even though they are infrequent. The islands also represent both the positive and the negative of wilderness. There is the beauty of the wild overgrowth of vegetation and the intensity of its colors. There is also the fear, the lack of safety, where law and order does not prevail. But once the characters move to England, readers confront dark, cold, sterile, and all but complete isolation.

Contrast and Similarity

Rhys uses contrast and similarity to construct not only her setting but also her characters. She compares the lives of the rich white people with the poor, the old white landowners with the new immigrant white families. She hints of the times when the white landowners used slaves and then shows the changes that occurred with the abolition of slavery. The conflict between the white people and the black people is demonstrated, but Rhys also mentions how many people are of mixed races, thus proving the sexual encounters between the two races. When Christophine uses voodoo in order to help Antoinette win back the affections of Rochester, Rhys has Rochester turn to the law, thus exposing the contrast between the beliefs of the local black population and those of white people's sense of rational order.

Similarities prevail throughout the story also. The major, and most obvious, one is that of Annette and Antoinette, who both suffer from a lack of love and understanding, which forces them to withdraw from reality. There is also a similarity between Mr. Mason, Annette's second husband, and Edward Rochester, Antoinette's husband. Both men do not understand their wives and appear to have little sense of their own emotions. Their attentions appear to be more on sex, money, and power. They also both had little respect for the black people who served them.

Historical Context

Dominica's Geography and Culture

Rhys was born and spent most of her childhood on the Caribbean island of Dominica. Most of Rhys's novel *Wide Sargasso Sea* is also set on this small island. Dominica is unique in that, because of its rugged landscape, much of the island has remained similar in appearance to the time that Christopher Columbus first saw it. Most of the island is covered in rain forest, receiving heavy rains each year. Dominica is the largest and most northerly of the Windward Island, with the Atlantic Ocean to its east and the Caribbean Sea to its west.

The culture of Dominica is unique. Before Columbus, the population was made up of Ciboneys people and Carib Indians. Most of them were killed when the European settlers arrived, beginning with the Spanish, followed by Great Britain and France. It was during the colonization of Dominica that slaves were brought to the islands to work on the massive sugar plantations. As a result of this combination of different cultures, Dominica's population contains characteristics that combine to make what is called Creole, or a mixing of cultures. These mixtures can be seen not only in the physical traits of its people but also in language, music, art, food, architecture, religion, dance, and dress. Many people of Dominica speak a patois, a mixture of French with other languages of the area, in particular different African languages and Spanish.

Slavery in Dominica

Between 1518 and 1870, the transatlantic slave trade dramatically increased in the Caribbean. As sugarcane began to dominate the agricultural business of the Caribbean, Africans were shipped to the island in dramatically increasing numbers to add to and replace those who had come before them. In the early sixteenth century, an average of about two thousand slaves a year were shipped to the Caribbean from Africa. At its height, which occurred between 1811 and 1834, the slave trade accounted for about thirty-two thousand additional people being brought to the islands each year. Besides providing free labor, thus giving the white population a chance to gather immense wealth, the slave trade also created a black majority in the Caribbean islands.

Due to the increasing popularity and power of antislavery societies in Britain, a bill to abolish the slave trade passed both houses in 1807. It would not be until 1834 that slavery was abolished through the entire British Empire, which included the Caribbean islands. To replace the free slave labor, many landowners imported indentured workers from Asia and India. Although these people had legal contracts, they fared not much better than the African slaves they replaced. In the meantime, sugar prices fell due to competition from other countries, and a large population of freed slaves was unemployed. Many freed slaves formed their own villages, some of them squatting on abandoned lands and growing the same crops their former owners had raised in addition to new crops such as coconuts, rice, and bananas.

Dominican Economics

After slavery was abolished, white people found themselves in the minority and were divided along status lines based on wealth. Basically, there were rich whites and poor whites. The most elite of the rich whites were the plantation owners and former slave owners. Next came the white merchants, government officials, and professionals such as doctors. The poor whites included owners of small farms, laborers, and service people, such as policemen. No matter how much money a white person had, any white person of European descent gained a privileged position over black people. The black population consisted of free persons of color, freed slaves, and slaves. Economically, most black people during this time found themselves at the bottom of the list.

Education in Dominica

In the mid-nineteenth century, rich landowners more than likely would send their children abroad to be educated, whereas the more native whites sent their children to local private schools, most of them religious based. Black children received not much more than religious training,

Compare
&
Contrast

- **1850s:** In Dominica, black elected officials make up the majority of the general assembly. A few years later, whites push blacks out of power by demanding the British government to assign whites to seats in the assembly.

  1960s: Universal adult suffrage is granted to every citizen over twenty-one years of age in Dominica, swinging the power back to the people, regardless of land ownership or wealth.

  Today: Dominica enjoys full independence with a prime minister elected by the citizenry.

- **1850s:** White children of rich landowners are sent to Europe to be educated. White children of the less elite attend religious schools locally. Black children seldom learn to read or write.

  1960s: Construction of roads throughout the island allow rural children to attend schools more easily. The development of a public school

  system run by the government is also begun. Education is available to all races.

  Today: Schools are available for all ages, from preschoolers through adults. However, there are no mandatory laws about attending school, and many children still do not attend, working full-time jobs instead.

- **1850s:** Although the land is relatively inexpensive (ten British shillings an acre), British laws demand that large tracts of land must be purchased. This keeps the land in the hands of the rich.

  1960s: Former land laborers are given a chance to purchase their own land for the first time in Dominican recent history, thus allowing them to build better houses and afford education for their children.

  Today: Dominica has the largest percentage of landowners per head of population than any other island in the Caribbean. This has provided the population with economic stability.

---

if anything at all. Some Caribbean island governments even made it illegal to teach blacks to read or write. Most local children who did attend school went there only until age sixteen.

The Sargasso Sea

The Sargasso Sea, the heart of the Bermuda Triangle, is a two-million-square-mile ellipse of deep-blue water adrift in the central North Atlantic. It was named after a Portuguese word for seaweed, *sargassum*, which is found in such abundance in this sea that Christopher Columbus feared his ships might become entangled in it. The waters in this floating sea are exceptionally clear and warm, but it unfortunately is relatively lifeless.

Ford Madox Ford

Ford Madox Ford played a substantial role both in Rhys's personal life and in her writing. He was an established writer and the influential founder of

the *Transatlantic Review*, for which Ernest Hemingway was the editor. This publication helped to promote many young writers of the day. According to some accounts, Ford had at least twenty major affairs with prominent women and budding stars of his time. Rhys was just one of them. Ford also encouraged Rhys's writing and wrote the introduction to her first collection of short stories. He would break off his affair with her, but Rhys used the material of their affair for one of her later novels. Ford's most important literary works include *The Good Soldier*, a story of adultery and deceit.

Critical Overview

The publication and wide critical acclaim of *Wide Sargasso Sea* returned Rhys to the spotlight. Her earlier popularity had faded, and her previous

Nathaniel Parker as Edward Rochester in the 1993 film depiction of Jean Rhys's Wide Sargasso Sea

publications had gone out of print, leaving Rhys so lost to her public that most people thought she had died. *Wide Sargasso Sea*, having won two prestigious awards and being praised by literary critics as well as Rhys's general readers, caught everyone by surprise. After that, *Wide Sargasso Sea* remained popular. It has become, wrote a *Christian Science Monitor* critic, "Rhys's most famous novel." The novel portrays the plight of women, a theme that is recurrent in many of Rhys's works. The same *Christian Science Monitor* critic, for example, went on to state that all Rhys's female protagonists could be described in a similar way: "[T]he typical Jean Rhys heroine is a feminist's nightmare: a textbook illustration of what not to be." This view has not dissuaded feminist critics from exploring Rhys's work, however. Quite the contrary, even though Celia Marshik, writing for *Studies in the Novel*, claims that Rhys is "an insistent anti-feminist" who nonetheless has "created texts that feminists have claimed as their own."

Although many describe Rhys's female characters as weak and prone to acting out the role of victim, critic Jan Curtis states otherwise. Writing for *Critique: Studies in Contemporary Fiction*, Curtis believes that "[e]ach Rhys heroine struggles to heave herself out of the wide Sargasso sea found in every Rhys novel." Curtis goes on: "It is not until *Wide Sargasso Sea* that the Rhys heroine overcomes the Sargasso and discovers her strength in a fallen world of fractured consciousness and failed relationships by overcoming what [Wilson] Harris's narrator [in *Palace of the Peacock*] describes as the 'need in the world to provide a material nexus to bind the spirit of the universe.'"

It is hard to define Rhys, Marshik found. And rather than pigeonhole the author, Marshik concluded that Rhys "is a writer who seems to belong everywhere and nowhere." The reason for a resurgent interest in Rhys and her works, according to Tara Pepper, writing for *Newsweek*, is due in part to the fact that Rhys's "contemporaries were uneasy about her morally ambiguous, fractured characters and the seedy world she dwelt in, as well as wrote about." Pepper believes that Rhys's characters were too strange for the general public (especially British readers) to accept at a time when "inhabitants of former colonies were still considered culturally inferior." Today, Rhys's characters are better understood.

Wide Sargasso Sea, writes Dennis Porter for the *Massachusetts Review*, is "unlike her other novels with a contemporary setting," because it is based on another work of art (*Jane Eyre*). Although this influence strongly affected the way Rhys wrote her novel and, therefore, is not a "fully autonomous novel," it does, however, achieve "its purpose because it is a remarkable work of art in its own right." The story is written, states Porter, in a language that is lyrical, "a functional lyricism that incorporates both beauty and terror and simultaneously defines the limited consciousness of the two narrators."

Criticism

Joyce Hart

Hart is a freelance writer and author of several books. In this essay, Hart discusses the concurrence of power and helplessness that flows through Jean Rhys's novel Wide Sargasso Sea.

Although an overall feeling of helplessness permeates Jean Rhys's *Wide Sargasso Sea*, there is a current of power that lies underneath the surface of the story. Each character, no matter how helpless he or she may seem, is touched by this current. Much like the real Sargasso Sea, whose mysterious forces gather all the wandering seaweed from miles around and hold them together in a haphazard mass, so does this underlying power align Rhys's characters. As each character tries to understand her or his relationship with the other, the surge of power pulsates amidst fear and vulnerability and moves the story forward.

Rhys's opening sentence is a perfect example of this juxtaposition of helplessness and power. The novel begins: "They say when trouble comes close ranks." Like a pod of whales swimming in the ocean and suddenly realizing danger, the white islanders tightened their circle to strengthen and protect themselves. As Rhys suggests, the old white families sought power and control by coming together. The white landowners did so to protect themselves from the threat of economic disaster that the lack of slave labor caused. But just as soon as Rhys mentions this demonstration of power, she counters it by stating that her family was not included in that circle. Her family members were considered outsiders and were therefore denied the strength of the enclosed group. This pattern of power and helplessness pulsates throughout the story as well as through the individual characters. Something threatens, and the power surges for a while, as long as there is a current that continues to reinforce it. But then, inevitably, the power fades, and helplessness once again returns.

Antoinette's mother, Annette, is the first to demonstrate this pattern. In the midst of her poverty, her power comes in the form of hope. "[M]y mother still planned and hoped," Antoinette narrates. Annette rides her horse as she always has every morning. The horse is powerful, and riding him makes Annette feel strong. For brief moments in her day, she is able to return to a time when her life was better, more carefree. But those moments are short-lived when the horse is poisoned and Annette is "marooned," forced to face the helplessness that her life has become." Her power has come and gone. But later it is again restored when Annette meets Mr. Mason, a man with money. He will provide her many outlets. He will fix up the house, feed and help care for her children. He will help Annette forget about the past. As long as the marriage is fresh, Annette is empowered. She can face her neighbors and even entertain them. She is buoyant and for a moment believes that her troubles are behind her. But the power soon fades again. The same man who gives her the power takes it away. He does not really like her, her children, her house, or the people who work there. He denounces Annette's wisdom and thus brings about disaster. Where hope once fills Annette with power, despair now leaves her as lifeless as a marionette without a master. She loses her home, her son, her husband, and her will to live.

Mr. Mason, on the other hand, is filled with power; but it is not grounded in anything more substantial than money. He has many false beliefs, one of which is that he can buy everything. He buys a wife. He buys her a home, which makes him think he is the lord of the manor, and invincible. He belittles the people who helped to build the family estate and had at one time made the place vibrant. Mason believes that because the black people had been at one time purchased, they were his possessions, even though they had recently been freed. As his possessions, he thinks he can do with them what he wants. He is proven wrong.

Most of the blacks in this story are freed slaves. Even though they have received their freedom, their lot has not improved much. But even so they are not completely helpless. For a brief moment, they are able to express their will and demand to be taken seriously. Once they come together, they discover their power as a group. Unlike the white landowners who use fear to direct them, the source of the blacks' power is anger. They are fed up with Mr. Mason's arrogance, and eventually they cut him down. They throw a torch into his house, burn his home to the ground, and destroy his family.

Antoinette's story is more complicated. She often hands over her power to a double, or alter ego.

First, Antoinette projects her power onto Tia, a childhood friend. As Antoinette describes her, "Tia would light a fire (fires always lit for her, sharp stones did not hurt her bare feet, I never saw her cry)." In other words, Antoinette sees Tia as stronger than she. When she bets all her pennies on her ability to turn a somersault under the water, Antoinette allows Tia to turn Antoinette's victory into a loss. Tia leaves not only with the pennies but also with Antoinette's dress. Tia is the only friend that Antoinette has. She is the liberated and more compelling version of Antoinette. Later, when Coulibri burns down, it is to Tia that Antoinette runs for solace. The destruction of the house brings Antoinette to her knees. The house is the only place that gives her strength. Tia, however, does not want to embrace Antoinette. Rather, she throws a stone and hits Antoinette on the head, knocking her unconscious. It is as if Tia is trying to knock some sense into Antoinette, as if she is saying, "Wake up and see who you truly are." But instead Antoinette falls unconscious and gives herself over to a fever. When she awakens, her life has completely changed. She has been torn away from everything familiar and is in a constant state of fear. She does not gain a sense of power until she marries.

Edward Rochester, to whom Antoinette is married, is somewhat like Mr. Mason. Rochester's power source is different, however, as he came to the island poor and only gained wealth through his marriage to Antoinette. Part of Rochester's strength is in his family name, which has made him a somewhat prestigious British gentleman. He did not gain this power on his own accord, though. The only strength that he can garner on his own is his urge to prove to his father that he has some self-worth. This urge, somewhat akin to Annette's hope, is fragile, though, and when it is tested, Rochester's only defense is to slowly destroy his adversary. Like Mason, Rochester belittles what he fears. Whereas Mason puts down the power of the black people around him, Rochester belittles Antoinette and Christophine. Antoinette has power over Rochester for a while. He lusts for her, melting at her touch. He does not like to admit this weakness and eventually becomes disgusted with himself, although he projects those feelings onto Antoinette. And when he sees that she too has a weakness for him, he breaks her spirit by having sex with Amelie, whom Rochester sees as Antoinette's double.

Amelie, unlike Antoinette, uses her body to control Rochester. After allowing him to make love to her, Amelie receives enough money from him to finance her escape from the island. Antoinette, in con-

> Much like the real Sargasso Sea, whose mysterious forces gather all the wandering seaweed from miles around and hold them together in a haphazard mass, so does this underlying power align Rhys's characters."

trast, makes love to Rochester and loses her soul to him. She becomes addicted to his affections. And she is helpless in his presence. To compensate for this, Antoinette pursues yet another alter ego, Christophine, and implores her to make a magic love potion. Antoinette loses power over her husband. She loses confidence in herself, believing that she is helpless in regaining her husband's love. Christophine intercedes and empowers Antoinette, making her believe in herself again. The power surges through Antoinette as she returns to the house, confident that she can once again seduce Rochester. She is successful, but only for one night. In the morning, Antoinette's dream of Rochester returning to her turns into a nightmare. Her power is not sufficient because she assumes that she can only gain access to it through the potion. Once her power source wears out, Antoinette is lost. If she had regained Rochester through a belief in herself, she might have enjoyed a longer period of strength and happiness.

In the meantime, not strong enough to face another bout with Christophine, Rochester threatens to turn her over to the police and have her locked away. Rochester does not want to come under any more spells, whether conjured by Christophine's potions or by Antoinette's charms. He senses that Antoinette gains her power from both Christophine and from the natural energy of the island. He also realizes that the more he withdraws from Antoinette, the more powerless she becomes. Once Rochester understands this, he becomes determined to regain his strength by putting Antoinette away forever.

But even locked in an attic, with her mind distorted by blinding illusions, Antoinette is not completely helpless. At the end of the story, when

What Do I Read Next?

- Rhys's *After Leaving Mr. MacKenzie* (1930) concerns a broken woman who is cursed by her highly sensitive personality and has turned to alcohol to cure her depression. The protagonist, Julia Martin, is in the throes of a failed affair with Mr. MacKenzie, who has been supporting her but refuses to continue to do so. She returns to England only to find that her mother is dying. The strength of this novel, as with most of Rhys's works, is the insight she offers into the psychology of women who claim the role of victim.

- Sasha Jensen is the protagonist of Rhys's *Good Morning, Midnight* (1939). Sasha is depressed and tends to make all the wrong decisions. She has little self-worth and looks to men to help build her confidence. Once again, Rhys is able to go into the deepest thoughts of her character, thus giving her readers an intimate look at depression.

- Maryse Conde's *Windward Heights* (1998) takes place on the West Indian island of Guadeloupe and is inspired by Emily Brontë's *Wuthering Heights*. The male protagonist, Rayze, becomes obsessed with his love for Cathy, the daughter of the man who takes Rayze, an orphan, into his home. Cathy dies after having been married to a weak but socially prominent man. Rayze, angered by his inability to marry Cathy, wreaks havoc on the next generation. This novel, with its exotic island setting and its complex social hierarchy based on the color of one's skin, puts an interesting spin on Brontë's classic work.

- *Mistress of Darkness* (1976) by Christopher Nicole is set in the late eighteenth century on the island of Haiti. The story concerns the relationships between white sugar plantation owners and slaves and recounts the slave rebellion that took place during that time.

- Charlotte Brontë's *Jane Eyre* (1847) is the novel that is said to have inspired Rhys's *Wide Sargasso Sea*. The story is about an unhappy orphan and her life as a governess at Thornfield. Her life is filled with continual challenge, but the story ends happily when she and her lover are finally reunited. This book is often credited with spawning the proliferation of romantic novels that followed it.

Antoinette is about to burn down Rochester's English mansion, Antoinette again thinks of her friend. It is with Tia, her childhood image of strength, that Antoinette wants to be reunited. It is through the power of the fire that Antoinette finally regains her strength.

Source: Joyce Hart, Critical Essay on *Wide Sargasso Sea*, in *Novels for Students*, Gale, 2004.

Elizabeth Dalton

In the following article, Dalton examines the elements of the novel that appeal "to the imagination and the emotions" that she says are often left out of discussions of the wider, more political implications of the novel.

Jean Rhys, in life apparently a quite unpolitical person, has become since her death a star of the feminist and postcolonial canon. In particular, *Wide Sargasso Sea*, Rhys's rewriting of *Jane Eyre* from the perspective of Rochester's mad Creole wife, is now discussed primarily in terms of postcolonialism and the politics of race. The novel's depiction of racial tension and violence in the West Indies, derived partly from Rhys's own childhood and family history in Dominica, offers the basis for this kind of reading and for the debate over the author's sympathies in the racial conflict. What tends to be left out of the political focus, however is virtually everything that appeals to the imagination and the emotions: the vivid, dreamlike atmosphere, the poignant account of childhood trauma and loss, the disturbingly masochistic sexuality.

Literature inevitably contains unconscious motifs and fantasies, but the traces are especially evident in this passionate novel, above all in the treatment of race and its connection with sex. The concern with racial identity and the fears and fantasies of miscegenation that pervade *Wide Sargasso Sea* can be interpreted psychoanalytically as well as politically. At the heart of the novel is an extraordinary scene of repressed sexual desire, a revelation that embodies a myth of origin not only for the heroine but for her Creole society as well. The political dimension of the text is complicated and rendered ambiguous by these unconscious fantasies and fears.

Rhys's novel recounts the early life of Antoinette Bertha Mason, here called Antoinette Cosway before her adoption by Mr. Mason. The Cosways are Creole planters, former slave-owners ruined by emancipation. Hated by the blacks, these "old-time white people" are also, paradoxically, despised as "white niggers" by the more recent English colonists because of their long intimacy with blacks. The lush, overgrown garden of Coulibri, the Cosways' estate, is a microcosm of the moral and sexual ambiguities of their situation, a kind of corrupted Eden: "the tree of life grew there. But it had gone wild ... a smell of dead flowers mixed with the fresh living smell." Recalled often in dream and memory, the garden is rich in symbolic overtones: "Orchids flourished out of reach or for some reason not to be touched. One was snaky looking, another like an octopus with long thin brown tentacles bare of leaves, hanging from a twisted root." Like the organs of some creature midway between plant and animal, these orchids, alluring and repellent, hint at forbidden fruit, the crossing of barriers, and an unruly fecundity. They hang from "a twisted root"—perhaps that of Creole society itself in its original sins of slavery and sexual exploitation.

The masochistic sexuality of the heroine has its own twisted roots in her childhood at Coulibri. Rejected by both whites and blacks, she suffers an even deeper injury from her mother, whose love she loses to an afflicted younger brother. This loss is evoked in a poignant image: "Once I made excuses to be near her when she brushed her hair, a soft black cloak to cover me, hide me, keep me safe." But now, "she pushed me away, not roughly but calmly, coldly, without a word. She wanted to sit with Pierre."

Antoinette's experience here is that of many a little girl rejected in favor of a brother; unconsciously the child attributes this rejection to a catastrophic defect in herself and her own body. *In Black Sun*, her study of depression, Julia Kristeva writes that the loss of a love object is experienced

> "At the heart of the novel is an extraordinary scene of repressed sexual desire, a revelation that embodies a myth of origin not only for the heroine but for her Creole society as well. The political dimension of the text is complicated and rendered ambiguous by these unconscious fantasies and fears."

by a woman as castration: "such a castration starts resonating with the threat of destruction of the body's integrity, the body image, and the entire psychic system as well."

The account of Antoinette's childhood contains many suggestions of this sort of mutilation. The male power of the family has been cut off by the death of the father, followed by the suicide of their only male friend and protector, and then by the poisoning of the mother's horse. Later the mother's second husband, Mr. Mason, clips the wings of her pet parrot. Frightening allusions to cutting and dismemberment appear in Antoinette's fantasies about the Obeah rituals practiced by her nurse, Christophine: "a dead man's dried hand ... a cock with its throat cut. ... Drop by drop the blood was falling." On the night when vengeful blacks set fire to Coulibri, Antoinette wishes "that I were very young again, for then I believed in my stick." This stick was just a pet piece of wood, but it had great significance: "I believed that no one could harm me when it was near me, to lose it would be a great misfortune." But this misfortune occurs: having lost her primitive confidence in her mother's love and in her own body, the girl sees herself as vulnerable, imperfect, castrated.

Antoinette's sense of herself as damaged goods also appears in her friendship with the black girl Tia. Here the motifs of racial impurity—the idea of the "white nigger"—and the impurity of the damaged female body are inextricably connected. The story of the relationship with Tia is also a symbolic account of Antoinette's traumatic passage through puberty and her assumption of a soiled and damaged female sexuality. Tia is a kind of double, at once the black part of Antoinette's divided identity and a fantasied other self through whom she might pass over into the feared and envied black majority. But the friendship ends in a quarrel at a forest pool, with overtones of sexual and racial humiliation and a foretaste of death. With Antoinette's few pennies as the stake, Tia bets her that she can't do an underwater somersault, then refuses to acknowledge that she's done it. "Tia laughed and told me that it certainly look like I drown dead that time. Then she picked up the money." Antoinette calls Tia "cheating nigger," and Tia insults her back, saying "Old time white people nothing but white nigger now, and black nigger better than white nigger." She makes off with Antoinette's clean dress, leaving her own soiled one behind.

The challenge of the underwater somersault may be seen as a promise of metamorphosis: immersion in water, as in baptism, signifies the death of the old self and the birth of the new. If Antoinette could do the somersault to Tia's satisfaction, perhaps she would emerge from the pool cleansed of her alienating whiteness, reborn black like her friend. But of course this does not happen. To get rid of her white self, Antoinette would literally have to "drown dead." Tia laughs at her for even trying. Paradoxically, she jeers at Antoinette for being her friend and thereby compromising further her precarious status as a white person. "Real white people, they got gold money," says Tia, "nobody see them come near us."

Back at Coulibri wearing Tia's soiled dress, Antoinette is laughed at again, this time by white people, her mother's elegant English visitors. Her mother, French via Martinique but "no white nigger either," refuses even to look at her. "She is ashamed of me," thinks Antoinette, "what Tia said is true."

The incident with the dress has sexual as well as racial implications. To be robbed of one's clothes, laughed at, and made to feel dirty, would be a severe social and sexual humiliation at any age, but perhaps especially for a pubescent girl. Morover, a dress is an image of the female body, a kind of second skin that both conceals and reveals, manifesting sexual status and desirability; indeed the dress—this one and others—is a recurrent trope in the novel. In putting on the dirty dress of a black girl, Antoinette is putting on her status. What seemed acceptable and even attractive in Tia means degradation and ridicule for Antoinette. Her mother has the dress burned, as if it carried the contagion of blackness. But the damage is already done: Antoinette has been contaminated by the soiled dress, representing not only her identification with Tia but also her family's ambiguous status and her own outcast condition as a girl unloved by her mother, therefore dirty, damaged, and unlovable.

The relationship with Tia reaches its violent climax on the night of the burning of Coulibri. Catching sight of Tia in the black mob, Antoinette runs to her as if to a part of herself: "We had eaten the same food, slept side by side, bathed in the same river. As I ran I thought, I will live with Tia and I will be like her." Once again she tries to resolve her divided identity by somehow fusing herself with Tia, and again this is impossible. Tia throws a stone at her, wounding her forehead. "We stared at each other, blood on my face, tears on hers. It was as if I saw myself, like in a looking-glass."

For some weeks after the fire, Antoinette lies ill and unconscious, perhaps signaling the onset of another kind of unconsciousness—that of repression. When she wakes up, she has indeed lost touch with something. With the separation from Tia, she is cut off from the "blackness" in herself—the innocent dirt and animality of childhood. The mingled racial world in which she has grown up has included intimacy and love as well as hatred. Now blackness and whiteness are sharply severed in her and what survives is mutilated and incomplete.

Moreover, the wound on her forehead may also signify the transformation of puberty. According to the chronology of the novel, Antoinette is about thirteen at this point. The bleeding wound suggests not only the severance from Tia and the childhood world of Coulibri, but also the bloody event that marks the end of childhood for every girl. When Antoinette regains consciousness with a bandaged head, she worries about having a scar, but her Aunt Cora reassures her, saying, "It won't spoil you on your wedding day." The illness, the blood, the bandage, the fear of bodily imperfection, and the doubts about the wedding day—all suggest menstruation, with its unconscious link with castration. And in fact, the first thing Antoinette sees on waking from her illness is her cut-off braid: "I saw my plait tied with red ribbon . . . I thought it was a snake."

The cut-off hair also echoes another severance—that from the mother, whose hair once enclosed the daughter in safety; now the daughter's hair is cut off. Antoinette's mother has broken down into madness after the fire and the death of her son. When Antoinette visits her, the mother flings her away, looking only for Pierre. With this renewed rejection in favor of the brother, Antoinette's sense of insufficiency is confirmed. Involved in this damaged sense of herself is the black girl in the dirty dress, a link that persists even in repression.

Concerns with sex, race, and the female body reappear in one of the most disturbing episodes in the novel, the scene in which Antoinette is harassed on her way to school by two bullies, a boy and a girl:

> The boy was about fourteen and tall and big for his age, he had a white skin, a dull ugly white covered with freckles, his mouth was a negro's mouth and he had small eyes, like bits of green glass. He had the eyes of a dead fish. Worst, most horrible of all, his hair was crinkled, a negro's hair, but bright red, and his eyebrows and eyelashes were red. The girl was very black and wore no head handkerchief. Her hair had been plaited and I could smell the sickening oil she had daubed on it.

Up to this point, blacks have been presented as variously appealing or frightening, but never as physically repellent. This unknown pair, however, provoke a kind of uncanny horror and revulsion. And yet they are perhaps not entirely unknown.

In the menacing black girl, there are echoes of Tia. After the fire, Tia disappears from the narrative, suggesting that the identification with her is repressed. In this encounter that repressed identification seems to come back in the form of a persecutor. Like Tia, the girl can be seen as a double of Antoinette, here transformed, after the crisis of adolescence, into a sort of negative anti-self-the feared and despised aspects of the female body projected outwards in the person of a bad-smelling black girl.

The final confrontation with Tia was above all visual: "I saw Tia. . . . I looked at her and saw her face . . . we stared at each other. . . . I saw myself. Like in a looking-glass." In contrast, the bad-smelling girl says to Antoinette, "Why you won't look at me. You don't want to look at me, eh, I make you look at me." This girl too is a reflection of Antoinette, but one she is afraid to look at. What draw her to Tia has become ugly and frightening in the dark mirror of the unconscious.

Even more terrifying than the girl is her companion, not only because he is sexually threatening—"You wait," he says, "one day I catch you alone"—but because of the way he looks. What seems so dreadful is an apparent anomaly: the boy is literally white, even freckled and red-haired; yet at the same time he is somehow not white. The boy is probably an albino, or perhaps a person of mixed race, descended like many West Indians from the encounters of Scottish and English slaveholders such as Antoinette's father with black or mulatto women. In either case, the disproportionate horror he inspires in Antoinette may come from his being in a sense the very thing she herself has been called, a "white nigger," and thus still another double, a disturbing image of her own anomalous status, and also an unsettling hint that white skin is no guarantee of unmixed ancestry. In "The Uncanny," Freud writes that the double embodies the return of the repressed. In the revulsion inspired by the boy and his companion, there is indeed something uncanny—the mingled dread and sense of familiarity that mark an encounter with repressed aspects of the self.

The incident with the boy and girl has a dream-like vividness and sense of portent; in fact, Rhys tried for a time to write the whole novel as the protagonist's dream, and three dreams remain in the final version. The most significant occurs several years after the fire, toward the end of Part I. Antoinette is boarding at a convent school, "a place of sunshine and of death" full of reminders of the dangers of female sexuality: the crypt holds the body of a fourteen-year-old saint named Innocenzia, and the girls hear of virgin martyrs and of "that flawless crystal that, once broken, can never be mended." Into this atmosphere of desperate repression comes a visit from Antoinette's stepfather, Mr. Mason, who hints at the arrival of a potential suitor from England.

That night, Antoinette dreams she is back at Coulibri, wearing a long white dress that she fears soiling, being led toward the forest by a man whose face is "black with hatred." Sick with dread, she follows him: "I make no effort to save myself. . . .This must happen." She is led into a garden and thinks, "It will be when I go up these steps." Stumbling on her dress, she holds onto a tree, which "sways and jerks" until the dream ends. The dream foretells the coming of Rochester and the loss of virginity. The fear of soiling the white dress makes clear the meaning of the exchange of dresses with Tia: to put on female sexuality is to be soiled and degraded, yet "This must happen." The garden in the dream is like that of Coulibri, but "the trees are different trees." The tree of life of the childhood Eden has become another kind of tree, a throbbing, jerking phallus, as the sexual act is finally accomplished in an atmosphere of fear and fatality.

The masochistic excitement of the dream is associated with indirect allusions to race and color, as if sex itself were somehow black: Antoinette's dress will be soiled like that of a black girl, and the face of the man is "black with hatred," connecting sex and race, desire and contempt. He may represent not only Rochester, who will both desire and hate her, but also the red-haired boy, the mob that burned Coulibri, the black man who will later be seen to dominate her mother. In this charged atmosphere, color has become the marker not only of conflict, but of difference, of meaning itself. The ambivalence of desire has become inseparable from racial attraction and repulsion, just as the division within the self is experienced in racial terms as the split between Antoinette and Tia.

In Part II of the novel, the narration passes from Antoinette to Rochester, although the man in Rhys's novel is not Charlotte Bronte's attractively turbulent hero, but a conventional upper-class Englishman very like male characters in Rhys's other fiction—hypocritical, coldly seductive, and fundamentally cruel. He is frightened of the place—"Not only wild, but menacing"—and repelled by the people: "I wouldn't hug and kiss them," he protests when Antoinette kisses Christophine, "I couldn't." Significantly, he criticizes Christophine for soiling her long dress by letting it trail on the floor: "it is not a clean habit." But despite his inhibitions, he is aroused by his wife's beauty and sensuality: "very soon, she was as eager for what is called loving as I was—more lost and drowned afterwards." The metaphor of drowning recalls the underwater somersault—"sure look like I drown dead that time"—and suggests the self-annihilating quality of Antoinette's erotic response.

Rochester treats her with lust unmediated by tenderness: "One day the sight of a dress she'd left lying on the bedroom floor made me breathless and savage with desire. When I was exhausted I turned away from her and slept, still without a word or a caress." The dress, separated from the woman herself, is emblematic of an empty and alienated desire.

In the honeymoon house, the couple are dangerously free. "Here I can do as I like," says Antoinette. Increasingly they liberate the dark undercurrents of sex, the sadistic and masochistic impulses held in its precarious equilibrium. For Antoinette, sexual surrender merges with the attraction to death that has haunted her since her childhood losses. "Say die and I will die," she whispers during sex, seeming to make herself dependent on Rochester for her very existence, as the child once depended on her mother. The marriage shows the deadly working of the repetition compulsion; with her husband Antoinette experiences again the coldness and contempt of that first love. To the girl convinced that she is damaged and dirty, a "white nigger," contempt and abuse mean love; they make her feel desired for what she really is. "Desire, Hatred, Life, Death came very

close in the darkness," Rochester writes. "Not close. The same."

This strange idyll is interrupted by a letter from Daniel Cosway, a man who claims to be the son of Antoinette's father by a black woman—"half-way house, as we say"—and thus Antoinette's half-brother. In the letter and a later visit, Daniel informs Rochester about Antoinette's family—"the bad blood she have from both sides." The story Daniel tells is one of drunkenness, miscegenation, and inherited madness—in other words, the standard nineteenth-century view of the "degeneracy" of the white Creole. Antoinette's mother is "a raging lunatic and worse besides"; her father was "a shameless man," with innumerable slave concubines and half-caste children. (Although Antoinette later disputes these allegations, they accord with gossip she overheard as a child.) As Rochester leaves him, Daniel says "Give my love to your wife—my sister . . . Pretty face, soft skin, pretty colour—not yellow like me. But my sister just the same."

Outside Daniel's house, Rochester is transfixed by something he sees: "a black and white goat . . . was staring at me and for what seemed minutes I stared back into its slanting yellow-green eyes." Symbol of lust, the goat with its mixed colors seems to stand for the sexual license of the men of Cosway's class and for the mixed race they produced. Their offspring can be of any color, as Daniel suggests: yellow like him, brown like the beautiful servant Amelie, white like the red-haired boy, perhaps even the "pretty colour" of Antoinette. This thought has already occurred fleetingly to Rochester: "Long, sad, dark alien eyes. Creole of pure English descent she may be, but they are not English or European either." Now he notices a resemblance between Antoinette and Amelie: "Perhaps they are related," he thinks. "It's possible, it's even probable in this damned place."

A similar suspicion is adumbrated in *Jane Eyre* in the description of Mrs. Rochester. Although the race of "the Creole" is never specified, the lurid glimpses of her are pointedly suggestive: Jane sees "a discoloured face . . . a savage face," "fearful blackened inflation of the lineaments," "lips swelled and dark." Rochester alludes to "the risks, the horrors, the loathings of incongruous unions." It seems unlikely that he would knowingly have married a woman of mixed race; the implication, therefore, is that even within the white Creole there lurks a germ of blackness, acquired through some secret impurity of the bloodline or perhaps, magically, through long proximity.

In Rhys's novel, Daniel Cosway's revelations cause Rochester to shun his wife's bed, driving Antoinette to seek an Obeah love charm from Christophine. The aphrodisiac works all too well, leaving Antoinette with bruises and a torn nightdress. But she is evidently not put off, quite the contrary: Christophine tells Rochester that what happened "make her love you more." For Antoinette, violence is intimacy, a confirmation of her own sense of herself as damaged, soiled, a "white nigger." But Rochester, horrified by what he has discovered about himself, takes revenge on his wife by going to bed with the servant who resembles her. The next morning, looking at Amelie, he thinks, "Impossible. And her skin was darker, her lips thicker than I had thought."

Amelie is another of Antoinette's dark doubles, and Rochester's ambivalence toward her parallels his feelings for his wife. He is repelled by the idea that Antoinette might have the fateful drop of black blood; yet unbeknownst to him, the love charm that excites him comes out of the heart of blackness—the hut in the forest where the "blue-black" Christophine does her Obeah magic.

Rochester's mingled repulsion and attraction for both Amelie and his wife echo Antoinette's own conflicted feelings about the possibility of blackness in herself: she both wants to be black and fears that in fact she might be. This paradox in turn grows out of ambivalence toward the elements represented for Antoinette, and indeed more generally for the Western imagination, by blackness: sex, dirt, animality, both the vitality and the violence of nature. The fact that these are largely projections of the content of the unconscious itself does not diminish their power—on the contrary. Blackness and all it represents is both frightening and irresistible. In his encounter with Amelie, perhaps even in his relationship with Antoinette, Rochester is tasting the guilty pleasures of old Mr. Cosway and the other slave-owners with their concubines: the forbidden fruit in the West Indian paradise is interracial sex.

All these strands of race and sex are tied together in one powerful scene involving Antoinette's mother, and thus Antoinette herself. In the series of doubles embodying the different aspects of Antoinette's fragmented being, the most important is her mother, whose name—Annette—resembles her daughter's, and whose fate—drunkenness, madness, confinement—prefigures Antoinette's. In Daniel Cosway's story, the mother is "a raging lunatic and worse besides"—the "worse besides" evidently something so shameful that even he is

unwilling to name it. On the night of the love charm, however, Antoinette tells Rochester the story of her mother's final degradation.

After the fire and the death of Pierre, Mr. Mason put the mother in the care of a colored couple. Antoinette goes to their house one day and hears crying; thinking her mother is being hurt, she runs onto the veranda and sees her mother inside: "I remember the dress she was wearing—an evening dress cut very low, and she was barefooted. There was a fat black man with a glass of rum in his hand. He said 'Drink it and you will forget.' She drank it without stopping." As Antoinette watches, the man lifts her mother up and kisses her. "I saw his mouth fasten on hers and she went all soft and limp in his arms and he laughed."

This scene depicts the nigthmare of whites in a society based on racial hierarchy: the violation of a white woman by a black man. The mother's degradation is evidently the culminating act of revenge on the owners of Coulibri: the white mistress, now broken and defenseless, is used as black women were used by their white masters. This account of the scene, however, leaves out its most disturbing aspect—the voluptuousness of the mother's response: she goes "all soft and limp" under the black man's kiss. The degrading details—the mother's captive, drunken, disheveled state and the man's coarse appearance—seem to contribute to that voluptuousness. The coercive circumstances appear not to force the mother against her own desire, but rather to allow her to give way to it. Her self-annihilating submissiveness is like that of Antoinette when she says to Rochester, "Say die and I will die." There is also an interesting slip or substitution: the mother's caretaker is originally referred to as "coloured"—mulatto—rather than "black," a distinction carefully maintained throughout the text. Here the man has become black, as though to intensify the outrage.

This scene, recounted by Antoinette years after it happens as though it were a dream, a nighttime flash of childhood memory or fantasy, has familiar meaning in psychoanalytic terms. The unseen child observer, the sexual embrace, the mother's cries, and the child's idea that the mother is being hurt all mark this as a sadomasochistic primal scene—the child's archetypal fantasy of sex between the parents as a scene of cruelty. Its most striking feature is the presence of the black man. The figures in such a fantasy need not be the real parents, but since Antoinette's real mother appears, why not her real father? The father's replacement by the black man may reflect the pervasive doubt about race and paternity in a Creole society. There is a kind of childish logic here: the father had many black women and mulatto children; here the mother has a black man—and if this one, why not others before him? (Indeed Christophine says "he take her whenever he want . . . That man and others.") And why not a child? The child's speculations about its own begetting are shaped here by the sexual and racial fears of her society, creating a primal scene that confirms Antoinette's notion of herself as "white nigger."

This is also, perhaps, a scene of founding or origin, not only for Antoinette but for her society. The varicolored Creole population originated mostly in sexual encounters between whites and blacks—although not of the kind depicted here, but rather between white men and black women. But what matters in this case is not historical reality but fantasy, both individual and social. Just as Antoinette is presumably the daughter of old Cosway and not of a black man, so too the origin of the colored population could be shown more accurately by an encounter between a white man like Cosway and a black slave concubine. But that scene would have nothing like the shocking force of this one. It would simply show the kind of nominality illicit sexual activity that poses no threat to the social structure.

A white man does not really degrade himself with a black woman, because the male is assumed to dominate the female as white dominates black. But a white woman who submits willingly to sex with a black man is seen as degrading her race as well as herself. And the possible result—pregnancy and a child of mixed race—is harder to hide and presents a greater threat to the "purity" of the white racial line than does the by-blow of a man. Had the kind of scene depicted here occurred more often in real life, white separateness and supremacy would soon have disappeared, along with white pretensions to moral superiority.

Thus this is a subversive scene of origin, a representation of what must not happen. It contains the one truly forbidden sin in this corrupt Creole paradise, and therefore in a sense its cornerstone, the fundamental taboo on which it is structured. The attraction of white men to black and brown women is openly acknowledged and everywhere evident in light-skinned offspring of uncertain paternity. The corresponding attraction of white women to black men must be entirely repressed. (Referring to this subject in a letter, Rhys writes "The men did as they liked. The women—never.") In a society founded on white hegemony, the act suggested in

this scene is the most degrading and anarchic—and thus the most erotically charged, the most capable of liberating repressed desire.

The scene of the mother with the black man is at the heart of *Wide Sargasso Sea*, in some sense a scene of origin for the novel itself, containing its central motifs of race and sex and the connection between them. Here the sexual domination inherent in slavery is represented, but with the races of the parties reversed, as if in fulfillment of an unconscious wish. The combined horror and excitement derive from this idea of eroticized enslavement, in which elements of sexual fantasy and historical reality converge. In a society barely beyond slavery, the sadistic and masochistic aspects of sexual feeling find ready to hand a pattern, a relationship, a vocabulary of images. The sadomasochistic primal scene becomes identified with a social institution in which sex is a transaction between masters and slaves. Female sexual pleasure is seen as enslavement, and powerlessness and submission are imagined as erotically exciting.

The relationship between slave and master is suggested throughout the novel in various forms. It appears, for instance, in the marriage of Antoinette's mother with Mr. Mason, to whom she sells herself to save her family from destitution. There is a powerful image of the mother bent backward in Mason's arms, her long hair touching the floor, that suggests the same voluptuous submissiveness that appears later with the black man, and also in Antoinette's relations with Rochester. All these pairings, as well as the encounter of Rochester with Amelie, are characterized by inequality of power, economic bondage, and hints of sadistic and masochistic pleasure. Even Rochester himself feels that he was sold by his father into bondage—that of a marriage for money—although it is Antoinette who ends up confined and penniless. The relation of master to slave, with its knot of race and sex, desire and hatred, power and dependence, excitement and shame, is a kind of shadowy template behind every sexual relationship in the novel. It is perhaps involved even in the tormented love of Antoinette for her mother.

The submissiveness of the slave, however, turns eventually to rage and rebellion. As the blacks burned Coulibri, so Antoinette, at the end of the novel, burns Thornfield Hall, fulfilling the destiny created for her in *Jane Eyre*. In Rhys's version, the act takes place in a dream of the past: as Antoinette leaps from the ramparts she calls Tia's name, in a final attempt to rejoin the lost black self of childhood.

1837 illustration of the island of Dominica, the setting of Wide Sargasso Sea

The issue of race in *Wide Sargasso Sea* goes beyond history and politics to the unconscious, where racial feelings have their deepest roots. The novel's most memorable images—the garden of Coulibri, the fire and Tia throwing the stone, the red-haired boy and the bad-smelling girl, the mother in the arms of the black man—are dream-like in their haunting power, and like dreams they represent the conflicts of the unconscious. In its fidelity to the unresolved nature of those conflicts, *Wide Sargasso Sea* has a kind of painful, masochistic integrity. It is disturbingly honest in its exploration of the fantasies and the tangled, contradictory desires not only of a Creole society, but of the Western imagination itself in its continuing struggle with the dilemma of race. Its political sympathies—whether with the oppressed black majority or the dispossessed white minority—are finally as profoundly ambiguous as the unconscious conflicts in which they are rooted.

Source: Elizabeth Dalton, "Sex and Race in *Wide Sargasso Sea*," in *Partisan Review*, Vol. 67, No. 3, Summer 2000, pp. 431–443.

Kathy Mezei

In the following article, Mezei examines the narrative structure and presentation of madness in Rhys's novel.

Very soon she'll join all the others who know the secret and will not tell it. Or cannot. Or try and fail because they do not know enough . . . She's one of them. I too can wait—for the day when she is only a memory to be avoided, looked away, and like all memories a legend. Or a lie . . . (*Wide Sargasso Sea*)

With these vengeful words, Rochester closes his narration, the disturbing story of his marriage in Jamaica to Antoinette Cosway (Mason), the first Mrs. Rochester. Soon enough Rochester has transformed Antoinette from a speaking subject into an object, an other, a locked-away madwoman—a lie. As a character and a narrator, Rochester has committed one kind of narratorial lie, but, according to Jean Rhys, the author of *Jane Eyre*, Charlotte Brontë, had engendered another, equally serious lie:

The Creole in Charlotte Brontë's novel is a lay figure—repulsive which does not matter, and not once alive which does. She's necessary to the plot, but always she shrieks, howls, laughs horribly, attacks all and sundry—*off stage*. For me (and for you I hope) she must be right *on stage*. She must be at least plausible with a past, the *reason* why Mr. Rochester treats her so abominably and feels justified, the *reason* why he thinks she is mad and why of course she goes mad, even the *reason* why she tries to set everything on fire, and eventually succeeds. (Personally, I think *that* one is simple. She is cold—and fire is the only warmth she knows in England). (*Letters, 1931–1966*)

> " Her very sanity is tied to her ability to narrate, and here being 'marooned' has consequences for both her narrative and her state of mind."

Rochester's sin was to impose his point of view on both the narrative and Antoinette: Charlotte Brontë's was a narratorial omission: in *Jane Eyre*, Antoinette (Bertha) is not permitted to speak. Instead, it is Jane who speaks for her when she admonishes Rochester, "you are inexorable for that unfortunate lady . . . she cannot help being mad." To rectify the situation, Jean Rhys in her novel, *Wide Sargasso Sea*, allows Antoinette to narrate her own story. Thus, despite Rochester's malediction, Antoinette does "tell it," and the telling of her secret, her memories, and her story mirrors her desperate effort to save herself from a lie.

How, as subject, does Antoinette tell her story? And does her narration hold a clue to her madness? In fact, Jean Rhys was uncertain how best to present Antoinette's point of view:

It can be done three ways. (1) Straight, Childhood, Marriage, Finale told in first person. Or it can be done (2) Man's point of view; (3) Woman's ditto both first person. Or it can be told in the third person with the writer as the Almighty. Well that is hard for me. I prefer direct thoughts and actions.

I am doing (2). (*Letters*)

As the novel reveals, Rhys decided to begin with Antoinette's narration, then to shift to Rochester's, and finally to close with Antoinette's disintegrating narration, introduced and contextualized by the disembodied voice of Grace Poole.

But, as Rochester feared, there are secrets shadowing Antoinette and her narration. Since the suspense in this essay lies in what I will say about the secrets, not in what they are, let me immediately alleviate the reader's suspense. First, hidden within the narrative is the textual secret representing the hidden or deferred meaning, which is the nature of Antoinette's ultimate "marooning," a secrecy as deep and seductive as the pools she swims in, but as dangerous as the madness in which she finally drowns. This "marooning" is gradually disclosed by the deliberate sequence of her opening narrative. The structural secret, which is the secret the reader must discover as he or she travels through the text, consists of Antoinette's desire (and need) for sequence. Her very sanity is tied to her ability to narrate, and here being "marooned" has consequences for both her narrative and her state of mind.

There is also, finally, the secret shaping the entire narrative—the secret of the narrative. In describing the tales of Henry James, Tzvetan Todorov observed:

we now know that Henry James' secret . . . resides precisely in the existence of a secret, of an absent and absolute cause, as well as in the effort to plumb this secret, to render the absent present. ("The Secret of Narrative")

Inevitably, the hunt for such a secret initiates, propels, and in effect creates the narrative. Quite simply the secret of *Wide Sargasso Sea* is Antoinette's valiant, heroic attempt to tell her story. The secret of the narrative is not her descent into madness in the figure of the madwoman locked in the attic, or her lack of madness and conventional society's excess of it, but her *reason* for engaging in the act of narration. Antoinette and the others "keep" their secret from Rochester (and perhaps the reader), because Rochester does not pause to unravel the story Antoinette is telling: he resists the structures and the function of her narrative, as well as its *histoire*; he is neither an ideal listener nor an ideal reader.

To prevent a false telling of her story by others—the lie—Antoinette must tell herself in the first person following the conventions of narrative order. When the narrative disintegrates, as it does in Part Three, so does Antoinette. When the narrative stops, Antoinette dies. By her act of narration, she retains her tenuous fragile hold on sanity, on life itself, since to narrate is to live, to order a life, to "make sense" out of it. If "narrative is a strategy for survival" (Daphne Marlatt, *How to Hug a Stone*), Antoinette survives only as long as she creates narratives.

Although, according to Kenneth Burke, the construction of symbolic actions such as the telling of stories is the "defining feature of human beings," (*Language as Symbolic Action*) for women narrators, this symbolic action may be a necessary strategy for survival. Antoinette joins Penelope, Scheherazade, the wicked stepmother in *Snow White*, and countless female narrators whose only form of control is through the weaving of words, the plotting of stories, the constructing of plots, and the telling of their own story in their voice as narrating subject, not narrated object. What is interesting about

Antoinette's narration is how desperately and ingeniously she uses narrative techniques such as the "illusion of sequence" (W. J. T. Mitchell, Foreword, *On Narrative*) and linear chronology to delay the final secret, climax, closure of her story—her descent into madness and death.

As long as Antoinette can remember and order the events of her memories into a temporal or causal sequence, create even an illusion of sequence and maintain a measured sense of space and time, then she can hold her life and self together. Her act of narration becomes an act of affirmation and cohesion, a nod to the world and its conventions, an attempt to prevent herself from dissolving. When, in Part Three, Antoinette lies encaged in Thornfield Hall's dark, cold attic, the threads that hold her to the reality that the world perceives as sanity finally break. These threads are the elements of conventional narrative: linear chronology, sequence, narratorial lucidity, distance. She herself admits at this point that "time has no meaning"; sequence disintegrates into a confusion of present and past and ultimately into a dream which narrates her future. The relation between text-time (*récit*) and story-time (*histoire*) blurs, creating anachrony (Gérard Genette, *Narrative Discourse*). She can neither "remember" what has happened in the past, nor what it is she must do in the future. Like her sense of time, her sense of space becomes distorted; "that afternoon we went to England" she says, describing a brief foray from her attic. Her attic is not England, a place, but a configuration of her mind, an enclosure. Finally, no longer in control of her narration, she must end it.

Rhys is a deliberately elusive writer, whose elusiveness differs from the lucid strategies of Joyce or Nabokov. She is also a modernist writer who polishes and hones her texts with a perfectionist's obsessions, and whose modernism is reflected in her method of paring away at authorial presence so that her characters may speak and act without intrusive authorial judgments and commentary. Unlike some of her contemporaries in the 1960s, she is not experimenting with the concept of narrative or narrator; her struggle with point of view and focalization concerns her desire to present a consciousness sincerely rather than to question the structures of presenting consciousness. We need, therefore, to dip and borrow and construct our own approach to her narrative, beckoned as it were by the text itself. With this in mind, we can now turn to narration in *Wide Sargasso Sea* and its relation to memory and madness.

An earlier version of Part One of *Wide Sargasso Sea* was published in *Art and Literature*, March 1964, and this and the endless agonizing revisions of this manuscript that took over ten years to complete, are witness to her search for perfection and purity of presentation. The changes to the earlier manuscript show her building a stronger case to justify Antoinette's state of mind and subsequent actions. Rhys removes verbs like "seem" or "thought" to allow Antoinette to speak directly, and omits "and," "but," and "then" in order to make Antoinette's discourse more disjointed and associative, to undermine the illusion of sequence. Certain deletions are indicative of her intention to allow Antionette to proffer her experiences with a greater immediacy through less commentary, therefore creating the sense of a highly impressionistic, troubled mind. For example, the earlier version had Antoinette commenting on her childhood. "I got used to a solitary life and began to distrust strangers . . .," which is unnecessary commentary whose signification is more effectively revealed by Antoinette's reactions to ensuing events. Similarly, the final version cuts "but it was understood that she would not approve of Tia," leaving "My mother never asked me where I had been or what I had done" to stand as an even more poignant indictment of her mother's neglect.

Rhys also adds several scenes in her final version—the poisoned horse, the first "forest" dream, a visit to her imprisoned mother, all of which strengthen the case of a troubled past for Antoinette. Despite Rhys' authorial elusiveness, by looking closely at the structures of these narrative acts, we can see how narrative becomes, for Antoinette, a strategy of survival, an attempt to maintain her hold on reality, to constrain dissolution into madness and how, finally, the act of retention helps her to remember what act (other than narration) she must commit in the future.

Part One is Antoinette's narration and the narrating (present) self seems to be speaking from the perspective (place and time) with which her narration closes—the convent, in the early hours of the morning as she falls asleep again. In this case, the narrating and experiencing self merge in the present time with which Part One closes. This first narration covers the period from Antoinette's childhood at Coulibri to age seventeen at the convent just prior to her marriage to Rochester. The narrating self is engaged in an act of memory, creating a pattern like Aunt Cora's colorful patchwork counterpane out of significant moments of her childhood. Although there is little dissonance between the two selves, for the narrating self rarely judges or comments on her younger self, there are several significant occasions in which the narrating self explicitly draws attention to her present state. At these moments, we are made aware of Antoinette's urgency, her hysteria, her desperation as if her world were closing in.

Since Antoinette is a child of silence, to whom communication, words, speech bring only unhappiness and rejection (her mother continually orders the child to leave her alone), it is a heroic effort for her to speak, even to herself. On two occasions—the poisoning of her mother's horse, and Mr. Mason's intimation of the prospect of her marriage—she shows her suspicion of words: "for I thought if I told no one it might not be true." To speak something raises it to the level of concrete reality. On the other hand, it is not her *passive* silence that causes her the greatest perturbation and the eventual division into two disassociated selves, but the act of being silenced. She is silenced first by her mother, who denies her existence, and then again by Rochester who refuses to be the reader of her story. He "reads" Daniel Cosway's letter-version, but is reluctant to listen to Antoinette's version. As the couple departs from Granbois, he refuses the healing act of communication: "No, I would say—I know what I would say 'I have made a terrible mistake. Forgive me.'" But he never says it, never releases her from her imprisoning silence.

Although Part One is narrated retrospectively in the past tense, it is in the moments when Antoinette slips into the present that we catch a glimpse of the older, narrating Antoinette and the secret of her narrative. The novel opens with the ominous "They say when trouble comes close ranks, and so the white people did." Although "say" is in the gnomic present, and functions as a reminder of the outside, anonymous world of clichés, it also serves to remind us that there is a present voice, a narrator who sometimes lapses into the present. Already the troubled presence of the present is felt.

At the beginning of her story, Antoinette describes her mother:

> Once I made excuses to be near her, when she brushed her hair, a soft black cloak to cover me, hide me, keep me safe. But not any longer. Not any more.

The repetition of "not any" and the slight change from "longer" to "more" implies that the second phrase is spoken by the present narrating self brooding on her loss—of her mother, of feeling "safe" and that, in the narrator's mind, past and present blur, a blurring which occurs repeatedly in Part Three and suggests a disassociated mind. Like conventional narrative, sanity apparently requires clarity of sequence and distinction.

Further along in her narrative, just before the burning of Coulibri, Antoinette slips again into a gnomic present:

> There are more ways than one of being happy, better perhaps to be peaceful and contented and protected, as I feel now, peaceful for years and long years.

"As I feel now" probably refers to her sense of the convent as a refuge (or possibly to the attic, where locked in the refuge of her mind, she feels safe). She digresses from retrospection again in that same section when she remarks in the only noticeable judgment of her younger experiencing self "All this was long ago, when I was still babyish and sure that everything was alive."

The most striking emergence into the present occurs as Antoinette describes her sojourn in the convent, after Coulibri was burned and her mother locked away: "Quickly while I can, I must remember the hot classroom." Why the sense of urgency? Why must she remember? The phrase "must remember" recurs in Part Three and is in fact the secret or hidden figure of her last narrative, her link to sanity, and the motivation of her entire narrative. Must it be told quickly because soon her narrative will be taken over by another narrator and/or because she is in danger of forgetting (losing) her mind?

After Mr. Mason hints that he has a suitor for her, Antoinette enters, for the second time, a recurring nightmare where she wanders in a menacing forest, pursued by someone characterized by the fact that he hates her. This dream is narrated in the present tense. It is then an *aide mémoire*, spoken by Antoinette in the attic, to help her to remember what it is she must do at Thornfield, since the dream clearly shifts from Jamaica to England: "We are no longer in the forest but in an enclosed garden surrounded by a stone wall and the trees are different trees." Or is the narrator, speaking from the convent, shifting from a past dream to a premonition of her future English nightmare? Then she wakes and continues in the present tense to describe Sister Marie Augustine giving her chocolate and their ensuing enigmatic discussion. Her recollection of chocolate causes a digression into the past to her mother's funeral, chocolate being the trigger of this memory. "Now the thought of her is mixed up with my dream." Antoinette's narration concludes as she goes back to bed to sleep, to dream; the last words she hears are the Sister's which lead into the future and into Rochester's narration: "Soon I will give the signal. Soon it will be tomorrow morning." This anticipation of the future is paralleled by the ending of Part Three which propels the reader into true closure only in *Jane Eyre*. The entire narrative ends with the future which remains, of course, to be narrated. The intertextuality of sequence between Brontë's and Rhys' novels is as significant as the intertextuality of the *histoire*.

Before we can leave Antoinette's narrative, there remain further secrets hidden in her story and in her telling that call for disclosure. First, her narrative appears to have certain characteristics of a monologue, of what Dorrit Cohn calls the "autobiographical monologue" in which "a lone speaker recalls his own past and tells it to himself—in chronological order" (*Transparent Minds*), or even of a "memory monologue." In order to describe the memory monologue Cohn quotes Claude Simon's remarks on his novel *La Route des Flandres*:

> this author undertakes less . . . to tell a story than to describe the imprint left by it on a memory and a sensibility. (*Transparent Minds*)

Cohn then suggests that the model is not autobiographical communication (telling one's story) but the self-involvement of memory and that this imitation of a solipsistic process imposes not only a fractured chronology but also a fragmentary coverage. Cohn again quotes Simon: "I do not fill in the blanks. They remain, like so many fragments." The movement of the narration is determined not by chronology but by associative memory.

Is then Antoinette's narration not a narrative but a monologue, an autobiographical or memory monologue? I think not. Antoinette has structured her narrative deliberately and, although as we shall see, the sequence of events are connected by associative memory rather than by temporality or causality, Antoinette's narrative is forcibly contained by a motif that determines her memories and her retelling of them. Conversely as stated earlier, she herself is held together by the act of narrating. Therefore, there is a deliberate narrative presentation and strategy. Moreover, as a narrator, she is always seeking to restrain her story within the boundaries of conventional narrative temporality such as sequence, linear chronology, plausible duration. This is why she so carefully sprinkles dates and sets out duration of time throughout her telling: a date of 1839 when she enters the convent, a reference to "the first day I had to go to the convent," and explanation that "During this time, nearly eighteen months my stepfather often came to see me." These are signposts of sanity. To measure time is a measure of how closely one is in touch with reality. Accordingly, Antoinette makes an effort to measure time and to progress from childhood, to school, to marriage. Rochester called her "a lunatic who always knows the time. But never does."

Pulling against chronology is her mind's tendency to work by association, to digress to the present, to compress time. After describing how she "knew the time of day when though it is hot and blue and there are no clouds, the sky can have a very black look," she pauses and begins a new section, a new time: "I was a bridesmaid when my mother married Mr. Mason." Surely this is the memory association of a bride who has learned to equate marriage with tragedy and blackness. The narrating self has invaded the experiencing self and imposed her perceptions upon the younger mind. While Antoinette's strategy as narrator is to compose a conventional narrative, the boundaries of the narrative are continually under threat of disintegrating—as is Antoinette herself. For Rhys and her narrator, freedom, iconoclasm, innovation imply danger, isolation, alienation: the tenets of modernism do not hold out liberation for a bound mind, they only release that mind into a further and more horrible entrapment, particularly if that mind is female, and by definition, not free.

A monologue, whether autobiography or memory, is suitable for a mad, rambling, or childish mind that free-associates and thus reveals itself (as Benjy does in *Sound and Fury*, or Vardaman in *As I Lay Dying*), but when a narrator like Antoinette makes such a formidable effort to structure a narrative and abide by the rhetorical principles of narrative, the difference between monologue and narrative becomes the difference between madness and sanity.

Rhys, in fact, originally intended to present Antoinette in monologue, but then changed her mind, her story, and as a consequence offered the reader a more complex fiction, a fiction with a secret to be discovered:

> The book began with a dream and ended with a dream (though I didn't get the last dream right for a long time). All the rest was to be a long monologue. Antoinette in her prison room remembers, loves, hates, raves, talks to imaginary people, hears imaginary voices answering and overhears meaningless conversations outside. The story, if any, to be implied, never told straight. . . . I remembered the last part of *Voyage in the Dark* written like that—time and place abolished, past and present the same—and I had been almost satisfied. Then everybody said it was "confused and confusing—impossible to understand, etc." and I had to cut and rewrite it (I still think I was right and they were wrong, tho' it was long ago). Still I thought "if they fussed over one part of a book, nobody will get the hang of a whole book written that way at all" or "A mad girl speaking all the time is too much!" And anyway there was a lot left to be done and could I do it? I think I was tired. Anyway after a week or two I decided to write it again as a story, a romance, but keeping the dream feeling and working up to the madness (I hoped). (*Letters*)

Because there is a psychological motivation for narrative, Antoinette's discourse, even if spoken, even if directed to herself (and really to whom else does she ever speak?) must be received as narrative.

Although her narrative unfolds primarily in the past, and although there is the appearance of consonance between the narrating and the experiencing selves, between the young woman of the present and the lonely child of the past, the heavy hand of present consciousness is felt throughout. But this is where Rhys is so elusive. Although in retrospective narratives, the relationship between narrating and experiencing selves varies from primary focalization on the experiencing self (and childhood) as in *Great Expectations*, to focalization on the present consciousness as it engages in the act of interpreting its past, and analyzing the present in the context of this past (Proust's *A la recherche du temps perdu*), Rhys' deliberate blurring of the two selves through allowing the present (and disturbed) consciousness of Antoinette to overtly and covertly intrude upon the narration, sows seeds of warning about the precarious state of the narrating consciousness. While Part One is evidently narrated in the past, we in fact learn as much about the present state of her mind. Antoinette's inability at times, particularly in Part Three, to distinguish between her past and present self is simultaneously a sign of her increased disturbance and of the breakdown of narrative presentation.

In Part One, Antoinette succumbs to certain narrative habits that are revelatory of her present disturbed mind. She repeats the adverbs "always" and "never." Within the opening pages, Mr. Luttrell "was gone for always"; Pierre's doctor "never came again"; Antoinette "never went near" the orchid in the wild garden at Coulibri; "The Wilderness of Coulibri never saddened me"; Christophine "never paid them"; "I never looked at any strange negro," "My mother never asked me where I had been or what I had done." In one sense the use of "always," along with the repetition of "still," ("she still rode about every morning") and "sometimes" ("sometimes we left the bathing pool at midday, sometimes we stayed till late afternoon") is iterative and durative, implying continuity over a certain duration of time in the past. However, the plaintive echo of "still," "sometimes," "usually," "always," and "never" intimates a presentness in that adverbs like "still" reach *into* the present, and that "always," and more strongly "never" affect the present narrating Antoinette who has suffered the consequences of the string of "always" and "never" in her childhood, and now exists in a state of neverness—always. Moreover the finality and negativity of "never"

(and, in the context of her discourse, of "always") imply a continual, progressing closure as her world narrows, closes in on her, and freedom, safety, and happiness are progressively cut off from her.

In other words, the repetition of adverbs (whose very repetition would connote iterativity) in fact implies the opposite—closure, a finality. The frequency and persistence of repetition evokes this sense of finality and desperate sadness.

With similar effect, Rhys often resorts to the verbal auxiliary "would." In reporting angry conversations between her mother and Mr. Mason, Antoinette describes their dialogue by reporting "he would say," "she'd speak,"; "would" is here used in the habitual mode. The impression the reader receives is again iterative—this argument occurred over and over again. Antoinette also creates this effect by remembering that "Mr. Mason *always* said." This use of the iterative has a psychological effect upon the reader, in that Antoinette's narration takes on a timeless urgency as if it were a universal or apocalyptic tale whose signification extends beyond the narrator and her experience, or to put it another way, the narrator's life and experience are not merely personal but also symbolic.

As Antoinette draws her narrative to its first conclusion, as she falls into her first sleep, and she seems to narrate from a region in which she is either just entering sleep or waking, a pre-or subconscious state where "only the magic and the dream are true," she sounds her most foreboding note. She has just woken from her nightmare, and asks the Sister who tends to her "such terrible things happen I said, 'why? why'?" If the reader reflects back on Part One, Antoinette's narrative has consisted entirely of the telling of "terrible things" one after the other; her narrative is obsessed with safety, her understandable desire to find refuge, the progressive diminishment of any feeling of safety, and conversely her increasing sense of isolation or, to use Antoinette's more poetic phrase, being "marooned." Rejected (and betrayed) by her mother, by Tia, the local blacks, and eventually by Mr. Mason, as first he abandons her to Rochester, and secondly, dies making her abandonment complete, Antoinette becomes increasingly marooned.

While Antoinette's narrative appears to follow a linear sequence, its deep structure is not linear but associative. Conscious of the need to present her story convincingly (even to herself), she appears to maintain a chronology, the illusion of sequence. Yet, if we look carefully at the sequence of events, we see their connexity is associative rather than temporal or causal, and that the associations are based on Antoinette's obsessions—her fear of the loss of safety, her sense of desertion and isolation—so that each episode she narrates becomes an amplification of these obsessions. She begins her story with an oblique reference to the Emancipation Act, "when trouble comes close ranks," continues with the anecdote of Mr. Luttrell's suicide, then recounts the poisoned horse incident (each episode "marooning" them further), and moves on to Pierre's feebleness, and a description to the wild garden. Eden destroyed. Safety for Antoinette implies evasion, burial, escape, enclosing oneself away from the world by assigning signs of safety to parentheses "(My father, visitors, horses, feeling safe in bed—all belonged to the past)." For a time, she feels safe in her bed, Coulibri, the convent, and Granbois. Gradually, however, each refuge is progressively destroyed: the safety of her bed and Coulibri ruined by fire and by her mother's marriage to Mr. Mason and the invasion of the blacks, the sanctuary of the convent by the imminent arrival of a suitor and another invasive marriage which, like her mother's, culminates in fire and madness. Her final evasion is within her own mind, disassociated from time, from people, even from her own self of which the attic, dark, cold and lightless, is a perfect sign.

Antoinette's narrative in Part One ends as she falls into sleep, and another narrator, Edward Rochester, who remains unnamed although his personal signature is strongly stamped on his discourse. Rhys wanted a "cold factual" narrator to contrast with Antoinette's "emotional" account (*Letters*); she also felt sympathy for Rochester's plight and gave him a chance to justify himself. His narration then, unlike Antoinette's is not a confession or a matter of survival, but a self-justification, an attempt at a rational, analytic explanation of the breakdown of his marriage and of his wife. It is appropriate that the narrative now falls into his hands since, at the point when Antoinette closes her narrative, she is experiencing greater and greater distress and disassociation. Like her mother, she is suffering a division of the self where she undergoes what she calls the real death, the death of the mind, and becomes blank, doll-like, inhuman, in waiting for the second death, the death of the body. Since she is now outside herself, her story, appropriately, is told from the outside by an outsider. Rochester has married her, taken possession of her, and made her *his* wife, and so he now tells *her* story and the story of their marriage which has become *his* story and no longer hers. Instead of narrating her own story, Antoinette becomes a character in his narration. She does, however, resist complete

marital and narratorial possession by Rochester for on two occasions she breaks into Rochester's narrative to present her point of view.

In contrast to Antoinette's narrative, Rochester's narrating self (and his narration takes the shape of a letter to his father that he will never send) is close in time to his experiencing self, and the immediacy of his language reflects the shocks suffered by his experiencing self. He speaks of "this morning" as he begins, slipping into the present because there is so little temporal distance between his two selves: "So this is Massacre," "Everything is too much." Despite Rochester's intention of presenting a reasoned explanation of the events, he is overwhelmed by the magic and sensuality of Granbois and his wife and crushed by his sense of betrayal by his own family and Antoinette's in saddling him with a mad wife. As a consequence, his mind loses its apparent clarity. His discourse, which in the beginning, although reflecting his unease, was at least ordered, becomes by the end of his narrative disjointed, wild, fragmented, impressionistic. "The tree shivers. Shivers and gathers all its strength. And waits." Unlike the Antoinette of Part One, he loses control of his narration and the structure of his narrative presentation disintegrates. This loss of control is manifested through Antoinette's invasion of his narration, first in what Rhys calls the interlude, but more pointedly, into his thoughts, her invasion is delivered in italics, between parentheses."

> (*I lay awake all night long after they were asleep, and as soon as it was light I got up and dressed and saddled Preston. And I came to you. Oh Christophine. On Pheena, Pheena, help me*).

If to narrate is a sign of lucidity, who then has lost his mind?

It is in Rochester's narration that the author's presence as manipulator and organizer is most strongly felt since Rhys permits Antoinette to interrupt Rochester's narrative and tell her story. After Rochester receives Daniel Cosway's incriminating letter condemning Antoinette and her mother to madness, Rochester turns against his wife. At that point, Antoinette wakes from one of her sleeps and temporarily takes on the telling of her own story. Here there is dissonance between the narrating and experiencing self; this narrating Antoinette is speaking from her English attic since, in a digression, she refers to England, focalizing on her experiencing self: "I will be a different person when I live in England," but then quickly reveals her knowledge of England, a knowledge that can only come from living there and thus from the narrating self: "Summer. There are fields of corn like sugar-cane fields, but good colour and not so tall. After summer the trees are bare, then winter and snow." Thus, the narrating self asserts its disturbing and disturbed presence. As she closes her interlude, it is the narrating Antoinette speaking in the present from her attic room, with its one window high up, who observes:

> but now I see everything still, fixed for ever like the colours in a stained-glass window. Only the clouds move.

Rhys also ensures that Antoinette's point of view and voice are heard even in the midst of Rochester's narrative, through extended passages of dialogue between the two that allow Antoinette to explain her past and clarify the sequence of events of her own life. Rochester reports one of their dialogues ("'Now come for a walk,' she said, 'and I will tell you a story'" in which Antoinette describes her dream of the watching rats and her moonlight sleep to explain her present state of mind.

Rochester's narration of their dialogues also becomes a mode for her clarification of sequence:

> "... Is your mother alive?"
>
> "No, she is dead, she died."
>
> "When?"
>
> "Not long ago."
>
> "Then why did you tell me she died when you were a child?"
>
> "Because they told me to say so and because it is true. She did die when I was a child. There are always two deaths, the real one, and the one people know about."

In a disturbed, fragmented state of mind, Rochester simultaneously concludes his own narrative (and Antoinette remains forever silenced and absent) and leaves that place with "its beauty and magic and the secret I would never know." Antoinette's mind is broken (to use Christophine's phrase) and Rochester vows:

> I too can wait—for the day when she is only a memory to be avoided, locked away, and like all memories a legend. Or a lie. . . .

His vow is prophetic, for in the end all Antoinette has is her memory which becomes her life line, her death, and almost the death of Rochester. Antoinette as a remembering consciousness absorbed not in retrospection, but in the *act* of recollection, acts out of that memory to burn Thornfield to the ground, and to die she has become another of the heroines killed into art, noted by Gilbert and Gubar in *The Madwoman in the Attic*. Once she has recollected the past (those moments that she wants and needs to recollect)—retention,

and recollected the future (that which she must do next)—protention, Antoinette transforms memory from a passive to an active mode.

In Part Three, after a brief narrative by Grace Poole, which brings the reader to England and into the darkness, prison, or shelter where Antoinette dwells, Antoinette once again takes up her own story. In contrast to her earlier narration, she now speaks in the present, digresses into the past (analepsis), and into the future through a dream (prolepsis) that foretells the events that follow after the narrative concludes, for a narrator presumably cannot describe her own death.

As she begins this her final narrative, she says: "In this room, I wake early and lie shivering for it is very cold." The present tense indicates that the judicious distance of her first narrative is obliterated. She has lost all sense of measured time and place for she refuses to believe "this is England," and of self for she does not recognize the woman with streaming hair, surrounded by a gilt frame as herself. The structures of narrative have broken down and she is faltering, shivering, an absence. Her memory which gave her a tenuous connection to reality and her narrative its surface structure, also eludes her. An Antoinette who can no longer remember is no longer Antoinette, she has lost her true self, her centre no longer holds. The narrating self has dissolved into a completely experiencing self. She had told Rochester "I am not a forgetting person." But here, in the attic, she has forgotten.

Her last narrative act is the story of her struggle to remember, and the phrases "to remember" and "must remember" recur continually. At first she remarks: "and to wonder why I have been brought here. For what reason? There must be a reason. What is it that I must do?" Then, "when I got back into bed, I could remember more and think again." Slowly, in a disjointed manner, she makes a tremendous effort to remember, to disclose the secret locked in her past, and to complete her story; her mind works again by feverish association—"Looking at the tapestry one day I recognized my mother ..."; "I remember watching myself"; "We lost our way to England. When? Where? I don't remember, but we lost it." Since her state of wakedness only seems to confuse her, she sinks into dream and when she wakes from it, she finally remembers: "Now at last I know why I was brought here and what I have to do." Through dreaming and submission to her subconscious, her memory has been restored. Now, by jumping to her death, she commits one of her few acts, other than narration, and closes her life and her story.

Deprived of light and warmth and love, she has made the supreme effort of will in sleeping, in dreaming, and in waking to narrate her own story, and to bring it to conclusion herself. The secret is thus told and the telling is the secret.

Source: Kathy Mezei, "'And It Kept Its Secret': Narration, Memory, and Madness in Jean Rhys' *Wide Sargasso Sea*," in *Critique: Studies in Modern Fiction*, Vol. 28, No. 4, Summer 1987, pp. 195–209.

Sources

Curtis, Jan, "The Secret of *Wide Sargasso Sea*," in *Critique: Studies in Contemporary Fiction*, Vol. XXXI, No. 3, Spring 1990, pp. 185–97.

"The Literary Life of Jean Rhys," in *Christian Science Monitor*, July 16, 1991.

Marshik, Celia, "Jean Rhys," in *Studies in the Novel*, Vol. 34, No. 1, pp. 116–18, Spring 2002.

Pepper, Tara, "Searching for a Home," in *Newsweek*, September 15, 2003, p. 58.

Porter, Dennis, "Of Heroines and Victims: Jean Rhys and *Jane Eyre*," in *Massachusetts Review*, Vol. XVII, No. 3, Autumn 1976, pp. 540–52.

Further Reading

Angier, Carole, *Jean Rhys: Life and Work*, Pubs Overstock, June 1991.
In this biography and study, Angier links events in Rhys's life to characters and events in her stories and novels.

Bender, Todd K., ed., *Literary Impressionism in Jean Rhys, Ford Madox Ford, Joseph Conrad, and Charlotte Brontë*, Garland Publishing, 1997.
After meeting with Joseph Conrad and then, twenty-five years later, with Jean Rhys, Ford Madox Ford is reported to have said that between these two writers, he saw the progression of modern literature toward impressionism. This text contains a collection of Ford's critical comments on impressionism, in particular the way in which Rhys's *Wide Sargasso Sea* forces readers to rethink Brontë's *Jane Eyre*.

Chesler, Phyllis, *Women and Madness*, Doubleday, 1972.
Chesler provides a definitive study of the mental health of women who live in a patriarchal society. Her work revolutionized psychiatry, providing new definitions of feminist therapy and demonstrating how women have often been controlled by conventional psychiatry.

Savory, Elaine, *Jean Rhys*, Cambridge University Press, 1998.
This is a critical study of Rhys's entire life's work, including her autobiography. Savory insists on looking at all of Rhys's work, keeping the author's Caribbean background in mind. This is an excellent study that keeps previous critical analyses on race, gender, class, and nationality in mind.

Williams, Eric, *From Columbus to Castro: The History of the Caribbean, 1492 to 1969*, Vintage Books, 1984.
Former prime minister of Trinidad and Tobago, Eric Williams outlines the common history of slavery in the Caribbean. In this book, Williams looks at the history of sugar and the free labor that provided wealth to a few and misery to over 30 million slaves.

Glossary of Literary Terms

A

Abstract: As an adjective applied to writing or literary works, abstract refers to words or phrases that name things not knowable through the five senses.

Aestheticism: A literary and artistic movement of the nineteenth century. Followers of the movement believed that art should not be mixed with social, political, or moral teaching. The statement "art for art's sake" is a good summary of aestheticism. The movement had its roots in France, but it gained widespread importance in England in the last half of the nineteenth century, where it helped change the Victorian practice of including moral lessons in literature.

Allegory: A narrative technique in which characters representing things or abstract ideas are used to convey a message or teach a lesson. Allegory is typically used to teach moral, ethical, or religious lessons but is sometimes used for satiric or political purposes.

Allusion: A reference to a familiar literary or historical person or event, used to make an idea more easily understood.

Analogy: A comparison of two things made to explain something unfamiliar through its similarities to something familiar, or to prove one point based on the acceptedness of another. Similes and metaphors are types of analogies.

Antagonist: The major character in a narrative or drama who works against the hero or protagonist.

Anthropomorphism: The presentation of animals or objects in human shape or with human characteristics. The term is derived from the Greek word for "human form."

Antihero: A central character in a work of literature who lacks traditional heroic qualities such as courage, physical prowess, and fortitude. Antiheroes typically distrust conventional values and are unable to commit themselves to any ideals. They generally feel helpless in a world over which they have no control. Antiheroes usually accept, and often celebrate, their positions as social outcasts.

Apprenticeship Novel: See *Bildungsroman*

Archetype: The word archetype is commonly used to describe an original pattern or model from which all other things of the same kind are made. This term was introduced to literary criticism from the psychology of Carl Jung. It expresses Jung's theory that behind every person's "unconscious," or repressed memories of the past, lies the "collective unconscious" of the human race: memories of the countless typical experiences of our ancestors. These memories are said to prompt illogical associations that trigger powerful emotions in the reader. Often, the emotional process is primitive, even primordial. Archetypes are the literary images that grow out of the "collective unconscious." They appear in literature as incidents and plots that repeat basic patterns of life. They may also appear as stereotyped characters.

Avant-garde: French term meaning "vanguard." It is used in literary criticism to describe new writing that rejects traditional approaches to literature in favor of innovations in style or content.

B

Beat Movement: A period featuring a group of American poets and novelists of the 1950s and 1960s—including Jack Kerouac, Allen Ginsberg, Gregory Corso, William S. Burroughs, and Lawrence Ferlinghetti—who rejected established social and literary values. Using such techniques as stream of consciousness writing and jazz-influenced free verse and focusing on unusual or abnormal states of mind—generated by religious ecstasy or the use of drugs—the Beat writers aimed to create works that were unconventional in both form and subject matter.

Bildungsroman: A German word meaning "novel of development." The *bildungsroman* is a study of the maturation of a youthful character, typically brought about through a series of social or sexual encounters that lead to self-awareness. *Bildungsroman* is used interchangeably with *erziehungsroman,* a novel of initiation and education. When a *bildungsroman* is concerned with the development of an artist (as in James Joyce's *A Portrait of the Artist as a Young Man*), it is often termed a *kunstlerroman.* Also known as Apprenticeship Novel, Coming of Age Novel, *Erziehungsroman,* or *Kunstlerroman.*

Black Aesthetic Movement: A period of artistic and literary development among African Americans in the 1960s and early 1970s. This was the first major African-American artistic movement since the Harlem Renaissance and was closely paralleled by the civil rights and black power movements. The black aesthetic writers attempted to produce works of art that would be meaningful to the black masses. Key figures in black aesthetics included one of its founders, poet and playwright Amiri Baraka, formerly known as LeRoi Jones; poet and essayist Haki R. Madhubuti, formerly Don L. Lee; poet and playwright Sonia Sanchez; and dramatist Ed Bullins. Also known as Black Arts Movement.

Black Humor: Writing that places grotesque elements side by side with humorous ones in an attempt to shock the reader, forcing him or her to laugh at the horrifying reality of a disordered world. Also known as Black Comedy.

Burlesque: Any literary work that uses exaggeration to make its subject appear ridiculous, either by treating a trivial subject with profound seriousness or by treating a dignified subject frivolously. The word "burlesque" may also be used as an adjective, as in "burlesque show," to mean "striptease act."

C

Character: Broadly speaking, a person in a literary work. The actions of characters are what constitute the plot of a story, novel, or poem. There are numerous types of characters, ranging from simple, stereotypical figures to intricate, multifaceted ones. In the techniques of anthropomorphism and personification, animals—and even places or things—can assume aspects of character. "Characterization" is the process by which an author creates vivid, believable characters in a work of art. This may be done in a variety of ways, including (1) direct description of the character by the narrator; (2) the direct presentation of the speech, thoughts, or actions of the character; and (3) the responses of other characters to the character. The term "character" also refers to a form originated by the ancient Greek writer Theophrastus that later became popular in the seventeenth and eighteenth centuries. It is a short essay or sketch of a person who prominently displays a specific attribute or quality, such as miserliness or ambition.

Climax: The turning point in a narrative, the moment when the conflict is at its most intense. Typically, the structure of stories, novels, and plays is one of rising action, in which tension builds to the climax, followed by falling action, in which tension lessens as the story moves to its conclusion.

Colloquialism: A word, phrase, or form of pronunciation that is acceptable in casual conversation but not in formal, written communication. It is considered more acceptable than slang.

Coming of Age Novel: See *Bildungsroman*

Concrete: Concrete is the opposite of abstract, and refers to a thing that actually exists or a description that allows the reader to experience an object or concept with the senses.

Connotation: The impression that a word gives beyond its defined meaning. Connotations may be universally understood or may be significant only to a certain group.

Convention: Any widely accepted literary device, style, or form.

D

Denotation: The definition of a word, apart from the impressions or feelings it creates (connotations) in the reader.

Denouement: A French word meaning "the unknotting." In literary criticism, it denotes the resolution of conflict in fiction or drama. The *denouement* follows the climax and provides an outcome to the primary plot situation as well as an explanation of secondary plot complications. The *denouement* often involves a character's recognition of his or her state of mind or moral condition. Also known as Falling Action.

Description: Descriptive writing is intended to allow a reader to picture the scene or setting in which the action of a story takes place. The form this description takes often evokes an intended emotional response—a dark, spooky graveyard will evoke fear, and a peaceful, sunny meadow will evoke calmness.

Dialogue: In its widest sense, dialogue is simply conversation between people in a literary work; in its most restricted sense, it refers specifically to the speech of characters in a drama. As a specific literary genre, a "dialogue" is a composition in which characters debate an issue or idea.

Diction: The selection and arrangement of words in a literary work. Either or both may vary depending on the desired effect. There are four general types of diction: "formal," used in scholarly or lofty writing; "informal," used in relaxed but educated conversation; "colloquial," used in everyday speech; and "slang," containing newly coined words and other terms not accepted in formal usage.

Didactic: A term used to describe works of literature that aim to teach some moral, religious, political, or practical lesson. Although didactic elements are often found in artistically pleasing works, the term "didactic" usually refers to literature in which the message is more important than the form. The term may also be used to criticize a work that the critic finds "overly didactic," that is, heavy-handed in its delivery of a lesson.

Doppelganger: A literary technique by which a character is duplicated (usually in the form of an alter ego, though sometimes as a ghostly counterpart) or divided into two distinct, usually opposite personalities. The use of this character device is widespread in nineteenth- and twentieth-century literature, and indicates a growing awareness among authors that the "self" is really a composite of many "selves." Also known as The Double.

Double Entendre: A corruption of a French phrase meaning "double meaning." The term is used to indicate a word or phrase that is deliberately ambiguous, especially when one of the meanings is risqué or improper.

Dramatic Irony: Occurs when the audience of a play or the reader of a work of literature knows something that a character in the work itself does not know. The irony is in the contrast between the intended meaning of the statements or actions of a character and the additional information understood by the audience.

Dystopia: An imaginary place in a work of fiction where the characters lead dehumanized, fearful lives.

E

Edwardian: Describes cultural conventions identified with the period of the reign of Edward VII of England (1901-1910). Writers of the Edwardian Age typically displayed a strong reaction against the propriety and conservatism of the Victorian Age. Their work often exhibits distrust of authority in religion, politics, and art and expresses strong doubts about the soundness of conventional values.

Empathy: A sense of shared experience, including emotional and physical feelings, with someone or something other than oneself. Empathy is often used to describe the response of a reader to a literary character.

Enlightenment, The: An eighteenth-century philosophical movement. It began in France but had a wide impact throughout Europe and America. Thinkers of the Enlightenment valued reason and believed that both the individual and society could achieve a state of perfection. Corresponding to this essentially humanist vision was a resistance to religious authority.

Epigram: A saying that makes the speaker's point quickly and concisely. Often used to preface a novel.

Epilogue: A concluding statement or section of a literary work. In dramas, particularly those of the seventeenth and eighteenth centuries, the epilogue is a closing speech, often in verse, delivered by an actor at the end of a play and spoken directly to the audience.

Epiphany: A sudden revelation of truth inspired by a seemingly trivial incident.

Episode: An incident that forms part of a story and is significantly related to it. Episodes may be either self-contained narratives or events that depend on a larger context for their sense and importance.

Epistolary Novel: A novel in the form of letters. The form was particularly popular in the eighteenth century.

Epithet: A word or phrase, often disparaging or abusive, that expresses a character trait of someone or something.

Existentialism: A predominantly twentieth-century philosophy concerned with the nature and perception of human existence. There are two major strains of existentialist thought: atheistic and Christian. Followers of atheistic existentialism believe that the individual is alone in a godless universe and that the basic human condition is one of suffering and loneliness. Nevertheless, because there are no fixed values, individuals can create their own characters—indeed, they can shape themselves—through the exercise of free will. The atheistic strain culminates in and is popularly associated with the works of Jean-Paul Sartre. The Christian existentialists, on the other hand, believe that only in God may people find freedom from life's anguish. The two strains hold certain beliefs in common: that existence cannot be fully understood or described through empirical effort; that anguish is a universal element of life; that individuals must bear responsibility for their actions; and that there is no common standard of behavior or perception for religious and ethical matters.

Expatriates: See *Expatriatism*

Expatriatism: The practice of leaving one's country to live for an extended period in another country.

Exposition: Writing intended to explain the nature of an idea, thing, or theme. Expository writing is often combined with description, narration, or argument. In dramatic writing, the exposition is the introductory material which presents the characters, setting, and tone of the play.

Expressionism: An indistinct literary term, originally used to describe an early twentieth-century school of German painting. The term applies to almost any mode of unconventional, highly subjective writing that distorts reality in some way.

F

Fable: A prose or verse narrative intended to convey a moral. Animals or inanimate objects with human characteristics often serve as characters in fables.

Falling Action: See *Denouement*

Fantasy: A literary form related to mythology and folklore. Fantasy literature is typically set in non-existent realms and features supernatural beings.

Farce: A type of comedy characterized by broad humor, outlandish incidents, and often vulgar subject matter.

Femme fatale: A French phrase with the literal translation "fatal woman." A *femme fatale* is a sensuous, alluring woman who often leads men into danger or trouble.

Fiction: Any story that is the product of imagination rather than a documentation of fact. Characters and events in such narratives may be based in real life but their ultimate form and configuration is a creation of the author.

Figurative Language: A technique in writing in which the author temporarily interrupts the order, construction, or meaning of the writing for a particular effect. This interruption takes the form of one or more figures of speech such as hyperbole, irony, or simile. Figurative language is the opposite of literal language, in which every word is truthful, accurate, and free of exaggeration or embellishment.

Figures of Speech: Writing that differs from customary conventions for construction, meaning, order, or significance for the purpose of a special meaning or effect. There are two major types of figures of speech: rhetorical figures, which do not make changes in the meaning of the words, and tropes, which do.

Fin de siecle: A French term meaning "end of the century." The term is used to denote the last decade of the nineteenth century, a transition period when writers and other artists abandoned old conventions and looked for new techniques and objectives.

First Person: See *Point of View*

Flashback: A device used in literature to present action that occurred before the beginning of the story. Flashbacks are often introduced as the dreams or recollections of one or more characters.

Foil: A character in a work of literature whose physical or psychological qualities contrast strongly with, and therefore highlight, the corresponding qualities of another character.

Folklore: Traditions and myths preserved in a culture or group of people. Typically, these are passed on by word of mouth in various forms—such as legends, songs, and proverbs—or preserved in customs and ceremonies. This term was first used by W. J. Thoms in 1846.

Folktale: A story originating in oral tradition. Folktales fall into a variety of categories, including legends, ghost stories, fairy tales, fables, and anecdotes based on historical figures and events.

Foreshadowing: A device used in literature to create expectation or to set up an explanation of later developments.

Form: The pattern or construction of a work which identifies its genre and distinguishes it from other genres.

G

Genre: A category of literary work. In critical theory, genre may refer to both the content of a given work—tragedy, comedy, pastoral—and to its form, such as poetry, novel, or drama.

Gilded Age: A period in American history during the 1870s characterized by political corruption and materialism. A number of important novels of social and political criticism were written during this time.

Gothicism: In literary criticism, works characterized by a taste for the medieval or morbidly attractive. A gothic novel prominently features elements of horror, the supernatural, gloom, and violence: clanking chains, terror, charnel houses, ghosts, medieval castles, and mysteriously slamming doors. The term "gothic novel" is also applied to novels that lack elements of the traditional Gothic setting but that create a similar atmosphere of terror or dread.

Grotesque: In literary criticism, the subject matter of a work or a style of expression characterized by exaggeration, deformity, freakishness, and disorder. The grotesque often includes an element of comic absurdity.

H

Harlem Renaissance: The Harlem Renaissance of the 1920s is generally considered the first significant movement of black writers and artists in the United States. During this period, new and established black writers published more fiction and poetry than ever before, the first influential black literary journals were established, and black authors and artists received their first widespread recognition and serious critical appraisal. Among the major writers associated with this period are Claude McKay, Jean Toomer, Countee Cullen, Langston Hughes, Arna Bontemps, Nella Larsen, and Zora Neale Hurston. Also known as Negro Renaissance and New Negro Movement.

Hero/Heroine: The principal sympathetic character (male or female) in a literary work. Heroes and heroines typically exhibit admirable traits: idealism, courage, and integrity, for example.

Holocaust Literature: Literature influenced by or written about the Holocaust of World War II. Such literature includes true stories of survival in concentration camps, escape, and life after the war, as well as fictional works and poetry.

Humanism: A philosophy that places faith in the dignity of humankind and rejects the medieval perception of the individual as a weak, fallen creature. "Humanists" typically believe in the perfectibility of human nature and view reason and education as the means to that end.

Hyperbole: In literary criticism, deliberate exaggeration used to achieve an effect.

I

Idiom: A word construction or verbal expression closely associated with a given language.

Image: A concrete representation of an object or sensory experience. Typically, such a representation helps evoke the feelings associated with the object or experience itself. Images are either "literal" or "figurative." Literal images are especially concrete and involve little or no extension of the obvious meaning of the words used to express them. Figurative images do not follow the literal meaning of the words exactly. Images in literature are usually visual, but the term "image" can also refer to the representation of any sensory experience.

Imagery: The array of images in a literary work. Also, figurative language.

In medias res: A Latin term meaning "in the middle of things." It refers to the technique of beginning a story at its midpoint and then using various flashback devices to reveal previous action.

Interior Monologue: A narrative technique in which characters' thoughts are revealed in a way that appears to be uncontrolled by the author. The interior monologue typically aims to reveal the inner self of a character. It portrays emotional experiences as they occur at both a conscious and unconscious level. Images are often used to represent sensations or emotions.

Irony: In literary criticism, the effect of language in which the intended meaning is the opposite of what is stated.

J

Jargon: Language that is used or understood only by a select group of people. Jargon may refer to terminology used in a certain profession, such as computer jargon, or it may refer to any nonsensical language that is not understood by most people.

L

Leitmotiv: See *Motif*

Literal Language: An author uses literal language when he or she writes without exaggerating or embellishing the subject matter and without any tools of figurative language.

Lost Generation: A term first used by Gertrude Stein to describe the post-World War I generation of American writers: men and women haunted by a sense of betrayal and emptiness brought about by the destructiveness of the war.

M

Mannerism: Exaggerated, artificial adherence to a literary manner or style. Also, a popular style of the visual arts of late sixteenth-century Europe that was marked by elongation of the human form and by intentional spatial distortion. Literary works that are self-consciously high-toned and artistic are often said to be "mannered."

Metaphor: A figure of speech that expresses an idea through the image of another object. Metaphors suggest the essence of the first object by identifying it with certain qualities of the second object.

Modernism: Modern literary practices. Also, the principles of a literary school that lasted from roughly the beginning of the twentieth century until the end of World War II. Modernism is defined by its rejection of the literary conventions of the nineteenth century and by its opposition to conventional morality, taste, traditions, and economic values.

Mood: The prevailing emotions of a work or of the author in his or her creation of the work. The mood of a work is not always what might be expected based on its subject matter.

Motif: A theme, character type, image, metaphor, or other verbal element that recurs throughout a single work of literature or occurs in a number of different works over a period of time. Also known as *Motiv* or *Leitmotiv*.

Myth: An anonymous tale emerging from the traditional beliefs of a culture or social unit. Myths use supernatural explanations for natural phenomena. They may also explain cosmic issues like creation and death. Collections of myths, known as mythologies, are common to all cultures and nations, but the best-known myths belong to the Norse, Roman, and Greek mythologies.

N

Narration: The telling of a series of events, real or invented. A narration may be either a simple narrative, in which the events are recounted chronologically, or a narrative with a plot, in which the account is given in a style reflecting the author's artistic concept of the story. Narration is sometimes used as a synonym for "storyline."

Narrative: A verse or prose accounting of an event or sequence of events, real or invented. The term is also used as an adjective in the sense "method of narration." For example, in literary criticism, the expression "narrative technique" usually refers to the way the author structures and presents his or her story.

Narrator: The teller of a story. The narrator may be the author or a character in the story through whom the author speaks.

Naturalism: A literary movement of the late nineteenth and early twentieth centuries. The movement's major theorist, French novelist Emile Zola, envisioned a type of fiction that would examine human life with the objectivity of scientific inquiry. The Naturalists typically viewed human beings as either the products of "biological determinism," ruled by hereditary instincts and engaged in an endless struggle for survival, or as the products of "socioeconomic determinism," ruled by social and economic forces beyond their control. In their works, the Naturalists generally ignored the highest levels of society and focused on degradation: poverty, alcoholism, prostitution, insanity, and disease.

Noble Savage: The idea that primitive man is noble and good but becomes evil and corrupted as he becomes civilized. The concept of the noble savage originated in the Renaissance period but is more closely identified with such later writers as

Jean-Jacques Rousseau and Aphra Behn. See also Primitivism.

Novel of Ideas: A novel in which the examination of intellectual issues and concepts takes precedence over characterization or a traditional storyline.

Novel of Manners: A novel that examines the customs and mores of a cultural group.

Novel: A long fictional narrative written in prose, which developed from the novella and other early forms of narrative. A novel is usually organized under a plot or theme with a focus on character development and action.

Novella: An Italian term meaning "story." This term has been especially used to describe fourteenth-century Italian tales, but it also refers to modern short novels.

O

Objective Correlative: An outward set of objects, a situation, or a chain of events corresponding to an inward experience and evoking this experience in the reader. The term frequently appears in modern criticism in discussions of authors' intended effects on the emotional responses of readers.

Objectivity: A quality in writing characterized by the absence of the author's opinion or feeling about the subject matter. Objectivity is an important factor in criticism.

Oedipus Complex: A son's amorous obsession with his mother. The phrase is derived from the story of the ancient Theban hero Oedipus, who unknowingly killed his father and married his mother.

Omniscience: See *Point of View*

Onomatopoeia: The use of words whose sounds express or suggest their meaning. In its simplest sense, onomatopoeia may be represented by words that mimic the sounds they denote such as "hiss" or "meow." At a more subtle level, the pattern and rhythm of sounds and rhymes of a line or poem may be onomatopoeic.

Oxymoron: A phrase combining two contradictory terms. Oxymorons may be intentional or unintentional.

P

Parable: A story intended to teach a moral lesson or answer an ethical question.

Paradox: A statement that appears illogical or contradictory at first, but may actually point to an underlying truth.

Parallelism: A method of comparison of two ideas in which each is developed in the same grammatical structure.

Parody: In literary criticism, this term refers to an imitation of a serious literary work or the signature style of a particular author in a ridiculous manner. A typical parody adopts the style of the original and applies it to an inappropriate subject for humorous effect. Parody is a form of satire and could be considered the literary equivalent of a caricature or cartoon.

Pastoral: A term derived from the Latin word "pastor," meaning shepherd. A pastoral is a literary composition on a rural theme. The conventions of the pastoral were originated by the third-century Greek poet Theocritus, who wrote about the experiences, love affairs, and pastimes of Sicilian shepherds. In a pastoral, characters and language of a courtly nature are often placed in a simple setting. The term pastoral is also used to classify dramas, elegies, and lyrics that exhibit the use of country settings and shepherd characters.

Pen Name: See *Pseudonym*

Persona: A Latin term meaning "mask." *Personae* are the characters in a fictional work of literature. The *persona* generally functions as a mask through which the author tells a story in a voice other than his or her own. A *persona* is usually either a character in a story who acts as a narrator or an "implied author," a voice created by the author to act as the narrator for himself or herself.

Personification: A figure of speech that gives human qualities to abstract ideas, animals, and inanimate objects. Also known as *Prosopopoeia*.

Picaresque Novel: Episodic fiction depicting the adventures of a roguish central character ("picaro" is Spanish for "rogue"). The picaresque hero is commonly a low-born but clever individual who wanders into and out of various affairs of love, danger, and farcical intrigue. These involvements may take place at all social levels and typically present a humorous and wide-ranging satire of a given society.

Plagiarism: Claiming another person's written material as one's own. Plagiarism can take the form of direct, word-for-word copying or the theft of the substance or idea of the work.

Plot: In literary criticism, this term refers to the pattern of events in a narrative or drama. In its simplest sense, the plot guides the author in composing the work and helps the reader follow the work. Typically, plots exhibit causality and unity and have a beginning, a middle, and an end. Sometimes, however, a plot may consist of a series of disconnected events, in which case it is known as an "episodic plot."

Poetic Justice: An outcome in a literary work, not necessarily a poem, in which the good are rewarded and the evil are punished, especially in ways that particularly fit their virtues or crimes.

Poetic License: Distortions of fact and literary convention made by a writer—not always a poet—for the sake of the effect gained. Poetic license is closely related to the concept of "artistic freedom."

Poetics: This term has two closely related meanings. It denotes (1) an aesthetic theory in literary criticism about the essence of poetry or (2) rules prescribing the proper methods, content, style, or diction of poetry. The term poetics may also refer to theories about literature in general, not just poetry.

Point of View: The narrative perspective from which a literary work is presented to the reader. There are four traditional points of view. The "third person omniscient" gives the reader a "godlike" perspective, unrestricted by time or place, from which to see actions and look into the minds of characters. This allows the author to comment openly on characters and events in the work. The "third person" point of view presents the events of the story from outside of any single character's perception, much like the omniscient point of view, but the reader must understand the action as it takes place and without any special insight into characters' minds or motivations. The "first person" or "personal" point of view relates events as they are perceived by a single character. The main character "tells" the story and may offer opinions about the action and characters which differ from those of the author. Much less common than omniscient, third person, and first person is the "second person" point of view, wherein the author tells the story as if it is happening to the reader.

Polemic: A work in which the author takes a stand on a controversial subject, such as abortion or religion. Such works are often extremely argumentative or provocative.

Pornography: Writing intended to provoke feelings of lust in the reader. Such works are often condemned by critics and teachers, but those which can be shown to have literary value are viewed less harshly.

Post-Aesthetic Movement: An artistic response made by African Americans to the black aesthetic movement of the 1960s and early '70s. Writers since that time have adopted a somewhat different tone in their work, with less emphasis placed on the disparity between black and white in the United States. In the words of post-aesthetic authors such as Toni Morrison, John Edgar Wideman, and Kristin Hunter, African Americans are portrayed as looking inward for answers to their own questions, rather than always looking to the outside world.

Postmodernism: Writing from the 1960s forward characterized by experimentation and continuing to apply some of the fundamentals of modernism, which included existentialism and alienation. Postmodernists have gone a step further in the rejection of tradition begun with the modernists by also rejecting traditional forms, preferring the anti-novel over the novel and the antihero over the hero.

Primitivism: The belief that primitive peoples were nobler and less flawed than civilized peoples because they had not been subjected to the tainting influence of society. See also Noble Savage.

Prologue: An introductory section of a literary work. It often contains information establishing the situation of the characters or presents information about the setting, time period, or action. In drama, the prologue is spoken by a chorus or by one of the principal characters.

Prose: A literary medium that attempts to mirror the language of everyday speech. It is distinguished from poetry by its use of unmetered, unrhymed language consisting of logically related sentences. Prose is usually grouped into paragraphs that form a cohesive whole such as an essay or a novel.

Prosopopoeia: See *Personification*

Protagonist: The central character of a story who serves as a focus for its themes and incidents and as the principal rationale for its development. The protagonist is sometimes referred to in discussions of modern literature as the hero or antihero.

Protest Fiction: Protest fiction has as its primary purpose the protesting of some social injustice, such as racism or discrimination.

Proverb: A brief, sage saying that expresses a truth about life in a striking manner.

Pseudonym: A name assumed by a writer, most often intended to prevent his or her identification as the author of a work. Two or more authors may work together under one pseudonym, or an author may use a different name for each genre he or she publishes in. Some publishing companies maintain "house pseudonyms," under which any number of authors may write installations in a series. Some authors also choose a pseudonym over their real names the way an actor may use a stage name.

Pun: A play on words that have similar sounds but different meanings.

R

Realism: A nineteenth-century European literary movement that sought to portray familiar characters, situations, and settings in a realistic manner. This was done primarily by using an objective narrative point of view and through the buildup of accurate detail. The standard for success of any realistic work depends on how faithfully it transfers common experience into fictional forms. The realistic method may be altered or extended, as in stream of consciousness writing, to record highly subjective experience.

Repartee: Conversation featuring snappy retorts and witticisms.

Resolution: The portion of a story following the climax, in which the conflict is resolved. See also *Denouement*.

Rhetoric: In literary criticism, this term denotes the art of ethical persuasion. In its strictest sense, rhetoric adheres to various principles developed since classical times for arranging facts and ideas in a clear, persuasive, appealing manner. The term is also used to refer to effective prose in general and theories of or methods for composing effective prose.

Rhetorical Question: A question intended to provoke thought, but not an expressed answer, in the reader. It is most commonly used in oratory and other persuasive genres.

Rising Action: The part of a drama where the plot becomes increasingly complicated. Rising action leads up to the climax, or turning point, of a drama.

Roman a clef: A French phrase meaning "novel with a key." It refers to a narrative in which real persons are portrayed under fictitious names.

Romance: A broad term, usually denoting a narrative with exotic, exaggerated, often idealized characters, scenes, and themes.

Romanticism: This term has two widely accepted meanings. In historical criticism, it refers to a European intellectual and artistic movement of the late eighteenth and early nineteenth centuries that sought greater freedom of personal expression than that allowed by the strict rules of literary form and logic of the eighteenth-century neoclassicists. The Romantics preferred emotional and imaginative expression to rational analysis. They considered the individual to be at the center of all experience and so placed him or her at the center of their art. The Romantics believed that the creative imagination reveals nobler truths—unique feelings and attitudes—than those that could be discovered by logic or by scientific examination. Both the natural world and the state of childhood were important sources for revelations of "eternal truths." "Romanticism" is also used as a general term to refer to a type of sensibility found in all periods of literary history and usually considered to be in opposition to the principles of classicism. In this sense, Romanticism signifies any work or philosophy in which the exotic or dreamlike figure strongly, or that is devoted to individualistic expression, self-analysis, or a pursuit of a higher realm of knowledge than can be discovered by human reason.

Romantics: See *Romanticism*

S

Satire: A work that uses ridicule, humor, and wit to criticize and provoke change in human nature and institutions. There are two major types of satire: "formal" or "direct" satire speaks directly to the reader or to a character in the work; "indirect" satire relies upon the ridiculous behavior of its characters to make its point. Formal satire is further divided into two manners: the "Horatian," which ridicules gently, and the "Juvenalian," which derides its subjects harshly and bitterly.

Science Fiction: A type of narrative about or based upon real or imagined scientific theories and technology. Science fiction is often peopled with alien creatures and set on other planets or in different dimensions.

Second Person: See *Point of View*

Setting: The time, place, and culture in which the action of a narrative takes place. The elements of setting may include geographic location, characters' physical and mental environments, prevailing cultural attitudes, or the historical time in which the action takes place.

Simile: A comparison, usually using "like" or "as", of two essentially dissimilar things, as in "coffee as cold as ice" or "He sounded like a broken record."

Slang: A type of informal verbal communication that is generally unacceptable for formal writing. Slang words and phrases are often colorful exaggerations used to emphasize the speaker's point; they may also be shortened versions of an often-used word or phrase.

Slave Narrative: Autobiographical accounts of American slave life as told by escaped slaves. These works first appeared during the abolition movement of the 1830s through the 1850s.

Socialist Realism: The Socialist Realism school of literary theory was proposed by Maxim Gorky and established as a dogma by the first Soviet Congress of Writers. It demanded adherence to a communist worldview in works of literature. Its doctrines required an objective viewpoint comprehensible to the working classes and themes of social struggle featuring strong proletarian heroes. Also known as Social Realism.

Stereotype: A stereotype was originally the name for a duplication made during the printing process; this led to its modern definition as a person or thing that is (or is assumed to be) the same as all others of its type.

Stream of Consciousness: A narrative technique for rendering the inward experience of a character. This technique is designed to give the impression of an ever-changing series of thoughts, emotions, images, and memories in the spontaneous and seemingly illogical order that they occur in life.

Structure: The form taken by a piece of literature. The structure may be made obvious for ease of understanding, as in nonfiction works, or may be obscured for artistic purposes, as in some poetry or seemingly "unstructured" prose.

Sturm und Drang: A German term meaning "storm and stress." It refers to a German literary movement of the 1770s and 1780s that reacted against the order and rationalism of the enlightenment, focusing instead on the intense experience of extraordinary individuals.

Style: A writer's distinctive manner of arranging words to suit his or her ideas and purpose in writing. The unique imprint of the author's personality upon his or her writing, style is the product of an author's way of arranging ideas and his or her use of diction, different sentence structures, rhythm, figures of speech, rhetorical principles, and other elements of composition.

Subjectivity: Writing that expresses the author's personal feelings about his subject, and which may or may not include factual information about the subject.

Subplot: A secondary story in a narrative. A subplot may serve as a motivating or complicating force for the main plot of the work, or it may provide emphasis for, or relief from, the main plot.

Surrealism: A term introduced to criticism by Guillaume Apollinaire and later adopted by Andre Breton. It refers to a French literary and artistic movement founded in the 1920s. The Surrealists sought to express unconscious thoughts and feelings in their works. The best-known technique used for achieving this aim was automatic writing—transcriptions of spontaneous outpourings from the unconscious. The Surrealists proposed to unify the contrary levels of conscious and unconscious, dream and reality, objectivity and subjectivity into a new level of "super-realism."

Suspense: A literary device in which the author maintains the audience's attention through the buildup of events, the outcome of which will soon be revealed.

Symbol: Something that suggests or stands for something else without losing its original identity. In literature, symbols combine their literal meaning with the suggestion of an abstract concept. Literary symbols are of two types: those that carry complex associations of meaning no matter what their contexts, and those that derive their suggestive meaning from their functions in specific literary works.

Symbolism: This term has two widely accepted meanings. In historical criticism, it denotes an early modernist literary movement initiated in France during the nineteenth century that reacted against the prevailing standards of realism. Writers in this movement aimed to evoke, indirectly and symbolically, an order of being beyond the material world of the five senses. Poetic expression of personal emotion figured strongly in the movement, typically by means of a private set of symbols uniquely identifiable with the individual poet. The principal aim of the Symbolists was to express in words the highly complex feelings that grew out of everyday contact with the world. In a broader sense, the term "symbolism" refers to the use of one object to represent another.

T

Tall Tale: A humorous tale told in a straightforward, credible tone but relating absolutely impossible events or feats of the characters. Such tales were commonly told of frontier adventures during the settlement of the west in the United States.

Theme: The main point of a work of literature. The term is used interchangeably with thesis.

Thesis: A thesis is both an essay and the point argued in the essay. Thesis novels and thesis plays share the quality of containing a thesis which is supported through the action of the story.

Third Person: See *Point of View*

Tone: The author's attitude toward his or her audience may be deduced from the tone of the work. A formal tone may create distance or convey politeness, while an informal tone may encourage a friendly, intimate, or intrusive feeling in the reader. The author's attitude toward his or her subject matter may also be deduced from the tone of the words he or she uses in discussing it.

Transcendentalism: An American philosophical and religious movement, based in New England from around 1835 until the Civil War. Transcendentalism was a form of American romanticism that had its roots abroad in the works of Thomas Carlyle, Samuel Coleridge, and Johann Wolfgang von Goethe. The Transcendentalists stressed the importance of intuition and subjective experience in communication with God. They rejected religious dogma and texts in favor of mysticism and scientific naturalism. They pursued truths that lie beyond the "colorless" realms perceived by reason and the senses and were active social reformers in public education, women's rights, and the abolition of slavery.

U

Urban Realism: A branch of realist writing that attempts to accurately reflect the often harsh facts of modern urban existence.

Utopia: A fictional perfect place, such as "paradise" or "heaven."

V

Verisimilitude: Literally, the appearance of truth. In literary criticism, the term refers to aspects of a work of literature that seem true to the reader.

Victorian: Refers broadly to the reign of Queen Victoria of England (1837-1901) and to anything with qualities typical of that era. For example, the qualities of smug narrowmindedness, bourgeois materialism, faith in social progress, and priggish morality are often considered Victorian. This stereotype is contradicted by such dramatic intellectual developments as the theories of Charles Darwin, Karl Marx, and Sigmund Freud (which stirred strong debates in England) and the critical attitudes of serious Victorian writers like Charles Dickens and George Eliot. In literature, the Victorian Period was the great age of the English novel, and the latter part of the era saw the rise of movements such as decadence and symbolism. Also known as Victorian Age and Victorian Period.

W

Weltanschauung: A German term referring to a person's worldview or philosophy.

Weltschmerz: A German term meaning "world pain." It describes a sense of anguish about the nature of existence, usually associated with a melancholy, pessimistic attitude.

Z

Zeitgeist: A German term meaning "spirit of the time." It refers to the moral and intellectual trends of a given era.

Cumulative Author/Title Index

Numerical

1984 (Orwell): V7

A

Absalom, Absalom! (Faulkner): V13
The Accidental Tourist (Tyler): V7
Achebe, Chinua
   Things Fall Apart: V2
Adams, Douglas
   The Hitchhiker's Guide to the Galaxy: V7
Adams, Richard
   Watership Down: V11
The Adventures of Huckleberry Finn (Twain): V1
The Adventures of Tom Sawyer (Twain): V6
The Age of Innocence (Wharton): V11
Alcott, Louisa May
   Little Women: V12
   Sense and Sensibility: V18
Alexie, Sherman
   The Lone Ranger and Tonto Fistfight in Heaven: V17
Alias Grace (Atwood): V19
Alice's Adventures in Wonderland (Carroll): V7
All the King's Men (Warren): V13
Allende, Isabel
   Daughter of Fortune: V18
   The House of the Spirits: V6
Allison, Dorothy
   Bastard Out of Carolina: V11

All Quiet on the Western Front (Remarque): V4
Alvarez, Julia
   How the García Girls Lost Their Accents: V5
   In the Time of the Butterflies: V9
Always Coming Home (Le Guin): V9
The Ambassadors (James): V12
An American Tragedy (Dreiser): V17
Anaya, Rudolfo
   Bless Me, Ultima: V12
Anderson, Sherwood
   Winesburg, Ohio: V4
Angelou, Maya
   I Know Why the Caged Bird Sings: V2
Animal Dreams (Kingsolver): V12
Animal Farm (Orwell): V3
Annie John (Kincaid): V3
Appointment in Samarra (O'Hara): V11
As I Lay Dying (Faulkner): V8
Atlas Shrugged (Rand): V10
Atwood, Margaret
   Alias Grace: V19
   Cat's Eye: V14
   The Handmaid's Tale: V4
   Surfacing: V13
Auel, Jean
   The Clan of the Cave Bear: V11
Austen, Jane
   Persuasion: V14
   Pride and Prejudice: V1
The Autobiography of Miss Jane Pittman (Gaines): V5
The Awakening (Chopin): V3

B

Babbitt (Lewis): V19
Baldwin, James
   Go Tell It on the Mountain: V4
Ballard, J. G.
   Empire of the Sun: V8
Banks, Russell
   The Sweet Hereafter: V13
Bastard Out of Carolina (Allison): V11
Baum, L. Frank
   The Wonderful Wizard of Oz: V13
The Bean Trees (Kingsolver): V5
The Bell Jar (Plath): V1
Bellamy, Edward
   Looking Backward: 2000–1887: V15
Bellow, Saul
   Herzog: V14
   Seize the Day: V4
Beloved (Morrison): V6
Betsey Brown (Shange): V11
The Big Sleep (Chandler): V17
Billy Budd, Sailor: An Inside Narrative (Melville): V9
Black Boy (Wright): V1
Blair, Eric Arthur
   Animal Farm: V3
Bless Me, Ultima (Anaya): V12
The Bluest Eye (Morrison): V1
Body and Soul (Conroy): V11
Borland, Hal
   When the Legends Die: V18
Bowen, Elizabeth Dorothea Cole
   The Death of the Heart: V13
Bradbury, Ray
   Fahrenheit 451: V1

Cumulative
Nationality/Ethnicity Index

African American

Angelou, Maya
*I Know Why the Caged Bird
Sings:* V2
Baldwin, James
Go Tell It on the Mountain: V4
Cleage, Pearl
*What Looks Like Crazy on an
Ordinary Day:* V17
Ellison, Ralph
Invisible Man: V2
Gaines, Ernest J.
*The Autobiography of Miss Jane
Pittman:* V5
A Gathering of Old Men: V16
A Lesson before Dying: V7
Haley, Alex
*Roots: The Story of an American
Family:* V9
Hurston, Zora Neale
Their Eyes Were Watching God: V3
Kincaid, Jamaica
Annie John: V3
Morrison, Toni
Beloved: V6
The Bluest Eye: V1
Song of Solomom: V8
Sula: V14
Naylor, Gloria
Mama Day: V7
The Women of Brewster Place: V4
Shange, Ntozake
Betsey Brown: V11
Toomer, Jean
Cane: V11
Walker, Alice
The Color Purple: V5

Wright, Richard
Black Boy: V1

Algerian

Camus, Albert
The Plague: V16
The Stranger: V6

American

Alcott, Louisa May
Little Women: V12
Alexie, Sherman
*The Lone Ranger and Tonto
Fistfight in Heaven:* V17
Allison, Dorothy
Bastard Out of Carolina: V11
Alvarez, Julia
*How the García Girls Lost Their
Accents:* V5
Anaya, Rudolfo
Bless Me, Ultima: V12
Anderson, Sherwood
Winesburg, Ohio: V4
Angelou, Maya
*I Know Why the Caged Bird
Sings:* V2
Auel, Jean
The Clan of the Cave Bear: V11
Banks, Russell
The Sweet Hereafter: V13
Baum, L. Frank
The Wonderful Wizard of Oz: V13
Bellamy, Edward
Looking Backward: 2000–1887:
V15

Bellow, Saul
Herzog: V14
Borland, Hal
When the Legends Die: V18
Bradbury, Ray
Fahrenheit 451: V1
Bridal, Tessa
The Tree of Red Stars: V17
Brown, Rita Mae
Rubyfruit Jungle: V9
Butler, Octavia
Kindred: V8
Card, Orson Scott
Ender's Game: V5
Cather, Willa
Death Comes for the Archbishop:
V19
My Ántonia: V2
Chandler, Raymond
The Big Sleep: V17
Chopin, Kate
The Awakening: V3
Cisneros, Sandra
The House on Mango Street: V2
Clavell, James du Maresq
Shogun: A Novel of Japan: V10
Cleage, Pearl
*What Looks Like Crazy on an
Ordinary Day:* V17
Clemens, Samuel
*The Adventures of Huckleberry
Finn:* V1
The Adventures of Tom Sawyer: V6
Conroy, Frank
Body and Soul: V11
Cooper, James Fenimore
The Last of the Mohicans: V9

Greene, Graham
The End of the Affair: V16
Hardy, Thomas
Far from the Madding Crowd:
V19
The Mayor of Casterbridge:
V15
The Return of the Native: V11
Tess of the d'Urbervilles: V3
Huxley, Aldous
Brave New World: V6
Ishiguro, Kazuo
The Remains of the Day: V13
James, Henry
The Ambassadors: V12
The Portrait of a Lady: V19
The Turn of the Screw: V16
Koestler, Arthur
Darkness at Noon: V19
Lawrence, D. H.
Sons and Lovers: V18
Marmon Silko, Leslie
Ceremony: V4
Orwell, George
1984: V7
Animal Farm: V3
Rhys, Jean
Wide Sargasso Sea: V19
Shelley, Mary
Frankenstein: V1
Shute, Nevil
On the Beach: V9
Stevenson, Robert Louis
Dr. Jekyll and Mr. Hyde: V11
Swift, Graham
Waterland: V18
Swift, Jonathan
Gulliver's Travels: V6
Thackeray, William Makepeace
Vanity Fair: V13
Tolkien, J. R. R.
The Hobbit: V8
Waugh, Evelyn
Brideshead Revisited: V13
Scoop: V17
Wells, H. G.
The Time Machine: V17
Woolf, Virginia
Mrs. Dalloway: V12
To the Lighthouse: V8

European American

Hemingway, Ernest
The Old Man and the Sea: V6
Stowe, Harriet Beecher
Uncle Tom's Cabin: V6

French

Camus, Albert
The Plague: V16
The Stranger: V6

Dumas, Alexandre
The Count of Monte Cristo: V19
The Three Musketeers: V14
Flaubert, Gustave
Madame Bovary: V14
Hugo, Victor
Les Misérables: V5
Japrisot, Sébastien
A Very Long Engagement: V18
Voltaire
Candide: V7

German

Hesse, Hermann
Demian: V15
Siddhartha: V6
Mann, Thomas
Death in Venice: V17
Remarque, Erich Maria
All Quiet on the Western Front: V4

Hispanic American

Cisneros, Sandra
The House on Mango Street: V2
Hijuelos, Oscar
*The Mambo Kings Play Songs of
Love:* V17

Hungarian

Koestler, Arthur
Darkness at Noon: V19

Indian

Markandaya, Kamala
Nectar in a Sieve: V13

Italian

Machiavelli, Niccolo
The Prince: V9

Irish

Bowen, Elizabeth Dorothea Cole
The Death of the Heart: V13
Joyce, James
*A Portrait of the Artist as a
Young Man:* V7
Murdoch, Iris
Under the Net: V18
Stoker, Bram
Dracula: V18

Japanese

Ishiguro, Kazuo
The Remains of the Day: V13

Mori, Kyoko
Shizuko's Daughter: V15
Yoshimoto, Banana
Kitchen: V7

Jewish

Bellow, Saul
Herzog: V14
Seize the Day: V4
Kafka, Frank
The Trial: V7
Malamud, Bernard
The Fixer: V9
The Natural: V4
West, Nathanael
The Day of the Locust: V16
Wiesel, Eliezer
Night: V4

Mexican

Esquivel, Laura
Like Water for Chocolate: V5
Fuentes, Carlos
The Old Gringo: V8

Native American

Alexie, Sherman
*The Lone Ranger and Tonto
Fistfight in Heaven:* V17
Dorris, Michael
A Yellow Raft in Blue Water:
V3
Erdrich, Louise
Love Medicine: V5
Marmon Silko, Leslie
Ceremony: V4
Momaday, N. Scott
House Made of Dawn: V10

Nigerian

Achebe, Chinua
Things Fall Apart: V3
Emecheta, Buchi
The Bride Price: V12
The Wrestling Match: V14

Norwegian

Rölvaag, O. E.
Giants in the Earth: V5

Peruvian

Allende, Isabel
Daughter of Fortune: V18

Nationality/Ethnicity Index

Subject/Theme Index

*Boldface denotes discussion in
Themes section.*

A

Abandonment
  Babbitt: 36–37
  East of Eden: 141–142, 144–145
  Far from the Madding Crowd:
    173–174
  Wide Sargasso Sea: 315, 318
Abstinence
  Death Comes for the Archbishop:
    113, 115–117
Adultery
  Babbitt: 26, 33
Adulthood
  Tender Is the Night: 268, 270
Adventure and Exploration
  East of Eden: 146–147, 149–150
Alcoholism
  Tender Is the Night: 247
**Alcoholism, Drugs, and Drug
Addiction**
  Farewell My Concubine: 183,
    187, 189
  Tender Is the Night: 240,
    242–244, 249
Alienation
  East of Eden: 152–154
Allegory
  East of Eden: 133, 135
American Business
  Babbitt: 31
American Northeast
  Tender Is the Night: 240,
    243–244, 247, 249

American Southwest
  Death Comes for the Archbishop:
    94, 96–97, 99–105, 119–122,
    124–125
**American Versus European
Character**
  The Portrait of a Lady: 223
American West
  East of Eden: 127–130, 135
  White Fang: 286–287
Anger
  East of Eden: 129, 133, 152, 154
  Wide Sargasso Sea: 294–295, 299
Appearance vs. Reality
  Memoirs of a Geisha: 208–209
Art
  Tender Is the Night: 247
Asia
  Farewell My Concubine:
    181–184, 188–191, 198–202
  Memoirs of a Geisha: 204,
    211–213
Atonement
  Darkness at Noon: 73, 75, 79–81,
    83–84, 86–88, 90, 93
  Death Comes for the Archbishop:
    106, 110–111

B

Beauty
  Death Comes for the Archbishop:
    112–113, 115–117, 123–126
  Memoirs of a Geisha: 203–204,
    210–211
  White Fang: 276, 279, 282,
    284–286

Betrayal
  Alias Grace: 17, 19–20
  The Count of Monte Cristo: 48,
    50–51, 55

C

Capitalism
  White Fang: 290–291
Catastrophe
  Far from the Madding Crowd: 162
Childhood
  Wide Sargasso Sea: 306–312,
    314–315, 317–318
Christianity
  Death Comes for the Archbishop:
    112–114, 117, 120, 122–124,
    126
Class Structure
  Tender Is the Night: 247
Classicism
  The Count of Monte Cristo:
    67–70, 72
Comedy
  Far from the Madding Crowd:
    175, 177
Communism
  Darkness at Noon: 73–75, 78–87
  Farewell My Concubine: 181,
    183, 187–195
Conformity
  Babbitt: 26, 33–35
Courage
  The Count of Monte Cristo: 56, 70
  East of Eden: 148–150
  Far from the Madding Crowd:
    171, 173–174
  The Portrait of a Lady: 237

W

War

Tender Is the Night: 249

War, the Military, and Soldier Life

Babbitt: 38, 40–41, 44

The Count of Monte Cristo: 56–57, 67, 70–72

Darkness at Noon: 74–75, 82

East of Eden: 128–130, 135–136

Far from the Madding Crowd: 156, 158–159, 162

Farewell My Concubine: 183, 190–191

Memoirs of a Geisha: 205–206, 210–211

Tender Is the Night: 242, 249–251

White Fang: 287–288

Wealth

Babbitt: 26, 28, 31, 34–35

The Count of Monte Cristo: 48, 50–51

The Portrait of a Lady: 219–221, 225–227

Tender Is the Night: 240, 242, 247–251

Wildlife

The Count of Monte Cristo: 67–68, 70–72

Far from the Madding Crowd: 158–159, 164, 166

White Fang: 272–277, 279–286

World War I

Tender Is the Night: 247, 249–251

Subject/Theme Index

For Reference

Not to be taken from this room